Preventive Conservation in Museums

Preventive Conservation in Museums makes available and comprehensible the diverse literature and ideas of preventive conservation to an audience with a limited scientific background, principally those studying museum studies or engaged in the museum profession. It bridges the gap between the basic museum-generated literature and technical and detailed conservation literature.

The area of preventative conservation has developed greatly in recent decades adopting a far more holistic, collection wide approach. The development of the concepts of risk analysis, management of conservation and sensitivity to traditional beliefs and approaches to artefacts have all made an impact on the subject in recent years. The advance of instrumentation over the last thirty years has changed the emphasis from obtaining data on the museum environment to interpreting them. The next generation of ideas that will affect preventive conservation practice is just starting to emerge, including: detailed modelling of the environments of buildings and the sustainability of the artefactual and building heritage and an emphasis on preservation in situ.

Preventive Conservation in Museums highlights the wide variety of threats to the storage and display of objects in museums, it develops the concept of a holistic appreciation of these threats, and appreciates the need to prioritise the appropriate forms of response. It uses a careful balance of sources, some technical, some theoretical, some practical, as well as case studies to explore threats and their mitigation. For all those involved in preventive conservation, be they students or professionals, this volume will be an invaluable summary of the past, present and future of the discipline.

Chris Caple is Senior Lecturer in the Department of Archaeology at Durham University.

Leicester Readers in Museum Studies
Series Editor: Professor Simon J. Knell

Museum Management and Marketing
Richard Sandell and Robert R. Janes

Museums in the Material World
Simon J. Knell

Museums and their Communities
Sheila Watson

Museums in a Digital Age
Ross Parry

Forthcoming:

Museum Objects
Sandra Dudley

Preventive

Conservation

in Museums

Edited by

Chris Caple

 Routledge
Taylor & Francis Group

LONDON AND NEW YORK

First published 2011
by Routledge
2 Park Square, Milton Park, Abingdon, Oxon OX14 4RN

Simultaneously published in the USA and Canada
by Routledge
711 Third Avenue, New York, NY 10017

Routledge is an imprint of the Taylor & Francis Group, an informa business

British Library Cataloguing in Publication Data
A catalogue record for this book is available from the British Library

Library of Congress Cataloging in Publication Data
A catalog record for this book has been requested

ISBN: 978–0–415–57969–8 (hbk)
ISBN: 978–0–415–57970–4 (pbk)

Typeset in Perpetua
by Swales and Willis Ltd, Exeter, Devon

Printed and bound in Great Britain by
CPI Antony Rowe, Chippenham, Wiltshire

Contents

Section Three: Pests

Section Four: Contaminants (Gases, Dust)

Section Five: Radiation (Light)

Figures

Tables

List of Contributors

Jonathan Ashley Smith (Prof.), Head of Conservation at the Victoria and Albert Museum (1977–1994)

Mary W. Ballard, Senior Textile Conservator, Smithsonian Institution

Janet Berry, Course Director for the MSc Sustainable Heritage at University College London (2004–2009), editor of the *Journal of the Institute of Conservation* and a collections care consultant

Julian Bickersteth, Freelance conservator, director of International Conservation Services

Sharon Blank, Conservator specialising in plastics and modern works of art

Valerie Blyth, Preventive conservator dealing with Pest Management at the Victoria and Albert Museum

Sue Bradley, Retired Head of Conservation Research at the British Museum

Peter Brimblecombe, Professor in Atmospheric Chemistry in the School of Environmental Sciences, University of East Anglia

Linda Bullock, Preventive Conservation Advisor to the National Trust

Chris Caple, Senior Lecturer in Archaeological Conservation, Department of Archaeology, at Durham University

Julian Carter, Zoological Conservation Officer, National Museum of Wales

May Cassar (Prof.), Director of the Centre for Sustainable Heritage at University College London

Bob Child, Recently retired Head of Conservation at the National Museums of Wales

Miriam Clavir, Conservator Emerita and Research Fellow, University of British Columbia Museum of Anthropology, Vancouver

Sarah Clayton, Senior Textile Conservator at the Australian War Memorial

Charlie Costain, Director of Conservation and Scientific Services at the Canadian Conservation Institute

Claire Dean, Freelance conservator, director Dean & Associates Conservation Services

Diane Dollery, Keeper of Collection Services, National Museum of Wales

Ann Drumheller, Registrar, National Museum of the American Indian

Dave Erhardt, Senior Research Chemist in the Smithsonian Institution

Kate Frame, Historic Royal Palaces, Head of Conservation and Collection Care

Linda Hillyer, Head of Textile Conservation, Victoria and Albert Museum

John Hunter, Curator, US National Parks Service

Amy de Joia, Executive Director of Development and Communications for National Museums, Liverpool

Sophie Julien-Lees, Senior Preventive Conservator at Historic Royal Palaces

Marian Kaminitz, Head of Conservation at the National Museum of the American Indian

Suzanne Keene, Emeritus Reader in Museum and Heritage Studies at University College London

Helen Kingsley, Conservation Manager, Science Museum London

Barry Knight, Head of Conservation Research at the British Library

Lorna Lee, Conservation scientist with the Conservation Research Group of the British Museum

Katy Lithgow, National Trust's Head of Conservation and their wall paintings conservation advisor

Helen Lloyd, Deputy Head Conservator and Preventive Conservation Advisor (Housekeeping) to the National Trust

Paul Marcon, Mechanical engineer with the Conservation Research Division of the Canadian Conservation Institute

John Martin, Freelance writer on museum topics

Cathy Mathias, Head of Conservation Memorial University of Newfoundland

Marion Mecklenburg, Senior Physical Research Scientist in the Smithsonian Institution

Stefan Michalski, Senior Conservation Scientist at the Canadian Conservation Institute

Gwen Miles, Director of Somerset House, previously a conservator at the Victoria and Albert Museum

Catherine Nightingale, Conservator who specialises in liaising between conservation department and exhibition project teams, Museum of London

Douglas Nixon, Archaeologist, Newfoundland, Canada

Robert Payton, Head of Conservation, Museum of London

Robyn Pender, Senior Architectural Conservator with English Heritage

Fiona Philpott, Director of Exhibitions, National Museums, Liverpool

Dave Pinniger, Independent consultant advising on pest management and control

Lim Chong Quek, Conservator, National Museum of Singapore

Kristen Ramsdale, Collections Technician (conservator), Canterbury Museum

Muhammadin Razak, Conservator, National Museum of Indonesia in Jakarta

Sue Renault, Head of the Conservation Unit, St Fagan's National History Museum of Wales

Martin Robinson, Architectural historian

Christopher Rowell, National Trust Historic Buildings representative

Theo Skinner, Recently retired conservator at the National Museum of Scotland

Sarah Stanniforth, Head Conservator and subsequently Historic Properties Director at the National Trust

Jim Tate, Head of the Department of Conservation and Analytical Research in the National Museums of Scotland

Fiona Tennant, Preventive conservator working for International Conservation Services
Jean Tétreault, Conservation Scientist, Canadian Conservation Institute
Dave Thickett, Senior Conservation Scientist at English Heritage, Collections Division
Garry Thomson, retired Scientific Advisor, the National Gallery, London
Siobhan Watts, Conservation Scientist at the National Museums and Galleries on Merseyside
Glenn Wharton, Conservator (time-based media) Museum of Modern Art (New York) and Research Scholar New York University
Peter Winsor, Collections Link Project Director
Young Hun Yoon, Senior Research Associate in the School of Environmental Sciences, University of East Anglia

Series Preface

Leicester Readers in Museum Studies provide students of museums – whether employed in the museum, engaged in a museum studies programme or studying in a cognate area – with a selection of focused readings in core areas of museum thought and practice. Each book has been compiled by a specialist in that field, but all share the Leicester School's belief that the development and effectiveness of museums relies upon informed and creative practice. The series as a whole reflects the core Leicester curriculum which is now visible in programmes around the world and which grew, forty years ago, from a desire to train working professionals, and students prior to entry into the museum, in the technical aspects of museum practice. In some respects the curriculum taught then looks similar to that we teach today. The following, for example, was included in the curriculum in 1968: history and development of the museum movement; the purpose of museum; types of museum and their functions; the law as it relates to museums; staff appointments and duties, sources of funding; preparation of estimates; byelaws and regulations; local, regional, etc. bodies; buildings; heating, ventilation and cleaning; lighting; security systems; control of stores and so on. Some of the language and focus here, however, indicates a very different world. A single component of the course, for example, focused on collections and dealt with collection management, conservation and exhibitions. Another component covered 'museum activities' from enquiry services to lectures, films, and so on. There was also training in specialist areas, such as local history, and many practical classes which included making plaster casts and models. Many museum workers around the world will recognise these kinds of curriculum topics; they certainly resonate with my early experiences of working in museums.

While the skeleton of that curriculum in some respects remains, there has been a fundamental shift in the flesh we hang upon it. One cannot help but think that the museum world has grown remarkably sophisticated: practices are now regulated by equal opportunities, child protection, cultural property and wildlife conservation laws; collections are now exposed to material culture analysis, contemporary documentation projects, digital capture and so on; communication is now multimedia, inclusive, evaluated and theorised. The museum has over that time become intellectually fashionable, technologically advanced and developed a new social relevance. *Leicester Readers in Museum Studies* address this change. They deal with practice as it is relevant to the museum today, but they are also about expanding horizons beyond one's own experiences. They reflect a more professionalised world and one that has thought very deeply about this wonderfully interesting and significant institution. Museum studies remains a vocational subject but it is now very different. It is, however, sobering to think that the Leicester course was founded in the year Michel Foucault published *The Order of Things* – a book that greatly influenced the way we think about the museum today. The writing was on the wall even then.

Simon Knell
Series Editor

Preface

This reader attempts to make some of the key publications of the diverse literature on preventive conservation more readily available. It is an updated version of Simon Knell's *Care of Collections*, published in 1994. This latter book successfully drew together information, largely from the museum literature, on the subject of collections care. Since that date the literature on this subject has grown considerably. A large number of papers are now published by groups of museum scientists in the specialist conservation literature. There are also an increasing number of books on different types of collectable object, from military vehicles to medals, which contain chapters on 'the basic care of . . .'. The problem with much of the 'care of . . .' literature is that, although it gives sound advice, it avoids technical terms, symbols and explanations of the chemical basis for the decay or prevention of decay processes. To be able to read and understand this subject at anything beyond the most basic level, these technical terms, the relevant symbols and basic scientific explanations need to be understood. This reader seeks to bridge the gap between the very basic museum 'care of . . .' literature and the technical and detailed conservation literature.

To provide a picture of the practice of preventive conservation in the initial decade of the twenty-first century, the papers are drawn from the last 20 years of research and publishing on the subject. They are a mixture of seminal books and papers in the subject, such as Thomson (1986) and Michalski (1993), clear introductions to and expositions of the topic, such as Keene (1996), or case studies which demonstrate current practice, such as Nightingale (2005–6). The observant reader may note that many of the papers are drawn from the mid-1990s. This reflects the influential nature of the research undertaken and publications written in this period. Whilst further research has taken place, leading to more recent detailed appreciation of a number of topics, such as airborne pollutants by Tétreault (2003), in many cases the developments of the mid-1990s are still being implemented in museums. Consequently, a significant number of the case studies and summaries from that period remain highly appropriate. One significant change since 1994 is the availability of information on preventive conservation from websites.[1] Many national and international heritage organisations, such as the Canadian Conservation Institute (CCI), the Getty Conservation Institute (GCI) and the Collections Trust, now make information on preventive conservation available via their websites as well as through publications. Their aim is to raise the standards of care of historic and artistic artefacts throughout the world.

One subject that is crucial to the practice of preventive conservation, which is not covered by this book, is that of materials identification. To apply preventive conservation measures effectively it is important to know what materials you are dealing with. Is this metal object lead and thus vulnerable to the organic acid vapours from oak cabinets, or iron and subject to corrosion at high humidity? Is this object plastic likely to lose plasticiser and develop a cracked and crazed surface or ivory and likely to react poorly to changes in relative humidity? Materials identification is a large subject which is not currently appropriately covered in a succinct published form aimed at museum curators or museum studies students. Though there are a number of basic identification books on individual materials, such *What Wood Is That?* (Edlin 1977), there is nothing comprehensive for the full range of materials in objects collected by museums. It is also, arguably, not a subject that can be adequately learnt solely from textual sources: you need to handle the actual materials and gain a 'feel' for them if you are to identify them accurately. Unfortunately there is not normally room available in the curricula of most museum courses for this type of time-consuming 'skilling'. Consequently, it is a key aspect of preventive conservation that students must develop themselves.

Finally, it will be noted that the title of the book has changed from *Care of Collections* to *Preventive Conservation*. This reflects:

- the narrower focus of this reader on the different agents of artefact decay, their monitoring and control
- the existence of many other books which cover subjects such as conservation ethics (Richmond and Bracker 2009) and collections management (Fahy 1995, British Standards Institute 2009), which were included in Knell's original *Care of Collections* book.
- the widespread adoption of the term 'preventive conservation' since the 1994 IIC Ottawa conference on this subject
- the increased volume of research and the increasingly scientific basis for the work undertaken in this area
- the importance of conveying to both the public and decision makers the high degree of education and training that museum professionals, whether curators, conservators or collections managers are required to possess in order to practise preventive conservation at a competent level. There is an increasing need to distinguish preventive conservation from the sometimes unspecific activities and attitudes which the term 'care' can evoke.

Notes

1   http://www.collectionslink.org.uk/

References

British Standards Institute (2009) *PAS197:2009 Code of Practice for Cultural Collections Management*, London: BSI.

Edlin, H. L. (1977) *What Wood Is That?* London: Stobart and Son Ltd.

Fahy, A. (ed.) (1995) *Collections Management*, Abingdon: Routledge.

Keene, S. (1996) *Managing Conservation in Museums*, London: Butterworth-Heinemann, pp. 112–135, 136–158.

Michalski, S. (1993) 'Relative Humidity: A Discussion of Correct/Incorrect Values', in *ICOM-CC 10th Triennial Meeting, Washington, DC, USA*, pp. 624–629.

Nightingale, C. (2005–6) Designing an Exhibition to Minimise Risks to Costume on Open Display, *The Conservator* 29: 35–50.

Richmond, A and Bracker, A. (2009) *Conservation Principles, Dilemmas and Uncomfortable Truths*, London: Butterworth-Heinemann.

Tétreault, J. (2003) *Airborne Pollutants in Museums, Galleries and Archives: Risk assessment, Control Strategies and Preservation Management*, Ottawa: CCI.

Thomson, G. *The Museum Environment* (2nd edn), London: Butterworths, 1986, pp. 2–33.

Acknowledgements

I wish to express my thanks to many colleagues who have helped develop my understanding of this subject and who have helped bring this reader into existence.

- Simon Knell for his invitation to create this reader, which made me look again at this subject with a much more critical eye.
- Janet Berry and Mary Brooks made many valuable suggestions for papers for inclusion in this reader.
- David Leigh and David Watkinson, who provided my initial schooling in this subject, so, so long ago.
- Colleagues at York Castle Museum 1984–1988 for helping me appreciate how beneficial and how challenging it can be to put preventive conservation measures into place and how important colleagues and teamwork are in achieving the consistent care of collections.
- Colleagues and students at Durham University, especially the students on the MA in Conservation of Historic Objects (Archaeology) (1990–2004), MA in Conservation of Archaeological and Museum Objects (2009–)and MA in Museum and Artefacts courses, for the opportunity to learn about the subject through teaching them preventive conservation courses for over 20 years.

The papers selected for this reader, their appreciation and that of the subject as a whole, remain my responsibility, mine alone.

The following are reproduced with kind permission. While every effort has been made to trace copyright holders to obtain permission, this has not been possible in all cases. Any omissions brought to our attention will be remedied in future editions.

Chris Caple

1. Holistic Approach to Preventive Conservation

Charlie Costain, 'Framework for Preservation of Museum Collections', *CCI Newsletter* No. 14 (1994), pp. 1–4 and Canadian Conservation Institute, *Framework for Preservation of Museum Collections* (a poster) (Ottawa, CCI, 1994). © All rights reserved. Reproduced with the permission of the Canadian Conservation Institute of the Department of Canadian Heritage, 2011.

Jonathan Ashley-Smith, 'Risk Analysis', in S. Bradbury (ed.), *The Interface between Science and Conservation*, British Museum Occasional Paper No. 116, London: British Museum Press, 1997, pp. 123–132. By kind permission of The Trustees of the British Museum.

2. Agents of Deterioration

2.1. Physical Forces (Handling, Moving) and Security

Gwen Miles, 'Object Handling', in J. M. A. Thompson (ed.), *Manual of Curatorship* (2nd edn), Oxford: Butterworth-Heinemann, 1992, pp. 455–458. © Elsevier.

Paul Marcon, Six Steps to Safe Shipment, CCI website, www.cci-icc.gc.ca/crc/articles/sixsteps-sixtapes/index-eng.aspx. © All rights reserved. Reproduced with the permission of the Canadian Conservation Institute of the Department of Canadian Heritage, 2011.

Chris Caple, *Conservation Skills: Judgement, Method and Decision Making*, London: Routledge, 2000, pp. 152–160. © Routledge/Taylor and Francis.

James Tate and Theo Skinner, 'Storage Systems', in J. M. A. Thompson (ed.) *Manual of Curatorship* (2nd edn), Oxford: Butterworth-Heinemann, 1992, pp. 459–467. © Elsevier.

Peter Winsor, 'Which Conservation Materials to Use at Home?', in Museums and Galleries Commission (ed.), *Ours for Keeps?*, London: MGC, 1997, pp. 7.07–7.10. By kind permission of the author and the Collections Trust.

IIC, Before the Unthinkable . . . Happens Again, IIC website, http://www.iiconservation.org/dialogues/IIC_tokyo_transcript.pdf. By kind permission of the IIC, Jerry Podany (IIC President), and the panellists.

Rob Payton, 'Safety by Numbers', *Museum Practice* 22 (2003), pp. 40–42. By kind permission of the Museums Association.

2.2. Fire and Water (Disasters)

Christopher Rowell and Martin Robinson, *Uppark Restored* (Chapter 1: The Fire and Salvage), London: The National Trust, 1996, pp. 15–31. By kind permission of The National Trust.

John Martin, 'Emergency Planning', *Museum Practice* Spring 2005, pp. 43–59. By kind permission of the Museums Association.

John E. Hunter, 'Museum Disaster Preparedness and Planning', in S. Knell (ed.), *Care of Collections* (London, Routledge, 1994), pp. 60–79 (originally in B.G. Jones (ed.), *Protecting Historic Architecture and Museum Collections from Natural Disasters* (Oxford, Butterworth-Heinemann, 1986), pp. 211–230.

2.3. Pests

Dave Pinniger and Peter Winsor, *Integrated Pest Management*, London: Museums and Galleries Commission, 1998. By kind permission of David Pinniger, Peter Winsor and the Collections Trust.

Linda Hillyer and Valerie Blyth, 'Carpet Beetle – a Pilot Study in Detection and Control', in S. Knell (ed.), *Care of Collections* (London, Routledge, 1994), pp. 217–233 (originally in *The Conservator* 16 (1992), pp. 65–77. This is an article whose final and definitive form has been published in *The Conservator*, Volume 16 © 1992 Institute of Conservation. Reproduced with permission from the Institute of Conservation.

Lim Chong Quek, Muhammadin Razak and Mary W. Ballard, 'Pest Control for Temperate vs. Tropical Museums: North America vs. Southeast Asia', in *ICOM-CC 9th Triennial Meeting, Dresden, German Democratic Republic 26–31 August 1990*, Los Angeles: ICOM-CC, 1990, pp. 817–821. By kind permission of the authors.

2.4 Contaminants (Gases, Dust)

Sarah Stanniforth, Sophie Julien and Linda Bullock, 'Chemical Agents of Deterioration', in National Trust, *Manual of Housekeeping*, London: Butterworth-Heinemann, 2006, pp. 69–79. By kind permission of the authors and The National Trust.

L. R. Lee and D. Thickett, *Selection of Materials for the Storage and Display of Museum Objects*, British Museum Occasional Papers 111, London: British Museum Press 1996, pp. 3–8, 12–17, 37–39. By kind permission of The Trustees of the British Museum.

Susan Bradley and David Thickett, 'The pollution problem in perspective', in J. Bridgeland (ed.), *ICOM-CC 12th Triennial Meeting Lyon 29 August – 3 September 1999*, London: James & James, 1999, pp. 8–13. By kind permission of the authors.

Jean Tétreault, *Airborne Pollutants in Museums, Galleries and Archives: Risk Assessment, Control Strategies and Preservation Management*, Ottawa: CCI, 2003. © All rights reserved. Reproduced with the permission of the Canadian Conservation Institute of the Department of Canadian Heritage, 2011.

Helen Lloyd, Katy Lithgow, Peter Brimblecombe, Young Hun Yoon, Kate Frame and Barry Knight, 'The Effects of Visitor Activity on Dust in Historic Collections', *The Conservator* 26 (2002): 72–84. This is an article whose final and definitive form has been published in *The Conservator*, Volume 26 © 2006 Institute of Conservation. Reproduced with permission from the Institute of Conservation.

C. Mathias, K. Ramsdale and D. Nixon, 'Saving Archaeological Iron using the Revolutionary Preservation System', in J. Ashton and D. Hallam (eds), *Metal 04*, Canberra: National Museum of Australia, 2004, pp. 28–42. By kind permission of the National Museum of Australia.

2.5. Radiation (Light)

Garry Thomson *The Museum Environment* (2nd edn), London: Butterworths, 1986, pp. 2–33. © Elsevier.

Stefan Michalski, 'The Lighting Decision', in CCI (eds), *Fabric of an Exhibition: An Interdisciplinary Approach – Preprints*, Ottawa: CCI, 1997, pp. 97–104. © All rights

2.6. Incorrect Temperature and Relative Humidity

David Erhardt and Marion Mecklenburg, 'Relative Humidity Re-examined', in A. Roy and P. Smith (eds), *Preventive Conservation: Practice, Theory and Research, IIC Ottawa Congress 12–16 September 1994*, Ottawa: IIC, 1994, pp. 32–38. © All rights reserved. Reproduced with the permission of the Canadian Conservation Institute of the Department of Canadian Heritage, 2011.

Stefan Michalski, 'Relative Humidity: A Discussion of Correct/Incorrect Values', in *ICOM-CC 10th Triennial Meeting, Washington, DC, USA*, Paris: ICOM-CC, 1993, pp. 624–629. By kind permission of the author and the CCI.

Stefan Michalski, 'Relative Humidity and Temperature Guidelines: What's Happening', *CCI Newsletter* 14 (1994): 6. © All rights reserved. Reproduced with the permission of the Canadian Conservation Institute of the Department of Canadian Heritage, 2011.

3. Managing Preventive Conservation

3.1. Environmental Management

May Cassar, *Environmental Management*, London: Routledge, 1995, pp. 39–41, 77–87, 94–108. © Routledge/Taylor and Francis.

Suzanne Keene, *Managing Conservation in Museums*, London: Butterworth-Heinemann, 1996, pp. 112–135, 136–158. © Suzanne Keene.

Helen Kingsley and Robert Payton, 'Condition Surveying of Large Varied Stored Collections', *Conservation News* 54: 8–10. This is an article whose final and definitive form has been published in *Conservation News*, Volume 54 © 1994 Institute of Conservation. Reproduced with permission from the Institute of Conservation.

Diane Dollery 'A Methodology of Preventive Conservation for a Large, Expanding and Mixed Archaeological Collection', in A. Roy and P. Smith (eds), *Preventive Conservation: Practice, Theory and Research, IIC Ottawa Congress 12–16 September 1994*, Ottawa: IIC, 1994, pp. 69–72. By kind permission of the author.

3.2. Ethical Considerations

Miriam Clavir, 'Preserving Conceptual Integrity: Ethics and Theory in Preventive Conservation', in A. Roy and P. Smith (eds), *Preventive Conservation: Practice, Theory and Research, IIC Ottawa Congress 12–16 September 1994*, Ottawa: IIC, 1994, pp. 53–57. By kind permission of the author.

Ann Drumheller and Marian Kaminitz, 'Traditional Care and Conservation, the Merging of Two Disciplines at the National Museum on the American Indian', in A. Roy and P. Smith (eds), *Preventive Conservation: Practice, Theory and Research, IIC Ottawa Congress 12–16 September 1994*, Ottawa: IIC, 1994, pp. 58–60. By kind permission of the authors.

Robert Child, 'Conserving a Coal Mine: Keeping our Industrial Heritage Working', in C.

Butler and M. Davis (eds), *Things Fall Apart . . .*, Cardiff: National Museum of Wales, 2006, pp. 24–31. © Amgueddfa Cymru – National Museum Wales.

Glenn Wharton, Sharon D. Blank and J. Claire Dean 'Sweetness and Blight: Conservation of Chocolate Works of Art', in J. Heuman (ed.), *From Marble to Chocolate: The Conservation of Modern Sculpture*, London: Archetype, 1995), pp. 162–170. By kind permission of the authors.

3.3 *All Together Now*

Museums and Galleries Commission, *Levels of Collections Care: A Self-Assessment Checklist for UK Museums*, London: MGC, 1998. By kind permission of the Collections Trust.

Suzanne Keane, Information for Preservation, *Managing Conservation in Museums*, London: Butterworth-Heinemann, 1996, pp. 112–135. © Suzanne Keene.

Catherine Nightingale, 'Designing an Exhibition to Minimise Risks to Costume on Open Display', *The Conservator* 29 (2005/6): 35–50. This is an article whose final and definitive form has been published in *The Conservator*, Volume 29 © 2005/6 Institute of Conservation. Reproduced with permission from the Institute of Conservation.

Siobhan Watts, Janet Berry, Amy de Joia and Fiona Philpott, 'In Control or Simply Monitoring? The Protection of Museum Collections from Dust and Vibration during Building Works', in R. Vontobel (ed.), *ICOM-CC 13th Triennial Meeting Rio de Janeiro 22–27 September 2002*, London: James & James, 2002, pp. 108–115. By kind permission of the authors.

Sue Renault, 'Make Yourself at Home: Looking after an Open-Air Museum', in C. Butler and M. Davis (eds), *Things Fall Apart . . .*, Cardiff: National Museum of Wales, 2006, pp. 6–14. © Amgueddfa Cymru – National Museum Wales.

4. Preventive Conservation: the future

Julian Bickersteth, Sarah Clayton and Fiona Tennant, 'Conserving and Interpreting the Historic Huts of Antarctica', in D. Saunders, J. H. Townsend and S. Woodcock (eds), *Conservation and Access, Contributions to the London Congress 15–19 September 2008*, London: IIC, 2008), pp. 218–220. By kind permission of the authors.

Julian Carter, 'Breaking the Code: Conserving DNA – New Demands on Natural Science Collections', in C. Butler and M. Davis (eds.) *Things Fall Apart . . .*, Cardiff: National Museum of Wales, 2006, pp. 16–22. © Amgueddfa Cymru – National Museum Wales.

May Cassar and Robyn Pender, 'The Impact of Climate Change on Cultural Heritage: Evidence and Response', in A. Paterakis, et al. (eds), *ICOM-CC 14th Triennial Meeting The Hague 12–16 September 2005*, London: James & James, 2005, pp. 610–616. By kind permission of the authors.

The History of and an Introduction to Preventive Conservation

Chris Caple

What is preventive conservation?

ARTEFACTS,[1] WHETHER TOOLS FOR cutting or pictures for viewing, are functional objects (Caple 2006: 8–13). They are maintained during their working lives by their owners to ensure they remain functional and effective. Thus, the good carpenter ensures that his tools are cleaned, sharpened and, if stored, have a light coat of oil to prevent corrosion. This ensures that they can continue to function effectively in this initial 'use' phase of their life. When the carpenter's tools enter a museum collection, they cease to fulfil their original function and become part of collections which are to be preserved in perpetuity. Their new role (function) is to preserve and display evidence of the past. This is invariably the final or curation phase of the object's life (Caple 2006, Figure 1.3). If any object is to function effectively as part of a museum collection then it must be prevented from corroding or decaying; preserved in its present state, since loss or deterioration would reduce or eliminate its ability to perform its museum functions of being a research subject or display item. It is the efforts to preserve, balanced with the needs to reveal (display) and investigate (research) the object and its values which can be understood as conservation (Caple 2000: 33–35). Activities, particularly those associated with preserving the object, that occur without physical interaction with the object can be regarded as preventive conservation. Preventive conservation can be defined as any measure that reduces the potential for, or prevents, damage. It focuses on collections rather than individual objects, non-treatment rather than treatment. In practical terms handling, storage and management of collections (including emergency planning) are critical elements in a preventive conservation methodology (Getty Conservation Institute 1992)

Preventive conservation absorbs products and ideas from the world of modern industry and commerce and applies them, where appropriate, to museum objects.

Ideas such as oxygen-free storage come from the food-preservation industry, products like bubble wrap from the packaging industry, disaster planning from the fire-prevention industry, air conditioning from the building industry. All these products and ideas have to be assessed for application to precious artistic and historic works. Whilst they must be effective, crucially there is an ethical requirement that no element or valued aspect (tangible or intangible) of the original artefact should be altered or lost in the preserving process. In practical terms they also need to be cost-effective, as the museum and heritage industry invariably has limited resources.

Preventive conservation has also looked back to 'traditional' practices, in a range of cultures. Traditional methods often have the benefit of being low-energy solutions, using natural materials and sympathetic to other aspects of human existence. Whether closing a country house over the winter, using blinds or curtains, keeping objects in boxes or chests, such practices are often highly effective in minimising decay rates. The evidence of surviving objects which have been the recipients of such practices demonstrates their effectiveness, especially over the long term.

Regardless of whether new or traditional methods and materials are used, only if artefacts are valued are resources made available to preserve them. So the first requirement for preventive conservation is to ensure that society, or someone in it, values the object.

History: preventive conservation – prehistory to the nineteenth century

The idea that ancient artefacts have always been valued by humankind appears well attested by archaeologists who have found significant numbers of ancient objects in more recent contexts, such as Roman jewellery in Saxon graves (White 1988, 1990). Some of the earliest surviving structures of human settlement in Europe, megalithic tombs on the western seaboard of Spain, France and Britain, appear to be made deliberately using stones which have been decorated by earlier peoples (Bradley, R. 2002). Some artefacts preserve evidence which goes beyond being valued and thus collected: they display evidence of veneration (retained, cleaned, repaired and restored). The Coppergate Anglian helmet was retained and used for well over 100 years after its manufacture; it shows clear evidence of continued and extensive cleaning through the nature of its worn decoration (Tweddle 1992: 980–982). The Saxon brooch from Harford Farm, Caistor St Edmund, Norfolk shows evidence of careful repair by a Saxon metalsmith called Luda (Tudda?) (Hinton 2005: 79), who inscribed his work. It could be suggested that the cleaning and repair of this and even 'older' objects could be interpreted as maintaining their initial (original) function. However, some older artefacts, such as the examples of shattered Roman Samian pottery vessels which have been held together with lead strips and rivets (Marsh 1981, Ward 1993) or broken seventeenth-century wine glasses held together with wire (Willmott 2001), demonstrate a desire to maintain an object as an heirloom, since in its repaired form it no longer has the strength or integrity to fulfil its initial function. Its age and original appearance (shape) have now become its key values; it functions as an heirloom, acting as a mnemonic to draw viewers into remembrance (Jones 2007; Haug 2001: 112).

From the point that we ceased to be hunter-gatherers and became settled agricultural communities living in permanent dwellings, we have retained objects that have become symbols of personal and cultural identity (Rowlands 1993). Artefacts have become powerful totems, endowed with social, religious or personal significance: from the crown jewels to parts of the 'true cross', possessing them gives the holder power. Steps have invariably been taken to safeguard and to care for these artefacts; it appears that we always look after the things we love (value). By the time of the Greek and Roman civilisations, artefacts such as the prized possessions of conquered peoples were routinely held in the temple treasuries of victorious Greek and Roman cities as 'physical proof' of the power of their gods. In Rome these collections were cared for by senate-appointed officers. In the Roman Republican period these officials were known as *censors* and *aediles*; the *censors* primarily catalogued and distributed the objects, the *aediles* were responsible for the maintenance and security of the buildings and their contents. From the Augustan period onwards both functions were performed by the imperially appointed *curators* (Strong 1973). Written sources from this period indicate that the Romans had both knowledge and appreciation of art and a good understanding of the processes of decay.

- Seneca reminds his readers that a bad light can ruin pictures (Strong 1973: 258).
- Vitruvius recommends north light for pictures, since it is steady and does not alter through the day (Strong 1973: 258).
- Pausanias records that the ivory parts of the statue of Zeus were treated with oil to prevent damp, whilst the ivory of the Athena Parthenos was deliberately kept damp (to avoid drying out and presumably cracking) (Strong 1973: 261).
- Pausanius also mentions treating bronze shields in the Stoa Poekile with pitch, presumably to preserve them against water and prevent them corroding (Strong 1973: 261).
- Pliny the Elder remarks that in the third century BC the Greek artist Apelles of Cos applied a thin black varnish to his paintings, since it 'enhanced the brilliance of the colours and protected from dust and dirt' (Abey-Koch 2006: 32)
- Pliny describes four types of wood-boring insect and suggested making objects out of cypress, as the bitterness of this wood deterred wood-boring insects, or hardwoods such as boxwood, as they prevented the birth of these insects (Abey-Koch 2006: 28). He also suggests treating papyrus with citrus oil to deter insect pests (Pye 2001: 40).
- Pliny wrote of the corrosive effects of timber on lead (Rackham 1968: 253).
- The problem of loss and damage of collections from fire was evident to many ancient writers. Fire destroyed the Forum Pacis and its ancient statues in AD 191; it also badly damaged the Forum Caesar and the Theatre of Pompey and their associated works of ancient art (Strong 1973: 26). In AD 483 an inscription records the restoration of a statue of Minerva, the goddess protector against fire, which had, ironically, been badly damaged by fire (Strong 1973: 263).

Educated ancient Romans were thus well aware of the processes of decay and the potential loss of artefacts from disasters such as fire. The active roles of cleaning, coating and restoration have subsequently developed into the processes of interventive or remedial conservation. Those of protecting objects from light, insects, damp, fires and theft have evolved into preventive conservation. The names of a number of the *censors*, *aediles* and *curators* have come down to us. A *curule aedile*, T. Septimus Sabinus, who is referred to by Pliny as returning a statue of Hercules to public view (Strong 1973: 252) is one of the earliest named individuals we can identify as practising preventive conservation.

The concept of preserving valued artefacts from the ravages of the natural world continued in the medieval period; paintings of the late medieval period often had shutters or curtains in front of them to protect from the effects of light (Campbell 1998: 17). There was also recognition of the risks involved in moving objects. In 1454 the artist Neri sold a panel painting to Antonio dalla Lastra, who took it away packed in a pair of large baskets; but on the journey home he collided with a mule who kicked the baskets and broke the panel painting into 12 fragments, which the artist then had to piece back together for his client (Thomas 1998: 5). This, and no doubt many other incidents, caused at least some owners and artists to take great care when transporting works of art. In 1399 the artist Brederlam, when dispatching the newly painted wing panels of a triptych to his client, packed them in a crate made of elm wood, lined with leather and stuffed with cotton. The crate was also wrapped in 22 ells of waxed cloth (presumably to make it waterproof) (Campbell 1998: 18). By the Renaissance the creation of purpose-built containers to protect (and display) art had developed to the point that the earliest galleries and museums were being constructed, such as the upper floor of the Uffizi constructed by Francesco I (1541–87) and the art gallery (1563–67) and museum (1569–73) built by Albrecht V, Duke of Bavaria.

The closable container, such as the box, has long been appreciated as one of the most effective forms of preventive conservation. A box excludes light, is a barrier against pests, provides insulation against temperature and relative humidity (RH) change and, crucially, provides physical security and some measure of protection against disasters such as fire and flood. Boxes of strong-smelling woods such as cedar or containing herbs such as lavender have a long tradition of repelling insects such as moths and were thus used for storing clothing in the late and post-medieval periods. Containers such as portfolio made of pasteboard or thin wood are identified as early as 1439 for protecting prints and drawings (Hicks 1988: 7); other forms of physical protection such as the use of mounts, frames with and without glazing, date from the seventeenth century and become widespread by the eighteenth (Hicks 1988: 8). Weapons such as swords were kept in fleece-lined scabbards, which gave the iron blade a coating of water-repellent lanolin (the natural grease of wool) every time it was drawn or inserted, so keeping the blade from corroding (Nissan 1999: 111).

Though emperors, kings, lords and princes took great pride and interest in their treasured processions and lavished resources on them, the basic tasks of care and cleaning were often done by household servants; indeed some of the early *censors* and *aediles* were public slaves. In the absence of courses and books, from the Roman period to the eighteenth/nineteenth century it was through practice and oral tradition that the skills of cleaning, storing, de-infestation and repair were routinely passed on from one generation of household servants/slaves to the next. The late medieval period, like the late Roman Republic period, was a time when displays of wealth through possessions such as furniture, paintings, books and clothing were important to the ruling elite, and by the sixteenth century this information began to be written down, e.g. *The Jewel House of Art and Nature* by Sir Hugh Platt (1594). Books on caring for household possessions become more common in the eighteenth and nineteenth centuries, such as *The Housekeeping Book of Joanna Whatman 1776–1800* and Mrs Beeton's *Housewife's Treasury of Domestic Information*, published in 1865 (Abey-Koch 2006). These publications made available a large volume of knowledge based on empirical observation and provided a wealth of practical 'how to clean and care for' information. They demonstrate that environmental phenomena and their effects, such as damp and moulds, light and fading, were well understood on a cause-and-effect basis.

In summary, from prehistory to the mid-nineteenth century, artefacts were collected and preserved principally by private individuals. A small number of powerful organisations also acquired objects: the Roman state, religious organisations such as the Catholic Church, late medieval towns such as Basel (which acquired Amerbach's collection in 1661) and, from the late eighteenth century, the emergent European nation-states, which started to found national museums. In most cases the collected objects are either curiosities, related to family ancestry, are evidence for religious belief or secular power, or are art (valued as a display of wealth and sophistication as aesthetic pleasure). As materials were scarce and valuable, efforts were generally made to preserve all types of artefacts, weapons, tools, even clothing. The same techniques and ideas were used to protect and maintain ancient artefacts as to preserve and maintain functional tools and weapons. Preservative measures were invariably applied by servants or craftsmen to the artefacts of their masters or clients. Measures were applied to valued artefacts in order to maintain the artefact's visual appearance and involved active cleaning and mending as well as protection from agents of decay. Natural agents of decay were clearly understood and, although literature on this subject was limited, understanding may have been widespread. Whilst the origins of preventive conservation lie in this period, it is not yet clearly distinguishable as preventive conservation, since the objects are often not distinguished from any other functional objects and there is no differentiation between interventive and preventive measures.

Preventive conservation in Britain – the nineteenth century to the 1990s

The development of rational thought, observation of the natural world and experimentation from the seventeenth century onwards had, amongst other things, led to the foundation of scientific principles and the establishment of museums by the nineteenth century. Collection and classification, initially applied to the natural world, had also been utilised in the study of artefacts of the ancient past, leading to an understanding of human development and the creation of a material and culture classification sequence of the past. This is exemplified by C. J. Thomson's 'Three Age System' (Stone, Bronze and Iron Ages) and Pitt-Rivers' ideas of cultural evolution reflected in artefacts such as weapons (Thompson 1977). By the mid-nineteenth century science was being applied to provide a chemical, physical or biological explanation for the numerous phenomena of the natural world, including the mechanisms of decay. By 1843 Michael Faraday was publishing research into the decay of leather book bindings in the vicinity of gas lamp burners (Caldararo 1987), whilst in 1861 Brewster and in 1880 Fowler had published papers on glass decay. In 1888 Russell and Abney studied the effect of light on watercolours and by 1921 Alexander Scott had identified acetic acid as the cause of active corrosion of lead (Bradley, S. 2002: 3) and was aware that lead white was blackened by the presence of sulphurous gases (Lee and Thickett 1996: 3). These observations emphasised how damaging the gaseous environment could be to works of art, a topic which was also highlighted in the parliamentary enquiry of 1853 into the cleaning of pictures in the National Gallery. An awareness of the damaging effect of the atmosphere was not new. Brimblecombe has shown (1977, 1978) that as early as the thirteenth century people were aware of the damaging effect of coal burning. In 1661 Evelyn, in his book *Fumifugium*, could write:

> the weary traveller, at many Miles distance, sooner smells than sees the City to which he repairs. This is that perniscious Smoake which sullyes all her Glory, superinducing a sooty Crust or Furr upon all its lights, spoyling the movables, tarnishing the Plate, Gildings and Furniture, and corroding the very Iron-bars and hardest Stones; and executing more in one year, than exposed to the Aer of her country it could effect in some hundreds . . . Finally it spreads yellowness upon our choicest Pictures and Hangings . . .
>
> (Brimblecombe 1978)

It was, however, the science of the nineteenth and twentieth centuries that provided explanations of how and why gases could damage artefacts. By the late nineteenth century, the deleterious effects of the environment were well understood, with the need to protect artefacts from light, damp and polluting gases being discussed in scientific journals. By the early twentieth century the first books on conserving ancient artefacts, such as Friedrich Rathgen's *The Preservation of Antiquities*, published in 1905 (Gilberg 1987), were starting to appear.

In the mid-nineteenth century the number of museums in Britain had started to increase, due to a growing belief in the benefits of education and self-improvement, and the passing of the Museums Act of 1845, which permitted local authorities to set up museums using local taxes (the rates). Though this led to the collection and protection of many artefacts, preventive conservation practices were not yet widespread because:

- there was a lack of trained personnel; there were no conservators or museum scientists, and curators, who rarely had a background in science, were not trained in artefact care
- there was a lack of resources
- preventive conservation was not considered a high priority for the limited resources available.

Events in the First World War led to a perception that there could be significant damage to national museum collections from aerial bombardment. Both the British Museum and National Gallery moved significant items in their collections into the museum/gallery basements. By 1917 the threat from high-flying Zeppelins and more powerful bombs was growing, so the National Gallery moved part of its collection to the new underground railway station at Aldwych, which was converted, by adding heating and ventilation to reduce the damp, into a store for small and medium-sized paintings (Saunders 1992). Early in 1918 part of the British Museum's collection was moved into the Holborn Post Office Tunnels; again, due to awareness of the risk of damp, electric radiators and ventilation were installed and temperature and relative humidity levels monitored (Caygill 1992). Harold Plenderleith has suggested that, despite these precautions, after the war the discovery of mould, corrosion and soluble salts damaging the collections of the British Museum resulted in the secondment of Dr Alexander Scott of the British Government's Department of Science and Industrial Research to the British Museum during the 1920s, to provide greater scientific input to the preservation of the collections (Plenderleith 1998), and ultimately in the establishment of the British Museum Research Laboratory in 1931.

Scientific work in European museums in the 1930s began to establish the basis for the standards and practices of the present. Thus, work on the moisture content of wood at the National Gallery in London led the building engineer, MacIntyre, to propose 55–60% as ambient RH for the display and storage of wooden artefacts in London. These standards entered the literature, were widely used and frequently quoted (Michalski 1993).

From the 1930s onwards, as a result of the First World War and the Depression, the role of governments and the regulation of populations increased. This led to increasing ownership of collections by the state and encouraged the development of defined standards of care for this public property. Thus, the period can be divided into two: the period before the 1930s and the period after the 1930s.

By the late 1930s, before the outbreak of the Second World War, institutions such as the British Museum and the National Gallery were concerned about the risk of bombing, and made preparations. Consequently, on 24 August 1939, before war was declared on 3 September, the British Museum started packing up its collections and moving them out to country houses such as Broughton (Oxfordshire). Library materials went to the National Library of Wales at Aberystwyth, where a tunnel store in the hillside was just becoming available, and the 'imperishable' antiques went into underground railway tunnel at Aldwych. Careful assessment of the conditions and risks at each venue had led to a selection of the most appropriate objects being moved to the most appropriate locations. At the same time, the National Gallery collection was evacuated to Bangor University and Penrhyn Castle in North Wales, as well as the National Library of Wales at Aberystwyth. In 1940 the collections were further dispersed, to Caernarvon Castle and a county house, 'Plas-yr-Bryn'. Following the intensive bombing of the Blitz, concerns were raised over the safety of all museum and gallery collections stored above ground. For the British Museum, caverns in the Bath stone quarry at Westwood near Corsham were prepared. Influenced by the problems experienced in the First World War, the museum created a stable mid-range RH environment by sealing the stone walls and installing air conditioning equipment, as well a backup system. In late 1941 the British Museum collections were moved from their various locations to this underground store, where they stayed in stable conditions (65–75°F, 60–65% RH) until the end of the war (Caygill 1992). For the

National Gallery, the slate caverns at Manod near Ffestiniog were prepared. A larger entrance was created and brick buildings were constructed within the giant caverns, where the air (a constant 8°C) could be heated to provide constant conditions of 58% RH and 17°C inside the brick buildings. The paintings stayed in this ultra-stable environment until they were returned to London at the end of the war. Impressed with this facility, the National Gallery retained the Manod site ready for evacuation of the collection to the safety of North Wales, if required, throughout the Cold War, until the early 1980s (Saunders 1992). At both Westwood and Manod excellent storage conditions had been created and the possibility of creating 'ideal' storage conditions had been shown to be achievable. Having fought for such conditions, the directors of the British Museum and National Gallery had effectively defined the 'appropriate' standards for the storage of their collections, not a position from which they could easily retreat. Subsequent years were spent trying to bring their own institutions up to those war-time standards.

After the Second World War independence was sought by many former colonies of European countries, and many of the emergent countries in North Africa, South America and Asia started to develop national museums. These continued the trend in the internationalisation of museums that had started in the 1930s. This emergent international museum community had begun to publish articles on aspects of the care and conservation of museum artefacts in the new museum journals such as *The Museums Journal* (UK) (est. 1901), *Museumhinde* (Germany) (est. 1905), *Museum News* (USA) (est. 1924) and *Museion* (Germany) (1927–47) later *Museum* (UNESCO) (1948–). By the 1950s the colonial practices of removing objects from all corners of the world to the great European treasure-house museums had largely ceased and museum staff increasingly found 'recognition' through exhibitions, publications, research and scholarship. Some of these publications related to developments in the care of museum artefacts.

In Britain the development of the welfare state saw a wide range of services and industries brought under state control. These developments were part of a conscious attempt to improve the quality of life for the public as a whole. Legislation such as the Clean Air Act of 1956, which prohibited the burning of coal in densely populated urban areas, was adopted in the UK as part of a series of measures to improve public health. Whilst this had the fortuitous effect of improving the environment surrounding works of art in British cities, other developments of this period, such as modern architecture that utilised large areas of glass, had a detrimental effect on museum artefacts, increasing light levels, RH and temperature fluctuations. Increases in leisure time and education in the 1950s and 1960s brought many people to view museums and historic houses. This resulted in many historic artefacts and artworks being brought into the limelight of display.

Technological developments of the twentieth century also brought mixed blessings. The polymers that had begun to be used in the early twentieth century as adhesives and consolidants for repair of museum artefacts increased in variety and availability after the Second World War. However, many polymers were found to be unstable and potentially damaging to the objects they were supposed to protect. The bulky scientific instruments of the nineteenth and early twentieth centuries used for monitoring and controlling the museum environment were replaced with smaller, reliable instruments, with developments such as the transistor and, later, the integrated circuit/microchip resulting in smaller, cheaper devices. Continued progress in science and technology and the experiences of environmental control at the British Museum and National Gallery in the Second World War led Sue Bradley, writing in 2002, to state 'most of the problems of collection care were elucidated by the 1950s' (Bradley, S. 2002: 3).

Whilst the principles may have been elucidated, there continued to be a lack of knowledgeable staff and a shortage of resources, which ensured that object care continued to remain a low priority. Consequently, implementation of preventive conservation measures remained limited. Only in 1967 did the IIC (the International Institute of Conservation for Historic and Artistic Works, founded in 1950, an international organisation for museum conservators) dedicate a whole conference to Museum Climatology (Thomson 1968). Knowledge in this sector was consolidated and brought to the attention of the wider museum and conservation world through the publication of Garry Thomson's book *The Museum Environment* in 1978. The establishment of Area Museum Services in the UK from 1963 ensured that advice, and monitoring equipment to implement preventive conservation, were available to all smaller and regional museums. The establishment of conservation courses in universities such as Cardiff and Durham in the mid 1970s increased the flow of qualified conservators. The presence of increased numbers of trained curators and conservators in museums encouraged the widespread adoption of standards for light and humidity which emerged from the experiences of British, European and North American Museums in the years after the Second World War. It is, however, Thomson's book, more than any other single measure, which has made a wider museum world aware of what needed to be done to safeguard museum collections.

In summary, in the emergent international museum culture of the twentieth century, preventive conservation was a minor topic until the world wars forced European museums to think seriously about continued preservation of their collections. Developing from the scientific progress of the nineteenth century, awareness of the chemical, physical and biological basis of decay had advanced significantly. The concepts of conservation and preventive conservation had emerged, with recognition of the value of the historic information present within artefacts and an awareness of the need for an ethical approach to their conservation (Caple 2000: 55; Pye 2001: 52). In Britain, it was, arguably, the increase in public ownership of works of art in the nineteenth and twentieth century and the social changes engendered by the world wars that created both the ability and the will to ensure that standards in the preservation of museum collections were developed and implemented. However, at the same time, the vast expansion of the collections and the increased expectation of seeing artefacts on display, created further challenges to the implementation of such standards.

Preventive conservation – 1990s to the present

By the 1980s knowledge of collections care was becoming well established throughout the museum world. A series of appropriate environmental (minima and maxima) levels for humidity and the lighting of different types of museum artefact had been established. This information was being disseminated through Thomson's book and an increasing number of conservators and curators well versed in the literature about preventive conservation were emerging from the university system. Insect problems were receding after several decades of using insecticides, the use of 'archival' materials was increasing and museums invariably had access to light and relative humidity monitoring equipment.

Continued developments in science and technology were, however, leading to an increasing number of new materials and devices. In particular there were considerable developments in the sensitivity and availability of devices for monitoring gases, humidity, light, etc. This increasing ability to monitor a wide range of gases at lower and lower levels inevitably led to suggestions that museums and archives should have clean air environments in which very low levels of pollutant gases were tolerated (Hatchfield 2002: 22–23). Examples include the National Air Filtration Association, which proposed limits for archives of 1ppb (parts per billion) for sulphur dioxide (SO_2), 2.6ppb for nitrogen oxides (NOX), 2ppb for ozone (O_3); whilst the Canadian Conservation Institute (CCI) proposed upper limits for general museum collections of 10ppb for NOX, 5ppb for O_3 and 15ppb for SO_2 (Grzywacz 2006: 109). The most significant technical development which changed the nature of the subject was computers. Initially large and expensive, they failed to have any significant role in museums in the decades after the Second World War. However, by the 1990s computers were sufficiently small and powerful to be present in every museum. Their ability to store and manipulate vast amounts of data meant that it was possible to continuously monitor and acquire data about the museum environment in many locations. Museums went from a situation in the 1950s of often having little or no data on their environments to having too much data by the 1990s. The computer was the tool that enabled museums to both monitor and manage their collections and environment. The large volume of RH and temperature data was not, however, the only problem. The widespread availability of data on RH levels and the constant use of such numbers encouraged those lending objects to request increasingly stringent RH levels. Such stringency articulated the 'value' of their objects, though such requests frequently failed to understand the inherent limitations in measuring and maintaining RH levels (Ashley-Smith et al. 1994). These stringent loan requirements were often not realistic and could not be achieved in the objects' 'home' institutions, let alone the institutions seeking the loans. Some of the specified light levels were also often so low that visitors with less than perfect eyesight could not distinguish the colour or detail in artefacts such as prints, drawings, textiles and manuscripts.

For many museums and heritage organisations the suggested air quality and RH levels were unrealistic, given the costs of the air-purification/air-handling plant required to achieve them and the staff needed to monitor and maintain such environment levels. Also, given the nature of the collections, the nature of the existing historic museum buildings and their internal fixtures and fittings, and the continued requirements for visitor access, many of the polluting gases and RH levels were simply unachievable in practice. An increasing separation of what was technically achievable and what it was realistic and affordable was emerging, and this prompted renewed research into what was really necessary. The question was increasingly why there was so much emphasis placed on measuring and controlling light and RH in very tight terms, when there were many other threats, from disasters such as fires, theft of artefacts, or damage through handling and moving objects between exhibitions.

A museum trying to achieve tight RH control when it lacked a smoke detector was clearly an absurdity. These and other concerns combined to lead to a major change of emphasis in preventive conservation around the mid-1990s.

In 1994 the IIC held its biennial conference in Ottawa, Preventive Conservation: Practice Theory and Research (Roy and Smith 1994). Several of the papers at that conference reflected recent developments in the approach to preventive conservation. Key concerns that have shaped research and practice in preventive conservation from the 1990s onwards have included:

- The need for the many threats to objects to be objectively appraised. This resulted in the quantification of risk and the application of risk analysis methodology to museum objects (Ashley-Smith 1999; Waller 2003). The concept of object 'loss per annum' (Chapter 2) enabled researchers to compare the threat of damage to objects from a wide variety of sources from, light to earthquakes.
- Utilising risk analysis as well as resource information for the full range of threats to artefacts, led to a far more holistic and realistic approach to the subject of preventive conservation. This is exemplified by CCI's *Framework for the Preservation of Museum Collections* (Chapter 1) and the Museum and Galleries Commission's *Levels of Collections Care* (Chapter 35). Most usefully expressed in table form, this has enabled resources to be prioritised to mitigate the greatest threats.
- A recognition that we were not measuring object damage, but the more easily measured quantity of deterioration agent (light level and wavelength, gas concentration, temperature and relative humidity). It was also appreciated that deterioration was a very complex phenomenon which depended on many variables that often acted together synergistically. Thus, the damage to an artefact from light depends not only on the wavelength and intensity of the light but also on the levels of oxygen present, as well as the nature of the recipient material (Chapter 23). Similarly, the damaging effects of polluting gases are often determined by the level of relative humidity (Chapter 18). Thus, measuring one chemical agent to a high level of accuracy is often not the most effective way of assessing the risk of damage to an object.
- Increasing social concerns about the hazards to human health from chemicals. Governments in Europe, North America and elsewhere in the world started to pass legislation banning certain chemicals, reducing exposure to others and, above all, raising awareness about the need to assess the risks from using chemicals. In the UK this was seen in the issuing of the 1986 Control of Pesticide Regulations and the 1994 Control of Substances Hazardous to Health Regulations. These led to significant re-appraisal of the risks to staff and museum collections, especially from fumigation for insect eradication (Chapter 13).
- An increase in the role of management practices, in particular the development of collections management. This led to the adoption of management and information systems, data analysis and the use of project management skills to manage museum activities and seek to exploit collections as a resource. From condition surveys to zonation, these techniques were developed to make best use of the museum's resources (heat, light, expertise) as well as to improve the care of the collection.

- Increased concern over the rights of indigenous peoples and their material culture. This was signalled through the passing of legislation such as the Native Graves Protection and Repatriation Act in 1994 in the USA, the frequently revised Burra Charter (1979–99) in Australia and the Nara Conference on authenticity in 1994. This signified an increasing awareness of other cultures on the part of museums and that other, 'non traditional', ways of looking at artefacts had validity (Chapters 31 and 32). This was also expressed in an increased appreciation of the importance of context in understanding artefacts. Consequently, we have seen far greater efforts being made to preserve archaeological and historic sites 'in situ' in recent years (Chapters 33, 39, 40).

Subsequent work in preventive conservation has embraced these ideas, with many museum scientists, conservators and curators moving from describing preventive conservation through a series of simple maximum limits for relative humidity, light and polluting gases to talking about increasing or reducing risk, using annual exposure limits (an idea from health and safety literature) and the problems of synergistic effects (as one decay agent influences another). This change has been portrayed by Waller and Michalski as a paradigm shift (Waller and Michalski 2004). Preventive conservation in the nineteenth to twenty-first centuries can thus potentially be divided into three eras: nineteenth century to the 1930s, 1930s to 1990s and the 1990s to the present (Table 0.1). The chapters in this reader are either key papers

Table 0.1 Developments in preventive conservation in museums

	Nineteenth and early twentieth century	1930s–1990s	1990s to the present
Light	Natural light provided through windows to view the collection. Some materials which are known to fade, such as textiles, prints and drawings, are kept in drawers or behind curtains, out of direct light.	Guidelines on light levels established. Technology provides accurate means of measuring light levels. Museum lighting is now largely electric, controlled to meet the approved levels as part of drive for professional standards.	Requirements of the visitor are considered increasingly important. Desire for increased visibility of collections leads to use of annual light dose concept. Management of the collection to rotate objects. Fluorescent lights for energy efficiency, plus LED and fibre optics for effect.
Insects	Reaction to insect infestations with large-scale chemical treatment, Arsenic dust or similar toxic insecticides used.	A range of newer chemicals, such as DDT and chlorinated hydrocarbons, replace arsenic. Gaseous fumigants such as phosphine, methyl bromide and ethylene oxide regularly used for complete insect eradication.	Integrated pest management systems developed; continuous monitoring, removal of all sources of succour dissuades insect activity. Eradication achieved through non-chemical anoxia or thermal treatments.

Incorrect humidity	Awareness of avoiding damp; objects located in appropriate areas of the building to minimise risk of mould. Regular cleaning and maintenance. Limited heating in winter means that low RH conditions are rare.	Awareness of the effect of high and low RH. Central heating from the 1960s leads to low RH problems in the winter. The ability to measure RH raises expectations and by the 1990s strict RH limits for loans. Air conditioning used where tight RH control required.	Revised RH limits mean that strict RH limits are rarely necessary. Costs and necessity of air conditioning questioned. Computer-based monitoring of the museum environment makes RH and temperature data increasingly available. Modelling of building microclimates starts.
Disasters (water and fire)	Reaction to individual disasters. Little or no planning until Second World War. Establishment of the emergency services reduces loss of life and property. Watchmen widely used.	Fire alarms and smoke detectors increase detection. Professional emergency services and improved fire resistance of materials and building designs by the 1980s reduce fire damage. Disaster/emergency planning established.	Disaster/emergency planning becomes the norm, proactive managed approaches to emergencies developed. Prohibiting smoking in public buildings, increased safety of electrical devices and use of earth-leakage circuit breakers reduces the number of fires.
Security	Museum objects have low value and are thus rarely taken, little security needed. Museum attendants and watchmen provide deterrents.	Museum object values rise sharply. Alarms installed in all museums and galleries. Some objects stolen to order, but the major increase is in opportunistic crime.	CCTV increasingly used, replacing attendants. Security sometimes high but focused on high-value items. Opportunistic crime continues.
Gases and Dust	Dust equated with a lack of care, so objects dusted and cleaned as a social norm. Deleterious effects of gases from burning gas and coal known to some, but lack of alternative heating sources means coal burning continues.	Damaging effects of a wider range of gases on museum objects appreciated. Problems created by some new polymers for museum materials emerge. Materials testing develops. In 1956 Clean Air Act reduces SO_2 and dust levels in Britain. Car pollution emerges as a problem.	Gas and dust monitoring increasingly used. Increasing use of safer materials, e.g. polyester sleeves, Plastazoate packaging and absorbers, e.g. activated charcoal and molecular sieves. Dust from smoking indoors ceases but NOX pollution levels from cars increase.
Incorrect temperature	Temperatures exclusively for human comfort. No attempt to maintain consistent temperature levels.	Expectations of higher temperatures for human comfort. Raised temperatures increase the season for and range of pests. Low RH levels result from high levels of heating in winter.	Heating still primarily for human comfort. Level of control is higher. Efforts to reduce heating costs. Some limited use of heating to control RH.

Table 0.1 Continued

	Nineteenth and early twentieth century	1930s–1990s	1990s to the present
Direct physical forces	Objects in glass cases, so handling limited. Limited concern over handling, professionals occasionally cavalier. No protection for objects in earthquakes. Limited object movement, since few loans. Levels of care variable.	Objects increasingly handled with gloves, awareness of careful handling and packaging. However, many objects increasingly loaned and travelling long distances. Objects in handling collections and on open display. Precautions against earthquakes. Vandalism increasing.	Greater number of exhibitions means increasing object movement and handling. Increasing protection from earthquakes and transit through improved materials, case and building design.

from this paradigm shift in the mid-1990s or they explore current practice in preventive conservation.

In summary, since the mid-1990s the subject of preventive conservation has started to evolve from simple dos and don'ts into a subject requiring considerable professional judgement where trade-offs and balances are exercised. Annual exposure limits for light are increasingly practised, rather than simple maximum levels. More realistic appraisal of relative humidity levels requires more detailed appraisal of each object and selection of some objects for loan, and not others. The simple minimum and maximum limits have not been abandoned, but they are capable of being traded in for more refined concepts such as 'increasing risk of damage as we approach extreme high or low RH'. Museums are increasingly relying on management systems, processes or procedures to ensure that risks are assessed and minimised. Integrated pest management relies on regular insect trapping, housekeeping and quarantine procedures (Chapters 13 and 14). Environmental control requires regular detailed RH, temperature, particulate and gaseous pollutants levels monitoring, interpretation of the data, analysis of any problems and the ability to change the control systems (Chapter 36). Oddy tests need to be performed for all new storage and display materials (Chapter 17). Increasingly this is a managed system, but all organisations change and all systems eventually fail. As this introduction has already shown, Roman *curators* knew many of the basics of preventive conservation over 2,000 years ago. Given high levels of staff turnover, variable skills, limited resources, short-term project funding, changing priorities and increasing expectations regarding the quality and duration of exhibitions, our ability to manage in the long term is highly questionable. Few management systems last a decade, few organisations last a century, but many of our objects have been in our care for thousands of years. Empires collapse but (some) artefacts endure.

Preventive conservation in the future

From this brief history it is clear that the deleterious effect of pollution, the effects of light or damp on our treasured possessions is not a modern subject that has emerged in the late twentieth century, but has ancient origins. This book has a long line of precedents that stretch back to the Roman Republic. However, the advent of scientific explanation in the nineteenth century moved the subject from one of empirical observation of cause and effect, to a science in which the exact chemical, physical and biological mechanisms of decay were identified. Since the 1990s preventive conservation has started to focus on a holistic approach, identifying the greatest threat and seeking to reduce it. Considered optimistically, museums may be slowly coming to grips with the preventive conservation problems presented by their present collections. Some of the next generation of ideas that will affect preventive conservation practice are already starting to emerge. These include:

- Predictive modelling of systems such as building environments (air movements and thermal masses) and their fluctuation over time. This is increasingly being done for historic building such as the Sistine Chapel or the Chiericati Palace (Bernardi and Camuffo 1995), in an effort to explore in what ways it is possible to minimise harmful effects such as condensation on windows, or high relative humidity and mould growth behind pictures, furniture or panelling. This detailed modelling relies in gathering large volumes of data from known conditions to construct a mathematical model which mimics the reactions of a building and its contents. Then the reactions to a series of proposed conditions are generated. Predictive modelling has already been used to explore likely changes in the planet's climate and postulate what effects these climate changes will have on the heritage (Chapter 42). This should enable mitigation measures to be planned well in advance, but raises problematic ethical and resource issues. Predictive modelling can also be adapted to consider risk and explore the levels of risk associated with small changes within the museum – even an individual object being moved from one wall of a gallery to another (Waller and Michalski 2004).
- The preservation of chemical, microscopic physical and biological evidence, such as DNA (Chapter 41), which is not visually obvious but which contains crucial information about the past is a new challenge for preventive conservation. Strategies will need to be found for identifying artefacts rich in the microscopic and molecular information, and effective preventive conservation methods will need to be developed for preserving it. This could require visually intrusive methodologies, such as freezing, which are not compatible with display. There is potentially a widening gulf in the requirements for preservation and display, especially display in more extreme 'in context' or 'in situ' locations. This problem already exists for many 'working' objects and open-air museums, such as Beamish. Working objects, such as Stephenson's *Rocket*, have been incorporated into several restorations, and the point has now been reached where the original material is no longer discernible. This loss of such valuable research material is of great concern (Mann 1994), as one aim of heritage (display/education) has obscured the other (research). Although we have many working examples of aircraft from the Second World War, such as the Spitfire, we increasingly lack any untouched examples, so how will we answer research questions about the materials and technology of the Second World War in the future? The solution requires that two objects are saved, one preserved as historic record, stored for future

investigation and research purposes, the second used for active display and capable of being restored.

Each generation values its museum collections in slightly different ways. The symbols of a conquered society, the aesthetic values of classical civilisations, the evidence of human development, and now the microscopic traces of use and the intangible beliefs and meanings associated with artefacts. Preventive conservation adapts to care for museum collections so as to ensure all aspects of the artefacts that society values are preserved. It also responds to improvements in technology, developments in social attitudes, transformations in organisation, reductions in resources and even alterations in the climate. As these change, so does preventive conservation.

Note

1   In this introduction I focus on archaeological and historic artefacts. Similar arguments can be advanced for the application of preventive conservation to all types of collected material; natural history specimens, works of art, devices or specimens for illustrating scientific principals or natural phenomena. In fact, anything that has an attribute which a society or an individual considers worthy of collection and curation, regardless of whether in a museum, mansion, house, hut or home.

     I also focus on the development of preventive conservation in the UK within an international context. Though many aspects of this history will be similar for other countries, the social, political and economic realities of each country will have determined the extent to which preventive conservation is practised within that country.

     The terms 'artefact' (anything made by human artifice, from a building to scratches made on a piece of bone) and 'object' (a physical entity, normally one capable of presentation, e.g. in a museum) are used interchangeably. Which is the most familiar depends on the culture from which you come or the academic tradition in which you have studied.

References

Abey-Koch, M. (1996) 'History of Housekeeping', in National Trust, *Manual of Housekeeping*, London: Butterworth-Heinemann.

Ashley-Smith, L. Umney, N. and Ford, D. (1994) 'Let's be Honest – Realistic Environmental Parameters for Loaned Objects', in A. Roy and P. Smith (eds), *Preventive Conservation: Practice, Theory and Research, IIC Ottawa Congress 12–16 September 1994*, Ottawa: IIC.

Ashley-Smith, J. (1999) *Risk Assessment for Object Conservation*, Oxford: Butterworth-Heinemann.

Bernardi, A. and Camuffo, D. (1995) 'Microclimate in the Chiericati Palace Municipal Museum, Vicenza', *Museum Management and Curatorship* 14: 1, 5–18.

Bradley, R. (2002) *The Past in Prehistoric Societies*, London: Routledge.

Bradley, S. (2002) 'Preventive Conservation: The Research Legacy', in J. Townsend, K. Eremin and A. Adriaens (eds) *Conservation Science 2002*, London: Archetype Publications.

Brimblecombe, P. (1977) 'London Air Pollution 1500–1900', *Atmospheric Environment* 11: 1157–1162.

Brimblecombe, P. (1978) 'Interest in Air Pollution among Early Fellows of the Royal Society', *Notes and Records of the Royal Society of London* 32: 123–129.

Caldararo, N. L. (1987) 'An Outline History of Conservation in Archaeology and Anthropology as Presented through its Publications', *Journal of the American Institute for Conservation* 26(2): 85–104.

Campbell, L. (1998) 'The Conservation of Netherlandish Paintings in the Fifteenth and Sixteenth Centuries', in C. Sitwell and S. Staniforth (eds) *Studies in the History of Painting Restoration*, London: Archetype Publications.

Caple, C. (2000) *Conservation Skills: Judgement, Method and Decision Making*, London: Routledge.

Caple, C. (2006) *Objects: Reluctant Witnesses to the Past*, Abingdon: Routledge.

Caygill, M. (1992) 'The Protection of National Treasures at the British Museum during the First World and Second World Wars', in P. Vandiver, J. Druzik, G. Wheeler and I. Freestone (eds), *Materials Issues in Art and Archaeology III*, Pittsburgh: Metals Research Society.

Getty Conservation Institute (1992) 'Preventive Conservation', *GCI Newsletter* 7(1): 4–7.

Gilberg, M. (1987) 'Friedrich Rathgen: The Father of Modern Archaeological Conservation', *Journal of the American Institute for Conservation* 26(2): 105–120.

Grzywacz, C. M. (2006) *Monitoring for Gaseous Pollutants in Museum Environments*, Los Angeles: Getty Conservation Institute.

Hatchfield, P. B. (2002) *Pollutants in the Museum Environment*, London: Archetype.

Hicks, H. (1988) 'Early Approaches to the Conservation of Works of Art on Paper', in V. Daniels (ed.) *Early Advances in Conservation*, British Museum Occasional Papers No. 65, London: British Museum Press.

Hinton, D. A. (2005) *Gold and Gilt, Pots and Pin*, Oxford: OUP.

Haug, A. (2001) 'Constituting the Past – Forming the Present: The Role of Material Culture in the Augustinian Period', *Journal of the History of Collections* 13(2): 111–123.

Jones, A. (2007) *Memory and Material Culture*, Cambridge: CUP.

Lee, L. and Thickett, D. (1996) *Selection of Materials for the Storage or Display of Museum Objects*, British Museum Occasional Paper 111, London: British Museum Press.

Marsh, G. (1981) 'London's Samian Supply and its Relationship to the Development of the Gallic Samian Industry', in A. Anderson and A. Anderson (eds), *Roman Pottery Research in Britain and North West Europe* (BAR Int. Ser. 123i), Oxford: British Archaeological Reports.

Mann, P. (1994) 'The Restoration of Vehicles for Use in Research, Exhibition, and Demonstration', in A. Oddy (ed.) *Restoration: Is It Acceptable?* British Museum Occasional Paper No. 99, London: British Museum Press.

Michalski, S. (1993) 'Relative Humidity: A Discussion of Correct/Incorrect Values', in *ICOM-CC 10th Triennial Meeting, Washington, DC, USA*: 624–629.

Nissan, K. (1999) 'The Sword and its Scabbard', in O. Owen and M. Dalland (eds), *Scar: A Viking Boat Burial on Sanday, Orkney*, East Linton: Tuckwell Press.

Plenderleith, H. J. (1998) 'A History of Conservation', *Studies in Conservation* 43(3): 129–143.

Pye, E. (2001) *Caring for the Past*, London: James & James.

Rackham, H. (trans) (1968) *Pliny's Natural History*, London: Heinemann.

Rowlands, M. (1993) 'The Role of Memory in the Transmission of Culture', *World Archaeology* 25(2): 141–151.

Roy, A. and Smith, P. (eds) (1994) *Preventive Conservation: Practice, Theory and Research, IIC Ottawa Congress 12–16 September 1994*, Ottawa: IIC.

Saunders, D. (1992) 'The National Gallery at War', in P. Vandiver, J. Druzik, G. Wheeler and I. Freestone (eds), *Materials Issues in Art and Archaeology III*, Pittsburgh: Metals Research Society.

Strong, D. E. (1973) 'Roman Museums', in D. E. Strong (ed.) *Archaeological Theory and Practice*, London: Seminar Press.

Thomas, A. (1998) 'Restoration or Renovation: Remuneration and Expectation in Renaissance "Acconciatura"', in C. Sitwell and S. Staniforth (eds) *Studies in the History of Painting Restoration*, London: Archetype Publications.

Thomson, G. (ed.) (1968) *1967 London Conference on Museum Climatology*, London: IIC.

Thomson, G. (1978) *The Museum Environment*, London: Butterworth.

Thompson, M. W. (1977) *General Pitt-Rivers*, Bradford on Avon: Moonraker Press.

Tweddle, D. (1992) *The Anglian Helmet from 16–22 Coppergate*, The Archaeology of York 17/8. London: CBA.

Waller, R. (2003) *Cultural Property Risk Analysis Model, Development and Application to Preventive Conservation at the Canadian Museum of Nature*, Goteborg: Acta Universitatis Gothoburgensis.

Waller, R. and Michalski, S. (2004) 'Effective Preservation: From Reaction to Prediction', *Getty Conservation Institute Newsletter* 19(1) (Spring 2004): 1–4.

Ward, R. (1993) 'A Survey of the Samian Ware from Excavations at Piercebridge', *Journal of Roman Pottery Studies* 6: 15–22.

White, R. (1988) *Roman and Celtic Objects from Anglo-Saxon Graves: A Catalogue and an Interpretation of Their Use*, BAR(British Series) 161, Oxford: British Archaeological Reports.

White, R. (1990) 'Scrap or Substitute: Roman Material in Anglo-Saxon Graves', in E. Southworth (ed.) *Anglo-Saxon Cemeteries: A Reappraisal*, Stroud: Alan Sutton Publishing.

Willmott, H. (2001) 'A Group of 17th Century Glass Goblets with Restored Stems: Considering the Archaeology of Repair', *Post Medieval Archaeology* 35: 96–105.

PART ONE

Holistic Approach to Preventive Conservation

Introduction to Part One

Chris Caple

Holistic approach to preventive conservation

AS THE CANADIAN CONSERVATION Institute (CCI) sought to support Canadian museums in caring for their collections, it was concerned that the risks of object damage and loss were not being properly evaluated. Too often museums, following the emphasis in the literature and on museum courses, focused their limited resources on measuring temperature and humidity rather than on installing smoke detectors or basic security measures. Fire and theft were in reality far greater threats to the museum collection than changes in temperature or relative humidity. This led Stephan Michalski and the CCI staff to create a framework for the preservation of museum collections; a 9 row x 7 column table in which threats (direct physical forces; thieves, vandals and displacers; fire; water; pests; contaminants; radiations; incorrect temperature; incorrect humidity) were cross-referenced against the museum situation (in storage; on display; in transit). Each cell in the table addressed the threat in each situation with actions to be taken to avoid, block, detect, respond to or recover from the threat.

This table was developed circa 1992/93 and, in bringing all the threats together, focused Canadian museums on a much more holistic approach to preventive conservation. This approach and CCI's framework were widely promoted in the mid-1990s (Costain 1994) (Chapter 1) and have had a significant impact, even to the point of suggesting the format for this and other books on preventive conservation. They promoted a far more pragmatic approach by museums, curators and conservators to threats to their collections. It is, however, not the whole story. The table does not assess the level of threat, it does not rate the extent or nature of deterioration and it does not look at the loss of value of the object. It is also somewhat idealised, suggesting that the museum can 'provide a conservation laboratory to treat damaged artefacts'; it does, however, provide a good starting-point.

In seeking to compare the extent of damage from gradual threats (light, relative humidity, gaseous pollutants, dust), episodic threats (insect attack) and occasional catastrophic threats (fire, flood), conservators such as Jonathan Ashley-Smith (1997) (Chapter 2) and Rob Waller (2003) found that the ideas, language and mathematical models of risk analysis provided the most appropriate mechanism. A series of important concepts emerged from their work:

- value of an object – recognising that damage reduces value of various types (Ashley-Smith 1999: Chapter 4)
- annual loss rate – which enables very different forms of object decay (gradual, periodic, occasional) affecting numerous different types of material to be compared, through using this single unit of damage/loss of value
- the use of decision trees and cost-benefit analysis as a means of decision making and resource allocation.

The concept and language of risk are being increasingly adopted by the practitioners of preventive conservation. In the foreseeable future the materials-decay information obtained by scientists will be incorporated with the object-loss data generated by conservators to provide increasingly accurate appreciation of the risk of object damage for curators and conservators to use in assigning the resources for object care and assessing the risks associated with actions such as loaning objects (Waller and Michalski 2004).

References

Ashley-Smith, J. (1999) *Risk Assessment for Object Conservation*, Oxford: Butterworth-Heinemann.

Ashley-Smith, J. (1997) 'Risk Analysis', in S. Bradbury (ed.), *The Interface Between Science and Conservation*, British Museum Occasional Paper No. 116. London: British Museum Press, pp. 123–132.

Costain, C. (1994) 'Framework for Preservation of Museum Collections', *CCI Newsletter* 14: 1–4.

Waller, R. (2003) *Cultural Property Risk Analysis Model, Development and Application to Preventive Conservation at the Canadian Museum of Nature*, Goteborg: Acta Universitatis Gothoburgensis.

Waller, R. and Michalski, S. (2004) Effective Preservation: From Reaction to Prediction, *Getty Conservation Institute Newsletter* 19(1) Spring: 1–4.

Chapter 1

Framework for Preservation of Museum Collections

Charlie Costain

A CHART ENTITLED "Framework for Preservation of Museum Collections" (Table 1.1) has been developed by the Environment and Deterioration Research Division of CCI. It is intended to assist conservators, collection managers, and other museum professionals in assessing the threats to their collections.

The chart was initially developed by Stefan Michalski to help individuals assess the dangers to their collections objectively. Since the 1960s, conservators have been concerned about the museum environment, in particular about relative humidity, light levels, pollution, and temperature. Pests are also a concern, but often are considered separately from environmental factors. However, none of these factors had traditionally been grouped with other serious threats to a collection, such as breakage, theft, fire, or water damage. This incongruity became apparent when CCI staff were carrying out "environmental surveys" of museums; there were some museums that had purchased hygrothermographs when they had no smoke or fire detectors, or that were concerned about ultraviolet light when they had inadequate locks on the museum doors.

The "Framework for Preservation of Museum Collections" consists of a 9 row by 7 column matrix. Along the left-hand side of the chart, various threats to museum collections are grouped into nine agents of deterioration: direct physical forces; thieves, vandals, and displacers; fire; water; pests; contaminants; radiation; incorrect temperature; and incorrect relative humidity. The type of museum object that is vulnerable to each agent is identified, along with the type of damage that can occur. The columns outline methods of control that can be carried out at each of three different levels or scales: the building (architectural or engineering elements), portable fittings (items or modifications that are generally purchased on an operating budget), and procedures (actions that

Source: *CCI Newsletter* No. 14 (1994), pp. 1–4 and Canadian Conservation Institute, *Framework for Preservation of Museum Collections* (a poster) (Ottawa, CCI, 1994).

can be carried out by museum staff). Control at the building or portable fittings level is further broken down into actions that are suitable for storage, display, or transit situations. Each cell of the matrix lists stages for controlling an agent of deterioration under five general headings: avoid, block, detect, respond, and recover/treat.

In this article, I will restrict my discussion to the principal agents of deterioration that are outlined in the Framework, and will discuss some examples of how the Framework might be used.

Agents of deterioration

The nine agents of deterioration group together various active agents that threaten museum collections. The relative order of importance of these agents was generally determined by the severity of damage that each inflicts on an object and by the overall likelihood of this damage occurring. The actual order of importance of the agents may differ for a given institution or for a particular situation.

Direct physical forces can be either sudden and catastrophic or long term and gradual. Sudden damage usually results from a shock to the artifact while it is being handled or moved, during collapse of shelving or supports, or as a result of earthquakes or war. Long-term exposure to some force may result in the deformation of an object, and may be due to inadequate support in display or storage or to artifacts having been stacked. Vibration can also cause damage to artifacts in the short term or the long term, depending on the circumstances. The most common damages in this category result from improper handling procedures, and the type of damage varies from complete loss of the artifact to minor damage that can be repaired. Most museum artifacts are vulnerable to this type of direct physical force.

Most of the risks in the category of *thieves, vandals, and displacers* are traditionally covered by museum security services in large institutions. Thieves obviously are a great concern because museum objects have a high value, their location and existence are well known, and if an object is stolen the loss is total. Vandals tend to attack high-profile or noticeable items, and often inflict severe damage. The agent "displacers" addresses the problem of artifacts that are misplaced within the museum; this is usually done inadvertently by staff members in storage areas. If an artifact or specimen has been misplaced and cannot be found, the effect is the same as a theft.

Fire obviously poses a threat to all museum collections, although organic artifacts are particularly vulnerable. In addition, smoke from fires poses a particular threat, especially to porous specimens. Although fires are infrequent, they result in massive loss and extensive damage.

Water is a major threat to museum collections because of leaking roofs, skylights, or water pipes. Flooding or fire suppression equipment may also cause water damage. Porous organic materials, metals, and composite materials (i.e. materials that are layered or joined) are particularly susceptible to water damage. In addition, many artifacts have some component that is wholly or partially soluble in water.

There is an obvious relationship between the risks from the threat of fire and the risks of water damage from having a sprinkler fire suppression system. Although the risk of a sprinkler malfunction may be greater than that of a fire, the damage caused by a fire is much more extensive and devastating to the collection than that caused by water. The Fire Protection Advisor at Heritage Services, CCI, who has inspected hundreds of museums and has seen the results of a number of museum fires, strongly recommends installing sprinkler systems.

The agent of *pests* includes attack by insects, vermin, or mould. The threat here is primarily to organic materials, which can be damaged either because they are a food source to the pest or because they represent a barrier that the pest wants to cross. Damage can be extensive if pests become established (i.e. begin to live, eat, excrete, and die) in the museum collection. Problems with mould and microbes are related to problems with relative humidity.

Contaminants is the term used to describe chemical agents from the museum environment that can cause some alteration of museum objects. Contaminants can be in the form of gases, liquids, or solids. Gaseous contaminants are frequently considered to be pollutants, although the source of the gas may be external industrial and vehicle emissions (e.g. sulphur dioxide or nitrogen dioxide), gases emitted by materials within the museum (e.g. vapours given off by wood, coatings, or other artifacts), or oxygen present in the atmosphere. Liquids that might contaminate museum objects include plasticizers migrating from plastics, and grease deposited by improper handling. The most common solid contaminants are salt (either airborne or from handling) and dust. Contaminants can result in complete destruction of an artifact over a prolonged period of time, but more often result in some disfigurement of the artifact.

Radiation includes ultraviolet and visible light. Ultraviolet radiation can cause disintegration and discolouration of the outer layers of organic objects, and visible light can cause fading (or, less often, darkening) of the outer layers of coloured components in artifacts. Ultraviolet light is not necessary for humans to view museum objects, and so should be avoided or eliminated in museum display and storage areas. Some visible light is necessary to allow visitors to see objects on display, but this must be balanced against the stability of the colorants in the objects. Fugitive colorants will change noticeably after just a few years of display, even if they are displayed at low light levels (50 lux). Light damage will not cause complete physical destruction of an artifact, but can affect the relevance of or the interest in an object and can reduce its value considerably. Discolouration caused by light damage cannot be repaired or reversed.

Temperature is a measure of a physical property and by itself cannot directly cause damage to museum objects. However, damage to museum collections does result from *incorrect temperatures*, which can be broken down into three different types: temperatures that are too high, too low, or fluctuating. High temperature can result in accelerated degradation rates of chemically unstable components, low temperature can cause embrittlement of some materials, and fluctuating temperatures can cause materials to fracture or delaminate. Although temperature levels within museums are usually dictated by human comfort levels, low-temperature storage areas are used for certain unstable artifacts such as colour photographs. Temperature can be very important in determining the useful life of chemically unstable artifacts such as photographic films and acidic paper.

Incorrect relative humidity can be broken down into four subgroups: damp (over 75%), above or below a critical value, above 0%, and fluctuations. Mould growth can occur when the relative humidity is over about 75%, and certain minerals or contaminated metals deteriorate above or below critical relative humidity values. Some chemical deterioration reactions slow as the relative humidity is reduced, and stop when the relative humidity drops to 0%. Relative humidity fluctuations cause swelling or shrinkage of organic components, which can result in fracture, crushing, or delamination of organic components. Although incorrect relative humidity can result in considerable damage to vulnerable artifacts, in most cases it does not lead to complete destruction of artifacts.

We have found the "Framework for Preservation of Museum Collections" to be an extremely useful tool in assessing the risks posed by particular situations. The Framework's usefulness is not only due to its comprehensive nature, but also because it identifies potential areas of risk rather than directly identifying deficiencies.

Example 1

Consider a hypothetical situation where a large gallery receives a loan request from a small community museum nearby for a series of graphite pencil sketches on white rag paper that are of particular historical significance to the district. To make the situation more interesting, suppose that the director of the large gallery would like to agree to the loan but the curator involved has grave concerns about the risks to the works of art, and that the conservator is receiving subtle pressure from both sides. One method of resolving this predicament would be for the conservator to meet with the responsible person from the requesting institution and to use the Framework to describe the range of potential dangers to the works of art, identify the agents of deterioration that are pertinent in this situation, and then find ways of reducing the risks.

If the large institution is concerned about direct physical damage occurring during transit and handling, it may be possible to arrange for staff from the large museum to deliver and install the works. Security will clearly be a major concern, so arrangements must be made for securing the museum building, for exhibiting the works (i.e. display case, alarms), and for the presence of security personnel. Concerns about fire suppression, leaky roofs, and pest control will have to be discussed. Because the works in question are on untinted rag paper and are in stable condition, light levels are not a major concern within the range of 50 lux to 300 lux, as long as the ultraviolet component is filtered out. A discussion of the temperature and relative humidity within the borrowing museum shows that the temperature control is moderately good (between 18°C and 24°C), but that the relative humidity can only be maintained at 25%. Because the works are properly hinged and matted and because no thick paints are present, this will not pose any serious risk. Therefore, it may turn out that the only major risk that needs to be addressed is security. Further discussion between the borrowing institution, the reluctant curator, the director, the conservator, and possibly a security expert may be necessary to determine whether or not this risk can be safely controlled. No matter what the outcome, at least the decision will have been made on a factual, rational basis that can be clearly understood by all involved.

Example 2

Museums are under increasing pressure to allow more public access to their collections. The Framework may be useful in addressing the risks involved with this access.

Let us consider another hypothetical situation where a curator is planning to include a number of pieces of nineteenth- and twentieth-century furniture in a public session to let members of the public interact more closely with the collection. In addition to security and transit concerns, there may be an increased risk of artifacts being broken and contaminated (i.e. soiled) due to improper or unauthorized handling. Also, in this case, it is possible that a number of the pieces are quite vulnerable to relative humidity fluctuations, in which case humidity control is essential. All of these considerations may result in a decision to have the public session take place in an available gallery within the museum rather than in some outside location.

Conclusion

The nine agents of deterioration outlined on the "Framework for Preservation of Museum Collections" make up a comprehensive list of the various situations that can threaten museum, gallery, or archival collections. CCI staff members have found the Framework to be an extremely useful tool for identifying risks to museum collections and for suggesting appropriate methods of control.

Table 1.1 Framework for Preservation of Heritage Collections

The "Framework for Preservation of Heritage Collections" outlines various methods that can be used to avoid or control potential deterioration to museum objects.

    The rows list nine agents of deterioration that affect museum objects, and include the type of damage that each can cause. The first five agents (direct physical forces; thieves, vandals, displacers; fire; water; and pests) are widespread throughout the world. The last four agents (contaminants; radiation; incorrect temperature; and incorrect relative humidity) are of particular concern to museums. The agents are listed in rough order of importance according to their potential for damaging artifacts. Each term chosen describes a destructive agent. For example, "temperature" in and of itself does not cause damage, but "incorrect temperature" does.

    The columns present three different levels at which the agents of deterioration can be controlled: Building Features, Portable Fittings, and Procedures. Building Features and Portable Fittings are listed separately because they usually have different budgets and personnel, and because they are dealt with at different times in the life of a museum. Building Features and Portable Fittings are further subdivided by location of artifacts: on display, in storage, or in transit. The Procedures column outlines actions that can be taken by staff or contractors once the building features and portable fittings are in place.

    It may not be necessary or feasible for every museum to implement all of the control measures. Each museum must decide on the most effective combination for its particular collection, purpose, and resources.

    Each square within the matrix is broken down into five stages: Avoid, Block, Detect, Respond, and Recover/Treat. These stages are indicated within each square by the appropriate initial: A., B., D., R., and R.T. They are listed in decreasing order of preference. If an agent is successfully avoided, it will not have to be blocked, detected, responded to, or recovered from. If, however, an agent of deterioration cannot be avoided or blocked, then the other stages must come into play. The first four stages constitute preventive conservation. The last stage of recovery or treatment involves repair, conservation, and restoration of the affected artifact.

A. Avoid
Each agent of deterioration has the potential to harm museum objects. Therefore, sources and attractants of each agent must be avoided. It is always preferable, but not always possible, to avoid the agent rather than having to deal with it and with its consequences by other means of control.

B. Block
"Block" is frequently the most practical stage of control. If an agent cannot be avoided, then it should be prevented from reaching or affecting artifacts. For example, fire walls and compartments block fire, exclusion methods can be used to block pests, and vapour barriers block moisture and contaminants.

Table 1.1 Continued

Enclosures have special significance for museums. The building enclosure can be designed in such a way that it not only blocks fire, criminals, and water, but also pests, outside contaminants, UV and unnecessary light, incorrect temperature, and incorrect relative humidity. Portable enclosures such as cases, cabinets, crates, boxes, bags, and bottles are just as important as building features for blocking agents from reaching individual artifacts.

D. Detect

If an agent of deterioration has not been avoided or blocked, then its presence will have to be detected within the collection, either directly or by its effects. For example, one can detect either the source of direct physical forces or the new damage caused by them.

Regular inspection of the collection is necessary to detect new damage early. The frequency of inspections depends on the rate and risk of each agent. For example, constant monitoring is required to detect fire and criminals as soon as they are present because they act quickly and are major risks to the collection. However, only periodic monitoring is necessary to detect slower agents, such as pests and contaminants, or agents that do not present as great a risk, such as small water leaks.

R. Respond

Once the agent's presence has been detected, action must be taken. Establish response strategies in advance. Appropriate response time depends on the rate and risk of the agent. Minutes count when responding to fire or criminals, but museum staff may have a day or more before having to respond to damage by water, pests, or damp. Continue response activities until the agent is eliminated.

R.T. Recover/Treat

If all attempts at controlling damage from an agent of deterioration fail, then steps must be taken to recover from this damage by treating the affected artifacts. Usually, this involves cleaning, consolidation, and repair. However, much damage is impossible to undo. Some museum collections include the building. When damaged, new buildings and facilities may be repaired or rebuilt, but rebuilding is a less acceptable or feasible option with historic buildings. In all cases, it is better to establish control strategies so that this stage is never reached.

Framework for preservation			
Agents of deterioration (affect particular artifacts in specific ways)	**Building features** (include features that are permanently attached to or that are part of the main structure of the building)		
	Storage	Display	Transit
Direct Physical Forces (shock, vibration, abrasion, and gravity) *Cumulative* (improper handling or support/ *Cumulative* (e.g. earthquake, war, floor collapse, improper handling): • break, distort, dent, scratch, and/or abrade all types of artifacts.	A. Avoid areas of high seismic activity. Avoid building on soft, loose soils. Ensure adequate floor strength, smooth and soft interior wall finish, and adequate access. B. Construct earthquake-resistant buildings. Ensure adequate space for collection storage.	A. As for storage. B. As for storage. D. As for storage. R. As for storage. R.T. n/a	A. As for storage, plus ensure smooth floor surfaces; smooth ramps; and slow, smooth lifts. B. Allow adequate space for unloading. Install impact-absorbing perimeter around doors (e.g. rubber surround). D. n/a R. n/a R.T. n/a

	D. Leave adequate space to allow for inspection of artifacts. R. n/a R.T. Provide a conservation laboratory to treat damaged artifacts.		
Thieves, Vandals, Displacers *Intentional* (criminals): • steal small or portable artifacts. • disfigure valuable, popular, or symbolic artifacts. *Unintentional* (staff, users): • lose or misplace any type of artifact.	A. Avoid high-risk building sites. B. Block access by having a strong roof and strong exterior and interior walls. Have an open perimeter, no hidden entrances, and study areas outside storage areas to deter intruders or displacers. D. Detect intruders by ensuring clear sight lines and appropriate lighting. R. Provide offices and security posts for security staff. R.T. n/a	A. n/a B. Block entry with strong/barred windows and strong walls. Provide secure walls, ceilings, and doors. D. Detect intruders or displacers by ensuring clear lines of sight. R. Include offices and security posts for security staff. R.T. n/a	A. n/a B. Block entry by enclosing and securing loading bay. D. Establish security post to detect intruders or displacers. R. n/a R.T. n/a
Fire • destroys, scorches, or deposits smoke on all types of artifacts, particularly those that contain organic materials.	A. Avoid work areas or unnecessary electricity in collections areas. Store flammable liquids in a separate storage area. B. Block spread of fire with fire-resistant structural elements, compartments, and fire separations. Use smoke-control systems. D. n/a R. Install sprinkler system with automatic shut-off and with protective cages around heads (preferably a pre-action system). R.T. Provide a conservation laboratory to treat damaged artifacts.	A. Avoid unnecessary electricity in display areas. B. Block fire with fire-resistant compartments of moderate size. Install smoke-control systems. D. n/a R. Install sprinkler system with automatic shut-off and with protective cages around heads (preferably a pre-action system). R.T. n/a	A. n/a. B. n/a D. n/a R. Use fire suppression systems in loading bay that are designed for fires involving vehicles and shipping materials. R.T. n/a

Table 1.1 Continued

Water			
• causes efflorescence or tide marks in porous materials. • swells organic materials • corrodes metals. • dissolves some materials (e.g. glue). • delaminates, tents, and/or buckles layered components of an artifact. • loosens, fractures, or corrodes joined components of an artifact. • shrinks tightly woven textiles or canvases.	A. Avoid sites within flood plains and floors below ground level. Provide a reliable, pitched roof. Route plumbing around collection areas (use a services corridor). B. Block water with watertight floors that have drains. Provide dams around mechanical rooms. Build in drains for every floor. D. n/a R. Allocate space to store emergency supplies for floods. R.T. Provide a conservation laboratory to treat damaged artifacts.	A. As for storage, plus avoid skylights. B. n/a D. n/a R. Allocate space close to display area to store emergency supplies for floods. R.T. n/a	A. Avoid locating loading bay area below grade. B. Ensure adequate drains in loading bay. D. n/a R. n/a R.T. n/a
Pests *Insects:* • consume, perforate, cut, graze, tunnel, and/or excrete, which destroys, weakens, disfigures, or etches materials, especially furs, feathers, skins, insect collections, textiles, paper, and wood. *Vermin, birds, and other animals:* • gnaw organic materials and displace smaller items. • foul artifacts with faeces and urine. • gnaw through or foul inorganic materials if they present an obstacle to reaching the organic material. *Mould and microbes* (see also "Incorrect Relative Humidity, Damp"): • weaken or stain organic and inorganic materials.	A. Avoid creating pest habitats inside and outside the building. Contain and isolate food and garbage areas. Use non-attractant lighting. B. Use mineral and metal building fabric. Pay attention to seal details. Establish separate HVAC zones for eating areas and workshops. Maintain sanitary perimeters. D. Provide a quarantine room for incoming artifacts. R. Keep all spaces easily accessible to simplify pest control. Provide space for pest control equipment (e.g. freezer, fumigator). R.T. Provide a conservation laboratory to treat damaged artifacts.	A. Avoid creating pest habitats. Contain and isolate food and garbage areas. B. As for storage. D. n/a R. Keep all spaces easily accessible to simplify pest control. R.T. As for storage.	A. Avoid garbage in loading bay. Provide an exterior site for garbage. B. Pay attention to seal details around loading bay door and interior access doors. Have loading area on separate HVAC zone. D. Provide an adequate quarantine room close to loading bay. R. n/a R.T. n/a

Contaminants *Indoor and outdoor gases* (e.g. pollution, oxygen) / *Liquids* (e.g. plasticizer, grease) / *Solids* (e.g. dust, salt): • disintegrate, discolour, or corrode all artifacts, especially reactive or porous materials.	A. Avoid locations with high pollution or dust and with high local emissions (e.g. roadways). Avoid building materials that are sources of contaminants. B. Block external contaminants with an airtight building. Have separate ventilation to smoking areas and parking facilities. Filter fresh air intake. D. n/a R. Recirculate and filter air. R.T. Provide a conservation laboratory to treat damaged artifacts.	A. As for storage. B. As for storage. D. As for storage. R. As for storage. R.T. As for storage.	A. n/a B. Block contaminants with an adequate extraction system for vehicle exhaust. D. n/a R. n/a R.T. n/a
Radiation *Ultraviolet:* • disintegrates, fades, darkens, and/or yellows the outer layer of organic materials and some coloured inorganic materials. *Unnecessary light:* • fades or darkens the outer opaque layer of paints and wood to a typical depth of 10 µm to 100 µm, or to greater depths on more transparent layers.	A. Avoid windows. Establish area lighting that can be switched on over specific locations (e.g. task lighting in inspection areas). B. n/a D. n/a R. n/a R.T. Provide a conservation laboratory to treat damaged artifacts.	A. n/a B. Block radiation with UV filters on windows. Use small windows, solar screens, louvres, etc. Separate bright public access areas from display areas, and provide adaptation paths between the two. D. n/a R. n/a R.T. n/a	A. n/a B. n/a D. n/a R. n/a R.T. n/a
Incorrect Temperature *Too high:* • causes gradual disintegration or discolouration of organic materials, especially if they are chemically unstable (e.g. acidic paper, colour photographs, nitrate and acetate films). NOTE: Most materials	A. Avoid solar exposure (e.g. attics, skylights). B. Block incorrect temperature with extremely well-insulated walls, floors, and roof. Avoid windows. Build well-insulated walls around special collections (e.g. cold rooms). D. n/a	A. Avoid solar exposure (e.g. skylights). B. Block incorrect temperature with well-insulated walls, floors, and roof. Use double or triple glazing on windows. D. n/a R. Ensure HVAC	A. Enclose loading bay, if possible. B. Block incorrect temperature from spreading to other areas by providing a separate HVAC zone for loading area. D. n/a R. Ensure HVAC system is of adequate size for

Table 1.1 Continued

decompose gradually at room temperature, but the time scale for complete destruction is in millennia. *Too low:* • causes embrittlement, which results in fractures of paints and of other polymers. *Fluctuations:* • cause fractures and delamination in brittle, solid materials, especially if they are layered. • cause RH fluctuations (see "Incorrect Relative Humidity").	R. Provide a reliable HVAC system. Design mechanical rooms and equipment for easy maintenance. R.T. Provide a conservation laboratory to treat damaged artifacts.	system has multiple zones, is of adequate size for load conditions, and provides good distribution of conditioned air. R.T. n/a	worst load conditions. R.T. n/a
Incorrect Relative Humidity (RH) *Damp (over 75% RH):* • causes moulds (which stain and weaken organic and inorganic materials), corrosion (of metals), and shrinkage (of tightly woven textiles). *RH above or below a critical value:* • hydrates/dehydrates some minerals and corrodes metals that contain salts. *RH above 0%:* • gradually disintegrates and discolours organic materials, especially materials that are chemically unstable (e.g. acidic paper). *Fluctuations:* • shrink and swell unconstrained organic materials. • crush or fracture constrained organic materials. • cause layered organic materials to delaminate, tent, and/or buckle. • loosen joints in organic components.	A. Avoid storing collections in basements, in attics, or near windows or exterior walls. B. Block incorrect RH with continuous vapour barrier in walls, roof, and floors. Install zoned RH control. D. n/a R. Provide a reliable HVAC system (desiccant systems must not be LICI). Include back-up humidification and dehumidification systems. R.T. Provide a conservation laboratory to treat damaged artifacts.	A. Avoid windows. Use double or triple glazing on windows. B. Block incorrect RH with a good vapour barrier. D. n/a R. Ensure HVAC system has multiple zones, is of adequate size for load conditions, and provides good distribution of conditioned air. R.T. n/a	A. RH control is provided by packing case. B. Block incorrect RH with an independent HVAC zone for loading area. D. n/a R. n/a R.T. n/a

Portable fittings

(include fittings and equipment that are not integral parts of the building)

Procedures

	Storage	Display	Transit	Procedures
Direct Physical Forces	A. Avoid unstable shelves and cabinets. Immobilize and secure artifacts, especially if there is a high risk of earthquake. B. Block forces with cradles and fitted supports made of inert padding (e.g. Ethafoam). Ensure adequate shelf space. D. n/a R. n/a R.T. Provide conservation laboratory equipment to treat damaged artifacts.	A. Avoid unstable display cases, shelves, and pedestals. Immobilize and secure artifacts, especially if there is a high risk of earthquake. B. Separate artifacts from each other and from the public. Provide discrete cradles and supports made of inert padding. D. n/a R. n/a R.T. n/a	A. Avoid handles at incorrect heights. Transport artifacts in well-maintained air-ride trucks. Provide lifts and dollies to move artifacts safely. B. Block forces from all sides using adequate size and number of packing cases, proper foam to absorb shock and vibration and braces or restraints for vibration-prone components. D. Detect forces by using tipping indicators, shock detectors, and data loggers. R. n/a R.T. n/a	A. Train staff in techniques of handling artifacts. Plan movements of artifacts. Avoid unreliable art handlers. B. Train staff in techniques of supporting and packing artifacts. Keep artifacts separated from each other. D. Format condition reports compatible with museum catalogue. Record new damage. Take good photos. R. Implement disaster plan when warranted (e.g. earthquake, war). Reconsider all stages. R.T. Treat damaged artifacts.
Thieves, Vandals, Displacers	A. n/a. B. Block entry with controlled access system and with adequate locks on cabinets that hold valuable items. D. Connect electronic detectors to central annunciator panel. Provide clear lines of sight. R. Provide communicators and equipment for security personnel. R.T. Provide conservation	A. n/a B. Secure display cases and shelves. Provide separate access to light box. Deter vandalism by using psychological barriers (e.g. ropes, floor markings). D. As for storage, plus use proximity detectors, etc. to warn visitors crossing thresholds. R. As for storage. R.T. n/a	A. Avoid prominent labelling of packing cases. B. Use strong packing cases (locks optional). Hire secure, reputable carriers. D. Detect intruders and displacers by using electronic detectors. R. n/a R.T. n/a	A. Implement a security program appropriate to the scale of the institution. Integrate security program with museum services and with municipal security services. B. Maintain access and perimeter security systems. Keep doors and windows locked. Control the circulation of keys. D. Station personnel in public areas. Maintain a catalogue to identify losses. Routinely

Table 1.1 Continued

Thieves, Vandals, Displacers	laboratory equipment to treat damaged artifacts.			inspect collections and building. R. Train staff in appropriate response to intruders. Inform local police department of museum layout and of location of valuable artifacts. Reconsider all stages. R.T. Recover lost artifacts. Treat vandalized artifacts.
Fire	A. Avoid electrical services within shelves. B. Block fire with closed fire-resistant cabinets and with fire-resistant bulkheads in shelving. Leave adequate space (1.5 m) between walls and shelving to block spread of fire. D. Detect fire by using smoke and heat detectors connected to a central annunciator panel. R. Place enough portable fire extinguishers of adequate size capacity near exits. Consult fire authorities for details. R.T. Provide conservation laboratory equipment to treat damaged artifacts.	A. Use only approved and well-ventilated lights, audio-visual equipment, motors etc. B. Block fire with smoke-tight, fire-resistant display cases. D. As for storage. R. As for storage. R.T. n/a	A. n/a B. Block fire with smoke-tight, fire-resistant packing cases. D. n/a R. n/a R.T. n/a	A. Implement a fire safety program in consultation with local authorities. Train staff in fire prevention techniques. B. Maintain fire barriers and fire separations. Keep fire doors closed. Limit chaos and debris during exhibit installations. D. Establish whom to call in case of fire alarm. Test fire detection systems as required. R. Activate fire disaster plan. Inform authorities of museum layout and of location of valuable or flammable artifacts. Train staff in use of fire extinguishers. Reconsider all stages. R.T. Treat artifacts damaged by fire and smoke.
Water	A. Avoid placing shelves within 10 cm of the floor. B. Block water by	A. Avoid displaying artifacts within 10 cm of the floor. B. Block water by	A. Avoid packing cases that are not supported by skids or feet.	A. Inspect and maintain sprinkler system, roof, and plumbing. Keep all artifacts off the floor

Water	using water-resistant cabinets that have a watershed above the top shelf and a drain channel from the watershed. D. Detect water by using water detectors connected to a central annunciator panel. R. Stock clean-up equipment (e.g. pumps, mops, wet vacuum cleaner). R.T. Provide fans, drying rack, and other equipment to treat damaged artifacts.	using water-resistant display cases with tops that shed water and that will not collapse. Design light boxes to drain water away from artifacts. D. As for storage. R. As for storage. R.T. As for storage.	B. Block water by placing the wrapped object inside a water-resistant packing case. Design drain channels on the packing case lid to prevent water accumulation. D. n/a R. n/a R.T. n/a	and away from walls and water sources (e.g. air conditioning units). Inform cleaners of risks. B. Maintain barriers to water (e.g. watersheds on display cases). Protect artifacts with temporary waterproof covers if leaks are anticipated. D. Inspect collections for water, especially after heavy rain or periods of thaw. R. Activate flood disaster plan. Label and maintain cut-off valves. Store emergency supplies. Reconsider all stages. R.T. Establish emergency treatments for wet artifacts, dry, freeze, or keep wet. Treat artifacts damaged by water.
Pests	A. Avoid wool carpets and clutter. Use elevated cabinets to eliminate crevices and to ensure that the entire floor can be cleaned. B. Block pests by using well-sealed, insect-resistant storage cabinets and containers. D. Provide easy access between cabinets and between artifacts. Use appropriate traps. R. Design cabinets for easy cleaning. Stock pest control equipment (e.g.	A. Avoid using infested materials for display cases. Avoid wool carpets in exhibit halls. B. Block pests by using well-sealed, insect-resistant, vermin-resistant display cases and cabinets. D. Provide easy access for complete inspection (e.g. underneath and behind display areas). R. Design cases and shelves for easy cleaning. R.T. As for storage.	A. Avoid infested packing cases and packing materials. B. Block pests with sealed, insect-resistant, vermin-resistant packing cases. Bag artifacts. D. n/a R. n/a. R.T. n/a	A. Establish an integrated pest management (IPM) program suitable to the building and to the type of collection. Keep collections neat, clean, and free of foodstuffs. B. Maintain all seals, especially at ground level. Quarantine and examine incoming artifacts, building materials, and packing cases. Perhaps apply perimeter pesticides. D. Inspect collection and traps regularly. Identify pests and maintain a log. R. Respond to infestation based on

Table 1.1 Continued

Pests	freezer, controlled atmosphere chamber, polyethylene bags, traps). R.T. Provide conservation laboratory equipment to treat damaged artifacts.			IPM principles. Remove and quarantine infested artifacts on display or in storage. Consider health risks. Reconsider all stages. R.T. Treat artifacts damaged by pests.
Contaminants	A. Avoid materials and finishes that are sources of contaminants. B. Block external contaminants by using airtight cabinets, barrier, coatings, and barrier films (e.g. bags, shelf liners). D. Detect contaminants by using gas, particulate, and aerosol dosimeters. R. Place absorbents in cabinets. Supply filtered air to cabinets. Use portable filter/fan units for small rooms. R.T. Provide conservation laboratory equipment to treat damaged artifacts.	A. Avoid materials and finishes that are sources of contaminants. B. Block contaminants by using airtight cases and barrier coatings. D. Detect contaminants by using gas dosimeters. R. Place absorbents (e.g. activated charcoal) in cases. Slowly supply filtered air to cases. R.T. n/a	A. Use only clean, non-dusting packing case materials that are approved for museum use. B. Block contaminants by using inert, clean wrapping materials. D. n/a R. Place absorbents in packing cases. R.T. n/a	A. Identify susceptible artifacts. Establish a list of suitable building and display materials. Test unknown materials. Train staff to use appropriate gloves. B. Maintain barriers to contaminants. Measure enclosure leakages, and seal if necessary. D. Check for dust, changes in colour/patina, tarnish, fingerprints, and loss of strength. Use gas dosimeters. R. Maintain any filters and absorbers. Maintain cleanliness. Remove artifacts from problem areas. Ventilate. Reconsider all stages. R.T. Treat artifacts damaged by contaminants.
Radiation	A. Avoid general lighting; use task lighting instead. Avoid high sources of UV. B. Block UV radiation by placing UV filters on lamps. D. Detect radiation by using UV meters, light meters, and light dosimeters. R. n/a	A. Avoid unnecessary light on artifacts. Use timers and multi-level lighting. B. Block UV radiation by placing UV filters on lamps. If possible, place UV filters on glazing. Use curtains, shutters, and blinds. D. Detect radiation	A. n/a B. Block radiation by using opaque packaging. D. n/a R. n/a R.T. n/a	A. Establish optimum light levels, UV levels, and light sources. Estimate fading rates of various artifacts, and then establish exposure times and schedules. B. Close curtains, blinds, shutters, etc. when the museum is closed. Cover cases and turn off lights when no viewers are present.

Radiation	R.T. Provide conservation laboratory equipment to treat damaged artifacts.	by using UV meters, light meters, and light dosimeters. R. n/a R.T. n/a		D. Measure new installations for UV and light levels. Monitor any light dosimeters. R. Reconsider all stages. R.T. Treat artifacts damaged by light and UV, where possible.
Incorrect Temperature	A. Avoid locating cabinets near heat sources (e.g. radiators, heaters). Avoid placing light fixtures inside cabinets. B. Block incorrect temperature by leaving adequate space (1.5 m) between shelving and exterior walls. Use insulated cabinets, if necessary. D. Use thermohygrographs, thermometers, data loggers, temperature monitors, and alarms. R. Use portable heaters or air conditioners to correct local problem areas. Use freezers for cold storage. R.T. Provide conservation laboratory equipment to treat damaged artifacts.	A. Avoid placing lamps inside display cases. Ensure adequate ventilation in light boxes. B. Leave space between exterior walls and display cases, shelves, or cabinets. Use bulbs with dichroic reflectors or heat filters. D. Use thermohygrographs, thermometers, and data loggers. Provide a probe hole in display cases. R. Use portable heaters or air conditioners to correct local problem areas. R.T. n/a	A. Avoid vehicles that are not temperature controlled. B. Block incorrect temperature by using insulated packing cases. D. Place an electronic data logger, and a thermometer with external readout, in packing case. R. n/a R.T. n/a	A. Define the correct temperatures for various artifacts. Identify artifacts that require cold storage. B. Maintain insulation. Ensure adequate distance between artifacts and hot or cold surfaces D. Monitor measuring instruments and interpret the data. R. Plan response to HVAC system failures. Reconsider all stages. R.T. Treat artifacts damaged by incorrect temperature.
Incorrect RH	A. Avoid locating shelving too close to exterior walls. Avoid placing shelves within 10 cm of cold floors. B. Block incorrect RH by using airtight	A. Avoid locating artifacts near sources of incorrect temperature and humidity (e.g. lamps, damp floors, exterior walls). B. Block incorrect	A. Avoid vehicles that are not humidity controlled. B. Block incorrect RH by wrapping artifacts and by using	A. Define the correct RH range for various artifacts, and inform relevant staff. Allow time for packing cases to reach room temperature before opening.

Incorrect Relative Humidity			
cabinets, boxes, or bags. (If temperature changes more than 10°C, provide sufficient buffer in sealed enclosures.) D. Use thermohygrographs, psychrometers, coloured indicators, data loggers, and alarms. R. Use buffers such as silica gel, wood, cotton, and paper. Slowly supply controlled air to cabinets. R.T. Provide conservation laboratory equipment to treat damaged artifacts.	RH by using airtight cases. D. Use thermohygrographs, psychrometers, and data loggers. Provide a probe hole in display cases. R. Use buffers such as silica gel, wood, cotton, and paper. Supply RH-controlled air to display cases. R.T. n/a	airtight packing cases. D. Place an electronic data logger, or a hygrometer with external readout, in packing case. R. Use buffers such as silica gel, wood, cotton, and paper, if required. R.T. n/a	B. Maintain vapour barriers. Ensure adequate distance between artifacts and cold surfaces. Measure enclosure leakages, and seal if necessary. D. Monitor measuring instruments and interpret the data R. Plan response to HVAC system failures. Maintain buffers in cases. Reconsider all stages. R.T. Treat artifacts damaged by incorrect RH.

Chapter 2

Risk Analysis

Jonathan Ashley-Smith

Introduction

THE WORD 'RISK' IS USED loosely in everyday language and with several slightly different definitions in the technical literature. It relates to events in the future that are unwanted but not unforeseen. Phrases such as 'risk assessment' and 'risk analysis' are used to describe systematic approaches to identifying, quantifying and evaluating the relative importance of the risks associated with proposed activities. Quantification of risk involves predicting the probability of future one-off events or extrapolating current rates of change to predict future states. It also entails making estimates of the change in value or utility as the unwanted events occur. The use of risk assessment as a technique to aid conservation decisions was probably pioneered by Baer (1991). It has been given recent impetus in the area of collections management by Waller (1994) and Michalski (1994).

It is necessary to make assessments of risk in order to manage risk. Managing risk means taking steps to prevent or minimise the possibility of undesirable future states. Managing risk must also include devising procedures to deal with the effects of unwanted events that cannot be prevented. The various stages of risk analysis provide information for the decision-making necessary for risk management (Covello and Merkhofer 1993). This risk information is moderated by constraints such as budget priorities, the single-mindedness of museum directors and the stupidity of politicians.

Traditional interventive conservation/restoration has dealt with salvage following the absence or failure of risk management strategies in the past. Preventive

Source: S. Bradbury (ed.), *The Interface between Science and Conservation*, British Museum Occasional Paper No. 116, London: British Museum Press, 1997, pp. 123–132.

conservation through environmental control and disaster mitigation involves developing and implementing successful risk management strategies.

Potentially, the risk information needed to drive these strategies comes from two sources, scientists and conservators. Scientists, working inside and outside the conservation milieu, study the relationships of variables such as light intensity, temperature, and concentrations of moisture and acid gases on a variety of materials and constructions. These investigations can be used to derive 'damage functions', mathematical relationships that define the rate of deterioration under specific conditions. Conservators are repeatedly confronted by damaged objects and are in a position to build a formal or anecdotal database relating condition and probable cause of deterioration. They are also in a position to relate construction type to frequency of failure. Unfortunately the potential of these two groups is not fully realised and the information that is fed into the decision-making process is partial (in both senses of the word).

If the task in hand is solely to manage risk, then decisions can be based solely on risk assessments. Most conservators believe that this concentration on the down-side of any proposal is an appropriate professional attitude as they see themselves as the sole advocates of the welfare of the collections.

Viewed holistically, the task of management is to accomplish the success of a venture rather than control the factors that would lead to undesirable outcomes. The formal definitions of museums provided by international bodies such as ICOM (Anon 1990) or by Parliament (Anon 1983) give weight to increased utility of the objects through increased access to collections. Thus museum management decisions are likely to be about putting on a successful exhibition or arranging a successful loan, rather than specifically reducing damage to objects. The stages of option generation, evaluation, selection and implementation are likely to be influenced by the benefits that reward a successful decision. An assessment of the costs of achieving success is needed in addition to prediction of the costs of failure. This evaluation based on a balanced view of both the up-side and the down-side is a part of cost-benefit analysis (CBA). If risks are still the main subject of interest this balanced evaluation can be called risk-benefit analysis.

Cost-benefit analysis and risk-benefit analysis are expressions that are used loosely in non-technical speech and with a range of meanings in technical writings. Historically CBA has been used to inform decisions that would have a long-term impact on the welfare of large numbers of people not directly associated with the design or implementation of a scheme such as the building of a dam or a bridge (Zerbe and Dively 1994). The benefits considered are those to society as a whole in the long erm, rather than the rewards to the decision-maker in the short term. However, CBA can be used to describe any comparison of options based on calculation of costs and evaluation of rewards. It is often used when only costs are being compared, although this is more correctly described as cost-effectiveness analysis. It is profitable to think that decisions taken in boardrooms and conservation laboratories within museums will have long-term outcomes beneficial to members of society outside the museum. CBA is therefore an appropriate, but by no means simple, adjunct to conservation decision-making.

The study of risk allows a change of attitude from 'the safer the better' to 'how much can I achieve without causing damage?' which might be translated as 'how close can I approach damage without actually getting there?' 'Testing the envelope' of risk, which may have positive advantages in terms of display and interpretation, requires a trustworthy evaluation by conservators of their own observations and the observations of scientists who have studied related materials.

Decision analysis

It is possible to analyse the decision-making process by using diagrams called decision trees (Moore and Thomas 1988). The simplest decision consists of selecting one option from two. For either option the outcome may be what was hoped for, but there is a certain probability that it will be somewhat worse. A simple decision consists of consideration of four potential outcomes (Figure 2.1). The 'payoff', N_{1-4}, for each outcome is the difference between the sum of the benefits and the sum of the costs. (All the following equations will be written as though costs, benefits and values could be measured using the same units although no such units will be defined.)

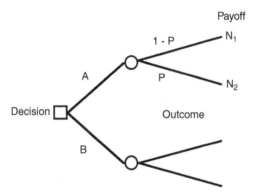

Figure 2.1 Decision tree showing a choice between two options, each of which has two possible outcomes

$$N = B - C$$

The difference in payoff between the good outcome and the less good outcome will usually result from a difference in the benefits. The costs are likely to be a function of the option and will be fixed irrespective of the outcome. The estimated value (EV) of each option is the average of the good and less good outcomes weighted by the probabilities of each. (If the probability of one outcome is the fraction P, the probability of the alternative is, by definition, 1–P.)

$$EV = N_1 (1-P) + N_2 P$$

In general, if the costs and the benefits are of the same order and P is small then the option of choice will be the one with the highest EV. In the following discussion it will be assumed that these conditions are met. High EV will not always be the appropriate deciding factor in museums where risk aversion is part of the job description. If

P is large and the benefits in the event of the poor outcome are considerably less than those for success, the option is only for risk lovers.

If one of the two options is 'doing nothing', that is failing to make a decision or to take any action, then we can define the value of doing nothing as EV_0 without considering in detail the possible outcomes that lead to this value. Any decision will then have a net estimated value (NEV) which is the difference between the EV of this option and EV_0, the estimated value of the status quo.

$$NEV = EV - EV_0$$

It is then possible to compare a number of different options by comparing their NEVs. (This has some advantages over comparing the EVs of all the options, one of which is doing nothing.) In CBA it is conventional to discount future costs and benefits, that is, give them lower values the further into the future they arise. A simple way of understanding why this is done is to ask yourself whether you would rather have £100 now or £105 in a year's time. It is assumed that most people would take the money now because they could do more with the cash than they could with just a promise of money. £100 now has greater present value than £105 later. There is considerable debate about an appropriate discount rate for CBA in the areas of health and ecology (Soby and Ball 1992; Hanley and Spash 1993) and one can imagine the same would be true for museum decisions. In the following discussion the symbols used to show future cost and benefit streams will be assumed to be suitably discounted at an undefined rate (which could be zero). The resulting NEV is then comparable to the more widely used Net Present Value (NPV). NEV looks at a position at a fixed time in the future, NPV looks at the present value of future flows of costs and benefits.

Decisions involving the conservation of objects

It is arguable that the purpose of preventive conservation (passive or interventive) is to maintain the value of an object and that the purpose of restoration is to restore value (add value to a devalued object). It is also arguable that the purpose of new galleries, exhibitions and loans is to increase the value of collections. If there is no aversion to considering museum collections as investments which provide a flow of benefits, then it could be argued that once the value of an object or collection has been increased it will continue to provide a higher rate of return. The words value, return and investment do not have to be interpreted in money terms. For instance, once an object has been made more famous by an exhibition more people will want to see it in the future. Its 'cultural' value is increased.

Adding value

Figure 2.2 shows a simple decision tree used to decide whether to go ahead with a treatment or event that should raise the value of an object. This could be a decision to send a collection of ceramics to an exhibition in Japan, to restore a painting or mass deacidify a library full of brittle books. The benefits of a good outcome will be the increase in value $V_1 - V_0$, immediate benefits B_1 such as a loan fee or entrance charges

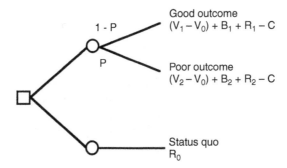

Good outcome
$(V_1 - V_0) + B_1 + R_1 - C$

$1 - P$

P

Poor outcome
$(V_2 - V_0) + B_2 + R_2 - C$

Status quo
R_0

Figure 2.2 Decision tree showing the payoffs for a good outcome and a poor outcome
of a decision compared with the option of doing nothing

for an exhibition, and the long-term return R_1 (net of maintenance costs) over a specified number of years. The costs C are the immediate costs of the treatment or event. There is a probability P that the operation will not be as successful as intended. In that case there will be a new lower value V_2 which could be less than V_0, or even zero if something goes disastrously wrong. The NEV for this operation is composed of the immediate and long-term net benefits $(V_1 - V_0) + B_1 + R_1 - C$ plus a number of terms that relate to possible losses of value and opportunity, $-P(V_2 - V_1) - P(B_2 - B_1) - P(R_2 - R_1)$. These terms represent the risk, that is, the probability of failure multiplied by differences in return and value between success and failure.

The key lesson this simplistic model teaches is that it is imperative to understand what the consequences of success or failure are and to have a clear idea of the chances of failure. The definitions of success and failure are for discussion amongst groups from the different disciplines within the Museum profession. Determination of the value of P, the probability that something will go wrong, comes from a scientific approach to the documentation and evaluation of unplanned occurrences. This puts a pressure on conservators to document failures, truthfully and retrievably. It also directs scientists to research mechanisms of failure to help quantify the risk.

Estimates of the various quantities can be put into a computer spreadsheet. Different assumptions can be tested and the sensitivity of certain changes on the NEV can be evaluated. Figure 2.3 shows a graph extracted from such a spreadsheet exercise. This shows the change in NEV for different values of P. A negative NEV indicates an unsound decision. In this case the largest probability of failure that is acceptable is 0.3, the value of P when NEV is zero, i.e. no net gain. Suppose it is not known what your chances of success are but you think they are between 90 and 95% (P = 0.05 – 0.1) then you know you have a considerable margin of 'safety'. The value of 0.3 is shown for graphical clarity; in many cases the critical value of P will be a very much smaller fraction and the actual probability smaller still. For example the probability of a road accident causing damage to an art object is considerably below 10^{-4}.

Maintaining value

The type of tree shown in Figure 2.2 can be used as a model for a spreadsheet to investigate proposals to increase capital and/or operation costs to maintain the state of a

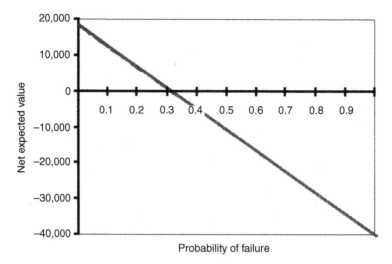

Figure 2.3 Graphic output from a specific spreadsheet scenario. The plot shows how the NEV of the option varies with the possibility of things going wrong. In this case NEV ceases to be positive when P is greater than 0.3

collection. For example, is it a wise decision to install air-conditioning to prevent deterioration? In this simple model it is assumed that there is a known relationship between deterioration and change in value; this may be linear, although I have argued elsewhere that this is often not the case (Ashley-Smith 1995). Table 2.1 shows typical values used in the calculations. The variables k_0, k_1 and k_2 are the annual fractional losses in value in different environments. A figure of -0.00001 indicates complete loss of value in 100,000 years, i.e. slow deterioration. Silk deterioration might have a value around $-0.002 \, y^{-1}$, decay of cellulose acetate negatives might be of the order of $-0.02y^{-1}$.

Table 2.1 Typical input to spreadsheet analysis to determine NEV. (Investing 1 million units of value in the environmental control of a collection worth 100 million.)

Benefit (interest on investment)		k	0.05
Original investment		Vo	100,000,000
Present rate of deterioration		ko	−0.000100
Proposed rate of deterioration		k1	−0.000010
Possible rate of deterioration		k2	−0.00005
Probability of ill fate		p	0.05
Capital outlay		c	1,000,000
Present maintenance	costs	mo	20,000
Proposed maintenance	costs	m	60,000
Discount rate		r	0.05
Year of first capital	outlay	0	(1−50)
Frequency of repeat			25 years

The model does not give a straight 'yes or no' but it does indicate what values of which variables make an expensive investment in plant seem a sensible option.

The aim is to radically decrease the rate of deterioration, however, this may not be achieved. The risk depends on the value of P and on the difference between k_1 and k_2, the difference between the hoped for rate of deterioration and the rate achieved if something goes wrong in the planning or execution.

Using realistically large values for capital and running costs the NEV only becomes positive if the present rate of deterioration is greater than about $0.001y^{-1}$, greater than 10% loss in value per century. More important, the certainty that intervention is going to cause a significant improvement in stability has to be about 90% or better. Thus low temperature storage for photographic materials is easy to justify, an air-conditioned gallery for stone sculpture might be more debatable. The conservator's desire to create clean, stable conditions has to be supported by an accurate scientific appraisal of rates of deterioration.

Such a scientific appraisal put in the form of an equation linking the rate of damage to variations in concentration or intensity of damaging agents is known as a damage function. Robert Koestler has summarised the different types of damage function (Koestler 1994). Relatively few have been derived and even fewer are published in the conservation literature (Lipfert 1988; Mirabelli and Massa 1991; Ware 1996).

Conservators who have seen damage caused by wrong environments might argue that such damage is not the result of slow progressive deterioration but of catastrophic failure. Mathematically the two mechanisms can be treated as the same. A catastrophic loss of 50% value with an annual probability of 0.001 can be modelled as a deterioration rate of $0.0005y^{-1}$ (Figure 2.4). Benarie has demonstrated the relationship between supposedly random isolated catastrophes and the first order rate law which determines many deterioration reactions (Benarie 1991).

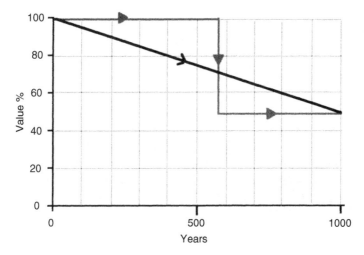

Figure 2.4 Graphical representation of the idea that a catastrophic loss in value at some unspecified point within 1000 years can be thought of as equivalent to a constant fractional loss

Uses of information

The examples above place risk in the area of general decision-making. In that context risk is the danger that a prediction will be wrong as a result of incomplete information. Most published work concentrates solely on risk as potential damage to objects.

Collections management

Waller (1994) has assessed the risk (probability of damage × change in utility resulting from damage) posed by each of a large number of agents of deterioration to different types of natural history collections. The results give differing risk profiles for different sorts of material, some being more prone to damage by light, others by physical forces or by changes in temperature. The profiles do not indicate what should be done next, but the implication is that effort would be directed to areas of high risk. The cost-effectiveness of risk reduction measures is then assessed. To minimise the dangers of giving absolute values to priceless or worthless objects Waller works only with proportional changes in value or utility.

A number of other tools devised to direct collections management decisions have used approximations of the probability/value estimation of risk. Most rely on construction of a matrix of importance versus condition. An object's priority for action or treatment is judged by its coordinates in the matrix. The Delta project in the Netherlands (Krikken 1996) used relevance to the collection as the measure of value. The assessment of damage, measured as conservation need, can be seen as a *post hoc* measure of probability.

Prediction and study

One area where scientists and conservators can work together for mutual benefit is in the design and interpretation of collection condition surveys. Full conservation surveys to a standard format are the potential basis for epidemiological studies of deterioration. If there are enough similar objects with the same environmental history then information about susceptibilities to particular agents can be derived from the survey data. If objects have entered a specific environment at known times there is the possibility of using survey data to derive a form of damage function. This can be used to predict future states of the collection. The methodology used by Mirwald and Buschmann (1991) in work on deterioration of gravestones can be extended to other collections such as libraries where there are large numbers of similar objects whose date of acquisition is known.

The survey places each object in a condition category. The percentage of objects in each category is plotted against the year of acquisition. The percentage of objects in the worst state will increase the older the objects are, as shown by the solid black line in Figure 2.5. To predict the state of the collection in say 50 years' time the line can be shifted horizontally to the right by 50 years. To predict the effect of improving the environmental factors the new line can be shifted vertically downwards. The damage function derived from the survey only includes the variables time and damage. To determine future states in future environments requires damage functions that include variables such as pollution levels. However, the method described above gives an indication of the possible effects of improvement.

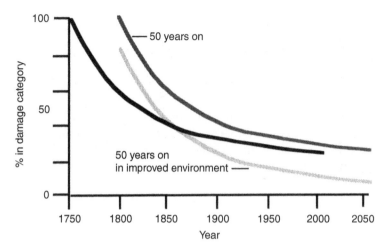

Figure 2.5 Data from a condition survey about categories of damage is plotted against the year that each object entered the specific environment. The resulting curve can be manipulated to give predictions about future states of the collection. (After Mirwald)

Conclusion

The main users of risk information will be conservators advising other museum professionals. The information used to assess risk is unnecessarily inexact and would be improved by more systematic studies leading to derived relationships between the progress of time and the progress of damage. In scientific experiments it is necessary to limit the number of variables so that interpretable and reproducible data can be collected. What has been studied is not directly related to the real world (Figure 2.6).

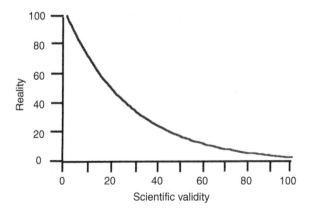

Figure 2.6 The more a scientific experiment is designed to be reproducible and scientifically valid the less it resembles what is observed in the real world

In the real world, and even in museums, the number of variables is large and uncontrolled. Most real-world observers do not make enough observations to form statistically valid conclusions, but this does not make the information they provide invalid. Nor does it stop them forming opinions which turn out to be correct.

There need to be people who operate at the interface between science and conservation acting as interpreters. The scientists need someone to explain what it is in the real world that actually matters, so that they can design their experiments more meaningfully. The conservators need someone to interpret the results of scientific experiment in the light of their experience of reality. There is a special need to explain that when two scientists disagree this does not mean that either or both are wrong, but merely that their experiments were different.

In other more mature areas of the study of risk, it has been noted that there are three stages in the dissemination and acceptance of risk assessments (Figure 2.7) (Funtowitz and Rautz 1985).

The boundaries between the three are determined by degrees of uncertainty about the methodology and information (systems uncertainty) and the importance of the outcome of decisions (decision stakes). At one end is 'consensual science' where there are reliable databases and there is agreement because there is no advantage in disagreement. At the other end is a system (total environmental assessment) which is permeated by qualitative judgements and value commitments. In the middle is an area termed 'clinical consultancy' which is determined by the use of quantitative tools supplemented explicitly by qualitative judgement based on experience. This reliance on personal judgement tends to accentuate differences of interpretation arising from competing institutional, educational and disciplinary cultures. It also leads to an unbalanced state where views on risk can oscillate wildly.

There can be no doubt that the conservation profession is at the stage of clinical consultancy. Unfortunately the profession is small and there are not enough clinical consultants.

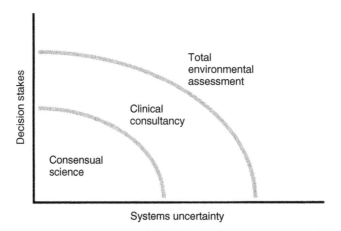

Figure 2.7 Three types of risk assessment determined by the state of knowledge and the personal or societal rewards of a particular viewpoint. (After Funtowitz and Rautz)

References

Anon (1983) *National Heritage Act*, Chapter 47, London: HMSO.

Anon (1990) *Statutes: Code of Professional Ethics*, Paris: ICOM.

Ashley-Smith, J. (1995) *Definitions of Damage*, AAH Conference, London (available online via http://palimpsest.stanford.edu/).

Baer, N. S. (1991) 'Assessment and management of risks to cultural property', in N. S. Baer, et al. (eds) *Science, Technology and European Cultural Heritage, Proceedings of the European Symposium, Bologna, Italy, 13–16 June 1989*, London: Butterworth-Heinemann for the Commission of the European Communities.

Benarie, M. (1991) 'The establishment and use of damage functions', in N. S. Baer et al. (eds) *Science, Technology and European Cultural Heritage, Proceedings of the European Symposium, Bologna, Italy, 13–16 June 1989*, London: Butterworth-Heinemann for the Commission of the European Communities.

Covello, V. T. and Merkhofer, M. W. (1993) *Risk Assessment Methods: Approaches for Assessing Health and Environmental Risks*, London: Plenum Press.

Funtowitz and Rautz (1985) 'Three types of risk assessment: a methodological analysis', in B. B. Johnson and C. T. Covello (eds) *The Social and Cultural Construction of Risk*, Dordrecht, Holland: D. Reidel.

Hanley, N. and Spash, C. L. (1993) *Cost-Benefit Analysis and the Environment*, Aldershot: Edward Elgar Publishing.

Koestler, R. J. (1994) 'How do external environmental factors accelerate change?' in W. E. Krumbein et al. (eds) *Durability and Change*, Chichester: Wiley.

Krikken, J. (1996) 'A Dutch exercise in the valuation of natural history collections', in *International Conference on the Value and Valuation of Natural Science Collections*, Manchester (a conference held in April 1995).

Lipfert, F. W. (1988) 'Atmospheric damage to calcareous stones: comparison and reconciliation of recent experimental findings', *Atmospheric Environment*, 23: 415.

Michalski, S. (1994) 'A systematic approach to preservation: description and integration with other museum activities', in A. Roy and P. Smith (eds) *Preventive Conservation: Practice, Theory and Research*, preprints IIC Ottawa Congress, London: IIC.

Mirabelli, M. and Massa S. (1991) 'Ancient metal objects in outdoor exposure: causes, mechanisms and measurements of damage', in N. S. Baer et al. (eds) *Science, Technology and European Cultural Heritage*, Proceedings of the European Symposium, Bologna, Italy, 13–16 June 1989, London: Butterworth-Heinemann for the Commission of the European Communities.

Mirwald, P. W. and Buschmann, H. (1991) 'Assessment of the stone inventory and weathering state of the tombstones of the old cemetery of Bonn FRG as a constraint for urban planning', in N. S. Baer et al. (eds) *Science, Technology and European Cultural Heritage*, Proceedings of the European Symposium, Bologna, Italy, 13–16 June 1989, London: Butterworth-Heinemann for the Commission of the European Communities.

Moore, P. G. and Thomas, H. (1988) *The Anatomy of Decisions* (2nd edn), Harmondsworth: Penguin Books.

Soby, B. A. and Ball, D. J. (1992) *Consumer Safety and the Valuation of Life and Injury*, Research Report No. 9, Norwich: Environmental Risk Assessment Unit, School of Environmental Sciences, UEA, Norwich, NR4 7TJ.

Waller, R. (1994) 'Conservation risk assessment: a strategy for managing resources for preventive conservation', in A. Roy and P. Smith (eds) *Preventive Conservation: Practice, Theory and Research*, preprints IIC Ottawa Congress, London: IIC.

Ware, M. J. (1996) 'Quantifying the vulnerability of photogenic drawings', in M. S. Koch et al. (eds) *Research Techniques in Photographic Conservation*, Copenhagen: Royal Danish Academy of Fine Arts.

Zerbe, R. O. and Dively D. D. (1994) *Benefit-Cost Analysis in Theory and Practice*, New York: Harper Collins.

PART TWO

Agents of Deterioration

Introduction to Part Two – Section One

Chris Caple

Agents of deterioration: physical forces (handling and moving) and security

THE MOST OBVIOUS THREAT to any object is the risk of physical damage from handling, moving the object, seismic activity; anything which results in the impact of a surface with the object. Care and protection against the threat of physical damage, whether it be a caress, the kick of a mule or an earthquake, is an essential component of preventive conservation.

Careful handling is the single most important skill which any curator or conservator can develop to minimise damage to objects. Whilst they may need to be moved for a museum to fulfil its display, storage and education functions effectively, objects broken during moving form part of every museum conservator's workload. Gwen Miles (1992) (Chapter 3) provides simple, sound, sensible advice about handling museum objects, including being practical about issues such as wearing gloves. There are no simple dos and don'ts; each situation must be assessed and appropriate precautions taken. As the loads to be lifted become heavier there is an increase in the level of organisation, equipment required and relevant legislation. In the UK, for example, the Manual Handling Operation Regulations (1992) have to be taken into account. The risk of damage increases, the greater the fragility of the object, the further the distance travelled, the greater its weight or volume; whilst the use of packaging and increasing the level of preparation will reduce the risk. More detailed information on packaging and moving artefacts, especially for historic objects, is available (Read and Hickey 2006).

Paul Marcon (undated) (Chapter 4) has summarised much of the practical information on moving objects over longer distances, between rather than within museums, on a website run by the Canadian Conservation Institute (CCI). Websites represent the medium through which basic museum information will normally be provided in the future; they have the advantages that they can be regularly updated as commercial products or advice changes and that they are potentially available almost anywhere in the world. This site takes its readers, step by step, through the decision-making processes that need to be addressed when packing and transporting objects, from selecting a carrier to the cushioning value of various materials and the different designs of packing case. It also makes the reader aware of the range of information already created by the CCI on this subject. Though many museums package and courier their own objects, there is also a great deal of knowledge about the safe transportation of objects embedded within the commercial shipping industry. Case studies on moving objects appear regularly in conferences (Ashley-Smith 2008) and journals, such as those in *Museum Practice* 28 (Winter 2004): 43–59.

Within the museum literature, discussions about storage often focus on its aim of providing objects to support the museum's display and education functions. Less is written about the aims of storage from the preventive conservation point of view. There is a clear objective in preserving collections in the 'as found' state to the point when they are required for use in research, display or education. But, is this actually achievable? Chris Caple (2000) (Chapter 5) explores that objective using two concepts:

- the aspiration of a 'black box' ideal of perfect object preservation and access, exploring some of the realistic steps which museums often made towards that objective
- use of a simple grading system of levels of storage, clarifying how individual actions grouped together in a series of logical steps can move a chaotic group of objects to a well-stored museum collection.

Good storage has a relatively high, even density of objects, in order to make maximum use of beneficial environmental conditions in the store and achieve the lowest cost per object for near ideal storage (Caple 2000: 152–154).

High-quality storage has been practised in museums for many years. Using examples drawn from the 1960s to the 1990s, Jim Tate and Theo Skinner (1992) (Chapter 6) describe some of the storage systems created in the National Museum of Scotland. Well-designed storage greatly reduces the risks from physical damage and, provided that appropriate materials are used, substantially reduces the risk from the environment around the objects. The range of variables that should be considered when improving storage and the practical activities involved in achieving it were reviewed by Proudlove (2000a, 2000b). In many areas such as textiles, photographs and transport collections, specialist articles or chapters in books on storage have been published and provide useful detailed advice on materials and methods of safe storage, such as those in the journal *Museum Practice* 10 (1999): 60–83.

The development of modern inert materials such as:

- polypropylene crates or boxes, which make excellent stackable rigid containers
- polyethylene foams such as Plastazote™, which can act as a cushioning material, can be used to make a cut-out for movement-free seating for objects and provides thermal insulation
- steel cupboards, drawers and shelving units with stoved-enamel or powder-coated finishes
- polyester sleeves for documents and photographs
- archival-quality papers and boxes
- bubble-wrap polythene sheet containing air bubbles, which provides a physical cushioning and vapour barrier when wrapped around an object

is leading to improved object storage. However, there is also continued use of 'cheap' materials such MDF, chipboard and lower-quality cardboard boxes, all of which emit volatile organic compounds (VOC) (Chapters 16 and 17) and lose strength over time. Short-term thinking remains prevalent in many heritage organisations, aided by the perennial problems of limited resources and a lack of awareness of the problematic nature of these materials on the part of senior managers.

Though conservators and curators normally focus on the collections in public museums, many culturally valued artefacts remain in private possession. In the book *Ours for Keeps?* the Museums and Galleries Commission (MGC) assembled a range of papers intended to be read by the public and private collectors as well as by museum volunteers and staff which provided basic information about care of collections. Information was provided on suitable storage and display conditions, techniques and materials for a large range of different object types. Pete Winsor's section on materials (1997) (Chapter 7) is one of the most useful, clearly explaining what the different materials are and why they are useful for preserving objects. The focus is on modern inert materials which have a good track record for safely storing artefacts. Similar information is available through websites.[1]

Physical damage to artefacts can be caused by vibration, whether on a small scale through road traffic and building work (Chapter 38) or on a large scale in the form of earthquakes. The IIC (International Institute for Conservation of Historic and Artistic Works) hosted a seminar on the threat of seismic activity (earthquakes) to cultural heritage in Tokyo in July 2009 (Chapter 8). It was hosted by Jerry Podany, President of IIC, and contains the thoughts of a number of speakers on this subject. Whilst information on precautions that can be taken against the risk of physical damage during seismic activity is available from a number of sources (Podany 2008),[2] the majority of the discussion focused on the improvements to, and availability of, maps of seismic activity and the risks of seismic activity to museum artefacts. Whilst some richer countries such as Japan and America have fitted isolators to protect some high-value objects in museums in zones of seismic activity, other museums have not yet installed even basic low-cost protection measures, such as mesh in front of their open museum shelves to prevent objects falling onto the floor during an earthquake. The devastation of the earthquakes in New Zealand and Japan in early 2011, when this reader was being written, has again reminded the profession of the potential damage of such events.

Though museums have concerns over the safety of objects, either from theft or from vandalism, they also have concerns over the safety of visitors, staff and buildings. Consequently, safety issues are dealt with in greater detail in collections management publications (Fahy 1995) and specialist publications on museum security (Hoare 1990, Resource 2003). However, consideration does need to be given when storing or displaying objects to measures to minimise the risk of theft of or damage to individual objects or groups of objects. As with other areas of preventive conservation, this means assessing the risk to the object. Rob Payton (2003) (Chapter 9) describes a simple method for assessing risk to the objects on display in the Museum of London. It shows how particular objects of value (financial or historic) which are at the greatest risk of theft or vandalism damage can be identified and then steps taken to safeguard them.

Notes

1   http://www.collectionslink.org.uk/index.cfm?ct=search.home/catList/2
2   http://www.eqprotection-museums.org/index.asp?lang=2

References

Ashley-Smith, J. (ed.) (2008) *Conservation and Access, Preprints of the 2008 IIC Congress, London 15–19 September 2008,* London: IIC.

Caple, C. (2000) *Conservation Skills: Judgement, Method and Decision Making,* London: Routledge, pp. 152–154.

Fahy, A. (1995) *Collections Management,* Abingdon: Routledge.

Hoare, N. (1990) *Security for Museums,* London: Committee of Area Museum Councils & Museums Association.

IIC (undated) 'Before the Unthinkable . . . Happens Again', IIC website (accessed 28 March 2011) http://www.iiconservation.org/dialogues/IIC_tokyo_transcript.pdf.

Manual Handling. Manual Handling Operations Regulations 1992 (as amended). Guidance on Regulations L23 (3rd edn), [Sudbury]: HSE Books, 2004. Also available at http://www. hse.gov.uk/contact/faqs/manualhandling.htm.

Marcon, P. (undated) 'Six Steps to Safe Shipment', CCI website (accessed 13 March 2009) www.cci-icc.gc.ca/crc/articles/sixsteps-sixetapes/index-eng.aspx.

Miles, G. (1992) 'Object Handling', in J. M. A. Thompson (ed.), *Manual of Curatorship* (2nd edn), Oxford: Butterworth-Heinemann, pp. 455–458.

Payton, R. (2003) 'Safety by Numbers', *Museum Practice* 22: 40–42.

Podany, J. (ed.) (2008) *Advances in the Protection of Museum Collections from Earthquake Damage,* Los Angeles: J. Paul Getty Museum.

Proudlove C. (2000a) 'The Perfect Package', *Museum Practice* 14: 40–43.

Proudlove, C. (2000b) 'Perfect Package in Practice', *Museum Practice* 15: 40–43.

Read, M. and Hickey, S. (2006) 'Transporting Objects', in National Trust, *Manual of Housekeeping,* London: Butterworth-Heinemann, pp. 764–773.

Resource (2003) *Security in Museums, Archives and Libraries: A Practical Guide,* London: Resource.

Tate, J. and Skinner, T. (1992) 'Storage Systems', in J. M. A. Thompson (ed.), *Manual of Curatorship* (2nd edn), Oxford: Butterworth-Heinemann, pp. 459–467.

Winsor, P. (1997) 'Which Conservation Materials to Use at Home?', in Museums and Galleries Commission (ed.), *Ours for Keeps?,* London: MGC, 7.07–7.10.

Chapter 3

Object Handling

Gwen Miles

Introduction

ANYONE WHO COMES INTO contact with museum objects during their work must appreciate that there is a real need for care when objects are handled. Damage to objects occurs in all museums. However, with forethought much of the damage caused by poor handling or transportation can be avoided.

All staff who work in a museum may need to handle objects at some point in their career; handling is not simply the prerogative of the Curator and Conservator. In a large museum there will be other specialist groups: technicians dealing with object handling and installation, designers, photographers and object cleaners who will come into contact with objects as part of their normal duties. However, in the event of unforeseen circumstances such as fire or flood, staff from other areas may be asked to assist. In smaller museums where roles are less specialized the attendant staff may assist the Curator to move or even clean objects. Whether it is part of the normal routine or only in exceptional circumstances, anyone working in a museum should understand the nature of the collection and the principles governing the handling of objects.

Most objects within a museum are inherently vulnerable. This may be due to their nature: their structure, size or shape: to the materials from which they are made; or they may become fragile as they age. The value of an object is immaterial; the same standards of care should be shown to all objects, which need to be handled in a safe way that is appropriate for their physical make-up and construction.

Failure to understand the nature of museum objects can lead to irreparable

Source: J. M. A. Thompson (ed.), *Manual of Curatorship* (2nd edn), Oxford: Butterworth-Heinemann, 1992, pp. 455–458.

damage. The object in a museum is not simply a thing of beauty; it is also a piece of evidence. Often this evidence lies on the surface of the object – patination on the surface of a bronze, gilding on the frame of a painting, gesso and paint on the surface of a medieval sculpture.

The simple answer would seem to be not to handle the objects, but no museum can run without object movement. Objects enter a museum, where they will be inspected and registered. They will then be moved into store before being photographed, conserved and displayed. Once in display they may be required for loan. Displays change. Objects that are never displayed will still be required for study. All these activities are part of the normal life of a museum. We do not simply preserve objects in museums; we preserve them in order to make them available to the public through display and study. The duty of the museum profession is to preserve objects for future generations while making them accessible to this one. We cannot stop deterioration of objects, but we can take all possible steps to slow it down and prevent careless damage.

When an object is moved it is at risk:

* from direct impact, e.g. dropping a pot;
* from pressure on its surface, e.g. lifting flakes on a painting; and
* from unnatural stresses, e.g. lifting a chair by its arms.

To minimize the risks from these factors an object should never be carried unprotected, but should be placed within a container. To guard against any damage being caused through friction or vibration the object should be protected by padding or packing.

Preparation

The key to successful object handling is preparation. This includes preparation of the handler, the object, the route and the destination. The basic principle of all object movement is to think through every stage involved in the move before you start; then the move itself should be undertaken calmly and smoothly. Object movement should not be ill prepared and hurried – that way mistakes are much more likely.

The first step is to inspect the object. Ask yourself the following questions.

* What is it made of?
* Will it stand lifting?
* By which part should the object be lifted?
* Are there any loose parts which could become detached?
* How heavy is the object?
* How many people will be needed?
* What equipment is required?
* How heavy is the equipment needed?

If any of these questions are difficult to answer, get help from someone with more experience.

The second step is to decide how to move the object from A to B. Check the route and ask these questions.

- Will the object go through the doors?
- Will the object be able to make all the turns?
- Are there stairs, ramps or lifts to negotiate?
- What are the floor loadings permissible?
- Is the floor level, smooth, etc.?
- Will you damage the floor?
- How will you transport it?
- Does it need supporting, padding or tying?
- Will you clash with the public?
- Is the destination suitable and prepared?

The next step is to prepare yourself and the team who will move the object. It is wise to ensure that two people are always present when an object is moved. Thus one person can concentrate on the object while a second can make sure that the path is clear. If several people are needed to handle a given object the team must be disciplined. There can only be one team leader who will give instructions to the rest of the team. The responsibility for a safe move always rests with the team leader, who must ensure that everyone involved in the move understands exactly what is expected of them.

There should be no eating, drinking or smoking in the vicinity of the object. All handlers must have clean, dry hands and jewellery that could cause damage to an object must be removed. Ink or felt-tip pens should not be used near to objects; any notes that need to be made during a move should be taken in pencil. Any equipment to be used during the move, whether a pair of gloves, a basket or trolley, must also be clean and dry.

The use of gloves when handling objects is not as simple as might appear at first sight. It depends on the nature of the object to be handled.

Gloves must be worn:

- where acids from the hands can accelerate corrosion – this applies to metalwork, sick glass, lacquer and fine bindings and manuscripts;
- where heat from the hands can damage a surface – this applies to gilding; and
- where the health of staff is involved – this applies to dealing with soiled material for any reason such as a flood.

Gloves are optional:

- where staining or marking from fingerprints is a possibility; this may apply to unglazed ceramics, including terracotta, and the card mounts for prints, drawings, photographs or textiles.

Gloves should not be worn:

- where snagging may result – this is the case with paintings, fine jewellery, poly-chrome surfaces, un-mounted textiles and paper;
- where direct contact is essential for a secure grip – this is the case with stained glass panels, books and large furniture and sculpture.

The move

Once prepared and properly equipped, the object handlers must decide how to make contact with the object. Again you may find it useful to ask a series of questions:

Where do you grab hold of the object?

- Not at the top – to pick up any object such as a painting, pot or sculpture by the top is inviting disaster. The tension caused by the weight of the object can easily open up cracks and cause damage. Always lift from as low down on an object as possible and preferably with most of the weight balanced above the point of contact. To avoid this type of stress it is important not to drag an object – always push it.
- Not by any protrusions. All protrusions from an object are potential weak points and must be avoided at all costs. Never pick up a pot by its handle or a figure by its arms. Look for the most solid, stable area and use that as the point of contact.
- Maximize the area of contact. If you are manually lifting an object use the widest area of your hands possible as pressure increases if the area of contact is small. If moving a table try not to use only fingertip pressure, but lay your fingers along their length.
- Be aware of the centre of gravity. Remember that a high centre of gravity or a narrow base means that a small tilt could make the object unstable. If you are putting pots into a basket, it may be better to lay certain items on their sides, otherwise they could easily fall over. The centre of gravity of a supported object must be vertically over its base. If an object is suspended it will slip until its centre of gravity is vertically under the point of suspension.

How much force?

- The more force you use, the faster the object will move, or the quicker you may damage it.
- A weak force at the end of a long lever can do as much work (and, therefore, damage) as a strong force at the end of a short lever.
- If the speed of an object doubles, the amount of damage that could occur in the event of collision quadruples.

How do you transport the object?

- Never simply carry an object in your arms; it should be *in* something (e.g. a box or basket) or *on* something (e.g. a tray or trolley).

- Never overload a container or vehicles and make sure that the object fits properly within it without overhanging the sides.
- Never move objects of the same general type but of vastly different sizes or weights together.

Where do you put the object down?

- In a clean, stable environment, similar to the one from which the object was moved.
- Never leave an object sitting directly on the floor or in any kind of vulnerable position.
- Changes of environment should take place slowly; if an object is to move outside the museum the packing must provide reasonable insulation from outside conditions.

Safe lifting

It is important to remember that the law demands that we pay constant attention to health and safety at work; this is of particular relevance to the movement of objects. It should be seen as an area of mutual concern for both employers and employees. The employer is responsible for providing safe conditions of work, training and instruction and to make available all necessary safety and protective equipment for the tasks. The employee is responsible for using the equipment provided and to assist in making any improvement necessary to conform with safety standards.

Manual handling

Organize the work to minimize the amount of lifting necessary using mechanical means or other aids. When help is needed for lifting heavy or awkward loads, get everyone to work together, but make sure only one person gives clear and unhurried instructions. Provide protective clothing for hands and feet where necessary.

Make sure that everyone knows the correct lifting techniques.

- Do not jerk and shove, twisting the body may cause injury.
- Lift in easy stages, floor to knee, then from knee to carrying position. Reverse this lifting method when setting the load down.
- Hold weights close to the body. Lift with the legs and keep the back straight.
- Grip loads with palms, not fingertips and do not change your grip while carrying.
- Do not let the load obstruct your view; make sure the route is clear as you move.

When using equipment:

- always have a competent person operating any machinery or lifting gear;
- obey all instructions and procedures for using equipment, do not take short-cuts and never exceed safe working loads;

- never use make-shift, damaged or badly worn equipment; and
- always check even the simplest piece of equipment regularly to see that nothing is loose or dangerous (e.g. check that the tyres are firmly in position on a truck).

With regard to orderly placement of the object:

- do not allow items to protrude from stacks or bins into gangways;
- never climb racks to reach upper shelves, always use a ladder or steps;
- do not lean heavy stacks against structural walls; and
- never exceed the safe loading of racks, shelves or floors.

Once a move has been completed it is essential that the object's new resting place is recorded and that the personnel who will be responsible for the object are informed of its arrival. Check that no damage has occurred to the object, remember not to discard any packing material before searching it thoroughly for fragments which may have become detached in transit. If any damage has occurred it must be reported thoroughly and the cause of the damage investigated.

Policy on object handling

It is expected practice for museums to develop a Collections Management Policy, to provide guidelines for the body of museum practices and procedures which allow the sensible acquisition and disposal, care and preservation, security and accountability for objects, their movement (including loans) and documentation. The systems and procedures used for the handling of objects, both during routine operations and in 'disastrous' circumstances, should be established for every museum so that all staff understand what is expected of them.

Staff should be trained in the proper handling of objects so that they have an appreciation of the need for care and an understanding of the many dangers that face objects within the collections. Knowledge of the general principles of planning moves and handling objects is essential, as is the thorough grounding in the procedures for safeguarding objects and the welfare of the people who work with them. [. . .]

Safe handling of museum objects is easy if you apply good common sense; all that is needed is a sound knowledge of the material to be moved and good planning. Nevertheless, experience shows that if staff are provided with clear rules to be followed as they move objects the risk to those objects is reduced. The compilation of such rules depends on the nature of the museum.

Chapter 4

Six Steps to Safe Shipment

Paul Marcon

S HIPPING FRAGILE ITEMS SAFELY always presents a challenge. However, care and attention to a few important details can prevent unnecessary damage. The following information will guide you through the packaging process and provide a few pointers that can make a big difference. While this will substantially improve your prospects for safe shipment, exceptional challenges may still arise. Should you require additional assistance with your packaging problems, please contact CCI; we will be happy to provide further information and resources as well as detailed consultation and design services.

When shipping a museum object, the packaging will need to protect the object from the following hazards:

- shock and vibration
- punctures, dents, abrasion, grime, and distortion
- compressive forces (those acting on packages during shipment and in storage)
- environmental hazards (temperature and relative humidity (RH), water, pests, and pollutants).

The following steps provide a practical approach to packing fragile items:

- Step 1. Consider the type of shipment and the carriers.
- Step 2. Plan package weight and sizes to reduce shipping hazards.
- Step 3. Increase object durability (if possible).
- Step 4. Recognize the benefits of primary packaging (e.g. mounts, protective wrapping).

Source: CCI website, www.cci-icc.gc.ca/crc/articles/sixsteps-sixetapes/index-eng.aspx.

- Step 5. Use cushioning material effectively.
- Step 6. Find or construct good shipping crates.

Step 1. Consider the type of shipment and the carriers

When planning a shipment, take a few moments to consider the questions in Table 4.1.

Table 4.1 The answers to these questions will help you plan your shipment and anticipate the necessary packaging requirements

Question	Why the question is important
Who will transport the shipment?	Investment in reputable carriers (whether art handlers, commercial carriers, hand carriers/couriers, or delivery/postal services) is one of the best ways to avoid losses and major accidents during shipping. Reputable carriers have well-maintained fleets with sought-after features such as air ride suspension, temperature control, and the proper hardware to properly secure cargo in transport vehicles. Reputable carriers will answer your questions and maintain good communication over the course of the shipment. When selecting a carrier, ask about their level of experience moving the type of object you are shipping, confirm their ability to provide the service requested (e.g. service to a remote area), check that they have appropriate equipment/vehicles (e.g. air ride suspension), and ensure that they can meet site-specific facility requirements.
What do you know about the distribution network?	A door-to-door shipment without cargo transfers between vehicles can enable safe shipment with minimal, or substantially reduced, packaging – but this is generally the exception rather than the rule. Most shipments, whether by art handlers or other carriers, involve several loading and off-loading cycles. Typical art shipments involve air and truck transport. Other modes (e.g. rail and ocean) introduce additional hazards, e.g. high levels of shock due to slack between rail cars, high moisture levels during lengthy ocean voyages, and shifting of contents that are not properly secured in multimodal containers.
When will it travel?	It is important to anticipate and make provisions for summer heat and winter cold.
Where is it going?	Shipment in Canada and the United States offers flexibility in crating material choices, e.g. softwood lumber can be used in Canada and the United States but there are restrictions on its use in international shipments. Package design details for a multiple venue exhibition differ from those for a simple source-to-destination shipment. International shipments require attention to customs requirements and package designs that enable easy inspection if necessary.
Why are you shipping it?	If the object is being shipped for treatment, special protective measures may apply. Seek the advice of a qualified conservator. If it's a single source-to-destination shipment, a simple packing strategy may be appropriate. If it's a travelling exhibition, the package should be designed for easy packing and unpacking at each venue.

It also helps to know how and why damage occurs during shipment and what can be done to avoid it (see Table 4.2).

Table 4.2 Typical causes of damage during shipment and how to avoid them

Issue	How it causes damage	Remedies
Fundamental problems	Collision of loose object parts. Collision of loose objects with each other inside the package. Collision of loose objects with the packing crate. Abrasion. Deformation of crates that strains their contents; failure of crates that spills their contents. Distortion, mechanical damage, or soiling of objects during preparation for transit.	Take measures to improve the durability of an object (see Step 3). Use primary packaging to control collision and abrasion effects. Find or build crates that incorporate performance-enhancing construction details. Plan exhibit installation and removal carefully – ensure adequate time and space for the necessary handling operations and use qualified handlers.
Excessive force	Inadequate shock mitigation. Inadequate vibration mitigation.	Select and use the right cushioning material.
Lack of restraint in transit	Repetitive bouncing of cargo. Items falling off stacks in moving vehicles.	Ensure cargo is secured in the transport vehicle.
Environmental hazards	Extreme heat or cold. RH extremes. Water (e.g. rain or snow). Pests. Pollutants (chemicals from packing materials).	Specify temperature-controlled vehicles. Insulate cases. Wrap RH-sensitive items. Use suitable crates made of appropriate materials.
Extreme hazards	Intentional mishandling of packages. Vehicle accidents.	Choose reputable carriers and handlers.

Step 2. Plan package weights and sizes to reduce shipping hazards

It's a fact – smaller packages experience greater shipping hazards. For example, a package that weighs less than 15 kg might be dropped from a high height or thrown. Grouping one or more small items into a larger package that weighs 15–30 kg will subject each item to less force than if the items were packed individually. It may also save time and money by avoiding unnecessary packaging.

The distribution network is the carrier (or carriers) that get the package from Point A to Point B. Several distribution network scenarios are described in Table 4.3 in approximately increasing order of hazard intensity. The key to successful shipment is adapting the packing strategy to the worst-case hazards that can be expected in any given scenario.

Quality carriers can reduce shipping hazards and packaging requirements. However, when packaging a shipment, always plan for the worst leg of the journey. For example, even if quality carriers are involved in all but one leg of a journey, the

Table 4.3 Distribution network scenarios

Scenario	Hazard intensity	Packaging comments
Art handler door-to-door shipment without cargo transfers	Low	Use lighter crating or primary packaging alone (see Step 4 for information on primary packing). Reasonable cushioning is still advisable for high-value or very fragile items.
Art handlers and air cargo for long haul shipment	Low to moderate	Use heavier crating and moderate protection to accommodate cargo transfers.
Art handlers in combination with other art handlers or trusted commercial carriers	Moderate	Pack for the toughest leg of the journey (where the greatest hazards are expected) and the stresses of multiple cargo transfers.
Commercial carriers	Moderate to high	Use durable crating with good cushioning. Crates built according to recognized standards (e.g. ASTM, military, or other organizations) can be an asset. Worst-case hazards for commercial shipment can be anticipated.
Parcel post or courier shipments	High to very high	This scenario involves small packages and high hazard intensities so packages need to be designed accordingly.

packing needs to be designed for that leg of the journey where the greatest hazards are expected.

Step 3. Increase object durability (if possible)

Sometimes it is possible to make an object more durable by correcting the attributes that make it susceptible to forces:

- Attribute 1. Flexibility or looseness in the object or its parts.
- Attribute 2. Structural features that amplify the effects of forces encountered during shipment.
- Attribute 3. Materials that are already weak or damaged.

Table 4.4 provides examples of vulnerable objects and how to deal with them at the object level.

Improving the durability of an object can reduce dependence on packaging and can protect the object when it is packed, unpacked, or moved in-house.

Step 4. Recognize the benefits of primary packaging (e.g. mounts, protective wrapping)

Primary packaging ranges from simple wrapping to elaborate transit mounts that can restrain an object in all directions. This basic form of packaging is not intended to

Table 4.4 Examples of vulnerable objects and suggestions for preventing damage

Example	Attribute	Remedy(ies)
Small- to medium-sized canvas paintings with out-of-plane displacement (i.e. bowing out of the canvas perpendicular to the plane of the canvas)	#1	Backing boards (see CCI Notes 10/10).
Large canvas paintings with out-of-plane displacement	#1	Backing boards (see CCI Notes 10/10). Foam inserts (consult a conservator). Stretcher linings (see CCI Notes 10/10).
Stretched canvases with weak frames or stretcher bar structures that could scissor (deform)	#2	Backing boards will reinforce the stretcher structure (see CCI Notes 10/10). Frames with large pieces of loose ornamentation that could fall on the painting require special consideration.
Large items such as furniture and machinery with weak structural integrity	#2	Verification of connectors and attachments, and tightening if necessary. Blocking or bracing provisions for transit.
Paintings with fragile paint layers	#3	Stabilization for shipment (consult a conservator).
Contemporary art items with complex assembly (e.g. a skeleton)	#1, #2	Disassembly (if feasible) – the individual parts of an item are often less fragile than the assembled whole.

control shock or vibration directly. However, it can and does make a difficult object easier to handle and pack and can also reduce an object's overall susceptibility to force. This not only reduces dependence on the packing system during shipment, it also makes the object less susceptible to damage when it is handled in-house. Table 4.5 provides some examples of primary packaging treatments.

Primary packaging can also serve as a control measure against incorrect RH as well as dust, insects, water, and contact with incompatible materials. Table 4.6 provides some examples of useful primary packaging materials, although many more are available.

For additional material choices and guidelines on their use, see *Mount-making for Museum Objects*, Second Edition, and *Technical Bulletin 14 Working with Polyethylene Foam and Fluted Plastic Sheet*. The Packing, Art handling & Crating Information Network (PACIN) site also has an extensive material list. However, although many choices exist, most packers have their own short list of preferred materials.

Temperature and humidity

Temperature buffering during shipment can be achieved by lining the inside of a shipping container, or the inside surfaces of an inner case of a double case system (see Figure 4.1), with polystyrene plank insulation. Note that cushioning material is also a good insulator, so items completely wrapped in cushioning material will also be buffered from temperature changes.

Table 4.5 Primary packaging makes packing easier and can make an important contribution to the overall effectiveness of a protective package

Example	Function
Basic wrapping with an interleaf material followed by polyethylene (e.g. wrapping paintings as outlined in CCI Notes 10/16).	Avoids punctures, dents, and abrasion, and protects against minor impact. A reasonably tight-fitting polyethylene wrapping that encloses a cardboard-covered painting or painting/frame can buffer RH changes and protect the painting surface.
Armatures or other provisions to support an item with fragile surfaces at non-critical areas.	Avoids direct contact between the fragile item surfaces and the cushioning material. Avoids abrasion of a fragile surface against the cushioning material. Provides an intermediate structure or form that can easily be cushioned.
Mummy wrap for a fragile surface (use unbuffered tissue paper made of abaca fibres).	Gently protects a fragile surface enabling the object to be cushioned directly (not recommended for paintings).
Negative mount (a form fitting cut-out in a firm foam material such as polyethylene foam). An interleave material may be used between the object and the mount to improve the fit of the mount or to protect fragile object surfaces.	Creates a lower load per unit area than do individual support points, which is especially important for fragile object surfaces. Allows for voids to be carved around small projections that are easily damaged when wrapping/unwrapping or packing/unpacking. Because the object/mount combination is stiff compared to the cushioning system, it limits movement along the object/mount interface and associated problems such as abrasion.
Hard objects such as bottles or dishes packed together in a box and separated from each other and the inner box surfaces with an interleave material such as thin cardboard or thin sheets of polyethylene foam.	Avoids impact between hard objects.
Several items firmly packed together in a container with suitable interleaves between them, or partitions for heavy items, to ensure that they do not move relative to each other.	Enables multiple items to be protected with one cushioning system. Simplifies the design of the cushioning material. Assures good cushion performance. Allows for economical use of expensive cushion materials.
Filling/support for thin-walled items such as ethnographic objects (e.g. hats, boxes).	Restrains and immobilizes fragile items and helps them retain their shape during shipment.

Humidity control for organic materials during shipment can be achieved by wrapping them with an interleaf material and then with a polyethylene sheet, and closing the seams with tape. Note that this treatment is effective only if the contained air space around the object is minimal – which means that the object should be wrapped fairly closely (although it is not necessary to achieve a really tight fit). The wrapped object can then be packed into the inner case of a double case package.

Table 4.6 A collection of useful primary packaging materials and their applications

Material	Description	Applications
Polyethylene sheet (HDPE)	High-density polyethylene. Higher density than ordinary polyethylene sheet, offers better protection with thinner films. Few release agents and plasticizers. Available as small food-grade bags or in larger rolls from bag manufacturers. Can be found in home improvement centres, where it is sold as painters' plastic.	Wrapping irregular shapes (because it is thinner, smoother, and more flexible than low-density sheet, it is better able to conform to irregular shapes without excess bulk or folds).
Polyethylene sheet (LDPE)	Low-density polyethylene sheet. Chemically stable, but talc or other release agents may be present and surface may also have an oily residue.	Wrapping paintings (with an interleaf material between the polyethylene and the painting) and inner boxes.
Teflon thread seal tape	Synthetic fluoropolymer made by Dupont. Chemically stable and non-toxic. Very stretchable and able to conform to various shapes. Conforms easily to cavity shapes in mounts without adding bulk.	Covering foam pads. Use with polyester batting to line cavities in mounts.
Aluminum-coated polyethylene (Marvelseal 360)	Nylon-coated aluminum barrier bonded to polyethylene. Effectively blocks passage of water, gases, and pollutants.	Lining the interior of shipping crates – especially if long storage periods are anticipated. Making bags to encapsulate objects. Lining interior cases of double case packages.
Unbuffered abaca tissue paper	Unbuffered long-fibred tissues made from abaca fibres similar to Japanese paper. Expensive.	Cushioning very delicate materials. Interleaving delicate items where it is necessary to conform to intricate forms. "Mummy wrapping" objects with fragile surfaces by repeatedly wrapping the item with thin strips.
Tyvek soft structure fabric	Spun-bonded high-density polyethylene fibres woven into a fabric. Lightweight, chemically stable, non-abrasive, and tear resistant. Heat-weldable to itself or it can be sewn.	Placing over polyester batting material to form pads. Interleaving material for contouring cavities and covering foam pads.
Cross-linked polyethylene sheet (Volara)	Made by Voltek (Volara is the brand name of Voltek's closed-cell polyethylene foam).	Heat-welding to polyethylene foam mounts to provide a non-abrasive surface at contact points.

Table 4.6 Continued

Material	Description	Applications
	Smooth and non-abrading. Common density is 33 kg/m³ (2 pcf*). Thickness range is 3–12 mm (1/8–1/2 in.); commonly used thickness is 6 mm (1/4 in.).	Lining cases and crates. Padding small unframed paintings in transit frames.
Stretch wrap	Linear low-density polyethylene (LLDPE). Flexible; elongates to wrap around shapes. Best used with a barrier material. Comes in roll widths of 50 mm (2 in.) to 760 mm (30 in.). Can be obtained from moving or packing material supply outlets.	Holding delicate objects or object parts in place. Securing boxes together. Sealing packages against water, pests, etc.
Polyethylene foam sheet	Chemically stable closed-cell polyethylene foam; typical trade names are Ethafoam, Plastazoate and Polyplank. Easy to work with; can be heat-welded to itself. Most commonly used density is 33 kg/m³ (2 pcf). A popular thickness is 50 mm (2 in.).	Making long-term storage mounts and transit mounts.
Acid-free tissue, unbuffered	Acid-free tissue made from high-quality pulp that does not contain lignin.	Wrapping metals to avoid possible condensation. Wrapping thin organic materials to help stabilize humidity after they are enclosed.
Polyester quilt batting	Sold in rolls to make quilts. Can be layered.	Padding uneven or complex surfaces.
Extruded polystyrene foam plank (Styrofoam)	Typically sold for insulation purposes. Limited application for cushioning as it is non-resilient (does not return to its original shape after impact). Excellent insulator. Chemically stable.	Lining the interior of shipping cases or interior cases of double case packages to provide temperature buffering.

* pcf = pounds per cubic foot.

Step 5. Use cushioning material effectively

Cushioning items with simple geometry and durable surfaces is easy. These objects can be wrapped or covered with a suitable interleaf and then cushioned directly (placed in foam cut-outs). Objects with complex geometry, or those that are highly fragile, are harder to cushion directly. In this case, primary packaging or the use of a double

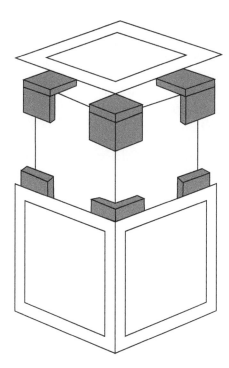

Figure 4.1 A double case package consisting of an inner box that is supported on corner pad cushions and placed in an outer crate

case system can transform difficult shapes into simple ones that are much easier to
cushion, and can provide additional protection for fragile projections or surfaces during packing and unpacking. Several examples of this are provided in Table 4.7.

Table 4.7 The addition of a mount, intermediate framework, or an inner box can
simplify packaging of items with irregular shapes or fragile surfaces. These measures
can save time and often result in a better performing package

Item	How to simplify complex shapes
Unframed painting	Add a travel frame that provides flat durable surfaces for cushion application (see CCI Notes 10/16).
Delicate ornate frame	Fix the object inside a handling, transport, and storage frame (HTS) with flat surfaces (see CCI Notes 10/16).
Fragile pottery item with projections	Use a carved negative mount that has voids carved around the small projections. This mount can then be cushioned or placed in a cushioned inner case.
Several fragile items that will be shipped together	Pack the items into the inner case of a double case system with suitable interleaves or mounts. Use partitions for heavy items.

Cushioning limits shocks and vibration to levels that objects can tolerate without
damage. However, the cushioning needs to be properly selected for good performance. Important features of cushioning include:

- material type
- material thickness
- material resilience (the material returns to its original shape after impact)
- correct loading (i.e. the cushion material is not too soft (overloaded) or too hard (insufficiently loaded) for a very fragile object)
- free movement of the cushioned item (i.e. the object is not tightly bound in the cushioning material).

Modern cushioning materials can provide very effective protection for fragile items when they are used correctly. Table 4.8 lists three material types that can be used in many cushioning applications.

Adequate cushion thickness is necessary for effective cushioning. As a general guide, use at least 50 mm (2 in.) of cushion thickness for fragile items in small- to

Table 4.8 The listed cushioning materials can solve many packing problems. Calculating the weight per unit area (W/A) on any given side of an object (see Figure 4.2) provides a basic assessment of material suitability for the cushion design under consideration

Material	Information	Applications	Typical W/A range for cushioning
Polyurethane ester	Dark grey coloured (usually) with open-cell structure. Most useful form has a density of 33 kg/m³ (2 pcf*) and a thickness of 50 mm (2 in.). Does not go by a trade name. Avoid direct contact with metals or other artifact surfaces.	Protective cushions. Good choice for cushioning double case packages.	For W in kilograms, A in square centimetres: W/A range is 0.003–0.06 kg/cm². For W in pounds, A in square inches: W/A range is 0.04–0.8 lb./in².
Polyethylene	White closed-cell polyethylene foam. Chemically stable. Commonly used density is 33 kg/m³ (2 pcf). Trade names are Ethafoam, Plastazoate and Polyplank. Thermoplastic, heat-weldable to itself.	Excellent choice for mount-making due to chemical stability. Easy to work with. Also used for cushioning heavier items.	For W in kilograms, A in square centimetres: W/A range is 0.015–0.1 kg/cm². For W in pounds, A in square inches: WA range is 0.2–2 lb./in².
Bubble pack	Air-encapsulated film. Use with an interleaf material to avoid deposits from release agents. Use a thickness of at least 50 mm (2 in.) on all sides.	Lightweight materials with simple or complex geometry and durable surfaces.	For W in kilograms, A in square centimetres: W/A range is 0.002–0.03 kg/cm². For W in pounds, A in square inches: W/A range is 0.03–0.4 lb./in².

* pcf = pounds per cubic foot.

medium-sized packages. Packages less than 15 kg (33 lb.), or exceptionally fragile objects, may benefit from additional cushion thickness – 75 mm (3 in.) or 100 mm (4 in.).

Resilience is the ability of a material to recover its shape when it is deformed, which makes it effective against repeated impacts. Polyurethane and polyethylene foams are both resilient materials.

Correct cushion loading can be achieved through material choice and pad geometry. Cushion designs may range from complete coverage, as in the case of wrapping and foam cut-outs, to individual pads. For any given cushioning method, the amount of cushion material in contact with the object will establish the load per unit area on the cushioning material. The suitability of a material for any given application can then be verified from cushion performance data (described below).

Note that cushioning is required on all sides of an object in small- to medium-sized packages. However, cushioning requirements decrease for very large packages. Base protection (padding the base of the object only) combined with suitable restraint against rebound can suffice for very large items.

For effective shock and vibration isolation, everything that floats on the cushioning system (i.e. the cushioned item) should be reasonably firm. The cushioned item will then move up and down on the cushioning as a single unit without any secondary movement of its own. To achieve this, gently restrain any loose or vibration-prone items and deal with object vulnerability by treatment, disassembly, or other means as discussed in steps 3 and 4. The cushioning system should be the most flexible part of the package.

Figure 4.2 illustrates the various forms that cushioning can take for several object geometries. A good material combination for many applications is polyurethane ester

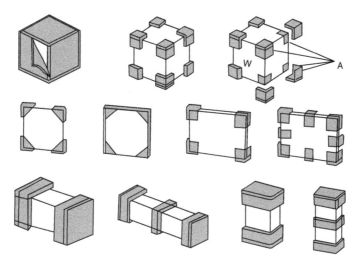

Figure 4.2 Protective cushioning systems for a variety of object geometries. Polyurethane ester foam can often be used with very good results. To verify that the material is being used correctly, the load per unit area on the cushions can be calculated by dividing the total object weight (W) by the total area (A) of foam contacting each side

[density 33 kg/m3 (2 pcf); thickness 50 mm (2 in.)] for pads and firm polyethylene foam for mounts. The cushion designs in Figure 4.2 involve straight cuts of foam. Polyurethane ester material can be cut easily on a band saw or with an electric carving knife. Polyethylene foam is chemically stable and can be carved and bonded, making it a popular choice for mount-making applications; it can also be used as a cushioning material for heavy objects.

To verify that a cushioning material is being used correctly, divide the total object weight (W) by the total area (A) of cushioning material on any given side as described in Table 4.8. If the result is outside of the indicated range, consider another material or change the pad geometry (e.g. increase or decrease the amount of cushioning material in contact with the object). *Corner Pads for Double Case Packages* provides instructions for making corner pads for double case packages without the need for calculations. A computer program for cushion design (PadCAD) is also available from CCI, and a trial version of the software can be downloaded from the CCI website. This software can be used to design all of the cushioning systems illustrated in Figure 4.2.

Step 6. Find or construct good shipping crates

Shipping crates are the first line of defence against shipping hazards. While it is easy to find good woodworkers, experienced crate builders are less common. A commercially fabricated crate that is built according to established industrial standards can be a good investment.

Two types of shipping crates can easily be constructed in-house: a triwall crate and a basic wood crate (Table 4.9). Construction details for triwall crates are published in CCI Notes 1/4. Construction and assembly details for wood crates are presented below.

Table 4.9 Two crating alternatives for in-house construction

Crate type	Description	Applications
Triwall crate	Triple wall corrugated cardboard with softwood framing. Detailed instructions for the triwall case are available in CCI Notes 1/4. Construction time can be as little as 20 minutes. Triwall crates are lightweight and surprisingly strong.	Local moves, long distance moves with high-quality transport.
Basic wood shipping crate	Plywood (sanded one side or sanded two sides), thickness of 9, 12, or 18 mm (3/8, 1/2, or 3/4 in.), with 19 × 64 mm (1 × 3) or 19 × 80 mm (1 × 4) cleats (framing). Handles and skids can be added. Design can be modified into other forms such as boxes.	A strong case suitable for domestic and international shipments of loads up to 450 kg (1000 lb.). For heavy loads use thicker plywood for the base and wall panels.

The panels of wood crates should be at least 9.5 mm (3/8 in.) thick. Many builders prefer to use thicker wood (12 mm, 1/2 in.) because the thicker sheets are flatter and easier to work with and the cost difference is small.

Features such as handles and skids can improve the ease of moving crates by manual and mechanical means, and careful handle positioning can reduce hazards by minimizing the height that a package is raised during manual handling.

For added protection, a layer of aluminum-coated polyethylene (e.g. Marvelseal) can be bonded to the case interior with an ordinary iron. This layer will:

- block the entry of water
- provide a barrier against organic compounds released by the wood
- enable the crate to be stored in uncontrolled environments
- allow cushioning material to slide easily into the case interior
- improve the thermal performance of the crate.

Painting the case interior provides a lower-cost alternative to Marvelseal, and is advisable if the contents will be stored inside the case for long periods of time. The following paints are suitable for this purpose:

- acrylic latex paint
- acrylic-urethane emulsion paint
- 2-part epoxy or 2-part polyurethane
- moisture-cured polyurethane.

Note that these paints will need to dry thoroughly (4 weeks is recommended) before the case is used.

Some paints and coatings should never be used inside shipping crates as they give off compounds that could react with artifact materials. Unless the package is a double case system, avoid using any coatings formed by oxidative polymerization. These include:

- oil-based paint
- alkyd
- 1-part epoxy
- oil-modified polyurethane.

The case interior may be left uncovered/unpainted if the objects placed inside it are wrapped and will not be stored in the case for long periods of time. However, for cases with uncovered/unpainted interiors, good construction detailing is essential to prevent the ingress of water, pests, or other agents.

Any paint or coating can be applied to the exterior of the shipping case.

N.B.: Wood packaging shipped to international destinations other than the United States may be regulated to avoid the spread of insect species that could harm agriculture and forestry industries. At the time of writing, there are no restrictions on the use of manufactured woods such as plywood, particle board, and wafer board; however, package components made of softwood lumber are subject to some regulations.

Features of a good crate

- Handles positioned for ease of handling and to minimize the height that the crate must be raised (ground to hand distance for standing male/female is approximately 825 mm/780 mm).
- Skids to keep the case off the ground and permit easy access for moving equipment if the case is heavy. (Figure 4.3)
- Screw or latch closures.
- Recessed hardware that won't break off.
- Good appearance.
- Discrete labeling as "Fragile" or "Handle with Care". Do not label as "Art".

Basic wood shipping crate

Figure 4.4 illustrates how the panels of a basic wood shipping crate are constructed, and how they are assembled to form the finished crate.

The lapped corner construction (detail A) adds substantial strength to the crate.

The large upper image shows the crate in a tall narrow orientation that would be suitable for paintings. The crate can be changed into a box by turning it on its back panel (opposite the removable cover shown) and relocating the skids. The result is shown in the lower left image.

Constructing a basic wood shipping crate

- Construct the panels first. Apply glue, position the cleats on the panels, and tack them in place with staples or nails at the ends not closer than 10 mm (⅜ in.) to the edge of the cleat.

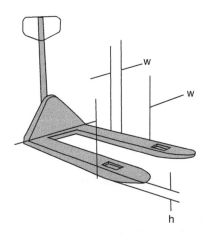

Figure 4.3 Consider pump truck access when building or specifying large or heavy crates. Allow a skid spacing width (W) of 710 mm (28 in.) for wide trucks and of 580 mm (23 in.) for narrow trucks. Allow a width (w) of 200 mm (8 in.) for tines. Skids must raise crates to a height (h) of 100 mm (4 in.) above ground level for easy access

DETAIL A

Figure 4.4 Basic wood shipping crate

- Turn the panel over and fasten the cleat from the panel side with two staggered rows of fasteners spaced about 150 mm (6 in.) apart and not closer than 10 mm (³⁄₈ in.) to the edge of the cleat.
- If nails are used, ensure that they are 12 mm (¼ in.) longer than the thickness of the panel plus the cleat. Drive them from the cleat side and bend them over. If staples are used, choose divergent staples (designed for increased holding power) and insert them on a 45° angle as shown.
- Assemble the panels with screws or staples. Ensure the fasteners are long enough to penetrate the plywood and anchor them securely into the cleats. Place fasteners in rows with about 150 mm (6 in.) between them. If cleats are more than 80 mm (2¼ in.) wide, use two fasteners at the ends.
- If the crate will be used for only one or a few shipments, screws can be used as a simple means of attaching the cover. However, if the crate will be used for multiple shipments, use captive nuts or latches to attach the cover.
- Edge cleats can be added to the inside of the cover (left) to improve the case seal details and to increase the crate's resistance to deformation.

Helpful resources

Primary packing and mount-making

CCI Technical Bulletin No. 14 — Working with Polyethylene Foam and Fluted Plastic Sheet by Carl Schlichting. ISBN 0–662–61042–3.

Mount-making for Museum Objects, Second Edition by Robert Barclay, André Bergeron, and Carole Dignard. ISBN 0–662–18843–0.

Cushion design

Corner Pads for Double Case Packages – Quickly make high-performance corner pads using a simple table. Available on the CCI website.

Pad CAD – A 30-day trial version of PadCAD, a computer program, can be downloaded from the CCI.

Pad CAD User Manual – Contains information on shipping hazards and practical aspects of protective cushion design.

Packing and transport of paintings

Art in Transit: Studies in the Transport of Paintings edited by M. F. Mecklenburg (Preprints for the International Conference on the Packing and Transportation of Paintings Sept 1991, London UK). Available in electronic format (pdf file) by request.

CCI Notes 10/10 – *Backing Boards for Paintings on Canvas*.

CCI Notes 10/15 – *Paintings: Considerations Prior to Travel*.

CCI Notes 10/16 – *Wrapping a Painting*.

Links of interest

APA, the Engineered Wood Association – an informative materials handling guide that includes practical information and step-by-step instructions for making large wooden shipping containers.

Canadian Food Inspection Agency – regulations for wood products.

CCI Newsletter 22 – packaging articles and some early case studies.

Packing, Art handling & Crating Information Network (PACIN) – information on crating and packing, material lists, publications.

Wooden crates and crating standards.

Chapter 5

Conservation Skills: preventive conservation – storage

Chris Caple

Storage

A S PART OF A MUSEUM collection, objects gain a value beyond their financial worth. As museum objects they are intended to be preserved for ever, for study, display or loan, and have information permanently associated with them. The term value is used, hereafter, to refer to the value of the object to the museum in terms of evidence of the past, a potential object for display and educative use.

The purpose of storage is to retain objects as a source of information, education and display, by preserving them in as near as possible their present condition. This can be seen at its simplest as putting a broken chair away in an attic to prevent further damage. If the chair is not valuable, the risk of loss or damage (stacking, dust, and insects) in the attic may be seen as acceptable. As the object rises in value then it becomes more important to store it carefully and safely, ensuring that it is both well preserved and readily retrievable.

Levels of storage

- Collection: Initially objects are collected. This prevents their loss, deliberate damage or disposal. There remains risk of environmental and physical damage to the objects, objects are difficult to find and they have little purpose or meaning.
- Catalogued Collection: Every object is uniquely identified and a written record of information about the object created. This enables the collection to be of use to a wide range of people. There remains a risk of environmental and physical

Source: *Conservation Skills: Judgement, Method and Decision Making*, London: Routledge, 2000, pp. 152–160.

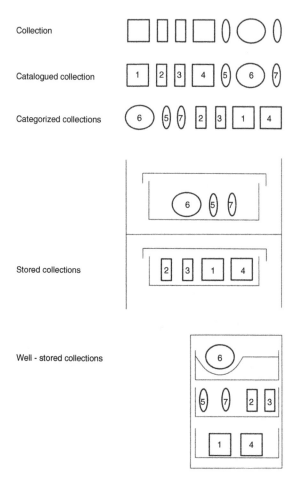

Figure 5.1 Levels of storage

damage. Objects are difficult to find but, through their unique identifier, can be correlated with their information.

- Categorised Collections: These collections are categorised to aid storage, object or information recovery, e.g. storing all the objects of a similar type, or from a single location, together. There remains a risk of environmental and physical damage, but objects and information are relatively easy to find.
- Stored Collections: These collections are given some protection against physical and environmental damage. Large objects are draped with dust sheets to prevent dust and light raining down on the object, smaller objects are boxed. Such measures reduce handling and physical damage to objects, insulate the object against changes in temperature and humidity and reduce accessibility for insect pests and unnecessary human inspection. Objects are placed on shelves or on pallets to lift them above the floor surface and the risk of flood damage. Improved security reduces the risk of theft. Storage locations are numbered (building, room, aisle, bay, shelf, box).

- Well Stored Collections: These collections will have their environment monitored and modified to meet the recommended conditions for storage. There will be an even density of objects through the storage space to maximise the modified storage environment. Storage materials used are inert and pose no threat to the collection. Often the object is stored, with regard to the material of which it is composed, in specialised conditions, e.g. archaeological ironwork stored at low humidities to prevent further corrosion. Many objects will sit in specifically made or shaped supports to provide the highest level of protection. This results in objects only being stored in a specific location. Such 'specific location storage' is most appropriate for high value objects, so that if an object is missing the loss is quickly noticed, or fragile items where specifically designed and constructed storage is crucial to the continued well being of the object. All storage locations are marked on object records and the contents of every box, shelf, bay, aisle and room are summarised of the exterior of the container.

The construction of a special storage container is always an important element in the conservation process. It provides a strong visual cue, emphasising to the curator or owner how valuable the object is and indicating the need to care for the object. Only through using the specifically shaped storage container will the object be stored 'in the approved manner'. If it is more difficult or awkward to store the object some other way, the simple correct method will be used, make it easy to do the right thing.

[. . .]

Black box standard

The theoretical ideal for storing any object is in a black box. Such a theoretical box represents secure storage, insulation against temperature and RH (relative humidity) fluctuation, a barrier against harmful gasses, light, insect pests and a barrier to being handled by human beings (Frost 1994). The box is labelled so the contents are known and can be retrieved. It represents the ideal environment for whatever it contains and every object's black box standard is potentially different. Any actual object storage environment can be compared against the black box standard. Though theoretically storage approaching absolute zero ($-273°C$), at which all chemical reactions cease, may be seen as the black box standard, such conditions are costly and not practical, and less extreme conditions are more usefully considered as a workable black box standard.

The need for human beings to interact with objects and the requirements for display have resulted in work to define modified ideal storage and display conditions where rates of decay are low enough to be barely perceptible. Probably the nearest to such environments were those created for storing Britain's national collections of art and artefacts during the Second World War. After initial storage in the Aldwych Underground tunnels the British Museum collections were moved to the Bath stone quarry at Westwood. It had taken many months to achieve a stable RH due to the porous limestone of the Westwood quarry, which had to be sealed and a refrigeration dehumidification system installed. Finally, when stable conditions had been established, the collections were moved during 1941/2. The National Gallery stored their collections in buildings specially constructed in the huge caverns of the slate quarry at Manod in North Wales. These buildings used heated air to control RH and managed to achieve a near constant 58% RH and 63°F. These conditions were very stable and regarded as far better than those at the National Gallery (Haynes 1993).

The clearest attempt to define such standards in scientific terms and bring them together into a coherent form was the work of Garry Thomson of the National Gallery in London, who published *The Museum Environment* in 1978. He proposed the first series of environmental conditions for objects, identifying that incorrect levels of: humidity, light, temperature, pollutant gases, etc. would damage objects. His recommendations have been widely adopted throughout the museum world. As a result of increased understanding of the nature of decay processes and advances in technology, research and management techniques, conservators should now be able to use their judgement to achieve better or more cost effective environmental conditions for objects.

- Though the concept of specification of environmental standards gained acceptance in the 1980s, concern for the welfare of objects often led to absurdly narrow levels being specified. These could not even be accurately monitored, let alone achieved (Ashley-Smith et al. 1994). In the early 1990s work by Michalski and colleagues at CCI (Canadian Conservation Institute) (Michalski 1993) and Erhardt at the Smithsonian Institution (Erhardt and Mecklenburg 1994) demonstrated that cycling of RH in the mid range does not damage most objects. Only extremely high or low RH will lead to direct damage of objects and materials, especially stressed jointed or composite objects.
- Work on environmental standards has led to the establishment of UK national standards for the storage and care of a range of types of museum object (Museums and Galleries Commission 1992, 1993a, 1993b, 1994, 1995, 1996, 1998a, 1998b) as well as for the contents of archives (BS 5454).
- It is the total dosage of light which determines the level of light damage to an object. There is increasing use of the concept of annual light dosage and lifetime light dosages, rather than merely using light levels. There is no need for objects to be illuminated when not on public display. A 50 lux light level for the viewing public's 8 hour day translates to 400 lux hours, a constant light level of 17 lux or an annual rate of 146 k.lux hours. For more robust objects, annual exposure limits of 600 k.lux hours (Saunders 1997) equate to display light levels of circa 200 lux for 8 hours per day.
- Thomson's initial limits for UV radiation: 75 micro-watts per lumen (Thomson 1978) were set to try and achieve a workable standard for museums in the 1970s. However, modern UV filters, lighting systems and monitoring devices mean that much lower levels of 20 micro-watts per lumen or lower are often readily achievable.
- The testing of materials used in museum display and storage has become routine and has indicated that a wide range of problems exist with the pollutant gases given off by modern materials: off-gassing as materials dry and harden, loss of plasticiser, degrading polymers, high levels of carbonyl pollutants from wood, fibre and particle boards, e.g. MDF (Thickett 1998). The need for greater

accuracy and a more rigorous approach by conservators using materials testing procedures such as the 'Oddy Tests' has been demonstrated (Blackshaw and Daniels 1979; Lee and Thickett 1996).

- Appreciation of the degradative effect of oxygen has led the development of specialised oxygen free storage (Lambert et al. 1992; Gilberg and Grattan 1994). Creating such conditions is expensive and is thus reserved for valuable objects and those, such as degrading polymers, for which it is the only solution.

- Insect pests are now monitored and managed through housekeeping regimes and quarantines rather than periodic mass extermination. This reduces risks to the collection and the risk, through fumigant and insecticide toxicity, to the conservator and others (Child and Pinneger 1994, 1987).

- As the detrimental effects of human beings on objects become more clearly appreciated, i.e. 'we are bad for objects', the level of contact between objects and human is increasingly managed and limited. Boxing, bagging and covering objects kept in dark stores discourages unnecessary contact. Providing easily accessible and informative records provides an alternative to examining objects. Ensuring the labelling of boxes, shelves, bays, aisles and rooms, the use of handling protocols, such as using gloves, limits human–object contact. Preventing any curator obtaining access to the objects needed for research or display purposes would negate the purpose of storing the object in the first place and thus is totally unacceptable. However, the suppression of casual unnecessary and unspecified use of objects greatly enhances their chances of survival.
  [. . .]

- Maximising the best storage and display conditions for the objects, which can be achieved for minimal cost, can be achieved through techniques such as:
  Zonation of Buildings – distributing objects through a building so they are in the most appropriate conditions which that building has to offer and improving the building's environments to offer an enhanced and extended range of storage and display environments (Cassar 1995).
  Building Envelopes – giving increased environmental protection to objects through increasing the number of barriers: building, room, case, box between the object and the exterior (Cassar 1995).

Bibliography

Ashley-Smith, J., Umney, N. and Ford, D. (1994) 'Let's Be Honest – Realistic Environmental Parameters for Loaned Objects', in A. Roy and P. Smith (eds), *Preventive Conservation Practice, Theory and Research, 1994 IIC Ottawa Congress*, London: IIC.

Blackshaw, S. M. and Daniels, V. D. (1979) 'The Testing of Materials for Use in Storage and Display in Museums', *The Conservator* 3: 16–19.

Cassar, M. (1995) *Environmental Management Guidelines for Museums and Galleries*, London: Butterworth-Heinemann.

Child, R.E and Pinniger, D. B. (1987) 'Insect Pest Control in UK Museums', in J. Black (ed.), *Recent Advances in Conservation and Analysis of Artefacts*, London: Summer Schools Press.

Child, R. E. and Pinniger, D. B. (1994) 'Insect Trapping in Museums and Historic Houses', in A. Roy and P. Smith (eds) *Preventive Conservation Practice, Theory and Research, 1994 IIC Ottawa Congress,* London: IIC.

Erhardt, D. and Mecklenburg, M. (1994) 'Relative Humidity Re-Examined', in A. Roy and P. Smith (eds), *Preventive Conservation Practice, Theory and Research, 1994 IIC Ottawa Congress*, London: IIC.

Frost, M. (1994) 'Working with Design Professionals: Preventive Conservators as Problem Solvers, not Problem Creators', in A. Roy and P. Smith (eds), *Preventive Conservation Practice, Theory and Research, 1994 IIC Ottawa Congress*, London: IIC.

Gilberg, M. and Grattan, D. (1994) 'Oxygen Free Storage Using "Ageless" Oxygen Adsorber', in A. Roy and P. Smith (eds), *Preventive Conservation Practice, Theory and Research, 1994 Ottawa Congress*, London: IIC.

Haynes, M. L. (1993) 'Buried Treasures: Wartime and Recent Uses of Underground Space for Artefact Storage', unpublished MA dissertation, Department of Archaeology, University of Durham.

Lambert, F. L., Vinard, D. and Preusser, F. D. (1992) 'The Rate of Absorption of Oxygen by "Ageless": the Utility of an Oxygen Scavenger in Sealed Cases', *Studies in Conservation* 37, 4: 267–274.

Lee, L. R. and Thickett, D. (1996) *Selection of Materials for the Storage or Display of Museum Objects*, British Museum Occasional Paper No. 111, London: British Museum Press.

Michalski, S. (1993) 'Relative Humidity: A Discussion of Correct/Incorrect Values', *ICOM-CC 10th Triennial Meeting, Washington, DC, USA, 1993*, Washington: ICOM-CC.

Museums and Galleries Commission (1992) *Standards in the Museum Care of Archaeological Collections*, London: MGC.

Museums and Galleries Commission (1993a) *Standards in the Museum Care of Biological Collections*, London: MGC.

Museums and Galleries Commission (1993b) *Standards in the Museum Care of Geological Collections*, London: MGC.

Museums and Galleries Commission (1994) *Standards in the Museum Care of Larger and Working Objects*, London: MGC.

Museums and Galleries Commission (1995) *Standards in the Museum Care of Musical Instruments*, London: MGC.

Museums and Galleries Commission (1996) *Standards in the Museum Care of Photographic Collections*, London: MGC.

Museums and Galleries Commission (1998a) *Standards in the Museum Care of Costume and Textile Collections*, London: MGC.

Museums and Galleries Commission (1998b) *Levels of Collection Care: A Self-Assessment Checklist for UK Museums*, London: MGC.

Saunders, D. (1997) 'Who Needs Class 1 Museums?', *IIC Bulletin* 2, April 1997: 3–6.

Thickett, D. (1998) 'Sealing of MDF to Prevent Corrosive Emissions', *The Conservator* 22: 49–56.

Thomson, G. (1978) *The Museum Environment*, London: Butterworth.

Chapter 6

Storage Systems

James Tate and Theo Skinner

Introduction

THE STORAGE OF OBJECTS can be greatly improved by the use of suitable storage systems. Such systems aid efficient object retrieval and help to eliminate physical damage to the objects. The implementation and use of good quality storage systems can be one of the most significant steps forward in the passive conservation of a museum collection.

For the storage of museum objects, it is necessary to identify, and perhaps design, the correct style of storage unit and system appropriate to the particular type of object, and to determine the space required using that system to house the collection. While this process is determined by factors general to all museums, the degree of variation and the constraints which apply are such that it is impossible to produce more than general guidelines. This chapter therefore gives examples of two aspects, a method of assessing storage requirements of a particular collection, and some of the successful storage systems which have been developed. No attempt is made to give a complete review of the types of storage system available, nor a comprehensive bibliography. Readers requiring such information are referred to Johnson and Horgan (1979) and the references therein.

Factors affecting the choice of storage system

Obviously, overall cost will be a prime consideration, and the availability and cost of space will be a major determining factor as to which systems can be considered

Source: J. M. A. Thompson (ed.) *Manual of Curatorship* (2nd edn), Oxford: Butterworth-Heinemann, 1992, pp. 459–467.

and eventually chosen. Storage facilities are not glamorous and are unlikely to attract sponsorship, but grants may be available to upgrade and provide facilities.

The choice of storage system will be affected by:

- The type and kind of use to which the collection will be put. How often will staff, both internal and external to the museum, wish to examine the various groups of objects in store?
- Can the objects be segregated by size/material/environmental requirements, or must they be kept in some sort of imposed order, e.g. chronological or typological, for curatorial reasons? (This is closely linked to the usage above.)
- Can the objects be boxed or otherwise enclosed, or must they be available to constant inspection? Boxes can be used to provide microclimate conditions for sensitive objects.
- Is the available space adequate, or will high density mobile storage units have to be used to maximize space utilization? Space can be very expensive, and high density storage units are often cost-effective, especially as they may also offer savings in travel, security, and environmental control costs. They may, however, require higher floor loadings.
- Would mechanical handling be an advantage? There may be savings in manpower costs within the store.
- How much will the collections increase in size or range over the probable lifetime of the store and/or of the storage units?
- Are there objects with unusual storage problems, e.g. extraordinary length, height, weight, or fragility, which will require special consideration?
- Will there be sufficient access to the store and within the store for the type of object intended?
- Must a particularly high level of security be provided for all or parts of the collection, e.g. coins or precious stones?
- Are the objects likely to be adversely affected by the materials of the storage system? Tarnishing of silver and corrosion of lead are well known examples. If possible the construction and finishing materials should be tested. Where known inert materials cannot be used, it may help to seal the surfaces: we currently use a vapour barrier produced for the building trade consisting of aluminium foil supported on a thin plastic backing.
- Are the storage systems able to give some primary protection against disaster, especially flooding? (Precautions against common damage, such as raising the storage units off the floor, are not covered here.)

By addressing basic questions such as these it should be possible to determine the precise type of system which best suits the overall needs of the collections.

Assessment of space requirement

One of the most difficult questions to answer, especially where large and diverse collections are held in inadequate storage conditions (a situation not unfamiliar to most museum Curators!) is just how much storage space is needed.

The storage needs of a particular collection should ideally be investigated quantitatively. In large collections, it may be possible to do this only by measuring the attributes of a sample of the objects, this technique being especially suitable for large collections of small objects. For large objects, particularly those of a fixed size, it may be more satisfactory to survey the whole collection, although if the collection is large this may prove an impossible objective in terms of available staff time. Very large objects will probable require individual consideration in any case.

For the purposes of surveying, the use of standard forms to record the required information is essential, prompting recording of the relevant information and allowing easy collation of the results. Collation is readily carried out on paper, or with fairly basic database or spreadsheet facilities, and should aim to provide information about the total areas required for each of the various classes of object previously decided upon.

The final choice of particular storage systems will be based on the type of object and the homogeneity of the collection, as well as the financial and use considerations outlined above. Some storage systems are more flexible than others with regard to the size and weight of objects they will house, and it is usually important to maximize efficient use of the available space.

Case studies

Assessment of the storage systems required for the reserve archaeological collections

In 1988, a rationalization of central storage provision within the National Museums of Scotland necessitated the rehousing of the reserve archaeological collections. At the start of this project the objects were stored in a number of locations, primarily in undercase cupboards in the display gallery. A survey of the material was instigated to determine storage requirements and, simultaneously, to assess the conservation needs.

Early consideration was given to the use of the material, essentially a study collection. It was decided not to enclose the objects individually, but to segregate objects according to their environmental requirements. The basic types of storage unit required for the different types and sizes of object were also decided on at this stage. For the smaller objects (flints, stone axes, metalwork, leather and other organic materials), drawers were considered to be the best storage system, whilst shelved cabinets were thought preferable for complete pottery vessels. Steel pallets were chosen to house the collection of large sculptured stones, allowing them to be easily moved within the store and thus be inspected from most sides by visiting scholars.

Examination of a range of different manufactured products led to the conclusion that the most useful units for this purpose were those made of metal rather than wood construction. These, whilst expensive, are made from conservationally sound materials, have a long lifetime, would allow a degree of flexibility in specifying the size of drawer combinations in each cabinet, have high weight-loading capacity in each drawer, and could be moved as complete units by a pallet truck if necessary.

The large size of the collections (estimated as 23,000 objects), the limited resources available, and the short time-scale made it necessary to undertake the survey by sampling. For this purpose, the collections to be rehoused were divided into categories expected to have similar properties and requirements, for example size and environment, as far as appeared possible from examination of the cataloguing system. This was intended to have the effect of reducing variations within the samples, thus increasing the efficiency of the sampling technique.

Standard forms were designed to record the relevant information, together with guidelines for recording data to ensure consistency between surveyors. Arrangements were made to obtain access to the objects chosen in the samples, and the survey carried out over a period of 3 weeks, by a team of four conservators. A total of 784 objects were examined, that is, some 3 per cent of the collection. The data relevant to storage were entered on a computer, and analysed using suitable software

The analysis consisted of calculating the height distribution of objects in each category and then determining the total storage area required for each of a selected series of height categories, chosen to fit in with the type of storage units envisaged for that category and size of object (Figures 6.1 and 6.2).

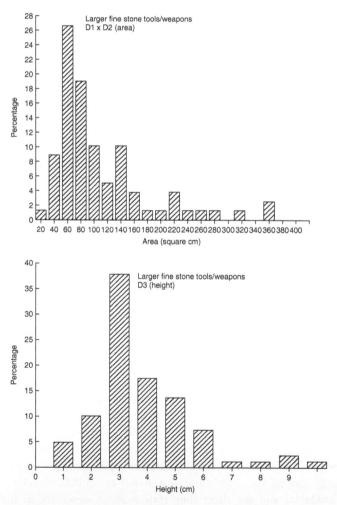

Figure 6.1 Size distribution of the sample of larger fine-stone tools/weapons

Areas

Total number of registrations	1905
Sample size	79
Total area of sample	7808 sq cm
Mean	98 sq cm
Calculated total area for whole population	10.82 sq m

Boxes

Optimal box sizes (areas)	%	Approx No.	% (cumulative)
20 cm	1	20	1
40	9	180	10
80	45	900	55
160	29	600	84
320	10	200	94

Optimal ratios (D2:D1)

1:1.5	2	40
1:2	16	320
1:3	45	900
1:4	13	260
1:4+	5	100

Optimal heights

1 cm	5	100	5
2	10	200	15
3	38	760	53
4	17	340	70
5	13	260	83
10	17	340	99

Drawers

83% of population can be stored in drawers 5 cm high.

A further 16% of population can be stored in drawers 10 cm high.
1% of population requires drawers of a greater height, say 18 cm.
Thus require 2 cabinets:
1 with 20 drawers at 54 mm (catalogue 101.02.703)
1 with 9 drawers at 104 mm (catalogue 101.02.705)
and 2 drawers at 179 mm (catalogue 101.02.707)

Environment	As for lithic assemblage
Shelf area	Zero

Figure 6.2 Estimation of storage system needed for the sample shown in Figure 6.1

An allowance of 20 per cent of the storage area was made for space between the objects, to allow access. This is a somewhat arbitrary figure, and it is hoped that it will be possible to calculate a more exact one when the units are filled with objects. Similarly, a factor was included to allow for the probable growth of the collection over the next 20 years. The figures were then used to itemize a series of cabinets and drawer combinations for the small metal, stone, organic objects and pottery sherds, as well as a series of shelved cupboards for the pottery collection and metal pallets to house the collection of large sculptured stones.

The itemized list of units was used as the basis for a quotation for fitting out the store and, eventually, the units were purchased, although it was not possible to purchase them all in one financial year. This turned out not to be a serious problem, as the time and manpower required to rehouse the material meant that the process took a very long time; indeed it has not yet been completed. The location of each item within the store will be logged on the National Museum of Scotland computer database, and retrieval of objects should then be a simple matter once the object registration number has been identified.

Storage of the ethnographic collection

Information about the storage of the ethnographic collections of the Royal Museums of Scotland has been published previously (Idiens 1973). Here the intention is to provide more detailed examples of the types of storage system used for particular aspects of the collection.

Weapons store

One room of the general store and all of the spear store have been fitted with sliding vertical panels, made of 50 mm expanded steel mesh within mahogany frames, 1930 mm × 1450 mm (larger frames in the spear store). There are 7 cupboards, each containing 7 such frames which hang from sliding channels similar to those used for garage doors. Each frame is separated by 160 mm, and can be slid out individually to examine the objects on it, which are fixed to the mesh with string or (preferably) cotton tape. Some of the panels have mesh made from unfinished metal and fairly sharp edges. Although this has not caused any problems since the system was installed our preference now is for plastic covered 50 mm square wire mesh.

Obviously this type of storage is only suitable for objects which have sufficient strength to be supported hanging and which are not liable to have component parts detach. Although the panels are fairly close together, and care has to be taken to ensure there is no danger of objects in adjacent panels rubbing or catching against each other, the system has proved very satisfactory in use since its installation in the 1970s (see Figures 6.3. and 6.4). Similar systems are used for other items both here and elsewhere in the museum, for example for firearms in the Scottish United Services Museum.

General small objects

The bulk of small items are kept in plastic trays within internally adjustable dustproof cupboards. The trays are commercially available bakers' trays with perforated

Figure 6.3 General view of the spear store

Figure 6.4 An open panel showing spears

Figure 6.5 View of open cupboards with one tray pulled out containing medium sized
objects

bottoms (731 mm long × 426 mm wide × 76 mm deep) (Idiens 1973). The trays are
sufficiently rigid to support a fairly wide range of items, and are supported within the
storage cupboards from side rails, that is they do not require individual shelves. An
alternative type of tray has been tried, consisting of an upper part of plastic of similar
dimensions, but mounted on a sheet of plywood to provide adequate support from
the shelf runners. There are two problems: firstly, the introduction of plywood into
the sealed cupboards may cause undesirable environmental factors; and secondly, the
tray plus plywood support are heavy and awkward to use.

Among the advantages of the system which is in use are: flexibility – the trays can
be left out to provide space for larger items, or the central upright of the cupboard
can be removed to allow the trays to be put in sideways; the trays can be drawn out
to see all items on that 'shelf' without having to handle or disturb them; in an emergency trays can be rapidly removed to an alternative location and the cupboard can
be emptied without having to repack or handle individual objects; the consistency of
storage units means that reorganization between cupboards is simplified; and absence
or movement of trays from the store can easily be recorded or noticed (see Figures
6.5 and 6.6). Objects can be stored individually within the trays or within specially
cut-out shapes in polyethylene foam lining the tray.

Skin and textile clothing

At present, part of the collections of skin and other costumes are stored in cupboards with
the items hung on individually padded coat hangers. This system was introduced some

Figure 6.6 View of open cupboards for storing irregularly shaped objects

years ago and we would not now recommend it, the aim now being to store all such costumes flat on large shelving, since it is felt that this gives far better support to items which may be fairly fragile and subject to damage when hanging side by side. There are disadvantages in storing the costumes flat, particularly the fact that some have to be laid on top of each other where individual shelving cannot be provided, so that examination of one has to involve moving other items. However, the benefits of improved support to the costumes are considered to outweigh this. Acid-free tissue paper is of course placed between individual items of costume, with additional padding if needed (see Figure 6.7).

Large textiles, etc.

Large flat textile, bark cloth and similar items are stored efficiently on large padded rollers, similar to those used for the storage and display of flooring materials in carpet warehouses. The rollers rest on adjustable side supports within shallow cupboards, and each can be individually removed (by two people) to be unrolled on a central table. Lack of space has meant that some rollers have to contain more than one item, protected by acid-free tissue paper and padding where necessary. The rolled textiles are held in place on the roller by suitably placed cotton ties (see Figure 6.8).

Large ethnographic items

The storage of large and irregularly shaped objects is generally an exercise in ingenuity for the Curator. Open shelving and storage bays are, of course, standard and

Figure 6.7 Present hanging system for skin and textile clothing

broadly useful solutions. In our ethnographic store we have found the use of padded slings particularly suitable for large but light objects, especially the undisplayed collection of skin canoes (Figure 6.9), both model and full size. The number of slings

Figure 6.8 Removal of a textile roller to a table

Figure 6.9 Padded slings used to store canoes

depends on the rigidity and fragility of the object, but could clearly be adapted in many ways.

Fragile and heavier large items pose other problems, particularly in terms of removing them from shelving without subjecting them to stress and without mechanical lifting aids. In the same cellar as the canoes, Egyptian sarcophagi are stored on simple racking, with each piece being placed on a rigid board with attached handles so that the whole unit can be slid forward and lifted out in one piece for study.

Other examples

Picture storage

Widely used systems for picture storage consist of wire mesh covering walls or other vertical surfaces, the pictures being suspended from the mesh. Such systems are simple but allow considerable flexibility. Higher packing density can be achieved by the use of mobile racking, or by the use of compactor storage (Figure 6.10). As with all mobile racking, the space between racks must be adequate to clear adjacent paintings, frames etc., while the effectiveness of sealing against dust must also be checked.

Geological specimens

Storage of geological specimens using efficient packing systems may raise a serious problem of weight, both in terms of floor loading and within the storage system itself. This may need specially constructed racking, such as the system illustrated in Figure 6.11 where specimens are housed in wooden boxes with hinged lids, each box sitting on a shelf in a frame made from 1 inch welded steel tubing.

[. . .]

Figure 6.10 High density picture storage

Figure 6.11 Example of storage of small specimens

References

Idiens, D. (1973) 'New Ethnographical Storage in the Royal Scottish Museum', *Museums Journal* 73(2): 61–62.

Johnson, E. V. and Horgan, J. C. (1979) 'Museum collection storage', *UNESCO Technical Handbooks for Museums and Monuments* 2: 34–56.

Chapter 7

Which Conservation Materials to Use at Home?

Peter Winsor

Introduction

MANY DIFFERENT PRODUCTS and materials are mentioned in the chapters in this book. These notes will give you a little more information about them and explain some of the terms used.

The terms 'acid-free', 'archival quality', 'conservation approved' are frequently used to describe materials you should select and use for the safe packing and storage of objects you wish to look after carefully. In particular, 'archival quality' is a non-technical term which implies that materials are durable or chemically stable and are most suitable for the purpose.

Good quality materials should be chosen for use in contact with, or in close proximity to objects. The use of boxes made from archival or acid-free materials or the wrapping of objects in acid-free tissue paper is recommended throughout this resource pack.

Many of the products described below meet the specific requirements of historic objects. They are available from the conservation suppliers listed. Their catalogues contain much useful information but if you are in doubt then contact a conservator.

Wrapping, boxing and protecting

'Acid-free' paper and board

Many products that are marketed as acid-free (tissue in particular) are made from cellulose fibre pulp derived from wood or cotton that is naturally acid but which is

Source: Museums and Galleries Commission (ed.), *Ours for Keeps?*, London: MGC, 1997, pp. 7.07–7.10.

buffered by the addition of chemicals (commonly calcium carbonate) to neutralise the acid. There are two important points to remember about materials that are manufactured to be acid-free, rather than being naturally pH neutral. These are:

- Buffering chemicals will lose their effectiveness over time (a few years) by the action of the natural acid in the paper or atmospheric pollutants. Once this process is complete, the paper will become acidified and potentially harmful to objects it surrounds;
- Some paper or board that is labelled as acid-free is, in fact, over-buffered to be alkaline (usually to pH 8.5) rather than neutral pH of 7.0 that you might expect, and these too could be harmful to some types of objects. The catalogues explain about this but you should also ask the supplier.

It is also worth remembering that paper and board can become acidified by the action of residual chlorine from bleaching, aluminium sulphate from sizing or pollutants in the atmosphere.

Although you should be aware of these facts, in most cases it is safe to use the much cheaper buffered type of acid-free wrapping paper, mounting board or boxes, though many museums will replace wrapping tissue every five to ten years. The signs of acidifying of the paper are that it discolours, turning yellow, and becoming brittle. You are probably familiar with the way newsprint discolours and becomes brittle over a relatively short time. This is the same process in action, but it is more rapid as newsprint is made from unrefined wood pulp that does not contain chemicals to buffer the natural acidity.

Wrapping paper and boards used for boxes or framing are available that are naturally pH neutral (i.e. pH of 7, neither acid nor alkaline) and which remain acid-free for much longer. Some are made from cotton rag and others are made from abaca fibre, derived from the Manila hemp plant (*Musa textilis*). This latter type is normally specified as the only paper or board suitable for use with the more sensitive items such as photographs and textiles. It is much more expensive than buffered materials.

Special papers are now available which can absorb pollutants (see 'Charcoal Cloth'). These too can lose their effectiveness over time and will need replacing with fresh.

Warning

Never be tempted to use the blue tissue paper that was traditionally used for wrapping textiles. This is quite acid and is not suitable for long-term storage.

Charcoal Cloth

This is one of a range of materials that actively absorb atmospheric pollutants such as acetic acid, formaldehyde, hydrogen sulphide and ammonia which are particularly harmful to polished metal surfaces, works of art on paper and textiles. The 'activated' charcoal is enclosed between layers of fibre which allows it to be cut and sewn like cloth. It is used inside the backing board of framed works of art and to line display cabinets and storage boxes to neutralise harmful vapours. These can be given off by new wood, fibre and particle boards, and newly painted surfaces which are just as common in the home as in museums. Charcoal Cloth is cheap, very easy to use and effective. It is available in rolls and as made-up bags. Like buffered acid-free tissue, its power to absorb will be used up eventually and it must be replaced with fresh.

Calico cloth and unbleached linen

These are light fabrics available from haberdashers. They are washed to remove size and proofing substances, and are used as covers for individual textiles or for racks of hanging costumes. This is an economical and very effective way of keeping dust from objects and protecting them from snagging etc. Covers should be washed regularly, at least once a year.

Tyvek

Tyvek is the trade name for spun-bonded, non-woven polyester fabric. It is non-abrasive, waterproof, rot-proof and dust-proof. Its original use in conservation was for labelling objects from archaeological excavations but it now has wider uses. These include individual covers for textiles and dust covers. It is available in wide rolls and as label tags, with or without perforation.

Polyester film

This plastic film is often specified for house documents and photographs. You will usually see it under one of its common trade names of Melinex or Mylar. It is crystal clear and chemically stable, and contains none of the fillers, plasticisers or other additives that are present in many other plastics. It is these additives which deteriorate or leach out, causing damage to sensitive objects. Polyester film is available as cut sheet, rolls or in a wide range of made-up sleeves and envelopes. Welded rather than glued seams are preferred for museum-type use and in some cases an unsealed, four-fold design is used. One of the advantages of polyester is that it can be heat or ultrasonically welded, and this property is used in the encapsulation of documents such as ephemera. Special equipment is necessary to do this.

Polyethylene film or sheeting

Bags, sleeves and envelopes made from polyethylene film are a cheaper alternative to polyester enclosures and will protect ephemera and matted prints or photographs from dust, abrasion and fingerprints. They are not as crystal clear as polyester film is and are not as tough or stable.

Plastazote or Ethafoam

This is dense, inert polyethylene foam which is available in a range of densities and thicknesses. It contains no harmful additives and the foaming agent is ozone-friendly.

It is used to line drawers and the base of cupboards to cushion objects and for packing. It is possible to cut out a shaped hole in which an object can 'nest'. This can be done using a sharp modelling knife or a special hotwire cutter. In many cases the object is further protected with several layers of acid-free tissue.

Bubble wrap

Bubble wrap is a protective cushioning material made from low-density polyethylene. Various bubble sizes are available, though the 9 mm size is probably most useful for normal packing purposes. It should not be used on objects that have a fragile surface unless these have been protected first with several layers of acid-free tissue. It is available as rolls of varying width.

Cotton gloves

These are used for safe handling of slides, negatives, documents and most other types of objects. They prevent oils, salts and acids present on the skin from damaging the surface of objects, and are recommended for general use though extra care is required when handling objects with hard, smooth surfaces such as porcelain. Here, a type of glove with rubber 'polka dots' (similar to the face of a table tennis bat) is recommended as they give an improved grip.

Silica gel

Silica gel is a porous form of amorphous silica which acts as a desiccant and is used to control humidity levels in storage containers and display cases. You may be familiar with the sachets containing silica gel that are often included in the packaging of a new camera, or pieces of electronic equipment. The silica gel is normally sold in the form of white granules, but a blue, self-indicating variety is available. This turns from blue to pink when it has absorbed moisture from the atmosphere and is no longer active. Both types can be regenerated by heating in an oven to 105°C–120°C. Silica gel is available loose or in a range of standard sized sachets. It is most effective when used to create a dry atmosphere in a well-sealed display case or a box such as the type made of polythene and sold as food storage containers.

Art-Sorb is a highly efficient form of silica gel which is available as beads or sheet, and in two sizes of sealed cassette suitable to control volumes of 1.0 and 0.7 cubic metres.

Tarnish inhibitors

Capsules and tablets containing a tarnish inhibitor that will protect polished silver for up to 12 months. Various sizes are available to protect volumes from 150 cubic inches to 33 cubic feet. Carosil is a commonly available brand. Variations on these are plastics, papers and cloths which contain chemicals which absorb tarnish forming chemicals. They are used to encase polished metals such as coins, medals, silverware.

Ultra-violet protection

Ultraviolet light can cause damage to textiles, paintings, prints and photographs, resulting in fading, discolouration and embrittlement. Daylight contains a significant amount of ultraviolet wavelength light and the content in electric sources varies with the type of lamp. Sensitive objects will need to be protected unless they are stored in light-proof containers.

Action you can take includes fitting filters to fluorescent lamp arrays or sleeves to the individual tubes. Ultraviolet absorbing sheet, film or varnish can be applied to protective glazing or windows. These are crystal clear and types include thin Perspex sheet and polyester film with a self-adhesive coating. The ultraviolet absorbing property of the films and varnishes has a limited life and the effectiveness needs to be monitored after 3–5 years' life.

Keeping pests at bay

Pests such as the common clothes moth and furniture beetle were once very common in the home. Modern cleaning methods and materials together with more efficient heating and ventilation systems have dramatically reduced the threats they pose. At the same time, health and safety, and environmental concerns have led to a re-appraisal of the techniques used to control pests. There are now far fewer commercially available products for dealing with pests and non-chemical methods are being devised. However, the most effective method of keeping pests at bay remains good housekeeping and sensible storage of your treasures using the materials described above. If you are worried that any of your heirlooms are being damaged by pests then contact a conservator.

Monitoring

Measuring the environmental conditions

It is always useful to know if the environment in which you are storing or displaying your treasures is possibly causing them harm. The increased use of central heating and air conditioning has resulted in our homes and work places having a much warmer and dryer environment than in the past. This has an impact on objects including causing wood to dry out and split, and paper to become brittle. A number of simple devices are now on the market which measure the moisture in the air, normally referred to as relative humidity. As this is closely related to temperature they often measure this too. It is difficult to specify the ideal conditions for an object but it is useful to know that mould and mildew can start to grow on organic materials at relative humidities of 70% and above and unprotected iron or steel will begin to rust at similar levels. On the other hand, organic materials should not be subjected to long periods at relative humilities of 35% and below. In general, lower temperatures are better for objects and rooms housing objects should ideally be kept at a stable temperature between 18 and 21°C. These figures are guidelines only and advice for specific materials and objects should be obtained from a conservator.

Humidity indicator cards

These are impregnated paper strips divided into nine sections which exhibit various colours from blue through lavender to pink. The position of the lavender section on the printed scale indicates the relative humidity of the surrounding air. They offer a very simple and cheap means of checking the relative humidity of your display cabinets or storage cupboards.

Dial hygrometers

The earliest and simplest device used to measuring relative humidity is the dial hygrometer. It is based on the principle that a hair expands and contracts proportionally as relative humidity increases and decreases. You will often see one of these round dials in museum display cases. They are cheap, easy to read and reasonably accurate if calibrated regularly.

Thermohygrometers

Inexpensive, hand-held digital devices are now available which use an electronic sensor to measure relative humidity and temperature of a room or display case. They are small, simple to operate, have an easy-to-read display panel and run off batteries. They give spot readings only and have an accuracy of about $+/-5\%$ for relative humidity and $+/-1-2°C$ for temperature.

Light meter

Excessive exposure to light is potentially harmful to materials such as paper, paintings and textiles, causing fading and embrittlement. For this reason, maximum levels of illumination are specified for their long-term preservation. Measuring the light level is done using a light (lux) meter. These operate on the same principle as a camera light meter. Battery operated electronic monitors which give an instant reading are inexpensive. They operate over several ranges to cope with light levels varying from full sun to near darkness.

Meters to measure levels of ultraviolet light radiation are also available, and a combined light/ultraviolet meter is produced. They are considerably more expensive than ordinary light meters.

[. . .]

Chapter 8

Before the Unthinkable . . . Happens Again

IIC: Jerry Podany and panel

AN EDITED TRANSCRIPTION OF AN INTERNATIONAL roundtable discussion, convened by the IIC, held in Tokyo on July 22nd, 2009 on the subject of earthquakes and cultural heritage.[1]

Panellists

Roberto Garufi: Centro Regionale per la Progettazione e il Restauro, Sicily, Italy; Kimio Kawaguchi: Conservator, The National Museum of Western Art, Japan; Charles A. Kircher: Principal at Kircher and Associates, United States; Vlasis Koumousis: Professor, School of Civil Engineering, National Technical University of Athens, Greece; Ugo Nizza: Centro Regionale per la Progettazione e il Restauro, Sicily, Italy; Paul Somerville: Principal Engineering Seismologist, URS, United States; Constantine Spyrakos: Professor, National Technical University of Athens, Greece; Bilgen Sungay: Bogazici Univ, Kandilli Observatory/Earthquake Research Institute, Turkey.

[. . .]

Our unsettled earth

Jerry Podany

[. . .]

If one glances at a seismic event map that records earthquake locations with small red dots of varying sizes depending upon the intensity of the earthquakes, it is clear that the surface of our world moves quite a bit. One cannot ignore the magnitude

Source: IIC website, http://www.iiconservation.org/dialogues/IIC_tokyo_transcript.pdf.

of the threat such movement presents to cultural heritage in all countries across our world. It should also be clear that these red dots appear to congregate more densely at certain locations, such as Japan. [. . .] It is no coincidence that we meet in a country where 10% of the world's earthquakes occur. [. . .]

This event is about vulnerability reduction. It is about reducing the risk to which our shared heritage, whether collections, archives, monuments or buildings, is exposed in areas of significant seismic activity. The challenge vulnerability reduction presents is quite significant since the focus of most seismic mitigation to date has been, appropriately enough, on life safety, the protection of essential services (power, water, roads, bridges, etc.) and on built structures. The effective protection of cultural property has lagged behind. Monuments, archives, and collections of works of art as well as historical and natural science materials, remain at great risk whether on exhibition or in storage. Research and implementation to protect "contents" is an area in great need of development. Such developments are complex in nature since artefacts do not always fit specific engineering categories. And the aesthetic concerns of presentation often restrict the degree to which restraints can be applied.

[. . .] Heritage professionals are often both uninformed and misinformed about what can be done to protect collections from earthquake damage. This is particularly unfortunate since so much that is both simple and inexpensive can be applied to avoid the significant loss of material experienced every year around the world. In every country, in every region, in every museum, site and storeroom one can see evidence of high vulnerability due to lack of information or denial. And after each earthquake one can witness significant damage [. . .]

If statistics are correct, many of the world's cultural centres will experience major earthquakes this decade and many have already suffered the effects of recent significant seismic events (the Abruzzo earthquake in Italy being only one). [. . .] Vulnerability reduction of cultural collections is a significant world challenge. Although seismic risk maps have been drawn up over large areas of the world, district by district, city by city, and region by region, most museums and indeed many historical districts find it difficult to know the level of threat they are facing. Specificity as to the exact nature of the threat aside, how can we do more to make such information available to these cultural institutions so that they might plan their mitigation efforts more effectively? Take a museum without the means to hire engineers, seismologists or geologists to undertake a specific site study and to develop a design spectra or a worse case statistical threat . . . how can they more effectively know the kind of earthquake threat they might face?

Paul Somerville

At the moment there is a global seismic hazard map, called the GSHAP map[2] which is good in some countries, and not so good in other countries. Now there is a new plan to build what is called the Global Earthquake Model (GEM) www.globalguake-model.org sponsored by a number of organizations within the insurance industry and some universities. This project will provide a much better seismic hazard map, but will also provide a seismic risk map. Some preliminary results might be available in about a year (GEM1) and then over the next few years the maps will be improved a great deal. So I think we should all look to the Global Earthquake Model Project as a resource for new and solid information. It is relatively easy to find the seismic hazard map for Japan online[3] and this of also true in the United States as well.[4]

[. . . .]

Charles A. Kircher

First of all Jerry said "risk maps" and I would like to explore that word "risk." We have heard a lot about risk management, particularly financial risk. I believe what was really being referred to is earthquake "hazard," and Paul Somerville just mentioned hazard maps. There is a big difference between "risk" and "hazard" mapping. Hazard mapping addresses the intensity of the ground motion in any given location. Risk, on the other hand, requires us to also understand the vulnerability of works of art and historical artefacts. For example, if it is a metal vase, as opposed to a porcelain vase, and it falls over, it may just be a small problem because the metal vase is less brittle and less likely to be damaged. If on the other hand the vase is porcelain, it may be a much larger problem because of the fragile nature of porcelain. Other issues to be considered are the relative values of the objects and this includes not only the monetary value but the religious, cultural, historical value. So when we say "risk" and consider the risk that these objects face, we have to consider both the vulnerability and the value of the objects, as well has the earthquake hazard. Seismologists and engineers can tell museums about the earthquake hazard (that is to say the character and potential of earthquake ground shaking) but not about the risk (without also incorporating additional information on museum vulnerability, collection value, etc.).

[. . .]

Bilgen Sungay

A loss scenario developed through engineering studies would be an effective tool and a good incentive to influence governments as well as funding agencies. However if an institution has the intention of mitigating its risks, specific information is not a must to understand the threat they face. We have been speaking with some of our colleagues, including mount makers, and it is clear from international research how categories of objects react to earthquake forces. And the possible mitigation methods to reduce risk are available in several printed and online resources such as www.eqprotection-museums.org and "Advances in the Protection of Museum Collections from Earthquake Damage".[5] We can start doing something now. We have examples from several museums in Turkey who have undertaken mitigation measures. It is not necessarily a must to hire engineers to undertake simple mitigation measures.

[. . .]

As an example, the museum professionals can begin with the storage areas where using padding between objects, adding simple restraints across open shelving and securing cabinets and shelving to walls and floors could be adequate precautionary actions. I don't mean we should set scientific studies aside, especially for those objects or groups of objects that would need specific solutions and in cases where more technical applications such as base isolation are needed. But we can start with published results and use them and build on them.

[. . .]

Vlasis Koumousis

[. . .] all the simple methods that combine the efficiency of seismic mounting,[6] together with the aesthetic demands of exhibition display, can be applied directly and immediately. As for more sophisticated techniques, like the use of intermediate lightweight isolators[7] under single artefacts or showcases, which is the next step, one needs specific designs and experimental verification to apply these approaches. At a medium cost, small scale isolators can provide adequate protection for single valuable objects or showcases. Then comes the question of unique and more massive pieces that require specific attention and efforts, such as Rodin's *Gates of Hell* here at the National Museum of Western Art, or the *Hermes of Praxiteles* at the new museum of Olympia in Greece. Descriptions of these projects can be found in "Advances in the Protection of Museum Collections from Earthquake Damage".[5] The ultimate protection of these objects should be based on seismic isolation, utilizing the maturing technology that exists for buildings and bridges, since isolation of entire buildings will offer the ultimate and safest approach. This is well understood in buildings like this one, the National Museum of Western Art in Tokyo (retrofitted with seismic isolation), and with new museum buildings we see around the world such as the recently inaugurated Museum of the Acropolis in Athens. Seismic isolation offers a solution.

[. . .]

Jerry Podany

Our experience in speaking with institutions and university engineering departments internationally is that a simple mount, a piece of monofilament used as a tie-down for an object, a bit of wax to stick a small object down, all work quite well if made and applied properly. But such simple approaches do not seem to engender much interest in most audiences, especially engineers. What has interested the engineering community is the discussion and development of base isolators. The complexities and technical challenges presented are much more of a draw to them. As long as this is the case, the very basic underlying issues of collections protection are going to lag behind. With reference to protecting individual objects or exhibition cases I must say that I have a sense from this discussion and others that there isn't really an agreement about what works and what doesn't in the area of isolators. [. . .]

Notes

1   http://www.iiconservation.org/dialogues/IIC_tokyo_transcript.pdf
2   http://www.seismo.ethz.ch/GSHAP/
3   http://wwwold.j-shis.bosai.go.jp/j-shis/index_en.html
4   http://earthquake.usgs.gov/research/hazmaps/

5 www.getty.edu/bookstore/titles/earthquake.html

6   Seismic Mounts: [. . .] In the context of preventing damage from earthquakes, the term "mounts" refers to any fixture or restraint that either adds strength to an object or restrains the motion of that object so that when earthquake forces are transferred those forces will have less dynamic effect upon the object than would otherwise be the case. That is to say, mounts safely keep an object from sliding, falling, tipping, turning over or colliding with other objects or with the object's surroundings. Contour mounts (also referred to as form fit mounts or spine mounts) are good examples of seismic mounts. These mounts are intimately fitting supports that follow the exact contour of an object and are attached to both the object (usually with monofilament ties) and to the deck of the exhibition case, to a pedestal or to the floor. Contour mounts can be made of metal, wood or plastic.

7   Base isolation: the term is used to define a wide range of energy-absorbing and/or decoupling mechanisms placed between the ground and the object (or building) being isolated. Columns of visco-elastic rubber, interleaved with lead sheets, are often used as isolators under building foundations. While some buildings, a few exhibition cases, objects and a variety of electronic, scientific and medical pieces of equipment have been protected by multistage isolators (whose individual stages travel freely on bearings within a predetermined distance), there are very few examples of works of art or artifacts isolated in this manner. The purpose of the base isolators is to absorb a percentage of the earthquake energy by essentially allowing the earth to move under the object or building with less of an effect upon the objects or buildings themselves.

Chapter 9

Safety by Numbers

Robert Payton

THE MUSEUM OF LONDON (MoL), like many museums, presents objects in various ways: on open display and in cases, behind barriers, in room settings and as part of interactive displays. The security of the objects varies considerably depending on the effectiveness of barriers, the type of mounts and security fixings, the upkeep of the displays, the presence of alarms and the level of invigilation.

The museum recently decided to review the security of its galleries in a way that was simple, quick and cheap. The project assessed the vulnerability of objects in the galleries and established a value for high-risk and rare objects. The results of the review allowed the museum to prioritise improvements in gallery security.

How we assessed security

We decided to score the value and vulnerability of objects on display using a simple security assessment form that we designed. The numerical totals of the scores indicated the displays that needed to be improved urgently and those that were a lower priority.

We decided to identify the most valuable object in a display and assess the value of the surrounding display by this item. This was because if a thief broke into a display case to steal a valuable item then all the other objects would be at risk. This meant we could complete the review in less time than if we had assessed each object separately.

The curators responsible for each gallery and I carried out the security assessments. The curators had an intimate knowledge of the importance of their collection and its monetary value. As a conservator I was able to assess the vulnerability of the

Source: *Museum Practice* 22 (2003), pp. 40–42.

displays. We wanted to have a consistent approach and we achieved this by having a standard form for reporting. I carried out the survey across the whole museum while the curators differed according to the gallery.

We saved more time because we had already given a unique location code to the displays. Using the survey forms, which included these location codes, it was relatively quick to go round the galleries filling in the information. Most galleries, which typically have about 30 displays, took between 45 and 60 minutes to complete. The whole of the museum's object-based displays were assessed in six and half hours. But we decided to assess the security of paintings, prints and drawings separately as their high financial value unbalanced our scoring system, see Table 9.1. The art curator and I completed this survey in about four hours and then the results were combined with the general survey, which took a day to complete. Apart from staff time no extra resources were needed.

Table 9.1 The scoring system for object risk assessment

Financial value	Historic value	Alarm	Protection
Less than £200 (1)	Low significance or set dressing (1)	Suitable alarm (1)	Secure case (1)
£200–£1,000 (2)	Important (2)	Poor alarm (2)	Insecure/easily opened (2)
£1,000–£10,000 (3)	Invaluable (3)	No alarm (3)	Barriered/not in reach (3)
More than £10,000 (4)			Open/vulnerable (4)

Recommended action: (add relevant figure from each column).
Totals: (4–8) Monitor and review only; (9–10) Consider improvements (11–12); Action required; (13–14) Immediate action.

Special cases

Some objects and displays were not straightforward. If detachable parts of an object were particularly vulnerable we chose the value of the whole object, as the theft of a part would detract from the value of the whole. When an object's value increased because it belonged to a group, such as a coin in a coin hoard, we decided that its value should be the higher group value. In a run of display cases with several doors we assessed the objects in front of each door. If someone had broken into the case, then the rest of the objects within their reach would be vulnerable.

Interpreting the results

Once we had combined the results from the two surveys we had a full picture of the galleries' security needs and a list of the displays that had the highest priority to improve. We also had the information needed to create an action plan and to start estimating the cost of making improvements. The survey showed a number of things, including:

* priorities for putting alarms on objects and displays
* priorities for improving physical barriers and fixings

- priorities for informing gallery staff about which displays should be monitored more closely
- where the most valuable items are placed for emergency planning.

Future uses

Risk assessment forms are the starting point for evaluating the wellbeing of people and processes in health and safety matters, but using similar forms to assess and improve the security of collections has considerable potential. We are considering assessing the security of the collections in our stores using this method, particularly stores with public access. We may also use it to assess security requirements in advance for new displays and loans. This simple method could be adapted easily by other museums.

Value

We calculated a display's value by adding its monetary value, or the cost of replacing it, to its historical value. The two are not necessarily the same as there are objects of high historical value that are worth little money, and vice versa. The curator valued the object on a scale of one (less than £200) to four (over £10,000). The valuation brackets were wide so that time was not wasted worrying about exact values.

The historical value of displays was scored from one (set dressing or low significance) to three (invaluable). Adding the two figures together gave the display's value rating, for example, six to seven was a high score and two to three was a low one.

Vulnerability

We assessed the vulnerability of the displays using two criteria: whether the display was alarmed and its physical protection. A well-alarmed display scored one, while a display with no alarm scored three. We also recorded whether alarms were poorly positioned and if they needed any maintenance.

Next we scored how well the display was protected on a scale of one, a secure case, to four, a vulnerable display within people's reach. A display in an insecure case that could be opened easily scored a two. Displays protected by barriers that would stop casual handling, because objects were out of reach, but not a determined person, scored a three. When the scores for alarms and protection were added together they might give a high score of six to seven, which meant that it was particularly vulnerable, or a low score of two to three for a secure display.

Recommending action

When the value and vulnerability scores were added together the result gave us a score indicating what kind of action we needed to take to improve security. The 'immediate action' score (13 to 14) showed that these displays should be given top priority for any remedial action to prevent damage or theft. An 'action required' score meant that remedial action was needed but not urgently. The next two categories were 'consider improvements' and 'monitor only' scores. The latter showed that there was an adequate level of security, or that only minor adjustments were required.

We used a comments space on the form to record details such as whether a lock needed repairing. We also used this space to identify high value objects within the display.

Paintings, prints and drawings

When we tested the assessment technique on displays featuring fine art we found that their consistently high monetary value and historical significance unbalanced the weighting of the scoring system. This gave an 'immediate action' recommendation for nearly all of these displays, whether it was fully justified or not. So we created a modified form by reducing the scoring of the historical value: an 'invaluable' painting was given a two instead of a three. We left out the 'important' category because it was irrelevant for artworks: they were either irreplaceable or other examples existed.

As far as the vulnerability of the art was concerned, we considered four different methods of fixing the artwork: mirror plates with security screws scored one, on chains screwed to the wall scored two, mirror plates with ordinary screws scored three and loosely hanging on hooks scored four.

In the comments space we recorded things such as whether the painting was glazed, or how portable it was. We found that we had to consider how valuable the works were when prioritising the recommended actions. A painting of high value, which scored 11 to 15, for example, fell into the immediate action list while a print of low value scoring a five would only require monitoring.

Introduction to Part Two – Section Two

Chris Caple

Agents of deterioration: fire and water (disasters)

THE IMPACT OF DISASTERS on museum collections goes back to the temple collections in early Rome, whilst the provision of documentation to prepare staff and thus mitigate damage from disasters can be seen in the 1939 publication *Air Raid Precautions in Museums and Picture Galleries and Libraries*, a 60-page booklet written by Sir John Fosdyke, Director of the British Museum (Caygill 1992), just before the outbreak of the Second World War. To appreciate the extent of the threat that disasters pose to the artefacts in a museum or a historic house, it is instructive to be reminded of the level of destruction of such events, hence the inclusion in this reader of Chapter 10 by Rowell and Robinson (1996) on the fire and salvage efforts at Uppark. The detailed analysis of many such events shows that the provision of appropriate equipment, planning and staff training can reduce the impact of disasters on collections. In the 1980s–90s there were a series of fires in the stately homes of Britain: Hampton Court in 1986, Uppark in 1989, Windsor Castle in 1992. It was the fire at Uppark and the visual impact of its damage, and the subsequent salvage operation, that gave renewed impetus in Britain to the creation of disaster plans for all museums and historic houses, the creation of disaster teams and the establishment of caches of emergency equipment to aid in dealing with emergencies. Preparations had been made, prior to 1989, by many organisations, including the National Trust, for dealing with disasters, but the extent of the devastation at Uppark brought home to organisations how catastrophic and costly such events could be. The fact that there was not one but a number of these events in the late 1980s reminded the heritage industry that, whilst such events are rare in the life of any one property, when one considers all the historic properties and museums in the world, a number of major incidents occur every year. This ultimately led to the incorporation of fire and flood (disaster and emergency planning) into the *Framework for Preservation* and an appreciation that reducing the likelihood and impact of fires and flooding was as much part of preventive conservation as reducing the levels of light.

The initial disaster plans of the 1980s and 1990s could often be long and detailed affairs. The advice given for disaster preparedness planning, such as that by John Hunter (1994) (Chapter 12), reflected this detailed, multi-step approach to the subject. Like other publications on this subject (Dorge and Jones 1999), its detail is useful for reminding people of the many things that should be considered. 'Disaster Plans' became widespread in the UK in the 1990s and were a formal requirement for all accredited museums and archives in England by 2004. As part of this effort to encourage museums, historic houses and even private collections to engage in disaster preparedness, a number of organisations provided information on disaster and emergency planning on websites.[1] However, these initial disaster planning documents were often very large and only limited sections, often the appendices, were needed in practice. The disaster teams and emergency equipment also consumed scarce resources. Consequently, in recent years their emphasis changed and the term 'emergency planning' has become more widely, used with a remit for dealing with any emergency situations that would arise in the museum. Three separate teams: emergency planning, emergency response and salvage team, are mentioned by David Martin in his updated review of emergency/disaster planning (2005). Though several members of these teams are the same, additional specialists are present in each one. In practice few organisations will be large enough to support three teams and a single team with additional members for specific situations is more usual. The broadening of the remit reflects a desire for more effective use of the resources and training consumed by disaster planning. However, as Martin's article shows, the heart of the emergency plan is still the same well-structured 'Disaster Plan' created in the 1990s. The slightly jaded statement that 'opinions vary about the value of kits of equipment and materials that might be needed in a disaster' reflects a decade of museum directors tripping over plywood sheets and polythene sheeting in the corner of a small museum, ready for a disaster which has yet to arrive.

Some of the more recent events, such as the damage and looting of museums caught up in conflicts in countries such as Kuwait, the former Yugoslavia, Chechnya and Iraq have emphasised the need for the emergency planning procedures of museums to engage with war or conflict situations. Most of these procedures are those outlined much earlier by Noblecourt (1956) and Stanley-Price (1997). However, the events of 11 September 2001 brought home to many museums outside 'traditional' conflict zones their unpreparedness for terrorism and the impact it could have on their collections (Heritage Preservation 2002).

Note

1   http://www.english-heritage.org.uk/professional/advice/advice-by-topic/climate-change/
     flood-risk-and-advice/,   http://www.getty.edu/conservation/publications/pdf_publications/

emergency_plan.pdf, http://www.chin.gc.ca/Applications_URL/icom/guide12A.html, http://
museum-sos.org/htm/index.html, http://www.collectionslink.org.uk/plan_for_emergencies.

References

Caygill, M. (1992) 'The Protection of National Treasures at the British Museum during the
    First World and Second World Wars', in P. Vandiver, J. Druzik, G. Wheeler and I.
    Freestone (eds), *Materials Issues in Art and Archaeology III*, Pittsburgh, PA: Materials
    Research Society, pp. 29–99.
Dorge, V. and Jones, S. L. (1999) *Building an Emergency Plan: A Guide for Museums and
    Other Cultural Institutions*, Los Angeles: Getty Conservation Institute.
Heritage Preservation (2002) *Cataclysm and Challenge: Impact of September 11, 2001 on
    Our Nation's Cultural Heritage*, New York: Heritage Preservation.
Hunter, J. E. (1994) 'Museum Disaster Preparedness and Planning', in S. Knell (ed.), *Care
    of Collections*, London: Routledge, pp. 60–79 (originally in B. G. Jones (ed.) (1986)
    Protecting Historic Architecture and Museum Collections from Natural Disasters, Oxford:
    Butterworth-Heinemann).
Martin, J. (2005) 'Emergency Planning', *Museum Practice* Spring 2005: 43–59.
Noblecourt, A. (1956) 'Protection of Cultural Property in the Event of Armed Conflict',
    Museums and Monuments VIII, Paris: UNESCO.
Rowell, C. and Robinson, J. M. (1996) *Uppark Restored*, London: National Trust.
Stanley-Price, N. (1997) 'War and the Conservator: 1 Preventive Measures and Recovery',
    Museum Management and Curatorship 16(2): 155–159.

Chapter 10

Uppark Restored: the fire and salvage

Christopher Rowell and Martin Robinson

WEDNESDAY 30 AUGUST 1989 was warm and windy. Although the sun was shining in a cloudless sky, there was a strong south-westerly breeze: typical August weather on this exposed crest of the South Downs in West Sussex. Uppark's brick and stone walls had been shrouded in scaffolding for over a year, but this was due to be dismantled the following day on completion of structural and roof repairs. A small team of leadworkers were sunning themselves and drinking tea on the lawn when they noticed a puff of smoke on the roof. The fire-alarms in the house sounded at 3.36 pm. There had been 270 visitors that afternoon; those remaining in the house were swiftly evacuated and the gates were opened on the north drive to allow the fire-engines to pass. The alarm was linked via a monitoring agency to the local fire stations at Petersfield, at Midhurst and to the county headquarters at Chichester. It seemed at first to be a practice – there was no evidence of a fire within the building. But the smoke was soon more pronounced. The leadworkers, subcontracted to Haden Young Ltd, had been welding sheets of lead on the roof adjoining the pediment; contrary to instructions, they had left the scaffolding prematurely, thereby failing to detect the ignition of the timbers beneath the lead. By the time they had returned, their fire extinguisher was powerless to arrest the progress of the fire, which was already spreading through the roof cavity.

A remarkable series of photographs taken by a visitor to the house charts the progress of the fire. Eight minutes after the fire-alarm had sounded, smoke was billowing from the east side of the pediment; soon afterwards the first flames were visible and then spread; by 4 o'clock a fireman's hose created clouds of steam. The first engine had arrived from Petersfield a few minutes earlier, and had immediately

Source: *Uppark Restored* (Chapter 1: The Fire and Salvage), London: The National Trust, 1996, pp. 15–31.

Figure 10.1 4.15 pm, visitors evacuated from the house watching helplessly. The house had been in scaffolding for almost a year, with the roof repairs practically complete (Photographs by Sheila Atkinson)

Figure 10.2 A swift response by staff, volunteer room stewards and the Meade-Fetherstonhaugh family, co-ordinated by the fire brigade, made possible the rescue of a remarkably large proportion of the contents of the house. Tragically, the private collection of the first floor was lost, as were several heavy and fixed pieces of furniture on the ground floor

radioed for two more. The Midhurst engine followed a minute later and summoned a further two. Within half an hour there were four fire-engines at Uppark and a further sixteen on their way. At the height of the fire, there were 27 fire-engines and 156 firemen, from West Sussex, Hampshire and Surrey.

Kenneth Lloyd, then Deputy Chief Fire Officer for West Sussex, took charge at 4.25 pm. He immediately realised that the fire would burn inexorably from the roof to the basement and bought time for the salvage of the contents. The evacuation of the pictures, furniture, textiles and fittings was already under way. The contents of the Little Parlour were cleared by a team of house staff and volunteer room stewards. The Saloon was next: the great glass doors to the south steps were thrown open and English and French furniture, books and porcelain were brought out and piled up on the grass.

Earlier on, a team of firemen had been led upstairs to the seat of the fire but were beaten back by the flames in the attic. As they rushed down the corridor, the ceiling collapsed in a shower of sparks and burning timbers. On their retreat, they snatched up an eighteenth-century portrait of a dog. This proved to be the sole survivor of the private collection, because by the time that it was clear that the fire would engulf the Meade-Fetherstonhaugh family's first-floor rooms it was too dangerous to evacuate their contents. Instead, tragically as it turned out, pictures were moved from one end of the first floor to the other rather than being taken downstairs. By 4.30 pm the fire was already breaking through from the attic, and half an hour later the family apartment was a mass of flames which were seen licking through the closed windows. The destruction of these magical panelled or wallpapered rooms, largely untouched since the eighteenth century, with their outstanding seventeenth-, eighteenth- and early nineteenth-century paintings, furniture and textiles, was the greatest disaster of the fire.

It was apparent, from the beginning of the desperate fire-fighting campaign, that Uppark's hill-top situation would create huge problems in the procurement of water. Uppark had depended upon wells and dew ponds until before 1746, when a water supply had been 'sometime since erected' by means of lead pipes and an engine within the existing pump-house at the foot of the steep hill on the outskirts of South Harting, over a mile away; in 1731 a payment was made for 'looking after the Water Engine'. By 4.30 pm on that August afternoon the water supply was already giving out. While the Dairy tank and the Meade-Fetherstonhaugh family's swimming pool were drained, five fire-engines and a hose-layer laid pipes down the hill to South Harting. But the South Harting main soon collapsed under the pressure and the firemen on the scaffold pouring water through the disintegrating roof saw their jets diminish into a trickle.

From about 5 o'clock and throughout the night, six fire-engines and two 5,000 gallon water-carriers shuttled between a 5 in (13 cm) main a few miles away and Uppark, where they off-loaded into holding tanks near the north drive gates. Also, firemen foraging for water found a private fishing lake in a wood near the village. The fire-engines could not reach it, so the water was transferred via a pipe through the wood to the line of fire-engines pumping water up South Harting hill. The following morning the lake was almost dry, and the shallow water was teeming with fish.

This resolute search for water did not hamper the rescue of the contents, but

worrying moments when the supply of water failed, and inevitably
s lost. Soon after 5 o'clock, fire-crews wearing breathing apparatus
north entrance and under a protective shower of water scooped up
s by Arthur Devis and a painting of Sir Matthew Fetherstonhaugh's
n Boultbee from the east wall of the burning Staircase Hall. Further
up the stairs, it was impossible to save a large painting of the Battle of Trafalgar,
whose surface was flayed from the stretcher in the searing heat. At ground-floor
level, despite the danger of falling timbers and showers of burning lead, the firemen,
wielding crowbars, prised Pieter Tillemans's huge pair of Uppark landscapes from
the panelling in which they had been set in the 1720s. Minutes later, the staircase collapsed in a welter of flame. Other salvage teams, an officer and four or five men, went
in continuously with designated paintings or other objects in view. In the Saloon, two
large paintings from Luca Giordano's *Prodigal Son* series were hauled down from their
positions high on the north wall. Luckily, the gilt fillets which held them in place were
easily detached, allowing the canvases to be swiftly removed from the plasterwork.
Until about 6 o'clock, the firemen made rapid sorties into the stricken building to
rescue what they could.

Earlier, a news cameraman in a helicopter had filmed the plume of smoke swirl-
ing to the north-east. The lens focused on the ant-like figures running in and out of
the house, fighting the flames or rescuing contents. These were the pictures that
appeared on that evening's television news. The footage clearly showed that the roof
had collapsed and that the attic was ruined, with its wooden floor in flames. The first
floor was also ablaze. The contents on the grass were gradually taken under cover
– into the Stables on the west side or into the former Orangery, Kitchen and Laundry
Block (the present tea-room) to the east. By 6 o'clock, when most of the obviously
portable objects had been removed, there was a lull. The ground-floor state-rooms
were still intact, the fire was raging above and it was obvious that it would soon break
through and destroy Uppark's grandest interiors.

At National Trust regional and national headquarters, the alarm had been raised
by press inquiries. Soon, switchboards were jammed with calls from reporters,
thereby hampering the communication of the disaster and the summons of help from
experts within and without the Trust. A disaster plan, revised since the 1986 fire at
Hampton Court, was put into operation. Telephone calls were made to an array of
conservators; supplies of equipment (bubble wrap, tissue paper, blotting paper) were
hurriedly amassed; a Land-Rover filled with salvage equipment was despatched from
Kingston Lacy in Dorset.

When David Sekers, Director of the National Trust's Southern Region and
Christopher Rowell, regional Historic Buildings Representative, arrived at Uppark
at about 6.30 pm, they were hoping that the unconfirmed news of the fire would turn
out to be a false alarm. On the drive their worst fears were confirmed as they first
smelled and then saw the smoke. Having reported immediately to Kenneth Lloyd,
they made a rapid circuit of the building to assess the success of the salvage operation. This had been an heroic effort, but it was clear that the state-rooms were on
the point of destruction, and that the less obviously portable objects – fixed furniture, pier-glasses and curtains, as well as fixtures and fittings, wallpapers and decorative woodwork – would be totally destroyed unless a second phase of salvage was

attempted. The interior had long been out of bounds to anyone other than firemen, and despite the increasing danger, the Chief Salvage Officer detailed a group of firemen to respond to National Trust requests for rescue attempts.

Still hanging at the windows were the red and yellow silk damask festoon curtains, believed to date from the eighteenth century. It was possible for individual firemen to reach up and tear down the curtains from the wooden pelmet boards to which they were close-nailed. The fact that most of these fragile curtains were robust enough to come down in one piece was due to their conservation in the 1930s by Lady (Margaret) Meade-Fetherstonhaugh, whose husband and son gave Uppark to the National Trust in 1954.

In the Red Drawing Room, firemen tore down the red flock wallpaper, first put up in c.1750 and papered over in 1851 or 1859. Because it was fixed to hessian and mounted on battens, rather than being stuck to the wall, it came away in huge strips and was hurled through the windows on to the lawn. Later that evening, at about 9.30 pm, the pair of magnificent mid-eighteenth-century rococo carved and gilded pier-glasses, attributed to Matthias Lock, was unscrewed from the walls and, with great difficulty because the room was by now in flames, manoeuvred sideways through the windows. One of them was already on fire as it was manhandled to safety. The original bevelled glass, already cracked by the heat, was smashed to lighten the load.

It was no longer safe to enter some ground-floor rooms after about 6.30 pm. The fire first broke through from above in the Stone Hall, the east (and original) entrance to the house. Here, National Trust staff could only look impotently through the glass doors as the room was rapidly ignited. Against the far wall, flanking the door into the Staircase Hall (a raging inferno for the last hour) stood the famous pair of scagliola-topped tables on English rococo supports. Two of the finest objects in the house, probably commissioned in Florence in 1750 by Sir Matthew Fetherstonhaugh, they were overlooked in the first phase of salvage due to their great weight and the fact that their bases were screwed to the panelled dado. Now, though only 15 ft (4.5 m) from the eastern steps, they were at the mercy of the fire. One of the bases was already burning when the ceiling collapsed at about 6.45 pm, and engulfed the tables in rubble and burning debris. A falling beam smashed the left-hand table into eight pieces. It seemed at the time that both tables must have been totally destroyed.

Since all the rooms, with the single exception of the Little Parlour, were by now ablaze, the salvage operation became increasingly sporadic. As night drew in, and Uppark became a picturesque bonfire, the endless drone of the fire-pumps, the tangled hoses snaking around the house, the shouting of orders to the fire-crews and, above all, the crackling and spitting of blazing wood made up an unforgettable miscellany of images, sounds and smells. Occasionally, the collapse of a large piece of masonry or a wooden beam shook the ground as it fell in a shower of sparks. Members of the Meade-Fetherstonhaugh family, who had lost their home and almost their entire inheritance and who were at the forefront of the initial salvage effort, bravely confronted the awful reality of the destruction of their beloved Uppark.

At this stage, there was not much more to be done in terms of rescue. At 3 am, National Trust staff were allowed for the first time into the north end of the building. In the company of the Chief Fire Officer, Martin Drury, then Historic Buildings

Secretary, and Christopher Rowell looked through the door from the North Corridor into the Staircase Hall. Piled high with burning debris, it was an infernal scene. Miraculously, a length of seventeenth-century balustrade was still visible through the smoke on the first-floor landing, which had somehow not entirely collapsed. Much of the plasterwork was undamaged, but the seventeenth-century panelling below was destroyed.

Returning into the corridor, and turning right into the Servery, the party was able to review the state of the Dining Room. The Servery, and its stained-glass window by Humphry Repton, was undamaged. The scene beyond the double doors was encouraging. This panelled Dining Room, constructed by Repton for Sir Harry Fetherstonhaugh in c.1815, was hardly damaged (its ceiling had not yet fallen in). The gilt overmantel mirror, contemporary with Repton's work, was still in place. The question was, could it be safely retrieved? As a fireman entered through the window, he called out, 'Do you want the glass?' Concerned for his safety and wishing to avoid any delay as the ceiling might have collapsed at any moment, Martin Drury shouted, 'No'. The fireman smashed the glass with a crowbar and carried the frame to safety.

Leaving the building once again, the group toured the exterior for the last time that night. At the south-east corner, the Little Parlour was empty but still unscathed. Its eighteenth-century glass chandelier, hanging from crimson cords and tassels supplied in 1836, was swinging in the heat below the Neo-classical compartmented ceiling. A fireman was playing his hose into the room, attempting to reduce the possibility of flames igniting it. He was asked to divert his water jet away from the chandelier – a futile request in view of the subsequent collapse of the chimneystack high above, which crashed through the ceiling carrying the plasterwork, the chandelier and the Parlour floor into the Housekeeper's Room beneath. A last vignette that night was the spectacle of the Prince Regent's Bed, now beyond rescue, in the Tapestry Bedroom at the north-western extremity of the ground floor. Martin Drury and Christopher Rowell took what they were sure would be their last sight of Uppark's state bed and retired for the consolation of whisky and eggs and bacon, greedily consumed at 4 am before three hours of fitful sleep.

Dawn revealed the full extent of the damage. The fire was still alight, but only smouldering by this time. An aerial photograph published in the *Portsmouth News* the following day, and then in several national newspapers, promoted the erroneous conclusion that Uppark had been 'gutted'. Gradually, it became evident that this was an exaggeration. The upper floors were indeed almost completely destroyed, but at ground-floor level, although all the ceilings had collapsed, much of the decorative plaster-work and woodwork had survived. The rooms were filled with wet smoking debris, but in the Saloon, where the paint and gilding of the walls and door-cases were remarkably untouched, the ormolu chandelier of c.1800 jutted out of the blackened rubbish, indicating the possibility of other survivals beneath. Here, and elsewhere, marble fireplaces had escaped damage. Although the Little Parlour had been destroyed in the course of the night, the Prince Regent's Bed still stood in the Tapestry Bedroom. There was no time to lose, as the ceiling looked precarious. At first, with shouted instructions from John Hart, one of the Trust's advisers on furniture conservation, firemen attempted to dismantle the bed. When they could not do it, John Hart and his assistant Gerard Bur joined them, lifted off the canopy, unscrewed the frame and passed everything through the windows. Twenty minutes later, at about 10.30 am, the ceiling collapsed.

Under the aegis of Sarah Staniforth, the Trust's adviser on paintings conservation, picture conservators from the Trust, the Royal Collection and in private practice had been working all night to consolidate canvases damaged by heat and water; this was done principally by laying down buckled paint and facing it with paper. A second shift relieved them at 8 am. The damage sometimes looked more dramatic than it actually was: great streaks of blanched varnish caused by fire water were easily removed in subsequent studio treatment. By that evening, all the paintings had left Uppark for storage and for eventual conservation elsewhere. As they entered the van, their inventory numbers were ticked off and transport forms compiled. For reasons of security as well as conservation, furniture and other contents in a fit state to be moved were also transported within the following two days. With the television, radio and newspaper coverage, there was a very real risk of theft, but fortunately these precautions prevented it. Later, the building was fenced off and a perimeter alarm installed. Petworth House, another National Trust property ten miles to the east, became the repository for most of the salvaged contents. Here, at first, the Square Dining Room and Chapel were closed to the public 'for repair', but were in fact secretly filled with Uppark's now homeless collection; later, former servants' quarters in the Domestic Block were converted into longer-term safe storage. Subsequently, the defunct Battery House, once the site of electric generators that had powered both the house and the town, was converted into a temporary laying-out area where damaged Uppark contents were assessed before repair.

The day after the fire inaugurated many weeks of determined action to preserve what could be preserved of the fabric and contents of Uppark. The walls were still standing but they needed buttressing. Scaffolding could not be introduced without clearing the surrounding slag-heaps that filled the carcass of the building. For nearly

Figure 10.3 The morning after the fire: flock wallpaper, torn down by firemen in the Red Drawing Room, is examined by Christopher Rowell and Mary Goodwin, then the National Trust's Adviser on Paper Conservation

Figure 10.4 In the Saloon much of the painting and gilding survived almost undamaged, as did the marble chimneypieces. Within the rubble lay fragments
of plaster, woodwork, and the room contents

five days until the fire was officially pronounced to be 'out', the fire brigade continued to 'damp down' the debris. Here and there small pockets of flame flared up
and were extinguished. Despite this, it was possible to begin the excavation almost
immediately. It was frustrating for those on site to be prevented from sifting through
the sludge, but meanwhile there was more than enough to attend to. Thought had to
be given not just to things but also to people. A home had to be found for the National
Trust's resident custodians Brian and Jan Smith, whose flat and a lifetime's possessions were no more. The staff and outside conservators had to be equipped and fed.
A system of regular, concise meetings was instigated to formulate a strategy for the
rescue of damaged fragments of the building and its contents. Communication and
co-ordination were essential, but conservators had to be given the time to proceed
efficiently with the work in hand rather than to attend meetings.

Day-to-day management was split between Peter Pearce, then Managing Agent
for Uppark (who dealt with general administration and had overall responsibility for
the rescue) and Christopher Rowell (whose curatorship of the Uppark collection
gave him a natural role in co-ordinating its conservation). A key figure, dubbed the
Quartermaster, was John Sursham, previously the regional volunteers' co-ordinator,
whose job was to procure anything that might be required, from voluntary help to
portable telephones and food. He proved adept at obtaining huge numbers of dustbins, baker's trays and other mundane items that were to prove invaluable for the
salvage operation. Three ballroom-sized marquees were pitched on the west lawn to
enable sodden textiles to be slowly dried. Previously, at the instigation of Jane Mathews, then the Trust's adviser on textile conservation, the filthy and charred curtains
had been interleaved with sheets of polythene. This dual process of keeping them
moist, followed by natural drying in airy marquees avoided permanent staining.

Before the fire was officially extinguished, the fire brigade deemed it safe to dig
out the several feet of debris in certain rooms. With watchers, armed with sirens

Figure 10.5 Rosalie Elwes, a National Trust volunteer, recording the departure of the paintings for studio repair. Essential emergency work by picture conservators had been completed within twenty-four hours of the fire

Figure 10.6 Nearly 4,000 dustbins stored the residue of debris excavated within the ruins of the house. This was later sifted on a conveyor belt, which passed the rubble over a sieve

to warn of any structural movement and stationed at a high level on the scaffolding, digging began. After most fires, even in important buildings, it had been the practice simply to cart away and dump the rubble, as, for example, after the 1980 fire at the National Trust's Nostell Priory, in Yorkshire. By contrast, after the fire at Hampton Court in 1986, investigation, recording and preservation of what was apparently rubbish had repaid considerable dividends.

At Uppark, teams of volunteers and staff under the supervision of the Trust's archaeological advisers and conservators systematically excavated the ruins. Each room (the sequence dictated by the condition of the surrounding walls) was

Figure 10.7 A tray containing a remnant of the Saloon ceiling plasterwork

separated into grid squares for the purpose of recording the location of each 'find'. The grid consisted of a chequerboard of ropes stretched above the workers with letters and numbers designating each compartment. As interesting fragments emerged from the sludge (a piece of carved woodwork or plasterwork, sherds of glass and porcelain) they were placed in plastic trays labelled with the grid references. Thus it was possible to determine that broken glass found in the Staircase Hall belonged to the mid-eighteenth-century Gothick lantern previously hanging there. In this way, the glass was replaced to the exact profile of the original.

This initial sorting had to be carried out at speed, due to the urgent requirement to shore up the weakened walls of the building. The residue was shovelled into dustbins, also marked with grid references, to be sifted later on a conveyor belt which passed the debris over a mesh. The 3,860 dustbins on the east lawn beside the house became a potent symbol of the scale of the salvage operation. Plastic 'polytunnels' with scaffolding and plank shelving gradually filled up with great baulks of charred timber, trays of plaster fragments, carved decorative woodwork, window catches, door knobs, picture hooks, chimneypots and anything that looked promising. The clear principle was that nothing should be discarded lest vital clues for the possible repair of Uppark should be lost. As each room was cleared, the scaffolders moved in, and a honeycomb of supports began to rise. This steadily grew into a giant roofed structure of interlocking supports that was completed by November 1989.

Between August and November, as digging continued and discoveries were made in the rubble, conservators worked under considerable pressure, handling a huge and ever-increasing volume of fragile material. As Jane Mathews, who was working with a large team of textile conservators, put it: 'I'd never worked in field conditions before.' Because of the principle that nothing should be discarded, every piece of charred textile – however apparently insignificant – was carefully dusted with a small brush to remove acidic ash and residue, and each item was labelled and recorded. There were some dramatic moments, when casualties were carried from the battle-front of the house into what increasingly resembled a field hospital with

white-coated conservators ministering quietly to their torn, scorched and bedrag-
gled textiles. From the Red Drawing Room and Little Parlour, stretchered out on
bread-trays, came the pathetic remains of four red silk chandelier tassels, supplied to
Uppark in 1836. Already fragile in 1933 when they were taken down and repaired by
Lady Meade-Fetherstonhaugh, they have once again been nursed back to life and now
hang in their old positions, despite being crushed by several tons of rubble. Beneath
the wreckage of the Red Drawing Room, against all reasonable expectations, lay
the Axminster carpet of c.1800, a totally unexpected product of the optimism that
had instigated the salvage operation. Hurriedly lifted and thrown over the Victorian
Broadwood grand piano in a last-minute attempt to protect the (much less important)
instrument from the fire, the piano had been incinerated, only its metal skeleton
surviving within the folds of the carpet. Blackened, stained and damaged, the carpet
responded well to emergency intensive care and was laid out to dry under canvas. It,
too, has now returned to its old place.

With such encouragement, those working on site up to fourteen hours a day,
seven days a week, began to feel that their efforts might not be in vain, and that
Uppark might indeed have a future. It soon became possible to see how much plaster
had been saved from the Saloon ceiling, how many lengths of gilt wallpaper fillet had
emerged from the Red Drawing Room and so on. Most encouraging of all was the
miraculous survival in situ of plasterwork, panelling, doors and chimneypieces. The
decision to repair the house was taken two months after the fire, but those battling
to save Uppark felt very quickly that this would be the likely outcome, and worked
all the harder with this hope in mind. As they worked, the pieces of the jigsaw were
increasing day by day, and an intense camaraderie developed. Everyone concerned
looks back to that time as a period of single-minded hard labour. They remember
how exhausted they were at night (and in the morning before another long day) but
they also recall the 'blitz' spirit of working together for something worthwhile. At
first, wartime analogies extended even to the food, which was not only reminiscent
of 1940s deprivation but also of the 'Monty Python' menu of 'spam, spam, spam or
spam'. Mercifully, cheese or spam sandwiches and Mars bars soon gave way to more
digestible alternatives.

Just as they had rallied to the emergency call, so the conservators in private
practice, many with a long history of working on Trust buildings and collections,
continued to work day after day with no thought of remuneration. No one waited
for an order to come through before beginning work, and the Trust's administrative
staff had to ensure much later that nobody was out of pocket due to this generosity
and selfless dedication. In the rescue and subsequent repair of Uppark the Trust's
conservation service came of age.

As the rooms were gradually cleared, not only did the scaffolding enabling emergency repairs to take place (only one chimneystack had to be pulled down) begin to
rise, but also the recording of the damaged interior was instituted. With the help of
the National Monuments Record, the Trust's archaeological department surveyed the
structure both as a possible preliminary to reconstruction and as an historical record.
This was later supplemented by photogrammetry (precision photography to scale),
which allowed the data to be incorporated on computer as an essential basis for architects' computer-assisted drawings. Computers were also brought in by the English

Heritage Archaeological Excavation Team that had pioneered their technique after the 1986 Hampton Court fire. In early November they joined National Trust rescuers and began the process of transferring manual records of over 12,000 finds on to their 'Delilah' computer programme. This was of considerable benefit, but its efficacy was qualified by the understandable misidentification of objects by inexperienced recording staff. Later, when the repairs were under way, only expert manual sorting would reveal how many eighteenth-century metal curtain cloakpins or window catches had survived, because they had been filed on the computer as 'miscellaneous metalwork'. As ever, automation proved not to be a panacea.

Research was also already in progress to establish the extent of pre-fire records that could serve to inform the possible renaissance of Uppark. Fortunately, Uppark had been extensively photographed since the late nineteenth century. The first *Country Life* article was illustrated in 1910, and family albums produced even earlier images. As well as the National Trust photographic archive, photographs were sent in by visitors, scholars, craftsmen and builders in response to the Trust's appeal for help. Later, the appeal became more specialised as the lacunae became more apparent. A snapshot of a pet owl perching on the shoulder of the Uppark Custodian's niece, for instance, proved to be the only evidence for the design of the attic kitchen in the Custodian's flat. On the first floor, Meade-Fetherstonhaugh family photographs solved the confusion about wallpaper colours and chimneypieces.

The principal rooms on the ground floor were, hardly surprisingly, more comprehensively recorded. There were also National Trust surveys of pictures and, more importantly, of picture and mirror frames. The latter proved to be of fundamental significance for the recarving of the destroyed base sections of one of the Red Drawing Room pier-glasses. There was also a series of general views of each room. None the less, there were gaps (which could usually be filled by resort to fragments recovered after the fire, or by comparative research), and some photographs were endlessly magnified and pored over in an endeavour to make sense of some missing detail. Needless to say, there is now a mandatory policy of architectural photography that, when completed, will provide a comprehensive record of all the Trust's buildings and collections.

From the first puff of smoke, Uppark's demise had been captured on film by amateurs and professionals. Thousands of photographs, hundreds of hours of film and tape recordings, as well as rooms full of documents, provide an exceptional opportunity for future study of what was done. Thanks to the generosity of Sun Alliance, which, as the Sun Fire Office, first insured Uppark in 1753, visitors see an introductory exhibition which draws upon this voluminous material. The educational potential is at least one silver lining to the catastrophe of 1989.

Chapter 11

Emergency Planning – Introduction

John Martin

DISASTER PLANNING IS ARGUABLY the museum equivalent of making a will or having a health check: one of those things that everyone knows they ought to do, but then puts off. But as the case studies in this issue show, having a robust, tested disaster plan is the single most important thing you can have to keep your staff, your visitors and your collections safe – or as safe as the situation allows.

Disasters can be divided into two kinds: the things you can plan for and aim to prevent; and the sort of cataclysmic and unusual events that you can't foresee – although your disaster plan will still be useful. In the latter case, a checklist anticipating how you might react to a disaster and the people you might need to contact will save time and help minimise the risks to staff, visitors and objects.

Our two case studies look at both types of disaster: the floods that affected the Perth Museum and Art Gallery in Scotland in 1993, and the fireworks factory explosion that damaged the Twenthe Museum in Enschede, the Netherlands, in 2000. The town of Perth had suffered from floods in the past, and the staff at its museum had a robust plan prepared. This was refined in the aftermath of the flood that finally penetrated the museum basement. The plan helped the staff to save most of the collection and prevent injuries to themselves and other people. In Enschede, a massive explosion in a fireworks factory that resulted in 22 deaths and the destruction of nearly 400 homes was not a disaster the Twenthe Museum could anticipate or prevent. But its disaster plan was vital in evacuating the museum and then securing it while the fires raged. [. . .]

Source: *Museum Practice* Spring 2005, pp. 43–59. By kind permission of the Museums Association.

Damage control

How to prepare

Disasters are unexpected events that cause or threaten damage to museum buildings and their contents and put staff and visitors at risk. They may be the result of natural forces such as fire, flood or subsidence; of unpredictable incidents such as accidents or explosions; or of criminal acts, ranging from theft to terrorism. Most museums have established procedures to protect or evacuate staff and visitors in a disaster, but far fewer are as well equipped to deal with the effects on their collections. In the UK, the Museum Accreditation Scheme, launched by the Museums, Libraries and Archives Council (MLA) in November 2004, has a mandatory requirement for museums to have an emergency plan (sometimes called a disaster plan) that covers:

* arrangements for staff and visitors
* arrangements for collections and museum buildings
* an assessment of the risk from threats such as fire, water, theft and vandalism, or other disasters
* procedures to be followed by staff on discovery of an emergency.

This article provides guidance on how to prepare for emergencies – but not the security measures that may be needed to prevent theft or other forms of criminal activity.

Step one: risk assessment

An essential first stage in producing an emergency plan is to carry out a thorough assessment of the risks most likely to affect the museum, its occupants and its collections. This will provide the basis for developing procedures and measures to:

* help minimise the likelihood of a disaster occurring in the first place (preventive or proactive planning)
* make sure there is a quick and effective response in the event of a disaster (reactive planning)
* help the museum return to normal as soon as possible.

The best way of going about this is to appoint one person as an emergency coordinator who will take responsibility for producing and implementing the plan. This coordinator should head a small emergency planning team of colleagues who between them are familiar with the key areas of the museum's operations, including:

* the building and site
* visitor services
* the collections
* collections care and conservation
* security, and health and safety.

Ideally, the same people will also be keyholders, live within easy reach of the museum and be the first points of contact in an emergency. The coordinator and team members may need training to enable them to carry out a risk assessment and use the results to prepare an effective emergency plan. An important part of the risk assessment is to consult widely within and outside the organisation to draw on other people's knowledge and experience. This will help make sure the risks and possible responses to them are considered from a wide range of perspectives.

Step two: preventing disasters

The aim of preventive planning is to use risk assessment to focus on the type of emergencies that are most likely to occur, or are most readily preventable, and develop appropriate procedures or measures to reduce the risk. Another aim is to minimise the impact of a disaster on people and collections. Preventive planning should include:

- regular liaison with the emergency services (fire, police and ambulance) for their advice and to agree response procedures in the even of a disaster. In some cases the emergency services will be needed for exercises involving mock disasters. The cooperation of the fire service is all-important – it will need to be familiar with the layout of your museum and your priorities in relation to the rescue of material from the collections
- finding out what local or regional resources and expertise are available. Local authority-run museums may have access to their council's emergency response facilities; and groups of museums might consider sharing their resources and experience in producing plans or responding to emergencies
- reviewing risks inherent in the location of the museum, such as vulnerability to flooding, subsidence, or associated with uses of neighbouring buildings
- routine inspection and maintenance of building fabric and services (to minimise risks such as leaking roofs, blocked gutters and drains, leaking joints in pipe-work, or hazardous electrical installations)
- inspection of weak spots or vulnerable areas of the building such as flat roofs (which may be prone to leakage) or basements (which may be prone to flooding). This might lead to the relocating of areas for functions such as storage or display to reduce the risk of water damage
- reviewing the adequacy and maintenance of detection and alarm systems for fire and water
- reviewing the provision and maintenance of fire extinguishers and fire suppression systems. In a fire, the water from localised sprinkler systems may be less damaging than that from fire brigade hoses
- backing-up and storage (in a separate building) of computer files and documentation
- reviewing insurance for public liability and for loss of, or damage to, the building and collections.

Step three: reacting to disasters

However thorough the preventive planning, disasters can still occur. So an effective response requires well-established procedures to deal with the immediate and longer-term effects of a disaster. Protection and safety of people must be the first priority. But an emergency plan must also include the procedures and information necessary to protect or rescue the collections and to restore the museum to a normal state of operation as soon as possible. The emergency planning team will need to:

- review the adequacy of evacuation procedures to get staff and visitors out of the building in an emergency. Do all staff receive regular training in evacuation procedures? How do visitors know what to do in an emergency – are escape routes clearly marked? Are written instructions provided? Is there a public address system? Do the arrangements take account of the needs of people with physical disabilities or learning difficulties? What procedures are in place for helping and sheltering people with injuries or in distress?
- review compliance with conditions for fire certification of the premises and the recommendations in BS 5454
- set up an emergency response team, headed by an incident controller, to provide an immediate reaction to first notification of a disaster (the response team may be the same people as the planning team). The controller should liaise with the emergency services and coordinate the response team's activities on site. Each member of the response team should be able to take on the incident controller's role if necessary, and there should be arrangements for cover for the controller and team members if they are ill or on leave
- set up an emergency salvage team (which may include members of the emergency planning and response teams), headed by a salvage controller. This group will be responsible for rescuing objects and removing them for treatment or temporary storage if the emergency services allow access to the building – and subject to health and safety and handling considerations. If possible, the salvage team should include people with some knowledge of the collections and their conservation and handling requirements. The team should be briefed about which objects should be salvaged as a priority and their location
- establish call-out procedures for the emergency response team, other key staff, the salvage team, and anyone else whose help would be required in an emergency. Procedures may vary depending on whether the emergency occurs within or outside opening hours and whether there is a security presence in the building during closed hours. Call-out methods range from telephone 'trees' (when each person called then calls one or more numbers from a pre-planned list) to (more reliable) auto-dialling arrangements initiated by a fire alarm control panel or carried out at a remote security monitoring station
- prepare floor plans showing the location of items to be salvaged as a priority, as well as features such as alarm control panels and switches and valves for isolating mains services – digitised plans can be easily revised
- consider arrangements, including liaison with the police, for access for emergency service vehicles; control of parking for staff, essential services, media and others arriving at the site; and controlling onlookers.

To support the salvage operation, the emergency planning team will also need to:

- liaise with the fire service over keyholding, main entry and exit points, and routes through the museum building
- consider the need for emergency kits of materials and equipment to be kept in or near the museum
- consider the equipment and services that may be needed by salvage teams (such as handling equipment, protective clothing and first-aid)
- decide in consultation with colleagues which objects (or other items such as documents or equipment) should be given priority in the salvage operation
- identify the most likely routes for removing prioritised items and other material from the building
- prepare outline guidance on how to treat damaged objects during the first 48 hours after a disaster
- investigate availability of spaces for temporary storage and initial treatment of salvaged objects
- identify sources of plant and equipment such as pumps, generators and temporary lighting
- identify sources of specialist help in areas such as conservation, remedial treatment, freezing facilities (for items such as wet books or works on paper), building repairs, training and media management
- consider procedures and equipment for recording damage to the building and objects, and for handling salvaged objects and transporting them to temporary storage or treatment.

Other tasks to be undertaken in parallel with any salvage operation may include:

- securing the building and collections
- clearing-up
- restoring services (power, lighting, communications, water supply, etc.)
- getting back to normal operation
- dealing with the media
- informing the public
- informing insurers.

Plan of action

Once you have analysed the possible risks and decided how you will react to them, it is time to write the museum's emergency plan.

How to write the plan

The purpose of a written plan is to set down as concisely as possible the information and procedures resulting from the planning and risk assessment process. Remember that in an emergency the people referring to the plan will not have time to read or even skim a lengthy document to find the information they need. You need to keep it clear and succinct and test it out on colleagues to see if they can grasp it quickly. A useful approach is to structure the plan in sections according to the urgency with which the information they contain is likely to be needed. This could typically be:

Immediate response

The information needed by the incident controller (or whoever has to respond first to the notification or occurrence of a disaster). This would include:

- call-out numbers for all the emergency services
- the name and call-out number for the emergency controller
- names, call-out details and responsibilities of the emergency response team
- names, call-out details and responsibilities of the salvage team
- names and call-out details of other staff members or people from other organisations whose assistance would be required
- call-out procedures (such as a call-out tree or contact details for external monitoring stations)
- evacuation and safety procedures for occupants of the building; location of assembly points; incident control points; and safe holding areas for people with injuries or in distress.

Follow-up response and salvage operation

The information needed by the salvage team and other people and organisations involved in dealing with the aftermath of the disaster once the emergency services allow access to the building or site. This is likely to be a more substantial section that includes:

- information on priorities and procedures for salvaging collections and other material
- contact details for individuals or organisations whose advice, equipment or services are needed for the salvage operation or to help restore the museum to normal operation
- location and contents of emergency kits kept on or off the site
- floor plans of the museum showing the location of prioritised items; floor plans kept on computers can also be linked to digitised images of the items
- location and contact details of any off-site facilities for storage or treatment of salvaged items
- information or guidance on arrangements for handling and transporting salvaged material to temporary storage
- responsibilities and procedures for contact with the media.

Risk reduction

Information on procedures and arrangements for regular reviews or management of the risks identified in the risk assessment process previously outlined. This may also be a substantial section, but one which staff are likely to refer to as part of their day-to-day work or as part of emergency training rather than immediately after an emergency. These three main elements of an emergency plan could be included in a single emergency manual, or as two or three separate volumes – one for an immediate response and one or two for follow-up responses and risk reduction – depending on how many people are likely to need access to the manual and its parts. Remember that the plan is likely to contain information about the museum and its collections, access to which will have to be restricted for reasons of security. Dividing it up into separate volumes means that the section on immediate response can be issued to members of the emergency response team or other key personnel to keep at home. The volumes containing confidential information can be kept at secure locations within (and outside) the museum.

As a general rule, the number of copies of the plan should be kept to minimum – for security and to make the updating process easier. A record should be kept of the location and holder of each copy of the plan, and out-of-date versions recalled when revisions are issued. A loose-leaf format, with sections of the plan held in ring binders, is the easiest way of distributing and updating the plan. The manual should be:

- readily identifiable, with a prominent cover and title
- robust and weatherproof – consider having the pages relating to immediate and follow-up responses encapsulated, or at least enclosed in clear polyester sleeves
- concise and easy to use, with a clear list of contents and prominent page and paragraph numbering
- printed in a minimum type size of 12pt, with prominent section for the headings
- easy to update as necessary – the date of amendments and revisions should be recorded in the manual
- regularly reviewed and updated. The Museums, Libraries and Archives Council's guidance on accreditation standards requires a review of emergency plans at least every five years. But a lot of the detailed information will need updating much more frequently to take account of changes within the museum and in outside organisations and agencies
- evaluated in the light of actual or mock emergencies and revised or improved as necessary.

Helping hands

After you have written the emergency plan, the next step is to train your staff to use it properly

Training

Training in preventive and reactive procedures is one of the most important elements of an effective and responsive emergency plan. The emergency coordinator and members of the emergency planning team may need training at the start of the planning process to give them the skills to carry out risk assessments, develop procedures for risk management, and incorporate them in the emergency plan.

The preparation of a plan can also be used as an opportunity to consult staff and volunteers from all areas and at all levels of the museum, and draw on their ideas and experience. This approach will raise the profile of emergency planning within the museum and help make sure that all staff — not just the emergency planning team — feel some sense of ownership of, and responsibility for, the plan. It may also help to promote a better understanding of what is meant by an emergency or disaster, the possible impact on the museum and its visitors, and the importance of preventive measures. Once a plan has been produced, training will continue to be essential to make sure that paid and volunteer staff are familiar with, and able to carry out, the procedures set out in it. Remember that in a real emergency, they may have to carry out tasks (such as salvage) or take on responsibilities (such as evacuating the building) unrelated to their day-to-day work in the museum. In an emergency, there is no time to waste thinking about what to do, and stressful situations are also likely to affect people's ability to make quick decisions. Training can help them function and respond as effectively as possible in difficult conditions. It can also help to:

- foster team-working — a key factor in responding to emergencies
- overcome people's natural tendency to be apathetic towards emergency preparedness and response procedures. People are often unconcerned about emergencies because they believe that disasters only happen to other museums.

Training might be necessary in:

- building evacuation procedures
- emergency call-out procedures
- use of fire-fighting equipment
- use of emergency kits
- procedures for bomb alerts
- security measures and key control procedures
- first aid
- object handling in emergency conditions
- using floor plans.

You will need to think about:

- who will be responsible for organising training and recording its delivery
- who will deliver training — and whether staff, once trained, can train other people
- who will need training in what skills
- how often it will be needed
- how its effectiveness will be tested and evaluated.

As well as drills and practice in emergency procedures, training can be varied to include, for example:

- team-based projects such as clear-up days to encourage staff to throw out rubbish or accumulations of unwanted materials that could be a fire risk

- discussion of day-to-day risks combined with advice on good housekeeping to minimise risks. This could include the storage of flammable materials; discouraging the use of ad hoc wiring arrangements involving trailing extension leads or adaptors for office equipment; and encouraging people to look out for and report warning signs such as a damp patch on the ceiling or overheating electrical equipment
- discussion of a range of typical emergency scenarios (such as a bomb alert or major power-cut) and how people would respond to them
- inviting outside speakers from the police or fire service, or the local council's emergency planning department, to talk about day-to-day risks and how to minimise or respond to them. Speakers from other museums can also talk about their approaches to emergency planning or experience of actual disasters.

Remember that talking about disasters or carrying out drills may alarm some people. As part of evaluating the usefulness of training, you should allow time for debriefing and for participants to share their feelings or make comments and observations. If necessary this can be done in confidence. Some museums also carry out mock-disaster exercises to test the effectiveness of disaster plans. These involve careful preparation, particularly if the plans are to be kept secret so that the exercise is as near as possible to a real disaster. These types of exercises may require the cooperation of the fire and police services as well as other outside organisations such as monitoring stations and alarm companies, and specialists such as conservators. If the exercise is to be carried out during open hours, thought must be given to how, if at all, to involve visitors – or whether to close the museum while it takes place. You may also want to record the exercise on video for evaluation or training purposes; or invite an independent observer – such as someone from the fire service or an emergency planner from the local council – to come and assess the event and make comments about its effectiveness. You should be clear about what you hope to achieve from the exercise and how you will use the results.

Objectives could include testing:

- the accessibility and effectiveness of your emergency manual
- the usefulness of equipment in emergency kits
- how familiar staff and volunteers are with emergency procedures and the location of mains switches, emergency exits and assembly areas
- the ability of staff members to work in teams and to take on unfamiliar responsibilities or carry out unfamiliar tasks in difficult conditions
- the practicalities of removing objects from galleries on upper floors or via unusual routes.

While such exercises can be useful – and some participants may find them exciting and even enjoyable – they take time and effort to organise. If resources are limited, it may be better to focus on risk management through preventive measures with the aim of minimising the likelihood that an emergency plan will have to be tested in a real disaster.

Order of merit

Deciding which objects should be given priority in a salvage operation is not an easy task, but it is a vital part of any emergency plan.

Priorities for salvage

An emergency plan should include a list of objects that are to be given priority in the salvage operation once the emergency services allow access to the disaster area. In a museum with large or diverse collections, the process of reaching a consensus on which objects should be given priority may be difficult. Remember also that priorities may change over time and any list should be regularly reviewed.

Under normal circumstances, priority might be given, for example, to items of national or international significance, of special significance in the context of the museum and its collections, or because of their intrinsic or financial value. But in emergency conditions, consideration must also be given to the safety and practicalities of removing objects, and whether the risk of damaging them in the process is greater than if they are given temporary protection and left in situ until later in the salvage and clean-up operation.

As well as being physically fit, members of a salvage team should have training in object handling. They should also be able to make on-the-spot decisions about whether to remove objects for immediate treatment and, if so, how to handle and transport them. Whatever the importance given to salvaging the museum's objects, the highest priority must always be to ensure the health and safety of the people involved in the salvage operation.

Once salvaged, objects should be logged, tagged and then removed from the site of the disaster to a suitable and secure area for immediate treatment or temporary storage. At this stage it is essential they are examined by a conservator who can decide what immediate treatment (such as drying, cleaning or freezing) is appropriate during the 48 hours following the disaster.

The emergency manual should include the names and contact details of conservators who can be called on to provide advice; the facing page has a summary of typical treatments for wet, soiled or damaged objects in a range of materials.

A continuous process

An emergency plan can never be considered finished. Emergency planning should be a continuous and active process at the core of day-to-day museum practice – and a key factor in the design, layout and operation of museums. Remember that:

- staff will need regular reminders about the existence of an emergency plan and training in procedures to make sure it is effective
- feedback from training and mock or actual disasters must be used to inform the future development of emergency plans
- regular reviews and continual updating are likely to be needed to take account of new risks and changing circumstances.

Emergency treatments

Summary of typical treatments for wet or wet and dirty objects in different materials.

Books and manuscripts

Wrap in polythene, freeze the object and then get specialist advice.

Paintings (oil on canvas)

Remove painting from frame (but not stretcher) and number frame and work. Blot off any excess water, insert blotting paper between canvas and stretcher, and dry out face down on pad of tissue paper. Blot excess water from frames and dry out slowly to ambient relative humidity.

Paintings (watercolours)

Freeze and get expert advice.

Wood and leather

Objects made from wood or leather should be dried slowly. If dirty, rinse and cover with polythene sheet to dry; you should not apply heat and do not rinse if the surface is unstable.

Textiles

Robust clothing, if clean, can be hung to dry on padded hangers. If wet and dirty or if colours are running, rinse in clean water, blot dry with towel or blotting paper, and air dry or dehumidify on padded hangers. If damp and dirty, keep in cool, well-ventilated space and get specialist advice. Dry delicate fabrics flat and out of sunlight; can be frozen.

Metals

Dry quickly. If dirty, rinse in clean water, blot off excess, and dry in air.

Photographs and film

If prints are wet or damp but separated, air-dry them with emulsion side up; if not readily separable, keep damp and get specialist advice. Immerse wet films or negatives in water, keep cool, and get expert advice.

Electrical items

Rinse if necessary, dry quickly without heating: open casings to assist drying if necessary.

Stone, ceramics and glass

Leave alone unless at risk of physical damage. If broken, make sure that all parts are kept together and any small pieces are bagged and labelled to avoid loss.

Sources

Disaster Planning, in *Manual of Curatorship*. Sue Cackett. Museums Association. 2nd edition. 1992.
    Salvage Manual for Carmarthen Museum, Anne Wright. 2004

Case study: the Perth Museum and Art Gallery

The flood

When the Scottish town of Perth suffered serious flooding in 1990, the highest water level was fortunately about one metre below the top of the sandbags stacked against the outside of the Perth Museum and Art Gallery. The incident, says Michael Taylor, the Head of Arts and Heritage at Perth and Kinross Council, was grounds for believing that the building was reasonably safe should flooding happen again. This guarded optimism was put to the test on 17 January 1993 when the River Tay burst its banks after a sudden thaw following four days of snow. Taylor and Jim Blair, the director of the Perth Museum, went to assess the situation. The museum was closed and the council had stacked sandbags against the exterior of the building. By midday the water was still below the level reached in 1990. But by 2 pm the water level was still rising and was expected to continue. Blair and Taylor telephoned as many of the museum staff as possible to come in and deal with an impending disaster.

The first floodwater entered the building at about 4 pm via door frames and internal drain covers. By early evening all of the museum's storerooms at ground level were flooded to 70 cm. Some members of staff had difficulty getting to the museum because of flooded roads, but those that reached the building concentrated on carrying portable items from the stores to the upper floors of the museum. Heavy and bulky items, including large paintings hung on vertical racking, had to be left behind. This work continued until late evening, but then the stores had to be evacuated because of the risk of electric shocks from saturated electrical circuits. At this point the security of the museum and its contents became a concern as staff had to hand over the building to the emergency services, who continued trying to pump out the floodwater.

Taylor says that about 50,000 items from the collections were affected by the flood. This included a large number of photographic negatives, but also books, archival material, costume, paintings, ceramics, sculpture, seals and social history items of many types. The floodwater was not polluted, but contained a lot of silt, which resulted in large deposits of sandy material as it dried out. The immediate remedial treatment of such a large volume and variety of material was well beyond the resources of the museum, even with specialist help. Instead, arrangements were made with a local cold store to freeze whatever could reasonably be frozen in its present condition and then to treat it in manageable batches as part of a planned recovery programme. Basic listings were made of items as they were packed and sent off by the van-load for freezing. Although they included material that would not normally be considered suitable for freezing (such as vellum), Taylor says the strategy resulted in a larger proportion of items being saved. A very small number of objects were lost altogether, and a small proportion suffered damage that is visible to an untrained eye (such as colour from bookbindings leaching into the pages). Many of the successfully treated items could probably not withstand further remedial conservation without being damaged.

The museum was closed to visitors for two months while the galleries were used as a temporary space for conservation work. The conservation programme took six years to complete at a cost of about £1m – of which £700,000 was covered by the insurance settlement and the balance by Perth and Kinross Council. Taylor says insurance claims can involve a hard fight when, for example, conservation work on damaged objects may cost more than their market value. Examples of uninsured losses included a large consignment of acid-free mounting board and the cost of repairs to storage cabinets and roller racking.

Since the flood

Taylor advises colleagues in other museums never to assume that a disaster could not happen to you – it could. Since 1993 the council has spent £23m on improving flood defences, upgrading its flood warning system, and now employs an emergency planning officer. Work to the museum building has included fitting water-resisting seals around external doors; seals on internal access hatches to the drainage system to prevent drains backing up into the building; and upgrading the electrical system to make it safer in a flood. The main measures now taken by the museum as part of its emergency plan are:

- an emergency manual – at the time of the flood, says Taylor, the museum's disaster plan was a lengthy document that did not give easy access to key information under disaster conditions. The current version is in the form of a disaster checklist, designed to provide all the information needed immediately after a disaster in an easily accessible format. The contents are updated annually. Evacuation plans are also fixed to the wall in storage areas
- liaison with emergency services – regular contact with the emergency services, especially the fire service, which needs to be familiar with the layout and contents of the museum
- emergency boxes – boxes of equipment for use in emergencies are now stored at strategic points in the museum. They include torches, tie-on labels, plastic bags, crowbars and absorbent booms (for containing minor floods or spillages). They have proved their worth in minor emergencies since they were introduced and their contents are checked annually
- training – all staff have annual refresher training in responding to emergencies, when they are reminded of the existence and location of the emergency manual and boxes, and practise emergency procedures and the use of key items of equipment.

Case study: the Rijksmuseum Twenthe

On 13 May 2000 a fireworks factory in the middle of a residential area in Enschede, the Netherlands, exploded – 100,000 kg of fireworks went up in the blast, 22 people were killed and about 950 injured. Between 350 and 400 houses were destroyed and thousands of homes were damaged. One of the damaged buildings was the Rijksmuseum Twenthe, a medium-sized art museum.

The Rijksmuseum Twenthe disaster plan

By Paul Knoll, the head of collections at the Rijksmuseum Twenthe.
Every self-respecting museum in the Netherlands is prepared for disasters. They usually have a disaster plan and the staff have been trained to prepare for one. But in general, plans are oriented towards a fire or an attack by a disturbed individual with a knife. But in our case an extreme disaster befell us – the sort that is very rare. I must also emphasise that the Rijksmuseum Twenthe is very aware that many residents around the museum suffered a great deal more than we did. Twenty two people died and almost 1,000 more were injured, some of them seriously; many families also became homeless. In comparison with this, we did not feel that we were the true victims.

All the visitors and most of the staff were taken downstairs after the first big explosion, following the procedure in our disaster plan. When no new explosions took place, the visitors were taken outside the museum and guided in a safe direction. The first steps were also taken to clear the exhibition rooms.

The heads of operational management and the technical department turned off the gas mains and informed various authorities of the situation, including the Ministry of Education, Culture and Science and the Department of Cultural Property Inspection. The Government Buildings Agency was also informed. While the police had the 'open' museum under close watch, the command centre could give no guarantee of safety. The heads of operational management and the technical department entered the building one more time, under police escort. They brought personal belongings out and locked as many windows and doors as possible. It was not until the following afternoon that the fire brigade gave staff permission to enter the building, through the cordon that had been placed around it.

According to the plan, the first area to be cleared was the modern art wing, which was most at risk of suffering water damage if it rained. We also felt we should take loan objects to safety first. It was decided to use a few safe working areas in the museum where the air conditioning still functioned. These areas were tidied up, the objects were taken there, cleaned if necessary, then packed as carefully as possible and taken to the storage depot of the Kröller-Müller Museum. On Sunday the museum's insurance company was informed of the estimated damage up to that point. A detailed inventory was made of the damage to the building. It was found that walls and roofs had been shaken loose, so that far-reaching reconstruction work would have to be carried out. A restoration plan was drawn up. After the report had been made, all the museum's contacts were informed of the situation in writing. It soon became clear that it would take a considerable amount of time before the museum could reopen, so the exhibition programme and other activities had to be cancelled. We were able to continue some activities; requests for loan objects were approved, where possible, for example. The museum took advantage of the opportunity to carry out a number of necessary renovations such as adjusting the air conditioning system, installing safe display cases and partially blocking the windows in the Old Masters department. The condition of the entire collection was checked. This took place at three places at once: the museum itself, the Kröller-Müller Museum and the Stichting Kollektief Restauratie Atelier in Amsterdam. As soon as it was clear how long the restoration of the building would take, a phased restructuring plan was drawn up. Eventually the museum reopened on 14 April 2001.

[. . .]

Emergency response kits

Opinions vary about the value of kits of equipment and materials that might be needed in a disaster. Especially in small museums, kits that may never be needed can take up valuable storage space. There is also the risk that items from the kits are gradually removed for other purposes and, if not replaced, compromise the usefulness of the kits in the event of a disaster. Kits may be more practical for larger museums or museum services that can store them off-site and transport them to the location of the disaster when needed. The East Midland Museums Service (EMMS) guide *Emergency Manual for Historic Buildings and Collections* includes checklists of equipment and materials often required in an emergency. An alternative approach to emergency kits for smaller museums is to:

- keep a small amount of equipment on site – this could include first-aid kits; protective clothing such as overalls, gloves, masks and hard hats; torches (and spare batteries) at strategic points around the building; a few key items such as basic tools and polythene sheeting; and materials and equipment for the rescue of specific objects prioritised for salvage
- provide in your emergency manual a list and contact details of sources from which materials and equipment that might be needed for salvage or clean-up operations can be obtained at short notice. This could include local stockists, equipment hire companies, council departments, and other museums in the area
- consider pooling resources with other museums in the area to assemble an emergency kit that can be stored at a mutually convenient location and transported to museums within the group as needed
- target resources on preventive measures such as alarms, smoke and water detectors, and effective procedures for housekeeping and building maintenance.

Emergency planning: contacts at a glance

Websites

National Preservation Office
The British Library/National Preservation Office website links to many organisations.
(http://www.bl.uk/blpac/index.html)

Conservation Online
Provides a portal to useful resources from around the world on disaster preparedness and response.
  (http://palimpsest.stanford.edu/bytopic/disasters/)

Conservation Register
Information on conservation practices in the UK and Ireland that might be helpful as sources of specialist advice or conservation treatment in the event of an emergency.
  (www.conservationregister.com)

The Environment Agency
The agency's website includes information about flood risk in England and general guidance about flood precautions.
  (www.environment-agency.gov.uk)

M25 Disaster Management Group
The website for the M25 Consortium of Academic Libraries contains helpful guidance and information on disaster control management.
  (www.m25lib.ac.uk)

Publications

Benchmarks in Collection Care for Museums, Archives and Libraries – A Self-assessment Checklist
Resource (now the MLA), 2002 (www.mla.gov.uk)
  This publication includes a short section on preparing for emergencies in the form of a checklist of basic, good and best practice.

BS 5454: 2000 Recommendations for the Storage and Exhibition of Archival Documents
British Standards Institution, 2000 (www.bsi-global.com)
  Includes authoritative general guidance on alarm and detection systems, fire suppression, and measures to minimise the risk of disasters.

Building an Emergency Plan – A Guide for Museums and Other Cultural Institutions
The Getty Conservation Institute, Los Angeles, 1999
  (www.getty.edu/conservation/institute)
  A clearly presented step-by-step guide to the preparation of emergency plans tailored to the needs of individual institutions and their collections. Includes examples of materials needed to be prepared for an emergency such as evacuation procedures, lists of equipment and services, and action checklists.

Emergency Manual for Historic Buildings and Collections
A useful CD-based interactive template for emergency plans for museums and historic buildings published by East Midlands Museums Service (EMMS). Order form is available on the EMMS website.
  (www.emms.org.uk)

Museum Accreditation Scheme
The accreditation scheme, launched by the MLA in November 2004 as successor to the Registration Scheme, includes emergency planning as a mandatory requirement. The accreditation standards and guidance are available as a PDF download.
    (www.mla.gov.uk)

Flooding and Historic Buildings
This English Heritage Technical Advice Note contains detailed guidance on disaster preparedness and dealing with flood damage. Available as a PDF download.
    (www.english-heritage.org.uk)

Testing a Disaster Plan
By J. Edmond, *Museum Practice*, issue 12, November 1999
    Account of the organisation and benefits of a mock disaster exercise held by Doncaster Museum Service in 1999.

Heaven Helps Those Who Help Themselves: The Realities of Disaster Planning
By P. Holden, *Journal of the Society of Archivists*, Carfax Publishing, 2004, Vol 25, No 1
    Account of an exercise to test the disaster plan at Lanhydrock House, a National Trust property.

Barrier-free Design – A Manual for Building Designers and Managers
By J. Holmes-Siedle, Architectural Press, 1997
    A useful guide to designing and managing buildings for people with physical and sensory disabilities, including guidance on signs, alarm systems and emergency escape procedures.

Chapter 12

Museum Disaster Preparedness and Planning

John E. Hunter

Why plan for disasters?

HILDA BOHEM OF THE University of California Library System provides the dictum that, 'A disaster is what happens only if you are not prepared for it' (Bohem 1978). Preparing for disasters may not prevent them but will lessen their impact. Preparing and following a disaster response plan can help to avoid costly or fatal damage and can prevent a disaster from becoming a tragedy.

Planning for museum emergencies and disasters is a four-phase process. The first phase requires identification of natural events that might threaten the institution, that is, conducting a multi-hazard vulnerability assessment, and determining what the effects of such hazards could be under varying circumstances. The second phase consists of designing and assessing strategies for coping with the identified events. Strategic goals should include disaster prevention where possible, minimization of damage during a disaster, mitigation of further damage or deterioration afterwards, and recovery and resumption of normal operations. The third phase entails writing a plan to guide the museum staff before, during and after a disaster. The fourth phase calls for regular reviews of the disaster plan to keep it current, training in the plan's execution, periodic drills to test the plan's effectiveness, and evaluation of the plan's performance after any disastrous occurrence.

Developing and implementing a disaster plan does not require a lot of technical knowledge. It does require the attention and dedication of at least one staff member. The planner must have full management support and access to all relevant

Source: S. Knell (ed.), *Care of Collections* (London, Routledge, 1994), pp. 60–79 (originally in B.G. Jones (ed.), *Protecting Historic Architecture and Museum Collections from Natural Disasters* (Oxford, Butterworth-Heinemann, 1986), pp. 211–230.

information on the museum's contents and operations. Developing a plan for a large or complex museum may take a year or more. Effective implementation of the plan – the training, testing and evaluation steps – will usually take longer than the design and production of a written plan.

The examination of the museum necessary to prepare a plan should make the museum's staff aware of the institution's vulnerabilities and may stimulate them to think about improvements that can be made in ordinary museum operations. For example, the survey required to identify the institution's most valuable assets can be carried out in conjunction with a conservation needs survey. The preventive actions that can be taken to prepare a museum for surviving an earthquake may also help protect it from burglary and vandalism and can enhance building maintenance and upkeep.

The plan

There are at least ten discrete steps or stages in the four-phase development, writing and evaluation of a disaster plan. The rest of this paper outlines what a disaster plan should contain and how an effective plan can be organized.

The first step in the preparation of a plan is designation of the person responsible for developing and writing the plan and the naming of an advisory committee. In a small institution, it is possible that everyone on the staff will play some role in developing the plan. In a large institution, a senior staff member will usually be in charge, assisted by individuals appointed from each department and perhaps from the museum's board. This planning team eventually may become the museum's Disaster Control Organization; its members would be the persons in charge of disaster mitigation and recovery efforts. Care in their selection is imperative.

Once the planning team has been selected, it should be given authority in writing and should enjoy the full support of management. Full support from the director, senior management, department heads and the board of trustees is vital to the success of the planning effort. Without enough support, the planning team may not get full cooperation from all departments and may not be able to implement any new policies or administrative changes needed to establish a disaster preparedness programme.

Once a team has been appointed and authorized to prepare a disaster plan, the second step is for them to locate sources of planning assistance and information. They should become familiar with disaster planning literature and should review plans developed by other museums. They should obtain as-built architectural drawings of the museum's building and, if possible, talk with the museum's architect and builder about its vulnerability to various disasters. They should find out what kinds of support local fire and building inspection offices can offer, not only in helping when disaster strikes but also in assessing the museum's vulnerability and helping with the planning effort. The team should contact other museums in the region to learn how they plan to deal with disasters and to explore the feasibility of mutual aid agreements. The team should also identify talents and capabilities possessed by the museum's own staff, trustees and volunteers. One of the museum's trustees or volunteers may have responsibility for corporate disaster planning in his or her business and could be invited to serve on the planning team.

The planning team must also contact state and local police, fire, and public health agencies, state and local civil defence agencies, the Red Cross, and state and regional museum organizations. Such contacts are advisable for two reasons. First, local organizations can provide planning assistance and technical advice and can explain the museum's place in existing community disaster plans. Second, local organizations must know of the museum's plans in order to incorporate disaster support for the museum into their own respective plans.

The third planning step is vulnerability assessment. I want to emphasize the importance of thoroughly assessing the total vulnerability of the museum before deciding how to protect it. Failure to consider the possibility of a particular disaster prevents planning for it. Faulty estimation of the damage that might result from a disaster will produce a disaster plan that falls short of affording full protection. Finally, inadequate vulnerability assessment may generate a false set of priorities for allocating the museum's resources to disaster prevention and mitigation.

The fourth step in the planning process is a survey to identify assets requiring protection against loss or damage from a disaster. This survey will produce an inventory or a summary of the museum's assets listed by importance to the museum and to its continued operation. Among the assets to be surveyed are: the collections and their catalogue and registration records; photograph and research files; the library and its card file; lab, shop and maintenance equipment and supplies; administrative files and records; the building and its operating systems; and sales shop merchandise. In conducting the survey, do not forget people, the museum's most important asset. Protection of visitors and staff must always come first in planning.

Evaluation of the museum's material assets will be based on the broad and somewhat subjective criteria of irreplaceability and value. The specific criteria used by a given museum will depend upon the nature of its assets, particularly the nature of the collections. Original works of art, natural history specimens, archaeological collections and most ethnographic specimens are unique and irreplaceable. Books, prints, copies of sculpture and taxidermic specimens may be replaceable, but only at great cost. Library materials, tools, equipment and supplies may also be considered. The building itself may be replaceable or economically reparable. If it is an important historic structure, however, this may not be true.

Criteria for determining the value of assets can include the following considerations:

- Intrinsic, sentimental or historic value
- Aesthetic or scientific value
- Legal and administrative value
- Research and documentary value
- Monetary value.

Considerations of monetary value may be inapplicable to cultural materials or may be determined by the other considerations. Nonetheless, monetary value has an important bearing on the practicality of replacing damaged or destroyed assets and thus must be included in relative evaluations of the museum's property.

Evaluation will classify the museum's contents into at least three broad categories:

- Priority 1: Assets of such importance that their safety must be guaranteed at all costs because their loss would be catastrophic.
- Priority 2: Assets of relatively great importance, the loss of which would be serious but not catastrophic.
- Priority 3: Assets of relatively little importance, the loss of which would not be a handicap.

In general, assets in the first group will be limited in number and will receive the maximum possible protection. The second group will be somewhat larger and will receive special protection only within the constraints of personnel availability, facilities, reasonable expense and time. The third group will include the majority of the museum's assets. These assets will initially receive only the protection offered by the museum building. Only after assets in the first two groups have been protected appropriately will resources be devoted to protection of third-priority assets.

The importance of prioritizing the museum's assets cannot be overemphasized. Just as an earthquake vulnerability assessment can result in false assumptions about disaster risk, so too can inadequate setting of priorities result in misapplication of scarce resources during disaster recovery.

After the planning team has identified threats to the museum and established priorities for protecting its assets against those threats, it is ready to determine specific methods of protection. This phase of the planning process contains two steps, protection of assets in advance of disaster and recovery of assets after a disaster. These two steps are among the most difficult, time-consuming and crucial in the entire planning process. The decisions made during these steps will determine the ultimate success and workability of the plan itself.

Step five is the design of protective measures. Selection of protective measures should be based on the following six considerations:

- The degree of danger to which the museum's assets would be exposed during and after a disaster.
- The level of protection currently afforded collections and other portable assets by the museum building and by the exhibit and storage cases in which they are kept.
- The physical characteristics of the assets; that is, the fragility of their materials and their susceptibility to various kinds of damage.
- How the assets are being used and whether such uses might contribute to risk. For example, objects on exhibition or left out for interpretive programmes may be at greater risk than objects in storage.
- The values assigned earlier when assets were being prioritized.
- The funds, personnel and other resources available for providing protection.

The sixth step in the planning process is formulation of recovery plans. In this step, the planning team determines how the museum is to recover from the unavoidable effects of disasters. When planning for earthquakes, floods, hurricanes and other major natural events, there are relatively few true preventive measures that can be taken. Planning aims to minimize the risk of asset losses to lessen the impact of losses that occur.

The kinds of measures selected by the planning team for incorporation into a recovery plan will depend upon the assets to be protected. More diversified collections will need a greater variety and complexity of recovery methods. Planning for recovery should provide for immediate and successful completion of certain tasks in the aftermath of disaster. Briefly, those tasks are:

- Assessment of damage to determine what has been damaged and the location and extent of damage.
- Assignment of specific priorities for recovery efforts, based on the general priorities established earlier in the planning process; these priorities will provide a basis for decisions about which assets to treat first.
- Selection of specific recovery methods from among the methods identified in advance as those the museum must be prepared to execute.
- Requesting assistance with recovery operations from outside the museum (e.g. other museums, outside conservators, local tradesmen and craftsmen, volunteers and local governmental authorities).

If the organization of recovery efforts has been well planned, recovery will be less difficult, less costly and more efficient. A critical part of the recovery plan will be providing for the protection of supplies and equipment that will be needed to begin the recovery effort. Such materials are much more valuable and much harder to obtain after a disaster than they might be under normal circumstances. Materials used for two primary purposes should be stockpiled: (1) materials for repair of the museum building, its operating equipment and protection systems and (2) supplies for emergency stabilization of the collections and collection records.

Stockpiled emergency materials must be given the same degree of protection from disaster as the collections themselves.

Emergency supplies and equipment can be classified into the following groups:

- Materials for removing dirt and debris
- Tools and equipment for demolition, repairs and rescue
- Construction materials
- Emergency lighting, communications and protection equipment
- Materials for protecting the health and safety of personnel
- Conservation supplies and equipment
- Miscellaneous supplies and equipment.

A suggested list of supplies and equipment is included at the end of this paper. Most museums probably keep most of these materials on hand routinely. If so, it remains only for the disaster plan to ensure their protection during a disaster so that they will be ready for use afterwards. Subsequent papers will address the topic of specific recovery supplies and techniques.

In step seven the planning team brings the first two phases of the planning process to their logical conclusion by writing out the plans it has developed. There are many good reasons why the museum's disaster plan must be written. Perhaps the most important reason is that a written plan shortens response time when disaster strikes and will minimize the number of decisions that have to be made. In the absence of a written plan, everyone with responsibility for emergency action would have to confer on the division of recovery tasks.

A written plan will define the museum's emergency command structure and the scope of each person's authority and will identify staff responsibilities. A written plan will include assessment and inventory of the resources needed to support the museum during and after a disaster. Rapid access to emergency supplies, equipment and personnel will be vital to the success of the plan; the written plan will help locate these resources. Finally, a written plan can and should be used to train all employees in carrying out their disaster recovery responsibilities.

The act of writing a disaster plan will point out gaps in the planning and will ensure that planning objectives have been met. Writing the plan will also suggest needed improvements in the museum's day-to-day operations, such as the need for more extensive fire protection, a more efficient organizational structure or better internal communications. The written plan will describe the museum's Disaster Control Organization and will determine whether that organization is sufficient to control disaster and to recover from it. Finally, a written plan may be required by the museum's insurers or by persons from whom it has borrowed objects for exhibition. A plan may also be required if the museum is part of a larger organization, such as a university or a city or county government. In such a case, the museum's plan will probably be part of the plan for the entire organization and must be compatible with that plan.

The written plan should be characterized by flexibility, simplicity, detail and adaptability. The plan should be flexible enough to allow for changes in the staff, in the availability of outside help and recovery supplies, or in threats to which the museum may be vulnerable. The plan should also allow for reduced vulnerability assessment following the implementation of disaster preventive measures. The plan should be simple enough to be understood easily and executed quickly. Yet it must be detailed enough to minimize the number of decisions necessary during an emergency. The plan should be adaptable to situations it is not specifically designed to cover. It should be oriented to the effects of disasters, not their causes. For example, instead of including one plan for floods, a second for broken water-pipes, and a third for water damage due to fire fighting, it ought to include a single, multipurpose plan for water damage in general. Similarly, a single plan for dealing with structural damage could be used for recovery from an earthquake, a tornado or an explosion.

There is no standard format for a museum disaster plan. Some authors have recommended seven to ten sections and I have seen plans with as many as thirty sections. I believe that most museums will find their needs met by a plan with six major sections and a series of appendices. The major sections would be: Introduction and Statement of Purpose, Authority, Scope of the Plan, Disaster Avoidance Procedures, Disaster Mitigation Procedures and Disaster Recovery Procedures.

Section 1, Introduction and Statement of Purpose, states why the plan has been developed and what it is intended to achieve. This is a good place to indicate how and by whom the plan was developed and how it is to be kept current.

Section 2, Authority, has three purposes. First, it documents the authority for preparation and implementation of the plan. Normally, the plan will be prepared under the authority of the museum's board of trustees or its director. Second, this section delegates responsibility for execution of the plan to a staff member designated Emergency Services Officer and placed in charge of the Disaster Control Organization. Third, this section establishes a Disaster Control Organization and indicates by name or title those responsible for co-ordinating all emergency activities.

Section 3, Scope of the Plan, identifies each of the emergencies and disasters the plan is intended to cover. It first lists and describes each of the events that could occur in the museum; these events will have been identified during the vulnerability assessment step of the planning process. Then this section indicates the probability of occurrence for each event, its expected frequency of occurrence, and the expected effects of the event on museum operations. The most likely events should be listed first. Vulnerability assessment must consider the 'trigger effect', wherein one event triggers others that create a more serious situation than that brought about by a single event. For example, in describing the potential impact of an earthquake, the plan should note that the losses may include not only structural damage to the building and its contents, but also death and injury, water damage, fire, contamination by chemicals and fuels, and looting. Planned responses to each of these events, including those 'triggered' by others, will be detailed subsequently in Sections 4 and 5.

A museum consisting of several buildings, particularly if they are widely scattered, may have an individual plan for each building or a single plan for the entire institution. If only one plan is written, Section 3 should describe its application to each building. This section should also describe how the disaster plan relates to any other emergency or operating plans that may exist, either within the institution or in the community (a medical emergency plan, a fire reaction plan or a general security plan). An explanation of how all plans relate to and complement each other and an indication of the circumstances under which they should be executed individually or simultaneously will enable a co-ordinated disaster response.

Sections 4, 5 and 6 are the heart of the disaster plan because they describe techniques for coping with every possible disaster. These sections will be based on the choices of protection and recovery methods made in Steps 5 and 6 of the planning process. They should assign responsibilities for implementing and executing each part of the overall plan, explain the circumstances dictating partial or complete execution of the plan, and detail necessary response procedures.

Section 4 will outline actions the museum can take to reduce disaster vulnerability such as structural modification to help withstand an earthquake or installation of fire protection systems. The actions outlined in the plan should be implemented as funds and other resources become available, ideally before the events whose effects they are to minimize.

Section 5 will treat disaster mitigation – response to unavoidable disasters normally preceded by a warning. Mitigation emphasizes reducing the impact of the events as they occur. For example, response to a hurricane warning will include weather-proofing buildings, relocating or evacuating artefacts and records to safer quarters, and covering objects that cannot be moved. The plan will also list procedures for recovering from the effects of the hurricane.

Recovery procedures may not have to be fully executed if predisaster mitigation is carried out successfully. Subsections should describe all activities to be carried out in response to each of the disaster events itemized in Section 3. If plans for the individual events share many features, a general subsection followed by a listing of the unique aspects of each event may suffice. The paramount goal is that the plans be accessible, understandable and workable.

Section 6 will cover disaster events for which there will normally be no warning. Plans in this section will place primary emphasis on recovery. For example, plans for recovering from major earthquake or flash flood damage will probably include: evacuating objects threatened by building collapse or looting; freezing water-soaked paper; drying metals subject to rusting; locating pieces of broken objects; securing the building against vandalism and theft; and, most importantly, evacuating and treating any injured people. The emphasis of this type of plan is not prevention of damage during the disaster event but protection from further damage afterwards.

These five sections will be the main part of the disaster plan. But these sections alone are not sufficient. They must be supplemented by appendices containing information necessary for execution of the plan but so subject to change that including it in the major sections of the plan would be impractical. The planning team will have to decide what kinds of information to include in the appendices. In most plans, the following appendices will be useful.

Appendix 1 should include an organization chart of the museum, showing all divisions and at least the key staff positions. If the museum is part of a larger organization, such as a university or a local government, the appendix should include a chart showing the museum's position within the larger organization. Reference to these charts during emergencies will facilitate communications and help to maintain the chain of command. The charts should be simple and clear. It will usually be sufficient to show only division and office names, functions, and the names and titles of their key personnel. Members of the Disaster Control Organization should be indicated on the organizational charts or perhaps on a separate chart. Coloured markers can be used to highlight the key personnel or activities.

Appendix 2 can consist of lists of key museum staff needed for execution of the plan. The list should include each person's name and title, home address and home telephone number. This list may also include a brief résumé of each person's responsibilities under the plan. The same appendix might well include a roster of the museum's entire staff in case there is an incident requiring a head count to determine whether everyone is safe.

Appendix 3 should list emergency contacts outside the museum. Such contacts would include: police and fire departments; the local Civil Defence organization; local utility companies, hospitals and ambulance companies; plumbers, electricians and glass companies; the museum's insurance agents; and any other organizations or persons the museum might have to contact in case of emergency. Both daytime and after-hours telephone numbers should be listed. Specific contacts in the listed agencies should be listed where appropriate.

Outside curators and conservators may be needed for advice and assistance. A list of various experts' addresses and specialities should be appended. If they must travel to the museum, transportation and compensation arrangements should be detailed. Previous arrangements may have been made to borrow personnel from nearby museums or sister organizations for assistance in evacuation or recovery operations. Record such arrangements and the appropriate contacts. List any volunteers you may need to call upon, along with their special skills. If anybody on the staff, including volunteers, has promised to bring certain equipment and supplies with him for personal or museum use, indicate what they are.

It is critical that this and all other call-up lists be kept current. They should be reviewed and revised at least once a month. Using a word processor can speed revisions.

Appendix 4 can be a description of the circumstances requiring a call to various outside agencies or persons and the kinds of services or assistance available from these outside sources. Appendices 3 and 4 might be combined if not too cumbersome.

Appendix 5 might include plans of the museum, its grounds and its immediate neighbourhood. Floor plans can indicate vulnerable parts of the museum or those containing the most valuable assets. They should show the locations of emergency exits and evacuation routes, gas and electric cutoffs, telephone closets, firefighting equipment, burglar and fire alarm devices and controls, emergency supplies and equipment stockpiles, and other such information.

Maps can show sidewalks, streets, driveways, gates, fences, buried and overhead utility lines, fire hydrants, manholes and other pertinent information. Certain floor plans might be posted at key locations around the non-public parts of the museum to facilitate movement during an emergency and to orient outside maintenance and service crews. Floor plans and maps will prove particularly useful if the museum depends upon volunteers or other non-staff personnel for help after a disaster. The inclusion of sensitive information in this appendix, like plans of the intrusion detection systems, may require restricting distribution of the museum's disaster plan or keeping the appendix in a sealed envelope or safe.

Appendix 6 might be an inventory of all collections, records and other valuable assets and the priority for their protection. With this record could be a floor plan that shows the location of each asset or group of assets on the inventory. A similar plan can be posted in museum storerooms and conservation labs to speed access to these assets by emergency evacuation personnel unfamiliar with your facility. Caution in including such details on a posted floor plan is prudent. It could become a shopping list for burglars. Some sort of private coding, such as with colours, might eliminate this problem.

Appendix 7 might be a summary of arrangements for evacuating and relocating the collections. This appendix would include packing and crating instructions and the location of available supplies and materials. This appendix would also indicate several possible sites for temporary storage in case the primary site suffers the same disaster that strikes the museum.

Appendix 8 could be instructions for emergency management of the building's utilities and for service and operation of vital building support systems. Such systems might include: burglar and fire alarm systems, fire suppression system, firefighting equipment, elevators and escalators, emergency lighting, emergency generator, heating and air-conditioning equipment, humidifiers and dehumidifiers. This appendix could either include information from manufacturers' instruction manuals or could refer to the manuals. If the vital information is only referenced, the cited manuals must be protected as well as the emergency plan itself.

Appendix 9 is one of the most important appendices; it contains an inventory of supplies, equipment and other local resources useful in time of disaster. Stockpiled emergency supplies and equipment should be described, as to purpose, quantity and location. Arrangements to borrow equipment like portable generators, power tools, fans and dehumidifiers should be recorded and delegated to certain staff for execution. Arrangements to procure supplies like plywood, nails, plastic sheeting, tissue-paper, cardboard boxes, tape and disinfectants should be in place and fully described. See the list of suggested materials at the end of this paper.

Appendix 10 might be a glossary of terms used in the disaster plan. A glossary will ensure that everyone using the plan will be speaking the same language.

An index would make a highly useful addition to the plan. However, because the plan will change fairly frequently, an index may be difficult to keep current. Nonetheless, an index should be considered and included if its usefulness would outweigh the effort required to keep it current.

Because the disaster plan will evolve, it can be kept most conveniently in a three-ring binder. The original should be stored in a secure, fire-resistant safe or vault. Each member of the Disaster Control Organization should have a copy of the plan. The Emergency Services Officer will be responsible for keeping the plan updated and should have a copy in which to make pen-and-ink changes. As he makes changes to his copy, a typist can revise the original. (This is another good application for a word processor.) If the museum occupies more than one building, at least one copy of the plan should be in each building. Additional copies should be placed at critical spots around the museum in disaster-resistant containers. Each copy of the plan should list the locations of all other copies. It is vital that the original and all copies be updated often. Changes should be posted as they occur, changed pages should be retyped, including the date of the change, and obsolete pages should be removed and destroyed.

At least one copy of the plan kept in the museum should be accompanied by selected publications for reference during emergency stabilization and conservation efforts following a disaster. For example, if you anticipate having to salvage and preserve wet paper, you would want to have Peter Waters's book *Procedures for Salvage of Water-Damaged Library Materials* published by the Library of Congress. If the museum has a staff conservator, he or she may prepare instructions tailored specifically for your collections, instead of using existing published instructions. If so, these special instructions would be kept with the plan or perhaps even made part of it.

The plan ought to be accompanied by a carefully selected assortment of blank forms, typing supplies and other materials needed for preparing purchase orders and reports during and after an emergency.

If the museum office is damaged during a disaster, these materials will permit the carrying out of vital administrative duties.

Training

The disaster preparedness process does not end with preparation and distribution of a written disaster plan. The effectiveness of the plan during a disaster depends upon training all personnel who will execute the plan and upon regular testing of the plan under simulated conditions. The continued usefulness of the plan will depend upon how well it performs during actual emergencies, as determined by post-event evaluations.

The eighth step in the disaster preparedness process is training of the museum staff. Three purposes to training are:

- to guarantee that every employee will react rapidly in an emergency;
- to ensure that each person on whom execution of the plan depends will know his or her responsibility;
- to ensure that each responsible person has acquired the skills and the confidence to do his or her job efficiently and without panic.

Two kinds of training are needed to achieve these purposes. The first is briefing everyone on the museum staff on the disaster plan's goals and on their individual roles and responsibilities in case of disaster. Such training can be held in conjunction with regular museum employee training and skills development programmes. New employees should be trained as soon as possible after joining the staff. Retraining should take place every time the plan changes enough to warrant it.

The second kind of training is for members of the Disaster Control Organization. They will need a higher level of training than the rest of the staff. They should probably take courses offered by local and state Civil Defence organizations; these courses are usually free and are excellent training opportunities. Major businesses and industries often have internal disaster preparedness courses and may be willing to train museum staff. Local public protection agencies, such as the fire department, offer training in such skills as fighting small fires with hand-held equipment and controlling crowds during an emergency. Reading as widely as possible on the subjects of emergency planning and disaster preparedness is also good practice. Particularly useful works are cited in the bibliography at the end of this paper.

The ninth step in disaster preparedness takes place after the plan is written and training of the museum's staff has begun. This step calls for testing the plan.

To ensure the plan's effectiveness under actual disaster conditions, the Disaster Control Organization must test it thoroughly under simulated disaster conditions. As Richard J. Healy warns, the effectiveness (or ineffectiveness) of the disaster plan should not be discovered first during an actual disaster (Healy 1969). Testing will reveal the plan's deficiencies and unrealistic features and may expose a need to add or revise procedures. In testing the plan, the Disaster Control Organization will receive valuable training in operation under emergency conditions.

Testing consists of holding periodic exercises covering the full range of expected emergency and disaster situations. The Disaster Control Organization can write test problems for each potential disaster event and present them for solution. Senior administrative and curatorial personnel should test the plan first, as soon as possible after the Disaster Control Organization itself is fully functioning. After they have participated in a series of exercises helping to improve the plan, the entire staff and the staffs of agencies supporting the museum in disaster can be tested. All exercises should be as realistic as possible and held with as little advance notice and preparation as feasible. Test exercises should be concerned with the full range of possible emergencies, from minor incidents to major disasters. Each exercise should conclude with a critique and suitable modification of the plan.

Constant evaluation of the disaster plan is essential to keeping it always up to date and fully capable of dealing with every event it is intended to. Evaluation is the tenth and last step in the disaster preparedness process. The most effective way to evaluate a plan is to examine how well it functions during actual disasters. For this reason, it is vital that the Disaster Control Organization keep records whenever any part of the plan must be executed. After the crisis has passed, all those involved in executing the plan should meet to discuss any problems they encountered. They should try to improve the plan so that similar problems do not arise in the future.

As part of the evaluation, it is very important to observe and record exactly what damage resulted from the disaster and why it occurred. Such records will enable the plan to be refined to focus on the kinds of damage that actually occur rather than on the kinds of damage predicted to occur. Analysing the causes of damage might permit the rebuilding or remodelling of the museum for greater resistance to the same kinds of damage in the future. Records of damage sustained may also be required by the museum's insurance carriers. Photographs are particularly useful as part of complete, graphic records. It is important that one or more cameras and accessories and a quantity of film be included in the museum's stockpile of protected emergency supplies.

Conclusion

Emergencies are a part of the life of a museum. You may never have been involved personally in a serious emergency, let alone a disaster. If so, count yourself lucky. On the other hand, you may already be prepared. If you are prepared, please keep vigilant and stay prepared.

The primary goal of emergency planning is to avoid or minimize loss of the museum's assets, and preparation is the key to achieving that goal. Reducing the impacts of a disaster and avoiding loss depend upon how well you have planned for meeting all possible emergencies and disasters, how well you and your staff react when a disaster occurs, and how much learning from experiences during actual disasters you apply to revising your plan and preparing for the future.

Some emergencies cannot be prevented. The impact of some disasters cannot be avoided. But, you can plan in advance. You can commit a plan to paper. You can keep the plan up to date, as you can train yourself and your staff to execute the plan. By taking these steps, you will be able to cope with any unavoidable emergency or disaster.

Appendix 12.1: suggested emergency supplies and equipment

The supplies and equipment listed here include a variety of items that may be needed to cope with emergencies or disasters; some items can be used to prevent or minimize damage and others can be used afterwards to clean up or recover from damage. Few museums will need to use all of these items. Each museum should acquire only those items that will be needed to cope with the range of emergencies and disasters that it can expect. On the other hand, this list is not all-inclusive; it is intended only as a guide. Any museum may find that it will require items not listed here.

Items listed here do not necessarily have to be obtained or stockpiled exclusively for use in an emergency. Some of the listed items will be found in all museums as a matter of routine. They can be diverted for use in cleanup and repair operations when they are needed. However, keep in mind that the items you may count on using in an emergency may be damaged or destroyed by the disaster. Therefore, those items that will be critical to the survival or recovery of the museum and that cannot be procured promptly from elsewhere after the disaster should be set aside or stockpiled in a safe place so they will be available if ever they are needed.

Remember, too, that some items – such as dry-cell batteries and certain first-aid supplies – have a limited shelf-life. Plan on replacing such items periodically so that fresh stock is always on hand in your stockpile.

Finally, remember always to include operating manuals or instructions with items of mechanical and electrical equipment in case persons not experienced with their operation are required to use them.

Supplies and equipment for debris removal and cleanup

Low foaming detergents
Bleaches
Sanitizers (such as chloride of lime or high-test hypochlorite)
Fungicides
Disinfectants
Ammonia
Scouring powders or other household cleaners
Rubber gloves
Brooms
Dust pans
Mops, mop buckets and wringers
Scoops and shovels
Scrub brushes
Sponges and rags or cloths
Buckets and tubs
Water hoses and nozzles
Throw-away containers or bags for trash
Wet/dry vacuum cleaner with accessories

Tools and equipment for demolition, repairs and rescue

Hammers (both claw and machinist's)
Wrenches (pipe, channel-lock and Vise Grips in various sizes)

Pliers (adjustable, lineman's and needle-nose in various sizes)
Screwdrivers (straight blade and Philips in various sizes)
Wood saws
Hand drill with bits
(Power saw and drills may be selected if a source of electricity can be assured)
Metal saw with blades
Utility knife with extra blades
Wire cutters with insulated handles
Tin snips
Pipe cutters and possibly pipe threaders
Bolt cutter
Pry bar or crowbar
Axes, including fireman's axe
Rope
Dollies or handcarts
Folding rule or retractable tape measures
3-ton hydraulic jack
Sledgehammer
Block and tackle
Pit-cover hood (if applicable)
Hydrant and post indicator valve wrenches (if the museum has a sprinkler or hose and standpipe system)
Staple gun and staples
Ladder(s) and step-stool(s)

Construction materials

Plywood for covering or replacing windows
Dimensional lumber
Nails, screws, and assorted fasteners
Tapes of various kinds (masking, duct, electrician's, etc.)
Glue
Twine and cord
Plastic sheeting for protection against leaks and splashes
Binding wire

Emergency equipment

Emergency gasoline-powered electrical generator
Portable lights (to be powered from the generator if electricity unavailable)
Emergency lights with extra batteries
Flashlights or lanterns with extra batteries
Fire extinguishers (ABC type recommended)
Battery-operated AM/FM radio(s) with extra batteries
Walkie-talkie radios with extra batteries
CB radio with extra batteries

Portable public address system or bullhorn, electrical or battery-powered
Geiger counter and dosimeters
Gas-masks with extra canisters
Air breathers with extra oxygen tanks
Resuscitation equipment
Gasoline-powered water-pump (or pump that can be powered from the electrical generator) with hoses
Extension cords, preferably equipped with ground-fault interrupters

Personal equipment and supplies (some of these items may be provided by the individual employees and volunteers who are to use them)

Necessary protective clothing
Rubber boots or waders
Hard hats
Rubber lab aprons
Protective masks
First-aid kits and medical supplies
Food and food preparation equipment
Potable water
Sanitation facilities
Changes of clothing
Sleeping-bags and blankets

Conservation supplies and equipment

Polyester (Mylar) and polyethylene film (in rolls)
Newsprint (unprinted)
Polyethylene bags, various sizes (such as Zip-Lock and produce bags)
Plastic garbage bags
Ethanol
Acetone
Industrial denatured alcohol
White blotter paper
Weights (such as shot bags)
Various sizes of thick glass or smooth masonite
Japanese tissue
Towels or clean rags
Clothes pins
Scissors
Sharp knives
Water displacement compound (such as WD-40)
Waxes and dressings (determined by nature of collection)
Other preservatives

Miscellaneous supplies

Boxes for packing and moving artefacts, records and equipment. (Record transfer boxes are the easiest to use, carry, and store. They come flat for storage and are set up as needed; they may be re-flattened for future use.)
Box sealing and strapping tapes
Tissue-paper, clean newsprint, plastic 'bubble pack', foam 'noodles' and other such materials for packing and padding artefacts for movement
Marking pens, preferably ones that are not water-soluble
Insecticides and rodenticides

Miscellaneous equipment

Fans
Space heaters, either electric or gas-operated
Portable dehumidifiers
Hygrometers
Photographic equipment (camera, lenses, flash, light meter, etc.)
Essential office equipment (manual typewriter, pocket calculator, pencil-sharpener, stapler, rulers, scissors, etc.)
Essential stationery and blank forms and other such supplies to ensure continuity of minimal administrative operations
This paper first appeared in B. G. Jones (1986) *Protecting Historic Architecture and Museum Collections from Natural Disasters,* Oxford: Butterworth-Heinemann, pp. 211–230.

References

Part 1: Emergency and disaster preparedness and planning

American Society of Corporate Secretaries, Inc. (1970) *Continuity of Corporate Management in Event of Major Disaster*, Washington, D.C.: Office of Civil Defense, Department of Defense.

Association of Records Executives and Administrators (1966) *Protection of Vital Records*, Washington, D.C.: Office of Civil Defense, Department of Defense.

Bahme, Charles W. (1976), *Fire Officer's Guide to Emergency Action*, Boston, Mass.: National Fire Protection Association.

—— (1978) *Fire Officer's Guide to Disaster Control*, Boston, Mass.: National Fire Protection Association.

Bohem, Hilda (1978) *Disaster Prevention and Disaster Preparedness,* Berkeley, Calif.: Office of the Assistant Vice President for Library Plans and Policies, Systemwide Library Administration, University of California.

Committee on Conservation of Cultural Resources (1942) *The Protection of Cultural Resources Against the Hazards of War,* Washington, D.C.: National Resources Planning Board.

Cox, David L. (1972) 'Training for facility self-protection', *Security Management*, reprinted by Defense Civil Preparedness Agency.

Disaster Operations: A Handbook for Local Governments (1981) Washington, D.C.: Defense Civil Preparedness Agency, Publication no. CPG 1–6.

Disaster Planning Guide for Business and Industry (1974) Washington, D.C.: Defense Civil Preparedness Agency, Publication no. CPG 25.

Disaster Response and Recovery Program Guide (1980) Washington, D.C.: Federal Emergency Management Agency.

Fennelly, Lawrence J. (ed.) (1982) *Museum, Archive, and Library Security*, Woburn, Mass.: Butterworth Publishers.

Healy, Richard J. (1969) *Emergency and Disaster Planning*, New York: John Wiley & Sons.

Local Government Emergency Planning (1978) Washington, D.C.: Federal Emergency Management Agency, Publication no. CPG 1–8.

Myers, James N. and Bedford, Denise D. (1981) *Disasters: Prevention and Coping*, Stanford, Calif.: Stanford University Libraries.

Noblecourt, Andre F. (1958) *Protection of Cultural Property in the Event of Armed Conflict*, Paris: UNESCO, Museums and Monument Series VIII.

Tillotson, Robert G. and the International Committee on Museum Security (1977) *Museum Security/La Sécurité dans les musées*, Paris: International Council of Museums.

Upton, M. S. and Pearson, C. (1978) *Disaster Planning and Emergency Treatments in Museums, Art Galleries, Libraries, Archives, and Allied Institutions*, Belconnen, A.C.T. Australia: Institute for the Conservation of Cultural Materials, Canberra College of Advanced Education.

Part 2: Salvage and recovery

Agricultural Research Service (1971) *How to Prevent and Remove Mildew: Home Methods.* Washington, D.C.: US Department of Agriculture, Home and Garden Bulletin no. 68 (Rev.).

Cohen, William (1975) 'Halon 1301: library fires and post-fire procedures', *Library Security Newsletter* (May) 5–7.

First Aid for Flooded Homes and Farms (1972) Washington, D.C.: US Department of Agriculture, Agriculture Handbook no. 38.

Fischer, David J. (1975) 'Problems encountered, hurricane Agnes flood, June 23, 1972 at Corning, NY and the Corning Museum of Glass', in George M. Cunha, *Conservation Administration*, North Andover, Mass.: New England Document Conservation Center.

Fischer, David J. and Duncan, Thomas (1975) 'Conservation research: flood-damaged library materials', *AIC Bulletin* 15(2): 27–8.

Haas, J. Eugene et al. (eds) (1977) *Reconstruction Following Disaster*, Cambridge, Mass.: MIT Press.

Keck, Caroline K. (1972) 'On conservation: instructions for emergency treatment of water damage', *Museum News* 50(10): 13.

Koesterer, Martin G. and Getting, John A. (1976) 'Restoring water-soaked papers and textiles: applying freeze-drying methods to books and art objects', *Technology and Conservation* (Fall) 20–2.

McGregor, L. and Bruce, J. (1974) 'Recovery of flood damaged documents by the Queensland state archives', *Archives and Manuscripts* 5(8): 193–9.

Martin, John H. (1975) 'Resuscitating a waterlogged library', *Wilson Library Bulletin* 241–3.

—— (1977) *The Corning Flood: Museum Under Water*, Corning, N.Y.: Corning Museum of Glass.

Minoque, Adelaide (1946) 'Treatment of fire and water damaged records', *American Archivist* 9(1): 17–25.

Montuori, Theodore (1973) 'Lesson learned from Agnes', *Journal of Micrographics* 6(3): 133–6.

Morris, John (1979) *Managing the Library Fire Risk* (2nd edn), Berkeley, Calif.: Office of Risk Management and Safety, University of California. (Available only from author at 333 Nutmeg Lane, Walnut Creek, Calif. 94598.)

Sellers, David Y. and Strassberg, Richard (1973) 'Anatomy of a library emergency', *Library Journal* 98 (17): 2824–7.

Spawn, Wilman (1973) 'After the water comes', *Bulletin [of the Pennsylvania Library Association]* 28(6): 243–51.

Surrency, Erwin C. (1973) 'Guarding against disaster', *Law Library Journal* 66(4): 419–28.

Walston, S. (1976) 'Emergency conservation following the Darwin cyclone', *ICCM Bulletin* 2(1): 21–5.

Waters, Peter (1975) *Procedures for Salvage of Water-Damaged Library Materials*, Washington, D.C.: Library of Congress.

Whipkey, Harold E. (1973) *After Agnes: A Report on Flood Recovery Assistance by the Pennsylvania Historical and Museum Commission*, Harrisburg, Pa.: Pennsylvania Historical and Museum Commission.

Introduction to Part Two – Section Three

Chris Caple

Agents of deterioration: pests

PRIOR TO THE 1980S, insect infestations of museum objects or collections were normally dealt with in a reactive manner. Upon discovery of an infestation, the object or collection was fumigated, sprayed or dusted with chemical agents that were toxic to insects, and could potentially be deleterious to human health. Prior to the 1970s these had included arsenic and DDT. However, by the 1990s a far more proactive approach was being adopted, with prevention recognised as more cost-effective than cure. This approach, known as 'integrated pest management' (IPM), is here described by Dave Pinniger and Peter Winsor (1998) (Chapter 13); an updated version of this book was produced in 2009 (Pinniger 2009). It has now also been adapted to use the same avoid, block, detect, respond (recover) as the *Framework for Preservation* (Strang and Kigawa 2009). To be successful, integrated pest management relies on an effective museum management that can, for example, ensure that a member of staff remains responsible for maintaining insect trapping information, that quarantine and housekeeping procedures are maintained and that museum-wide assessments for, and elimination of, food sources, access points and harbourage for insects are regularly carried out.

It is no coincidence that integrated pest management systems were being adopted, and non-chemical approaches to eradicating insects such as freezing, heating and anoxia became increasingly used, in the museum community in the 1980s, as this was the period when legislation that restricted the use of chemical insecticides was being enacted in Britain, Europe and North America. The use of integrated pest management techniques does require a higher level of organisational control than the mass-fumigation approach of earlier years, and in most museums increasing levels of managerial control were evident in the 1980s. It should also be noted that the demise of wild animals through the loss of their habitats was the subject of increasing awareness and concern from the 1960s onwards. It is ultimately this loss/denial of habitat that was adopted and developed as 'housekeeping' and forms a key part of the integrated pest management systems which began to be applied in museums from the mid-1980s (Story 1985). Since the 1980s we have continued to move away from the chemical treatments of the nineteenth and early twentieth centuries to the management and control approach that characterises the late twentieth and early twenty-first centuries.

Freezing has been used for treating insect infestations since the 1970s (Zycherman and Schrock 1988; Florian 1997; Strang 1992) and integrated pest management systems have been in use since the mid-1980s. However, case studies reporting such 'routine' activities have only rarely been submitted or published in journals or conferences in recent years (Berry 2001). Chapter 14, by Hillyer and Blyth, first appeared in *The Conservator* in 1992 and was later reprinted in Simon Knell's *Care of Collections* (1994). It is a good example of the implementation of an integrated pest management strategy and of the use of freezing as a method of insect eradication. However, a product of its time, the work involved the use of pesticides, a number of which have now been withdrawn from use.

Much of the literature selected for this reader refers to the problems faced by objects in the museums and historic houses of the UK and North America; this reflects the large volume of literature produced in Britain and North America on preventive conservation, as well as the experiences of your editor. Elsewhere in the world similar problems exist, but the details vary. Lim Chong Quek, Muhammadin Razak and Mary Ballard (1990) (Chapter 15) describe the differences between museum insect pests in North America and South-East Asia. Their work provides a timely reminder that all the advice and information provided in this reader should be evaluated by readers with reference to their local conditions, the resources available and with regard to the objects with which they are working.

References

Berry, J. (2001) 'Battle of the Beasts: Treatment of a Pest Infestation of the Mounted Mammal Collection at Liverpool Museum', in H. Kingsley, D. Pinniger, A. Xavier-Rowe and P. Winsor (eds), *2001 Pest Odyssey: Integrated Pest Management for Collections*, London: James & James (Science Publishers) Ltd, pp. 130–134.

Chong Quek, L., Razak, M. and Ballard M. W. (1990) 'Pest Control for Temperate vs. Tropical Museums: North America vs. South East Asia', in *ICOM-CC 9th Triennial Meeting, Dresden, German Democratic Republic 26–31 August 1990*, Los Angeles: ICOM-CC, pp. 817–821.

Florian, M.-L. (1997) *Heritage Eaters, Insects and Fungi in Heritage Collections*, London: James & James.

Hillyer, L. and Blyth, D. B. (1994) 'Carpet Beetle – a Pilot Study in Detection and Control', in S. Knell (ed.), *Care of Collections*, London: Routledge, pp. 217–233 (originally in *The Conservator* 16: 65–77).

Pinniger, D. (2009) *Pest Management: A Practical Guide*, Cambridge: Collections Trust.

Pinniger, D. and Winsor, P. (1998) *Integrated Pest Management*, London: Museums and Galleries Commission.

Story, K. O. (1985) *Approaches to Pest Management*, Washington, DC: Conservation Analytical Laboratory, Smithsonian Institution.

Strang, T. J. K. (1992) 'A Review of Published Temperatures for the Control of Insect Pests in Museums', *Collections Forum* 8(2): 41–67.

Strang, T. and Kigawa, R. (2009) *Combating Pests of Cultural Property*, CCI Technical Bulletin 29, Ottawa: CCI.

Zycherman, L. A. and Schrock, J. R. (1988) *A Guide to Museum Pest Control*, Washington DC.: Foundation of the American Institute for Conservation of Historic and Artistic works and the Association of Systematics Collection.

Chapter 13

Integrated Pest Management

Dave Pinniger and Peter Winsor

Introduction

ALL TOO OFTEN, pest control in museums is a reaction to the discovery of evidence of pest activity, such as damage to objects or elements of the building. The aim of this booklet is to provide practical, safe and cost-effective advice on the prevention and control of pests. It will explain what a museum needs to do to protect its collections, furnishings and buildings from harm by pests. It will describe some of the options for controlling infestations should they occur; but concentrates on the strategies that will reduce the risks.

What is integrated pest management?

Integrated pest management (IPM) is a term originally adopted to describe the development of pest control methods for fruit and cereal crops that do not rely on the regular and systematic use of pesticides. The approach is one of using non-invasive methods to prevent or at least minimise the risk of pest infestation. The main principles of IPM – monitoring, discouraging pests, modifying the environment and targeting treatments – have been adapted for use in museums. The approach has considerable advantages regarding health and safety, being less harmful to both humans and the environment, and once established is also likely to be more cost-effective than a passive or reactive approach.

Why IPM in a museum?

The care of collections and historic buildings involves many different disciplines, including conservation and management of both collections and buildings. The major

Source: *Integrated Pest Management*, London: Museums and Galleries Commission, 1998.

factors causing deterioration are the environmental effects of light, humidity and temperature, and agents of decay such as insects, mould and rodents. All of these factors are inter-related and IPM seeks to approach all pest problems using a holistic approach rather than reacting to each separate crisis. The expertise currently available in the field of collection care in the museum sector can readily be applied to develop an IPM programme tailored to the specific needs of a collection or historic house. A well planned and executed IPM programme will prevent problems or crises occurring and, in times of restricted budgets, will make much more effective use of limited human and cash resources. The reduced use of pesticides will lessen the risk of chemical damage to objects.

Developing an IPM strategy

An IPM programme should be relevant to the needs of the museum building and the collections, as well as to the variety of activities that take place within a museum. It should use as much local information and expertise as possible, and it needs to be practical and achievable, as it is all too easy to devise a grandiose IPM scheme that turns out to be unworkable. The programme should be considered as a process of evolution rather than revolution, and those developing it should encourage participation by all those working on the site. With the full involvement of staff at all levels, an IPM programme has a much surer chance of success.

The key management issues relating to an IPM programme are:

* Recognising and identifying priorities for action;
* Identifying an IPM co-ordinator and other responsible staff;
* Taking action on the high priorities;
* Establishing procedures for forward planning, financing and review.

In order to develop an IPM strategy, it is important to understand and recognise the key elements of successful pest control.

The key to successful pest control

Avoiding pests

– by denying them safe havens where they can live and reproduce (commonly referred to as 'harbourage') and developing procedures to keep them out of the building.

Preventing pests

– by blocking their access to the building and collections.

Identifying pests

– the most harmful species and the signs of their presence.

Assessing the problem

– based on inspection and trapping, and identifying the high-risk parts of the collection and building. It is also essential to understand the life cycle of pests, especially insects.

Solving pest problems

– by improving the environment to discourage the pests and carrying out appropriate treatments.

Reviewing the IPM procedures

– periodic assessment of the effectiveness of the strategy and modifying in order to improve it. This should include pest identification, documentation, training and funding resources, as well as surveys and treatment of infestations.

Common pests found in UK museums

Vertebrates

- Rodents – rats, mice, squirrels (Table 13.1)
- Birds – sparrows, pigeons, starlings
- Other vertebrates – rabbits, feral cats

Vertebrates can damage museum objects by eating them, shredding them for nesting material and staining from their urine and faeces. Their nests contain organic detritus such as fur, feather and plant material that will attract insects, which can then spread to the museum collections. Dead bodies of pests, whether death occurred naturally or through a pest control programme, pose a similar threat.

Insects

- Furniture beetle
- Booklouse
- Powderpost beetle
- Silverfish
- Wood weevil
- Death-watch beetle
- Carpet/Fur beetle
- Carpet beetle
- Biscuit beetle
- Case-bearing clothes moth
- Cigarette beetle
- Webbing clothes moth
- Spider beetle

Beetles and moths cause most insect pest problems, although other insects such as cluster flies, ants and cockroaches can cause great nuisance. The potential for damage to collections is great; entire collections of entomological specimens have been lost. More common is damage such as holes or 'grazing' on the surface of textiles. An object's value for display can be lost and important decorative or aesthetic features destroyed. Important information about the identity of objects can be lost through damage to paper labels. Museums have a duty to care for the collections, something that is enshrined in the accepted definitions of a museum. Signs of pest activity are an indication that this is not being done to a sufficiently high standard.

Avoiding pests

It is not usually practical to totally exclude all pests from a building, so it is important that they are denied a suitable environment in which to feed and breed when they do get in. The key to avoiding pest infestations is an understanding of the conditions under which they thrive. By denying them the four things they need – food, warmth, humidity and harbourage – it is possible to prevent them from becoming established. The four factors are often inter-linked and achieving the right balance is not always straightforward. It is also important to develop procedures, such as quarantine of incoming material, so that a pest is not introduced as a result of normal museum activities.

Food

The search for food is often what attracts pests into a museum. Pests are normally wild creatures but they are opportunistic, and if material is available that resembles their preferred natural food or nesting, they will readily adapt and possibly thrive. The material that attracts them is normally organic, such as paper, wood, leather and wool, though insects can make do with dust and fluff derived from these. The foods consumed by humans are also attractive to a wide range of pests. The key to avoiding pests is to deny them food and nesting materials by ensuring the cleaning regime, both inside and outside of the building, is of a high standard.

Special attention should be paid to areas where food is prepared, consumed or disposed of, and waste of all types must be removed regularly from the site and the disposal points (and containers) cleaned and disinfected. Ideally, human food should be kept out of the museum but as this is unrealistic, aim to keep to a minimum the number of sites where it may be stored, prepared, consumed and disposed of. Hygiene conditions in cafeterias and public areas should already be high, but do not forget areas where staff take tea or coffee and eat sandwiches.

Cleaning is probably the most important part of any IPM programme. Many cleaning schedules are targeted on public areas which may appear to be superficially clean. However, a close examination with a good flashlight will usually show accumulations of organic dirt and debris in corners, wall/floor angles and behind fittings that will support insect pests. Unused rooms and storage areas are often neglected and dirt and debris will provide food and an ideal harbourage for pests. It is advisable to initiate an additional programme of cleaning that focuses on the less accessible dead spaces such as ducts and chimney voids. This can be carried out on a rolling programme so that each of these areas is cleaned once every few years. Periodic deep cleaning of stores is recommended. This involves systematically emptying all drawers, cupboards and shelving, cleaning these and then ensuring that everything that is put back (objects or packing) is as clean as is reasonable. All horizontal surfaces where dust and rubbish can accumulate should be cleaned, including the tops of storage and display units, light-fittings and ledges, etc. Special care should be taken with less accessible areas such as beneath shelving units, cupboards, pallets and large objects. Vacuuming is the best method, but you may need to supplement this by cleaning using a damp cloth, though care should be taken to avoid causing the relative humidity to rise to high levels for any extended period.

Vertebrate pests need water to live just as humans do, so eliminate potential sources of drinking water such as leaking pipes and taps, and cover all open drains with securely fitted wire mesh screens.

Warmth and humidity

Temperature

Cool conditions will discourage insects from breeding and any areas with temperatures of 20°C and above will encourage insect breeding. Although it may not be possible to lower temperatures in public areas, object stores should be at as low a temperature as is practical, provided that the relative humidity levels are not permitted to rise to unacceptable levels. Remember that direct sunlight can cause local hotspots even in cool areas, and preventive measures such as providing shading should be taken. Also, uneven temperatures can result in localised condensation.

Vertebrate pests are much more tolerant of high or low temperatures than insects as they have much better temperature regulatory systems and so have more potential nesting sites available to them.

Humidity

Although insects can tolerate a wide range of relative humidity (RH) and will survive for long periods in a very dry or humid environment, they often require very particular conditions to complete all phases of their life cycle and so thrive. The biscuit beetle will breed at low relative humidity but other species, such as the furniture beetle, need a damper environment. The number of furniture beetle infestations has declined in recent years due to the increased use of central heating which has reduced the average relative humidity levels in homes and public buildings. This beetle will only successfully complete its life cycle when wood is in an environment above 60% relative humidity (RH). It is usually only found infesting wood in basements or attics, or in objects that have been stored in outbuildings. Silverfish will only breed rapidly and cause serious problems in conditions of above 70% RH. Booklice also need higher levels of humidity than is normally found in libraries and archives. They are often found in damp basements or in localised damp areas.

By establishing appropriate environmental conditions, it is possible to limit the threat from a large number of potential insect pest species. This can be achieved by mechanical means, but you also need to ensure that condensation, poor damp-proofing, broken or missing damp-proof courses, or leaks from gutters or water, sewage and heating pipes are not causing localised areas of high humidity where some pests will thrive.

Vertebrates are less likely to be inhibited by extremes of relative humidity, though high humidity is typical of the neglected parts of buildings that they exploit.

Relative humidity (usually abbreviated to RH)

RH is a measure of the amount of moisture that a volume of air can hold, expressed as a percentage of the total amount of moisture that the same volume of air can hold at the same temperature. Humans are tolerant to a wide range of relative humidity but feel most comfortable in the range 45–65%. Some insects have a strong preference for environments with a higher RH. This is because at these levels moulds and fungi have begun to attack their food sources such as wood, making it easier to digest.

In general, low temperatures and drier conditions are less attractive to most pest species.

Harbourage

The type of harbourage preferred by pests, whether vertebrate or insect, is one where they are undisturbed by human activity. Common sites where pests hide within buildings include:

- Unused chimney flues and blocked fireplaces (these often contain old birds' nests that attract insects such as carpet beetles);
- Heating and ventilation ducts (especially disused ones);
- Cavity walls and floors;
- Cracks between floorboards;
- Unused or little frequented rooms and cupboards, particularly in attics and basements;
- Gaps between walls and floors;
- Dead spaces behind and under storage cabinets, shelving units, display cases and plinths (and even large objects);
- Felt lining on boxes and felt sealing strips on doors;
- Old or discarded display material, particularly when covered by wool felt;
- De-accessioned material which has not been removed from the site;
- Flowers and plants.

Many of these situations are difficult to inspect, so you may consider a programme of adaptations such as fitting inspection hatches to give access to display case plinths, the space behind fitted cupboards etc., and to include these in the briefs for any improvement scheme.

Quarantine

An essential part of any pest prevention policy in a museum is to keep pests out of collections (Figure 13.1). Insects can be introduced from many sources, including new acquisitions, objects on loan from other museums and objects returned from loan.

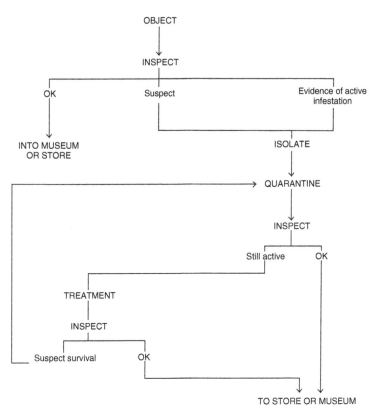

Diagram of quarantine strategy for museum

Figure 13.1 Diagram of quarantine strategy for a museum

Objects must be checked for infestation before being allowed into the main collection areas, whether storage or display. Inspection may reveal insect damage and clothes moth webbing, but insect eggs or small larvae are more difficult to see. Similarly, the emergence (flight) holes of wood-boring insects may be obvious, but any developing larvae will be hidden in the wood. This means that some incubation period may be necessary to determine whether an infestation is active or long dead. Because it is sometimes difficult to identify when insect damage occurred, it is important that a condition report is made for all objects loaned to other organisations, and this is used when checking the objects on their return.

Inspection area

All organic material and objects coming into the museum must initially be placed in a designated area and checked for signs of infestation. This area must be physically isolated from collection storage and display areas. If there is active infestation, then the objects should be further isolated by bagging, clearly labelled as having an active pest, and treated as soon as possible. Pests may also be living semi-dormant in packing materials, waiting for an opportunity to emerge when the conditions are suitable. These materials will also need to be checked and possibly treated or disposed of.

If there is no direct evidence of live insects, but there is reason to suspect that there may be active infestation, then the objects should be isolated and incubated over a summer period. If adult insects are seen to emerge, then remedial action can be taken.

Some simple treatments can be carried out on objects in the quarantine area by museum staff. Some museums have established procedures that treat all appropriate items using one of these methods, when they are first acquired or on return from loan. Routine treatments are most commonly applied to natural history, social history and textile items.

An IPM programme should seek to identify and resolve problems such as those described as soon as possible. The key to this is a good standard of cleanliness and maintenance, and adopting procedures such as quarantine for objects and other materials entering the museum.

Keeping pests out

Many modern buildings successfully prevent the entry of pests by careful design and detailing of potential entry points such as doors, windows and vents. Building standards and the improvements to heating and ventilation systems have also played a part in creating environments that are generally less attractive to insect pests. If you are planning a new building, it is worth discussing the special needs of your collection with the architect and including this in the initial design brief. Excluding pests from older and historic buildings is often far more difficult (Figure 13.2) because of the

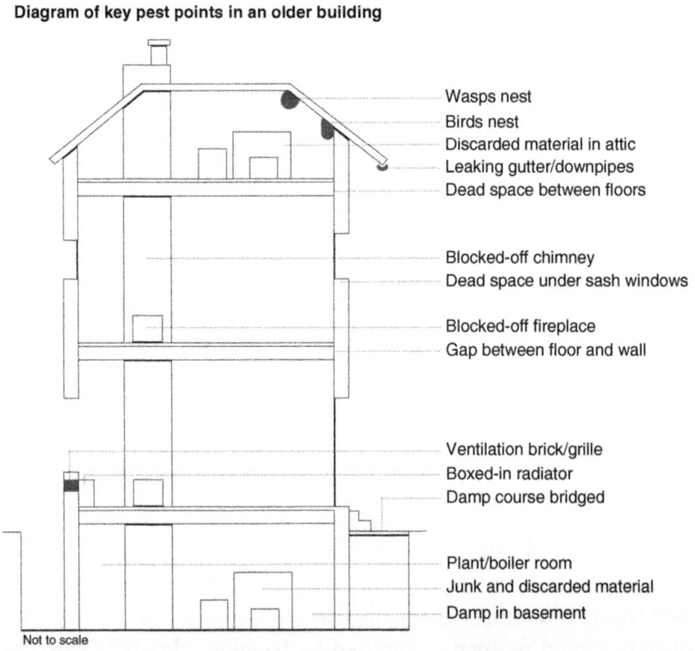

Diagram of key pest points in an older building

Wasps nest
Birds nest
Discarded material in attic
Leaking gutter/downpipes
Dead space between floors

Blocked-off chimney
Dead space under sash windows

Blocked-off fireplace
Gap between floor and wall

Ventilation brick/grille
Boxed-in radiator
Damp course bridged

Plant/boiler room
Junk and discarded material
Damp in basement

Not to scale

Figure 13.2 Diagram of key pest points in an older building

unacceptable appearance of some proofing methods. You may need to take advice from a pest control consultant who has experience of dealing with such situations.

Good building construction practice and subsequent maintenance is essential if pests are to be kept out of museum buildings. Check brickwork for cracks and damaged pointing and initiate remedial work, if required, as soon as possible. Ill-fitting window frames, broken ventilation grills, poorly sealed unused openings (such as where old extraction fans were once fitted or at pipe—wall junctions) all provide easy access for a variety of pests, yet are relatively simple and inexpensive to remedy. Ensure that all doors and windows are well-fitting and kept securely closed as much as possible. In older buildings, rubber or brush seals can be rebated into door edges to provide a flexible seal. Seals suitable for larger gaps around loading bay and roller shutter doors are also available. All unnecessary openings should be blocked using appropriate building materials and techniques, but ensure that essential ventilation openings are left unsealed. Pay particular attention to ground, basement and roof areas. It is worthwhile cutting back vegetation for at least three metres around the perimeter of buildings and any overhanging branches, as these are often home to many potential pests. If the standard of maintenance of the outside of the building is to be high, then it must be included as part of your annual planning and budget cycle.

Open-air sites and vernacular buildings may require alternative strategies such as trapping or using residual pesticides.

The following describes the typical exclusion methods for different types of pests.

Vertebrates

Rodents

Specific measures to exclude rodents include:

- Sheet metal cladding fixed to the base of wooden doors, windows or walls in high-risk areas or where there are signs of gnawing. This can only be done if it is aesthetically acceptable;
- Wire mesh screens and grills fitted to louvres and vents, or other openings that cannot be sealed. Steel mesh screens can usually be designed and made by a local steel fabricator. Hot-dip galvanising will extend the life of the barrier;
- Insert steel mesh into gaps around pipes and in eaves to prevent access but without restricting ventilation;
- Ensure that exterior drain covers and rodding caps are sound and close-fitting;
- Fitting metal cones or screens around exterior pipework, cables and poles. A barrier with a diameter of 200–250 mm will prevent rodents climbing around it and gaining access to entry at higher level. Barriers should only be fitted to telephone and power cables and their supports with the permission of the appropriate utility company.

Ultrasonic repellent devices are available against rodent pests, but many experts consider them to be ineffective.

Table 13.1 Rodent pests found in the UK

Rodent	Size	Appearance	Droppings	Habitat	Food
House mouse *Mus domesticus*	Length 17–18 cms. Weight: 25 grams.	Colour: brown-grey with grey belly. Tail is only slightly longer than body and head. Nose: pointed. Ears: large. Tail: dark in colour.	Thin and cylinder-shaped. 6 mm long	Range only 10–15 metres from nest. Can squeeze through 10 mm size gaps. Good climber and swimmer, and can jump up to 30 cms. Prefers gaps behind walls and beneath fitted cupboards.	Omnivores, but prefer cereals
Brown rat *Rattus norvegicus*	30–45 cms. Tail is shorter than body. Weight: 200–550 grams.	Colour: brown to reddish grey, light grey belly. Nose: blunt. Ears: short and thick. Tail: rough, thick and lighter on underside.	Capsule-shaped. Approx. 20 mm long.	Range up to 500 metres. Prefers lower levels and builds burrows underground.	Omnivores
Black rat *Rattus rattus*	40–45 cms. Tail is longer than head and body. Weight: 300 grams.	Colour: Black or brownish grey with lighter belly. Nose: pointed. Ears: thin and large. Tail: slender.	Curved with pointed ends. 12 mm long.	Range only 100 metres. Good climber and swimmer, and can jump up to 1.5 metres. Prefers upper levels of buildings.	Omnivores

Birds

Measures to discourage birds from nesting or roosting include:

- Netting or wire screens fitted over balconies, alcoves, light wells and other openings;
- Steel mesh fitted into the gaps in eaves to prevent access but without restricting ventilation;
- Preventing perching on ledges and sills by fitting sharp metal wire spikes and strip. Specially designed products are now readily available and may be fitted by museum staff or a commercial firm contracted in. Anti-perching gel is an alternative, but this requires thorough site preparation and regular cleaning as it rapidly

becomes unsightly and ineffective. Spikes (pins) and wires are more expensive but more durable;

- Chimney capping to prevent nesting and access. This must be designed so that any essential natural ventilation is not restricted.

Other methods such as using silhouettes of birds of prey are rarely effective in the long-term. Devices using loud noises or distress calls are only likely to be applicable in rural areas and in situations where the staff and visitors are extremely tolerant.

Insects

The highest standards of maintenance and building practices are essential if insects are to be excluded. The following methods will improve the effectiveness:

- Doors and windows can be fitted with unobtrusive sealing barrier strips to prevent the entry of larger insects. This has the added advantage of reducing dust levels and also provides good draught proofing, so reducing energy costs;
- Windows and doors can be fitted with fly mesh screening, though this is usually only acceptable on more modern buildings or where appearance is not a priority;
- Splits and holes in wooden doors and windows or their frames should be caulked using builders' mastic or other appropriate materials.

Insects, once in the building, can penetrate small cracks and crevices, but display and storage furniture can act as a further barrier to pest attack, if well-designed and maintained. Money spent on fitting insect-proofing seals to drawers for entomological collections may prevent serious problems in the future. Cupboards, cabinets and drawers, which may appear to be sound, should be inspected because they may have hidden cracks that can allow insect access. Rubber or fibre systems for doors are available.

Identifying pests and pest activity

An important element of any IPM programme is the correct identification of pests and signs of their presence. Vertebrate pests are relatively easy to identify, but if the problem is insects, then you may need the expertise of an entomologist. You should aim to have someone in your organisation competent in identifying the common insect pests encountered in museums. Time and money should be set aside for the appropriate training.

Rodents

The signs of a rodent infestation are difficult to ignore easily. They include profuse droppings and gnaw marks. Infestations of brown rats, *Rattus norvegicus*, are rare in museums and usually only found associated with considerable and accessible sources of human food such as farm feed stores, and catering facilities with poor refuse disposal systems. The black rat, *Rattus rattus*, is now extremely rare in the UK. The house mouse, *Mus domesticus*, is the main cause of concern, although in many museums and houses the fear of infestation is far greater than the reality. Given undisturbed areas with access to food supplies, mice will breed rapidly and create serious damage by shredding paper and textiles to make nest bedding. They will not discriminate between valuable objects, packaging or rubbish. Their faeces and urine also present a health hazard.

Typical signs of a rodent problem are:

- Gnaw marks near the base of doors and cabinets. Rodents need to gnaw to wear down their incisor teeth, which are constantly growing. To reach food or nest sites they can gnaw through wood, particleboard, plaster and asphalt, as well as soft metals such as zinc, lead and aluminium;
- Faecal droppings and urine stains;
- Nest made from shredded paper and textiles, normally situated in dry, well-concealed spaces, where they are least likely to be disturbed;
- Rat access burrows are dug in soft earth around foundations and are approximately 100 mm in diameter and may be a metre deep;
- Paw prints on dusty surfaces. Tracking powder such as talc can be sprinkled to confirm suspected runs;
- Noises of scampering, squeaks and gnawing – usually only at night or during low-occupancy levels;
- Rats do not normally have a distinctive odour, but mice have a musty smell reminiscent of stale biscuits.

Birds

Roosting or nesting birds can be a nuisance on windowsills, ledges and other architectural features. Their droppings, which are actually mostly urine through which they excrete uric acid, cause unsightly stains and can damage the building fabric. Church towers and decorative elements on the top of older buildings are regularly colonised by birds, and huge quantities of excrement and nesting material can build up over a very short period of time. These pose a health hazard to humans, as birds such as pigeons carry parasites and disease. The nests, feathers and other debris attract insect pests such as clothes moths and carpet beetles, and these can move into the building and cause damage to the collection.

Birds such as pigeons and sparrows will occasionally find their way inside a building and be unable to escape. The bird's response is to panic, resulting in a mess of excrement, feathers and usually a dead bird. The amount of damage caused to furnishings can be extensive, and it is also distressing to staff and visitors. Birds can also become trapped in chimney flues, where they quickly die and become an attractive food supply for several insect pest species. The insects often spread into the building, and bird corpses are one of the most common sources of insect pest infestations in museums.

The most common bird pests are:

- Pigeons, starlings and sparrows are the most troublesome in urban areas;
- Gulls, rooks and geese may also cause serious problems of roosting and fouling in specific locations.

Insects

Although it is often the adult insects that are found, it is the larvae that do the most serious damage. Adults will be more active and obvious during the summer months but the larvae, which hatch from the eggs laid by the adults, will feed and grow throughout the rest of the year (Figure 13.3).

Many of the insects found in museums are not active pests but have simply strayed into the building.

Although the dead bodies of flies, wasps and ground beetles may not present a direct risk to the collection, they can provide a substantial source of food for pests such as carpet beetles. It is not intended that this booklet should be an identification guide, as there are more comprehensive sources of information, some of which are listed at the end of the publication. The following summary (Table 13.2) will help you to focus on the main insect pest problems, although some expert help may be required to confirm the identity of suspected pest species and the level of activity. [. . .]

Entomologists working in museums and universities may be willing to help, or you could contact pest control consultants.

There are many excellent reference guides describing insects and their habits. The article by John M. Kingsolver, 'Illustrated Guide to Common Insect Pests in Museums', included in Zycherman and Schrock (1988), the Natural History Museum's publication, 'Mound' (1989) and *Insect Pests in Museums* by David Pinniger (1994) are all recommended. The illustrations in these, and most similar publications (Figure 13.4) show complete, undamaged specimens. It requires considerable experience to identify damaged specimens or fragments, which are typical finds of a pest inspection programme. A good magnifier ($\times$ 5 or $\times$ 10) and light are essential tools when trying to identify insects.

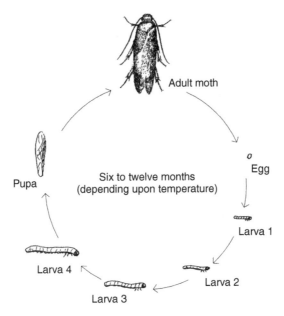

Figure 13.3 Life cycle of the common clothes moth

Table 13.2 Most common insect pests and damage in UK museums

Pest	Type of damage	Materials damaged
Woodworm / Furniture beetle *Anobium punctatum*	Small 2 mm round exit holes, gritty frass* in tunnels	Sapwood of hardwoods, ply with animal glue, some composite cellulose materials and books
Death-watch beetle *Xestobium rufovillosum*	Large 3 mm exit holes, rounded frass in tunnels	Structural hardwoods, particularly when in contact with damp walls
Powderpost beetle *Lyctus brunneus*	Small 2 mm round exit holes, fine talc-like frass in tunnels	Starchy wood
Wood weevil *Euophryum confine*	Surface damage and holes on damp wood	Damp wood, paper and books
Carpet beetle *Anthrenus sp*	Irregular holes in textiles, loose fur, short hairy cast skins of larvae	Bird and mammal skins, insect specimens, wool textiles
Carpet/Fur beetle *Attagenus sp*	Irregular holes in textiles, loose fur, long banded cast skins of larvae	Bird and mammal skins, insect specimens, wool textiles
Webbing clothes moth *Tineola bisselliella*	Large irregular holes with quantities of silk webbing tubes and gritty frass	Wool, fur and feather textiles, bird and mammal skins
Case-bearing clothes moth *Tinea pellionella*	Irregular holes and grazed fabric with loose silk bags	Wool, fur and feather textiles, bird and mammal skins
Biscuit beetle *Stegobium paniceum*	Round exit holes and gritty dust	Dried food and spices, starchy plant specimens and seed heads, papier-mâché, freeze-dried animal specimens
Cigarette beetle *Lasioderma serricorne*	Round exit holes and gritty dust	Dried food and tobacco, starchy plant specimens and seed heads, freeze-dried animal specimens
Spider beetle *Ptinus sp*	Some holes or cavities, spherical silk pupal bags	Starchy dried plant specimens and seed heads, animal specimens
Booklouse *Liposcelis sp*	Scratched and eroded surface of materials	Starchy paper and glues
Silverfish *Lepisma sp*	Irregular scratched and eroded surface of materials	Damp paper and textiles, animal glue. Silverfish are very partial to paper labels on objects

* Frass is the fine powdery debris left by insects and is mostly excrement, with fragments of the material it is boring through or eating.

Assessing the problem

In order to have a full appreciation of the situation it is essential that you collect as much information as possible. This requires regular and systematic inspection of the building, both inside and outside, paying particular attention to all collection storage and display areas, and the objects housed in them. A programme of trapping can supplement this information. The results of all surveys and trapping should be documented in a central logbook, together with a record of pest control treatment to museum spaces.

Some common insects found in museums

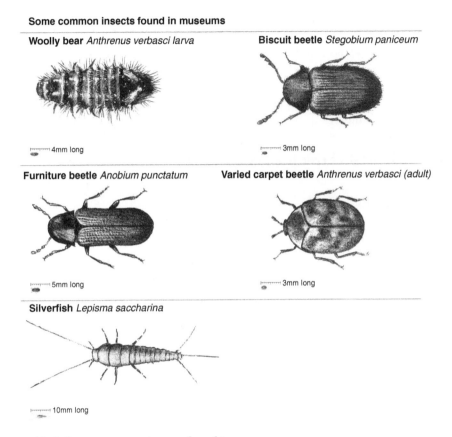

Woolly bear *Anthrenus verbasci larva*

⊢⋯⋯⋯⊣ 4mm long

Biscuit beetle *Stegobium paniceum*

⊢⋯⋯⋯⊣ 3mm long

Furniture beetle *Anobium punctatum*

⊢⋯⋯⋯⊣ 5mm long

Varied carpet beetle *Anthrenus verbasci (adult)*

⊢⋯⋯⋯⊣ 3mm long

Silverfish *Lepisma saccharina*

⊢⋯⋯⋯⊣ 10mm long

Figure 13.4 Some common insects found in museums

As part of your pest control strategy you will need to identify:

- The parts of your collection that are most at risk;
- The parts of the building that are most at risk;
- Museum activities that might present an opportunity for pests.

By reviewing the above, you should be able to determine the pests most likely to be attracted to the museum. Next, investigate their life cycle, seasonal activity and habits. Only then can you decide on priorities and any action that is needed. It is useful to go through the following basic checklist of pest activity:

- Is there any damage?
- Are there signs of insects or droppings from birds or rodents?
- If there are insects, are they alive or dead?
- What species are the insects?
- How many insects are there?
- Are they breeding?
- Where are they?

- How many objects are affected?
- Are they in display material?
- Are they elsewhere in the building?

Some of these questions may be difficult to answer because it is not normally possible to inspect all objects, particularly when they are in storage, and the many hidden areas in older buildings.

Materials most at risk from insect attack

- Fur
- Dried plants and seeds
- Feathers
- Seeds
- Animal skins
- Dried food such as pasta or flour
- Hair
- Freeze-dried natural history specimens
- Wool
- Papier-mâché
- Silk
- Materials rich in starch
- Insect specimens
- Sapwoods
- Parchment and vellum
- Any damp organic material.

Materials such as cotton are not attacked unless, for example, insects eat through cotton covering when they emerge from infested upholstery.

Paper is rarely attacked unless it is dirty and damp.

Where to look

In general, dirty and neglected objects in dark places will be more at risk than those that are clean and in well-lit areas. Look for insects in:

- Dark areas (a good flashlight is an essential tool for anyone checking for pests);
- Inside folded textiles or where they are touching walls or floors.

It is important to check the materials used by education and school liaison sections; they sometimes use de-accessioned objects, and products such as pasta and wool felt for creative and hands-on sessions with school groups. These are all potential food sources for pests.

Remember to check all food storage and preparation areas, including canteens, cafeterias, mess rooms and waste disposal areas, as these may be sources of pests.

The presence of rodents is usually clear from their droppings and the damage they cause. You should check the perimeter of the building and basements for burrows, runs or signs of nests. It is sometimes worth laying traps to determine the level of activity. If you are aware that rodents are present in the building and want to check their activity, you can put down a tracking powder such as talc and look for paw prints.

Even a thorough inspection may fail to find insects that are hidden away. This is why all museums and collections should have a programme of monitoring using sticky traps to detect and find insects.

The use of traps

Traps are used to detect the presence of insects and not to control them. A range of sticky traps (Figure 13.5) are available that work on the principle of the wandering insect blundering into the trap and becoming stuck on the non-toxic adhesive surface. These are designed to be placed on the floor and are most effective when placed in corners and wall/floor angles rather than in open areas (Figure 13.6). Most traps will remain effective for at least a year and need to be checked at regular intervals. It is better to check regularly every two months than to start by checking every week and then finding that the workload is too great. A minimum regime would be to check traps four times a year, in March, June, September and December. It is also important to check the stickiness of the trap at the same time as you check for pests. Dust can quickly build up on the adhesive and render it useless.

The greater the number of traps used, the greater is the chance of finding insects. However, the workload should not be underestimated and trapping programmes should be designed to be manageable. Traps should be placed in a regular grid pattern and all traps date-labelled and their position marked on a plan. Insects caught on traps should be identified and the information recorded in a log. It is important to record whether the insects caught are larvae or adults. An adult beetle may simply have wandered in from outside. If it is a larva then it is almost certain that the species is breed-

Typical 'blunder' or 'sticky' type of insect trap

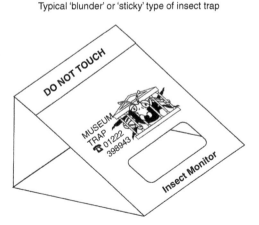

Figure 13.5 Typical 'blunder' or 'sticky' type of insect trap

Diagram to show placement of traps in a museum store

▦ Position of blunder traps (all at floor level)
■ Position of moth pheromone trap (suspended)

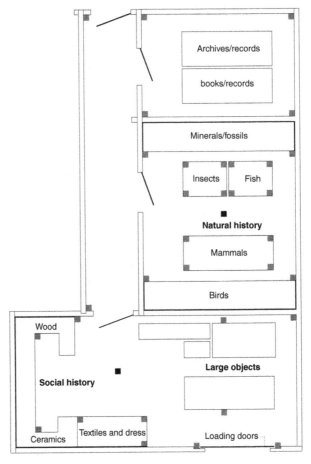

Figure 13.6 Diagram to show placement of traps in a museum store

ing within the building. Over a period of time, careful monitoring of the traps will enable a picture to be built up of insect distribution. Additional traps can be placed in areas where pests need to be more accurately pinpointed.

Large numbers of non-pest insects may be caught on traps, for example, if they are near an outside door. When this happens, the traps should be replaced as the trapped insects can act as a food source for pest species.

Pheromone traps

Many insects use chemicals called pheromones to attract mates when they are ready to breed. These chemicals are now being used as lures in traps. Pheromone lures are currently available for the furniture beetle, *Anobium punctatum*, and the webbing clothes moth, *Tineola bisselliella*. The lures are extremely effective, but will only attract the males of the target species and have no effect on other insect species. Because they attract only males, there is no risk of the pheromone traps causing an increase in insect numbers through breeding. These lures and traps are more expensive than the small, sticky blunder traps, but have a value for accurate monitoring and early warning of these two species in sensitive areas. The placing of pheromone traps is more complex than for blunder traps and advice from a specialist should be sought.

Traps should be used as a supplement to visual inspection, and the information they provide used to identify what preventative and remedial measures are required, and to establish priorities. Trap catches can show:

- The presence of a pest species;
- An increase in insect numbers in a specific area;
- The spread of a pest from one area to another;
- An invasion of the adult insects in summer;
- Localised infestation in a problem area;
- The failure of a control treatment.

One trap catch may not mean much. It is only by recording results over a period of time that a full picture of the insect distribution will emerge.

Because pheromone traps are far more effective than blunder-type traps, their large catch may be disconcerting. This may cause panic until it is realised that this is reflecting trap efficiency, and not a real increase in pest numbers.

Solving pest problems

The most effective pest control measures are preventive; the avoidance and exclusion methods described should be the priority. Only when these methods prove ineffective should chemical treatments or trapping (for removal from site or killing) be considered. If pests are found in objects or in the building, then a decision must be made on whether some remedial action is necessary and, if so, what it should be. In the first instance action should be taken to:

- Isolate any objects suspected of being infested, to prevent spread of infestation to other objects;
- Clean infested areas and remove insect bodies, droppings and debris from the museum in a sealed container;
- Dispose of debris in such a way that it does not become a potential food source for new pests that might then re-infest the museum site. Incineration is probably the best method;
- Decide on the most appropriate treatment.

This booklet is not intended to provide an exhaustive review of all possible treatments, but to provide a summary of the control options currently available.

Dealing with vertebrate pests

- Rodents – chemical treatment for control of rodents is best left to professional pest control companies. But you do need to ensure that the techniques and chemicals they use are safe for your staff, visitors and the collections. You may need to take advice from a pest control consultant who has experience of working in a museum environment. Trapping has the advantage over poisoning that the rodents do not die in inaccessible places, so causing a nasty smell and acting as a food source for numerous insect pests. Great care should be taken when handling the traps and the dead rodents. Large spring traps can break a human finger and rodents are carriers of parasites and disease. Local regulations may restrict the ways you can dispose of dead rodent pests.
- Squirrels – trapping for squirrels can be with 'live' traps. [. . .]
- Bats – in the UK these are protected species, so if they are a problem contact the Bat Conservation Trust. The presence of bats may preclude the use of certain control measures, such as chemical treatment for woodworm or dry rot in roof spaces or the sealing of access points. This is covered by legislation in the Wildlife and Countryside Act, 1981.
- Birds – the trapping or poisoning of birds requires a licence and is likely to provoke a hostile response from staff and visitors. It is not recommended. Use methods that exclude them from the building and discourage them from roosting nearby.
- Feral cats – these have proved to be a nuisance at a number of large museum sites in urban areas. The most effective strategy is to manage the situation and use the staff's love of animals. Appoint someone to be responsible for the feline population and give them an appropriate budget. Establish a feeding point and latrine area and keep these clean. Employ humane methods to trap the animals. The captured animals should be examined and treated by a vet, and neutered. This will stabilise the situation and it may be possible to reduce the population by moving individual cats that have been re-domesticated to new homes. In large institutions it is important to keep all staff informed and to encourage their co-operation. This proved a successful strategy for several large museums, and had the support and encouragement of staff and trustees.

What if there are insect pests in the museum?

Targeted treatment using an approved insecticidal dust or spray can be very effective in reducing the numbers of insects. However, insects mostly live in places where it is difficult to apply insecticides and will only come into contact with it when they wander across treated surfaces. Locations to pay particular attention to include:

- Wall/floor angles, cracks in woodwork:
  these can be treated with a residual insecticide;
- Dead spaces in ducts and under cabinets:
  can be treated with an insecticidal or desiccant dust. These are both very useful for little frequented areas as it is important that the dust is not disturbed by

pedestrian traffic. Desiccant dusts have the advantage of being low hazard to humans;
• Structural timber:
• can be treated for infestations of woodworm by application of a suitable insecti-cidal fluid;
• Carpets, wool felt underlay and curtains:
infested textiles that are not museum artefacts can be treated in situ with an appropriate insecticide.

The use of aerosols or airborne sprays is not recommended as they achieve little con-trol of most museum pests and cause indiscriminate contamination of objects and the general environment. Museum staff can safely carry out many localised treatments, but a competent contractor should carry out large-scale treatments.

Residual insecticides are formulated to be effective when applied and for some period afterwards. The duration of their efficacy varies. Some examples are listed in Table 13.3. Available types include:

• Desiccant type insecticide, which is an inert siliceous powder that absorbs part of the insect's outer protective wax coating. This causes dehydration and eventual death.
• Encapsulated formulations that incorporate the insecticide into microscopic porous plastic beads. The insecticide slowly diffuses out or is released on being ruptured.
• Wettable powder formulations mix an insecticide with an inert powder and a wetting agent. Water is added to form a suspension that can be sprayed.

Table 13.3 Examples of residual insecticides which can be used

Insecticide	Type	Formulation	Use	Examples of brand name
Permethrin	Pyrethroid	Dust	Dead spaces	Coopex
		Microemulsion	Wood, textiles	Constrain
Bendiocarb	Carbamate	Dust Wettable powder	Dead spaces Wall/floor angle spray	Ficam D Ficam W
Chlorpyrifos	Organophosphorus	Encapsulated	Wall/floor angle spray	Empire 20
Silica aerogel	Desiccant	Dust	Dead spaces	Drione

Treating objects

The choice of remedial treatment will depend upon the severity of the infestation, the type of material and the value of the object. The treatment of objects should only be carried out after taking the advice of a conservation or collections care specialist.

In many situations, the application of an appropriate residual insecticide such as permethrin micro-emulsion will be sufficient to tackle an isolated outbreak of insect infestation in a wooden object. This treatment will kill emerging furniture beetle adults and may kill larvae and pupae near the surface of the wood. Such treatments may be appropriate for bulky and robust wooden objects, but may be less suitable for delicate objects and fine furniture, or if the outbreak is severe or deep-seated.

Recent developments in the food preservation industry and by museum researchers mean that museums now have a number of options for treatments that will kill all pests in objects, if they are carried out correctly.

Low temperature

This method will kill all stages of an insect's life cycle and is being used routinely in some museums to treat textile, social history and natural history collections. The objects are sealed in polythene (other plastic films such as polyester can be used but not PVC) and exposed to temperatures of −30°C for three days or at −18°C for at least seven days. It is not necessary to treat objects through two freeze–thaw cycles at −18°C, as was once recommended. A domestic chest freezer is more efficient than an upright type, but neither will normally reach a temperature lower than −18°C. Commercial freezers operate at around −30°C. It is not advisable to rely on a freezer's built-in thermometer but to use a separate device. Objects should not be removed from the bag until they have returned to room temperature and there is no risk of condensation. Some large museums own freezer chambers, and the National Museums and Galleries on Merseyside now offers this form of pest control treatment as a commercial service.

Elevated temperature

All insects will be killed at temperatures above 45°C. Objects can be treated in 24 hours without bagging in a special humidity-controlled chamber at 52°C in the Thermo Lignum process. Some less sensitive objects can be treated in an oven at 52°C if they are bagged in the same way as for freezing.

Carbon dioxide

This treatment involves placing objects in an environment with a concentration of at least 60% carbon dioxide. It is usually carried out in a special gas-tight plastic bubble or tent. Carbon dioxide has no deleterious effect on objects at normal temperature and relative humidity. Long exposures of three weeks or more may be needed to kill all pests.

Nitrogen

The treatment involves placing the object in a nitrogen atmosphere and kills the insects by depriving them of oxygen. Insects require oxygen to live, but they can tolerate very low concentrations so the treatment is effective only at nitrogen concentrations of greater than 99%. The treatment must be carried out in specially constructed chambers or in cubicles made from a barrier film that has low oxygen-permeability. The nitrogen must be humidified, and the oxygen levels carefully monitored and controlled using an oxygen meter. As with carbon dioxide, exposure times need to be longer at lower temperatures. Nitrogen gas is used extensively in industrial processes so it is relatively inexpensive and readily available.

A variation on the nitrogen anoxia treatment that is suitable for smaller objects is to seal the item in bags constructed from the barrier film together with an oxygen scavenger such as Ageless™. This product contains finely divided iron compounds that react with the oxygen and remove it from the atmosphere. The insects die through lack of oxygen. The procedure is only useful for small items, as the oxygen scavenger is expensive. Ageless™ is produced by the Mitsubishi Company and different grades are available for different situations.

[. . .]

Fumigation

In the past museum collections were treated, usually by commercial companies with toxic gasses such as methyl bromide, ethylene oxide and phosphine. Use of many of these gasses is now prohibited. For up-to-date information on available fumigation options, consult a reputable pest treatment company.

Insect repellents

Substances such as naphthalene and paradichlorobenzene have been used in mothballs or moth flakes for many years to repel insects such as clothes moths and carpet beetles. There is some insecticidal effect at very high concentrations and both chemicals will repel adult clothes moths. [. . .] Following concern about the hazards to humans of long-term exposure to these chemicals, their use in the UK by untrained personnel is now prohibited.

Insects are repelled by high doses of some traditional plant-derived materials such as cedarwood oil and aromatic herbs including lavender, bay, rosemary and wormwood. These are currently being re-examined for efficacy and repellency. It is worth noting that some chemicals derived from plants are as toxic as synthetic pesticides and the oils may have deleterious effects on objects.

Implementing IPM

An IPM programme should not be seen as a rigid set of rules and procedures that are immutable once established. It is essentially an evolving process that should apply your knowledge of the local situation and be adaptable to changing needs and priorities.

Implementing an IPM programme in a large museum or collection can be a daunting task. It is therefore important to identify priorities and plan to cover the museum in achievable steps. In many cases it has taken several years to develop and implement a programme in a large collection. It has been achieved by initially selecting one department or collection area, demonstrating that IPM is effective and achievable in that area, and then adapting the programme for other areas until all parts are covered.

A suggested plan of action is as follows.

Survey the situation

- Obtain a plan of the building and grounds or make survey sketches. Include galleries, stores and any other areas such as outbuildings;
- Carry out a preliminary survey to identify pest access points, and high-risk areas and objects. Record this on the plan;
- Place monitoring traps;
- Plan a detailed inspection schedule for all areas.

Develop or assess IPM procedures

- Check cleaning regimes and modify if necessary;
- Review existing pest control contracts;
- Examine the pattern of movement of objects into and out of the museum;
- Establish a quarantine strategy, if one is not in place;
- Explain to key personnel the objectives of IPM and encourage their co-operation;
- Form a small team to aid communication and spread the IPM load. This can, for example, include conservation, collection management, buildings management and gallery staff;
- Identify training/awareness needs;
- Write an outline strategy for short-term and long-term IPM;
- Identify budgets that may contribute funding for IPM. For example, training, buildings maintenance, collections care, storage furniture, etc.

The problem of budgeting for IPM should not be underestimated. It is essential to find out what is currently being spent on existing pest control contracts and any fumigation treatments. In many cases, a good IPM programme can use this money more effectively and efficiently. It is also important to consider the overall costs relating to caring for collections. An IPM programme will help avoid the neglect and resulting deterioration of objects, and consequently increased expenditure on remedial conservation.

Training

Successful IPM involves all staff. Training can range from an intensive five-day IPM course to a 30-minute awareness talk for cleaners and warding staff. One person should be identified as the co-ordinator and chief contact for IPM matters. Some IPM tasks such as monitoring can be shared by several members of staff, depending upon the size of the collection and staff structure. If contractors are involved, then it is important to monitor that the work is being done as specified and their staff are adequately trained.

Buildings' and Estates' Officers normally deal with pest control contracts. It is essential that these contracts be examined closely to ensure that they are geared to the needs of a museum. The contractor may not fully understand the limitations imposed by the specialised needs of the collection and some treatments may be ineffective or harmful to objects. If you are in doubt about priorities, surveying, treatments or implementing IPM, you can obtain specialist advice from a pest management consultant.

Documentation

All pest treatments of areas within the museum and all monitoring data should be recorded by the IPM co-ordinator. This can be done in a central logbook, on customised forms or using a spreadsheet programme such as Excel. Plotting insect pest occurrences on to a plan of the building (best of all on transparent film) will help you to visualise the situation and show how it develops over time. An annual summary of pest incidence and attack should be produced and sent to all relevant staff and trustees.

Any control treatment for pests on museum objects should be recorded in the object's documentation. The occurrence of an insect pest on returned loans or newly acquired objects should, of course, be documented, and the previous owner or the borrower informed.

Health and safety

The IPM co-ordinator should be responsible for ensuring that all monitoring and treatments are undertaken safely. Ensure that you and all of your colleagues are aware of the following:

- The use of chemicals must be justified and recorded. This is required under the Control of Substances Hazardous to Health Regulations (COSHH) 1994;
- Hazard data-sheets should be obtained from the supplier for all of the chemical products used, and their contents noted;
- Under the Control of Pesticides Regulations 1986, many chemicals are approved for use only by licensed, professional operators;
- Instructions and information on pesticide container labels relating to application and use of protective clothing must be read and followed;
- All pesticides and other chemicals must be stored safely and securely.

If your museum has stocks of pesticides then check that they are within any 'use-by' limit and that they are still permitted pesticides. Some may now be banned and must not be used. These should be disposed of correctly as stated in the Control of Pesticides Regulations 1986. Your local authority may have special arrangements for disposing of such material. Otherwise, a commercial waste disposal contractor must be used.

IPM and the future

Because of the effects of some chemicals on staff, objects and the environment, there will be increased pressure to move away from persistent and toxic pesticides. The development of an IPM programme based on the principles outlined in this booklet will enable collections and buildings to be cared for in ways that are safe and effective.

There are exciting new developments that are becoming available for the detection, prevention and control of pests and it is important that those responsible for developing IPM in museums do not work in isolation, but share their experiences with others.

Reading list

Books

Florian, M. (1997) *Heritage Eaters: Insects and Fungi in Heritage Collections*, London: James & James.
Mound, L. (ed.) (1989) *Common Insect Pests of Stored Food Products: A Guide to Their Identification*, London: British Museum (Natural History).
Pinniger, D. B. (1994) (3rd edition) *Insect Pests in Museums*, London: Archetype Press.
Zycherman, L. A., and J. R. Schrock (eds) (1988) *A Guide to Museum Pest Control*, Washington DC: Foundation of the American Institute for Conservation of Historic and Artistic Works and the Association of Systematics Collection.

Papers

Canadian Conservation Institute (CCI) (1991) 'Controlling vertebrate pests in museums', *Technical Bulletin 13*, Ottawa: CCI.
Child, R. E. and Pinniger, D. B. (1994) 'Insect trapping in museums and historic houses', in A. Roy and P. Smith (eds) *Preventive Conservation: Practice, Theory and Research*, preprints, IIC Ottawa Congress, London: IIC.
Hillyer, L. and Blyth, V. (1992) 'Carpet beetle – a pilot study in detection and control', *The Conservator* 16.
Linnie, M. J. (1996) 'Integrated pest management: a proposed strategy for natural history museums', *Museum Management and Curatorship* 15(2).
Pinniger, D. B. and Child, R. E. (1996) 'Insecticides: optimising their performance and targeting their use in museums', in *Proceedings of 3rd International Conference on Biodeterioration of Cultural Property, Bangkok, Thailand 1995*.
Rossol, M. and Jessup, W. C. (1996) 'No magic bullets: safe and ethical pest management strategies', *Museum Management and Curatorship* 15(2).
Rust, M. K., Daniel, V., Druzik, J. R. and Preusser, F. D. (1996) 'The feasibility of using modified atmospheres to control insect pests in museums', *Restaurator* 17(1).
Scott, G. H. (1991) 'Design and construction: building-out pests', in R. Gorham (ed.) *Ecology and Management of Food-Industry Pests*, Arlington: Association of Official Analytical Chemists.
Strang, T J. K. (1992) 'A review of published temperatures for the control of pest insects in museums', *Collection Forum* 8(2).
Strang, T. J. K. (1996) 'The effect of thermal methods of pest control on museum collections', in *Proceedings of 3rd International Conference on Biodeterioration of Cultural Property, Bangkok, Thailand 1995*.
[. . .]

Integrated pest management checklist

In the beginning

- Appoint an IPM co-ordinator
- Put together a team to prepare, co-ordinate and implement the pest control programme
- Tell the rest of the staff what you are doing and why

Survey the situation

- On a plan of building and grounds indicate galleries, stores and any other areas such as catering points, refuse disposal points, etc.
- Make a preliminary survey to identify pest access points, and high-risk areas and objects, and record this information on the plan
- Make an initial survey of building, adjacent grounds and collections for signs of pest activity, and assess level of activity

Initial steps

- Isolate any infested material or areas that are at immediate risk and arrange for remedial treatment
- Determine cause and origin of infestation
- Identify funds and resources for immediate preventive works

Preventive measures

- Screen windows and ventilation openings, eaves etc. and install bird netting if necessary
- Undertake necessary repairs and maintenance to building fabric
- Check cleaning regimes and modify if necessary
- Examine the pattern of movement of objects into and out of the museum
- Review existing pest control contracts

Ongoing activities

- Inspect all areas, and record and report findings
- Enhance your monitoring by instituting a trapping programme
- Operate a quarantine programme
- Take action to eradicate the inevitable minor pest infestation
- Maintain records of monitoring and treatments
- Keep staff and volunteers up to date with what is happening and encourage their co-operation
- Operate training and awareness-raising programmes
- Monitor and review IPM programme and consolidate into forward planning process

Longer-term initiatives

- Write down your IPM strategy and include it in your Collections Management Policy
- Formulate plans to deal with serious outbreaks

Chapter 14

Carpet Beetle: a pilot study in detection and control

Lynda Hillyer and Valerie Blyth

Introduction

A SERIES OF HOT SUMMERS and mild winters over the last few years has contributed to an increase in the activity of carpet beetle (*Anthrenus* spp.) particularly in the south of England.[1] Museum collections containing proteinaceous material such as wool, fur, feathers or mounted specimens provide potential food sources for the larvae (woolly bear) of carpet beetle which, unchecked, can cause widespread damage. Dramatic examples have been found in museums containing natural history specimens where entire entomological collections can be destroyed within months.[2,3]

South Kensington, where the Victoria and Albert Museum (V&A) is situated, is a recognized high-risk area for Guernsey carpet beetle (*Anthrenus sarnicus*).[4,5] It is a complex site of approximately 12 acres with 7 miles of galleries and stores, many of which contain material vulnerable to insect attack. Reserve collections of tapestries, carpets and theatre costume are stored at Blythe Road in West Kensington, 3 miles from the main museum site. Insects know no boundaries and what might appear to be a localized problem in one gallery or store is likely to occur in adjacent areas containing material from other collections. Evidence of insect activity, identified as Guernsey carpet beetle, was discovered in a textile gallery in the autumn of 1989 and resulted in the formation of a strategy for pest detection and control throughout the museum. Early on in the V&A project it became clear that successful detection and prevention of potential infestation could be achieved only with the collaboration of many different sections of the museum. One of the primary responsibilities of the

Source: S. Knell (ed.), *Care of Collections* (London, Routledge, 1994), pp. 217–233 (originally in *The Conservator* 16 (1992), pp. 65–77. This is an article whose final and definitive form has been published in *The Conservator*, Volume 16 © 1992 Institute of Conservation.

team initiating the pest control strategy was to heighten awareness throughout the museum by distributing basic information in the form of guidelines (Appendix 1), backed up by training sessions to staff most actively involved with the handling of objects. A second key element of the strategy was the recognition that on a large and complex site there is the likelihood of some level of continuous insect activity. In order to maintain a threshold which is as low as possible, parts of the strategy have to be repeated annually. Inevitably this leads to a shift in museum priorities as a greater proportion of time is spent on preventive conservation. Some of the work can be incorporated into other essential operations such as surveys or store moves, but there remains a core of routine, systematic and labour-intensive work which has to be built into each year's work programme.

Insect behaviour as the key to strategic planning

Integrated pest control policies are established practice in some museums in the United States, for example in parts of the Smithsonian Institution such as the Museum Support Centre and the National Museum of Natural History, and some excellent publications are available on strategies.[6,7] The initial stages of planning, however, can be daunting, particularly on a large site. The advice and guidance of an entomologist with expertise in current detection and control methods was available throughout the V&A project.[8]

It is essential that conservators are familiar with the life cycle and habits of the insect that they are trying to control and are able to communicate relevant information to a wide cross-section of museum staff. The biology of the insect and particular aspects of the life cycle of *Anthrenus* spp. proved relevant in planning a monitoring and detection policy (Appendix 1). More detailed descriptions of *Anthrenus verbasci*, a similar, related species, can be found in Hinton,[9] Busvine,[10] and Pinniger:[11]

- Insects are unable to regulate their body temperature. Their life cycles are dependent to a large extent on external (or seasonal) changes in temperature and relative humidity. However, a stable museum environment can provide conditions which may facilitate emergence of adult populations throughout the year[12] and an enclosed environment free of predators. Particularly favourable conditions may speed up the span of the life cycle of the carpet beetle, which can vary between ten months and two years.
- Adult beetles are phototropic and are attracted to short wavelength ultraviolet radiation. They fly from the safety of a dark area where pupation has taken place towards the light in order to leave the building to mate. Thus adults may be found on window-sills, particularly of north-facing windows, during peak emergence months of June, July and August.
- Female adults re-enter a building through chimneys, airvents and cracks in order to lay eggs. However, adults do not always have to leave the building to mate. Thus an infestation may become established and spread despite meticulous sealing of entry and exit points.
- Eggs are laid in dark crevices, usually close to a food source for the newly emerging larvae. Breeding reservoirs inside buildings are usually associated with poor

hygiene although it is not unknown for objects to be breeding reservoirs too. Typical external reservoirs are birds' nests, since feathers, bird droppings and broken birds' eggs provide a rich source of food for larvae. Nests can also be found inside a building under the eaves of the roof.

- Because carpet beetle larvae are small and can exist on dust, hair, fibres from clothing and dead insects they do not have to move far for food. However, larvae are highly mobile although their migration patterns are not fully understood. There is evidence that they are attracted to some food sources. They can gain access to storerooms, display cases, vulnerable areas through cracks and crevices.

- Within a major infestation, larvae may be found at several different developmental stages. A characteristic of new local infestations is the predominance of small larvae.

- As the larvae grow, they shed their skins six to eight times and these skins or moults may be one of the first signs of infestation. In adverse conditions where there is an insufficient food supply the number of moults may be much higher. The insect pupates in the last larval skin, which is left behind when the adult emerges. These large moults may be found in places which are some distance from infestation centres because the larvae have moved away to find a safe pupation site.

- *Anthrenus* spp. are able to tolerate humidities as low as 20–30 per cent RH.[13]

Detection

The development of a monitoring programme

The monitoring programme in the museum developed in the initial stages as a response to larval moults found by chance in a textile gallery in the North-East quadrant of the museum when a case display was being dismantled. This kind of evidence can indicate that infestation has already reached damaging levels. A detailed inspection of surrounding galleries revealed this to be so. Larvae were found in typical habitats: protected from light under a wool-upholstered chaise longue; concealed between the underside of a chair and the metal supports of its legs and hidden inside a sofa bed. Clues were provided by large numbers of moults in surrounding areas. This particular series of galleries, which include the main Tapestry gallery, Textile Study Room, Far Eastern Study Room, part of the carpet collection and furniture galleries containing wool upholstery, was recognized as a high-risk area and a trapping programme was initiated. The routine established in this suite of galleries served as a model for other galleries and stores throughout the museum.

Traps

Three types of sticky traps are in current use in the museum and in off-site storage areas at Blythe Road. The window trap capitalizes on the known preference of larvae for enclosed spaces and crevices. It has a central sticky area surrounded with corrugated borders. It is useful for display cases where trapped insects can be seen without moving the trap. It is also recommended for dusty areas since the sticky area is protected by a transparent cover. The Lo Line Roach trap (a cockroach trap with a roach bait) was used in preliminary trials but has been superseded by the smaller and more discreet Detector or Trappit trap. Both offer an enclosed environment with a sticky base. The Detector trap can be placed in any high-risk area. It is used under objects or directly on floors of galleries and stores. Lasiotraps (originally designed for the detection of cigarette beetles) are used on window-sills at Blythe Road in the summer months to intercept adult beetles flying towards the light; sticky tape laid across sills can be equally effective.

The traps are placed in a grid formation (the recommended interval is from 2 to 6 metres), numbered, dated and entered on a floorplan of the area. Dark hidden locations, for example in corners or under furnishings, are likely to produce better results. Traps should be changed every six months, or more frequently if they contain large numbers of insects, since larvae can avoid the sticky surface, moult, and escape from the trap. Care must be taken to check that the more exposed sticky areas of the Lo Line Roach trap and the Detector trap have not become clogged with dust, which makes them ineffective. At the V&A, checking by both conservation and curatorial staff takes place weekly in the spring and summer months and fortnightly in the autumn and winter. All finds are recorded on forms which are collected centrally and the information is compiled onto a spreadsheet programme.

Monitoring

Monitoring has two functions. Its primary purpose is to detect and identify insect activity. Since there is no bait or pheromone (sex attractant)[14] in these traps, insects only enter them by random or investigative movement. Thus preliminary inspection may indicate that an area needs closer investigation. For example, the discovery of one larva in a trap in the Textile Study Room led to a supplementary search in the surrounding area and twenty live larvae were discovered in a nearby heating duct, an area already recognized as a likely breeding reservoir. Where an infestation has already been identified, traps can highlight clusters of activity, seasonal activity and to some extent indicate the scale of the infestation. By careful documentation of finds, some clues as to the stage that the infestation has reached may be given. Sizes of larvae, for example, can reveal whether the infestation is new or is well established. If more information is needed about the intensity of an infestation in a particular area, the grid of traps can be tightened and more intensive searches can be organized. Some museums use bait, e.g. wheatgerm or fishmeal in sticky traps.[15] Dead insects, particularly silverfish, are attractive bait for *Anthrenus* spp.

Valuable and often surprising information about types of insect activity can be obtained. A localized infestation of brown carpet beetle (*Attagenus smirnovi*), a comparatively unusual type of beetle, was discovered in one gallery of the museum through the use of traps. Meticulous recording is essential. All insects and all stages of insect life need to be identified. The advice of an entomologist is vital, particularly in the early stages of monitoring. With experience, staff can soon become familiar with a range of common pest species.

Monitoring in the period from autumn 1989 to the summer of 1991 has revealed a variety of species active on the main museum site and at Blythe Road. At the

V&A site, Guernsey carpet beetle *Anthrenus sarnicus*, dermestid beetle *Anthrenocerus australis*, two spot carpet beetle *Attagenus pellio*, brown carpet beetle *Attagenus smirnovi*, hide beetle *Dermestes* sp. (probably *D. lardarius*) and wharf borer *Nacerdes melanura* were detected.

At the Blythe Road site, Guernsey carpet beetle *Anthrenus sarnicus*, varied carpet beetle *Anthrenus verbasci*, two spot carpet beetle *Attagenus pellio*, brown carpet beetle *Attagenus smirnovi*, plaster beetle *Cartodere filum*, Australian spider beetle *Ptinus tectus*, biscuit beetle *Stegobium paniceum*, common clothes moth *Tineola bisselliella*, brown clothes moth *Hofmannaphila pseudospretella* and silverfish *Lepisma saccharina* were found.

The second function of monitoring is to assess the broad picture of activity in the museum over several seasons. Migration patterns can be plotted. Monitoring has revealed levels of activity in what would normally be considered improbable areas. Moults have been found in cases containing metalwork and ceramics. Neither the case linings nor the adhesives used in the lining of the cases were a source of nutrition. Evidence of large moults suggested that the larvae had entered these cases in order to pupate. In a store containing theatre museum material, a disproportionate percentage of moults were collected from the calico cover of a dress rail which housed costume containing virtually no proteinaceous materials. Some live larvae were recovered but were very small. The larvae had been insufficiently nourished and had become progressively smaller. In such cases monitoring over a longer period may reveal whether there is a breeding reservoir still to be discovered in the vicinity or whether larvae have hatched in these areas by chance.

Monitoring allows the effectiveness of control methods to be evaluated. Data have now been collected for two years. At Blythe Road, where monitoring has been systematic and the site is easier to manage, levels of activity are much lower and have been eliminated from some areas. On the main museum site, activity of Guernsey carpet beetle *Anthrenus sarnicus* appears to be more widespread. However, the monitoring programme has been doubled since its start in the spring of 1990 and is now supported by regular routine inspections. Although the programme is well established, not enough consistent data has yet been accumulated to draw significant conclusions.

Methods of control

Elimination of the causes of infestation as the key to long-term pest control

Good housekeeping and hygiene

Carpet beetle infestation is almost always associated with poor hygiene. Initial inspections in the North-East quadrant of the museum revealed dust and debris in dark corners of galleries, areas which had been neglected because of their inaccessibility or because the necessary attachments for vacuum cleaners were not readily available. Given that larvae can survive on fibres from clothing, hair and dead insects, the importance of cleaning and the disturbance created by cleaning cannot be stressed enough. Training sessions have been organized both for cleaning staff and for specialist staff trained in object cleaning to inform them of the habits of carpet beetle and thus the need for vigilant and thorough cleaning. Vacuum cleaners can be transmitters of infestation if their bags are not changed after each cleaning session. The contents of a dust bag provide a virtual banquet for woolly bear larvae. Bags need to be sealed and destroyed to prevent transportation of infestation to other parts of the museum.

Deep cleaning of galleries and storage areas is essential to target possible breeding reservoirs and areas which are completely inaccessible for surface cleaning. Grilles covering cavities for heating pipes, where warm, dark and often very dirty conditions provide ideal breeding grounds, are one example. In two galleries it has been necessary to dismantle cases in order to gain access to covered heating pipes. Dead spaces under and behind cases are often neglected sources of infestation. Gaps between strips of parquet flooring can accumulate enough fibre and dirt to support growing larvae. Such crevices also provide attractive sites for egg-laying females. They need to be cleaned out thoroughly and sealed.

A new awareness of potential insect problems has been incorporated into the design of new galleries in the museum. Accessibility to all dead spaces for cleaning and/or treatment is now seen as an essential part of environmental planning.

The building

The South Kensington site is a particularly complex building. It was developed over a period of fifty years from 1857 'as a result of a tortuous and elaborate construction programme'.[16] This piecemeal development makes it extremely difficult to isolate the root causes of infestation. In summer months entry of adult beetles may be through open windows or doors. Museums surrounded by gardens or trees are particularly vulnerable. The most common entry points, however, are from the roof. Birds' nests, feathers, bird droppings and dead birds are typical habitats of *Anthrenus* spp. Entry is through chimneys, air vents, air-conditioning ducts and poorly fitting skylights. Regular inspections of the V&A roof and the roof area at Blythe Road have resulted in the removal of nests and the renewal of pigeon netting. Ducted air vents have been cleaned and blocked, fireplaces and chimneys sealed with fine-gauge metal mesh. Many windows in the museum are built over airbricks so standard prefilter mesh will be used to filter air flow necessary for the internal spaces.

Monitoring can often highlight a weakness in the building structure. The cause of infestation in a Blythe Road store was traced to redundant air vents which enabled adult beetles to enter. Findings in one basement area of the V&A could be related to a large number of sparrows' nests constructed into a nearby outside wall. The wall needs repointing and provides good anchorage for nests.

At least twice a month the museum site is inspected by a contract pest control company, Southern Pest Control, for dead rats and mice. *Dermestes* spp. (hide beetle) as well as *Anthrenus* spp. can thrive on rodent carcasses.

Insecticides

[Note from the editor: In 1992 when this article was written the use of chemical insecticides was legally permitted and standard museum practice.]

Deep cleaning of suspect areas is augmented by a six-monthly programme of treatment with residual insecticides. Coopex WP™ is a wettable power containing permethrin (3-phenoxybenzyl-3-(2,2-dichlorovinyl)-2,2 dimethylcyclopropanecarboxylate), a synthetic pyrethroid related to pyrethrin, a naturally occurring insecticidal compound which occurs in flowers of the single-flowered chrysanthemum (C. cinerariifolium).[17,18] It is not readily soluble and forms a suspension in water. When it is used as a surface spray it is deposited as a thin layer of particles on treated areas. These particles adhere to any insects which come into contact with them. The effects are rapid knockdown and subsequent kill. Where a wet application is inappropriate, an insecticidal dust containing the same formulation is used. Typical applications include crevices behind skirting-boards, dead spaces under cases, roof voids, cracks between wooden flooring, gaps between original flooring (as in a room setting) and the gallery floor and areas under heating grilles. Heat and ultraviolet radiation will reduce the effective life of this insecticide, so areas near heating pipes may need to be retreated frequently.

The disturbance created by building works is a major inhibitor of infestation and treatment with insecticide in such cases is primarily a preventive measure to eliminate any survivors. For example, as building work proceeded on the ground-floor level of the North-East quadrant of the museum in preparation for the 'Visions of Japan' exhibition which opened in September 1991, the site was treated with Coopex WP™. This area has particularly complex ventilation systems,[19] a common source of entry for *Anthrenus* spp. The recently opened Nehru Gallery of Indian Art and the Tsui Gallery of Chinese Art have also been treated.

Bendiocarb, 2.2 dimethyl-l,3-benzodioxol-4yl N-rnethylcarbamate, produced under the trade name Ficam™ (active ingredient – 80 per cent bendiocarb) has been used on the Blythe Road site. It is a wettable powder, although a dust formulation is also available. Areas treated have included air vents, window bays, floor ducts, fireplaces, water-tank lofts and cupboards under eaves. Application of both Coopex™ and Ficam™ has been undertaken by the consultant pest control company.

[. . .]

[Note from the editor – Bendiocarb is no longer available in the USA, due to health concerns. Dichlorvos, which was also used as a knockdown insecticide in the original paper and was legally used in 1992, is no longer (from 2002) available for public sale or use in the UK.]

[. . .]

Treatment of objects from suspect areas

Procedures have been established in the museum for action following the discovery of active insect infestation in or near objects. The underlying principle is that of confining the infestation by isolation. This may involve the isolation of an object by sealing it in polyethylene bags or sheeting or treating a particular space, for example a showcase, as a local isolation area.

Objects found to contain evidence of infestation are inspected by a conservator. Evidence in the form of larval moults may or may not be a sign of recent activity. Moults can survive intact for many years before finally disintegrating. In such cases the object is rigorously examined and particular attention is paid to those areas known to be typical habitats of larvae or attractive sites for egg-laying, for example inside folds, seam allowances and linings on garments. Good torches are essential and a magnifying glass is often useful since eggs can rarely be seen with the naked eye. After inspection the object is cleaned using a vacuum cleaner to remove the moults. Record-keeping is vital. If moults are left in situ it is impossible to determine at a later date whether infestation is recent or not. The object may be returned to its case or store depending on the picture presented by monitoring and inspection. If a store cannot be guaranteed free of infestation, the object must be protected and it is returned to the store in a sealed package. Where a gallery cannot be guaranteed free of infestation, the showcases may have to be emptied for a prolonged period.

If the object presents positive evidence of insect activity it is sealed in polyethylene or Tyvek (a polyethylene material which permits air exchange through minute apertures) and placed in a quarantine area. Ideally this is a sealed room where isolated objects can be inspected, usually after a period of at least ten days, to determine whether any eggs have hatched. Objects awaiting further treatment are stored and sealed in this quarantine area. Loan objects may be included in this category. Both incoming objects from other institutions and objects returned from loan requests are subject to scrupulous examination. Occasionally it may be appropriate to treat the display case as an isolation area. After inspecting, cleaning and recording the condition of the case, any dead space under the case is treated with an appropriate insecticide. [. . .]

Freezing as a method of control

Freezing at the appropriate temperature and exposure time is a simple and effective method of pest control and is particularly suitable for textile objects. Unlike alternative chemical means of control, for example fumigation by methyl bromide or sulfuryl fluoride, it is both environmentally safe and safe for operators. No residue can be left in the object. More work is needed on the effects of freezing on degraded organic materials but current research[20] does not indicate any damage to fibres as the result of exposure to low temperatures.

Two freezing projects have been carried out at the V&A. The first, in the summer of 1990, was organized in response to the preliminary findings of larval activity in textile galleries in the autumn of 1989. The second, carried out in the summer of 1991, was largely a preventive measure. Five hundred tapestries and carpets were moved from a suspect store on the main museum site to new storage at Blythe Road which monitoring had shown to be pest-free.

Insects have mechanisms which enable them to survive very cold temperatures. They can build up sugars and glycerols in the tissue of their cells which lower their freezing-point in preparation for the winter months. If an insect which has been acclimatized to warm temperatures or to the relatively stable environment of a museum is exposed to a sudden drop in temperature, it is generally unable to survive. The speed of the drop in temperature is critical, although it is not known what specific temperatures are needed to kill each development stage of particular species of museum pests. Pupae and eggs are known to be more resistant than adults and larvae and it has been noted that the feeding stages of insect life are the least resistant to freezing.[21] Much of the research carried out on freezing as a method of control for pest infestation has been carried out in the stored food industry. Mullen and Arbogast[22] found that survival times of the eggs of five common insect pests of stored food products decreased rapidly in direct relationship to the lowering of temperature or to the length of exposure time. Exposure to −20°C achieved 95 per cent mortality for all five species within a few hours.

Freezing is a well-established practice in some museums in the United States, Scandinavia and Australia. One of the first large-scale freezing projects to be undertaken was at the Beinecke Library at Yale University in 1977 to eradicate an infestation of Gastrallus sp. (Anobiidae).[23] Using a blast freezer (a food storage freezer which has fans behind the freezing coils which can move the cooled air very quickly around the chamber) a total of 37,000 books were treated over a period of thirteen months at a temperature of −29°C and an exposure time of seventy-two hours.

The most relevant information on the effect of using freezing as a control method for infested museum artefacts is contained in a Canadian publication.[24] It states:

When living cells (90 per cent water content) are subjected to low temperatures, depending on the rate of cooling and thawing and the time at the final temperature reached, specific physical and chemical changes occur, some of which may be lethal. The actual cause of death is not known − whether a combination of events or a single factor is involved has not been conclusively shown.

The literature review on the lethal effects of freezing on living cells includes dehydration, osmotic swelling, loss of bound water and formation of ice crystals.

A common practice is double exposure of infested material to temperatures of −18°C or −20°C. Objects are frozen for a period of forty-eight hours, taken out of the freezer and left to return to ambient temperature for forty-eight hours. They are then replaced in the freezer unit for a further forty-eight hours. The effect of this freeze–thaw–freeze cycle ensures that any insect life not killed in the first exposure will be eradicated in the repeat exposure. It is thought that eggs respond to the interim rise in temperature and humidity and hatch. Few insects would be able to withstand the extreme fluctuation in temperatures used in this method. Most domestic freezers operate within these parameters. For small collections and as an emergency measure for larger collections this method is useful although the size of the objects that can be treated is necessarily limited.

This approach was considered when planning the first freezing programme at the V&A but the logistics of handling a large number of fragile tapestries twice were daunting and most of the textiles included in this first project were too large for a chest freezer. Recent research by the Danish entomologist Toke Skytte, at the Museum of Natural History in Aarhus, Denmark, confirmed the effectiveness of the Yale method.[25] Skytte found that a temperature of −30°C was lethal to all stages of insect life tested. Freezing at −30°C has also been practised for several years at the Museum of Textile History in Boras, Sweden.[26]

The freezing programmes at the V&A were organized on this basis. A cold storage unit capable of reaching a temperature of −30°C was hired for both projects. Although not classified as a blast freezer, the unit is fitted with a fan which accelerates circulation of cold air. A defrost cycle operates for one hour every six hours, causing

a rise in temperature to –18°C. This fluctuation is of immense benefit for the eradication of insects since it simulates a freeze–thaw–freeze cycle at very low temperatures.
A temperature of –20°C can be reached within five hours and –29°C can be reached
within ten hours. The total exposure time between the first drop to –29°C and the
last recorded temperature of –30°C within a seventy-two-hour cycle averages at sixty
hours.

The internal measurements of the cold storage unit are 2.20 m (height), 2.20 m
(width) and 5.30 m (length), large enough to accommodate tapestries on 5 m length
rollers. It was fitted with Dexion™ shelving in various arrangements according to
sizes of objects being treated. Each shelf was covered with a layer of plastazote. In
order to work at low temperatures, staff were equipped with protective clothing:
polar suits, balaclavas, gloves and freezer boots.

Exposure of common museum pests to low temperatures in the cold storage unit

Since so little published research exists on the exact temperature and time exposure
needed to kill each stage of particular species of insect life, bioassays using live insects
were carried out during both freezing projects. Where possible different developmental stages of insect life found in the museum were included in the experiments
in order to establish the efficiency of using a single exposure treatment at a lower
temperature.

In August 1990, ten treatment tubes containing mixed-age larvae of *Tineola bisselliella* (webbing clothes moth) were placed in sealed bags and placed in the cold storage unit. They were exposed to temperatures of –30°C within a seventy-two hour
period and then returned to the laboratory and incubated at 25°C. No adult moths
emerged from any of the tubes. Seventy per cent emergence was observed from a
control group of moth larvae.

In August 1991, during a seventy-hour exposure cycle to temperatures of
–29.5°C, the following insects were placed in treatment tubes in the cold storage
unit: webbing clothes moth *Tineola bisselliella* (larvae, adults), casemaking clothes
moth *Tineola pellionella* (larvae), furniture carpet beetle *Anthrenus flavipes* (eggs,
adults), Guernsey carpet beetle *Anthrenus sarnicus* (larvae), brown carpet beetle *Attagenus smirnovi* (larvae, adults), varied carpet beetle *Anthrenus verbasci* (larvae, adults)
and two spot carpet beetle *Attagenus pellio* (adults).

All insects appeared to be dead on removal from the cold storage chamber.
No recovery was apparent and inspection after seven days confirmed 100 per cent
mortality.

Types of objects suitable for freezing

Many organic materials can be treated by freezing. Objects must be able to withstand
minor changes in relative humidity and consequently minor dimensional changes
which occur as the inevitable result of the decrease in temperature on cooling and the
increase in temperature as conditions in the cold storage unit rise towards ambient
levels.

Objects must be dry. Ice damage cannot occur when dry materials are subjected to low temperatures. None of the moisture content of the dry object including the intercellular bound water is frozen at low temperatures.[27]

It is not advisable or necessary to treat non-adsorbent materials (i.e. those that cannot take up moisture vapour) by freezing because of the danger of surface condensation. Such materials include metals, ceramics, glass. Textiles with metal attachments or metal-thread embroidery or with glass or ceramic components, however, can usually be exposed to low temperatures providing there is enough textile to act as the adsorber. A buffer material such as cotton-wool or thick acid-free paper can be included with the object. Silica gel can be included but it has not been used in this way in either freezing project.

Organic objects which are desiccated or very degraded and materials with a high water content such as gelatin may not be suitable for freezing. Objects with stratified layers, for example paintings on canvas and furniture with inlaid surfaces or veneers, are unsuitable for treatment by freezing. Many twentieth-century textiles may have plastic components. Polymers may be taken below their glass transition temperature (Tg) at low temperatures and become brittle. This is a reversible effect but care must be taken when handling objects which contain plastics at low temperatures. Empirical tests carried out in the cold storage unit using Mowilith DNC2 poly(vinylacetate), a copolymer of PVAC and dibutyl maleate, Beva ethylene-vinylacetate copolymer-Ketone resin N, and a silicone adhesive, FS2, showed no loss of flexibility or bond strength after exposure to low temperatures.

Procedures for the treatment of objects at low temperatures

The details of these procedures were worked out experientially during the course of the two projects but they closely followed those adopted by colleagues in the United States and Scandinavia. Objects are prepared for treatment by wrapping in medium-weight polyethylene to form a reasonably close-fitting bag. The purpose of the bag is to protect the object from condensation when it is removed from the cold storage unit. Where the polyethylene needs to be joined to create a bag, it should be folded over twice to form a secure and airtight seam. The seam can then be sealed with aluminium ducting tape. Care must be taken to ensure that there are no apertures in the bag.

A quarantine area must be created for this procedure in order to prevent the possible spread of infestation. For the first project which was carried out in an off-site storage area at Battersea, a polyethylene tent was erected containing two air-conditioning units. For the second, the bagging of objects was carried out in the main V&A site using the suspect storage area which was being vacated.

Objects are placed in the cold storage unit when it has reached a temperature of at least −10°C. Because of the defrost cycle of the unit it was not always possible to predict the exact temperature at the loading for each run. When the doors of the unit are opened there is an inevitable rise in temperature, usually to 0°C. Objects must be loaded at ambient temperature. It is essential that insects are not given an opportunity to acclimatize to a cooler temperature. Acclimatization can occur within the relatively short time span of eight to eighteen hours. Objects must remain in the cold storage unit for seventy-two hours.

The cold storage unit is switched off six hours before the objects are removed. One hour before the objects are removed the doors of the unit are opened to ensure that objects are brought back to ambient temperature slowly.

Objects are left in their sealed bags for at least forty-eight hours. There should be no condensate on the outside of the polyethylene bag when it is opened.

The object is inspected for any signs of insect life. Any moults or dead larvae must be removed using a vacuum cleaner. Left in situ, they provide misleading evidence for further inspections and a food source for future infestation. The object is repacked for storage in a safe area.

Changes of temperature and relative humidity during the cold storage cycle

The complexity of the relationship between temperature, relative humidity and the moisture content and moisture regain capacity of the object warrants greater study, which is beyond the scope of this paper. However, it is worth commenting on the observations of these complex relationships during this work.

A data logger capable of operating to a lower temperature limit of −50°C was used to monitor several cycles of temperature and humidity for several cycles of the cold storage unit during both projects.

Changes occur in the moisture equilibrium of objects when subjected to freezing. As the temperature is lowered during the cold storage cycle, the air in the sealed package containing the object is unable to retain its moisture content and excess moisture is adsorbed onto the object. Some conservators recommend partial evacuation of air from the package in an attempt to modify this effect. This was tried but found to be difficult to achieve. As objects are removed from the cold chamber, they experience an inevitable and sudden rise in relative humidity. Objects can be placed in an interim refrigerated unit to adjust the temperature more slowly or the unit can be switched off several hours in advance of removal.[28] Blast freezers are reputed to operate at constant temperature and humidity.[29]

Readings were taken at the core and on the surface of a dense object, an upholstered couch, in a short experimental cycle in the cold storage unit during the 1990 project. A time lag of one hour was observed before the core temperature started to drop. The total exposure time to temperatures lower than −28°C was longer (nine hours in a twenty-two hour run) at the core than at the surface (seven hours) due to the thermal mass of the object.

During the 1991 project the cold storage unit was unable to reach a temperature of −30°C with a full load of twenty tapestries. The project was carried out in hot summer months, which undoubtedly affected the efficiency of the unit when it was fully loaded. The timing of the 1991 project was dependent on the store move which had been planned to take place from June to September. The unit reached a temperature of −29.5°C at its lowest point. It took eighteen hours to reach −20°C and forty hours to reach −28°C. External factors probably exacerbated the rise in RH, as the objects encountered the warm ambient conditions on removal from the unit. The surface of the object will be most affected by these changes. In every case each object was protected by a covering of M tissue, a thick acid-free paper, which acts as a buffer to humidity fluctuations. There was no condensation at any time during either project.

More work needs to be done on controlling the final rate of the rise in relative humidity. The subjection of an object to temporary changes in humidity has to be weighed against the dangers of leaving objects exposed to potential insect damage.

Conclusion

The mechanics of an integrated pest control strategy are now well established in the museum but it is still too early to evaluate its long-term success. The pilot study has acted as a blueprint for future applications but has been recognized as a learning process. Key factors are the detection and monitoring programme and the collaboration of staff from different sections of the museum in implementing the policy. Future developments include plans to adapt the methyl bromide chamber in the museum for use with CO_2 gas so that objects not suitable for freezing can also be treated with a non-toxic method. Freezing projects will in the future be carried out in late spring so that external factors do not hinder either the workings of the unit or the return of objects to ambient temperature. The continuity of any of the aspects of the strategy is dependent on maintaining consistently high levels of communication, vigilance and co-operation. Some indication of the spread of responsibility across the museum is given in Appendix 1. The monitoring programme is to be expanded with the help of a wider section of museum staff to obtain a more comprehensive picture of insect activity.

The strategy is labour-intensive and can disrupt other work programmes. The combined store move and freezing programme in 1991, for example, employed twenty people on a rotation basis for three months. Detection of pests, however, is now recognized as a priority in collection management. This collaboration with the Conservation Department in a shift towards preventive conservation for at least a proportion of the year's work programme is a significant step for future success. One of the difficulties of monitoring a complex site is discovering what constitutes an acceptable level of insect activity. Despite numerous insect sitings the actual proportion of insect-damaged objects has been very small. Out of 600 objects selected for treatment by freezing, only 2–3 per cent showed positive signs of insect infestation and the rest were from suspect or high-risk areas.

Safety

Under the Control of Substances Hazardous to Health Regulations, institutions or companies must make a written assessment of the risks, precautions and emergency procedures associated with the work they will be undertaking.

[. . .]

Under the Control of Pesticides Regulations (1986)[30] it is now illegal for unskilled or untrained staff to use pesticides. Applications of Coopex™ and Ficam™ were undertaken by a contract pest control company.

Training sessions were organized for staff working in the freezer unit, and staff involved in loading and unloading the unit were issued with protective clothing.

A written safe system of work, to comply with the Health and Safety at Work Act (1974),[31] was issued to staff working at low temperatures. The main points are:

- Staff must be medically fit with no minor ailments and no heart or lung conditions. Staff taking prescribed medication should seek advice from their doctor on their suitability to undertake this work.
- No member of staff must spend longer than twenty minutes in any thirty-minute period in the refrigerated area. A first-aider conversant with the identification and treatment of hypothermia and frostbite must be on hand at all times that cold temperatures are encountered.
- Staff must not consume alcohol before or during the work cycle.
- Staff must not work alone in the refrigerated area.
- Protective clothing must be worn and must be kept dry.

In addition, caution must be taken in entering the freezer unit at low temperatures, since the surface of the floor can be slippery. Caution must be taken when lifting heavy objects into or out of the freezer unit.

Appendix 1: Victoria and Albert Museum guidelines

Woolly bear – carpet beetle infestation

The museum has a serious carpet beetle infestation. Detection, monitoring and control depend on the vigilance and co-operation of all staff involved in the care of collections and in the care of the building: conservation and curatorial staff, manual attendants, object cleaners and the Department of Building and Estates.

Textile objects constructed of wool are at risk throughout the building, also any museum object of which wool is a component. Wool-felt in display cases may also harbour larvae and eggs.

Basic habits of the woolly bear carpet beetle

Adult carpet beetles enter the museum from May to September through:

- open doors and windows;
- ventilation shafts;
- air-conditioning ducts;
- 'dead' spaces in roof areas;
- pot plants and cut flowers indoors;
- shrubs and plants outdoors.

The warmer the summer the greater is the risk. One fertilized female can lay enough eggs to begin an infestation. Birds' nests and dead pigeons on roof areas provide breeding grounds for pests.

Each adult lays from 20 to 100 eggs. Eggs and emerging larvae are very difficult to detect. Emerging larvae can penetrate crevices and tiny cracks.

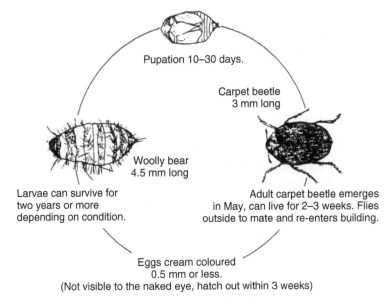

Pupation 10–30 days.

Carpet beetle
3 mm long

Woolly bear
4.5 mm long

Larvae can survive for
two years or more
depending on condition.

Adult carpet beetle emerges
in May, can live for 2–3 weeks. Flies
outside to mate and re-enters building.

Eggs cream coloured
0.5 mm or less.
(Not visible to the naked eye, hatch out within 3 weeks)

Figure 14.1 Life cycle of the woolly bear carpet beetle

Larvae are voracious feeders. They will attack wool, felt, fur, feathers, hide and silk. They will eat through other materials to reach these materials. They prefer:

- gloomy, dusty and dirty conditions;
- crevices and enclosed spaces, e.g. behind hangings, at the side of upholstery, under cushions, etc.;
- soiled areas and soiled objects.

They can survive for up to two years or more. Emergence as adults depends on conditions (e.g. food, temperature, disturbance). Warm summers and mild winters speed up development and can lead, if unchecked, to large-scale infestations.

As the larvae grow they leave moults, i.e. fine cast skins. One larva can deposit up to six or seven moults. Detection of moults may be the first sign of infestation.

CONTROL OF INFESTATION REQUIRES CO-OPERATION AND VIGILANCE.

INSECTS DO NOT LIKE TO BE DISTURBED.

Inspection

This must be part of an on-going programme. A system must be worked into each year's cycle.

Where should one inspect?

'Dead' spaces, dark corners, areas of poor hygiene, storage areas, display cases and textile objects on open display should be inspected.

How should one look?

A methodical system should be established. A good torch should be used. Anything suspicious should be reported to the Textiles Conservation Department.

Vacuum cleaning is essential:

- to improve hygiene in galleries;
- to diminish the spread of infestation;
- to create disturbances in the life cycle of carpet beetle by vacuum cleaning. When using a vacuum cleaner:
- ensure all nozzles are thoroughly washed in hot water and detergent afterwards. Nozzles can pick up eggs and redeposit them elsewhere in the museum.
- make sure the bags used in the vacuum cleaners are sealed and disposed of after each cleaning session. Change the bag after each session.
- be vigilant about crevices, dark corners, areas with access to roof space.

Traps

Sticky insect traps have been distributed by Conservation to be placed in galleries, stores, display cases. These traps monitor the extent of the infestation. PLEASE LEAVE THEM IN SITU. It is very important that findings on traps (positive and negative) are recorded on the form devised by staff from the Textiles Conservation and Collections Departments.

Division of observation and cleaning

Conservation and curatorial staff, object cleaners, Buildings and Estates Department

To monitor insect traps using insect pest control form to record findings. Storage and gallery areas need to be observed regularly.

Manual attendants

Please help by meticulous cleaning of galleries, particularly those containing woollen objects (e.g. upholstered furniture, carpets) on open display. Better hygiene and disturbance of these areas by cleaning is basic to pest control. Please observe guidelines regarding the cleaning of nozzles on vacuum cleaners and sealing and disposing of vacuum cleaning bags after each gallery session.

Please ensure that traps are retained in the galleries.

Object cleaners

Please be meticulous about cleaning under and behind objects, and in crevices on upholstered furniture as outlined in gallery training. Please observe the guidelines regarding the cleaning of nozzles and disposing of vacuum cleaning bags after each gallery session.

Buildings and Estates

Please make periodic checks of 'dead' roof spaces and areas with openings to the roof. Be alert to evidence of birds' nests.

THE MUSEUM IS A HUGE AND COMPLEX SITE.

THIS INFESTATION NEEDS THE CO-OPERATION OF ALL SECTIONS INVOLVED.

Notes and references

1 Shaw, M. R. (1991) 'New threats from museum beetles', *SSCR Journal* 2(3).
2 Armes, N. J. (1984) 'Aspects of the biology of the Guernsey carpet beetle, *Anthrenus sarnicus* and control of dermestid beetle pests in museums', *ICOM Committee for Conservation 7th Triennial Meeting, Copenhagen* 84.13.1.
3 Dr George McGavin, Head of Entomology Collection, Oxford University Museum, personal communication.
4 Armes, op. cit., p. 1.
5 David Pinniger, consultant entomologist, personal communication.
6 Story, K. O. (1985) *Approaches to Pest Management in Museums*, Washington, D.C.: Conservation Analytical Laboratory, Smithsonian Institution.
7 Zycherman, L. A. and Schrock, J. R. (eds) (1988) *A Guide to Museum Pest Control*, Washington, D.C.: Foundation of the American Institute for Conservation of Historic and Artistic Works and the Association of Systematics Collection (joint publication).
8 David Pinniger, consultant entomologist, MAFF Central Science Laboratory, London Road, Slough SL3 7HJ.
9 Hinton, H. E. (1945) *Monograph of the Beetles Associated with Stored Products*, London: British Museum (Natural History).
10 Busvine, J. R. (1980) *Insects and Hygiene: The Biology and Control of Insect Pests of Medical and Domestic Importance*, London: Chapman & Hall.
11 Pinniger, D. (1990) *Insect Pests in Museums,* Denbigh, Clwyd: Archetype Publications.
12 Armes, op. cit.
13 Child, R. E. and Pinniger, D. B. (1987) 'Insect pest control in museums', in J. Black (ed.) *Recent Advances in the Conservation and Analysis of Artifacts*, London: Institute of Archaeology, University of London, p. 305.
14 Pheromones are specific to each insect species. The pheromone for varied carpet beetle (*Anthrenus verbasci*) has been identified but it is unlikely to be developed for specialized museum use. See Pinniger, D. (1991) 'New developments in the detection and control of insects which damage museum collections', *Biodeterioration Abstracts* 5(2): 126.
15 Zycherman and Schrock 'Trapping techniques for dermestid and anobiid beetles', op. cit., p. 109.
16 Physick, J. (1982) *The Victoria and Albert Museum: The History of the Building*, Oxford: Phaidon & Christies, p. 13.
17 Pinniger, *Insect Pests in Museums*, pp. 34–35.
18 Linnie, M. J. (1990) 'Professional notes', *Museum Management and Curatorship* 9(4): 421.

19 Physick, op. cit., Chapter IV.
20 Florian, M. L. (1986) 'The freezing process, effects on insects and artifact materi-
    als', *Leather Conservation News* 3(1): 1.
21 Salt, R. W. (1970) 'Analysis of insect freezing temperature distributions', *Canadian
    Journal of Zoology* 48: 205–8.
22 Mullen, M. A. and Arbogast, R. T. (1978) 'Time-temperature-mortality relation-
    ships for various stored product insect eggs and chilling times for selected commodi-
    ties', *Journal of Economic Entomology* 72(4): 476–8.
23 Nesheim, K. (1984) 'The Yale non-toxic method of eradicating book-eating insects
    by deep freezing', *Restaurator* 6: 147–64.
24 Florian, op. cit., p. 1.
25 Richter, J., Lecturer, Det Kongelige Danske Kunstakademi, Copenhagen, personal
    communication.
26 Haggren, A., Conservator, Textil Museet, Boras, Sweden, personal communica-
    tion.
27 Florian, M. L. (1987) 'The effect of artifact materials of the fumigant ethylene oxide
    and freezing used in insect control', *ICOM Committee for Conservation 8th Triennial
    Meeting, Sydney*, Marina del Ray, CA: ICOM-CC, GCI.
28 Florian, 'The freezing process', p. 9.
29 Smith, R. D. (1984) 'Background, use and benefits of blast freezers in the preven-
    tion and extermination of insects', *Biodeterioration* 6, Papers presented at the 6th
    International Biodeterioration Symposium, Washington, D.C.
30 The Control of Pesticides Regulations (1986).
31 The Health and Safety at Work Act (1974).

Chapter 15

Pest Control for Temperate vs. Tropical Museums: North America vs. Southeast Asia

Lim Chong Quek, Muhammadin Razak and Mary W. Ballard

Introduction

PESTS WHICH DAMAGE ART WORKS and artifacts are a cause of concern to museums and archives throughout the world. The aggregation of large numbers of similar objects in a single collection space can attract and maintain a large pest population. Similarly, the conditions for the optimum preservation of the objects can be simultaneously the preferred climate for pest growth. Climate itself can affect the type and species of most prevalent pest, and thus, which museum objects are most at risk. In order to develop a pest control strategy, the types of pests that threaten a collection need to be identified and reviewed.

Climate and collection specific pests

Table 15.1 summarizes the major differences between North American and Southeast Asian museum pest problems. A great deal of North American and European litera-ture on pest control in museums involves the control of textile pests.[9] These textile pests are divided into two families: the dermestids called carpet beetles (*Anthrenus* and *Attagenus*) and the clothes moths (*Tineola bisselliella H.* and *Tinea pellionella L.*) These insects attack keratin, the sulfur containing amino acids found in wool, hair, and camelid fibers (sheep wool, llama, alpaca, vicuna, camel, and goat hair products).

Because of the climatic conditions of the Americas and Europe, both wool and camelid fibers are seasonally used today in clothing and furnishings and were used in the past. Thus, not only do museum staff and visitors wear wool clothing subject to

Source: *ICOM-CC 9th Triennial Meeting, Dresden, German Democratic Republic 26–31 August 1990*, Los Angeles: ICOM-CC, 1990, pp. 817–821.

Table 15.1 Common museum pest control problems

Object	Insect	North America	ASEAN Region
Basketry	Cigarette beetle	rare	critical
Paper	Silverfish	rare	critical
	Cockroach:		
	American	occasional	common
	Asian (southern USA)	occasional	N.A.
	Brown-banded	occasional	N.A.
	Brown	occasional	N.A.
	German	occasional	common
	Oriental		
Structures	Termites:		
	Subterranean	occasional	critical
	Drywood	rare	critical
Textiles (wool, hair)	Carpet beetles	critical	rare
	Clothes moths	critical	rare
Wood:			
Softwood	Furniture beetle	Occasional	N.A.
Hardwood	Furniture beetle	Occasional	N.A.
	Powder-post beetle	occasional	N.A.*

Notes: N.A. means Not applicable, i.e. not indigenous.
* Not listed as indigenous to ASEAN countries, but capable of attacking bamboo.
References: 1, 2, 4, 9, 10.

infestation, but also large portions of American and European textile collections have such fibers – tapestries, carpets, folk art and archeological objects, military uniforms and flags – as their principal component, or as part of the object – as the batting inside quilts and as stuffing in upholstered furniture.

These collections are constantly threatened by the infestation of keratin-eating insects, particularly those objects with soiled fabrics or those with brushed (napped) surfaces. Staff and visitors can inadvertently introduce such pests to the museum environment and also provide the keratin-based fiber dust to support the initial growth.

Consequently, it is extremely important for museums in temperate climates to maintain a dust-free environment. This concept is so engrained that the museum staff and the general public alike associate dust with insects and vermin. Textile objects are routinely examined and vacuumed to reduce the hazard of insect infestation. Isolating textiles by means of storage containers (i.e. wrapped in acid free tissue paper and then boxed) is oftentimes the preferred textile storage method.

In Southeast Asia, keratin-containing fibers are not an indigenous fiber source for fabrics. Both modern usage and antique collections are restricted largely to cellulosic materials (cotton, abaca, ramie, hemp) or silk. The latter does not contain a significant cysteine or methionine amino acid content. Thus, dust in the Southeast Asian domestic environment and in the museum environment does not foster the same pest control problem.

By contrast, silverfish, a minor pest for most American libraries, archives, or museums, can constitute a more sizable problem in ASEAN[11] countries, where they can threaten paper, books, textiles, and basketry. Open aggregations of materials like library stacks or archival collections are particularly at risk. Tropical conditions do not provide a cold season "kill" of the insects in their outdoor harborages. This is also true of cockroach harborages. While American museums can often restrict pest control operations to specific basement or food handling areas, ASEAN museums have formulated several policies and procedures to reduce this threat of infestation. Restrictions on the use of photocopies, extraneous paper files, and memoranda are routine.

In ASEAN countries these precautions are natural to everyone there: coffee and tea cups are lidded when not in use; waste-paper baskets are emptied twice daily; desks are wiped down, as are floors. Gallery openings are catered with food located outside the museum building. In Singapore, the common species are the American cockroach (*Periplaneta Americana*), the German cockroach (*Blatella Germanica*), and the Oriental cockroach (*Blatta Orientalis*).[1, 2, 5]

Although wood-boring beetles (*Anobium punctatum DeG.* and *Lyctus* spp.) are major pest problems in European museums and historic buildings, they have not been a serious problem for collections in the United States. With the ban of chlorinated insecticides, however, this type of insect infestation is an increasing concern. Painting stretchers as well as furniture have been infested; American furniture conservators are trained to identify the characteristic frass and bore-holes of these pests. ASEAN conservators are rarely faced with those wood-boring beetles because of the extensive use of the insect resistant woods traditionally employed by artists and craftsmen. This extensive use of tropical hardwoods, like teak, both in the museum furnishings such as cabinets and display cases and in the antiques themselves, including the Chinese furniture, has meant that the ASEAN collections are largely free of this hazard.

Termites, however, can attack structural components of the tropical museum buildings and Western-type wood display cases. Anecdotal evidence of rapid damage continues to be exchanged among Southeast Asian conservators. This damage may be caused by subterranean or drywood termites (e.g. *Coptotermes curvignathus H.* and *Cryptotermes cynocephalus L.*). Historic structures in North America are most likely to be damaged by the Eastern subterranean termite (*Reticulotermes flavipes*, Kollar) where the average minimum winter temperatures do not reach –29°C.[4, 10]

Another major hazard to ASEAN museum collections is a small (2mm) insect, the "cigarette beetle" (*Lasioderna serricorne F.*), which routinely attacks tropical collections of bamboo and rattan. The breadth of the infestation threat that these insects pose is most readily apparent when Western observers remember that, historically, Southeast Asia was prized for its spice growing: these *Anobiidae* not only feed on spices but are also characterized as the most destructive members of the *Anobiidae* family.[7] Pest control for cigarette beetles, therefore, includes chemical treatment. Insecticides, with their residual protection, are preferred by conservators over fumigation for basketry.[3]

Implications for treatment and international loans

Objects and packing materials transported from one museum to another within a single climatic region bring certain entomological risks. With similar collections and similar climates, the prevalent and most serious infestation problems will be similar. At both the origin and the destination, conservators and registrars will examine the crates for the same insect problems. Otherwise, untreated infestations could spread to the host museum's collections.

When objects and packing materials travel abroad, particularly across climatic boundaries, the entomological implications may be more difficult to recognize. The conservators and registrars may be unfamiliar with the signs of infestation; they will certainly be less familiar with treatment. While the host museum's collections may be at a lower risk due to its dissimilar materials and external climate, the incoming loan may be less well monitored. For example, the protocols for woolen textiles would not be familiar to staff at the National Museum, Singapore nor would the characteristics of incipient infestation. Any carpet beetle or moth infestation that arrived with a loan shipment might not be an issue for the Singaporean collections, but could cause serious damage to the loaned textiles. Similarly, textiles being returned to an ASEAN museum from the West might be carefully rolled on acid free tubes, wrapped in acid free paper, and packed in acid free cardboard containers. Such a shipment is standard and acceptable in temperate regions, but would be an ideal harborage for local pests in Southeast Asia.

Perhaps more important, such loans may be subject to minor repairs with inappropriate materials. Thus, a tropical museum's basketry loaned to a temperate climate museum might be repaired without consideration of the need for close monitoring in its ASEAN home; textiles might be permanently mounted with corrugated acid free board, a procedure acceptable in North America where the cockroach and silverfish problems are not severe. Temperate climate conservators cannot predict the possible synergism between their "safe" conservation materials and unknown pest populations.

Conclusion

The conservation field must be prepared to recognize not only the insect hazards to collections in their home institutions, but also the implications of these hazards to other institutions abroad. Particularly important, with the present tendency for loans and exhibitions across climates, is the need for recognition of inherent differences. Museum construction, policies, monitoring, laboratory activities, gallery design, storage, and exhibitions, and even preventive measures may well have been created to deal with specific indigenous insect problems. Conservation treatment programs developed locally must be evaluated in light of their response to specific biodeterioration threats characteristic of the climate within which the local museum, its collections, and its conservators live and work. Registrars and conservators are oftentimes surprised at the choice of packing materials from cross-climate institutions. Rarely are they aware that the selection may be due to knowledge of local insect proclivities, rather than a lack of more "appropriate" supplies.

Museums in both climatic conditions need to be more observant and more forthright about the potential insect hazards in their climatic zone. It is not enough to request permission to fumigate nor is it useful to recommend a particular type of pesticide, unless the insect pest is actually identified and the dosage necessary to eradicate that particular species is clearly determined. Long-term effects of even relatively benign agents can be serious.[6,8] The actual chemical treatment technology can only be properly transferred under carefully prescribed conditions. The conservation treatment preparatory to an exhibition cannot be effectively transferred without careful assessment of the potential biodeterioration mechanisms of the climatic zones involved. The museum environment exists within a larger climatic and biological zone; that larger zone may be forgotten only at the risk of irreparable damage to cultural patrimony.

Notes and references

1 Chew, Tee Sim. National Museum, Singapore, personal communication, December, 1988 and January, 1989.

2 Chong, Patrick. Rentokil Pte Ltd., Singapore, personal communication, December, 1988 and September, 1989.

3 *Core Manual, Maryland Pesticide Applicator Training Series* (1986/7) College Park, Maryland: University of Maryland.

4 Dynamac Corporation (1984) *Structural Pest I: Termites*, National Park Service Information Package.

5 Lee, R. Managing Director, SGS AllPest Management Pte Ltd., Singapore, personal communication, December, 1988.

6 *"Naphthalene" Chemical Fact Sheet* (1983), Cambridge, MA, USA: University Health Services, Environmental Health and Safety, Harvard University.

7 Meltzer, J. Technical Services, Smithsonian Institution, personal communication, April, 1989.

8 *"P-Dichlorobenzene," Chemical Fact Sheet* (1983), Cambridge, MA, USA: University Health Services, Environmental Health and Safety, Harvard University.

9 Story, K. O. (1985) *Approaches to Pest Management in Museums*, Washington, D.C.: Smithsonian Institution, Conservation Analytical Laboratory.

10 Supriana, N. (1988) 'Studies on the Natural Durability of Tropical Timbers to Termite Attack', *International Biodeterioration* 24: 337–341.

11 ASEAN = Association of Southeast Asian Nations: Singapore, Indonesia, Malaysia, Thailand, the Philippines, and Brunei.

Introduction to Part Two – Section Four

Chris Caple

Agents of deterioration: contaminants (gases, dust)

THE ENVIRONMENT WHICH SURROUNDS an object is composed of the storage or display materials and the gaseous environment including the fine particles (dust) suspended in that gas. Sarah Stanniforth, Sophie Julien and Linda Bullock (2006) (Chapter 16) provide a simple, straightforward introduction to gaseous pollutants, a topic which can quickly become highly technical and very scientific. Their article describes the gases that react with artefacts, their origin, their damaging effects and the methods used in monitoring and minimising the concentrations of these gases. More detailed information, especially on storage and display materials and the gases they can emit, is available in books by Tétreault (2003) and Hatchfield (2002).

Following the initial development of the Oddy Test in the British Museum in the 1970s, Lee and Thickett (1996) (Chapter 17), in *British Museum Occasional Paper 111*, produced a 'standard' work on the principal gaseous pollutants in museums, their reactions with the artefacts in the collections and the application of the Oddy Test. It provides full details of the Oddy Test, the industry standard test for storage and display materials, used to ascertain the extent to which they emit gases that could be harmful to museum artefacts and specimens. It also provides, like a number of other publications, information on materials that are considered safe for storage and display, as well as methods to minimise the risk from pollutant gases from less safe materials. *British Museum Occasional Paper 111* also provides details of a number of 'instant' tests, such as the iodine-iodate, azide and Beilstein test for the chemical composition of materials and thus an indicator of their possible reaction with museum objects, though these tests are far less accurate regarding the degree of threat to artefacts than are Oddy Tests. Details of materials and their suppliers which the

British Museum has tested and found to be safe for use in storing and displaying museum artefacts and specimens are also found in this publication.

Research work on gaseous pollutants has been carried out at the British Museum for over 30 years. The results of this testing were published by Bradley and Thickett (1999) (Chapter 18). They provide a particularly detailed look at the reduced sulphur gases and VOCs (volatile organic compounds), such as formaldehyde and ethanoic (acetic) acid pollutants, present in the galleries of the British Museum. This study shows that the situation is more complex than decay triggered by the presence of a polluting gas. There are synergistic effects, where one decay promoter/product influences another. The concentration of the gas, the relative humidity, the nature of the artefact and the history of the artefact (whether it has undergone conservation or not) are all shown to affect the likelihood of decay.

Whilst monitoring and/or eliminating damaging gases is the defensive approach to the subject, the knowledge of the reaction between artefacts and gases allows the creation of a proactive approach, deliberately creating microclimates and storing objects in a gaseous environment that will have a benign or beneficial effect. Boxes, frames and other containers have been used since antiquity to give protection to paintings against physical, insect and light damage. During the last few decades objects have begun to be sealed in gas-tight enclosures to prevent contact with harmful gases. These microclimates have been used for some time, such as storing archaeological ironwork at low relative humidity (RH) or storing silver in enclosures which exclude sulphurous gases. However, in recent years there has been particular interest in creating anoxic (oxygen free) environments. In 1994 Gilberg and Grattan (1994) outlined the use of Ageless™ and oxygen-impermeable polymers for creating oxygen-free storage for museum artefacts. This system has been used on a range of historic artefacts, in particular, decaying plastics for which there are few other storage options available. In recent years the Ageless™ system has been superseded by the Revolutionary Preservation (RP) System™. Mathias, Ramsdale and Nixon (2004) (Chapter 21) explore the use of the RP System™ for storing archaeological ironwork. A number of conservators in the USA and Europe are currently experimenting using the RP-A System™ for storing corroded ironwork (Guggenheimer and Thickett 2008), since they believe that its ability to create both low RH and anoxic conditions is the best for preserving corroded ironwork.

Dust is a perennial problem for historic houses and museums. It both damages and obscures the surfaces of objects. Research continues into the nature of dust, its rates of deposition and sources. These vary from museum to museum. Two different approaches to minimising the exposure of objects to dust have been taken. Tétreault (2003) (Chapter 19) describes the approach of museums with air conditioning, seeking to remove dust through filtering. Since air conditioning is not feasible in most historic buildings in Britain the National Trust has become active in monitoring the rate of dust deposition at a range of properties and drawing lessons that it can apply more generally. There is now a heightened level of consciousness evident at the Trust regarding the nature of dust and its deposition. Simple 'remove it' attitudes have been superseded by awareness of the damage that removal can do, and the greater need to understand how and where dust is deposited and what steps can be taken to reduce that deposition and minimise the damage during the removal process (Lloyd and Lithgow 2006). The move to a proactive rather than reactive approach is again clearly evident. The benefits of knowing the distribution and level of dust deposition are demonstrated through a series of case studies at National Trust properties and a royal palace, described by Helen Lloyd, Katie Lithgow, Peter Brimblecombe, Young Hun Yoon, Kate Frame and Barry Knight (2002) (Chapter 20). These demonstrate that although there are different vertical and horizontal dust distribution patterns at each site, some factors appear relatively constant. Visitors are a clear source of dust: the closer to the objects they are, the more the objects are soiled. Soiling (dust) can normally be reduced by raising objects 30 cm above the floor, moving them further away from the entrance to the property and further away from the visitor route. Drugget and entrance mats are effective at reducing dust. External surfaces can also have a significant effect on the amount and nature of dust. The beneficial role of individual property analysis is clear and the mechanism for undertaking basic dust distribution surveys is shown to be relatively simple.

References

Bradley, S. and Thickett D. (1999) 'The Pollution Problem in Perspective', in J. Bridgeland (ed.), *ICOM-CC 12th Triennial Meeting Lyon 29 August–3 September 1999*, London: James & James.

Gilberg, M. and Grattan, D. (1994) 'Oxygen Free Storage Using "Ageless" Oxygen Absorber', in A. Roy and P. Smith (eds), *Preventive Conservation Practice Theory and Research, IIC 1994 Conference, Ottawa*, London: IIC.

Guggenheimer, S. and Thickett, D. (2008) 'Investigation into the Potential of Low Oxygen Storage for Freshly Excavated Iron Artefacts: Fundamental Research Using the Revolutionary Preservation System (RP-System)', *VDR Beitrage* 1: 75–86.

Hatchfield, P. B. (2002) *Pollutants in the Museum Environment*, London: Archetype.

Lee, L. and Thickett, D. (1996) *Selection of Materials for the Storage of Display of Museum Objects*, British Museum Occasional Papers 111, London: British Museum Press.

Lloyd, H. and Lithgow, K. (2006) 'Physical Agents of Deterioration', in National Trust, *Manual of Housekeeping*, London: Butterworth-Heinemann, pp. 62–67.

Lloyd, H., Lithgow, K., Brimblecombe, P., Hun, Y., Frame, K. and Knight, B. (2002) 'The Effects of Visitor Activity on Dust in Historic Collections', *The Conservator* 26: 72–84.

Mathias, C., Ramsdale, K. and Nixon, D. (2004) 'Saving Archaeological Iron Using the Revolutionary Preservation System', in J. Ashton and D. Hallam (eds), *Metal 04*, Canberra: National Museum of Australia, pp. 28–42.

Stanniforth, S., Julien, S. and Bullock, L. (2006) 'Chemical Agents of Deterioration', in National Trust, *Manual of Housekeeping*, London: Butterworth-Heinemann.

Tétreault, J. (2003) *Airborne Pollutants in Museums, Galleries and Archives: Risk Assessment, Control Strategies and Preservation Management*, Ottawa, CCI.

Chapter 16

Chemical Agents of Deterioration

Sarah Stanniforth, Sophie Julien and Linda Bullock

Introduction

THE CHEMICAL AGENTS of deterioration are 'aggressive' chemicals in the form of gases, liquids or solids, which react or interact with materials and cause changes in their composition, nature or appearance. Where artefacts are affected it may only be their surface that is altered, often resulting in visible change. But with porous materials, chemicals can penetrate and cause alteration deeper within the structure, which often leads to physical weakening – especially if the material is not particularly thick. Most chemical agents cause deterioration by reacting with materials and so changing their composition irreversibly; but solvents are liquid chemical agents that do not react with materials, 'dissolving' them instead. That means they change the nature of the material from a solid into a liquid, which may reform if the solvent evaporates. Water can act as a solvent, but more usually 'solvent' refers to organic liquids, that is, those which contain carbon compounds such as methanol, ethanol and acetone.

Chemical agents in the form of gases which endanger artefacts in historic houses are classified as 'pollutants'; these, like liquids and solids, are considered 'contaminants'. These agents may come from the atmosphere or from local surroundings, including visitors, cleaning products and even other artefacts. In such cases they can be 'avoided' or at least 'minimized' by control. But the control of chemical agents which occur in some historic materials is much more problematic. As chemical reactions are accelerated by heat, light and the presence of moisture (in the process known as 'synergy') it is important to look as well at control of chemical agents in relation to these other agents of deterioration. Although it is impossible to arrest

Source: National Trust, *Manual of Housekeeping*, London: Butterworth-Heinemann, 2006, pp. 69–79.

chemical deterioration completely, slowing it down is an important part of preventive conservation.

Gaseous pollutants

Introduction

The first chemical agents of deterioration to be considered are gases. Liquids and solids are discussed later in the chapter.

Definition of gaseous pollutants

The term 'gaseous pollutants' is used to describe those, often man-made, gases such as sulphur dioxide that are present in the air in higher concentrations than its normal composition. Most of us are familiar with the damage gaseous pollutants do to natural environments and human health. Less obvious is the irreversible deterioration they cause to collections in indoor environments.

Sources of gaseous pollutants

Some gaseous pollutants are the by-products of industry and combustion. Although concentrations are usually higher in urban or industrial areas, such gases can also be produced much closer to home, for example by a furnace or machinery, or even given off by new or historic materials.

Pollutants mainly generated externally

- Sulphur dioxide (SO_2) is a product of fuel combustion, but there are natural background levels in the air. Fortunately, industrial output of the gas has significantly reduced over the last twenty-five years, and the fossil fuels that are burnt, including coal, oil and low-sulphur motor vehicle fuel, have a reduced sulphur content. Through chemical changes in the atmosphere, sulphur dioxide converts to the even more destructive sulphurous and sulphuric acid, better known as 'acid rain'. Inside a building gas lighting was a local source of sulphur dioxide.
- Nitrogen oxides (NOx) are produced by petroleum fuel combustion, notably in car engines and appliances like gas heaters and cookers. Concentrations are usually higher in towns and near busy roads. A degrading cellulose nitrate object can be a local source of nitrogen oxides.

Pollutants mainly generated internally or locally

- Ozone (O_3) is naturally present in the atmosphere and is also generated externally by the conversion of combustion fumes in strong sunlight, as well as internally by photocopiers, laser printers and ionizers.
- Hydrogen sulphide (H_2S) and carbonyl sulphide (COS) are given off by degrading organic matter, including wet wool, and near wet coats. They are also emitted by

a variety of construction materials, vulcanized rubber (including rubber bands), and from some paints and sealants. Artefacts too can be a source of these gases: they can be given off by archaeological objects from wet burial sites, for example. They can also be externally generated as by-products of industrial activity and from sewers.

- Volatile organic compounds (VOCs) are pollutant gases of organic or petroleum origin. The compounds are found in certain materials and, because they are volatile, can be given off in a process known as 'off-gassing', polluting the local environment. Most commonly encountered are formic acid, acetic acid (as in vinegar) and formaldehyde. They off-gas from a range of products, including woods (particularly unseasoned oak), fresh paints, sealants and textiles. Medium Density Fibreboard (MDF) is a well-known source in the museum environment. But historic materials such as cardboard and degrading plastics can also be sources of VOCs. Solvents, such as acetone, which can be present as locally generated vapours from drying paint, modern adhesives and perfume, etc. are another type of VOC.

Damage caused by gaseous pollutants

Chemical deterioration caused by gaseous pollutants can take place at remarkably different rates. In many cases, the rate of deterioration is slow and may not cause any noticeable change except over many decades. But a sudden exposure to high concentrations of a harmful gas can cause rapid deterioration. For instance, the off-gassing of new wooden display or storage cases or fresh paint can cause damage in a few weeks. As mentioned earlier, rates of deterioration are also governed by light, temperature and RH. The presence of particulates is also critical: dust and dirt, even when inert, can trap harmful gases, so increasing deterioration at points where they collect on a surface. However, the most frequently encountered problems caused by each gas are given here.

- Sulphur dioxide causes embrittlement of paper and parchment, 'red rot' of certain leathers, weakening of textiles and, in the presence of moisture, corrosion of metals. In the form of acid rain, it is said to slowly dissolve plaster and calcareous stone, materials which are also thought to be attacked directly by sulphur dioxide (Figure 16.1).
- Nitrogen oxides cause fading of pigment and dyes (in synergy with light), weakening of textiles, breakdown of early plastics and fading and embrittlement of film and photographic materials.
- Ozone attacks many materials, causing fading of dyes and pigments, fading and embrittlement of photographic materials and cracking of rubber and plastics.
- Sulphides (hydrogen sulphide and carbonyl sulphide) are the main agents responsible for tarnishing silver. They can also cause fading and yellowing of photographs.
- VOCs corrode metals, particularly lead and its alloys, and react with calcareous materials, as found in shell and mineral specimens, to form powdery crystals.
- Organic-solvent vapour – for example, from recently applied paints and varnishes – can damage many solvent-based organic substances in historic materials

Figure 16.1 Detail from a limestone urn. Calcium carbonate in limestone is transformed into gypsum (calcium sulphate). In sulphate-rich polluted environments (acid rain) thick black crusts can be formed on limestone. These
are a combination of soluble gypsum and black carbon-based pollution
particles and tend to form in areas sheltered from rainwash. (Credit:
Rupert Harris Conservation)

such as varnishes and lacquers, often present on furniture, paintings, lacquer-
ware or metals, as well as plastics, films and modern adhesives. They may cause
opacity, but depending on their interaction and concentration, can also cause
surfaces to become dull, tacky or crazed.

Realistic minimum levels of gaseous pollutants

The aim should be to have zero levels of gaseous pollutants. However, while zero
levels of externally generated gaseous pollutants would be ideal, they are unrealistic
in historic houses, or indeed anywhere. In museums, air conditioning is often used
in an attempt to approach such levels. It relies on passing outside air through chemical filters, which trap harmful gases within their molecular structure (absorption)
and/or fix them onto their surface (adsorption). However, air conditioning is neither
appropriate nor desirable in historic houses, due to the disruption caused to the fabric
of the building by the installation of the machinery and ductwork. So the aim must
be to keep the level of these gases as low as can be done using the means of control
described below.

Monitoring gaseous pollutants

Smell can be a useful indicator of the presence of high concentrations of gaseous
pollutants. However, the gases are harmful to historic materials in concentrations

below those our noses can detect. Thus deterioration may be the first sign that there is a gaseous pollutant problem. To avoid this situation, best practice in preventive conservation is the routine monitoring for the presence of gaseous pollutants of any location housing collections.

Monitoring methods fall into two broad categories: first, 'sampling' methods which determine the presence and concentrations of specific gases or group of gases; and second, methods which investigate the combined effect of gases in synergy with other environmental factors on test samples of materials.

Before methods of monitoring are selected, the particular questions to be addressed must be clearly set out. These questions might include: what gases are present; what their effects might be; what the sources could be; whether concentrations vary over time; or whether local pollution control is proving efficient in the house. To be able to check that any control methods introduced are effective, it is important to compare monitoring results with those from a parallel environment. Thus concentrations of pollutants in air indoors should always be compared with measurements of pollutants in the atmosphere outside (available publicly). Likewise, concentrations of pollutants or their effects in a sealed case should be compared with those of the room in which the case stands. For reliable comparison, and in order to include the effects of synergy, measurements must be carried out simultaneously.

Sampling methods

Air can be 'sampled' in various ways. It can then be analysed using various chemical or instrumental techniques. 'Active' sampling involves drawing air through an analytical device using a pump, whereas 'passive' sampling relies on diffusion and absorption of gases onto chemically reactive materials. The active devices give a snapshot of levels of pollutant gases at a particular moment in time. Passive devices normally give integrated (and therefore average) pollutant levels. A sampling tube for a particular pollutant is placed in a room for a period of time and then analysed for the amount of pollutant absorbed. By knowing the rate of diffusion and absorption across the absorber, it is possible to calculate the average pollutant concentration in the room over that period.

Those commonly used are:

- Air pumped through an analytical device. This gives an 'on-site' snapshot of the number of gases present and their concentrations.
- Sample tubes and badges known as 'passive samplers', some of which have been developed specifically for the heritage field. These can be exposed from between twenty-four hours and several months, but have to be sent away for laboratory analysis.
- Draeger™ tubes (used either passively or with a pump), each for a specific gas. Each tube gives a rapid, on-site visual result for the selected gas.
- Detectors attached to elaborate instrumentation. These give readings of gaseous concentrations at regular intervals but, due to cost, are not widely used in historic houses.

Testing effects on materials

In this approach individual gaseous concentrations are not looked at; instead, the overall potential ('Overall corrosive load') of a given environment to affect material is investigated. Samples of materials ('marker materials') which are representative of the collection are placed within the environment in question for a period of time and then assessed for chemical change. These marker materials can be:

- Metal coupons (silver, copper, zinc, lead and iron), either commercially available or made in-house (Figure 16.2). Assessment of the degree to which the metal corrodes is made either in-house or through specialist services.
- Eggshells. In the same way, but less accurately, these can be used to detect gases harmful to calcareous materials by the formation of powdery white crystals on their surface.
- Paint or plastic-based 'dosimeters' (to measure the dose of exposure). These have been developed to assess the combined effect of light, RH, temperature and pollution on a variety of traditional pigments and media. However, interpretation of some of the changes to these dosimeters requires highly specialized analytical equipment.

To test whether a new material will give off gaseous pollutants, metal coupons and a sample of the material in question can be sealed in a test tube and subjected to a standard procedure (the 'Oddy test').

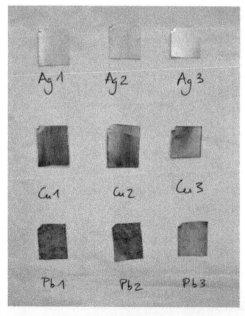

Figure 16.2 Small pieces of silver, copper and lead foil deployed to act as early warning indicators of corrosive environments. (Credit: Sophie Julien)

Controlling gaseous pollutants

Simple, economic solutions to help control gaseous pollution can be categorized under various approaches: avoidance, exclusion, removal (including adsorption and absorption), ventilation and synergy.

Avoidance

A solution which can be adopted in most situations to control levels of internally generated pollution is 'avoidance', i.e. avoiding the introduction of any new internal sources of gaseous pollutants. This means that new materials likely to off-gas should not be used, especially inside sealed enclosures. Specialist museum advice is usually available to advise on alternative inert materials, or on how long a material must be allowed to off-gas before it can be used. Paint, for example, must be allowed to dry fully before materials vulnerable to solvents are introduced to the area. Among many other things, avoidance also means that equipment likely to generate harmful gases, such as laser printers, should not be used near vulnerable objects, and car parks should be located away from the house.

Exclusion

In most situations the building envelope plays a crucial role in the exclusion of externally generated gaseous pollutants: the building itself and our management of it provides a barrier against them. Keeping windows and doors shut (or not leaving them open) will reduce air exchange and thus exposure to high levels of external pollutants. It may even be possible to seal openings in a building near a busy road or machinery. However, such steps have to be balanced against the need for a certain level of ventilation. In an historic house it might be possible to put particularly vulnerable materials in sealed showcases or storage containers. The former are widely used in museums to reduce pollution levels to near zero, but they are often inappropriate in historic houses. Exclusion can also be used for display and storage materials that might off-gas over a long period. This time it is the source itself which is sealed: this is done with inert varnishes or metal barrier foils. As it is obviously not possible to seal objects which are sources of local pollution in this way, such objects might have to be placed in sealed containers or put somewhere where there is good ventilation, away from other objects.

Removal

Gaseous pollutants can be removed to some extent from the air by 'passive adsorption'. Internal building surfaces made of certain materials have been shown to reduce levels of pollutants, especially sulphur dioxide, by passive adsorption. Most effective are porous materials such as plasters and cements, textured renders or textiles. Textiles, acid free tissue and alkaline-buffered card can provide protection by acting as sacrificial absorbers. Alternatively, objects can be placed in sealed spaces, such as display cases or storage containers, with materials which passively absorb pollutant gases. These pollution 'scavengers', such as activated carbon (available impregnated into cloth or boards or as pellets), can be used to prevent build up of internally generated pollutants such as VOCs. Bags are also available which contain activated copper particles bonded into a polymer: this neutralises all corrosive gases that come into contact with it, protecting objects inside from external pollutants such as H_2S, SO_2, NOx and O_3, as well as internally generated ones such as COS and VOCs. (See, for example, Corrosion Intercept® bags available from Conservation by Design.) More commonly, silver objects can be placed in bags whose fabric contains activated carbon to scavenge sulphide gases. Pollution scavengers are also used in 'active' air filtration systems, which absorb harmful gases as they pass through the activated carbon or potassium permanganate filters. (See, for example, the gas-phase filtration systems developed by Purafil Inc. to remove gaseous contaminants and particulates.) Freestanding units have been shown to reduce levels of gaseous pollutants. However, they are not as efficient as full air conditioning, since unfiltered outside air enters the building first, and they rely on the effective sealing of a particular room or building.

Ventilation

When avoidance, exclusion and removal fail to reduce a build up of internal gaseous pollutants, the circulation of air and the introduction of fresh air are possible solutions. This is especially useful for display cases where there are internally generated VOCs including solvents. Cases can be opened when the house is shut, or, if appropriate, extra holes or gaps made in the case to increase ventilation. Ventilation is also useful in removing the VOCs given off after a room or display case is decorated with solvent-based paints or sealants. As a rule of thumb, a minimum of two weeks should be allowed before any sensitive artefacts are placed in the room or case. (This also allows time for solid particulate matter, such as plaster dust or fragments of paint from 'rubbing down', to settle on dust sheets and be removed.)

Synergy

If levels of pollutants cannot be reduced sufficiently, then at least the rate of deterioration they cause can be reduced by keeping light levels, temperature and RH low.

Summary

Some important and easily achievable steps to combat internally generated gaseous pollution are:

- Avoid the use of new materials that are likely to generate pollutants.
- Ventilate spaces where materials that generate gaseous pollutants have been introduced.
- Keep vulnerable objects away from sources of local pollutants.
- Site printers and photocopiers away from vulnerable objects.
- Avoid engine fumes or ensure fumes are well vented to the outside.

- Use varnishes or metal barrier foils to encapsulate new materials that are likely to off-gas.
- If necessary, place objects in micro-environments where pollutants are removed by scavengers.

Oxygen

As a principal component of the atmosphere, oxygen cannot be called a pollutant, but it is a principal agent of chemical deterioration. While materials are attacked by oxygen at various speeds, these are greatly increased by synergy with other agents of deterioration. Thus light accelerates the oxidation of organic materials ('photo-oxidation'), and moisture speeds up the oxidation of metals ('corrosion'). By reacting in this way, oxygen is responsible for much of the 'ageing' (slow deterioration) of materials, resulting in visual and structural changes. Oxygen can also cause deterioration by reacting with materials to produce gaseous pollutants: for example, ageing cellulose nitrate oxidizing to form nitrogen oxides.

This means that much deterioration can be reduced by the removal of oxygen from the environment. This can be done by placing objects in sealed enclosures, whether for storage or display, and either using scavengers to remove the oxygen or displacing the air with nitrogen. Such environments are known as 'anoxic' and have been used in museums to preserve very vulnerable materials such as badly corroding iron and unstable rubberized textiles. Expert advice should be taken before using anoxic environments, as a few materials, including Prussian blue and some lead-containing pigments, deteriorate when oxygen is excluded.

Liquid and solid contaminants

Introduction

Liquid and solid contaminants can most obviously be introduced either as splashes, spills or leaks or by contact (from hands for example). However, liquid and solid contaminants can also be carried in the air, either as airborne particles or tiny droplets from sprays. When liquids (spills/splashes/sprays) dry out, they may leave behind solid contaminants. Chemical contaminants may not 'be introduced' at all: they can already be present in historic materials from their processes of manufacture or from their previous history.

Definition of liquid and solid contaminants

Many liquid and solid contaminants that come into contact with historic materials are inert and often simply stain or soil the materials. But when these contaminants are acids, alkalis, salts or metal particles, they can be chemically reactive. Solvents in liquid form or even solid form (as in polishes), as contaminants can interact with materials. Specific effects of these contaminants are discussed in later chapters, but generalities are introduced here.

Sources of liquid and solid contaminants

Particulate pollution

The main source of solid chemical contaminants is airborne particulate pollution, which is chemically active. As with gaseous pollutants, externally generated particulate contaminants, such as soot from the combustion of fossil fuels (including diesel fuel), metal particles and sea salts in coastal areas, may be carried indoors by movement of air. External particles may also be carried in and shed by people, either from their clothing or through exfoliation of skin. Particulate contaminants may also be generated internally, either in a cumulative fashion as when a lime-washed ceiling (alkaline) slowly powders, or else by an occasional event such as building work that produces cement or plaster dust (which may be alkaline) or wood dust (which may be acidic).

Handling and using

When surfaces are touched, accumulation or occasional deposits of mildly acidic perspiration can occur. Even greater contamination results if historic costume and shoes are worn, the perspiration becoming alkaline as it ages. Physical contact can also result in the deposition of salt on floors from soiled footwear. The preparation and consumption of food and drink in an historic house is a major source of chemical contamination. Contact contamination will occur if historic plates, vessels and cutlery are used. Food and drink, especially fruit and wine, can be acidic, and eggs are a source of sulphur, which tarnishes silver. Spills of food and drink are notorious causes of chemical contamination. However, vapour contamination may go on completely unnoticed, as happens during cooking, by the evaporation of oils or the dispersion of droplets during frying. Aerosols of any sort, including air fresheners, and artificial smells, also indiscriminately introduce chemicals including solvents. Smoke (another aerosol) from open fires may be both acidic and alkaline. Spills or splashes of paint or chemical treatments during building works, or of fake blood on film sets, or leaks of oil or grease from machinery, etc. can also occur. Vandalism can be in the form of the deliberate introduction of chemical agents, including acids, alkalis and solvents, which can cause catastrophic deterioration; if it occurs emergency action will need to be taken.

Misguided care

Misguided care can also introduce chemicals in any of the three ways described above. In general, introduction can be through the ill-advised use on vulnerable material of cleaning solutions, whether these be acidic, alkaline or solvent-containing; or the inadequate removal of a recommended solution such as 'silver dip'. Even the wrong choice of a surface protection coating, such as mildly acidic beeswax on bronze, can prove damaging in the long term. Proprietary aerosols introduce solvents as well as the chosen polish (or insecticide), and both of these can be unintentionally distributed over vulnerable surfaces nearby. Inappropriate first aid can also cause contamination:

the need to react rapidly after a spill can result in damaging chemicals, such as solvents in stain removers or salt, being introduced.

Damage caused by liquid and solid contaminants

Depending on the particular contaminant and the historic material in question, deterioration can either occur immediately or, more usually, over the long term. In the longer term, a build up of contaminant – for example, residues of food or cleaning products on silver – may often go unnoticed. If not removed these can cause chemical deterioration at these specific locations. Even if the residues are inert they can absorb harmful pollutant gases or liquids and so cause deterioration of the surface.

Acids or alkalis

The strength of the acidity and alkalinity of a liquid is measured by its 'pH': less than 4 is very acidic, 7 is neutral and more than 10 is very alkaline. Depending on their strength, reactions of acids or alkalis with vulnerable materials may be instantaneous or slow, ongoing over many years. This means even mild acids and alkalis can cause harm in the long term. Acids may corrode or etch into the surface of certain metals and calcareous materials. This means, for example, that touching metal surfaces, whether bright or patinated, or displaying fruit on pewter dishes, is inadvisable. In the longer term, acids will also weaken most organic materials: for example, they cause paper to become brittle. Alkalis can also damage some metals, particularly those containing lead, as well as proteinaceous organic materials, including wool, parchment and leather.

Metal particles

Metal particles, often in dust in industrial or urban areas, speed up the deterioration of paper and leather by acting as a catalyst, accelerating the action of other agents like sulphur dioxide. Thick dust and dirt deposits containing metal particles, which regular cleaning may have been unable to reach, can focus the deterioration on one particular area of the object.

Salts

Chemically active salts in perspiration, sea air or from manufacture are principally a problem to copper alloys and iron, as they increase the corrosion of these metals.

Solvents

Water is a solvent, causing water-soluble dyes to run, glues to dissolve and varnishes to bloom. The damage caused by organic solvents when vaporized has previously been discussed. Similar, if more extreme, damage can be caused by liquid solvents and sometimes results in complete dissolution. Some organic solvents also have the capacity to remove water, and thus when used in large quantities on organic materials such as wood and textiles, tend to 'dry' them out. That is, they remove water, reducing the moisture content of the wood or textile, which becomes excessively dry and may shrink and/or crack.

Realistic minimum levels of liquid and solid

Where there are internally generated liquid and solid contaminants it is possible to aim for zero levels by avoidance. Whilst zero levels would also be ideal for externally generated solid airborne contaminants, these are virtually unobtainable. This is because the reduction of external particulate pollution to zero inside a house would require impossibly high levels of technology to filter all incoming air, and 'air curtains' to cleanse visitors of any particles they might shed during a visit. So, as with gaseous pollutants, the level of external particulate pollutants to aim for must simply be the minimum that is practicably obtainable using the methods described below.

Monitoring solid and liquid contaminants

The most appropriate form of monitoring is by eye and vigilance. If vulnerable materials are present where there is a risk of reactive pollutants or residues, then regular monitoring of build up, or failing this, signs of damage, is essential for timely responsive action. This monitoring does not tell us if the particles are chemically active. It should at least be possible to determine the pH of a deposit by removing a sample, slightly dampening it and testing it with litmus paper.

Controlling contamination by liquids and solids

Most of the control measures to prevent chemical contamination involve the common-sense reduction of risks through avoidance and exclusion. While these are generally the same as those used to control dust and dirt, some specific points are added here.

Avoidance and exclusion

The preparation and consumption of food and drink in historic houses is best avoided altogether. Otherwise it must be kept to a minimum and well controlled. Certainly, significant items from collections should not be used for storing or serving food. It is also obviously useful to avoid having sources of fumes from machinery and smoke near historic surfaces. Using gloves or very clean hands when touching surfaces is of great importance, as is the choice, use and removal of housekeeping products. Procedures to circumvent acts of vandalism are dealt with elsewhere.

Removal, stabilization or synergy

Where chemicals have got onto historic surfaces, it may well be possible to remove them by cleaning. On occasion it may even be possible to remove them when they have got into a material. This could be in the form of the washing of robust materials such as linens and white-work. An alternative approach is to stabilize the chemicals in situ. For example, if the threat is from acidic contaminants in paper, control may be through adding a neutralizing buffer such as calcium carbonate. It should be noted that in these examples interventive conservation treatments are being used to prevent future deterioration and can thus also be considered to be a form of preventive conservation. However, specialist advice will be needed in carrying out any of these treatments, as they are interventive. If existing levels of chemicals cannot be reduced or neutralized, the rate of the deterioration they cause can be slowed down by exploiting synergies, i.e. reducing light exposure, temperature or high RH.

Summary

Some important and easily achievable steps to combat internally generated liquid and solid contaminants are:

- Avoid the preparation and consumption of food and drink in rooms with vulnerable surfaces and contents.
- Avoid fumes from machinery and smoke from open fires.
- Use gloves or very clean hands when touching vulnerable surfaces.
- Prevent particulates from entering historic houses (Lloyd and Lithgow 2006).
- Remove particulates by cleaning (Lloyd and Lithgow 2006).
- Consult a specialist about the use of interventive treatment to reduce the impact of chemical contaminants in objects.

Chemical contaminants already in materials

Aggressive chemicals may be present from the manufacturing process of the material: cheap paper with its high acidity is a case in point. Some objects may be inherently chemically unstable even though not manufactured, as for example certain geological specimens. Chemicals may also have got into objects before they were taken into historic house collections, as in world culture and archaeological collections. It may well be impossible or even inappropriate to remove these aggressive chemicals, in which case they have to be treated by stabilization or exploiting synergies as described in the preceding 'Removal, stabilization or synergy' section.

Further reading

Blades, N., Oreszczyn, T. and Cassar, M. (2000) 'Guidelines on pollution control in museums and archives', *Museum Practice*, 15 (Supplement).

Gibson, L. T., Cooksey, B. G., Littlejohn, D. and Tennent, N. H. (1999) 'Pollution from showcases: a passive sampler for acetic and formic acid vapours', *Museum Practice*, 1 (2): 46–47.

Hatchfield, P. (2002) *Pollutants in the Museum Environment – Practical Strategies for Problem Solving in Design, Exhibition and Storage,* London: Archetype Publications.

Indoor Air Quality in Museums and Archives (IAQ). Website: www.iaq.dk.

Lloyd, H. and Lithgow, K. (2006) 'Physical agents of deterioration', in National Trust, *Manual of Housekeeping*, London: Butterworth-Heinemann.

Tétreault, J. (1994) 'Display materials: the good, the bad and the ugly', in J. Sarge (ed.) *Exhibitions and Conservation*, Edinburgh: Scottish Society for Conservation and Restoration. (Available online via www.iaq.dk.)

Tétreault, J. (2003) *Airborne Pollutants in Museums, Galleries and Archives: Risk Assessment, Control Strategies and Preservation Management*, Ottawa: Canadian Conservation Institute.

Thomson, G. (1986) *The Museum Environment* (second edition), London: Butterworths.

UK National Air Quality Information Archive, Website: www.airquality.co.uk/archive.

Chapter 17

Selection of Materials for the Storage and Display of Museum Objects

L. R. Lee and D. Thickett

Effects of pollutants

A IR IS COMPOSED MAINLY OF nitrogen and oxygen, but also contains a complex mixture of many different gases present at much lower concentrations, for example ozone, sulphur dioxide and oxides of nitrogen. These low background concentrations can cause slow deterioration of objects; outdoor stone sculpture will form a sulphate crust and bronze statues become covered with a patina of corrosion products, particularly in an industrial or maritime area. However, these 'outdoor' pollutants are generally present at much lower levels inside a building (Graedel and McGill 1986), and the indoor environment often possesses its own characteristic range of pollutants. For example it may contain higher levels of organic acids, particularly formic (methanoic acid) and acetic acid. This is because they are emitted by materials such as timber and timber-composites. The problems arise when such materials are used in confined spaces, where any emissions become trapped and their concentration increases. If enclosed with inappropriate materials, metal artefacts can corrode, inorganic objects can suffer adverse reactions such as the formation of mixed salts and organic materials can become brittle. In this section, effects of various pollutant gases on each of these types of object will be explored in turn. At this point it is worth mentioning the deleterious effects of particulate matter; this absorbs moisture and pollutant gases, and therefore a layer of dust on an object can exacerbate any of the following effects. The importance of clean storage and display areas cannot be over-emphasised.

If silver is placed on open display, it will become dull and eventually acquire a tarnished appearance. This is due to reaction with low background levels of sulphide

Source: *Selection of Materials for the Storage of Display of Museum Objects*, British Museum Occasional Papers 111, London: British Museum Press 1996, pp. 3–8, 12–17, 37–39.

gases, for example hydrogen sulphide and carbonyl sulphide. However, if enclosed on display or in storage with inappropriate materials such as woollen felt, silver can tarnish rapidly. Although silver sulphide is the major corrosion product found on tarnished silver, other compounds such as sulphates, nitrates, hydroxides and chlorides have been identified (Rice et al. 1980; Lee 1996). The silver sulphate may have formed due to oxidation of atmospheric carbonyl sulphide (Wayne 1985). The disruptive effect of sulphide gases on silver chloride patinas has also been found (Shashoua and Green 1990). Objects made of alloys of silver with metals other than gold are less resistant to corrosion than pure silver.

Silver artefacts can be polished to remove disfiguring silver tarnish, although excessive polishing is undesirable as a small amount of the silver is removed. Repeated polishing can lead to loss of detail where the surface is decorated, or complete loss of the surface where an object is silver plated. However, in some situations, cleaning is not feasible and the tarnishing is permanent, as with silver leaf on manuscripts and scrolls. Silver-based photographic media can also be irreversibly damaged by sulphide gases, resulting in darkening and loss of contrast of the image. It is also reported that formaldehyde (methanal) will discolour photographs (Weyde 1972).

High purity gold is considered to be resistant to most pollutant gases. However, where gold exists in combination with other metals, for example as silver gilt or as a low purity alloy, the effects of pollutants on the associated metals must be considered.

Polished copper is susceptible to attack by sulphides, organic acids, chlorides and formaldehyde, which oxidises to formic acid (Hatchfield and Carpenter 1987). Copper and its alloys can also be disfigured by 'black spot', which was originally thought to be due to microbiological attack (Madsen and Hjelm-Hansen 1979). However, subsequent research has shown that 'black spot' is due to reaction of atmospheric sulphur compounds (Oddy and Bradley 1989), often due to unsuitable display or storage materials. The copper alloys are converted into copper sulphides, for example brown digenite, $Cu_{1.8}S$, and black chalcocite, Cu_2S (Green 1992a). However, copper and its alloys tend to be less sensitive to sulphide attack than polished silver. Copper often possesses an oxide patina or a more extensive corrosion layer, which can be protective against atmospheric attack. If prolonged exposure to harmful gases has occurred, the patina/corrosion layer can itself be affected. Several occurrences of the black sulphide formation on copper carbonate patinas have been seen in museum collections (Oddy and Meeks 1982).

Pure lead is particularly vulnerable to atmospheric corrosion if stored inappropriately. Volatile organic acids such as acetic and formic acids, and aldehydes cause extensive disruptive corrosion, often producing hydrocerussite, basic lead carbonate (Rance and Cole 1958). In some instances, lead formate has also been identified as the major corrosion product on lead artefacts. This may be due to attack of formic acid or formaldehyde rather than acetic acid. One of the problems with lead objects in a collection is that they may be visually identified only as a 'white metal'; their true composition may often be discovered only when corrosion occurs. Alloys of lead with copper or tin are more resistant to corrosion than pure lead, but heavily leaded bronzes may contain discrete particles of lead, which can corrode independently of the bronze matrix if stored in a corrosive environment.

When considering the effects of pollutant gases on metals, one generally focuses on silver, copper and lead, but these are not the only metals in museum collections. Iron is generally thought to rust in high humidities, and in the presence of chlorides. However, ferrous metals are also susceptible to attack by sulphur dioxide and nitrogen dioxide, and it has been reported that other pollutants, particularly acetic acid, are corrosive (Gilroy and Mayne 1965; Green and Bradley 1997). Zinc has been known for many centuries, for example in Bidriware from India. It will corrode in the presence of organic acids, formaldehyde, chlorides and sulphur dioxide. Zinc formate hydrate has been identified on zinc coins which have been stored in unsuitable wooden cabinets (Oddy and Bradley 1989; Oddy 1993). On a separate occasion, a number of corroding zinc coins were analysed and the presence of chloride was identified in some of the corrosion products (Green and Thickett 1991). This may have been due to their environment prior to acquisition, for example, they may have been recovered from the sea. Other sources of chlorides may have been from handling, or volatile chlorides from storage materials.

Artefacts made from modern metals such as aluminium and magnesium are now being collected by museums. Aluminium is generally stable due to the presence of a film of aluminium oxide. Formic acid, however, peptises this oxide film, producing a gelatinous layer that is no longer protective. It is reported that organic chlorides and hydrogen chloride also disrupt the oxide layer. Alloys of aluminium with small concentrations of other metals, such as copper, have a reduced corrosion resistance. An examination of a number of aluminium objects housed in a variety of storage situations in the British Museum in 1991 revealed very little corrosion. Magnesium normally possesses a protective film of carbonates and sulphates but will corrode in the presence of organic acids (Green and Thickett 1991). Other modern metals such as nickel, cadmium and chromium are also generally corrosion resistant in normal atmospheres but with more of these metals being collected by museums the effects of pollutants need to be elucidated. Cadmium, for example, is corroded by organic acids (Rance and Cole 1958).

Non-metallic inorganic materials are also adversely affected by pollutants; glass can deteriorate if exposed to high levels of formaldehyde (Hatchfield and Carpenter 1987). Soluble salts, for example in stone and ceramics, can react with volatile organic acids to form mixed salt compounds such as calclacite, $Ca(CH_3COO)C_{1.5}H_2O$ (West FitzHugh and Gettens 1971). Carbonate-based materials, such as shells, also react with organic acids, producing a crystalline alteration product, which has commonly been referred to as Byne's Disease, which was reported as early as 1899 (Byne 1899). Inorganic pigments can become discoloured, for example, lead white and red lead react with sulphide gases, resulting in black lead sulphide (Harley 1982; Daniels and Thickett 1992).

Organic materials suffer adverse effects when exposed to some pollutants. Cellulose-based materials such as paper and some textiles may degrade due to acid or alkaline hydrolysis. This breaks the cellulose chains, thus lowering the strength of the material, which eventually becomes brittle and susceptible to damage by handling. Certain components of paper may cause it to be acidic, or become acidic on ageing. Paper may be sized with an acidic alum/rosin size, and papers made with a high proportion of groundwood pulp will contain lignin. Lignin has been reported to become acidic on ageing, and thus lignin-free papers are generally recommended for archival use. However, recent evidence has shown that the mechanical ageing properties of paper containing lignin are not significantly different to those of lignin-free papers. It has been suggested that many of the papers used in previous trials contained alum/rosin size in addition to the lignin, and the increased acidity was due to the size and not the lignin (Priest and Stanley 1994). It was concluded that in a neutral or alkaline environment lignin will not degrade. However, papers containing lignin may discolour with time, and effects of atmospheric pollutants are not known. Low level concentrations of both sulphur dioxide and nitrogen oxides have been reported to affect cellulosic materials (Morris et al. 1964; Brysson et al. 1967; Lyth Hudson and Milner 1961; Langwell 1976). If textiles contain metal threads then these can be affected by pollutants as discussed earlier. Paper may also contain metallic inclusions. Reaction of these with sulphur-containing pollutants can be one cause of the spots known as foxing (Daniels and Meeks 1992, 1995). Ozone does not pose a significant risk at ambient levels present in air, but at greater concentrations, such as could build up in a storage area, it can increase the deterioration rate of cotton and rubber, and induce fading of dyes (Bogarty et al. 1952; Shashoua and Thomsen 1993; Shaver and Cass 1983). The risk of prolonged exposure to low levels of organic acids needs to be elucidated. Synthetic fabrics and plastic materials are now being collected by museums. Nylon suffers accelerated degradation in the presence of low levels of sulphur dioxide (Zeronian et al. 1973). Polymethylmethacrylate and polystyrene are reported to be affected by acetic acid (Fenn 1995).

Sources of pollutants

Table 17.1 summarises the major sources and effects of common indoor pollutants.

In a museum situation a wide range of materials are used to construct and dress showcases, and in fitting out a store. Wood is one such material as it is versatile, comparatively inexpensive and easily worked. It also has the advantage of buffering changes in relative humidity (RH), an effect which may be beneficial to certain types of artefact. However all wood emits varying levels of organic acids and formaldehyde. As wood is a natural, non-homogeneous material, it is difficult to be specific about properties regarding outgassing of certain species or products, and lists of results from previous tests are of minimal use. General statements can however be made, for example oak and sweet chestnut emit higher levels of organic acids than beech or spruce (Arni et al. 1965; Blackshaw and Daniels 1978). Variations in emissions from the same species can be influenced by several factors, including time of felling, whether the wood is heart or sapwood and treatment after felling; kiln drying has been found to produce higher levels of free organic acids in a sample of wood than air drying. The moisture content of wood and timber products also affects their corrosive nature. Certain woods have been found to be emitting significant levels of volatiles after twenty years (Grzywacs and Tennent 1994).

In addition to structural components, timber-based products are often used for internal fittings of a showcase, i.e. baseboards and mounting boards. Plywood, chipboard, hardboard, blockboard and medium density fibreboard (MDF) are composite materials of timber and adhesive, the latter often formaldehyde based (Sparkes 1989). Products manufactured for internal use are generally bonded with urea

Table 17.1 Sources and effects of common museum pollutants

Pollutant	Main source		Affects
Sulphur-containing species, e.g. hydrogen sulphide H$_2$S, and carbonyl sulphide COS	wool rubber	fabrics, e.g. felt adhesives draught sealant	silver and copper
Organic acids, e.g. formic acid, CHOOH, and acetic acid, CH$_3$COOH	timber timber composites paints adhesives, varnishes sealants moth and rot proofing	all, especially oak MDF*, plywood, blockboard, chipboard often oil-based polyvinyl acetate, some polyurethanes some silicones	lead, copper, zinc, cadmium magnesium, salt-laden stone and ceramic, shells, possibly paper
Formaldehyde CH$_2$O	adhesives timber timber composites fabrics, paints	urea and phenol formaldehyde all MDF*, plywood, blockboard, chipboard	high levels can attack most metals and organic artefacts
Chlorides	plastics fire retardants	PVC†, PVDC‡ inorganic salts	copper, aluminium, zinc and iron
Nitrogen oxides, NOX	plastics	cellulose nitrate	copper and iron

* medium density fibreboard
† poly vinyl chloride
‡ poly vinylidene chloride

formaldehyde resin, whereas those for external use utilise phenol formaldehyde resin. Urea formaldehyde adhesives emit more formaldehyde, due to hydrolysis; phenol formaldehyde resins are more stable, resulting in a lower release of formaldehyde (Pickrell et al. 1983). Therefore, phenol formaldehyde products are more desirable for use in a museum environment. Due to health and safety regulations in the furniture industry, there are limits to the maximum formaldehyde content of timber products such as MDF. MDF labelled 'E1' grade conforms to legislation for a lower formaldehyde content. Products which are manufactured using a formaldehyde-free adhesive component are available, but have the inherent problem that it is not only the adhesive which gives off formaldehyde but also the wood particles. Therefore although a formaldehyde-free adhesive can be used, this will not result in a completely formaldehyde-free product.

Fabrics are often used in a showcase display, and can also be a source of pollutants. Wool is known to be a source of sulphide gases, mainly carbonyl sulphide (Brimblecombe et al. 1992). However, although many other natural fibres may not be a major source of pollutants themselves, a fabric often has additions such as crease-resistant finishes or fire retardants, which may be a source of harmful substances such as formaldehyde or organic acids. Dyes can also be a source of pollutants. Since testing of display and storage materials was instigated in the British Museum in the early 1970s (Oddy 1973), examples of corrosion on display in its galleries have been minimised. However, on rare occasions, deterioration has been observed, as illustrated by the three following case studies.

In a recent gallery project, large fragments of stucco were displayed, along with three small lead objects. Panels of medium density fibreboard were used to line the back of the large showcase (approximately $2 \times 0.5 \times 3.5$ m). These panels were originally coated with a suitable decorative finish to blend with the colour scheme of the gallery. However, when placed in position, the colour of the board was found to be unacceptable, and due to pressures of time the untested gallery paint was used to recoat the board. Therefore there was insufficient time for the paint to fully cure before the panels were installed in the display case. After a few months white corrosion was noted on the lead pieces; this was identified as a mixture of basic lead carbonate and lead formate. Levels of acetic acid and formaldehyde inside the showcase were over twenty times higher than levels measured in the gallery. When the paint which had been used inside the showcase was tested, it was found to be a source of organic acids, and therefore corrosive to lead. MDF board is also a known source of formaldehyde and organic acids. This highlights two potential problem areas; last minute decisions being taken without full consultation and the need for full testing of materials intended for use in an enclosed display case.

Where corrosion of objects due to pollutant gases does occur, it should be borne in mind that this may not always be due to inappropriate storage or display materials. It has been shown that human beings can 'outgas', producing sulphur-containing gases (Brimblecombe et al. 1992). Although human beings rarely form part of a display, they can be found in research rooms. Objects themselves may also outgas, and affect associated materials. A silver-copper alloy necklace was found to be corroding in the early 1980s, and after conservation, degraded again in storage within a few years, resulting in severe green copper nitrate corrosion. Yellow beads on the same necklace had originally been catalogued as amber and copal, but analysis revealed they were in fact cellulose nitrate (Green and Bradley 1988). Due to loss of plasticiser, the cellulose nitrate beads had become unstable, and degraded to produce nitric acid. This had attacked the silver-copper alloy components of the necklace to produce the copper nitrate corrosion product. Eventually the cellulose nitrate beads were isolated from the necklace to avoid further decay of the silver alloy, and also to minimise effects on other artefacts in the same storage area.

Low-fired ceramics excavated from anaerobic sites have also been found to outgas, producing sulphide gases. This resulted in black deposits of copper sulphide forming on bronze objects in the same display case (Green 1992b). The ceramic vessels could have become impregnated with sulphur-rich or sulphide-producing materials during burial. Recently, it has been shown that iron artefacts from a similar site can also be a source of sulphides. This potential source of sulphide gases should be borne in mind when mixed media displays are planned.

Removal of harmful pollutant gases from museums with an air conditioning system is a costly approach, and not normally effective at reducing levels of gases generated inside enclosed showcases or storage units. In the first instance, it is more effective to ensure that materials used for the storage or display of artefacts are not a source of these pollutants. This is achieved by testing the materials.

Testing for pollutants

Introduction

In this section, detailed procedures for the tests used to assess the suitability of a storage or display material in the British Museum are given. The 'Oddy' test is used where possible to evaluate the effects of a material on metal artefacts. However this takes four weeks and therefore a range of shorter tests has also been developed. These shorter tests have some disadvantages which will be discussed before each test method is described. The tests have been found to cover the various types of material found within the collections at the British Museum. However, other applications may require different tests, for example the photographic activity test (ISO 10214 1991; Nishimura 1990). This particular method is not used at the British Museum as it necessitates a sample of the type of photographs being stored; this may be difficult to obtain. If the photographs are silver based, an Oddy test for silver can be undertaken. The primary object of a test is to be able to know with confidence that a material will not cause any deterioration if used in either the same air space or in direct contact with artefacts. In the event of one of the tests giving the 'wrong' result, e.g. due to contamination of the test material or a species interfering with the test, it is important that it 'fails safe', i.e. that the test gives a positive result and the material is considered unsuitable for use. Although this may mean more materials need to be tested, it is far more preferable to potentially corrosive materials passing a test.

Sampling

Before undertaking any tests it is important to obtain a representative sample of the intended display material, preferably from the batch of material being considered for use. Materials can vary from batch to batch and manufacturers may change their formulations without notification. Storage conditions can cause a material to become more or less corrosive with time. This is due to outgassing or absorption of gases from the storage environment.

Many materials are non-homogeneous and it is important that the sample tested contains all of the different components. For example, a patterned textile may contain threads treated with different dyes. Samples should always be presented to the tests in the form in which they are intended for use. For example, paints or lacquers should be tested as thin, dry films, which have been allowed to cure on glass or Melinex according to manufacturers' instructions. Such materials often emit corrosive gases as they cure. In some circumstances, a longer cure time can be allowed, to reflect that which will occur in practice when the material is used. Details of the time allowed for curing should be recorded with any test results.

Selection of tests

The flowcharts, Figures 17.1 and 17.2, provide a swift method to decide which tests need to be applied to a storage and display material proposed for use with specific groups of artefacts.

Many materials emit gases which may cause deterioration of artefacts. Since the corrosive species are gases, then a material does not need to be in contact with an artefact to cause deterioration, but only needs to be in the same airspace.

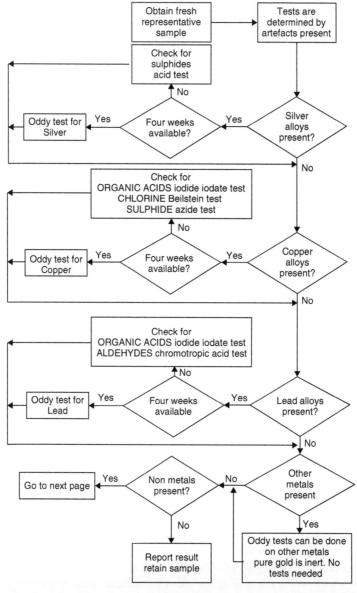

Figure 17.1 Flowchart to determine tests: metal artefacts

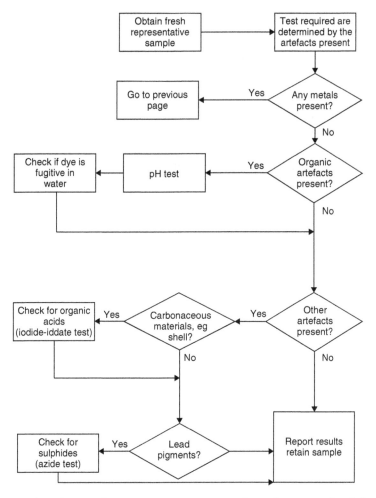

Figure 17.2 Flowchart to determine tests: non-metal artefacts. Details of these tests are to be found in Lee and Thickett (1996: 22–36)

The Oddy test[1] – an accelerated corrosion test for effects on metals (Green and Thickett 1995)

Introduction

The 'Oddy' test is an accelerated corrosion test where the material under test is enclosed in a sealed glass boiling tube with a metal coupon. Corrosion of the metal is accelerated in a number of ways:

- the ratio of test material to airspace is much higher than would be encountered in a display case or storage area. Therefore the concentration of any volatile corrosive gases is higher;
- the metal coupon is abraded to expose a reactive metal surface;

- the relative humidity in the tube is raised to 100%, which generally accelerates the corrosion;
- the temperature is elevated to 60°C, which increases the rate of emission of any volatile degradation products from the material, and accelerates any corrosion reactions.

After 28 days the test is disassembled. The amount of corrosion on the metal coupon is used to classify the material as being:

- suitable for permanent use (no corrosion);
- suitable for temporary use – up to six months only (slight corrosion);
- or unsuitable for use (obvious corrosion).

Metal coupons are chosen to represent the composition of artefacts of concern. Copper, silver and lead have been found to be the most susceptible metals of those used in antiquity. Copper may be used to represent copper alloys (bronze, brass etc) although certain heavily leaded bronzes contain discrete lead particles and proposed storage or display materials should also be tested for their effects on lead. The test has been applied to magnesium, zinc and aluminium (Green and Thickett 1991), and also to iron (Green and Bradley 1997) with some success.

Although the Oddy test has been developed for use with metals, it is possible to deduce the effects of a display/storage material on non-metallic artefacts. As previously described, the pollutants which cause corrosion of certain metals are also known to be the cause of deterioration of various non-metal substrates. Therefore if a material passes the Oddy test, it is not producing the harmful species known to corrode the chosen metal coupon. For example, shells are attacked by organic acids; if a material passes the Oddy test with lead it cannot be a source of organic acids, and is therefore suitable for the display or storage of the shells.

The major advantage of the Oddy test is that it will detect the effects of ALL corrosive species emitted from the sample. Many of the species found to cause corrosion on display are in fact degradation products of display materials. As the Oddy test accelerates the degradation of the test material it will detect if any of them are corrosive.

A drawback of the Oddy test is that 28 days are required before the results are available. If the chosen material fails, i.e. the metal coupon corrodes, an alternative material needs to be found and tested, and the full testing period required can be extensive. The Oddy test method needs to be followed rigorously, as even small changes can lead to differing results (Green and Thickett 1993). The test is designed to be as sensitive as possible and should indicate if a material has any potential to accelerate or cause corrosion of metals. This may lead to a small number of materials failing the test that under normal museum conditions may not cause corrosion. However, the many factors involved in a display case can be difficult to determine and can change with time and it is therefore important to have a sensitive test. Cleanliness of the apparatus is vitally important to avoid cross contamination between samples leading to erroneous results. It should be noted that such contamination would cause material to fail the test, which is far preferable to an unsuitable material passing the test. The coupon assessment stage has been found to be subjective (Green and Thickett 1993). Notes and reference photographs showing levels of corrosion from various tests have previously been published to help with assessing the metal coupons (Lee and Thickett 1996, Plates 4–6). The Oddy test can accommodate any type of solid sample. The size is limited by the neck of the reaction vessel; 24 mm diameter Quickfit glass tubes are used in the British Museum. Bulky materials, e.g. wood and plastics, will require cutting to size. Note that certain materials can swell in the 100% humidity atmosphere and this should be taken into account when sampling. It has been suggested to the authors that solid samples should be powdered to allow all corrosive vapours to escape. However, the elevated temperature of the test will accelerate diffusion of gaseous degradation products from solids and it is unlikely that, given 28 days, such materials will remain trapped. It is therefore not thought necessary to prepare samples as powders.

Test method

The following recommended method should be followed exactly. Care should be taken to ensure all equipment is clean and that it does not become contaminated during preparation of the test. This can lead to erroneous results. The cleaning procedure used for the glassware at the British Museum involves cleaning in chromic acid, washing with hot detergent solution, rinsing with distilled water, drying and passing through a Bunsen flame.

A prepared Oddy test is shown in Figure 17.3.

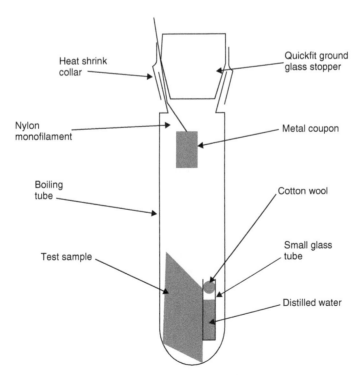

Figure 17.3 Diagrammatic representation of an Oddy test

- AnalaR (99.5% pure or better) metal foils, 0.1 mm thick, should be used: copper to assess the effects of the test material on copper-based artefacts, silver for silver-based artefacts and lead for lead-based artefacts. If artefacts are made of high-lead bronze, which can contain discrete particles of lead, then both copper and lead tests should be carried out. It is recommended that metal foils of the desired thickness are purchased, as processing of a thicker foil may introduce impurities and inconsistencies in the coupons, leading to irreproducible results.
- A 10×15 mm coupon is cut from the metal foil. Both faces of the coupon are lightly abraded using a glass bristle brush. Care should be taken to keep the coupons as flat as possible, as physical distortion can lead to problems at the assessment stage. A separate glass bristle brush should be reserved for each metal to avoid contamination.
- A small hole is pierced in each coupon, close to one edge. It has been found that this can be done effectively by using the guide pin on a pair of dissecting tweezers.
- Nylon monofilament (maximum diameter 0.053 mm) is threaded through the hole in the coupon and tied in place.
- The coupon is degreased in a glass dish of acetone for a few minutes with slight agitation. Using tweezers, the coupon is removed and allowed to dry between tissue paper. The coupon is subsequently handled using only tweezers and while wearing gloves.
- Approximately 2 g of the test material are added to a 50 ml glass boiling tube with a ground glass seal, which is a convenient 'reaction vessel'. Bulky materials should be cut into pieces approximately $10 \times 10 \times 5$ mm. When it is impossible to fit 2 g of certain materials in the tube, e.g. expanded foams, as much test material as is reasonably practical should be used, i.e. without causing contact with the metal coupon.
- A 0.5 ml test tube is filled with distilled water, stoppered with a small plug of cotton wool and added to the boiling tube.
- The nylon monofilament holding the cleaned coupon is trapped in the ground glass joint of the boiling tube. A collar of heat shrink tubing (type NMW360), approximately 15 mm in length, is shrunk onto the ground glass joint using gentle heat from a hot-air blower.
- A control is set up for each type of metal used, i.e. with a metal coupon and water but no test material.
- The assembly is placed in an oven at 60°C. If possible, the boiling tube should be placed at a slight angle from the horizontal to avoid condensation settling on the metal coupon.
- After 28 days the metal coupon is removed from the test and compared with the control coupon. In order to reduce reflections from silver and copper coupons it is recommended that a sheet of white paper is held at an angle of approximately 60° to the horizontal, over the coupons. The level of any corrosion is used to classify the test material as suitable for permanent use (P), temporary use (T) or unsuitable for use (U). See reference photographs and notes (Lee and Thickett 1996, Plates 4a–c).
- It is recommended that occasionally the tests are set up in duplicate, to act as a measure of reproducibility.

- It is recommended that results should be recorded along with manufacturer's/ supplier's details, date of the test and the intended location of the material. A sample of the test material should also be retained.
- A manufacturer may change the processes by which a material is made, which may affect the suitability of that material for use with certain artefacts. Results on most materials are considered to be valid for up to four years, although this is an arbitrary value.

Health and safety information

Consult suppliers' health and safety sheets for further information.

- Acetone is extremely flammable; can cause serious damage on contact with the eyes; may cause dermatitis. The vapour has an occupational exposure standard of $2400 \ mg/m^3$ under the UK COSHH regulations.
- Lead is harmful if ingested. The dust has a maximum exposure standard of $0.15 \ mg/m^3$ under the UK COSHH regulations. Gloves should be worn when handling this material.
- Glass bristle brushes produce many small fragments of glass fibre when used. Contact with the skin should be avoided to reduce risk of penetration into the skin.

   [. . .]

Practical methods of display and storage

[. . .] The purpose of this section is to provide a practical approach to selection of materials for use in the storage or display of museum artefacts. Every material which is proposed for use with an object should first be tested to ensure that it is not a source of harmful gases.

Often, objects have been stored in what may be considered non-ideal areas for many years without any visible change. Conversely, more sensitive objects may deteriorate within a few weeks in the wrong environment. Some of the initial research into effects of outgassing was undertaken due to deterioration of metal components in packing cases which occurred after transit to the tropics (Rance and Cole 1958). Although the components had been in the packing cases for a limited time only, the emissions from wood, combined with exposure to high relative humidity and temperature, resulted in corrosion. It is therefore essential to undertake a risk assessment process in order to identify the needs of different groups of artefacts and to prioritise necessary action regarding their environment, having consideration for the period of display or storage. A permanent display requires a more rigorous approach than, say, a three month temporary exhibition. The potential of a material to outgas within the airspace of a showcase is dependent on its surface area; for example a fabric used to line the baseboard of the case has a larger surface area exposed within the showcase and therefore the capacity to outgas more than an adhesive used to adhere labels where little, if any, surface area of the adhesive is exposed.

In most situations an open gallery will have sufficient natural ventilation to avoid the build up of any gases emitted from materials such as wall paints or carpets, and in such circumstances a more liberal approach may be taken when choosing materials used to furnish and decorate the gallery. However, it is advisable to avoid a pure wool carpet, not only because it will emit sulphide gases but also for factors including durability and pest control. In a more enclosed situation, such as a store room or display case, choice of materials requires more rigorous selection. Floor coverings in storage areas should be inert and easy to clean; suitable materials are quarry tiles or concrete sealed with a tested and approved epoxy coating.

It may be suggested that the ideal museum store or display case is made out of totally inert materials, i.e. glass and metal. However, metals for panels or cupboards are often coated, and care should be taken as some coatings may themselves emit gases. Stove-enamelled polyester or epoxy-based coatings are generally considered to be inert, although, on occasions, problems have occurred due to insufficient curing of the coating during manufacture (Grzywacs and Tennent 1994). Oil-based coatings have been shown to emit higher levels of acids after oven baking (Padfield et al. 1982). Another disadvantage of metal storage systems is that they may corrode if used in areas with elevated humidity.

Complete refurbishment of a gallery or store is not always an option but there are ways of avoiding some of the potential problems. If timber products have to be used for storage or display, or existing wooden fixtures are being reused, it is advisable to try and reduce concentrations of pollutant gases within the area holding the object. One method would be to produce a positive pressure inside the case, to ensure any pollutants inside the case were constantly being driven out. However, it may be more feasible to include ventilation holes to allow free movement of air and hence reduce the opportunity for build up of harmful gases. Ingress of particulates, which themselves can promote degradation, can be minimised by use of a suitable paper or fabric filter over the ventilation holes. If humidity control is required, ventilation in this manner will not be suitable.

Another option to reduce emissions is to 'seal' the wood. However, it should be borne in mind that a coating does not eliminate volatiles but simply delays their egress from a source (Hatchfield and Carpenter 1987). Products are sold for use as wood 'sealants', but this terminology often refers to preparation of a surface to receive further coatings, and is not particularly related to the ability of the 'sealant' to reduce emissions from the wood. Also, wood is an efficient material for buffering changes in relative humidity. A showcase containing wooden components can help stabilise the environment against changes in ambient RH, which is important for artefacts that are susceptible to damage by fluctuating RH. Since the application of a coating is intended to reduce gaseous emissions from the wood by providing an impermeable barrier then it is probable that it will also provide a barrier to moisture movement into and out of the wood and hence reduce the buffering abilities of the wood (Miles 1986). Additionally, several types of paint and varnish will outgas, and could compound the problem (Sparkes 1989). For example, many polyurethane varnishes and oil-based paints will emit organic acids. Consideration should be given to the properties of a coating which may change as it ages and through wear and tear during use. Therefore, it may become less effective with time. Manufacturers often quote lifetimes of a few years only for coatings and recommend regular reapplication.

An alternative method to reduce emissions from timber-based case inserts may be to wrap each board in an inert and impermeable polymer film, such as Melinex (polyester), Moistop or Marvelseal (aluminium/polythene laminates). This is most effective when the barrier film is heat-sealed to form a bag around the board which can subsequently be covered with a suitable display fabric. The relative effectiveness of barrier films is currently being investigated at the British Museum, a series of coatings have also been evaluated, but to date none have been found to be suitable sealants.

To facilitate display, objects may be pinned onto a board. At the British Museum, Sundeala K quality fibreboard is used for this purpose due to its physical properties; it accepts pins readily and holds them firmly in position. However, as Sundeala is a timber-based product it can cause corrosion of lead and it is therefore enclosed in a barrier film, to avoid harmful emissions into the showcase. The barrier film will be pierced if mounting pins are used, and the resulting holes have been found to reduce the effectiveness of the film; care should be taken to minimise perforations. Inert foams have been considered as an alternative to Sundeala as a case insert, but trials with these have shown that minor adjustment of the position of pins cannot be undertaken, as a hole is eventually produced in the foam. In order to avoid scratching of the pinned artefact or galvanic corrosion occurring between a metal pin and metal objects, all pins should be covered with plastic tubing; polythene catheter tubing has been found suitable for this purpose.

Existing stores can be improved on a limited budget using acid-free paper or board as a temporary barrier against emissions from wooden fixtures such as shelves or drawers. However, with prolonged exposure the paper will become acidic and eventually it will have to be replaced. An improvement may be to use an archival quality paper which contains additives, usually alkaline substances. These neutralise the absorbed acidic emissions and will thus increase the time before it requires replacing. However, acidic gases will still permeate through the paper to some extent but the addition of other materials such as zeolite scavengers to paper can minimise this to virtually nothing (Hollinger 1994). Such papers are relatively expensive. Paper will also offer buffering against fluctuations in relative humidity and some provide physical protection. Closed cell foams can be used as a barrier against emissions from wood.

Where the pH of a display or storage material falls outside the accepted range of 5.5–8.5, or it is shown to have the potential to transfer colour to an artefact, then a physical barrier may be used locally to isolate the artefact from the material. This can be effected by using Melinex or Perspex (polymethylmethacrylate) sheet cut to the profile of the base of the artefact, and placed between the artefact and the material of concern. Of course, such a barrier is completely ineffective if the display or storage material is a source of air-borne species, as these can affect all objects within the same air space, not only those in direct contact.

In order to mitigate the effects of low levels of background pollution such as sulphur compounds, or when old cases containing unsuitable materials must be used, then an absorbent material can be included in the case. However, sorbents should be additional to the correct choice of materials where possible, and not used as an alternative. The efficiency of a range of such materials, including molecular sieves and activated carbon, for removal of air pollution from showcases has been investigated (Grosjean and Parmar 1991).

Activated carbon is a broad range sorbent available as a powder or, more conveniently, as a fabric made of woven activated carbon fibres (for example 'Charcoal Cloth' and 'Kynol Activated Carbon Cloth'). The former has been used with some success to protect lead coins and medals which, although housed in an inert metal cabinet, were stored in a room containing a large amount of wooden furniture. Charcoal Cloth has also been used as a temporary measure beneath the display fabric in a showcase made from poor quality materials. Recently at the British Museum, it has been shown that Charcoal Cloth contains chlorides, and therefore direct contact with silver- or copper-based artefacts should be avoided. Zinc oxide pellets (Puraspec 2040 and 5040 made by ICI Katalco) are made specifically for removal of hydrogen sulphide from natural gas. Trials with silver objects in showcases in the British Museum have shown a marked reduction in tarnishing when a tray of Puraspec pellets was placed adjacent to each object (Bradley 1989). A range of products which are designed to remove the pollutant gases from the environment have been evaluated to assess their effectiveness at preventing the tarnishing of silver. Apparatus has been specifically designed to provide background levels of gases naturally present in the ambient atmosphere, to measure the rate of tarnishing of silver coupons, each enclosed with one of the products being evaluated. In addition to the Charcoal Cloth and Puraspec materials, the products under examination include vapour phase inhibitors, impregnated cloths and papers. Results to date suggest that Charcoal Cloth and zinc oxide pellets are the most effective materials, of those tested, in reducing the rate of tarnishing (Lee 1996).

All exposed sorbent materials will eventually become exhausted and need to be renewed. The time for this to occur is difficult to project as it depends on variables such as rate of air change, pollutant concentration, relative humidity and temperature. Although the air can be sampled and analysed to assess the levels of specific pollutant gases, and thus assess the effectiveness of an enclosed sorbent material, this can be extremely costly. An alternative method of evaluating the environment is to monitor the corrosion of exposed metal coupons in a showcase or store, for example silver could be used to monitor sulphide gases and lead to monitor organic acids or formaldehyde. If the metal coupon has a freshly cleaned surface it will be more reactive than the artefacts and will show corrosion at an earlier stage.

To conclude, materials which are intended for use in the storage or display of museum objects must be carefully chosen, to avoid any increased risk of damage to the objects. However, there is room for flexibility of approach in some circumstances, determined by the vulnerability of the particular object(s), site of intended use and period of exposure. [. . .]

Note

1 This test was developed at the British Museum by Andrew Oddy and co-workers in the early 1970s and the method has been through several improvements in later years; it is now referred to as the 'Oddy' test.

References

Arni, P. C., Cochrane, G. C. and Gray, J. D. (1965) 'The emission of corrosive vapours by wood II. The analysis of the vapours emitted by certain freshly felled hardwoods and softwoods by gas chromatography and spectrometry', *Journal of Applied Chemistry* 15: 463–8.

Blackshaw, S. M. and Daniels V. D. (1978) 'Selecting safe materials in the display and storage of antiquities', *ICOM Committee for Conservation 5th Triennial Meeting, Zagreb*, Zagreb: ICOM-CC.

Bogarty, H., Campbell, K. S., and Appel, W. C. (1952) 'The oxidation of cellulose by ozone in small concentrations', *Textile Research Journal* 22: 81.

Bradley, S. M. (1989) 'Hydrogen sulphide scavengers for the prevention of silver tarnishing', in *Environmental Monitoring and Control*, Dundee: SSCR.

Brimblecombe, P., Shooter, D. and Kaur, A. (1992) 'Wool and reduced sulphur gases in museum air', *Studies in Conservation* 37: 53–60.

Brysson, R. J., Trask, B. J., Upham, J. B. and Booras, S. G. (1967) 'The effects of air pollution on exposed cotton fabrics', *Journal of Air Pollution Control Association* 17: 294–8.

Byne, L. (1899) 'The corrosion of shells in cabinets', *Journal of Conchology* 9: 172–8, 253–4.

Daniels, V. D. and Meeks, N. (1992) 'An investigation into foxing phenomena with particular attention to the inorganic components', *Biodeterioration of Cultural Property 2, 2nd International Conference, Yokohama, Japan*: 292–305.

Daniels, V. D. and Meeks, N. (1995) 'Foxing caused by copper alloy inclusions in paper', in H. D. Burgess and J. Krill (eds) *Symposium 88 – Conservation of Historic and Artistic Works on Paper, Ottawa*, Canada: CCI.

Daniels, V. D. and Thickett, D. (1992) 'The reversion of blackened lead white on paper', in S. Fairbrass (ed.) *The Institute of Paper Conservation, Manchester 1992*: 109–15.

Fenn, J. (1995) 'Secret sabotage: reassessing museum plastics in display and storage', in M. Wright and J. Townsend (eds) *Resins Ancient and Modern*, Aberdeen: SSCR.

Gilroy, D. and Mayne, J. E. O. (1965) 'The inhibition of the corrosion of iron in the pH range 6–9', *British Corrosion Journal* 1: 107–9.

Graedel, T. E. and McGill, R. (1986) 'Degradation of materials in the atmosphere', *Environmental Science Technology* 20(11): 1093–100.

Green, L. R. (1992a) 'Investigation of black corrosion on bronze', *British Museum Conservation Research Section Report 1992/8*.

Green, L. R. (1992b) 'Low fired ceramics and H_2S', *Museums Journal* November 1992: 36.

Green, L. R. and Bradley, S. M. (1988) 'An investigation into the deterioration and stabilisation of cellulose nitrate in museum collections', in L. Eaton and C. Meredith (eds) *Modern Organic Materials*, Edinburgh: SSCR, 81–96.

Green, L. R. and Bradley, S. M. (1997) 'An investigation of strategies for the long term storage of archaeological iron', in I. D. MacLeod, S. L. Pennec and L. Robbiola (eds) *Metal 95: Proceedings of the International Conference on Metals Conservation*, London: James & James.

Green, L. R. and Thickett, D. (1991) 'Modern metals in museum collections', in D. Grattan (ed.) *Saving the Twentieth Century – The Conservation of Modern Materials*, Ottawa: CCI.

Green, L. R. and Thickett, D. (1993) 'Interlaboratory comparison of the Oddy test', in N. Tennent (ed.) *Conservation Science in the UK*, Edinburgh: James & James Science Publishers Ltd.

Green, L. R. and Thickett, D. (1995) 'Testing materials for the storage and display of artefacts – a revised methodology', *Studies in Conservation* 40(3): 145–52.

Grosjean, D. and Parmar, S. S. (1991) 'Removal of air pollutant mixtures from museum display cases', *Studies in Conservation* 36: 129–41.

Grzywacs, C. M. and Tennent, N.H. (1994) 'Pollution monitoring in storage and display cabinets: carbonyl pollutant levels in relation to artefact deterioration', in A. Roy and P. Smith (eds) *Preventive Conservation: Practice, Theory and Research,* preprints IIC Ottawa Congress, London: IIC.

Harley, J. D. (1982) (2nd edn) *Artists Pigments c.1600–1835*, London: Butterworths Scientific.

Hatchfield, P. and Carpenter, J. (1987) *Formaldehyde: How Great is the Danger?*, Cambridge, MA: Harvard University Art Museum.

Hollinger, W. K. Jr (1994) 'Microchamber papers used as a preventive conservation material', in A. Roy and P. Smith (eds) *Preventive Conservation: Practice, Theory and Research,* preprints IIC Ottawa Congress, London: IIC.

ISO 10214 (1990) *Processed Photographic Materials – Filing Enclosures for Storage*, Geneva: International Organization for Standardization.

Langwell, W. H. (1976) 'Measurement of the effects of air pollution on paper documents', *Journal of the Society of Archivists* 5: 372–3.

Lee, L. R. (1996) 'Investigation of materials to prevent the tarnishing of silver', *British Museum Conservation Research Group Report 1996/1*.

Lee, L. and Thickett, D. (1996) *Selection of Materials for the Storage of Display of Museum Objects*, British Museum Occasional Papers 111, London: British Museum Press.

Lyth Hudson, F. and Milner, W. D. (1961) 'Atmospheric sulphur and the durability of paper', *Journal of the Society of Archivists* 2: 166–7.

Madsen, H. B. and Hjelm-Hansen, N. (1979) 'Black spots on bronzes – a microbiological or chemical attack?', in *The Conservation and Restoration of Metals*, Edinburgh: SSCR.

Miles, C. E. (1986) 'Wood coatings for display and storage cases', *Studies in Conservation* 31: 114–24.

Morris, M. A., Young, M. A. and Tove, A. M. (1964) 'The effects of air pollution on cotton', *Textile Research Journal* 34: 563–4.

Nishimura, D. W. (1990) 'Improvements to the photographic activity test', in K. Grimstad (ed.) ANSI IT9.2, Dresden: ICOM Committee for Conservation.

Oddy, W. A. (1973) 'An unsuspected danger in display', *Museums Journal* 73: 27–8.

Oddy, W. A. (1993) 'The conservation of coins – is it art, craft or science?', *Images for Posterity. The Conservation of Coins and Medals*, Leiden: National Museums of Coins and Medals.

Oddy, W. A. and Bradley, S. M. (1989) 'The corrosion of metal objects in storage and on display', *Current Problems in the Conservation of Metal Artefacts*, Thirteenth International Symposium on the Conservation and Restoration of Cultural Property, Tokyo.

Oddy, W. A. and Meeks, N. (1982) 'Unusual phenomena in the corrosion of ancient bronze', in N. S. Brommelle and G. Thomson (eds) *Science and Technology in the Service of Conservation*, preprints IIC Washington Congress, London: IIC.

Padfield, T., Erhardt, D. and Hopwood, W. (1982) 'Trouble in store', in   N. S.

Brommelle and G. Thomson (eds) *Science and Technology in the Service of Conservation*, Preprints IIC Washington Congress, London: IIC.

Pickrell, J. A., Mokler, B. V., Griffis, L. C. and Hobbs, C. H. (1983) 'Formaldehyde release rate from selected consumer products', *Environmental Science Technology* 17: 753–7.

Priest, D. J. and Stanley, J. (1994) 'The ageing of paper containing chemithermomechanical pulp', *Environment et Conservation de l'écrit, de l'image et du son*, Paris: Association pour la Recherche Scientifique sur les Arts Graphique.

Rance, V. E. and Cole, H. G. (1958) *Corrosion of Metals by Vapours from Organic Materials. A Survey*, London: HMSO.

Rice, D. W., Cappell, R. J., Kinsolving, W. and Lawskowski, J. J. (1980) 'Indoor corrosion of metals', *Journal of the Electrochemical Society* 27(4): 891–901.

Shashoua, Y. and Green, L. (1990) 'Analysis of corrosion on a silver bead', *British Museum Conservation Research Section Report 1990/32*.

Shashoua, Y. and Thomsen, S. (1993) 'A field trial for the use of Ageless in the preservation of rubber in museum collections', in D. Grattan (ed.) *Saving the Twentieth Century – The Conservation of Modern Materials*, Ottawa: CCI Ottawa.

Shaver, C. L. and Cass, G. R. (1983) 'Ozone and deterioration of works of art', *Environmental Science Technology* 17: 748–52.

Sparkes, T. (1989) 'The effect of surface coatings on formaldehyde emission', *Environmental Monitoring and Control*, Dundee: SSCR.

Wayne, R. P. (1985) *Chemistry of Atmospheres*, Oxford: Oxford Science Publications, Clarendon Press

West FitzHugh, E. and Gettens, R. J. (1971) 'Calclacite and other efflorescent salts on objects stored in wooden museum cases', in R. H. Brill (ed.) *Science and Archaeology*, Massachusetts: MIT Press.

Weyde, E. (1972) 'A simple test to identify gases which destroy silver images', *Photographic Science and Engineering* 16(4): 283–6.

Zeronian, S. H., Alger, K. W. and Omaye, S. T. (1973) 'Effects of sulphur dioxide on the chemical and physical properties of nylon 66', *Textile Research Journal* 43: 222–37.

Chapter 18

Pollution Problem in Perspective

Susan Bradley and David Thickett

Introduction

THE ADVERSE EFFECTS OF indoor-generated pollutant gases on artefacts in museums are well known. The gases of concern are the reduced sulphur gases which
tarnish silver and cause blackening of some pigments; and organic acids and aldehydes
which corrode lead and other metals and can affect non-metals. The gases are given
off by many materials which have been, and in some cases still are, used in the construction of storage units and showcases. The reduced sulphur gases are present in
the atmosphere at reactive levels (Brimblecombe 1990), whereas the organic acids
and aldehydes are present in the ambient atmosphere at negligible levels but can be
present inside store cupboards and showcases at high levels (Leissner et al. 1996).

In the British Museum the effect of indoor pollutants on artefacts in the collection has been studied since 1919. Although the tarnishing of silver and corrosion of
lead were recognised problems, no specific research on prevention and the dangers
of out-gassing of materials was undertaken until the 1960s (Werner 1972). Since
1972 research has been carried out on methods of evaluating materials for use with
the collection, evaluating sorbents, identifying alteration products on objects, and
monitoring pollutant levels.

One of the advantages of working in a Museum with direct access to the
collection is that it is possible to monitor the stability of the collection long-term,
and to review the effects of both conservation treatments and preventive
strategies.

Source: J. Bridgeland (ed.), *ICOM-CC 12th Triennial Meeting Lyon 29 August–3 September 1999*,
London: James & James, 1999, pp. 8–13.

Testing materials for use in display and storage

Between 1972 and 1975 a standard corrosion test was developed in the Museum (Oddy 1975). The test was used to establish whether materials being considered for use in the construction of showcases gave off gases that were corrosive to metals. The materials tested included wood, fabrics for lining showcases, adhesives, sealants, paints and varnishes (Blackshaw and Daniels 1978). The test has since undergone a series of modifications and different workers have used different versions – sometimes devising their own methodologies – leading to inconsistency in the results. An inter-laboratory comparison was carried out (Green and Thickett 1993a), resulting in a definitive methodology (Green and Thickett 1995). The standard corrosion test should be carried out as described in the 1995 publication to ensure reproducibility between operators in different laboratories. In the Museum internal controls are run to ensure the validity of the testing.

The advantages of the test are that it takes into account the ageing of the material being tested and the potential for emissions to change with time; and that any conservator with an oven and basic laboratory equipment can carry it out. A potential disadvantage is that the test takes 28 days to reach completion.

The test is essentially failsafe. Since 1975 to the date of writing we have tested 4080 materials. During this period there have been no instances of materials that passed the test causing the corrosion of objects. When corrosion has occurred it has been caused by the use of a material that failed the test or as a result of out-gassing from other objects in the showcase. In 1982 white spots of corrosion were noticed on two Chinese bronzes (1960 2–20.1 and 1936 11–18.66). The corrosion was identified as lead methanoate. On investigation it was found that the showcase lining fabric had been mistakenly replaced with a fabric that had failed the test for lead. In 1995 several bronze objects in a showcase of Celtic objects were found to be covered with a black powdery corrosion which was identified as copper sulphide. All of the materials used in the construction of the showcase some 15 years earlier had been passed for use. Several ceramic objects in the showcase smelled of sulphide and in tests were found to be emitting a gas which caused the formation of silver sulphide on silver test coupons. The ceramic objects were from a waterlogged site (Green 1992).

The test has proved extremely useful in reducing incidents of corrosion of objects on exhibition in the Museum. However, there is one material which we continue to use inside showcases simply because we can find no satisfactory replacement – wood.

Design of showcases

Until the mid-1980s showcases in the Museum were constructed with wood frames, backboards and case inserts. As wood was corrosive towards lead, conservation was keen for the amount of wood in the construction to be reduced. The Museum exhibition designers were also keen to change the showcase design because the wood frames were heavy and intrusive. In 1988 a metal and glass showcase was introduced. Because no stable alternative that was easy to work with and to pin into could be found wood still had to be used in the case inserts and back boards. For pinning of objects a composite particleboard is used, laminated to a medium-density fibreboard

(MDF) support for structural strength. To reduce emissions the boards were wrapped in Melinex, presenting a barrier to vapour movement, and then covered with fabric. Experimental work has shown that Melinex is not the best barrier and that pinning reduces the level of protection obtained. As a result the boards are now covered with an aluminium/polyethylene laminate, sold as a moisture barrier (Thickett 1998).

Other materials used in the construction of the showcases are tested. If a material does not pass all of the tests carried out and an alternative is not available, the proximity of the material to the objects and the surface area exposed are taken into account in making a decision on use.

The showcases now in use substantially meet both conservation requirements and design requirements.

Reduced sulphur gases

The reduced sulphur gases hydrogen sulphide, H_2S, and carbonyl sulphide, COS, are present in the atmosphere at levels high enough for sulphides to form on the surface of silver and other metals, and for pigments such as lead white (hydrocerussite) to be converted to black lead sulphide. The rate at which silver tarnishes at these background levels is slow and more or less constant. In the Museum newly cleaned silver objects exhibited inside showcases can take between one and three years to re-tarnish. If materials which give off reduced sulphur gases, such as wool and polysulphide adhesives, are used inside a showcase the rate of tarnishing is substantially increased.

Because the majority of galleries in the Museum are not air-conditioned (Bradley 1996) the background levels of hydrogen sulphide and carbonyl sulphide are not removed from the gallery environment. Showcases are well sealed but there is still an exchange of air between the cases and the gallery. An evaluation of the effectiveness of sorbents for sulphide gases in preventing silver tarnishing has recently been carried out. The method of discrimination used was a visual assessment of silver metal test coupons coupled with analysis of the surfaces by X-ray photoelectron spectroscopy (Lee 1996). This analysis revealed that sulphide was only one component of the silver tarnish; oxide, sulphate and chloride were also present. The sorbents activated charcoal and zinc oxide slowed down the formation of silver sulphide, but alteration of the silver surface was not prevented.

Carbonyl pollutants

Lead and other metals including copper alloys, copper alloys containing lead, zinc and magnesium; calcareous stone and ceramics containing soluble salts; and glass are potentially at risk from the carbonyl pollutants methanoic (formic) and ethanoic (acetic) acid and methanal (formaldehyde) (Green and Thickett 1993b; Tennent and Grzywacz 1994). The corrosive carbonyl pollutants are not present in the atmosphere at levels that initiate corrosion (Leissner et al. 1996). Hence by using construction materials which do not emit these gases the problem can be avoided. However, since wood products are still used in showcases and the Museum has many stores with shelving and cupboards constructed from wood, the problem still exists.

Within the Museum levels of these pollutants have been monitored using passive diffusion sensors. In non-air-conditioned galleries, some with wood floors, levels have been at or below the limits of detection for the analytical method. In showcases, monitored levels have been higher than expected, given the precautions taken to minimise the effects of out-gassing from wood. Levels of carbonyl pollutants have been monitored in some wood store cupboards and found to be very high (see Table 18.1).

Table 18.1 Carbonyl pollutant levels at locations in the British Museum

Location	Objects	Methanoic acid µg/m³	Ethanoic acid µg/m³	Methanal µg/m³	Ethanal µg/m³
Gallery 34, case 23	leaded brass, leaded bronze, silver	ND	303±41	24±1	N/A
Gallery 42, ambient		ND	<153	18	N/A
Gallery 42, case 5	enamel, gold, silver	797±47	2094±60	631	N/A
Gallery 46, ambient		ND	ND	14±1	N/A
Gallery 46, case 15	lead, copper, alloy pewter, silver	ND	262±41	171±9	N/A
Gallery 68, ambient		ND	ND	16	N/A
Gallery 68, case 3	lead, copper alloy	ND	317±41	470±24	N/A
Gallery 73, ambient		ND	ND	23±1	14±1
Gallery 73, case 69	silver, copper alloy	401	ND	255	80
Store, ambient		ND	143±41	42	40
Wood cupboard R	lead, bronze	ND	1404±39	16	87
Wood cupboard S	lead, bronze	ND	1201	13	76
Wood cupboard G	lead, bronze	149±63	2473±43	11	
Wood cupboard U	lead, bronze	139±63	2745	6	

ND = not detected, N/A=not applicable

During collection surveys and the conservation of objects, analysis of salt efflorescence, corrosion products and surface deposits is often carried out. Between 1972 and 1998 over 2000 samples have been analysed, and less than 1% have contained methanoates and ethanoates. For analysis relating to objects mentioned in this paper see Table 18.2.

The largest incidence of corrosion attributable to carbonyl pollutants was on Egyptian bronzes stored in wood cabinets (Thickett et al. 1999). The salt was a complex mixture of sodium, copper, carbonate and ethanoate and was present on 6.4% of the collection of 3500 objects. Sodium was not present in the composition of the bronze, but many of the affected objects had previously undergone conservation treatments with sodium-based chemicals. Levels of ethanoic acid in the cupboards were high (see Table 18.1) and the cause of the corrosion was attributed to its reaction on the corroded surface of the bronzes. The corrosion product was present on the bronzes 20–25 years ago and has not been actively forming in recent years. Lead coupons placed in the cupboards to monitor the environment have not corroded, despite the high levels of ethanoic acid present. Also, lead objects stored in the

Table 18.2 Alteration products attributed to the effects of carbonyl pollutants

Object	Registration number	Date of analysis	Form	Identification
Chinese Bronze	OA I960 2–20.1	March 1982	White crystals	Lead methanoate $C_2H_2O_4Pb$
Chinese Bronze	OA 1936 11–8.66	March 1982	White crystals	Lead methanoate $C_2H_2O_4Pb$
Zinc coins	Private collector	July 1982	White corrosion	Zinc methanoate hydrate $C_2H_2O_4Zn.2H_2O$
Marble relief	MLA OA 10562	Sept. 1995	White efflorescence	Calcium ethanoate methanoate hydrate
Egyptian bronzes		1997	Turquoise blue corrosion	sodium copper carbonate ethanoate
Glass weight	EA 1990 2–7.26	June 1997	White crystals	sodium ethanoate
Glass unformed matrix	EA6665	August 1998	White crystals	White crystals sodium ethanoate hydrate $CH_3COONa.2H_2O$
Enamel plaque	MLA AF 2763	August 1997	White crystals	sodium methanoate CH_2OONa

cupboards with the bronzes have not corroded, even though lead is normally more readily corroded by ethanoic acid than copper-based metals. The relative humidity (RH) in the cupboards has been below 45% since monitoring started some five years ago. It appears that a higher RH is required to promote the corrosion reaction on the bronzes. Ambient RH levels in the Museum have fallen during the last 25 years – particularly in winter – due to the improved heating system.

Experimental work has indicated that ethanoic acid is more corrosive than methanoic acid and methanal is the least corrosive species (Thickett et al. 1999). This work also showed that lead was the metal most readily corroded by ethanoic and methanoic acids at 50% RH. Copper was not affected at 50% RH and ambient temperature. These findings confirm observations on the collection. Other instances of corrosion of copper alloy objects have been limited to periods of high ambient RH and temperature and have occurred on uncorroded copper alloy objects displayed in wood-framed showcases with painted backboards or stored in oak drawers.

Efflorescences containing ethanoate or methanoate have been found on stone and glass (see Table 18.2). Approximately 2000 Egyptian stele and other stone objects are stored in oak boxes with glass fronts. The marble relief MLA OA 10562 had evidence of water staining on the reverse which had caused the migration of colour from the box. A surface efflorescence was identified by Fourier transform infrared (FT-IR) spectroscopy as a calcium ethanoate methanoate hydrate; the presence of ethanoate and methanoate was confirmed by ion chromatography.

The Egyptian stela EA 1332 had on the surface a salt efflorescence which contained methanoate, nitrate and chloride in a 3:2:1 ratio. The stela had undergone previous conservation, which included removal of soluble salts. The stela had been returned to its box before adequate drying time had elapsed. The extent to which the stela was contaminated with organic acids was determined by drilling almost through the depth of the stone (85 mm rear to obverse) and sampling in 15 mm aliquots. Ion chromatography was used to analyse the aqueous extracts obtained from the drillings. Methanoate and ethanoate ions were present at 0.01–0.05% w/w concentration in each aliquot. Chloride ions were present at 0.18–0.28% w/w and nitrate ions at 0.64–0.72% w/w. The uniform distribution of the anions was attributed to the salt removal treatment.

For comparison the investigation was repeated on a stela (EA 646) which had not undergone conservation treatment. Again methanoates and ethanoates were present in all the aliquots of the stone at concentrations in the range 0.01–0.06% w/w and the chlorides and nitrates were also uniformly distributed within the stone (Bradley and Thickett 1995). This indicated that wetting was not responsible for the distribution of the anions; and the volatile acids emitted by the oak boxes had migrated throughout both stele. The absence of efflorescence on EA 646 suggests that residual moisture in EA1332 promoted the reaction between the organic acid, soluble salts and calcite matrix.

Analysis has been carried out on the droplets from the surface of weeping glass. The results of this analysis suggest that methanoates and ethanoates are present and may promote weeping. White crystals on the surface of an enamelled plaque, MLA AF 2763, were identified by ion chromatography as sodium methanoate. The plaque was exhibited in a wood-framed island showcase and the baseboard was not covered with a barrier film to limit out-gassing. The environment in the showcase was monitored. Methanoic acid and methanal levels were high, 797 and 631 $\mu g/m^3$, respectively, but the ethanoic acid level was very high, 2094 $\mu g/m^3$. The identification and the pollutant levels raised several questions. Why was methanoate formed when ethanoic acid was present at such high levels? Do methanoic acid and methanal act in a synergistic manner to promote the formation of methanoates? Why were carbonates and sulphates which have been reported on the surface of deteriorated glass by others (Organ and Bimson 1957; Pilz and Troll 1997) not found?

Discussion

Methanoates and ethanoates have formed on objects in environments containing high levels of methanoic and/or ethanoic acid. The measures taken since 1989 to reduce levels of emissions within showcases have been effective and objects made of, or containing lead have not undergone alteration on exhibition. If the showcase environment is corrosive, alteration is normally seen in less than one year. These observations suggest that up to 40C$\mu g/m^3$ of the organic acids can be present within a showcase, or other closed environment at the normal ambient RH (up to 60%) and temperature in the Museum without alteration of metal objects. Observations within the Museum suggest that in wood showcases and storage, corrosion due to out-gassing is promoted at periods of high RH and temperature. In experimental work the rate of out-gassing was found to be both RH and temperature dependent; and levels of organic acids monitored in showcases are normally higher in the summer than in the winter.

Examples of alteration due to carbonyl pollutants on non-metals have been found where high levels of organic acids have been present. The take-up of organic acids by porous stone objects is not unexpected as they have been stored in oak boxes for periods of up to 100 years. The probability that the reaction between the acids and the objects is linked to moisture from a conservation process is of concern, since many Egyptian limestone stele have undergone desalination treatments in the past. It seems probable that as long as the objects are now not exposed to a high RH the formation of mixed salt efflorescence on the surface of the objects can be controlled.

On glass objects there is a need for more investigation to fully understand the long-term effects of the organic acids, and the effects of the chemicals used in previous conservation treatments. This work is being planned.

For all types of objects the composition is an important consideration, as is the conservation history. Lead is the most vulnerable metal but leaded bronzes can be equally vulnerable because of their metallurgy. At high concentrations of organic acids and aldehydes, corrosion on leaded bronzes can occur at RH levels as low as 30% (Eremin and Wilthew 1998). Unleaded copper alloy objects only undergo alteration at an RH >70%; but residues from previous conservation, such as the sodium ions present on the Egyptian bronzes may promote a reaction at a lower RH.

Conclusions

The effects of the reduced sulphur gases are extremely difficult to prevent by passive means as they are present in the atmosphere. Corrosive carbonyl pollutants can be completely eliminated by using materials that do not emit them. However, wood is still used in the construction of showcases. From observation of the objects on exhibition and monitoring levels of carbonyl pollutants inside showcases it has been concluded that levels of ethanoic acid below 400 $\mu g/m^3$ can be present and corrosion does not occur at normal ambient conditions. The composition of an object (e.g. lead in a bronze, and soluble salts in limestone) and the conservation history (e.g. residues of a treatment on Egyptian bronzes and residual moisture in a limestone following desalination) both affect the reactivity of an object to the carbonyl pollutants. Relative humidity and temperature also affect the rate of corrosion since at high levels they promote out-gassing and hence reactions.

Pollutant gases are a problem in museums but one that can be contained by good management of the environment and the collection.

[. . .]

References

Blackshaw, S. M. and Daniels, V. D. (1978) 'Selecting safe materials for use in the display and storage of antiquities', in *Preprints of the 5th Triennial Meeting of the ICOM Committee for Conservation*, Paris: International Council of Museums: 78/23/2/1.

Bradley, S. M. (1996) 'The development of an environmental policy for the British Museum', in J. Bridgland (ed.) *Preprints of the 11th Triennial Meeting of the ICOM Committee for Conservation*, London: James & James.

Bradley, S. M. and Thickett, D. (1995) 'The study of salt and moisture movement in porous stone at the British Museum 1993–1995', in N. Tennent (ed.) *Conservation Science in the UK 1995*, London: James & James.

Brimblecombe, P. (1990) 'The composition of museum atmospheres', *Atmospheric Environment* 24B(1): 1–8.

Eremin, K. and Wilthew, P. (1998) 'Monitoring concentrations of organic gasses within the National Museums of Scotland', *SSCR Journal* 9: 15–19.

Green, L. R. (1992) 'Low fired ceramics and H_2S', *Museums Journal* November 1992: 36.

Green, L. R. and Thickett, D. (1993a) 'Interlaboratory comparison of the Oddy test', in N. Tennent (ed.) *Conservation Science in the UK,* London: James & James.

Green, L. R. and Thickett, D. (1993b) 'Modern metals in museum collections', in D. Grattan (ed.) *Saving the Twentieth Century, the Deterioration of Modern Materials.* Ottawa: CCI.

Green, L. R. and Thickett, D. (1995) 'Testing materials for the storage and display of artefacts – a revised methodology', *Studies in Conservation* 40(3): 145–152.

Lee, L. R. (1996) *Investigation of Materials to Prevent the Tarnishing of Silver*, British Museum, Department of Conservation, Conservation Research Group Internal Report: 1996/1.

Leissner, J., Beuschlein, S., Pilz, M., Martin, G., Blades, N. and Redol, P. (1996) *Assessment and Monitoring the Environment of Cultural Property. Environment programme 1991–1994: Topic II.4: Environmental protection and conservation of Europe's cultural heritage*, CEC-Contract EV5V–CT92–0144 "AMECP".

Oddy, W. A. (1975) 'The corrosion of metals on display', in D. Leigh et al. (ed.) *Conservation in Applied Archaeology and the Applied Arts*, London: IIC.

Organ, R. and Bimson, M. (1957) 'The safe storage of unstable glass', *The Museums Journal* 56: 265–272.

Pilz, M. and Troll, C. (1997) 'Simulation of gold enamel deterioration', in S. Bradley (ed.) *The Interface between Science and Conservation, British Museum Occasional Paper 116.* London, The British Museum: 193–202.

Tennent, N. and Grzywacz, C. M. (1994) 'Pollution monitoring in storage and display cabinets: carbonyl pollutant levels in relation to artefact deterioration' in A. Roy and P. Smith (eds) *Preventive Conservation: Practice, Theory and Research*, preprints IIC Ottawa Congress, London: IIC.

Thickett, D. (1998) 'Sealing of MDF to prevent corrosive emissions', *The Conservator* 22: 49–56.

Thickett, D., Bradley, S. M. and Lee, L. R. (1999) 'Assessment of the risks to metal artefacts posed by volatile carbonyl pollutants', in W. Mourey and L. Robbiola (eds) *Metal 98, Proceedings of the International Conference on Metals Conservation*, London: James & James.

Werner, A. E. A. (1972) 'Conservation and display: environmental control', *Museums Journal* 72(2): 58–60.

Chapter 19

Airborne Pollutants in Museums, Galleries and Archives – Particulates

Jean Tétreault

Sources of airborne pollutants – particles (fine and coarse)

- *General*: aerosol humidifier, burning candles, concrete, cooking, laser printers, renovations, spray cans, shedding from clothing, carpets, packing crates, etc. (due to abrasion, vibration, or wear), industrial activities, outdoor building construction, ozone-generating air purifiers, soil.
- *Ammonium salts*: ammonium sulphate and nitrate: reaction of ammonia with SO_2 or NO_2 in indoor or outdoor environments or on solid surfaces.
- *Biological and organic compounds*: micro-organisms, degradation of materials and objects, visitor and animal danders, construction activities.
- *Chlorides*: sea salt aerosol, fossil combustion.
- *Soot* (organic carbon): burning candles, fires, coal combustion, vehicle exhaust.
  [. . .]

Adverse effects of airborne pollutants – particles

- *General*: abrasion of surfaces (critical for magnetic media), discoloration of objects (especially critical for those with surfaces with interstices that entrap dust, e.g. with pores, cracks, or often micro-irregularities), may initiate or increase corrosion processes due to their hygroscopic nature, or may initiate catalysis forming reactive gases.
- *Ammonium salts*: corrosion of copper, nickel, silver, and zinc, blemishes on furniture varnished with natural resins and on ebonite.
- *Chlorine compounds*: increase of rate of metal corrosion.

Source: *Airborne Pollutants in Museums, Galleries and Archives: Risk Assessment, Control Strategies and Preservation Management*, Ottawa: CCI, 2003.

- *Soot*: discoloration of porous surfaces (painting, frescoes, statues, books, textiles, etc.), increase of rate of metal corrosion.

  [. . .]

Fine particles

It is common to characterize particulate matter (dust) in terms of diameter. This property is important because it determines behaviour and control. Particles have been divided into a few groups based on their aerodynamic diameter (*see Glossary on pp. 277–8). For the control of pollutants, the fine particle (PM$_{2.5}$: suspended particle matter having an aerodynamic diameter equal or less than 2.5 μm) and the coarse particle (PM$_{10}$: aerodynamic diameter between 2.5 and 10 μm) are commonly used as indicators. Figure 19.1 shows size and mass distribution, formation processes, and the deposition velocity* of different particles. Sulphate and nitrate compounds, organic carbon, crustal* materials, and salts are the major harmful compounds from fine particulate matter (PM$_{2.5}$) from outdoors (EPA 2001). They are discharged directly into the atmosphere or formed in the atmosphere from secondary reactions. Canada and the United States show decreasing levels over the last 15–20 years (EPA 2000; EC 1999). Because smaller particles can lodge in the smaller interstices on an object's surface, PM$_{2.5}$ is the most harmful particle size, and its control will also reduce significantly the levels of gaseous pollutants which tend to be grouped by nucleation or be adsorbed by the particle. As shown in Figure 19.1, fine particles having a diameter between 0.05 and 2 μm tend to accumulate in the environment due to their low deposition velocity. They can be in the ambient air for a few days. Due to their small size, they are also the most challenging particle size to control. Any attempt to control the level of PM$_{2.5}$ must consider *a priori* the control of levels of PM$_{10}$ and some super coarse particles (>10 μm) which still contain some potentially reactive compounds, such as combustion residues, human danders, and microbiological specimens. Compared to fine particles, particles larger than 10 μm have a short suspension time*. They are found close to their sources if not carried by strong winds. Fine particles are particularly damaging, because they discolour or soil surfaces. Soiling changes the visual perception of objects. The more fragile, porous, or altered the surfaces, the more difficult they are to clean. Any control strategy designed to maintain low levels of particles is beneficial to objects since cleaning fragile or porous objects can be difficult. Object cleaning is a delicate process that requires time and trained conservators. An ivory sculpture or a delicate First Nations hat made of feathers and down are two good examples of objects that are challenging to clean. Another example would be filamentous mineral specimens, which are probably impossible to clean using conventional methods.

Deposition of hygroscopic, oily, or metallic particles on a surface can initiate or accelerate deterioration as well as the formation of harmful compounds, such as acids. Except for particles generated by cooking activities in a museum's cafeteria or burning combustibles (candles), most indoor-generated particles are composed of soil, dust, and carpet and cloth fibres. Fibres are not generally considered to have direct adverse effects on a collection, with the exception of magnetic media such as audio and video tapes where abrasive dusts are an issue during handling and

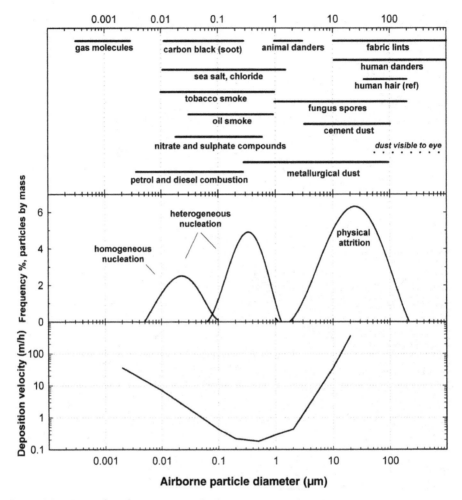

Figure 19.1 Dust distribution. Particle diameters are taken from various sources. The diameter of a human hair is shown for reference only. Deposition velocity adapted from Slinn et al. (1978)

playing. Dust accumulation can also provide an attractive foraging place for insects and mould. Another adverse consequence from a wider viewpoint is the impact of the perception by visitors, including potential donors, that there is a basic lack of care for the collection.

Filtration of outdoor fine particles should be considered as an important control strategy. However, not all particle sizes are evenly controlled. The most dense and the biggest indoor-generated particles (probably bigger than an aerodynamic diameter of 50 μm) do not easily reach filters of an HVAC system. Their suspension times (a few seconds) are too short to be trapped by the air filter system and they fall with gravity. These dust particles can eventually resuspend with air movement from human activity. Dust can also be released by objects and products due to vibrations and dimensional changes from RH fluctuations. Periodic vacuum cleaning is needed and the vacuum cleaner should have a high-efficiency filter. Airtight enclosures and those with a positive pressure system are two good options to prevent dust deposition on objects.

[. . .]

Quantification of the exposure–effect relationship

To establish defensible exposure guidelines, it is essential to determine the quantitative relationship between a given pollutant and its effect on materials. Two approaches have been chosen to determine the exposure–effect relationship: the no and lowest observed adverse effect levels (NOAEL and LOAEL) of an airborne pollutant surrounding an object, and the doses (concentration × length of time). These approaches are the foundation of contemporary quantitative risk assessment (ACS 1998). The notion of deterioration of objects needs to be defined precisely in the context of these concentrations and doses. First, deterioration is a complex function involving many environmental parameters. Fortunately, in indoor environments, many parameters can be considered as pseudo-constant. This assumption simplifies the determination of the effect over time of a single parameter, such as the main airborne pollutant. The second point relates to which chemical and physical characteristics of the objects are the most significant expression of an adverse effect or loss of value. This is a subjective notion and depends on the pollutant–object system. The characteristics and the method used must be the most reliable and meaningful for the decision-makers in the museum. For a comprehensive evaluation of a specific pollutant–object system, more than one characteristic may need to be monitored.

[. . .]

The linear reciprocity principle allows for the estimation of the time required to observe an adverse effect on a material at lower pollutant concentrations. For example, copper has a significant tarnish layer after being exposed to an average level of 1 µg m^{-3} of hydrogen sulphide for 1 year. Based on the reciprocity principle, it takes about 10 years to obtain the same deterioration at a level of 0.1 µg m^{-3}. Figure 19.2 illustrates a good correlation between fine particle soiling and the time required to observe visible signs of soiling over 3 orders of magnitude of fine particle concentrations. The approach of LOAED has some potential for the assessment of the deposition of particles and for the adverse effects of a gaseous pollutant on materials.

[. . .]

Dirt on objects

Even without supportive data, it is safe to assume that depositions of salt, oils, metal particles, and cleaning product residues have a significant affect on the NOAEL and LOAED. In many cases, corrosion begins when a particle is deposited on a metal surface. Salts are hygroscopic and are active in corrosion or efflorescence processes. Salt-contaminated seashells can probably have a NOAEL of acetic acid vapour that is

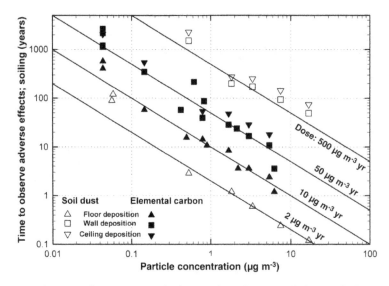

Figure 19.2 Estimated time (years) before soiling due to soil dust and elemental carbon deposition is observed. Adapted from a model. Because elemental carbon is the most important fine particle, $PM_{2.5}$ will give the same darkening (less than 5–20%) as elemental carbon alone. The model assumes homogeneous air distribution (Nazaroff et al. 1993; Bellan et al. 2000)

3–100 times lower than that for "clean" shells. Decontamination of shells and low-fire ceramics can eventually become an important specification for their preservation. Oily residues tend to absorb airborne pollutants, and metal particles can behave as catalysts in the deterioration process.

[. . .]

Controls at building/room level

The main issues at the building level are the infiltration of outdoor gaseous and particulate pollutants, and the emissions from indoor products, visitors, and, in some cases, the collection itself. Common or important control strategies are discussed below.

Avoid

There is usually very little that can be done to control the levels of pollutants outside buildings. However, some measures that can be applied locally include having paved parking spaces and a paved entrance way to avoid resuspension of dust, and limiting heavy traffic close to the museum. For indoor sources, there are many more possibilities.

Control of visitor density

In a crowded exhibit room with inadequate ventilation, the level of pollutants such as ammonia, hydrogen sulphide, dust, and water vapour may increase; likewise the temperature may rise. For the comfort of both visitors and the collection, limiting the maximum density of visitors per room is recommended. For popular exhibits, this can be done by allowing only a certain number of visitors to enter the exhibition every half hour.

Selection and use of products

Due to the high dilution capacity of a room (from natural or forced ventilation), pollutants generated by products do not tend to reach high levels beyond a few weeks following their application. [. . .]

Block, dilute, filter, or sorb

Control with an HVAC system

Large new buildings control the level of pollutants through a central HVAC system especially designed for this purpose. Such systems must fulfil requirements for human health and for the preservation of the collection at a minimum cost. Basic HVAC systems (Figure 19.3) tend to concentrate on a stable and uniform climate with modest control of dust (Table 19.1). In historic houses, the climate control performance depends not only on the HVAC system but sometimes even more on the vapour/gas barrier and thermal isolation capacities of the building and on human activities. Accurate control of pollutants requires expert assessments to determine the combined performance of the HVAC system and the building envelope.

Table 19.1 Parameters of HVAC systems related to the control of pollutants

Parameters	Advantages	Limitations
Use of high-performance particle filters	• Allows better filtration of fine particles. • Delays the need for cleaning HVAC components.	• Performance can be lower than predicted if inadequately installed. • Indoor-generated dense particles are not trapped by the HVAC system due to their short suspension times. • A more powerful pressure fan may be needed for higher efficiency filters (more energy consuming). • Electrostatic air cleaners cannot be used because they generate ozone.
Filtration of the return air	• In addition to the filtration of outdoor pollutants, indoor-generated pollutants such as H_2S, ammonia, and particles emitted or shed from visitors will be filtered.	• More energy consuming.

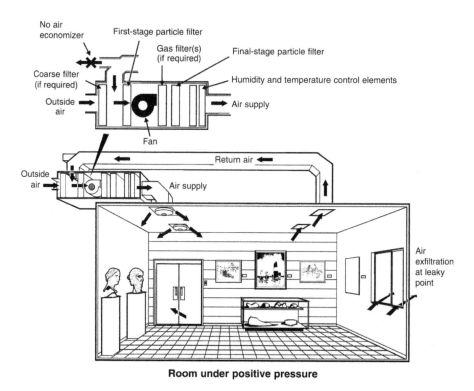

Room under positive pressure

Figure 19.3 Typical HVAC system

Filter systems are important in the control of pollution in new or retrofit buildings. An HVAC filter system can have different filter configurations ranging from a simple water spray with a coarse particle filter to a complex series of specialized gas and high-performance particulate filters. ASHRAE and the European Committee for Standardisation (CEN) have developed new performance standards for dust filters: the ANSI/ASHRAE Standard 52.2 (ASHRAE 1999) and the EN 779 (CEN 2002). Unfortunately, there is no direct equivalency between these two standards. The previous standard dust spot test and the (old) EN 779 (ASHRAE 2001) are based on the same measurement method and can be used to make approximate correlations between the two new standards. Figure 19.4 shows the typical efficiency of filters for different particle sizes based on the dust spot test. These efficiencies serve as estimations, since the real efficiency varies depending on such physical parameters as airflow and saturation of the filter. For example, a filter with an efficiency of 80% blocks half of the 0.3 µm particles and more than 95% of the 2.5 µm particles. As shown in Figure 19.4, blocking infiltration of fine particles is important since the most harmful particles for museums are those having an aerodynamic diameter between 0.01 and 1 µm, such as carbon black, salt, and sulphate and nitrate compounds.

The performance of the filter system should be proportional to the building capacity and the function of the room. Even with the most efficient filter system,

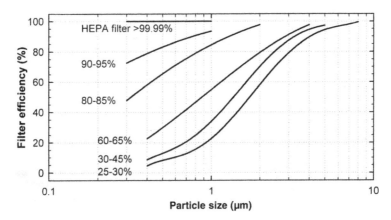

Figure 19.4 Efficiency of filters versus particle size based on the dust spot test (ASHRAE 2001)

the deposition of fabric lints or human danders will remain an issue if there is too much human activity or circulation in the room. Table 19.2 shows five progressive specifications related to the performance of filter systems. When a museum has a centralized HVAC system, a final-stage filter with at least 70–75% efficiency (dust spot test) should be specified. This filter performance corresponds to Level D, and represents a performance slightly above that expected for office buildings. However, at this level only about 40% of the fine particles are filtered. Subsequent classes represent more progressive, balanced performance levels. At Level B, a gas filter should be considered for more global pollutant control. Level A is the optimum level. It provides superior control of fine particles (a reduction of more than 80%, with an acceptable pressure drop). Different configurations of filters are also possible as long as the minimum performance required is respected.

Due to the high cost of high-performance filters, a lower-performance, first-stage filter is often installed upstream to extend the useful life of the high-performance final filter. The final filter must be installed downstream of the fan for optimal efficiency in positive pressure. It is also possible to add, before the first-stage filter, a prefilter for very coarse particles such as sand, insects, and dead leaves. However, the use of medium-performance first filters is more common, partly because the price of these filters has fallen but also due to the long-term benefit of postponing the need to clean the climatization unit (e.g. heat exchanger or cooling coils). Reasonable energy consumption, the extended life for the final-stage filter, and dust abatement procedures leading to finer particles with less mass have all promoted the use of medium-performance filters. Furthermore, air intakes are most often placed at the roof level rather than close to the dust-loaded ground level. The use of medium-performance filters as first-stage filters has been well documented in some engineering standards, such as the Swiss (SWKI 96–4), German (VDI 6022), and Canadian guidelines (Société Suisse 1998; Verein 1998; Nathanson et al. 2002).

With increasing concerns about viruses, bacteria, and metallic toxic dust, HEPA filters have become more popular and readily available. A true HEPA filter removes

Table 19.2 Specifications for HVAC filter systems

Class of specification	First-stage particle filter, minimum efficiency based on				Final-stage particle filter, minimum efficiency based on			
	ASHRAE 52.2 (MERV)[a]	Dust spot efficiency[b]	EN 779[c]	Gas filter[d] (stages)	ASHRAE 52.2 (MERV)	Dust spot efficiency	EN 779	Return air[e]
AA	≥12	≥70%	≥F6	1 or 2	≥16	>99%	≥H10	filtered
A	11	60–65%	F6	1	15	>95%	F9	filtered
B	10	50–55%	F5	1	14	90–95%	F8	filtered
C	9	40–45%	F5	none	13	80–85%	F7	filtered
D	8	30–35%	G4	none	12	70–75%	F6	unfiltered

a: MERV: Minimum efficiency reporting value from ANSI/ASHRAE Standard 52.2 (ASHRAE 1999).
b: Performance of the filter based on the atmospheric dust spot test ASHRAE 52.1.
c: EN 779 from the CEN (CEN 2002).
d: See Table 11 for the selection of gas filters.
e: Return air is filtered when it is recirculated through the filter system.

99.97% of all 0.3 µm particles while a near-HEPA filter removes particles with an efficiency between 90 and 99.97%. Because of the high pressure drop, HEPA filters are very energy demanding. HEPA filters are mainly used for the pharmaceutical or semi-conductor industries, where staff must wear special clothing and masks. Obviously, this is not the case for museums offering public access to their collection. In some special cases, restricted access collections will benefit by having very high-performance filters if the use of enclosures is not an option. This performance is referred to as specification Class AA in Table 19.2. If the gas filter releases sorbent particles, it is recommended to include a pre-final-stage filter in front of the expensive final filter. [. . .] It is usually easy to know when particle filters are saturated and need replacement: the pressure of the HVAC system drops, the filter gains substantial weight, or dust can be seen on the filter. [. . .]

Electrostatic air cleaners incorporated into HVAC systems are not appropriate for museums. With this type of cleaner system, particles acquire a charge as they pass through a high voltage. Negatively charged particles are then attracted by oppositely charged surfaces from which they may be removed later. However, the ionization produces substantial amounts of ozone, a strong oxidant. A wet scrubber or water spray system incorporated into an HVAC system partly removes particles and gases by bringing them into contact with water. Such a system, by itself, does not reduce the water vapour infiltration into the building. It has an uneven efficiency for gaseous pollutants but it does reduce the level of fine particles (PM2.5) by about 50% and particles having a diameter of more than 10 µm by more than 99% (Air Pollution Training Institute 2000). The main disadvantage of wet scrubbers is that they need periodic cleaning to avoid calcareous deposition and mould contamination.

[. . .]

Vacuum cleaning

Proper housekeeping is important. When vacuuming floors, be sure to use proper filter bags as vacuum cleaning can resuspend about half of the fine particles ($PM_{2.5}$) when the filter's efficiency is below 75%. This means that, in a museum without an HVAC system, each time vacuuming is done only about half the deposed fine particles will be captured while the others may settle down in hard-to-clean places such as an object's surface. Fortunately, it is now easier to get vacuum cleaners designed for high-efficiency filtration (Stavroudis 2002a, b).

[. . .]

Protective wrapping

When an object is in storage and does not have to be visible, wrapping it with sorbent fabrics is a low-cost, very efficient way to provide long-term protection against outdoor pollutants such as particles and oxidants. As shown in Figure 19.5, textiles can be rolled with two or three layers of cotton fabrics or acid-free tissues. An alkaline-buffered cardboard box is adequate to maintain low levels of outdoor acids even if the box is just moderately airtight. Silver objects wrapped with sorbent fabrics such as Pacific Silvercloth or activated charcoal cloth remain untarnished for more than 10

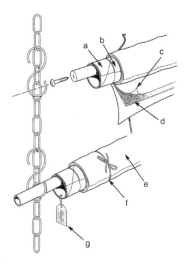

Figure 19.5 Textiles wrapped with cotton or acid-free tissues are well protected
against airborne pollutants: (a) Mylar (Melinex) type D or type 516
covering a plastic or cardboard tube; (b) acid-free tissue or prewashed
cotton sheeting over Mylar; (c) interleaving of neutral pH tissues or prewashed cotton sheeting; (d) textile with pile on outside; (e) prewashed
cotton cover; (f) cotton tape; (g) identification tag

years. Even in a simple polyethylene plastic bag, the protection of silver or any metal
object is greatly improved (Figure 19.6). The polyethylene bag is probably the most
cost-effective solution. However, the lifetime of plastic sheets for indoor use is usually limited to 10–20 years.

[. . .]

Figure 19.6 A jet and space rockets wrapped in plastic during renovations

* Glossary

The following terms are defined on the basis of the way in which they are used in this book and/or the field of preservation. Some terms may have wider or alternate meanings in other fields.

[. . .]

Aerodynamic diameter
The diameter of a sphere with a unit density that has an equivalent aerodynamic behaviour to that of the particle in question; an expression of aerodynamic behaviour of an irregularly shaped particle in terms of the diameter of an idealized particle. Particles with different dimensions and shapes may have the same aerodynamic diameter.

[. . .]

Crustal particles
Particles emitted directly from a non-industrial surface (e.g. paved roads and traffic, construction, agricultural operations, high wind events) and some industrial processes.

Deposition velocity (or mass transfer coefficient)
A measure of the rate at which a pollutant reaches the surface of a material. A common unit is metres per second (m/s) or per hour (m/h). Visualize the time it takes a particle to fall a distance of 1 m. If it takes 2 h, the particle has a deposition velocity of 0.5 m/h (1 m/2 h). This number is determined experimentally and is used as a constant to simplify modelling. The deposition velocity refers only to mass transfer from the ambient air to a surface. The mass transfer coefficient refers to mass transfer from the ambient air to a surface, or from a surface to the ambient air. Its value will be positive or negative depending on the direction of the transfer.

[. . .]

Electrostatic precipitator
A type of air pollution control system that uses high voltage fields to give particulate matter an electrical charge. When the charged particles approach an electrically grounded collection plate they accumulate as a dust layer, which is mechanically removed (at least partially) on a routine basis.

[. . .]

HVAC system
A heating, ventilating, and air-conditioning system that includes any interior surface of the facility's air distribution system for conditioned spaces and/or occupied zones.

[. . .]

Nucleation
A process by which gases or fine particle compounds interact and form aggregates with the same molecules (homogeneous) or with different molecules (heterogeneous).

[. . .]

Suspension time
The average period for which an emitted or resuspended pollutant stays in the ambient air or is carried in the atmosphere without chemical conversion. Also referred to as atmospheric residence time.

[. . .]

References

ACS (American Chemical Society) and Resource for the Future (1998) *Understanding Risk Analysis: A Short Guide for Health, Safety, and Environmental Policy Making.* Internet edition (1998), pp. 6–27. <www.rff.org/misc_docs/risk_book.pdf>

Air Pollution Training Institute (2000) 'Control Techniques', Module 6, in *Air Pollutants and Control Techniques, Basic Concepts in Environmental Sciences.* <www.epin.ncsu.edu/apti/o1_2000/module6/mod6fram.htm>

ASHRAE (2001) 'Air Cleaners for Particulate Contaminants', Chapter 25, in *Heating, Ventilating, and Air-Conditioning: Systems and Equipment*, ASHRAE Handbook. Atlanta: ASHRAE, pp. 25.3–25.5.

ASHRAE (1999) *Methods of Testing General Ventilation Air-Cleaning Devices for Removal Efficiency by Particle Size*, ANSI/ASHRAE Standard 52.2–1999, pp. 35–39.

Bellan, L. M., Salmon, L. G. and Cass, G. R. (2000) 'A Study on the Human Ability to Detect Soot Deposition onto Works of Art', *Environmental Science & Technology* 34: 1946–1952.

CEN (European Committee for Standardisation) (2002) *Particulate Air Filters for General Ventilation: Determination of the Filtration Performance*, EN 779. Brussels: CEN.

EC (Environment Canada) (n.d.) *Climate Trends and Variations Bulletin.* <www.msc-smc.ec.gc.ca/ccrm/bulletin/>

EC (Environment Canada) and HC (Health Canada) (1999) *National Ambient Air Quality Objectives for Ground-level Ozone: Science Assessment Document.* Hull: Environment Canada, pp. 7–1–7–32. <www.hc-sc.gc.ca/hecs-sesc/air_quality/publications/ground_level_ozone/part1/toc.htm>

EPA (2001) *Latest Findings on National Air Quality: 2000 Status and Trends,* EPA-454/K-01-002. Research Triangle Park, pp. 6–13. <www.epa.gov/oar/aqtrnd00/brochure/00brochure.pdf>

EPA (2000) *National Air Pollutant Emission Trends, 1900–1998*, EPA-454/R-00-002. Research Triangle Park, pp. ES-3, ES-5, 2.3, 2.12, 3–27, 3–29.

Nathanson, T., Morawska, L. and Jamriska, M. (2002) 'Filter Performance Guidelines for Good IAQ', in H. Levin (ed.) *Proceedings of the 9th International Conference on Indoor Air Quality and Climate*, Santa Cruz: International Conference on Indoor Air Quality and Climate, pp. 1082–1087.

Nazaroff, W. W., Ligocki, M. P., Salmon, L. G., Cass, G. R., Fall, T., Jones, M. C., Liu, H. I. H. and Ma, T. (1993) *Airborne Particles in Museums. Research in Conservation No. 6*, Marina del Rey: The Getty Conservation Institute, pp. 38–41, 91–103. <www.getty.edu/conservation/resources/reports.html>

Slinn, W. G., Hasse, N., Hicks, L., Hogan, B. B. A. W., Lai, D., Liss, P. S., Munnich, K. O., Sehmel, G. A. and Vittori, O. (1978), 'Some Aspects of the Transfer of Atmospheric Trace Constituents past the Air–Sea Interface', *Atmospheric Environment* 12, 2055–2087.

Société Suisse des ingénieurs en chauffage et climatisation (1998) *Directive 96–4 pour l'utilisation des filtres dans les installations aérotechnique,* Bern: Société Suisse des ingénieurs en chauffage et climatisation.

Stavroudis, C. (2002a) 'HEPA HEPA HEPA', *AIC Newsletter* January (2002a), 24–25. <aic.stanford.edu/health/hepa.html>

Stavroudis, C. (2002b) 'Never Mind the Bollocks, Here's the HEPA Chart', *WAAC Newsletter* 24, 13–16.

Verein Deutscher Ingenieure (1998) *Hygienic Standards for Ventilation and Air-Conditioning Systems Offices and Assembly Rooms,* VDI 6022. Dusseldorf: Verein Deutscher Ingenieure.

Chapter 20

The Effects of Visitor Activity on Dust in Historic Collections

Helen Lloyd, Katy Lithgow, Peter Brimblecombe, Young Hun Yoon, Kate Frame and Barry Knight

Introduction

D
UST DEPOSITION INDOORS is an atmospheric process that poses a significant risk to cultural property on open display. The increasing desire for open display in museums raises concerns that have always been present in historic houses. Apart from exacerbating deterioration, the accumulation of particles detracts from the visual appearance and necessitates cleaning to maintain the artistic worth and public appreciation of objects as well as their survival. The particles in such accumulations are often rather coarse and include large fibres (Schneider et al. 1996), so are usually considered easy to remove by gentle brushing or vacuuming. But each time an object is cleaned, especially those with fragile surfaces, there is a risk of damage, for example removing original silk fibres. If the dust is left in place, damage of a different kind may result. Dust appears to become more strongly bound to surfaces over time, a process that worried housekeepers of the late eighteenth century who wrote that '. . . places where the dust lodges should be attended to. Otherwise, if left too long, it takes a long time and much labour to get it off . . .' (Hardyment 2000). Even apparently resistant surfaces such as porcelain gradually become dull over decades, with the formation of strongly bound films of deposited particulate material.[1]

[. . .]

Current housekeeping regimes in the properties investigated

The challenges faced by conservators and other staff working in historic houses differ from those faced by their colleagues in museums. Fragile materials more usually

Source: *The Conservator* 26 (2002): 72–84.

seen in glass cases are instead on open display within their original historic context (National Trust 1996; Sandwith and Stainton 2001). As a result, careful regimes of housekeeping have been developed to ensure the day-to-day prevention of damage and deterioration, especially from visitors and dust. Simple ropes and stanchions prevent visitors from touching tactile materials, and traditional floor covers ('drugget') prevent footwear from eroding or soiling carpets and floors (Lloyd 2002). Entrance matting is used to remove grit, gravel and mud from outdoor footwear. Daily cleaning on open days includes vacuuming of floors accessible to visitors, and dusting robust polished surfaces, while fragile surfaces within sight of visitors are only occasionally lightly cleaned to maintain standards of presentation.[2] To reduce cumulative damage caused by cleaning, less accessible surfaces are inspected annually and cleaned only when necessary, not as a matter of habit (National Trust 1991; Lloyd 1997; Lloyd and Staniforth 2000). Glass display cases are used in exceptional circumstances to provide greater environmental protection and security for particularly vulnerable materials, such as fragile textiles and silver.

Dust monitoring methods used

Studies of soiling concern the rate of deposition of particles on surfaces, rather than the concentration of particles in the air, so instead of concentration, deposition was measured. There is at present no standard method of measuring deposition of particles in museum environments, but two common methods involve collecting deposits either on glass slides or on sticky samplers (Adams et al. 2001). To minimise accidental loss of larger particles, sticky samplers were adopted for this study (Figure 20.1). Samplers were arranged at 20 cm intervals to monitor profiles of deposition. Vertical

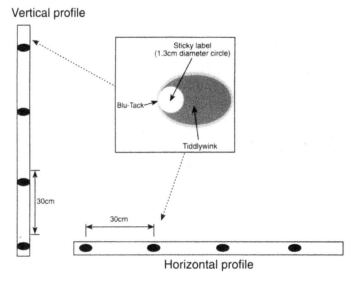

Figure 20.1 Sticky sampler made from Teflon™ labels attached to a tiddlywink counter with Blu-Tack™. © UEA/Y. H. Yoon

Figure 20.2 Detail showing samplers attached to cotton tape laid between the visitor
barrier and the State Bed. © National Trust/K. Lithgow

profiles up walls, tapestries, bed hangings and window curtains, and horizontal profiles across bedspreads and floors, were monitored (Figure 20.2).

[. . .]

The dust deposited was studied in two ways.

Manual method

The number of dust particles collected on each of the sticky samplers was counted
visually using a light microscope at 40× to 200× magnification (Yoon and Brimblecombe 2000a). Although laborious, this method allowed particles of a size greater
than 2.25 μm to be classified as fibrous or non-fibrous dust, and their likely source
to be identified.

Automatic method (image analysis)

Digital images were analysed using Adobe PhotoShop 4.OK (410 × 299 pixels) to
calculate the soiling, i.e. the fraction of the total area of the sticky samplers that was
covered by particles during the 8 weeks the samplers were exposed. The soiling rate
could then be expressed as the percentage of the area covered by particles for every
second of exposure. In order to provide measurements in numbers of a manageable
size, the units reciprocal gigaseconds (Gs^{-1}) were chosen. As 1 Gs is a billion seconds,
or roughly 31.7 years, the unit can be thought of as equivalent to dust covering 100%
of a surface in 31.7 years, or 1% of a surface in 4 months. A coverage rate of 2 Gs^{-1}
would therefore be twice as fast and 0.5 Gs^{-1} twice as slow.

Case studies

Four historic houses, Knole, Hampton Court Palace, Osterley Park, Audley End
were subject to dust monitoring in a variety of rooms.

Knole

[. . .]
During 2001, the closure of the deer park to prevent spread of foot-and-mouth disease provided an unexpected opportunity to measure dust levels when there were no visitors to the house. The results were then compared with those collected when the house re-opened and attendance rose to 400 per day. During the closed period, dust deposition in both the King's Bedroom and Brown Gallery was minimal (Figure 20.3). After reopening, dust deposition in the Brown Gallery increased 20-fold, while in the King's Bedroom, where the King's Bed is protected by a glass enclosure, the dust hardly increased after re-opening. The route through the Gallery took visitors past two of the samplers C and E twice, and the higher measurements demonstrated that repetitive visitor activity causes more rapid coverage of dust. The vertical profile of dust deposition on the visitor side of the glass barrier in the King's Bedroom (Figure 20.4) showed that some dust was deposited at floor level. This dust consisted mostly of large mineral and soot particles, with some fibres from the carpet (15–100 µm diameter, 5 mm long). However, little of this dust was found to rise above 30 cm. Most dust was deposited between 80 and 150 cm above floor level, roughly between hip and shoulder height. Whilst after reopening dust levels increased at both floor level and waist height, dust levels remained low between these two points, showing that dust was being stirred up from the floor and also generated at waist height by visitors' clothing. If the dust deposited at 80–150 cm had been stirred up from the floor, the graph would have shown a straight line. Particles at waist–shoulder height were generally smaller than those found at floor level. While again containing some soil dust and soot, they mostly comprised large clothing fibres (5–20 µm diameter, 0.3–1 mm long) that were presumed to come from upper garments.
[. . .]

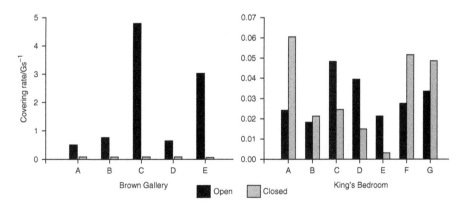

Figure 20.3 Covering rates of dust when Knole was closed and then open, to illustrate the impact of visitors in accessible and inaccessible areas. © UEA/ Y. H. Yoon

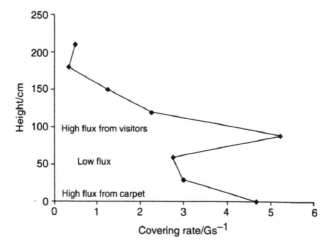

Figure 20.4 Covering rate of dust, with height above floor. The organic particles were mostly carpet fibres at floor level, and clothing fibres at higher levels. ©UEA/Y. H. Yoon

Hampton Court Palace

[. . .]

Hampton Court Palace has much more visitor activity than the other sites studied. The palace is open 363 days per year and receives annually more than 600,000 visitors during daytime (averaging over 11,500 visitors per week) and up to 10,000 guests at evening functions. Within the display rooms, richly costumed interpreters perform lively events for the visiting public and hundreds of catering staff serve the evening receptions and dinners. In the Tudor kitchens an open fire is lit daily, generating soot.

[. . .]

The palace was found to have rates of dust deposition two to three times greater than the other sites. All but a few samplers showed similar patterns of horizontal dust deposition that illustrated a significant decrease in dust as the distance between visitor and sample point increased. For example, on the Campaign Bed, positioned 1 m from a visitor barrier, the greatest amount of dust deposited horizontally was found up to 1.50 m from the barrier, from where it gradually decreased to approximately 80% less dust at 2.40 m. A similar decrease in dust levels was found on a State Bed situated 2 m from a visitor barrier. Slightly greater levels of dust at the Campaign Bed site were attributed to the warders' daily adjustment of the floor-mounted alarms nearby. This horizontal distribution is similar to that found at Knole. In the small Pages' Chamber it was interesting to note that especially high levels of inorganic dirt were found at the greatest distance from the visitors, by the fireplace. This could be explained as having been generated by an uncapped chimney in the room.

[. . .]

Osterley Park House

[. . .]
    Monitoring of dust at Osterley Park House focused on three beds. The two first seen by visitors are on the first floor. The Yellow Taffeta Bedroom is named after the fragile painted silk hangings of the Adam bed, conserved in 1998. The earlier mahogany bed in Mr Child's Bedroom retains only the valances and bed cornice of its original 1759 embroidered Indian silk hangings. At the end of the visitor route, on the principal floor, the State Bed forms the centrepiece of a 1776 suite of three rooms symbolising natural elements and decorative styles.
    [. . .]
    Visitors are kept at least 1 m away from all three beds by ropes and stanchions. The highest dust readings were found to occur beside the visitor route, declining to nearly half by 0.8 m away from the route (Figure 20.5). On all three beds, levels rose to a peak at 1.75–2 m from the visitor route and then declined to their lowest point 2.75–3 m away. The lower readings at the end of the bed beside the visitor route may indicate that the foot curtains help to shield the bed cover from dust, with levels rising again as visitors lean over the barrier to examine embroidery details. The least dust was detected on the State Bed at the end of the visitor route, and the most in the Entrance Hall at the beginning. About 40 times more dust was found on the tester of Mr Child's Bed than on the Yellow Taffeta or State Beds (Figure 20.6).
    [. . .]

Audley End House

[. . .]
    The house is open between April and November, and receives about 118,000 visitors per year. The windows are kept closed, and shutters and blinds are used to

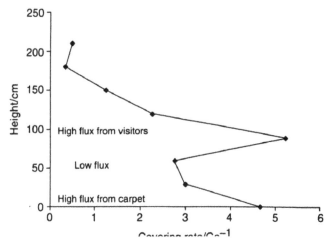

Figure 20.5 Covering rate of dust, with distance from a visitor route, in three bedrooms at Osterley Park House. © UEA/Y. H. Yoon

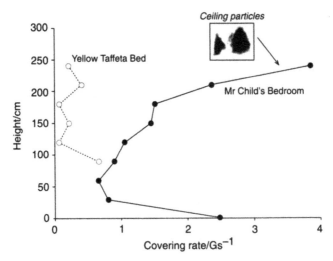

Figure 20.6 The results from Mr Child's Bed show the usual peak in dust deposition at floor level, but that even more dust is being deposited on the tester. Micro-photograph of paint particle from ceiling. © UEA/Y. H. Yoon

control light levels. Ambient pollution levels are low but gravel paths surround the house, and dust brought in on visitors' feet is known to be a problem. Visitors follow a set route round the house, marked by stanchions and drugget. Dust was monitored in five rooms on the first floor: the Saloon, the South Library, the Library, the Neville Bedroom and the Howard Bedroom.

[. . .]

Results from the Saloon, South Library and Library duplicated those seen in the Brown Gallery at Knole. The deposition rate was highest in the Saloon, which is the first furnished room on the visitor route. It was lower in the South Library, where visitors walk straight through, than in the Main Library (the next room), where visitors make two turns. This suggests that increasingly complex visitor routes with many turns increase dust deposition rates. In the Neville Bedroom, the deposition rate at 240 cm was only one-quarter of that at 120 cm (Figure 20.7). Vertical monitoring inside and outside the bed curtains found that outside the curtains deposition reduced continuously from ground level up to about 175 cm, after which it was more or less constant at about one-tenth of its value at ground level. Inside the curtains the deposition rate was lower and hardly affected by height from the floor (Figure 20.8).

[. . .]

Results and discussion

[. . .]

In all four sites monitored, dust deposition caused by visitors tended to be more marked in turbulent areas, for example at entrances to historic houses where dust may be stirred up from ground level (0–30 cm) and where visitors remove outer garments. It was less marked in the last rooms of the visitor route. Although complex

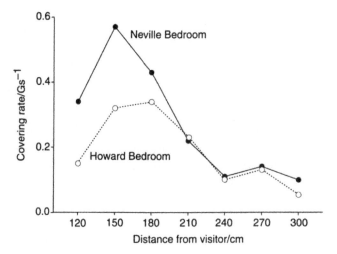

Figure 20.7 Horizontal covering rates for Neville and Howard Bedrooms, Audley
End House. © UEA/Y. H. Yoon

and lengthy visitor pathways within each room seemed to increase dust deposition
rates, dust coverage was halved with each additional metre of distance between visitors and furnishings. Dust particles were shed from visitors only up to heights of 1.5
m, and clothing fibres generated from upper garments were typical of those particles
found at waist–shoulder height (80–150 cm). These studies confirmed previous findings that dust and dirt brought in or stirred up by visitors' shoes rose only to 30 cm,
and consisted of a high proportion of mineral and plant material (Yoon and Brimblecombe a, b).

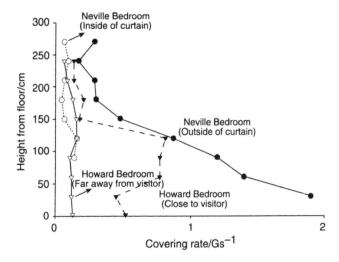

Figure 20.8 Vertical covering rates for Neville and Howard Bedrooms, Audley End
House. © UEA/Y. H. Yoon

This project showed that visitors have a strong impact on soiling rates within historic buildings. While visitors add to the income of properties they also impose costs, in terms both of damage and of increased need for cleaning. Nevertheless this work suggests that there are management choices that can reduce the impact of dust deposition from visitors.

[. . .]

Rope barriers or well-defined pathways, already used to enhance security and viewing conditions in crowded rooms, can also keep visitors at a reasonable distance from dust-sensitive objects. Each additional metre of distance between visitors and furnishings halves the soiling rate, so that optimum protection of fragile materials can be provided at distances greater than 2 m. More solid barriers can also be effective, but may intrude on the visitors' experience. Shoulder-height barriers may provide dust control equally effectively as screens that rise from floor to ceiling, although the latter provide other advantages, such as localised environmental control and greater scope for artificial lighting. However, within a historic context any form of glass barrier is intrusive, and only considered as a last resort when all management and traditional housekeeping measures have been exhausted.

[. . .]

Although carpets could be a reservoir of dust, the deposition of dust in the first 30 cm above the floor is not especially sensitive to floor covering (Yoon and Brimblecombe 2000b). However, it is clear from this study that entrance matting, if well designed and properly maintained by daily vacuuming, is extremely useful in collecting soiling from visitors' shoes and in preventing its transfer to floors further within the building. Although these studies took place in historic buildings in rural sites, where environmental control is achieved without air-conditioning, the results may interest those working in air-conditioned museums where collections are now on open display and where the effectiveness of air filters in reducing dust levels varies considerably.

[. . .]

Notes

1   Observations made since 1982 by Helen Lloyd, Ceramics Conservation Adviser, National Trust.
2   In unpublished course notes, edited by H. Lloyd for Housekeeping Study Days, National Trust, 2002.

References

Adams, S. J., Brimblecombe, P. and Yoon Y. H. (2001) 'Comparison of two methods for measuring the deposition of indoor dust', *The Conservator* 25: 90–4.
Hardyment, C. (2000) *The Housekeeping Book of Susannah Whatman*, London: National Trust.
Lloyd, H. (1997) 'The role of housekeeping and preventive conservation in the care of textiles in historic houses', in K. Marko (ed.) *Textiles in Trust*, London: Archetype Publications and the National Trust.

Lloyd, H. (2002) 'Strategies for visitor management at National Trust properties', in A. Brandt-Grau, S. Perez-Vitoria, M. Chapuis and J. Leissner (eds) *Research for Protection, Conservation and Enhancement of Cultural Heritage: Opportunities for European Enterprise*, Luxembourg: European Commission and French Ministry of Culture and Communication, Office for Official Publications of the European Communities.

Lloyd, H. and Staniforth, S. (2000) 'Preventive conservation and "a madness to gaze at trifles": a sustainable future for historic houses', in A. Roy and P. Smith (eds) *Tradition and Innovation: Advances in Conservation, Preprints IIC Melbourne Congress*, London: International Institute for Conservation (IIC).

National Trust (1991) *Keeping House* (training video), London: National Trust.

National Trust (1996) *Historic Buildings: The Conservation of Their Fixtures, Fittings, Decorations and Contents, Policy Paper*, London: National Trust.

Sandwith, H. and Stainton, S. (2001) *The National Trust Manual of Housekeeping*, London: National Trust.

Schneider, T., Petersen, O. H., Kildeso, J., Kloch, N. P. and Lobner, T. (1996) 'Design and calibration of a simple instrument for measuring dust surface in the indoor environment', *Indoor Air* 6: 204–10.

Yoon, Y. H. and Brimblecombe, P. (2000a) 'Contribution of dust at floor level to particle deposit within the Sainsbury Centre for Visual Arts', *Studies in Conservation* 45: 127–37.

Yoon, Y. H. and Brimblecombe, P. (2000b) 'Dust monitoring at Felbrigg Hall', *Views* 32: 31–2.

Chapter 21

Saving Archaeological Iron Using the Revolutionary Preservation System

C. Mathias, K. Ramsdale and D. Nixon

[. . .]

Introduction

THE FERRYLAND ARCHAEOLOGICAL SITE is located approximately 80 km south of St. John's on the Avalon Peninsula of the Island of Newfoundland within Canada. Located on the Atlantic Ocean this temperate zone provides a moist, acidic soil with a high salt content.

Historical documents indicate that George Calvert, later Lord Baltimore, established the colony of Avalon in 1621. At Ferryland colonists constructed a mansion house, brew house, salt works, forge, hen house, kitchen, fishing stores and dwellings around the "Pool". Lord Baltimore visited his colony in the summer of 1627 and returned with his family in 1628. Sir David Kirke was granted the Island of Newfoundland in 1637 and took control of the colony in 1638. The Dutch attacked the area in 1673 inflicting significant damage on several plantations, especially Ferryland (Lovelace 1675). The colony recovered from this attack, but after the French captured and burned the settlement in 1696 activity at the site ceased until the 1700s.

The present Ferryland Project began excavations in 1992. The site itself is believed to cover an area of approximately 30,000 m². To date about 1,100 m² have been excavated and designated as Areas A through G. Briefly described, these areas represent the landward palisaded edge of the colony (Area A), the houses of middling planters (Areas B and D), a waterfront warehouse complex (Area C), defensive works (Area E), a high status house, possibly the Kirke residence (Area F), and

Source: J. Ashton and D. Hallam (eds), *Metal 04*, Canberra: National Museum of Australia, 2004, pp. 28–42.

another waterfront area with an early eighteenth-century domestic structure (Area G). Artefact assemblages including textiles, glass, ceramics, ferrous and non-ferrous metals, brick and wood are concentrated in areas defined by structures. To date catalogued artefacts number about half a million, with many numbers representing two or more objects. Of this group about 20% are made of iron. Each year of excavation uncovers about 7,000 iron nails and 1,000 to 2,000 iron objects. Though we are required by permit to document and retain the nails, conservation of these object types is not a requirement. We are required, however, to fully conserve and store all non-nail iron objects. The cost of conserving artefactual remains, for the Ferryland project, is equal to that of excavation. [. . .]

By the early modern period iron was used for a variety of objects from structural hardware, to blacksmith's tools, to snuff boxes. For this reason iron artefacts are numerous on any historic site and scattered through all areas of excavation. For the thousands of iron objects excavated each year at Ferryland condition varies greatly by object and area of excavation. Some are better preserved than others. Because the site's soils are coarse in texture and allow easy movement of water and dissolved salts objects appear to always be exposed to the corrosive environment of a maritime climate.

Geochemical analysis of the soil solution indicates a range of chloride concentrations from 635 ppb to 33,109 ppb. Soil pH ranges from 3.81 (H20) to 5.74 (H20). Corrosion rate measurements range from 0.02–0.22 millimetres per year. After some 350 years of burial this means that an object's corrosion layer could vary from 7 mm to 77 mm.

[. . .]

Treatment

At Memorial, iron artefacts have been treated with aqueous sodium hydroxide solutions of either 0.5 or 1.0% (w/v) through at least six changes of solution. Most treatment times average two years. This treatment method has been developed based on work by Scott and Seeley (1987), Costain (2000) and Mathias (1994). Mathias worked with Costain on the holding solution experiments while interning at the Canadian Conservation Institute (CCI). Realizing the ability of sodium hydroxide to remove chlorides, after monitoring solutions for chloride concentrations, Mathias felt this would be a suitable treatment for the bulk treatment of iron at Memorial University. This decision was made in consultation with Judy Logan, archaeological conservator working at CCI. After treatment some mechanical cleaning is conducted, but no such cleaning is performed during treatment because of the limited availability of personnel. In many instances it appears that chlorides remain within the pores of the artefacts and will not move into solution if a thick silica-rich corrosion layer is still present during and after chemical treatment. It is these artefacts for which the RP/ESCAL system is used. Because chlorides are potentially still trapped in the iron they will begin to re-corrode during the summer months when the relative humidity can exceed 65% in June, July or August and akaganeite will form. Figure 21.1 presents the change in RH for the collections storage area from 1993 to 2003.

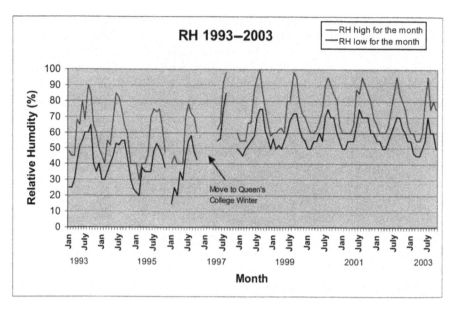

Figure 21.1   RH for collections storage area from 1993 to 2003

During the winter of 1996/97, the conservation lab and collections storage were moved from the Ingstad building to the lower level of Queen's College, several city blocks away. Queen's College is located next to a large pond, which seems to have had an adverse effect on the ambient environment inside the building. Data collected over a ten year period at both buildings shows an average increase in relative humidity of over 10% at Queen's College as compared to the Ingstad Building.

The archaeological iron collection is currently stored either in baked enamel, gasket sealed, metal cabinets, if a non-nail iron object, or in large plastic tubs, for nails. The cabinets are conditioned with silica gel sachets, but given the limited availability of staff these are not well maintained. Individual items are wrapped in acid-free tissue and placed in hard plastic boxes or in polyethylene bags. Ethafoam supports are made for delicate items. Humidity is controlled only through the use of portable dehumidifiers.

Overall it was found that the interesting iron objects stored in the larger collections storage area in the storage cabinets were at greater risk of physical breakage because of the appearance of akaganeite. To date we have not observed the akaganeite phase on freshly excavated iron (Mathias 1999 and Turgoose 1985). Akaganeite appears only after an object has been treated, dried and in storage for a period of at least one year. This observation may be specific to the burial environment from which the archaeological iron was excavated and the storage environment, in terms of both relative humidity and air pollutants (Turgoose 1982 and Jones 1992). As stated above, accelerated deterioration because of corrosive processes occurs with an increase in relative humidity within the storage environment. Humidity is necessary for this type of atmospheric corrosion. Condensed water forming with an increase in relative humidity on the surface of the metal will provide the electrolyte needed for electrochemical corrosion (Jones 1992). Contaminants near the surface layer, such as chlorides, enhance the effectiveness of the electrolyte (Jones 1992). Thus uncontaminated iron would not corrode as the humidity increased; however, this is not the case for the Ferryland iron (Mathias 1999). The ESCAL/RP will slow the deteriorating effects of the environment by reducing humidity and oxygen until these objects can be retreated. Therefore, to prevent corrosion from occurring, archaeological iron should be stored in an oxygen free environment with an RH of less than 15%.

Revolutionary Preservation (RP) system

The RP agent is available in two different forms – RP-A, for use with metal artefacts, and RP-K, to be used with non-metal items. The use of RP-A will result in a micro-environment with an RH of less than 10% and an oxygen concentration of below 0.1%. RP-A is available in three sizes – 3A, 5A, and 20A. The numbers correspond to the volume of air each packet can condition – 3 = 300 ml, 5 = 500 ml, 20 = 2000 ml. The RP-A packets contain mordenite, calcium, oxide, polyethylene and activated carbon, along with unsaturated organic compounds, the makeup of which is propri-etary information.

The heat-sealing layer of ESCAL film is linear low density polyethylene (LLDPE). In rolls of ESCAL that are pre-sealed on two sides, the LLDPE layers are already oriented to the inside, where they will melt together when heat of an appropriate temperature is applied. In ESCAL film, the plastic must be folded correctly or the heat will not seal the bag. Although heat-sealers are recommended for use with the ESCAL film and RP system, they can be quite expensive. Heat sealing using a tacking iron has also been suggested as a low-cost option to the more expensive heat sealers. As an alternative, the conservation lab at Memorial has used a conventional iron for heat-sealing the ESCAL bags. The strength of the seal created by the iron was tested by pulling on the film to try and separate the newly joined layers. It was impossible to tear the seal by hand, indicating that the iron creates a sufficiently strong seal.

The microenvironment created using ESCAL and the RP agent can last from four to six years assuming: a good seal has been obtained, that the film remains undam-aged, and the proper amount of RP agent has been added. After this time, the RH will begin to rise, although the oxygen-free environment can last much longer (Conserva-tion by Design 2003).

To determine how much and how long the RH drop takes in the microenviron-ment using the RP system, a datalogger was enclosed to chart the decline of the RH. A HOBO LCD Temperature/Relative Humidity datalogger was used, set at a sam-pling interval of two minutes. The logger has an operating range of 0–95% RH, but a measurement range of only 15–95%. The ambient RH at the time of placement in the enclosure was 42%. In just over two hours, the RH within the package dropped to 15% (lowest range for the logger).

Although the temperature in the enclosure is not directly affected by the RP agent, there was a temperature spike noted on the logger graph. It is possible that the oxygen-scavenging reaction caused by the RP agent is exothermic, resulting in a small rise of 1°C in temperature during the first two hours of enclosure.

Working with the RP system

The following points illustrate the method used in packaging the artefacts:

- The appropriate size ESCAL film is chosen (either 160 mm or 480 mm wide).
- The ESCAL is cut (with ordinary scissors) to fit the object, making sure to leave enough room for the RP packets and sufficient plastic to seal the enclosure on both ends.
- One end of the bag is sealed with the iron set to the 'nylon' setting.
- The object is protected if needed – delicate objects may be placed in small, hard plastic boxes with microfoam padding, and objects with sharp projections may be padded with microfoam to prevent the possibility of puncturing the bag.
- The object is then placed inside the bag, along with its catalogue tag. If the objects are small, more than one may be placed in each enclosure. They can be placed in polyethylene bags within the ESCAL to separate them.
- The appropriate number of RP packets are placed in with object, then the end is sealed with the iron. This is determined by calculating the volume of the bag and subtracting the volume of the object. It is much easier to measure only the volume of the enclosure and disregard the volume of the object – this may result in adding slightly more RP agent than is necessary. This will not harm the object, and the manufacturer has suggested adding 25–50% more RP agent to each enclosure. Through trial and error we have found that for wrought iron one bag of the RP-5A is needed per 100 gram of weight.
- The artefact's catalogue number can be recorded on the white strip on the ESCAL film.

Previous studies of the RP system using archaeological metal indicate that there should be no change in the appearance of the objects. Research has been conducted in which excavated iron nails were used as samples to show that objects stored using the RP system do not corrode while in storage, and in fact have a slight decrease in weight, due likely to a loss of moisture (Lampel 2003). Nails stored only in polyethylene bags suffered an average weight gain of 7.4% after three years, due to the formation of corrosion products.

After working with the system, it was possible to determine easier methods of working, and several problems were also discovered. The bag of RP agent contains 25 packets, and these should be exposed to air for only 30 minutes before being resealed in their new enclosures. Because most artefacts are small and use only one packet per enclosure it is most efficient to design a working session where 20 artefacts will be bagged. In this way, the entire bag of RP agent could be used.

Heat sealing the ESCAL film with an iron is a fairly straightforward task, though several problems were encountered. If the object is large a bag formed from the large tube (480 mm in width) of ESCAL is difficult to seal. Because several passes have to be made with the iron to seal the end, it is difficult to seal without incorporating any air channels. Also the corrosion 'dust' created by the iron artefacts can actually prevent a complete seal.

When the oxygen is removed from the enclosure, the bag does suck down about

20%. In most cases, this is a visible change, and it indicates that the seal was successful and the correct number of RP packets was enclosed.

Why is the use of ESCAL/RP system advantageous to archaeologists?

From the perspective of field archaeology the use of the RP/ESCAL system is advantageous for a number of reasons including: its relatively low cost; its ease of use in the field; the accessibility of the artefacts following their enclosure; and the opportunity to stabilize artefacts while alternate conservation strategies are considered. Figure 21.2 shows stored iron objects in RP/ESCAL bags. These enclosures make access easy as they support the object and allow for close examination of the object while still providing a stable environment free from the contaminants of handling.

The relatively low cost of the RP/ESCAL enclosure system derives, on the one hand, from the low cost of the enclosing materials themselves, and on the other, from savings in terms of labour in a field laboratory. In our experience with the purchase of some $3,000 (Canadian dollars) worth of materials, which may at first glance seem overly expensive, we have managed to enclose more than 200 iron objects of various sizes and still have more than half of the original materials left for additional enclosures. Although other barrier films may be used with the RP agent, ESCAL is recommended for long-term storage as it has very low rates of migration for both water vapour and oxygen – it is 2,000 times more effective as a barrier than polypropylene bags, and it is transparent, so that objects can be viewed without opening the package (MGC 2003). A carefully planned strategy for the initial processing of the artefacts themselves (for example, a light cleaning followed by the documentation of the object and its condition post-excavation) combined with the careful and judicious use of the enclosing materials, makes a little go a long way. The labour savings in a field lab derive from the relatively "light" handling an artefact receives prior to its being enclosed in a relatively sturdy environmentally-appropriate enclosure. The

Figure 21.2 Storage of iron in RP/ESCAL bags

light handling of the objects not only protects them, but reduces the number of laboratory staff required to process the objects themselves.

The ease with which enclosures can be created in the field is likewise advantageous in terms of time, effort, and materials. In our experience, it is more efficient to enclose a number of objects at once where attention can be focussed specifically on cutting ESCAL enclosing tubes to size, estimating the number of RP sachets to be included, placing the artefacts within the enclosure and then heat-sealing it. It doesn't take long to get the feel for estimating the size of tube to be cut and the number of sachets to be added. Once the iron is up to heat, sealing the enclosures is quick. A team of two can easily enclose some 20 objects an hour. Laboratory requirements for creating the enclosures are meagre: a clean work area; a flat surface upon which to iron the ends of the enclosures; and an electrical outlet for the iron.

Once enclosed in the RP/ESCAL system the artefacts can be easily visually examined not only for purposes of additional identification, but also to monitor their condition. For the purposes of transportation and storage, the semi-rigid nature of the enclosure allows the objects to be packed more readily, albeit carefully, for travel, while in storage the enclosure provides ongoing environmental protection for the object. If an artefact requires closer examination or additional stabilization, it is as easy as cutting the end of the ESCAL tube and removing the object. In this sense, the RP/ESCAL system is readily reversible, unlike most other chemical treatment strategies. Following examination or additional stabilization, a new enclosure can be made and the artefact returned to a stable storage environment.

Perhaps the most important advantage of the RP/ESCAL system for field archaeologists is that it provides us the opportunity to consider alternate stabilization strategies – in a real sense it buys us time. It is abundantly clear that a variety of conservation strategies have been undertaken in various circumstances and that some have been more successful than others. Depending on the degree and nature of the corrosion experienced by ferrous objects, different conservation strategies are appropriate. This system allows archaeologist to take the necessary first steps, in the field, to stabilize objects until the best long-term strategy is selected. Because the objects themselves have not been otherwise "treated", this system reduces the likelihood that inappropriate and irreversible treatments will be performed by archaeologists who lack the specific knowledge that is the realm of the conservator.

Methods

A small research project was begun in December 2003 in an effort to determine the efficiency of the RP/ESCAL system in reducing the re-corrosion of iron nails recovered from the Ferryland archaeology site. The total sample included 150 nails, half of which had received 2.5 years of treatment in sodium hydroxide to remove chlorides, the other half had received no post-excavation conservation treatment. Each group of 75 nails was subdivided into three groups of 25 nails each. These three groups of treated and untreated nails were then stored differently. The first group of 50 nails (25 treated and 25 untreated) was stored in individual RP/ESCAL enclosures, the second group of 50 nails (25 treated and 25 untreated) in individual polypropylene bags, and the third group of 50 nails (25 treated and 25 untreated) stored without enclosure. The total sample of 150 nails has been stored in an ambient environment. Our intention is to visually monitor the condition of the three groups three times each year for the next five years.

Additionally it was decided to select a group of objects (not nails) from four areas of excavation, and make observations about the RP/ESCAL packaging technique over the course of the experiment. A total of 55 objects were sealed in the RP/ESCAL system, some with microfoam for support and protection against film puncture. Once bagged the initial weight was recorded. The quality of the bag seal was visually assessed as good, fair or poor. The initial bagging occurred March, 2004. Objects were monitored in April and June of 2004.

Results

The first monitoring interval for the nail experiment has revealed the following. All nails treated with sodium hydroxide appear stable regardless of method of enclosure. Some untreated nails show signs of continued deterioration and this varies by method of enclosure. After being bagged for 5 months:

> 12% of those nails in RP/ESCAL enclosures are visibly cracking;
> 60% of those nails in polypropylene bags are visibly cracking; and
> 56% of those nails with no enclosure are visibly cracking.

The nails were monitored again in June. Though the time interval between examinations, in this case, was short, we were entering the first period of increased humidity and felt we might see changes. The treated nails remained stable. However, within the untreated nail group an additional nail in each of the polypropylene and RP/ESCAL groups appeared cracked. The results are presented in Table 21.1 The second group of objects being monitored showed that for three samples the protective microfoam had moved off the intended area of protection. This will probably result in bag damage. Overall, however, the seals were good.

Discussion

It is too early to know yet how effective the bagging of corroding iron in the RP/ESCAL system will be but at this point it does look promising. Experiments, to date,

Table 21.1 Total nails showing signs of deterioration

Date	Untreated nails			Treated nails		
	No enclosure	Polypropylene	RP/ESCAL	No enclosure	Polypropylene	RP/ESCAL
Dec. 15/03	0	0	0	0	0	0
May 20/04	14	15	3	0	0	0
June 11/04	14	16	4	0	0	0

* Samples for untreated nails were excavated in 2003

do reveal that it is important to have a good seal and that for archaeological objects with sharp edges and irregular three dimensional shapes maintaining the seal will be the greatest challenge. I know that over the past 24 years that I have been involved in the preservation of our heritage there has been a move away from bench conservation treatment to preventive conservation. Institutions can no longer afford a conservator who may spend one year on one object. To justify the conservation position they must have one conservator stabilizing hundreds or thousands of objects per year. This preservation system, if it proves successful, will help archaeological conservators meet their goal of stabilizing thousands of objects. However, I must emphasize that archaeological materials will require some form of chemical stabilization prior to storage and the use of the RP/ESCAL system. The ESCAL packaging system will, however, continue to protect these fragile objects once removed from chemical treatment and make them easily accessible to researchers.

Additionally the RP/ESCAL system can be used for fragile artefacts being excavated and as an emergency intervention. In the former case, objects excavated from a wet saline environment can be bagged and held in a stable state until aqueous treatment for chloride removal can begin. The Ferryland cross made of iron, brass and gold, provides an example for the latter. This seventeenth-century artefact began re-corroding while on exhibit in 2003.

One of the orbs cracked off as a result of this damage, the corrosion had progressed from the metal surface inward to the core. This object is currently bagged in RP-5A/ESCAL awaiting further treatment.

Conclusions

Collections storage issues are becoming more challenging for institutions worldwide. Within academic units, issues such as budget cuts and increasing numbers of students are forcing administrators to carefully monitor space usage. Archaeology departments with ongoing research projects will require significant space for collections storage. Because the RP-5A/ESCAL system provides a constantly low RH and oxygen free environment it may be ideally suited for the metal artefacts in these collections. It is a relatively low cost solution compared to air-conditioning the larger collections storage space. Additionally these enclosures provide support to archaeological objects which may be moved many times in their post-excavation period.

[. . .]

Suppliers

The RP Agent and ESCAL Barrier Film are manufactured by
Mitsubishi Gas Chemical Company
5–2, Marunouchi 2-chome, Chiyoda-ku, Tokyo 100–8324, Japan
www.mgc-a.com

The RP System is supplied to Canada and the USA by
Keepsafe Systems
570 King Street West

Suite 400
Toronto, Ontario
M5V 1M3
www.keepsafe.ca

and in the UK by
Conservation by Design Limited
Timecare Works, 5 Singer Way
Woburn Rd. Ind. Estate
Kempston, Bedford
MK42 7AW
www.conservation-by-design.co.uk

References

Conservation by Design. (2003) *Oxygen-Free Storage and Display*, Conservation by Design Limited, Kempston, Bedford.

Costain, C. G. (2000) 'Evaluation of storage solutions for archaeological iron', *Journal of the Canadian Association for Conservation* 25: 11–20.

Jones, D. A. (1992) *Principles and Prevention of Corrosion*, New York: Macmillan Publishing Company.

Lampel, K. (2003) *Long-Term STorage of Archaeological Iron Using an Oxygen-Free Microclimate*, Poster, NOOX[3] Conference, London, England.

Lovelace, D. (1675) *An Account of the Dutch Fleet upon the Coast of Newfoundland in the Year 1673*, Great Britain, Colonial Office, CO 1/34 (37), 85. MHA 16-C-2–024. Transcribed by P. E. Pope.

Mathias, C. (1994) 'A conservation strategy for a seventeenth century archaeological site at Ferryland, Newfoundland', *Journal of the International Institute for Conservation – Canadian Group* 19: 14–23.

Mathias, C. (1999) 'Examination of the interaction between ferrous metals and the archaeological burial environment for a seventeenth century plantation site', in *Proceedings of the 6th International Conference on "Non-Destructive Testing and Microanalysis for the Diagnostics and Conservation of the Cultural and Environmental Heritage"* 3, Rome: Euroma.

Scott, D. A. and N. J. Seeley (1987) 'The washing of fragile iron artifacts', *Studies in Conservation* 32: 73–76.

Turgoose, S. (1982) 'Post excavation changes in iron antiquities', *Studies in Conservation* 27: 97–101.

Turgoose, S. (1985) 'The corrosion of archaeological iron during burial and treatment', *Studies in Conservation* 30: 13–18.

Web site referenced

MGC (2003) Mitsusbishi Gas Chemical America, Inc., www.mgca.com/rpsystem/mgca.html

Introduction to Part Two – Section Five

Chris Caple

Agents of deterioration: radiation (light)

THE PARADOX THAT LIGHT IS ESSENTIAL in order to see artefacts but that it damages many artefacts made of organic materials has been understood since antiquity. Conservators, scientists and curators have all recognised the need to gain clear and accurate information about the nature of light, its interaction with materials, accurate measurements of light in terms of wavelength and amount (flux) and information on a full range of options for minimising exposure, if the best possible viewing conditions are to be obtained with a minimum of damage to the object. Chapter 22 of this reader is an edited version of Garry Thomson's chapter on light from his influential book *The Museum Environment*, which is where many conservators and curators first learnt about the beneficial use of 50 and 200 lux maxima when lighting objects in museums. It is appropriate to have at least one section in this reader from *The Museum Environment*, given the importance of this work to the subject of preventive conservation. Originally written in 1978, though revised in 1986, it does focus on older illuminance sources such as tungsten filament bulbs and does not include details of more recent sources such as light-emitting diodes (LEDs). It provides a useful outline of the subject and focuses on practical problems such as the monitoring of light and UV levels and the steps that can be taken to control them, but avoids the complex chemistry of the interactions between light and materials that is covered in more detailed textbooks (Schaeffer 2001).

Whilst annual light dose is often now the preferred approach to controlling the exposure of artefacts to light in historic buildings, in museums there is still an emphasis on using the 50 and 200 lux maxima, since they have the ability to group together objects, such as textiles or natural history specimens, with similar light sensitivity in the same gallery. A comprehensive list of materials and recommended exposure levels is provided by Linda Bullock (2006) in her excellent outline on light in the National Trust's *Manual of Housekeeping*. In museums there is also less emphasis on daylight and greater use of electric illuminance sources. The spectral distribution and questions of colour rendering become important in such museums and galleries. Though the lighting industry is constantly evolving new illuminance sources, details of which are covered in dedicated textbooks (IESNA 1996), these always need to be assessed for their suitability for use in museums, galleries and historic houses.

Early museum lighting recommendations, light level maxima of 50 and 200 lux (Thomson 1986), were proposed because the amount of light falling on the object was much more easily measured than the rate of damage, such as fading (Michalski 1990). Subsequent research has continued to show that these maxima values are a reasonable compromise between visual acuity and damage. However, as Michalski (1997) (Chapter 23) shows, factors such as the age of the viewer, the colour of the object being viewed and the detail to be observed all affect the ability to read and understand the image. Thus, complex detail in dark objects is not visible at 50 lux light levels, especially to older viewers, and in such circumstances there is good reason for considering higher light levels for shorter periods of time. This more complex set of sensitivities, which requires awareness of the nature of each individual object being viewed and the visual abilities of the viewer, is outlined in Table 23.1.

In order to achieve this more refined approach to lighting museum exhibits, the need again emerges to know what artefacts are made of. Michalski (1997) explores this issue in terms of the light-fastness of dyes. It is a complex issue, with the nature of the dye molecule, the exact wavelengths of light to which it is exposed and other factors all affecting the rate of fading. Recent work by Boris Pretzel (2006) has shown that developments in colour-monitoring technology now enable light damage, as fading, to be accurately measured. Developments in levels of human visual perception mean that there is a working model of how much a colour can change (i.e. fade) before it is noticeable (JND – just noticeable difference). This means that for the first time, through testing the rate at which the different colours of a specific object will fade, an estimate of the light dose an object can receive before a detectable fading has occurred can be made. Key ethical issues still remain, as individual museum authorities still need to specify/agree the rate of noticeable fading they consider acceptable. As many factors are unique to each object and each museum display, and accurate measurements are only obtainable from experimentally fading a small representative area of the object, this system will probably only be used on a small number of high-profile objects in the foreseeable future. However, when such information is available and integrated with accurate records of display history, preventive conservation will, potentially, have moved a step closer to being an object-specific, objective, proactive preservation process.

References

Bullock, L. (2006) 'Light as an Agent of Decay', in National Trust, *Manual of Housekeeping*, London: Butterworth-Heinemann, pp. 92–101.

IESNA (1996) *Museum and Art Gallery Lighting: A Recommended Practice*, New York: Illuminating Engineering Society of North America.

Michalski, S. (1990) 'Towards Specific Lighting Guidelines', in *Preprints of the 9th ICOM-CC, Triennial Meeting, Dresden*, Marina del Ray, CA: ICOM-CC and GCI, pp. 589–592.

Michalski, S. (1997) 'The Lighting Decision', in CCI (eds), *Fabric of an Exhibition: An Interdisciplinary Approach – Preprints*, Ottawa: CCI, pp. 97–104

Pretzel, B. (2006) 'Ephemeral or Permanent: Environmental Decisions for Textiles', in F. Lennard and M. Hayward, *Tapestry Conservation*, London: Butterworth-Heinemannn, pp. 213–218.

Schaeffer, T. T. (2001) *Effects of Light on Materials in Collections, Research in Conservation*, Los Angeles: Getty Publications.

Thomson, G. (1978) *The Museum Environment*, London: Butterworth-Heinemann.

Thomson, G. (1986) *The Museum Environment* (2nd edn), London: Butterworths.

Chapter 22

The Museum Environment – Light

Garry Thomson

Surface deterioration

N O ONE NEEDS TO BE TOLD THAT light can change colours and rot materials, though with the fastness of modern dyes and the affluent tendency to throw away rather than repair this common knowledge has no longer the practical importance that it once had – except in the museum.

Light and heat energy

A chemical reaction, for us, means deterioration. [. . .] A certain definite quantity of energy must be supplied in order to start the (chemical) reaction; this is known as the activation energy of the reaction. In the museum the activation energy may be brought to an object by heating it or illuminating it. [. . .]

Quanta of light energy are called photons and most of them are very much more potent than room-temperature heat quanta. [. . .] Photons of red light cause very little physical damage, while those equivalent to photons of blue and violet light would be the worst. However, of shorter wavelength than the violet and invisible to the eye, ultraviolet radiation photons are the most damaging of all.

[. . .]

The spectrum

[. . .] Light is that form of radiation which we can see. Since we are also concerned with 'colours' invisible to the human eye – the ultraviolet and the infrared – we will from now on frequently use the term radiation instead of light.

Source: *The Museum Environment* (2nd edn), London: Butterworths, 1986, pp. 2–33.

The radiation from white-light sources, such as daylight, tungsten and fluorescent lamps, can be split by a prism into all the colours of the rainbow with wavelength shortest in the violet and longest in the red. Beyond the visible at the short end lies the ultraviolet (UV), and beyond the red at the long-wavelength end lies the infrared (IR). All these are emitted to various extents by white-light sources.

We now assign wavelengths so that we can deal in numbers instead of colours. Energy arrives in separate packets, which, for all forms of radiation, as well as for light, are called photons. But now we are talking of waves. We have come up against a central conundrum of modern physics: light behaves like particles but also like waves. The figures work out beautifully, but they seem to have no objective reality. We must be content to talk in terms either of waves or photons, whichever is the most convenient.

At the long-wavelength end of the visible spectrum, the longest wavelength red which we can see is at about 760 nm, though red beyond 700 nm is barely visible. Beyond this the radiation is called IR. All radiation, if it is absorbed by any material, causes a rise in temperature, so we would be quite correct to call light a form of radiant heat. But in practice the term 'radiant heat' is very often confined to IR radiation, because we can regard heating as its only effect. There is no definite wavelength limit to the IR radiation in museum light sources, since it falls off gradually as the wavelength increases.

[. . .] Unlike IR, UV is confined within a band, in the light-sources we are considering, stretching between 300 and 400 nm. From the exhibit's point of view there is no line dividing UV from violet (or IR from red) – the 400 nm division is made entirely by our eyes' inability to see anything shorter. The 300 nm limit is set by the daylight spectrum. Wavelengths below 300 nm cannot penetrate the atmosphere. The radiation then has to pass through the glass of the museum window (or the glass envelope round a tungsten or fluorescent lamp). This removes some more UV, so that the effective limit is near 325 nm. Thus glass removes some UV, but the band between 325 and 400 nm gets through.

We have now divided radiation from light sources into three regions, the UV, the visible and the IR, and we have added a wavelength scale. This scale has already been used to show the transmission of window glass, and it has many other useful functions. The vertical scale can be assigned to measure any quantity which varies with wavelength. Consider the colour of light reflected from a brushstroke of green paint. White light falls on the brushstroke and green light is reflected. In practice all colours are reflected, green merely more than others. The light which is not reflected is absorbed and thereby heats up the paint by a small amount. A very tiny proportion of this absorbed light may even be used up in causing a chemical change to take place in the pigment. Green is in the middle of the spectrum, so less of the light at either end, blue and red, is reflected. If we measure the amount of light reflected at each wavelength as a percentage of the light falling on the brushstroke at that wavelength, we can plot our figures in the form of a 'reflectance curve' (Figure 22.1a). This states quantitatively what we have already described. Purple colours do the opposite to green: they reflect light predominantly at both blue and red ends of the spectrum, with less reflected in the middle (Figure 22.1b). Consequently, if the two pigments, green and purple, are mixed, light from all parts of the spectrum will be partly reflected and partly absorbed, so that one could get a fairly neutral grey (Figure 22.1c). For this reason green and purple are said to be complementary colours. A white-light source emits energy throughout the spectrum: there are wavelengths of all colours. Following a similar procedure to our reflectance spectrum, if we now plot the amount of energy emitted by some particular white-light source at each wavelength through the spectrum we might expect to get a more or less level line. [. . .]

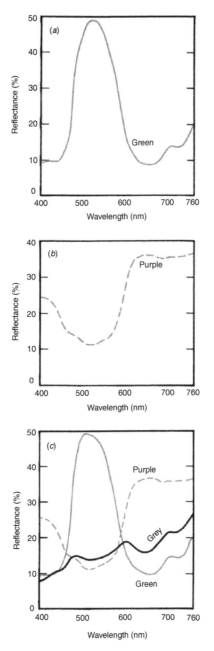

Figure 22.1 Reflectance curves of three watercolours[1]

The basic light sources

At the time of writing (1978 revised 1986) there are three types of light source suitable for general lighting in museums: tungsten, fluorescent and metal halide lamps.

At one time artificial light could only be produced by burning, as in a candle. But non-inflammable materials can be made to give out light if they are heated strongly enough. The ordinary domestic electric light bulb (circa 1930–2009) is referred to as the tungsten or incandescent lamp because it gives out light from a coiled tungsten filament heated to about 2700°C by passing an electric current through it. The tungsten lamp comes in a great variety of forms and powers, some with clear glass and some with opal glass envelopes, some with built-in reflectors [. . .] the addition of a small quantity of iodine or halogen [. . .] allowing the production of a more efficient, slightly whiter lamp, the tungsten-halogen lamp. [. . .] Because of the high operating temperature, quartz must be used in place of glass for the envelope. But quartz is transparent to the emitted UV, and a small amount of this is of wavelength less than 300 nm. This is very potent and must be eliminated. [. . .]

Light can also be produced by passing electricity through a gas such as mercury vapour or sodium vapour or neon. [. . .] They are not sufficiently white to be used for lighting exhibits. However, if a tubular lamp containing mercury vapour has the inside of its glass coated with a mixture of powders capable of fluorescing in the radiation emitted by the mercury vapour we get a fluorescent lamp. A substance is said to fluoresce if it absorbs radiation and re-emits it at a longer wavelength. In this case the UV radiation emitted by the mercury is absorbed by the fluorescent powders and re-emitted as visible light. Some fluorescent lamps are good at colour rendering, but others are bad.

[. . .]

A third type of lamp, the metal-halide lamp, is basically a modification of the high-pressure mercury bulb lamp to improve its colour. [. . .] They are economical in electricity and have become suitable for museum use. The colour-rendering improvements are obtained by adding small amounts of metal halide to the mercury. [. . .]

Damage caused by UV and visible radiation

Light can only damage what it reaches, and since most objects are opaque to light its major effect is on surface deterioration. But the surface is the very essence of many exhibits, above all of paintings and drawings. We can say that all organic material is at risk under light. The term 'organic material' includes all things which originated in animals or plants – for example, paper, cotton, linen, wood, parchment, leather, silk, wool, feathers, hair, dyes, oils, glues, gums and resins – and in addition, because of similarities in chemical structure, almost all synthetic dyes and plastics. It must be remembered that light can cause not only colour change but strength change, as in the weakening of textiles and the destruction of paint medium.

[. . .]

Stone, metal, glass and ceramics, with some exceptions, are not affected by light, and we need not worry too much about wood, bone or ivory if their surface colour is not important. But this section on light is concerned to a greater or lesser extent with just about every other kind of museum material.

To reduce surface deterioration to a minimum we must control the lighting. But before we deal with ways and means it will help to examine the nature of light.

If we had a tunable light source which we could adjust to emit its radiant energy at any wavelength, and if we wanted to fade a colour as quickly as possible we would in the average case tune it to emit all its energy in the UV. This is because damage is related to wavelength. UV radiation causes more damage in general than the same amount of blue radiation, which causes more damage than yellow radiation. One can confidently assume that in the museum red light never causes any photochemical damage (damage due to chemical change by radiation). There is much less UV than visible radiation in all light sources, even in daylight. Balancing these two factors, the extra potency of UV against the smaller quantity of UV, it is still not possible to answer with any confidence the question, 'Which causes more damage, visible or UV radiation?' because many materials are only faded by radiation at certain wavelengths. However, it is safe to assume that, under unfiltered daylight through glass, more damage will be caused in general by the small quantity of UV than by the whole of the visible radiation.

One may also generalise along the following lines. A very fugitive material will be damaged by either visible or UV radiation, and, since visible radiation is more plentiful, most of the damage will be done by the visible. A material which is fairly fast but nevertheless susceptible in the long run may be secure against most of the visible spectrum, and therefore will be changed mainly or wholly by UV radiation. This has been shown true of a large number of dyes.

A colourless material such as a varnish or paint medium, by virtue of its colourlessness, hardly absorbs any visible radiation but may absorb UV quite strongly. In such cases deterioration is also likely to be caused mainly by UV.

Thus, for the more sensitive dyes and pigments, though UV protection is important, this measure will not get us very far. Of much greater importance is the reduction of visible radiation. In contrast, the more stable exhibits, such as oil paintings, stand to benefit very greatly by elimination of UV radiation, though visible radiation should obviously be controlled to reasonable levels, especially since the occasional fugitive material is to be found in them.

[. . .]

UV radiation and how to deal with it

[. . .] There is much higher proportion of UV energy in daylight radiation through glass than in tungsten (light bulb) radiation, characteristically about six times as much.

If an exhibit is lit during the day by daylight and after dark by tungsten light to the same brightness, it will be receiving about six times as much UV energy during an hour of daylight as it does in an hour of tungsten light. Tungsten lamps emit too little UV to require a filter.

Nearly all fluorescent lamps emit more UV than does a tungsten lamp, but none – except for a special high-UV lamp called 'Artificial Daylight' – emit as high a proportion as does daylight.

Therefore for UV protection we tackle first the daylight then the fluorescent lamps. We remove UV radiation by passing the light, before it reaches the exhibits, through a material transparent to visible light but opaque to UV.

The ideal UV-absorbing filter will prevent all the UV down to 400 nm from passing through, but will not hinder the passage of any visible light (Figure 22.2a). This is a lot to ask, and there is no filter made only of glass which will do this job well. However, several kinds of plastic UV-absorbing filter of very satisfactory quality are available (Figure 22.2b and c). The filters available vary from country to country. [. . .]

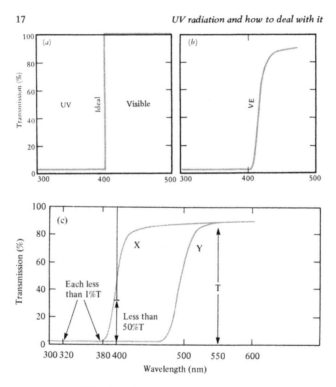

Figure 22.2 (a) The ideal UV-absorbing filter would transmit no radiation of wavelength shorter than 400 nm, while being completely transparent to all visible radiation. (b) ICE VE Perspex, an acrylic filter which eliminates UV radiation. Because it also removes a little violet light it has a slight yellow tint. (c) Curve X is of a typical satisfactory UV filter. This passes a suggested specification: Transmission at 400 nm should be less than half of transmission in the middle of the visible range: at 550 nm. Transmission at 320 and at 380 nm should be less than 1/100th of that at 550 nm. Y is of a filter which removes all UV and also all blue light. It can be used to give extra protection to delicate material whose colour is not important (e.g. black on white documents): it has a strong yellow colour

Note: CIE proposals to define two UV bands, UV-A from 380–315 nm and UV-B from 315–280 nm, are useful in emphasising that short-wavelength UV is more damaging than long. But a good UV-absorbing filter should cut off at 400 not 380 nm. The residual sensitivity of the eye between 380 and 400 nm is too small to affect colour rendering in adapted situations.

These filters must extend completely across windows, skylights or light fittings so that all light passes through them. They are principally manufactured in two forms:

- Self-supporting acrylic or polycarbonate sheet 3–6 mm thick, either clear or diffusing, which can be used in place of glass in windows and skylights (if fire regulations allow) and for fluorescent lamp diffusers.
- Thin foil, usually acetate, which can be cut to shape with knife or scissors and laid on glass, or adhered to glass.

Another useful form, but less easily available, is a sandwich of glass with a plastic interlayer. The interlayer contains the UV absorber. The glass can be made in security grades. Glass is less easily damaged by cleaning, and also the sealing of the plastic interlayer from air should increase its permanence.

[. . .]

It is useful to know that white paint, which contains titanium dioxide, is itself a fairly good UV absorber. In some cases, especially in the Tropics, it may be possible to ensure that all light entering a room is reflected at least once from a white wall. This will solve the UV problem. Titanium dioxide is the usual white pigment, but lead and zinc white are also good absorbers. Whitewash (chalk) is not effective.

The acrylic and polycarbonate sheets seem to be of high permanence, and can be expected to last at least ten years, even in moderately exposed situations. Foil filters, to err on the safe side, should be regarded as having the same sort of permanence as the paint on the walls, and should therefore be checked at not more than five-year intervals, using a UV monitor.

It has been mentioned that most fluorescent lamps also emit worrying amounts of UV radiation, though less strongly than daylight. The present situation is that all fluorescent lamps require UV filters. Some of the diffusing plastics used in fluorescent-lamp fittings act as reasonable UV filters. The only way to check whether this is so in any particular case is to use a UV monitor.

Occasionally UV radiation is actually used in museums for fluorescent effects: to show for example the fluorescence of minerals in a geological museum or to brighten pigments in some modern works of art. The advantages in these special cases must be balanced against the dangers. In all other situations UV radiation contributes nothing to appearance and can cause irreparable damage. It should therefore be eliminated in the ways described above.

[. . .]

Measuring UV and visible radiation

Since both UV and visible radiation are forms of energy, any scientist would point out that the most direct way of measuring either kind of radiation is to measure the rate at which the energy, whether UV or visible radiation, falls on a standard area (a square metre for example) where the exhibit is. In practice this is not done.

For visible radiation we use an instrument, the light meter or lux meter, which measures energy not directly but as the eye sees it. The eye does not see UV or IR so the meter does not respond to these ranges. The eye is more sensitive to green than to blue or red and so is the meter. This is because the instrument is most commonly used for relating light to visual tasks such as office work or learning at school. The best meters correspond very closely to the human eye in sensitivity.

The scale of the instrument is graduated in lux² and the measurement thus made is called the illuminance.

A light meter consists of a suitably protected sensitive surface, or photocell, connected electrically to a meter. [. . .]

The UV monitor is designed to complement the light meter. We have already measured the illuminance and now we want to find out the proportion of UV in the light. The UV monitor will answer such questions as: 'Does this light source need a UV filter?', 'Does this filter need replacing?', 'How does the UV in this light source compare with the UV in tungsten light?' Furthermore we want to get this measurement irrespective of the distance we are from the light source.

The measurement is actually in microwatts of UV radiation per lumen, but this need not concern most users. Readings for tungsten lights are around 60–80, and since we have said that tungsten lamps do not require UV filters, this is the highest tolerable level. Any source with a reading above about 75 therefore requires filtering.

The reciprocity law

There is an acceptable rule-of-thumb which says that the same amount of damage will be produced whether by a strong light in a short time or a weak light in a long time: if we halve the illuminance we halve the rate of damage. This is a loose statement of the reciprocity law.

More precisely, the reciprocity law teaches us that light, like high-energy radiation, acts cumulatively, so that it is the total dose, the exposure, which matters. The exposure is the simple product of illuminance and time. For light to produce a given effect the exposure must be constant. If illuminance is measured in lux and time in hours, 100 lux on a painting for 5 hours gives it an exposure of 500 lux hours; 50 lux for 10 hours would give it the same exposure.

We use the reciprocity law every time we take a photograph, and in many experimental situations it holds exactly, though it may break down at very high or very low illuminances. In the museum, although there must be individual cases where the law does not hold, we are justified in using it for the general lighting situation.

Note that the reciprocity law does not state that twice the exposure will cause twice the amount of fading. Rates of fading commonly decrease with time, until there comes a point when no more fadeable material is left. The rate of fading is then obviously zero.

[. . .]

Controlling visible radiation

Both UV and visible radiation can cause colour change and surface deterioration. It is not sufficient only to remove UV radiation. We cannot eliminate the visible radiation as we have done the UV because we would then be left in darkness. We have to accept that a certain amount of damage is caused by the very act of display. And since we have to balance, by judgement rather than by scientific formula, two incommensurables – the amount of light needed for looking at exhibits against the damage which it causes – we are now in the realms of controversy. To be prepared for this controversy we should have a good understanding of the visual significance of the exhibits, of the way the eye sees things, of the way exhibits can be lit, and of the rates of damage actually caused by light. Our knowledge in some of these areas is very poor indeed, so it would seem that we are ill-equipped to make any recommendation. But meanwhile precious objects deteriorate, often under conditions of unconsidered illumination.

Two courses of action must be pursued together. First, reduce illumination to no more than is necessary for proper viewing and reduce time of illumination where possible. Second, find out more about rates of fading in museums.

Reducing illuminance

The 200/50 lux illuminance levels shown in Table 22.1, or figures close to them, are now recommended, among others, by the U.K. Chartered Institute of Building Services,[3] the French National Committee of ICOM,[4] ICCROM,[5] the U.S.S.R. Ministry of Culture,[6] and the Canadian Conservation Institute.[7, 8] See also Thomson,[9] Brommelle and Harris,[10] Brommelle,[11, 12] Harris,[13–16] Brawne[17] and Allen.[18] Since appreciation of museum objects is mediated mainly by our eyes, any sacrifice in illuminance must be considered very seriously.

The 50 lux illuminance level is not at the bottom of what would in the past have been regarded as the normal scale of artificial lighting. In fact in the days before fluorescent lamps 50 lux was supposed a good artificial lighting level. More recently the taste for bright lights has been boosted by cheap energy and industrial interests, so that the task of control is difficult. Museums are expected to be lit as brightly as

Table 22.1 Recommended maximum illuminances*

Exhibits	Maximum illuminance
Oil and tempera paintings, undyed leather, horn, bone and ivory, oriental lacquer	200 lux
Objects specially sensitive to light, such as textiles, costumes, watercolours, tapestries, prints and drawings, manuscripts, miniatures, paintings in distemper media, wallpapers, gouache, dyed leather. Most natural history exhibits, including botanical specimens, fur and feathers	50 lux

Notes

* Although objects insensitive to light (e.g. metal, stone, glass, ceramics, jewellery, enamel) and objects in which colour change is not of high importance (e.g. wood) may be illuminated at higher levels, it is rarely necessary to exceed 300 lux. Large differences in illuminance between rooms give rise to adaptation difficulties.

  Lighting for restoration, technical examination and photography is not limited by the above Table. 2500 lux is a reasonable upper limit for those relatively brief periods of exposure.

shops. Nevertheless it has been found that, provided glare is skilfully eliminated, 50 lux gives satisfactory lighting even of small objects with low contrast. The danger to fugitive materials in museums is so apparent that the 50 lux level has been fairly generally accepted as a necessary measure for conservation.

Criticism has been stronger against the maximum for oil and tempera paintings. Whereas many curators have actually seen fugitive colours disappear in the course of years, we have to rely on less direct evidence for easel paintings, though we know that big changes have occurred. There is also the feeling that, for example, with a fully browned copper resinate on an otherwise healthy painting, we may be 'locking the stable door after the horse has gone'. In contrast to examples where the frame has protected colours on the edge of a picture, there exist countless examples where no such differences are to be found. [. . .]

In the first edition of *The Museum Environment* the recommended figure was 150 lux. As a result of subsequent experience and particularly the work just quoted, this has been revised upwards to 200 lux.

The conservator, or curator, who does not wish to accept the 50/200 lux maxima uncritically should at least do one thing: they should arm themselves with a light meter and examine all kinds of lighting situations in their museum in order to judge for themselves the various levels of illuminance which they find, and how their viewing is affected by them, by their state of adaptation to the light in the room, by glare from light sources, and by other factors. They may conclude that these factors, glare in particular, are actually more important in determining viewing conditions than the level of illuminance itself, over a very wide range of illuminance.

50 lux – artificial light

Let us consider the low level first, since the options are simpler. They are simpler because experience shows that, for 50 lux, artificial light rather than daylight is appropriate. Control of daylight to a closely pre-set level is a difficult and expensive business. The 'coolness' of daylight when it has been reduced to 50 lux often gives the impression of gloom, especially when it is highly diffused. Ever since ancestors sat around fires, and later used oil lamps and candles, the human race has been accustomed to 'warm' light in the home after dark. As a result the warm 50 lux from tungsten lamps appears to be brighter, and certainly more cheerful, than 50 lux of diffused daylight. For the same reason warm rather than cool fluorescent lamps should be chosen for 50 lux situations.

Glare and the adaptation of the eye to the light have been mentioned as the most important factors to control in order successfully to create an apparently bright situation. Glare has been defined as 'the discomfort or impairment of vision experienced when parts of the visual field are excessively bright in relation to the general surroundings'. In practical museum terms glare has a narrower meaning, since no part of the exhibit itself is likely to be the source of glare. Glare to us means bright spotlights in the corner of the eye, a bright window beside an exhibit, reflections in glass or glossy surfaces which obstruct viewing, etc. Glare can only be avoided by planning and adjusting the position of the lights, masking lamps from shining in unwanted directions and the use of dark surfaces in critical positions. Many museums consider it justified to remove glass from paintings when air-conditioning is installed, and this is of very great benefit to appearance.

We speak of adaptation of the eye in two senses: adaptation to the strength of the light and adaptation to its colour. Here we are concerned with the former. In bright light the pupil of the eye becomes smaller so that less light reaches the retina. But the eye can adapt itself to brightness over a range of more than 10,000 to 1, which is far more than can be coped with by merely varying the size of a hole. An important part of adaptation lies in the processing which signals from the retina receive on their way to the part of the brain which interprets their message. In just the same way a closed-circuit television camera has two ways of adjusting the brightness of the image on the screen: a diaphragm in the lens of the camera and electronic circuitry for gain control.

The time taken for the eyes to adapt to a new lighting situation is a matter of seconds in the usual indoor or outdoor situation. But, coming into a building from bright sunshine or vice versa, adaptation may take a minute or so. All this should occur before the visitor sees the first exhibit. This implies that adaptation to the lighting of the exhibition room should take place not in the room but in the entrance area of the museum. Furthermore, since adaptation can easily be upset by a view of brighter areas, whether through windows or doors, this should not be allowed to occur. But this does not imply that windows should be banned. There are ways of using windows which avoid both glare and loss of adaptation. However, the exhibiting of material insensitive to light, such as unpainted stone sculpture, at high illuminance can cause trouble, and the attractive idea of being able to walk straight from an inside gallery to a sculpture garden raises almost insuperable difficulties in light control, even at 200 lux, let alone 50 lux.

The last matter to consider here is the distribution of the light. Designers have sometimes supposed that, if the viewer is kept in darkness and all the light is thrown on the exhibits, these will look brighter by contrast. They may look brighter, and this is certainly an excellent way to eliminate reflections in glass, but it is not the best way to make detail most visible.

To the doctor, a very slight shadow on a radiograph of the thorax may indicate tuberculosis. He therefore needs to view the radiograph in conditions optimised for visual acuity. The commonsense arrangement is to put the radiograph transparency on an illuminated viewer and mask it round the edge so that it becomes the only luminous object in view. Experiment shows, however, that visual acuity is improved if the area surrounding the radiograph is made about as bright as the radiograph itself. This fact should be borne in mind when choosing a wall-covering in the exhibition room. If we want the best conditions for seeing detail it should not be very much lighter or darker than the exhibits. A dark painting is not seen to best advantage on a white wall.

[. . .]

200 lux – daylight and artificial light

Once we accept the need to limit the amount of light which is allowed to fall on an exhibit the difficulties in controlling daylight as opposed to artificial light become apparent.

In the open air the expected illumination at 50° North latitude at midday in July is ten times that at midday in December. When the sun is shining it contributes as much illumination as the whole of an average sky, and much more if the sky is very clear. Indoors these differences may be exaggerated, and the variations in the resulting illuminance will be further compounded by the inequalities of light distribution round the room.

In other words any system aimed to provide indoor illumination at a set level must be capable of being continually and unobtrusively adjusted. There are a number of ways, partial and complete, in which we can do this:

1   The simplest system is to block out so much light that illuminance at the brightest times of the year rises to not much more than 200 lux. At all other times daylight is supplemented by artificial light. [. . .]
2   We can go to the other extreme of complexity by using a translucent ceiling through which daylight is highly diffused so as to light all exhibits at the agreed level, the daylight being admitted through shutters or blinds which are automatically controlled by photocell. As the daylight fails, artificial light is introduced, also by photocells, under dimmer control. Unfortunately what once seemed a neat – though expensive – solution to the problem has not lived up to its expectations. The constancy of the illumination and its high degree of diffusion have been widely found to have a depressing effect. [. . .]
3   Many existing daylight control systems, whether blinds or louvres, could be adapted, perhaps motorised, so that they were under the control of a room attendant. The output from a photocell on the wall could be led to a dial and the attendant would be required to reduce the light if the pointer on the dial moved onto a clearly marked part of the scale.

Annual light dose

4   Instead of aiming to achieve a steady illuminance of 200 lux we can work out the total annual dose of illumination, or exposure, equivalent to this. Eight hours a day plus a low level of adventitious and security lighting (say 10 lux) amount to an annual exposure of about 650 kilolux-hours. Similarly an annual exposure for the 50 lux level would be about 200 kilolux-hrs. Tables of illumination throughout the year at the locality of the museum can be obtained from meteorological organisations, and positions of blinds can be worked out to give 200 lux under average conditions. To carry out the scheme in detail requires the positions of blinds to be changed hourly (automatically) on a monthly schedule. This means a fair amount of computation, but simplifications will be evident. The result aimed at is a daylight illumination which retains some connection with the weather outside.
    [. . .]

The Blue Wool standards

By using the Blue Wool standards it is possible to estimate the lightfastness of a dyed fabric or paint. This measurement does no more than grade the material on a scale from 1 (fugitive) to 8 (of good lightfastness); it cannot give us a very good idea of how much exposure to light the material will stand in any situation.

The Blue Wool standards have been adopted as ISO (International Organisation for Standardisation) Recommendation R 105 and British Standard BS1006 (1961), so that sample cards are readily available. Each card contains 8 specially prepared blue dyeings on wool. They are so chosen that standard number 2 takes roughly twice as long to be perceptibly faded as standard 1, standard 3 roughly twice as long as standard 2, and so on through to standard 8.

To rate the lightfastness of our material we expose it together with a card of the Blue Wool standards, and from time to time check both our material and the standards for first signs of fading. This can most easily be done if one half of each patch of colour is covered with an opaque card throughout the test.

Attempts have been made to measure how much light exposure is required to fade the standards.[19] They have met with little success, since rates of fading are related to other factors besides the light, such as proportion of UV,[20] humidity, etc. The light may appear to be the same but the standards may be found to fade at quite a different rate, although they keep more or less in rank.

In the museum, however, we can limit our interest to an indoor situation where extremes of temperature and humidity are avoided and all the light comes through glass though without specifying UV-filtering. For this special situation Feller has found that the Blue Wool standards can be very useful in grading material into three categories (Table 22.2). It should be noted that the lifetimes estimated in the table are for an average annual exposure of about 1½ million lux hours (1½ Mlx h). Under conditions controlled to 150 lux the annual exposure is about ½ Mlx h so that the figures could be multiplied by three. With no UV the multiplying factor would be higher still: six or more.

Table 22.2 Standards of photochemical stability for materials in conservation

Class	Classification	Intended useful lifetime	Approximate equivalent standard of photochemical stability
C	Unstable or fugitive	Less than 20 years	BS1006 Class 3 or less
B	Intermediate	(20–100 years)	(3 to 6)
A	Excellent	Greater than 100 years	Greater than BS1006 Class 6

Notes and references

1   Thomson, G. (1986) *The Museum Environment* (2nd edn), London: Butterworths, plate 2.
2   An illuminance of 1 lux equals 1 lumen per square metre. This unit of luminous flux, the lumen, could be described as the radiant energy flux as perceived by the human eye.
3   Chartered Institute of Building Services (UK) (1980) *CIBS Lighting Guide: Museums and Art Galleries*, London: CIBS.
4   ICOM (1971) 'La Lumière et la Protection des Objets et Specimens exposés dans les Musées et

Galeries d'Art. Paris: L'Association Française de l'Eclairage (no date). Also in *Lux* 63, 235–64.

5 ICCROM (1975) *Catalogues of Technical Exhibitions, No. 1 – Lighting.*

6 Crollau, E. K. and Knoring, G. M. (1975) 'Standards of artificial light in museums of the USSR', *Preprints of the ICOM Committee for Conservation, 4th Triennial Meeting, Venice* (1975), 75/19/6.

7 Lafontaine, R. H. and Macleod, K. J. (1976) 'A statistical survey of lighting conditions and the use of ultraviolet filters in Canadian museums, archives and galleries', *J. Can. Conserv. Inst.*, 1: 41–4.

8 Macleod, K. J. (1978) (reprint), 'Museum lighting', *Technical Bull. No. 2, Canadian Conservation Institute.*

9 Thomson, G. (1961) 'A new look at colour rendering, level of illumination, and protection from ultraviolet radiation in museum lighting', *Studies in Conservation* 6, 49–70.

10 Brommelle, N. S. and Harris, J. B. (1961) 'Museum lighting', Parts 1 to 4. *Museums Journal* 61: 169–76; 61: 259–67; 62: 337–46; 62: 176–86.

11 Brommelle, N. S. (1968) 'Conservation of museum objects in the tropics', in G. Thomson, *1967 IIC London Conference on Museum Climatology*, London: IIC, 139–49.

12 Brommelle, N. S. (1968) 'Lighting, air-conditioning, exhibition, storage, handling and packing', *The Conservation of Cultural Property*, UNESCO Museums and Monuments series 11, 291–301.

13 Harris, J. B. (1964) 'Lighting problems in museums and art galleries', *Elect. Rev.*, 10: 175.

14 Harris, J. B. (1964) 'Art gallery and museum lighting', *Int. Ltg. Rev.* 15: 159.

15 Harris, J. B. (1964) 'Some aspects of art gallery lighting', *Int. Ltg. Rev.* 15: 170–9.

16 Harris, J. B. (1968) 'Practical aspects of lighting as related to conservation', in G. Thompson, *1967 IIC London Conference on Museum Climatology*, London: IIC, 133–8.

17 Brawne, M. (1965) *The New Museum*, London: Architectural Press, 170; and Brawne, M. (1982) *The Museum Interior*, London: Thames and Hudson, 102.

18 Allen, W. A. (1971) 'The new museum in Lisbon for the Gulbenkian Collection. A new approach to illumination', *Museums Journal* 71: 54–8.

19 Rawland, O. (1963), 'Fading of the British dyed-wool light-fastness standards in the U.K. – some energy measurements', *J. Soc. Dyers Colour.* 79: 697–701.

20 Tennent, N., Townsend, J. H. and Davis, A. (1982) 'A simple integrating dosimeter for ultraviolet light', in N. S. Brommelle and G. Thomson (eds) *Science and Technology in the Service of Conservation*, Preprints IIC Washington Congress, London: IIC, 32–38.

Chapter 23

The Lighting Decision

Stefan Michalski

Is there anything new under the sun?

T HE FUNDAMENTAL LIGHTING DILEMMA, visibility versus vulnerability, is the same today as it has been for centuries. It was never unique to museums, house-keepers have always known it. Can anything new be said?

Conservators can decide on intelligent negotiation rather than their 50 lux mantra. Although 50 lux can and will be justified as the fundamental benchmark, we must recover the flexibility Thomson intended, a flexibility that can bend towards more exposure, and bend towards less exposure, as circumstances demand. Vulnerability data is not so much new as unused by our (conservation) profession. It is not an exact or easy science, but it is the best answer to the most important question: how much damage will occur how soon for what lighting. A direct microscopic test for important artifacts is suggested for definitive predictions. Visibility, which has often been taken for granted by our profession, can draw on a new model from lighting research. It will explain the legitimate complaints aimed at museum lighting, and it will explain why bright lighting by scholars and conservators is not always, just sometimes, professional hypocrisy. A summary table of this "new" lighting decision has been developed at CCI, shown as Table 23.1. Note that there are no longer broad generalizations across artifact categories such as "50 lux for paper and textiles" and "200 lux for oil paintings."

Source: CCI (eds), *Fabric of an Exhibition: An Interdisciplinary Approach — Preprints*, Ottawa: CCI, 1997, pp. 97–104.

Table 23.1 Artifacts and lighting: visibility vs. vulnerability

	Basic rules for lighting	To adjust for visibility	To adjust for vulnerability
If total control of lighting is possible For rooms with total control of display lighting, where object lifetimes must be maximized.	**For all organic materials, and those inorganic materials that are light or UV sensitive:** *Light: 50 lux, only when viewers present* *UV: less than 10 µW/lm* Note: only those under 30 years of age will be content, and only when they are viewing light coloured surfaces without low contrast detail. **For all inorganic materials not sensitive to light or UV:** *Light level unlimited, but lighting must not raise the surface temperature of the artifact more than 5°C above ambient air temperature.* As a simple guide, the light-beam should not noticeably warm your hands.	For low contrast details – up to ×3 For dark surfaces up to − ×3 For older viewers up to − ×3 Limited time, complex search up to − ×3 For combinations of the above, multiply by each of the factors in turn. For example, if low contrast details in a dark surface are to be seen quickly and well by a 65 year old, then the calculation is: (50 lux) × 3 × 3 × 3 × 3 = 4050 lux, i.e. about 4,000 lux. In general, an older conservator, curator, scholar, or connoisseur, making a careful inspection of a dark artifact, but given ample time for the task, needs (50 lux) × 3 × 3 × 3 = 1350 lux. It makes sense to limit such activities by senior experts to brief periods of time, and to provide task lighting that can be adjusted to various angles. Only indirect daylight, fluorescent lights, and special cool incandescent lights can achieve such intensities without risk of overheating the object.	Determine the light sensitivities of the colorants in the artifacts. Given that determination, the following actions will reduce the rate of colour loss to a maximum of about one perceptible step per ten years, which will give almost complete colour loss in 300–500 years. To extend lifetimes beyond this will require proportionally greater reductions than those given below. *Fugitive colorants: (ISO 1, 2, 3)* Reduce all long-term adjustments for visibility to a total of ×3, i.e. 150 lux maximum and display for only 10% of the time. (Brief periods of inspection should not exceed 1500 lux for 1% of the time or equivalent). *Intermediate colorants: (ISO 4, 5, 6)* Reduce all long-term adjustments for visibility to a total of × 3, i.e. 150 lux maximum for permanent display. Any display at higher visibility levels will have to be proportionally reduced in time. (Brief periods of inspection should not exceed 1500 lux for 10% of the time, or equivalent). *Durable colorants: (ISO 7, 8,+)* Reduce all long-term adjustments for visibility to a total of ×30, i.e. 1500 lux maximum. (Brief periods of inspection should not exceed 4500 lux). *Permanent or absent colorants:* Given slow yellowing and disintegration of organic materials due to trace UV and unavoidable violet and blue light, follow guidelines for durable colorants above.

| If partial control of lighting is possible.

For rooms with limited control of lighting (historic houses, offices, homes), where object lifetimes must be maximized. | **For all organic materials, and those inorganic materials that are light or UV sensitive:**

Light: Avoid the range 1,000–100,000 lux, i.e. bright electric lights and daylight near windows.

UV: less than 75 µW/lm

For all inorganic materials not sensitive to light or UV:

Avoid direct sun on the artifact, especially if it has brittle components, such as aged enamel | Move artifacts, especially those with significant details, into locations that give acceptable lighting for whoever is meant to see the artefact. | Determine the light sensitivities of the colorants in the artifacts. Given that determination, the following actions will reduce the rate of colour loss to a maximum of about one perceptible step per ten years, which will give almost complete colour loss in 300–500 years. To extend lifetimes beyond this will require proportionally greater reductions than those given below.
Fugitive colorants: (ISO 1, 2, 3)
Place these away from any locations that exceed 150 lux average over a ten hour day, and display only 10% of the time. If average intensity exceeds 150 lux, exhibit proportionally less than 10% of the time.
Intermediate colorants: (ISO 4, 5, 6)
Place these artifacts away from any locations that exceed 150 lux average over a ten hour day. If average intensity exceeds 150 lux, then exhibit proportionally less.
Durable colorants: (ISO 7, 8,+)
Place these artifacts away from any locations that exceed 1500 lux average over a ten hour day. If average intensity exceeds 1500 lux, then exhibit proportionally less.
Permanent or absent colorants:
Given slow yellowing and disintegration of organic materials due to trace UV and unavoidable violet and blue light, follow guidelines for durable colorants above. |

Lighting and visibility of artifacts

Visibility and colour arguments

As shown in Figure 23.1, the transition from monochromatic night vision to colour vision is completely finished by about 2 lux. The exact nature of this transition has only recently been clarified.[1] In the 1961 article that established 50 lux as a museum benchmark, Thomson argued on the basis of common experience, and noted similar minimums in French and Japanese recommendations from thirty years earlier.[2] Thus

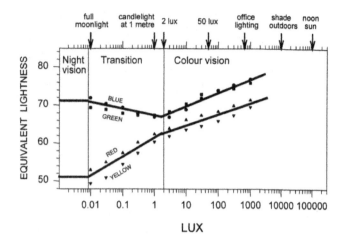

Figure 23.1 Transition of the human eye from monochromatic night vision to colour at differing light levels

conservation argued that at 50 lux we see well enough, particularly colours. Together with the widely invoked 1956 study by Kruithof that showed viewers preferred warm (2800°K) sources at low intensities,[3] the die was cast for museum lighting.

In 1973, Crawford showed that the boundary at which our eye lost its ability to see small colour differences did indeed occur near 2 lux[4] (Figure 23.2). By the 1987 Bristol Lighting conference, Boyce[5] could cite more colour discrimination data[6] that showed maximum performance by about 10 lux (Figure 23.2). Loe[7] described data on viewer satisfaction with lighting in a gallery. He fitted a soft curve with a knee near 200 lux, but one can also fit a sharp transition curve, and conclude that most of the satisfaction is reached by 50 lux. Thus 50 lux was proven to be well in excess of what was needed for colour perception, but it was a bare minimum for viewer comfort.

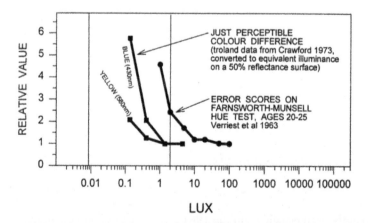

Figure 23.2 Ability of the human eye to detect small colour differences at low light levels

Scholarly dissatisfaction with 50 lux in museums has usually focussed on the "quality" of colours, or invoked the quagmires of historic or artistic "intent." Such dissatisfaction can often be traced simply to poor colour rendering sources, or competing colour temperatures across a single space, or poor gallery design for adaptation of the eye. On the other hand, there has been clarification of at least one real intensity effect: coloured materials are perceived as "brighter" in brighter light.[1] That is, their ranking relative to a non-coloured (grey) scale increases (equivalent lightness, in Figure 23.1). This effect may explain what some artists mean when they state that the colours in their works need lots of light, or conversely, when others state that their colours should not be "washed out" by too much light.[8]

Overlooked in the colour perception arguments, however, was the fact that the data concerned large patches of colour, viewed invariably by young students. Common experience tells us that seeing the details in our face is not just a little different with bright light but radically clearer, especially as we age.

Visibility, the lighting engineer, and the CIE

Unlike conservators, lighting engineers have always considered details as the primary criterion for visibility, not colours. By the 1970s, enough was known about the perception of detail for the Illuminating Engineering Society of North America (IESNA) to consider 50–100 lux as suitable only for "simple orientation for short temporary visits." "Visual tasks of medium contrast or small size" needed 500–1,000 lux while "tasks of extremely low contrast and small size" needed 10,000–20,000 lux.[9] In the 1996 IESNA *Museum and Art Gallery Lighting: A Recommended Practice*,[10] however, the traditional conservation rule of 50 lux for textiles, paper, etc. appears without explanation. The sole discussion of visibility states "there must be sufficient light on objects to make them visible to all visitors."

The rigorous basis for any discussion of visibility has its most recent version in the 1981 CIE publication *An Analytic Model for Describing the Influence of Lighting Parameters upon Visual Performance*.[11] The key concept, "visual performance," measures exactly what we mean by artifact visibility – the accuracy with which we see the artifact in all its details, as we stroll through an exhibition. CCI has considered the CIE model, and extracted the simplified rules shown under Adjustments for Visibility in Table 23.1. [. . .]

Contrast, the RCS curve, and visual performance

As light intensity increases, we can see details of lower contrast. The "relative contrast sensitivity" (RCS) curve plots this threshold for a simple dot, unambiguously presented in our line of sight. The curve was known by Thomson, but it did not offer optimistic transitions at low intensities, instead it climbed to full sunshine. (Contrast C and the RCS curves are actually in terms of luminance, but for our purposes reflectance (R) will do. Thus $C = |Rd–Rb|/Rb$, where d is detail and b is background.)

The CIE model begins with the RCS curve, but incorporates further studies on its deterioration with viewer age. The model then considers studies on dynamic viewing of clusters of details, where the difficulty of the viewer's task (D) can be increased by reducing the object exposure time, increasing the spread of the cluster, or asking for more information about the cluster. Visual performance is then the accuracy with which a detail of a certain size is seen (noted) as compared to the maximum accuracy possible for that detail when viewed by a young viewer, at maximum contrast, with maximum light (essentially full sunlight) and no task difficulty.

Visibility at the traditional 50 lux

In Figure 23.3 all curves are for moderately fine detail: 4 minutes arc, or 1.2 mm viewed at 1 metre. This is equivalent to the weave detail in a textile of 8 threads per cm (20 threads per inch) viewed at 1 m, or the period (full stop) at the end of this sentence (0.6 mm) held at arms length (50 cm).

In Figure 23.3, the heavy black line is visual performance for a viewer of age 25 (A25), on a low difficulty task (D30), and details of moderate contrast 0.5 (C0.5). For the textile example, it means the viewer is given ample time, and the interstices reflect 0.5 as much as the fabric. The CIE suggests a lighting design target of 80% of maximum performance (at full daylight) for a particular visual task. This is the diamond on the knee of the curve. If the artifact is of intermediate reflectance (R=50%) then the lower lux axis applies. Reading the lower lux axis, the diamond is near 50 lux. Thus we can confirm that the traditional benchmark of 50 lux gives good visibility for moderately fine details of moderate contrast for a young viewer given ample time.

Visibility rule for low contrast details

In Figure 23.3 the two thin solid curves differ from the benchmark conditions (A25, D30, C0.5) only in terms of contrast. The C0.9 line is for high contrast, such as the ink dot at the end of this sentence (ink about R = 10%, paper about R = 90%). The

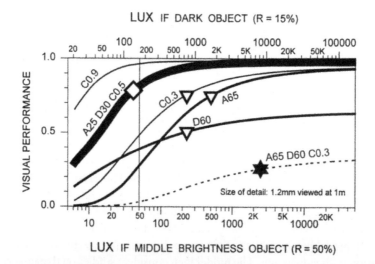

Figure 23.3 Differing visual performance with light level

C0.3 line is for low contrast, such as the textile weave example if the interstices reflect 0.7 as much as the fabric. Its knee at 80% of maximum, marked by a triangle, reads 250 lux on the lower axis, so five times 50 lux.

Lower contrast (or finer) details are possible, but for this size detail, C0.3 is the lowest contrast that gives a maximum visual performance near 1.0 for full daylight. It seems unreasonable to ask for a higher standard than those soft details that we see perfectly in sunlight in our youth. CCI has opted for only part of the ×5 factor needed to reach 80% performance on such details: a cautious "up to ×3" for low contrast details.

Visibility rule for darkness of the object

In Figure 23.3, the lower lux axis applies to intermediate brightness objects. The upper lux axis applies to dark objects, specifically R = 15%. Thus this axis reads just over three times the light compared to the lower axis, and gives rise to a rule of "up to ×3" for dark objects. Dark browns, dark blues, blacks, may fall as low as R = 5%, and would argue for ×10 lighting, but purposefully dark colours, such as textiles, are not meant to be seen in detail. Fortunately, inadvertently dark artifacts such as tarnished coins are not vulnerable to light, so plenty of light makes sense.

Visibility rule for age of the viewer

In Figure 23.3, the dotted line gives performance for the same conditions as the thick benchmark curve, except that the viewer is age 65, rather than 25. The maximum plateau still reaches close to 1.0, but the triangle at 80% maximum performance requires almost 500 lux on the lower axis, ten times that for the 25 year old.

This is not due to poor focus, which is assumed corrected. Part of the reason is that the fluid in our eye yellows, so that by age 65 we need four times the light to get the same light to our retina as in our youth. This is the ageing of the eye as camera. The eye as processor, as a dynamic searching system, also ages, hence the total lighting adjustment of ten times to maintain equal visual performance on clusters of details.

As noted in the CIE manual, it is unclear to what extent older viewers can compensate for their ageing visual performance. The simplest strategy is to spend longer looking. Much more difficult to assess are compensations due to experience. Thus a textile connoisseur may fill in details that a neophyte does not recognize, but does not need to!

For a cautious rule "up to ×3" is assigned to viewer age, but it must be recognized as only a partial answer to "equal visual access." Museums may need to consider "bright light tours" for seniors only, or for openings with ageing critics and executives.

Visibility rule for limited time, complex search

In Figure 23.3, the dashed line marked D60 is performance for the same conditions as the thick benchmark curve, except for increased task difficulty. Note that the maximum performance plateau has dropped to 0.6. The 80% knee at maximum performance, marked by a triangle, reads 250 lux on the bottom axis, five times 50 lux.

As noted under the rule for age, visual performance involves not just the eye as camera, but as a scanning processor too. In viewing artifacts with arrays of many details, irregularities, repairs, or defects, we need much more light to see them as readily as if they were pointed out to us.

A cautious lighting rule of "up to ×3" has been assigned for complex search in a limited time.

Visibility and the ethics of maximum adjustment

In Figure 23.3, the effect of age, difficulty and low contrast together is shown by the lowest curve. Note the low maximum. By reading the upper lux axis, we obtain the additional factor due to dark objects. To reach 80% of maximum shown by the star requires about 8,000 lux, so 160 times 50 lux. By using the simplified CCI rules, all four together yield $3 \times 3 \times 3 \times 3 = 81$, which is a cautious half of the 160 factor.

Senior scholars and conservators are older, and their visual tasks on artifacts are usually complex search of subtle details, but they can take their time, move closer, and use magnifiers. If we consider just the adjustments for low contrast, dark surfaces, and aged viewer, then $3 \times 3 \times 3 = 27$, so about 1350 lux gives excellent inspection for all ages. It is no surprise, therefore, that careful inspection has traditionally meant moving to a window to use daylight, or that the IESNA recommends 1,000–2,000 lux for "tasks of low contrast or very small size."

In the adjustments for vulnerability in the CCI guidelines, Table 1, it is suggested that study exposure never exceed display exposure. If display of an artifact with a fugitive colorant is controlled to an exposure of 10% of the time at 150 lux, then inspection at 1500 lux should not exceed 1% of the time. If a conservation lab examining or treating this important artifact once every hundred years takes a year from start to finish, and the artifact languishes in labs at 750 lux, they will be responsible for as much light damage as half a century of controlled display. If they want to avoid hypocritical use of the artifact as lab decor, they must use opaque covers whenever possible.

Visibility and the problem of large artifacts

With large objects, such as tapestries, the viewer stands back to see the whole thing. On the other hand, to see the authentic solid thing means to see its details. To see both together requires lighting similar to daylight. This phenomenon underlies the undeniable feel of daylight, the simultaneous experience of vast panorama and overwhelming detail. Museums must abandon such experience for light-sensitive materials, of course, but they must also recognize it as a desirable option for artifacts such as large metal and stone sculpture. There will, of course, be light adaptation problems to solve.

Visibility and raking lighting

It is an old lighting trick to enhance surface detail by raking the lighting from one direction, not at extreme disfiguring angles, but at 30°–45°. This can be understood now in terms of increasing contrast (C) of the detail. Part of the increased contrast is simply the creation of shadows, part is decreased reflectance to our eye for surfaces tilted away from the light. In textiles the interstices gain in darkness and apparent width, so weave becomes more visible. Contrast enhancement is stronger for point light sources than area sources. Raking light does nothing, however, for design details such as different coloured yarns.

Visibility and movement

For banners and costumes, movement of the fabric was intrinsic to the original visual experience. Movement not only gave rise to changes in conformation of the textile, but all the raking light phenomena outlined earlier also became dynamic for both weave and drape. For textiles with sheen, highlights become dynamic. And what worked well for sheen worked spectacularly for glitter. (Sheen and glitter elevate contrast to values many times above 1.0.) One could argue that such fabrics were developed expressly for the purpose of intensifying dynamic visibility in low intensity candlelight.

Overall, solid artifacts at low light levels will be seen in more detail if there is movement, such as slow rotation of a manikin under directional lighting, or rotation of the lighting itself. Such movement also reduces the uneven fading of draped textiles due to static lighting, and reduces exposure per unit area by about one half.

Vulnerability of textiles to lighting

Wavelength dependence and ultraviolet (UV)

Light sources emit light (visible radiation) and UV (ultraviolet radiation). In practical summary, UV yellows, weakens, embrittles, or disintegrates organic materials such as textiles. Light is incapable of most such damage. Light and UV fade colorants, but light is 10 to 50 times more plentiful than UV in light sources. Thus if light is capable of fading the colorant at all, as it is for most fugitive colorants, then it dominates fading. If light is not capable of fading the colorant, as it is not for durable colorants, then UV dominates the fading by default.

In a more precise argument, Figures 23.4 and 23.5 compile the relevant damage spectra. The border between UV and light lies between 380 nm and 400 nm. Our young eye sees out to about 380 nm, hence the glass industry prefers this boundary for calculating %UV transmittance. The museum world prefers 400 nm as a border, since UV type damage is still strong in the 380–400 nm band. Except for the curious yellowing blip at 520 nm, the wool data in Figure 23.4 is typical for paper, wood and oil media too: UV makes yellow colorant, and blue light bleaches it. The essential difference between the spectra in Figures 23.4 and 23.5 is obvious: disintegration and yellowing (Figure 23.4) follow steep, ascending lines in the UV/violet region, fading of colorants (Figure 23.5) follow flat or wavy lines across most wavelengths of light.

Researchers, starting with lighting engineer Harrison in 1953,[12] and continuing with others such as Krochman,[13] have calculated weighting functions using straight lines such as these in Figure 23.5. (The equation form: Damage rate at X nm = Dam-

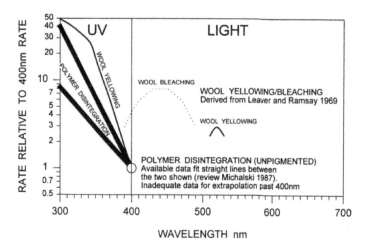

Figure 23.4 Differing rates of damage with variation in UV wavelength against the 400 nm damage rate

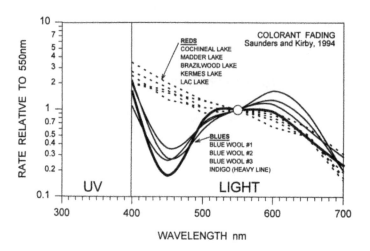

Figure 23.5 Differing rates of fading with variation in wavelength of visible light against the 400 nm damage rate

age rate at 400 nm*10^(400 nm − X nm)/C nm, where C is typically 100 nm.) This function is then used to calculate a relative damage rating for the spectrum of a light source. These light source damage factors are valid only for the types of damage associated with UV, and most of this damage is controlled by UV filtration. These "lamp damage ratings" must not be applied to colour fading by light. Saunders and Kirby[14] have shown convincingly that while red and yellow dyes (in lake pigments) may be slightly more vulnerable to blue light than longer wavelengths, blue dyes reverse this rule (Figure 23.5).

Lightfastness data

The most widely used international lightfastness scale is the ISO Blue Wools. Some of the rankings of historic textile colorants on this scale have been compiled in Table 23.2.[15–18] A few useful generalizations emerge from the literature. A given dye is more fugitive on silk and cotton than on wool, typically one or two steps worse on the scale. A pale tint (as new) is half or one step more fugitive than its standard depth shade, while a heavy dyeing may be one or two steps more durable. The mordant is very influential, one cannot estimate a dye's lightfastness without knowing it.

Unlike a new pale shade, a pale remnant of an already faded colour can be much more durable than the original colour. This small mercy comes about since a colorant forms a range of lightfastnesses so that the most fugitive components fade first, leaving the least fugitive components as the remnant. Kashiwagi and Yamasaki[18] have shown final fading of very fugitive dyes changes little from initial rates, but some dyes rated ISO#3 initially can jump three or more steps at final stages of fade. Table 23.2 measures this effect.

The practical problem for prediction of light damage in terms of exposure is the conversion of these lightfastness rankings to absolute sensitivities to light. This correlation has been the subject of much debate, and there is no doubt it is inherently messy for many reasons, but the approximate correlation derived by Michalski in his review,[19] and as used in the UV + scale on the CCI Light Damage Slide Rule, has been used for the scale in Table 23.2. This correlation is an idealized fit which spaces all eight standards evenly (dose in M1 $\times$ h to fade ISO Blue Wool number # to GS4 is: dose $= 0.22 \times 2.43^{\wedge}(\# - 1)$. This correlation is for daylight through glass (or xenon arc or fluorescent lamps that approximate the same), since almost all lightfastness data has been collected with this UV-rich spectrum.

In a museum that cares about light damage, one can assume UV filtration, so an exposure equivalence to the Blue Wool ratings for UV filtered light is needed. This equivalence, as used in Table 23.2, and in the UV-scale on the CCI Light Damage Slide Rule is based on the data of MacLaren on 400 direct dyes and the ISO Blue Wools themselves,[20] as well as the confirming trend of other data on historic colorants. The data show that ISO#1 and equivalent colours are helped very little, but each subsequent ISO number is helped more and more. The result is a dose increase of about $\times3$ between each ISO step, and a total span of 1000:1 between fugitive ISO#1, such as many greens, yellows and mauves on silk, and durable ISO#8, such as a heavy indigo on wool. This is the reason banners and ribbons fade early in military museums, while navy blue on wool seems to last longer than the wool itself.

Vulnerability assessment by analysis

Vulnerability analysis can be historical or chemical. History of textile technology will tell a knowledgeable curator or conservator whether a colour is likely to be one of the well known natural dyes, such as indigo or madder, or one of a group of known fugitive dyes, such as the anilines. For some colours, such as yellow, mauve, and green, the major historic dyes are all fugitive (Table 23.2), so analysis is only needed if one

Table 23.2 Lightfastness ratings of the natural dyes on wool, cotton, and silk

1	2	3	4	5	6	7	8
TIME FOR NOTICEABLE FADE AT 50 LUX: 1 Year=3000 hours=150 klx h. Noticeable=GS4. Full fade takes about 30 such steps.							
Daylight through window glass:							
1.5y	4y	10y	25y	60y	140y	340y	800y
Light with all UV removed: (Average behaviour. Some dyes benefit less from UV removal, so the scale above can be used as worst case.)							
2y	6y	20y	60y	200y	600y	1500y	4000y
BROWNS							
Wool (pl):	limawood.r24[cu]	sanderswood[cu,fe] ventilago.o1[cu,fe] camwood.r22[cu,fe] barwood.r22[cu,fe]			{cochineal.r4[cu,fe]; morinda.r18[cu,fe]; mang kudu.r19[cu, fe]} {chay root.r6[cu,fe]; munjeet.r16[cu,fe]; madder.r8[cu,fe]} {lac dye.r25[cu,fe]}	{dyes in categories 5–7 are not distinguished in the pl study}	
Wool (d):			crotile lichen.a				
REDS							
Wool (pl): orchil.r28 barwood.r22[al] sanderswood.r22[al]	limawood.r24[al, sn] barwood.r22[sn] sanderswood.r22[sn] camwood.r22[al, sn] ventilago.o1[al, sn]	cochineal.r4[al] kermes.r3[al]	lac dye.r25[al] munjeet.r16[al]	{cochineal.r4[sn]; kermes.r3[sn]; lac dye.r25[sn]} {madder.r8[al]; turkey red.r8} {dyes in categories 5–7 are not distinguished in the pl study}		
Wool (d):		cochineal.r4[sn] lac dye.r25[sn]	ladys bedstraw.r14[al]	alizarin.r8[al] ladys bedstraw.r14[sn]	alizarin.r8[sn]		
Cotton and Silk (ky):		cochineal[sn]r4 cot.init			cochineal[sn]r4 silk.init		cochineal[sn]r4 cot, silk final

	(init)	(init)	(final)	(final)
safflower.r26/ cot,silk init	madder[al]r8cot.init sappanwood.r2 4[alcl]cot.silk init. safflower.r26/cot,silk final	madder[al]r8 silk init sappanwood.r2 4[al]cot.silk init.	madder[al]r8 cotfinal sappanwood.r2 4[alcl]cot.silk final	madder[al]r8silk final sappanwood.r2 4[al]cot,silk final

ORANGES, YELLOWS

Wool (pl): annato.o4 saffron.y6 turmeric.y3 tesu.y28[al] gardenia.y6 coscinium.y18 evodia	kamala.o2[al] jak wood.y11[al,sn] old fustic.y11[al,sn] quercitron.y10[al, sn] tesu,y28[sn] persian berries.y13[al,sn]	weld.y2[al] morinda.r18	weld.y2[sn]	{munjeet.r16[sn]; morinda.r18[sn]; sophora. y10[sn]} {madder.r8[sn]; chay root.r6[sn]} {dyes in categories 5–7 are not distinguished in the pl study}
young fustic.br1[al]	young fustic.br1 [sn]			
Wool (d): ling heather tips.q.m[al] old fustic. y11 [sn]	persian berries. y13[sn]			
Silk (pl): kamala				
Cotton and Silk (ky):		oak.f[fe]cot.silk init		oak.f[fe] silk final, cot>8

Table 23.2 Continued

	pagoda tree.y10 [ala]silk init marygold.y27? [sn]cot.silk.init	myrica.m[cu] cot.silk init myrica.m[fe] cot.silk init pagoda tree.y10 [ala]cot.init	pagoda tree.y10 [ala]cot.final marygold.y27? [sn]cot.silk.final	pagoda tree. y10[ala]silk final	myrica.m[fe] cot.silk final	myrica.m[cu] cot.silk final
amur cork.y18 [ala]cot.silk init			amur cork.y18 [ala]cot.silk final			
BLUES, GREENS						
Wool (pl):	logwood.bk1[al]	privet berries.bk 5[al/fe]	ling heather tips. q.m[al/fe/cu] seaweed[cu]	indigo.b2	{indigo.b2; prussian blue.pb27}	foxglove.l[al/fe]
Wool (d): sulphonated indigo.b2 ling heather tips. q.m[al]						
Cotton (pl): lo kav.g1						
Cotton and Silk (ky):	indigo.b2 silk init	indigo.b2 silk init	indigo.b2 cot init			indigo.b2 silk final, cot>8
PURPLES						
Wool (pl): logwood.bk1[sn] elder berries.c.sc						
Wool (d): cudbear lichen.l						
Cotton and Silk (ky): shikone.s[alcl]cot. silk init	shikone.s[sn]silk. init	shikone.s[sn]cot. silk. init	shikone.s[alcl]cot. silk final			
shikone.s[sn]cot. init	shikone.s[sn]cot. init	shikone.s[sn]cot. silk. init				

BLACKS

Wool (pl):   limawood.r24[fe]   logwood.bk1[fe]

Wool (d):   water lily roots.t[fe]

The centre of each dye phrase is aligned with its published rating on the ISO blue wool standards, either 1 to 8, or midpoints, e.g. 1–2. Sources of data:

(PL): Padfield and Landhi, 1966, ref. 17. Daylight through glass. Their data table II has been abridged: Their rating "1–2" has been set as 2, their "4–5" as 4, since this agrees with their exposures for those columns, i.e. double the GS4 exposure of this table.

(D):   Duff, Sinclair and Stirling 1977, or Grierson, Duff and Sinclair, 1985, ref. 18, 19. Microscal lamp, simulation of daylight through glass.

(KY): Kashiwagi and Yamasaki, 1982, ref 20. Daylight through glass. Abbreviations: COT = Cotton. INIT = Initial fade rate, FINAL = Fade rate after significant fading has already taken place.

Only single dyes under "daylight" reported here, see original papers for some mixtures of these dyes, some studies with fluorescent lamps. Mordants: [AL: Alum] [ALCL: aluminium chloride] [ALA: aluminium acetate] [SN: tin] [FE: iron] [CU: Copper] Colour Index Natural Dye number given, if known, e.g. R8. (BR: Brown, R:Red, O:Orange, Y:Yellow, G:Green, B:Blue, BK:Black, PB:Pigment Blue). If not, then dominant constituents from authors (KY), or H. Schweppe, 1993 *Handbuche der Naturfarbstoffe*. A:Atranorin, C:Chrysanthemin, F:Fraxin, L:Luteolin, M:Myrecetin, Q:Quercetin (major but not sole component of Y10), S:Shikonin see Colour Index 75535, SC: Sambucyanin, T:Tannins

is hoping to find a more durable synthetic colorant. It is important for all chemical analyses to be shared, so that the pool of historic knowledge increases.

Vulnerability assessment by direct testing

For important artifacts, one may be looking for unequivocal predictions that analysis cannot provide. Besides, one may also be looking for more powerful evidence with which to influence disbelievers. A direct fading test of a tiny spot on the artifact will satisfy both. Textile artifacts in particular lend themselves to this approach, since colours can always be found in unobtrusive areas, such as the back of the textile, inside a hem or seam, even the back of a yarn. CCI has developed a simple technique using a standard fibre optic lamp that delivers about 200,000 lux.[21] A metal mask with a 2 mm hole is used to reduce the spot to even less than the fibre optic bundle diameter.

Notes

1 Ikeda, M., Huang, C. C. and Ashizawa, S. (1989) 'Equivalent lightness of colored objects at illuminances from the scotopic to the photopic level', *Colour Research and Application* (1989), 198–206.
2 Thomson, G. (1961) 'A new look at colour rendering, level of illumination, and protection from ultraviolet radiation in museum lighting', *Studies in Conservation* 6, 49–70.
3 Kruithof, A. A. and Ouweltjes, J. L. (1956) 'Colour and colour rendering of tubular fluorescent lamps', *Philips Technical Review* 18, 249–261.
4 Crawford, B. H. (1973) 'Just perceptible colour differences in relation to level of illumination', *Studies in Conservation* 18, 159–166.
5 Boyce, P. (1987) 'Visual acuity, colour discrimination, and light level', *Lighting in Museums, Galleries and Historic Houses*, London: UK Institute for Conservation and the Museums Association, 50–57.
6 Verriest, G., Buyssens, A. and Vanderdonck, R. (1963) 'Étude quantitative de l'effet qu'exerce sur les résultats de quelques tests de la discrimination chromatique une diminution non sélective du niveau d'un éclairage C', *Revue Optique* 428, 105–119.
7 Loe, D. (1987) 'Preferred lighting for the display of paintings with conservation in mind', *Lighting in Museums, Galleries and Historic Houses*, London: UK Institute for Conservation and the Museums Association, 36–49.
8 Rothko, Mark (1987) Letter to Bryan Robertson on how to hang an exhibition at Whitechapel Gallery, cited in the catalogue: Compton, M. *Mark Rothko*, London: The Tate Gallery, 59.
9 Kaufmann, J. E., and Haynes, H. (1981) *IES Lighting Handbook. 1981 Application Volume*. New York: Illuminating Engineering Society of North America, 2–5.
10 IESNA Committee on Museum and Art Gallery Lighting. Museum and Art Gallery Lighting (1996) *A Recommended Practice, RP-30-96*. New York: Illuminating Engineering Society of North America.
11 CIE (1981) *An Analytic Model for Describing the Influence of Lighting Parameters Upon Visual Performance*, CIE No.19/2 (volumes 1 and 2), Paris: Commission Internationale de l'Éclairage.

12 Harrison, L. S. (1953) *Report on the Deteriorating Effects of Modern Light Sources*, New York: Metropolitan Museum of Art.

13 Krochmann, J. (1985/6) 'Über die bestimmung der relativen spektralen lichtempfindlichkeit von Museumsgut', *Deutscher Restauratoren Verbard* 1985/86, 20–28.

14 Saunders, D. and Kirby, J. (1994) 'Wavelength-dependent fading of artists' pigments', in A. Roy and P. Smith (eds) *Preventive Conservation: Practice, Theory and Research*, preprints IIC Ottawa Congress, London: IIC, 190–194.

15 Padfield, T. and Landhi, S. (1966) 'The light-fastness of the natural dyes', *Studies in Conservation* 11, 181–196.

16 Duff, D., Sinclair, R. S. and Stirling D. S. (1977) 'Light-induced colour changes of natural dyes', *Studies in Conservation* 22, 161–169.

17 Grierson, S., Duff, D. G. and Sinclair R. S. (1985) 'The colour and fastness of natural dyes of the Scottish Highlands', *Journal of the Society of Dyers and Colourists* 101, 220–228.

18 Kashiwagi, M., and Yamasaki, S. (1982) 'The lightfastness properties of traditional vegetable dyes', *Scientific Papers on Japanese Antiques and Art Crafts* 27, 54–65. (English translation by Library of the Canadian Conservation Institute, Ottawa, 1984.)

19 Michalski, S. (1987) 'Damage to museum objects by visible radiation (light) and ultraviolet radiation (UV)', *Lighting, A Conference on Lighting in Museums, Galleries, and Historic Houses*, London: The Museums Association and the United Kingdom Institute for Conservation, 3–16.

20 McLaren, K. (1956) 'The spectral regions of daylight that cause fading of dyes', *Journal of the Society of Dyers and Colourists* 72, 86–99.

21 Costain, C. (1996) Cafnadian Conservation Institute, personal communication.

Introduction to Part Two – Section Six

Chris Caple

Agents of deterioration: incorrect temperature and relative humidity

AWARE OF THE DELETERIOUS EFFECT on many museum objects of either damp or very dry conditions, conservators and curators often set specific relative humidity (RH) limits for artefacts going on loan to other institutions. Over time, these RH limits became increasingly restrictive and by the late 1980s the specified conditions were not realistically achievable (Ashley-Smith et al., 1994). In the mid-1990s, Michalski (1993) (Chapter 25) and Erhardt and Mecklenburg (1994) (Chapter 24) suggested that the 'safe' limits for many objects and materials were much broader than had previously been suggested. Michalski's paper, in particular, provides the data to show that the likelihood of mould growth at RH below 75% is very low and that the mid-range fluctuation for unconfined organic materials does not lead to any significant mechanical damage over many thousands of cycles. However, objects that are formed from materials that respond at different rates to RH or are confined through rigid joints or fixings are much more at risk of failure (cracking or splitting) than unconfined objects. In many cases the size and shape of the object can be crucial in determining the likelihood of damage from RH changes or extremes. All this evidence demonstrated that many organic artefacts are less likely to be damaged by mid-range RH values between 25% and 75% than had previously been appreciated. The research demonstrated that there is a valid basis for assertions that the risks associated with RH should be evaluated on an individual object basis. The very limited range of acceptable RH values previously quoted for many objects was often not required and it could therefore be suggested that the money spent on achieving such controlled levels would be better spent on reducing other, greater threats to object safety and taking steps to identify high-risk objects. The research by Marion Mecklenburg on the relationship between materials and humidity continues at the Smithsonian Museum Conservation Institute, whilst Dave Grattan and Stefan Michalski at the Canadian Conservation Institute are exploring classifying (and grouping?) museum collections in terms of using the ASHRAE (American Society of Heating Refrigeration and Air Conditioning Engineers) five classes of control.

Although there has been considerable focus on RH, Michalski (1994) (Chapter 26) also reminds us that in addition to being the crucial driver of RH, temperature also has a wide range of effects on museum objects and materials, though extreme temperatures, like extreme RH, represent the greatest threat to objects.

References

Ashley-Smith, L., Umney, N. and Ford, D. (1994) 'Let's Be Honest – Realistic Environmental Parameters for Loaned Objects', in A. Roy and P. Smith (eds), *Preventive Conservation: Practice, Theory and Research, IIC Ottawa Congress 12–16 September 1994*, Ottawa: IIC, pp. 28–31.

Erhardt, D. and Mecklenburg, M. (1994) 'Relative Humidity Re-examined', in A. Roy and P. Smith (eds), *Preventive Conservation: Practice, Theory and Research*, IIC Ottawa Congress 12–16 September 1994, Ottawa: IIC, pp. 32–38.

Michalski, S. (1993) 'Relative Humidity: A Discussion of Correct/Incorrect Values', in *ICOM-CC 10th Triennial Meeting, Washington, DC, USA*, pp. 624–629.

Michalski, S. (1994) 'Relative Humidity and Temperature Guidelines: What's Happening', *CCI Newsletter* 14.

Chapter 24

Relative Humidity Re-examined

David Erhardt and Marion Mecklenburg

Introduction

T HE MOST IMPORTANT FACTOR in the preservation of collections is the maintenance of proper environmental conditions. What are the appropriate conditions
for museum objects? The museum environment has a number of components, including temperature, relative humidity, light, vibration, pollutants and particulates. Suitable values or limits must be determined for each. This is straightforward for some
factors, even if it is not practical to achieve the value. For example, vibration, pollution and particulates are all damaging and unnecessary and should be reduced to the
lowest practical levels.

Light is a more complex subject. Light, although damaging, is necessary for
viewing objects. Even the specifications for light, however, can be reduced to the
basic principle of using the minimum amount of visible light required to view an
object properly. The problems of determining how much light is required by viewers and providing the correct spectral distribution of visible light, while excluding
infrared and ultraviolet wavelengths, are largely technical and practical rather than
theoretical.

Temperature and relative humidity differ from other environmental factors.
They are interdependent and their effects on objects are more varied and complex
than those of the other factors. A temperature or relative humidity that is acceptable
for one object may be disastrous for another. Temperature and relative humidity cannot be eliminated; instead, satisfactory values for each must be determined. Objects
are also affected by the rate and magnitude of changes in temperature and relative

Source: A. Roy and P. Smith (eds), *Preventive Conservation: Practice, Theory and Research, IIC
Ottawa Congress 12–16 September 1994*, Ottawa: IIC, 1994, pp. 32–38.

humidity, making it insufficient simply to specify an average value for these factors. Relative humidity is a function of temperature, and the practical range within which it can be controlled is dependent on temperature.

The range of temperatures suitable for museums, except for special situations or long-term storage areas, is restricted to temperatures at which people are comfortable. This range is relatively narrow, at most 5 or 10°C. Therefore, relative humidity is the major variable of the museum environment for which there is no obvious optimal value or range.

Present standards for relative humidity

The title of this section is misleading. There are currently no universal official museum standards for relative humidity (RH). There are commonly accepted values, and general guidelines for certain types of objects. Many museums in the USA maintain 50% RH in general collection areas. European museums often use 55–60% as better replicating the local climate. Museums in colder climates tend toward lower values such as 40–45%, since higher values are difficult to maintain in heated buildings during extremely cold weather. Exceptions to these values are sometimes made for objects such as panel paintings (higher values) and corroded metal (the lower the better) because of their reported sensitivity to extremes of, or changes in, RH.

Such values are often mentioned without justification or references. Michalski traced the derivation of the generally recommended values, and showed that they originally were determined more by mechanical feasibility and the local climate than by any research designed to determine a value of relative humidity that minimized damage.[1] Early work led to settings in the range of 50–60% RH. In 1960, a survey by the International Council of Museums (ICOM) found that most of the curators, conservators and scientists who responded favored RH control either in or overlapping the 50–60% range,[2] with exceptions for materials such as corroded metals. This 50–60% range probably is accepted even more widely today.

Effects of relative humidity on individual objects or types of material have been studied, but few reports have attempted to derive an optimal value or range of values for either general or specific types of collection. Many references to an optimal value of relative humidity cite *The Museum Environment* by Thomson.[3] Thomson selected 55% RH as midway between an upper limit of 65–70% to prevent mold growth and a lower limit of 40–45% for the failure of materials such as wood and ivory. He emphasized that the relative humidity must be held stable, while acknowledging that there was little evidence as to how stable it must be.

The widespread, if unofficial, acceptance of values of relative humidity in the range 50–60% is because visible damage (cracking, flaking, distortion, mold) is greatly reduced by controlling the relative humidity in this range. However, the reduction of damage is at least partially due to the stabilization of relative humidity and the avoidance of damaging extremes, rather than to the specific value of relative humidity.

Effects of relative humidity

Consideration of specific effects

Many aspects of the degradation of museum objects are affected by relative humidity. Each factor should be considered in any attempt to determine an optimal overall value. A discussion of some factors affected by relative humidity follows.

Biological attack

Mold and mildew grow only at high relative humidity. Michalski concluded from an analysis of the literature that an upper limit of 60% RH should prevent all mold growth, with a real danger of mold growth above 75% RH.[1] Other forms of biological attack do not affect these limits. Bacterial growth requires even higher RH, while insects can survive all but extremely dry conditions[3]. In Figure 24.1, the caution and danger zones for mold growth are shaded light and dark, respectively.

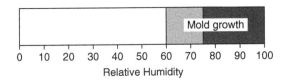

Figure 24.1 Relative humidity zones of possible and probable mold growth, shaded light and dark, respectively

Mechanical damage

The role of relative humidity in mechanical damage is complex. Changes in relative humidity produce changes in the dimensions and mechanical properties of organic materials and can lead to damage directly. At high RH, above about 80%, hide glue softens and loses adhesive strength.[4] Materials shrink and stiffen at low RH. This stiffening may be accompanied by fracture sensitivity or embrittlement. If the RH is stable, an object at equilibrium will experience damage only if components such as glue are too soft for proper adhesion or support, or so brittle that vibration or handling causes damage. Within an RH range in which an object is otherwise mechanically stable, most mechanical damage is due to RH fluctuations. Moderate changes in relative humidity produce minimal problems in materials that are free to expand and contract. Larger changes cause problems in objects, even those fully free to expand or contract, because moisture diffusion into or out of materials is not instantaneous, nor is it the same in different materials. Partial or differential moisture penetration results in the dry or less hygroscopic part of the object acting as a swelling restraint to the more moisture-reactive sections. The construction of an object tends to restrain the movement of its components, inducing stresses in the object. If changes in RH are severe enough, the induced stresses exceed the strength of the materials, resulting in cracking and flaking.

Effects of RH fluctuation

The behavior of wood illustrates these principles. Figure 24.2 plots stress against change in length for pine tested in a largely radial direction. The strength (maximum stress) rises as the RH is lowered until very low RH is reached. At 5% RH the wood is weaker and liable to fracture, because the strength has dropped from 3.79MPa at 48% RH to 2.41MPa at 5% RH. The ability to deform (maximum change in length) increases with increasing relative humidity. This increase in deformation allows the dramatic bending of wet and steamed wood for decorative furniture. Reversible, or elastic, stretching occurs during the initial linear portion of the plots. Plastic flow, or irreversible stretching, occurs at higher extensions. Its onset is indicated by curvature of the plot. Fracture can be prevented by avoiding the conditions at the ends of the plots, while irreversible deformation can be avoided by staying within the elastic zone indicated by the curved line connecting the plots.

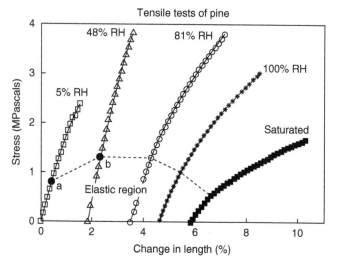

Figure 24.2 Stress-strain behavior of pine as a function of RH

The plots for each RH are separated on the x-axis by the differences in length due solely to changes in RH (with no restraint or stress applied). Moving along the x-axis from the 5% to the 48% RH plot shows an increase in length of 1.8% due solely to the change in RH. The 5% RH stress-strain test shows that the specimen breaks if stretched more than 1.5%. If a specimen of pine were restrained at 48% and desiccated to 5% RH, it would break, because it is being held at a length that exceeds that to which it can be stretched at 5% RH without breaking. A pine table-top, restrained by its frame, would be likely to split if subjected to a change in RH of this severity. Such data allow limits to be set that avoid breakage of pine objects. Narrower limits are required to avoid irreversible deformation, plastic flow and compression set.

Calculation of allowable RH fluctuations

The data suggest that the elastic limit, or yield point, is about one-third the maximum stress of the pine at each of the tested environments. The maximum stress that can occur without permanent deformation is therefore about one-third the measured breaking stress at all environments. This is shown in Figure 24.2 as the dotted line connecting the plots. The changes in length associated with these stresses are a function of the mechanical properties of the pine at each environment. At 5% RH the maximum allowable stress and its associated stretch is 0.79MPa at 0.42% extension (point a); at 48% RH, the allowable stress/stretch is 1.27MPa/0.45% (point b).

A drop of 10% RH from a starting point of 48% RH produces a shrinkage of approximately 0.44% in unrestrained pine. This is equivalent to moving from point c to point d in Figure 24.3, an expanded section of Figure 24.2. If the same pine is restrained and not allowed to shrink as the RH is lowered to 38%, it develops stresses (moving from point c to point e). These stresses are the same as if it were allowed to shrink freely at 38% RH (points c to d) and then stretched 0.44% (points d to e) at this new environment. The resulting stress would be around 1.17MPa (in tension) for the specimen at 38% RH, which is within the elastic region. Conversely, if the RH is raised by 10% to 58%, with restraint, stresses are produced equivalent to those required to compress unrestrained pine at 58% to the size it is at 48%. These compressive stresses would be about 1.27MPa, within the elastic range for 58% RH. The key to setting safe limits of RH fluctuation is to avoid stresses that exceed the yield point for a specific environment and that would produce plastic or irreversible deformation.

These data show that, at 48% RH, a piece of stress-free, restrained pine can experience fluctuations of ±10% without exceeding the yield points for these environments. This allowable fluctuation is not the same for all woods, or even necessarily for different starting relative humidities for the same wood. For pine the allowable fluctuation does remain constant at about ±10% RH over most of the RH range. Red oak, even though it can sustain considerably higher stresses, has approximately the same allowable fluctuation as pine because it has a greater dimensional response to

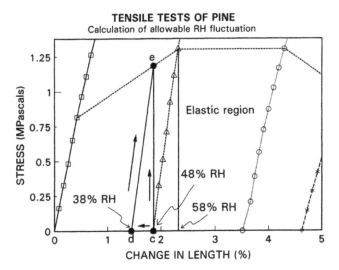

Figure 24.3 Calculation of maximum RH fluctuations within the elastic region

moisture. Spruce has allowable fluctuations in RH that are three or four times greater than either pine or red oak. Spruce has a smaller moisture response, and a larger elastic region, than the other two woods.

More complex analysis is required for objects such as furniture with inlays and veneers of various woods. Initial calculations show that the glue used in adhering the inlays and veneers is the component that determines the allowable limits. Adhesives are often more responsive than wood to RH. A similar analysis of the properties of sound rabbitskin-glue films shows that they can withstand fluctuations of $\pm 15\%$ RH at 50% RH, but only $\pm 8\%$ at 35% RH. Like many organic materials, the moisture response of glue is relatively flat at moderate (40–60%) RH, reducing both its response to RH fluctuations and the resulting stresses. Such analyses can be extended to composite materials whose properties are known. Calculations using data collected for a 13-year-old lead white pigmented oil-paint film indicate a tolerance to fluctuations of $\pm 30\%$ at 50% RH.

The magnitude of RH-induced stresses depends on several critical factors. These include the dimensional response to RH (the moisture coefficient of expansion), the change in stiffness as measured by the modulus of the material, the degree to which the material is restrained (the construction of the object), and the magnitude and rate of the change in relative humidity. The rate of change determines the depth of moisture penetration into a given material and the stress gradient resulting from the uneven moisture content. The potential for cracking is determined by the strength of the material, its ability to deform, the presence of defects in the material and the fracture sensitivity of the material.

By assuming conditions of full restraint and full equilibration as above, allowable RH fluctuations can be developed for materials for which appropriate data exist, and for composite objects that include these materials. The presence of degraded materials and existing flaws will certainly require a reduction in the allowable fluctuations. But calculations such as those above allow the development of rational guidelines, based on the measured physical and mechanical properties of the materials and the assembly of the object.

RH limits

The RH limits suggested by the above discussion are illustrated in Figure 24.4. The upper limit of 80% is determined by the softening of materials such as glue, with a value of 70% providing a margin of safety. Below 30–40%, materials such as glue become increasingly stiff and require increasingly tight RH control to prevent cracking. These limits assume that objects are at equilibrium and relatively stress-free

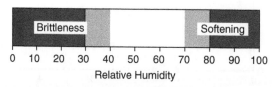

Figure 24.4 Relative humidity zones of possible and probable mechanical damage, shaded light and dark, respectively

at some moderate RH. Objects assembled at or acclimatized to very low RH may survive quite well at, and even require, drier conditions.

Deliquescent salts

Most properties of hygroscopic materials change smoothly over a range of relative humidities. Other changes, such as the deliquescence of salts, can occur over a very narrow RH range. Each deliquescent salt is stable up to a specific RH, above which it absorbs water vapor from the air and dissolves to form a solution. Common salt (sodium chloride) deliquesces at 76% RH. If the ambient RH is above 76%, then salt exists as an aqueous solution rather than a solid. If the RH varies over a range containing the deliquescence point, then the salt will alternately dissolve and crystallize. This can result in movement of the salt (crystallization on the surface is seen as efflorescence), or disruption and damage if the salt crystallizes within an object. Many objects, especially archaeological or previously submerged or buried materials, contain such salts, and examples are common.[5] Salt solutions can cause chemical damage. Their presence may increase the rate of corrosion of metals,[6] or make a material more susceptible to damage by pollutants.[7]

The deliquescence points of many pure salts are known.[8] A mixture of salts may deliquesce at a lower RH than either pure salt.[8] Hygroscopic materials impregnated with a deliquescent salt may absorb excess water at a relative humidity below the deliquescence point of the pure salt and form mobile ionic solutions of the salt. For example, silk containing 2.4% by weight of sodium chloride gained excess weight and increased in electrical conductivity when the RH exceeded about 55%.[7]

Some salts deliquesce at very low RH (lithium chloride at 15%, calcium chloride at 32%).[8] To prevent the deliquescence of salts in museum objects, the RH should be as low as possible. Other factors may rule out very low RH, but the deliquescence of sodium chloride, at least, can be prevented. To achieve this, the RH must be kept below 76%, the deliquescence point of the pure salt, and preferably below about 55%, a point at which the salt can form solutions in hygroscopic organic materials (Figure 24.5).

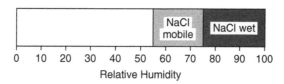

Figure 24.5 Relative humidity zones of salt deliquescence and mobility, shaded dark and light, respectively

Mineral hydrates

Mineral collections contain deliquescent salts and hydrates. If deliquescence is the sole concern, the RH need only be kept sufficiently low. Mineral hydrates are solid compounds that incorporate water in the crystalline lattice. Hydrates may be stable only within a specific range of relative humidity, losing water at lower RH or

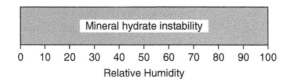

Figure 24.6 For any relative humidity, there are mineral hydrates that are unstable

gaining water at higher RH. Magnesium sulfate exists as the mono-, di-, tetra-, penta-, hexa- and heptahydrates, as well as the anhydrous form, depending on the RH.[9] Microenvironments must be maintained for collections containing minerals whose ranges of stability do not overlap. Waller compiled the stability ranges for a number of minerals.[9] Such a list shows that there is no value of RH at which all minerals are stable (Figure 24.6).

Building damage

Damage due to an inappropriate RH is not limited to objects. Condensation can occur in historic buildings that house objects if the outside temperature falls too low. With indoor conditions of 20°C and 50% RH, condensation can occur in exterior walls if the outside temperature falls below 10°C. Such condensates can cause damage, especially if they freeze. At 20°C, indoor relative humidities would have to be maintained at less than 10% to keep the dew-point above the winter temperatures of colder climates. It is difficult to prevent condensation within exterior walls. Effective vapor barriers are difficult to achieve in new buildings and almost impossible in old ones. Maintaining a negative pressure within the building may cause other problems. The construction of the building and the local climate determine the safe upper RH limit for a building, often no more than 50% in temperate climates and possibly much lower during cold weather (Figure 24.7). The interior RH may be allowed to vary seasonally, depending on other factors such as the RH range that the collection will tolerate. A year-long cycle through a limited RH range should cause little, if any, damage.

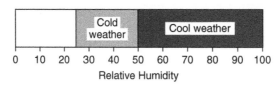

Figure 24.7 The colder the external temperature, the lower the internal relative humidity must be to reduce the possibility of condensation within the building structure

Chemical degradation

Many chemical processes depend on, or are accelerated by, the presence of water. Water may be present as absorbed water or may be incorporated from the vapor phase as a reaction proceeds. The amount of absorbed water increases as the RH increases. This added water is more available for chemical reactions, since each successive layer of water molecules is less tightly held.

Chemical degradation processes affected by relative humidity involve most types of material, including metals, glasses, inorganic and organic materials. The following examples will demonstrate the considerations involved in minimizing damage.

Metals

The corrosion of many metals is accelerated by high humidity, especially if corrosion or contaminants such as salts are present.[6] One example is bronze disease, in which small amounts of chlorides initiate the conversion of metallic copper to unstable copper chlorides and hydrated copper hydroxychlorides. Bronze disease is active at high RH, and slow or inactive at low RH. Low relative humidities are preferable for all metals that can corrode, especially those that already exhibit corrosion or that may contain salts due to burial or submersion. There is no lower limit on RH for the storage of metal objects. Scott found an upper safe limit of 46% RH for bronze disease[10] (Figure 24.8). Lower values would provide a greater margin of safety and help to prevent other corrosion reactions, such as the rusting of iron, that might have lower RH limits.

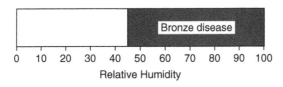

Figure 24.8 Bronze disease can be active above 46% RH

Glass

Certain highly alkaline glasses may decompose at all but very low relative humidities. Sodium and potassium ions leach from the glass to form alkali hydroxide solutions. These solutions pick up carbon dioxide from the atmosphere. The resulting sodium and potassium carbonates either crystallize out and cause delamination and flaking if the RH is below their deliquescence points (91% for sodium carbonate and 44% for potassium carbonate[11]), or appear as droplets on so-called 'weeping glass' at relative humidities above the lower deliquescence point. At high RH the glass may appear sound, with carbonate solution filling in the pores and spaces between delaminations. The glass looks normal while it rapidly decomposes. Relative humidities below the deliquescence point of the carbonates yield a less visually desirable (opaque) glass, yet still may not be low enough to prevent the leaching of sodium and potassium ions from the glass (Figure 24.9). Sodium and potassium hydroxide both have extremely low deliquescence points, respectively 6% and 5% RH,[11] values impractical to maintain in a general environment. Available data are inadequate to determine the RH at which such alkaline glass would be stable.

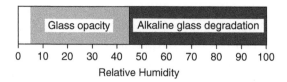

Figure 24.9 Alkaline glass becomes wet and deteriorates at high relative humidity, but deterioration may continue even down to very low values of RH

Minerals

Some inorganic materials react with water to form new compounds, rather than simply dissolving or changing hydration state. One example is barium sulfide, which reacts with water to form barium hydroxide and hydrogen sulfide. Others may undergo reactions more quickly in the presence of water. At high RH, pyrite (ferrous disulfide) oxidizes in air more quickly to form ferrous and ferric sulfates. Waller found that the rate rose exponentially as RH increased from 10 to 60%, but the rise was less drastic and approached a limiting value above 60% RH.[12] This work also indicated that the rate eventually slowed and approached zero when the RH was below 30%; above 50% RH the reaction would continue until the pyrite was consumed. Low RH, certainly below 50% and preferably below 30%, is required for pyrite (Figure 24.10). Though there are few, if any, such studies for other similarly reactive minerals, it is obvious that, in this case, the RH should be maintained as low as is practical.

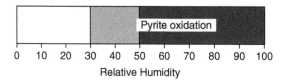

Figure 24.10 Pyrite continues to oxidize indefinitely at high relative humidity, and requires very low RH for stability

Organic materials

Most organic materials are hygroscopic, gaining and losing water with increases and decreases in RH so that their water content is a smooth (though not linear) function of RH. The effects of RH on the nature and rate of chemical reactions generally vary gradually with changes in RH, with no specific limiting values that determine whether or not a reaction occurs. Most of the RH-dependent reactions of organic materials will proceed, however slowly, at all practical values of relative humidity. The goal becomes one of minimizing, rather than eliminating, their effect. The degradation of organic materials is often slow, gradual, and more subtle than that of inorganic materials. Changes in inorganic materials, such as corrosion, dissolution and conversion to another compound, are more obvious and more easily measured than changes such as fading, loss of strength, crosslinking or hydrolysis in organic materials. Some changes were not measurable until recent developments in instrumentation. The relationship of relative humidity to the chemical degradation of organic materials was not obvious, and often was not considered when setting the RH. The effects of relative humidity on two common organic materials derived from plants and animals, respectively – cellulose and protein – will demonstrate.

Cellulose

The effects of relative humidity on the aging of cellulose (in the form of paper) were examined perhaps most thoroughly in the study by Graminski, Parks and Toth.[13] They found that effects on the aging of paper varied smoothly, increasing from 0 to 75% RH. Michalski re-examined their data and concluded that relative humidity has an effect down to 2–3% RH.[1] The hydrolysis of cellulose has been studied in this laboratory by measuring increases in the amount of free glucose in paper.[14] Hydrolysis continues, however slowly, even during dry oven aging. The temperature range of the study, 90 to 150°C, implies RH values of <2% to <1%, respectively. During water extraction of soluble reaction products from the samples, it was noticed that longer aging made samples more resistant to pulping, indicating that crosslinking was occurring. Samples aged at 90°C in air in sealed vessels containing water (high RH) developed much higher concentrations of glucose, and remained pulpable. This indicated that hydrolysis, rather than crosslinking, was the predominant reaction at high RH. Layers of absorbed water surround the cellulose fibers at high RH, inhibit the fibers from reacting with one another, and accelerate hydrolysis. The moisture absorption of cotton levels off above about 20% RH,[15] when water has covered most of the absorptive active surface sites of the cellulose fibers. Maintaining the RH above 25% should ensure the presence of enough water to inhibit crosslinking reactions between fibers.

The rate of hydrolysis is minimized by reducing the RH to as low a value as possible, while crosslinking reactions are probably minimized by maintaining the RH above 25% (Figure 24.11). Insufficient data exist to determine a range of relative humidity in which the total rate of change is minimized, but it is probably somewhere in the range 25–50%.

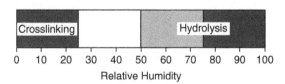

Figure 24.11 Lowering the relative humidity reduces the rate of hydrolysis of cellulose, but the rate of crosslinking increases if the RH falls too low

Proteins

Hansen, Lee and Sobel investigated the effects of relative humidity on the physical properties of vellum, reviewed relevant literature on the effects of RH on leather, and proposed an optimum RH range for the storage of leather and related protein-based materials.[16] Studies of the gelatinization (hydrolysis) of collagen in the range 40–100% RH showed that rates increased with increasing RH. The rate of gelatinization should slow further below 40% RH. Highly desiccated collagen does not completely rehydrate. This probably does not occur unless the RH is reduced below 25%. Above this value, strongly water-absorbing groups (those that might otherwise interact with each other to prevent rehydration) are saturated with water. The important reactions of collagen affected by RH therefore mirror those for cellulose: hydrolysis and crosslinking. For these and other reasons, Hansen et al. recommended a value of 30% RH as the optimum for the storage of materials composed of collagen, with outer limits of 25 and 40% (Figure 24.12).

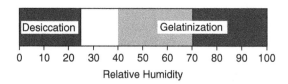

Figure 24.12 Gelatinization of collagen accelerates with increasing relative humidity, while irreversible desiccation occurs at very low RH

Type of collection

The purpose and use of the collection must also be considered.

Active collections

The section on 'Mechanical damage' examined environmentally induced static stresses. For a collection in active use, with objects moved on and off display, subjected to study or otherwise handled or moved with some frequency, the effects of RH on more dynamic processes such as vibration and impact must be considered. At low RH, materials lose ductility and are less able to withstand deformation, even though they might be stronger. Many materials become fracture-sensitive and prone to breakage, behaving more like a glass or ceramic. An impact that briefly distorts a painting at 50% RH might cause cracking at 15% RH. Pre-existing defects and cracks, present in most museum objects, represent sites of intense stress concentration from where further cracking or flaking can propagate.

Shock and vibration generated by different forms of transport have been characterized,[17] and the results applied to the transport of art.[18] Transport without proper packing protection is a hazard at any environment, but especially at low RH. Maintaining an RH above 40% should provide a reasonable margin of safety during transport.

Other sources of serious impact include accidents and improper handling within the museum. As with transport, moderate RH environments reduce the potential for damage during handling. Both extremes – flexible but weak at high RH and strong but brittle at low RH – should be avoided for collections in active use. Minimizing damage due to handling thus leads to the same RH limits as does minimizing damage from mechanical problems in general (Figure 24.13).

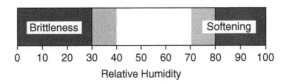

Figure 24.13 For active collections, both the extremes – flexible but weak at high relative humidity and strong but brittle at low relative humidity – should be avoided

Archival collections

Collections in which objects are infrequently moved from storage are less subject to damage by handling. Permanence is more important than durability and resistance to breakage. For objects that are not handled, brittleness caused by low RH is acceptable as long as stresses generated by low RH are not enough to cause direct damage. Objects can be slowly conditioned to moderate RH for the rare occasion when the object is to be handled or moved. High RH, and the resulting softening that leads to deformation due to the weight of the object, still should be avoided. Once mechanical damage is reduced or eliminated, chemical degradation is the major remaining concern. As discussed earlier, many chemical processes are slower at low RH, and only very low relative humidity (less than about 25–30%) should be avoided (Figure 24.14). Many long-term storage facilities maintain low temperatures to slow down chemical degradation processes. Low-temperature storage is beyond the scope of this paper, however, since it results in changes in the physical properties of materials that further complicate matters and may affect the choice of RH. For example, the effects of changes in temperature and RH on paintings have been examined.[19]

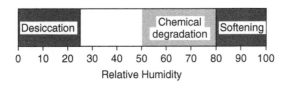

Figure 24.14 For archival collections, lowering the relative humidity reduces most types of chemical degradation. Only very low values of RH that promote crosslinking or irreversible desiccation or induce intolerable stresses should be avoided

Overall relative humidity

In Figure 24.15 the values and ranges in Figures 24.1 and 24.4–24.14 are collected and arranged in groups relevant to general collections, to special cases, and to specific

-ypes of collection. It is obvious that there is no 'ideal' RH for museums. Examining the effects of relative humidity does not lead to convergence on an ideal RH, but to a set of values and ranges (i) that may be more or less precise or accurate, (ii) that may apply only to specific types of material or object, and (iii) at which different types of damage may stop, start, increase or decrease. These values and ranges may or may not overlap, and often are in conflict. To choose an overall RH set-point for a collection it is necessary to determine the relevant factors, assess their importance, and select a value that is the best compromise in terms of minimizing overall effects. This may require separate macro- or microenvironments for some collections or objects, and special precautions in handling and conditioning if objects are kept at low RH. Costs and capabilities of available heating and air-conditioning equipment must also be considered.

The RH settings most common in museums, those in the range 40–60%, minimize biological attack, mechanical damage and the efflorescence of common salt. It is interesting to note that these are the most visible, and often the fastest, forms of damage seen in museums (other than for materials known to require separate treatment, such as corroded metals, weeping glass and mineral hydrates). It is easy to see how RH values around 50% have become so widely accepted. It is only when less

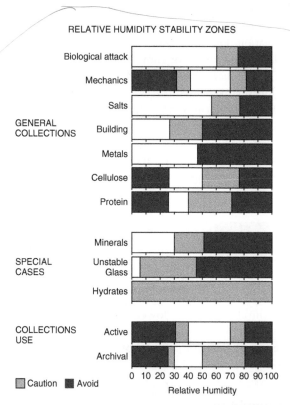

Figure 24.15 The ranges of relative humidity suggested by consideration of various factors. No one RH is ideal, and any value chosen must be a compromise

obvious forms of damage are considered, such as the slow but continuous degradation of organic materials, that lower values of relative humidity seem more desirable. In fact, the reduction of mechanical damage is the only major factor that would seem to argue against all but the lowest values of relative humidity, those below 25–30%. This conflict – mechanical damage versus chemical degradation, form versus content – is the main consideration in choosing a suitable RH, and one for which there is no obvious resolution.

Conclusions

There is no one 'ideal' relative humidity for museums, only values and ranges that minimize specific types of change in materials and objects. Extreme values and rapid or large changes in RH should be avoided. Within the range of moderate RH values (30–60%), high RH tends to minimize mechanical damage and low RH tends to minimize chemical change. Some objects will require, or would benefit from, separate microenvironments no matter what RH set-point is chosen.

References

1   Michalski, S. (1993) 'Relative humidity: a discussion of correct/incorrect values' in *Preprints of the 10th ICOM-CC Triennial Meeting, Washington, DC*, Marina del Ray, CA: ICOM-CC & GCI.

2   Plenderleith, H. J. and Philippot, P. (1960) 'Climatology and conservation in museums', *Museum* 13: 242–289.

3   Thomson, G. (1978) *The Museum Environment*, London: Butterworths.

4   Mecklenburg, M. F. and Tumosa, C. S. (1991) 'An introduction into the mechanical behavior of paintings under rapid loading conditions' in M. F. Mecklenburg (ed.) *Art in Transit: Studies in the Transport of Paintings*, Washington: National Gallery of Art.

5   FitzHugh, E. W. and Gettens, R. J. (1971) 'Calclacite and other efflorescent salts on objects stored in wooden museum cases' in R. H. Brill (ed.) *Science and Archaeology*, Cambridge, MA: MIT Press.

6   Evans, U. R. (1960) *The Corrosion and Oxidation of Metals: Scientific Principles and Practical Applications*, London: Edward Arnold Ltd.

7   Padfield, T. and Erhardt, D. (1987) 'The spontaneous transfer to glass of an image of Joan of Arc' in *Preprints of the 8th ICOM-CC Triennial Meeting, Sydney*, Marina del Ray, CA: ICOM-CC & GCI ICOM.

8   Weast, R. C. (ed.) (1973) *Handbook of Chemistry and Physics* (54th edn), Cleveland, OH: CRC Press.

9   Waller, R. (1980) 'The preservation of mineral specimens', in *Preprints of Papers Presented at the 8th Annual Meeting, American Institute for Conservation, Washington*.

10 Scott, D. (1990) 'Bronze disease: a review of some chemical problems and the role of relative humidity', *Journal of the American Institute for Conservation* 29: 193–206.

11 Meites, L. (ed.) (1963) *Handbook of Analytical Chemistry* (1st edn), New York: McGraw Hill Book Company.

12 Waller. R. (1989) 'Pyrite oxidation studies', *CCI Newsletter* (1989): 10.

13 Graminski, E. L., Parks, E. J. and Toth, E. E. (1978) 'The effects of temperature and moisture on the accelerated aging of paper', *NBSIR 78–1443, prepared for the National Archives and Records Service by the Polymer Division, Institute for Materials Research*, Washington, DC: National Bureau of Standards, US Department of Commerce.

14 Erhardt, D., Von Endt, D. and Hopwood, W. (1987) 'The comparison of accelerated aging conditions through the analysis of extracts of artificially aged paper' in *Preprints of Papers Presented at the 15th Annual Meeting, American Institute for Conservation, Washington*.

15 Morton, W. E. and Hearle, J. W. S. (1975) *Physical Properties of Textile Fibres*, London: Heinemann.

16 Hansen, E. F., Lee, S. N. and Sobel, H. (1992) 'The effects of relative humidity on some physical properties of modern vellum: implications for the optimum relative humidity for the display and storage of parchment', *Journal of the American Institute for Conservation* 31: 325–342.

17 Ostrem, F. E. and Godshall, W. D. (1979) *An Assessment of the Common Earner Shipping Environment*, General Technical Report FPL 22, Madison USA: Forest Products Laboratory, USDA.

18 Marcon, P. J. (1991) 'Shock, vibration, and the shipping environment' in M. F. Mecklenburg (ed.) *Art in Transit: Studies in the Transport of Paintings*, Washington, DC: National Gallery of Art.

19 Mecklenburg, M. F. and Tumosa, C. S. (1991) 'Mechanical behavior of paintings subjected to changes in temperature and relative humidity' in M. F. Mecklenburg (ed.) *Art in Transit: Studies in the Transport of Paintings*, Washington, DC: National Gallery of Art.

Relative Humidity: a discussion of correct/incorrect values

Stefan Michalski

Introduction

THE VERY WORDS "DAMP" AND "DRY" contain an ancient understanding of relative humidity (RH) that has proven very difficult to specify. Despite this, bureaucrats and designers needed a single "correct" relative humidity, and conservation obliged. The ensuing questions were inevitable: Why this number, and how important are deviations?

History of relative humidity specifications

By the turn of the last century, Rathgen had dismissed bacteria as the explanation of bronze disease and shown that an airtight case with desiccant would cure unstable patina.[1] As to organic materials, Church stated that "if a stream of warm and dry air enters a gallery . . . the canvases, frames, and panels become altered in shape and size each day . . . Thus the colored films . . . are submitted to an injurious strain, which may end . . . in a multitude of minute fissures, and the final flaking off of portions of the paint."[2]

In 1929, the National Gallery (London) instigated research on panel paintings. The wood scientists demonstrated damage with large RH fluctuations, but did not recommend a "correct" RH.[3] Instead, they looked for the best vapour barrier for the back, just as Buck did in the United States. It was left to the building engineer, MacIntyre, to propose a value: 55%RH–60%RH, based on London's climate and on feasibility. He noted an advantage of low RH (reduced pigment fading) and wondered what its effect might be on paper and canvas. He concluded that without this knowledge "optimum conditions for any particular class of paintings must be more or less

Source: *ICOM-CC 10th Triennial Meeting, Washington, DC, USA,* Paris: ICOM-CC, 1993, pp. 624–629.

arbitrary." Finally, he foretold that "the maintenance of the plant and control gear cannot be left to the ordinary attendant."[4]

During the 1930s, the National Gallery determined that their annual average for the moisture content of wood was 11%, so deduced an average RH of 58%.[5] Thus, the feasibility argument and the annual average argument had converged (for pre-war London). This became the set-point for wartime storage in a slate quarry, during which normal panel damage disappeared. After the war, the National Gallery installed control systems, 20 years after MacIntyre's proposal.

By the 1960s and 1970s, designers worldwide demanded specifications by which to build. The familiar numbers, 50% RH or 55% RH, emerged from many experts, but actual knowledge about humidity had not changed in 100 years. What about small fluctuations? As before, feasibility became the determinant that determined flucuations of ±2%, ±3%, or ±5%, depending on one's experience and one's concept of measurement (much of which was naive).

The numbers became standards: Class A, Class I, ideal! Museum users assumed that the values were scientific, based on a significant minimum in deterioration. The originators knew 50% RH emphasized mechanical phenomena and neglected chemical phenomena; they knew that it was a nice round number and that the specified fluctuations were not derived from artifact needs, but in the museum world at large, non-conformity became transgression.

The "best available" feasibility argument assumed that even if it did insignificant good, it could do no harm. Unfortunately, the mechanical systems were unorthodox, expensive to build and to maintain. Reliability was compromised. In cold climates, humidification was wrecking buildings. Historic walls were gutted in dubious attempts to install vapour barriers and machinery. Deviations from the specifications consumed inordinate amounts of staff time in detection and response. And what of the artifact loans denied, grants determined, and new buildings justified by the magic numbers? What, exactly, was it all in aid of?

Deterioration by incorrect relative humidity

For practical purposes, incorrect relative humidity can be divided into four types: (1) damp; (2) RH above or below a critical value; (3) RH above 0%; and (4) RH fluctuations.

Deterioration by damp

In 1933, Groom and Panisset published the one accurate study of RH effect on mould growth in museum materials (29 book materials, old and new).[6] The samples with the lowest minimum RH for growth amongst each of parchments, cellulosics, and leathers are shown in Figure 25.1 In 1968, Ayerst reviewed 40 years of industrial data.[7] Figure 25.1 shows his outer limit for growth of a wide variety of common species on a highly nutritive substrate. A few species have been shown to grow (very slowly) in the range 60–65% RH.[8, 9] It is incorrect to extrapolate plots like Figure 25.1 from one EMC, as Nyuksha did, thereby concluding paper could mould at 30% RH.[10] Within a single material, however, moisture content is the accurate parameter when comparing samples at different states of sorption hysteresis. In leather, mould that develops at 78% RH following a wet cycle will not develop after a dry cycle until 90% RH (13.5% EMC for both, 300 day test).[11] Within these limits, RH has a profound, practical effect: speed (see Figure 25.2). Speed varies logarithmically between days at 90% RH and years at 65% RH.[12]

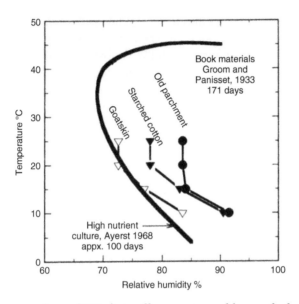

Figure 25.1 Lowest values of RH that will support mould growth (book study: one species; culture study: many species)

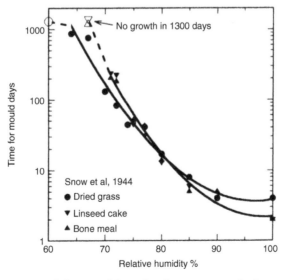

Figure 25.2 Time required for mould to develop on some high nutrient materials (first appearance of mycelium, many species)

Overall, several days of damp cause mould in leather and "dirty" (nutrient rich) artifacts only if RH exceeds 80%. Clean paper, paint, and textiles need over 90% RH. In the range of 90%–75% RH, a 10% RH reduction controls mould growth as much as dropping the temperature from 30 to 10°C. A conservative limit for no mould, ever, on anything, would be to stay below 60% RH, but the practical danger for most situations begins above 75% RH. In either case, an excursion to 90% RH is tolerable (in terms of mould) as long as it does not exceed a day or two.

The moisture diffusion coefficient of organic materials increases with moisture content. Capillary wicking of condensate penetrates faster than vapour. On the other hand, drying solids form a low permeability skin which slows drying. Thus, a 1-cm thick wood board takes one hour to get waterlogged and 10 to dry.[13] I believe this asymmetry explains the traditional insistence on openings in the backing boards of paintings. A closed but permeable board would push the back of the painting to an RH higher than the ambient average. After a damp night in an unheated building, only convection through large openings would dry the painting by late afternoon. With heated galleries, polluted air, and impermeable boards, such ventilation becomes counter-productive.

Deterioration by RH above or below a critical RH

Waller has recently compiled dozens of critical values available for RH-sensitive minerals, some of which apply to the patina on metals.[14] This precision leads away from a generalized "safe" RH towards an emphasis on particular conditions for particular artifacts (and decontamination treatments). Despite this, experience demands that a generalized region of rapid inorganic deterioration must be identified for the non-specialist: damp. Both metal surfaces and particulate dirt show the classic sigmoidal adsorption curve that bends sharply upwards at 75% RH, as the adsorbed water changes from 2–3 molecules to a liquid film.[15] Besides, the most ubiquitous salt contaminant, NaCl, deliquesces at 76%RH.

Deterioration by RH above 0%

I re-analyzed some of the data from the monumental study of paper by Graminski, Parks and Toth and fitted a two-stage linear decay to the fiber strength (zero span data).[16, 17] The rate of strength loss fits a simple power law of RH, exponent 1.35 (see Figure 25.3) The yellowing data fits a similar power law. The "zero" RH data point for both can be fitted to the power law at 2–3% RH, or considered an independent slow mechanism. (This is academic, since practical RH control will not go below 2–3% RH.)

The dark and light fading of dyes is much less profoundly influenced by RH (see Figure 25.4).[18,19]

Deterioration by RH fluctuation

For most organic materials, the EMC/RH curve is sigmoidal, with knees near 25% RH and 75% RH. For wood, the absorption coefficient almost doubles from 0.14

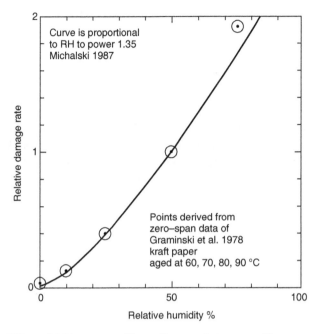

Figure 25.3 Effect of RH on rate of loss of strength in paper fibers

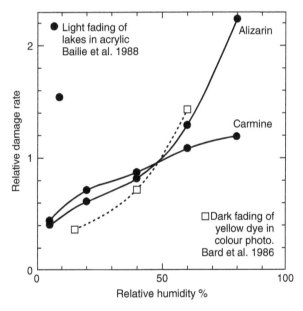

Figure 25.4 Influence of RH on fading of some colourants

in the range 40%–50% RH to 0.25 at 0%–10% RH and triples by 85% RH.[20] Thus, fluctuations of ±20% RH cause less than half the dimensional change of ±40% RH.

Fluctuations under one hour do not affect most museum objects. The outer layers of bare wood may have shorter response times than the whole; on the other hand, furniture with typical coatings does respond fairly uniformly throughout its thickness. Various charts have been produced at the Canadian Conservation Institute (CCI) to help estimation of response times. Figure 25.5 demonstrates the contributions of air leakage, wood coating, and textile buffering on the response of a chest of drawers. It shows that it is risky to display furniture empty and open, as compared to normal usage.

The most stressful fluctuations are longer than the response time, but shorter than the stress relaxation time. Glue, gesso, wood, paint, and varnish have very different relaxation times, and all are strongly increased by low RH and low temperature.[21] I have modelled the cracking of gilding and suggest that low RH causes more cracking than high RH because the relaxation time of the gesso changes from days to months.[22]

Animal glue is the most common historical adhesive, and it changes from a strong, glassy material at low RH to a weak, rubbery material above 80% RH. Glued veneer can either let go completely (buckle) at high RH or more subtly, slide to a new position and re-adhere there as the humidity drops. CCI has demonstrated this pre-stressing effect in veneer/frame assemblies made at 50% RH: a low humidity cycle caused no failure, unless it was preceded by a 90% RH cycle that caused slippage.[23]

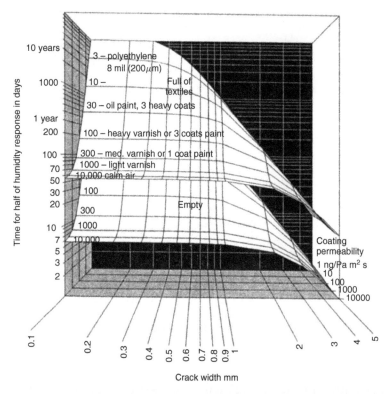

Figure 25.5 3-D chart of moisture half-time of a chest of drawers, with and without textile contents, as a function of various coatings or wrappings, and various cracks at top and bottom for natural convection

Stresses below the critical value necessary to fracture an assembly in one cycle can still cause incremental growth of cracks from microscopic flaws inherent in real materials. The resultant "fatigue" lifetimes depend logarithmically on stress reduction. They reach 1–10 million cycles between one half the stress in tough polymers (wood, skin) and one fifth the stress in brittle polymers (glue, gesso, paint, bone, for cycles shorter than relaxation times). If this fatigue dependence on stress/strain is transformed to a dependence on RH fluctuation, then a curve like Figure 25.6 emerges: a wide forgiving region and a sudden, steep climb to danger. Indeed, given that about ±25% RH daily was most common historically (given a house free of damp) the estimate for brittle materials conforms to the observation that paintings developed full craquelure in about a century (30,000 daily cycles) whereas areas of the painting protected from daily fluctuation by the stretcher bar often remained free of all but one or two cracks (100 seasonal cycles). Moderately vulnerable assemblies in wood (tough material) suffered very little in these conditions.

Aside from all of the above considerations about material response, humidity fluctuation damage depends greatly on the geometry of assembly. Constrained textiles show very little tension change between 75% RH and 0% RH, because of crimp in the yarns. Textiles can shrink dangerously in the region 75%–100% RH, especially above 90% RH.

Knowledgeable joinery is designed for movement: panels float, dovetails loosen and retighten. Most antique tabletops in Canada pass through wide humidity fluctuations without cracking, though many show permanent plastic compression ("shrinkage"). The attachment to the side rails underneath generally consists of a few large screws that slip or bend before the top breaks. Any short wood blocks that were glued have generally let go. These were purposeful "safety valves."

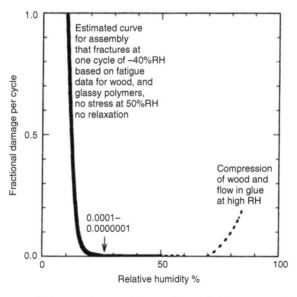

Figure 25.6 Estimated shape of curve for mechanical damage as a function of RH
      fluctuation from some middle value

Radial shrinkage of most woods for a drop of −25% RH is 0.5%, for −40% RH about 0.9%.[24] Mechanical studies show wide boards (Douglas fir) can be stretched only 0.2% before cracking if stressed over one day, but stretch 0.5% over one week and 0.8% over two months.[25] Thus, furniture that typically takes a week to reach 90% of response to a humidity change will face high risk only for drops in the range −25% RH to −40% RH. No one knows how much further wood can relax, but creep-rupture studies currently include plans for 10-year experiments. Creep will also be higher in boards or veneers held uniformly over their whole face, because the worst flaw no longer has access to all the elastic energy of the stressed assembly. Thus, veneers and lap joints are less vulnerable to cracking than panels jammed in their rebates.

The most common, highly vulnerable assembly in furniture is veneer (or coating) over a joint. As long as the joint remains solid, the veneer is only moderately vulnerable, but if the glued joint has loosened, then the veneer is sheared when the cross-grain piece shrinks (see Figure 25.7).

I have reviewed the data on RH effects on painting materials and glue grounds elsewhere.[26,27] Further valuable work by Mecklenburg has appeared.[28,29] Although tension change at low humidity has become fairly predictable, fracture has not (see Figure 25.8). Calculation and experiment to date indicate that these assemblies require a humidity drop of −50% RH before they reach a high probability of cracking when new. Ageing of the coatings, UV exposure, reduction in adhesion, cracks, and delamination from other causes will all reduce this value, probably to about −25% RH.

Some materials are already under tension at middle RH, e.g. plywood lamina, over keyed-out paintings, paints and gesso with curing stress. Large timbers and whole teeth are prestressed at middle RH because they have circular grain and formed at 100% RH. Figure 25.9 shows the probability of fracture of fresh teeth A as a function of decreasing RH, from Williams.[30] As with wood, a hollow center (molars) very much reduces constraint as compared to solid centers (canines). Such pre-stressing will relax out eventually in uncrosslinked constituents (e.g. lignin, collagen, cellulose), but it may take decades.

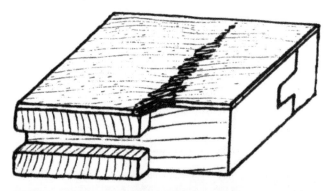

Figure 25.7 Common high vulnerability assembly: veneer over joint that has failed. The veneer shears as shown

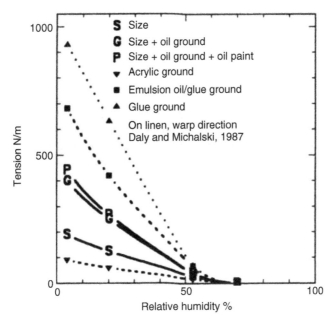

Figure 25.8 Effect of 0–70% RH on the tension in paintings. At 70–100% RH, the linen dominates and may rise in tension ("shrinker")

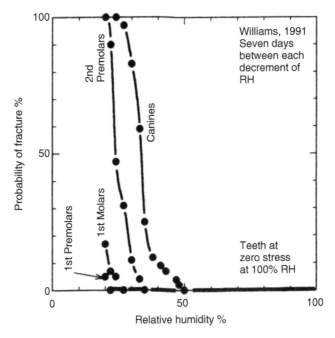

Figure 25.9 Fracture of fresh teeth in a natural history collection as humidity drops

Furniture and polychrome survived fairly well in Europe prior to modern heating. The problem was damp, not dryness. Sustained drops from the annual average rarely exceeded –25% RH, except next to the fire. Then, heating technology improved. Objects were shipped to cold North America. Drops of –40% RH could occur daily. Still, heating went down at night, the upstairs was cold most of the time, and room furnishings could buffer daily fluctuations. Then, central and overnight heating developed. Drops of –40% RH became sustained winter extremes. Many traditional assemblies that had survived intact until now cracked and delaminated. This all confirms that between –25% and –40% RH drop, the probability of single-cycle damage jumps in traditional assemblies. It also shows the danger in sustaining the fluctuation for the week or more necessary for 90% of response in furniture. I have carefully monitored several pieces of nineteenth- and early twentieth-century furniture, tools, books, and textiles, submitted to 10 winters near 10% RH, some for the first time below about 25% RH. The results confirm two important facts: vulnerable designs considered acceptable practice during their day can survive about –25% RH drop, but not –40% RH drop; on the other hand, many assemblies accommodate –40% RH without problems.

Conclusions

A middle RH makes sense for the rigid organic materials that inspired it, especially paintings. The definition of "small" fluctuations, still problematic, depends on mechanical fatigue. Fatigue shows a powerful decrease in damage per cycle as the fluctuation diminishes below the critical value. How to know the critical fluctuation? Two strategies occur: proofed value and analysis. Proofed value is the largest fluctuation to which the artifact has responded in the past, so any single-cycle damage has occurred for this value. If the material properties have not weakened much (e.g. centuries for wood, decades for paint not exposed to UV), then collections that have seen fluctuations of ±20% to ±40% RH must experience minute or zero damage at one half of this.

Artifacts from more benign conditions, as well as recently keyed-out paintings, have lower proofed values. Strong consolidation of fully developed cracks that used to open and close harmlessly will reset the critical value to less than the proofed value (e.g. old checks, sheared veneer). On the other hand, consolidation of partial cracks due to other effects (e.g. bending, damp, ultraviolet light, leaching, loss of adhesion) will reduce vulnerability to damage.

Analysis, though not precise, can set priorities. Well-designed joinery has only low to moderate vulnerability; incompetent designs are highly vulnerable. In historic houses, it would be possible to estimate which furniture was likely to suffer and which was not. Experiments for such an "atlas" of design vulnerability are planned at CCI.

The extension of the small fluctuation criterion to all artifacts has no merit except convenience. Drops of –40% RH do not constitute an emergency for loose skins, fur, textiles, costumes, metals, botanical specimens, or most archival material. In fact, it is a period of reduced decay.

For libraries and archives holding acidic paper bound with paper products, specifying 50% RH in cold climates simply doubled the rate of chemical decay, by eliminating the winter lull. Leather bindings on non-acidic paper are indeed a mechanical issue, but they can only be considered low to moderately vulnerable assemblies. Brittle inks on parchment are highly vulnerable.

For collections dominated by rigid organic materials (wood and paint), we must accept that the data supports common sense, not magic numbers. Safe RH is a broad valley, like that shown in Figure 25.6. The slopes may be defined by science, but locating them still depends on experience. Overall, high risk begins outside the range 25%–75% RH. Slight mechanical damage will accumulate on highly vulnerable assemblies at ±20% RH but this is virtually eliminated by ±10% RH in wood, ±5% RH in paint. Middle RH can be the local mean, or international norm. If tight control sacrifices long-term reliability of the 25%–75% RH limits, or other issues like fire and pests, I believe it is counter-productive to the total well-being of most collections.

References

1 Rathgen, F. (1905) *The Preservation of Antiquities,* Cambridge: Cambridge: University Press.
2 Prof. Church (c. 1872) 'Chemistry of the Fine Arts-VI', in *Cassell's Technical Educator 3*, London: Cassell, Petter and Galpin.
3 Stillwell, S. T. O. and Knight, R. A. G. (c. 1934) 'An Investigation into the Effect of Humidity Variations on Old Panel Paintings on Wood', in *Some Notes on Atmospheric Humidity in Relation to Works of Art*, London: Courtauld Institute.
4 MacIntyre, J. (c. 1934) 'Some Problems Connected with Atmospheric Humidity', in *Some Notes on Atmospheric Humidity in Relation to Works of Art,* London: Courtauld Institute.
5 Rawlins, F. I. G. (1951) 'Air Conditioning at the National Gallery, London', *Museum* 4 (3): 194–200.
6 Groom, P. and Panisset, T. (1933) 'Studies in Penicillium Chrysogenum Thorn in Relation to Temperature and Relative Humidity of the Air', *Annals of Applied Biology* 20: 633–660.
7 Ayerst, G. (1968) 'Prevention of Biodeterioration by Control of Environmental Conditions', in A. H. Walters and J. J. Elphick (eds) *Biodeterioration of Materials*, Amsterdam: Elsevier.
8 Corry, J. L. (1978) 'Relationships of Water Activity to Fungal Growth', in L. R. Beuchat (ed.) *Food and Beverage Mycology*, Westport, Conn.: AVI Publishing.
9 Ohtsuki, T. (1990) 'Studies on Eurotium tonophilum Ohtsuki', *Scientific Papers on Japanese Antiques and Art Crafts* 35: 28–34.
10 Nyuksha, J. P. (1979) 'Biological Principles of Bookkeeping Conditions', *Restaurator* 3 (1979): 101–108.
11 Rose, C. D. and Turner, J. N. (1951) 'Mould Growth on Leather as Affected by Humidity Changes', *Journal of the Society of Leather Trades' Chemists* 35 (2): 37–42.
12 Snow, D., Crichton, M. H. G. and Wright, N. C. (1944) 'Mould Deterioration of Feeding Stuffs in Relation to Humidity of Storage', *Annals of Applied Biology* 31: 102–110.
13 Kouali, M. El, Bouzon, J. and Vergnaud, J. M. (1992) 'Process of Absorption and

Desorption of Water in a Wood Board, with 3-Dimensional Transport Beyond the FSP', *Wood Science Technology* 26: 307–321.

14 Waller, R. (1992) 'Temperature- and Humidity-sensitive Mineralogical and Petrological Specimens', in F. Howie (ed.) *The Care and Conservation of Geological Material*, London: Butterworth-Heinemann.

15 Graedel, T. E. (1993) Review in preparation for postprints of the Dahlem Konferenzen, Berlin 1992, London: Wiley.

16 Graminski, E. L., Parks, E. J. and Toth, E. E. (1978) 'The Effects of Temperature and Moisture on the Accelerated Aging of Paper', *NBSIR 78–1443, prepared for the National Archives and Records Service by the Polymer Division, Institute for Materials Research*, Washington, DC: National Bureau of Standards, US Department of Commerce.

17 Michalski, S. (1987) 'Correlation of Zero-span Strength, Fold Endurance, RH and Temperature in the Ageing of Paper: A Review of Published Data', in Book and Paper Specialty Group Abstracts, in *AIC Conference Preprints, Vancouver 1987*, Washington: American Institute for Conservation.

18 Bard, C. C., Larson, G. W., Hammond, H. and Packard, C. (1980) 'Predicting Long-term Dark Storage Dye Stability Characteristics of Color Photographic Products from Short Term Tests', *Journal of Applied Photographic Engineering* 6 (2): 42–45.

19 Bailie, C. W., Johnston-Feller, R. M. and Feller, R. L. 'The Fading of some Traditional Pigments as a Function of Relative Humidity', in E. V. Sayre et al. (eds) *Material Issues in Art and Archaeology,* Pittsburgh: Materials Research Society.

20 *Wood Handbook* (1987), revised edition, Washington: U.S. Department of Agriculture.

21 Michalski, S. (1991) 'Paintings – Their Response to Temperature, Relative Humidity, Shock and Vibration', in M. F. Mecklenburg (ed.) *Art of Transit*, Washington: National Gallery of Art.

22 Michalski, S (1991) 'Crack Mechanisms in Gilding', in D. Bigelow et al. (eds) *Gilded Wood*, Madison, Conn.: Sound View Press.

23 Marcon, P. (1988) unpublished study, Ottawa: Canadian Conservation Institute.

24 *Wood Handbook* (1987), revised edition, Washington: U.S. Department of Agriculture.

25 Madsen, B. (1975) 'Duration of Load Tests for Wood in Tension Perpendicular to the Grain', *Forest Products Journal* 25 (8): 48–53.

26 Michalski, S. (1991) 'Paintings – Their Response to Temperature, Relative Humidity, Shock and Vibration', in M. F. Mecklenburg (ed.) *Art of Transit*, Washington: National Gallery of Art.

27 Michalski, S. 'Crack Mechanisms in Gilding', in D. Bigelow et al. (eds) *Gilded Wood*, Madison, Conn.: Sound View Press.

28 Mecklenburg, M. F. (1991) 'Some Mechanical and Physical Properties of Gilding Gesso', in D. Bigelow et al. (eds) *Gilded Wood*, Madison, Conn.: Sound View Press.

29 Mecklenburg, M. F. and Tumosa, C. (1991) 'Mechanical Behaviour of Paintings Subjected to Changes in Temperature and Relative Humidity', in M. F. Mecklenburg (ed.) *Art of Transit*, Washington: National Gallery of Art.

30 Williams, S. L. (1991) 'Investigation of the Causes of Structural Damage to Teeth in Natural History Collections', *Collection Forum* 7 (1): 13–25.

Chapter 26

Relative Humidity and Temperature Guidelines: what's happening?

Stefan Michalski

THERE IS A RUMOUR going around that CCI no longer cares about temperature and humidity specifications! [Note from the editor – this was written in
1994.] That there's no need to worry about those impossible standards! Well, the
truth is that our approach has changed, but the issue has not gone away. Conservation research scientists at CCI have shifted from defining a single, simplistic standard
to identifying degrees of correctness or, more accurately, degrees of incorrectness.
We try to estimate the benefit of basic control of the environment and the benefit of increasing sophistication. The following paragraph summarizes CCI's current
approach to temperature.

Temperature

Many artifacts will tolerate extreme cold (−30°C). Low winter temperatures indoors
can reduce such problems as chemical self-destruction, pests, mould, energy consumption, and condensation in walls. At the other extreme, many artifacts will also
tolerate brief excursions to 50°C. Aside from this general tolerance, three forms of
incorrect temperature can be identified for a museum: temperatures that are too
low, temperatures that are too high, and temperature fluctuations. Temperatures
that are too low are a problem for plastics and paints because these materials become
brittle at low temperatures. Acrylic paints, for example, are quite leathery and robust
at temperatures that are comfortable for humans, but turn glassy and increasingly
brittle below 5°C. All paintings and coatings may crack at Canadian winter temperatures (below 5°C) either simply by contraction or by accidental blows to the paint.

Source: *CCI Newsletter* 14 (1994): 6.

Temperatures that are too high are incorrect for materials that self-destruct chemically within a human lifetime, such as acidic paper, nitrate and acetate films, celluloid, and rubber objects. The only practical solution for large quantities of these items is cold storage. Each 5°C drop will roughly double the lifetime of such materials, e.g. they will last a millennium at 0°C instead of a few decades at 25°C. Temperatures that are too high are also a problem for those artifacts that contain waxes or resins that soften above 30°C, such as lined paintings or artifacts that contain pitch. Temperature fluctuations can be incorrect for artifacts that contain restrained brittle layers (e.g. enamels). Generally, however, temperature fluctuations by themselves rarely cause problems.

Managing Preventive Conservation

Introduction to Part Three – Section One

Chris Caple

Environmental management

THE ABILITY TO MONITOR AND RECORD information about the museum environment improved throughout the twentieth century, especially from the 1960s, with the development of electronic sensors. After the development of desktop and personal computers in the 1980s much greater emphasis was placed on using the information from such sensors to manage the collections and mitigate the museum environment.

The humidity and temperature in museums and historic houses can be controlled to different levels, depending on the nature of the building, its contents and the desired level of relative humidity (RH) and temperature. Though there was considerable development of central heating systems and air conditioning systems in the period after the Second World War, it has proved expensive to use air conditioning systems to maintain the precise levels of RH. The oil crisis of 1973 and the dramatic increase in the price of energy first raised interest in reducing energy costs by using natural ventilation, zonation, buffering, insulation and the thermal mass of the building to make best use of the building's natural ability to control its own environment. May Cassar (1995) (Chapter 27) explores the mechanisms used to create the desired museum environment, from individual humidifiers and de-humidifiers to full air conditioning and building management systems. The high cost of energy, the cost of the plant, revised ideas about the need for such tight RH controls and the development of sustainability (reducing carbon footprints etc.) have encouraged many museums, galleries and historic houses to explore more natural and cost-effective ways of controlling their environments since the 1990s. Some of the pitfalls of large, expensive air conditioning systems (capital and running costs) and the problems of ensuring that they perform to the agreed specifications are highlighted by Cassar.

The assessment of collections and their physical condition occurred only very occasionally prior to the 1990s, usually triggered by the arrival of a new curator or conservator who was keen to know the state of the collections for which they had become responsible. Spurred on by the publication of one or two surveys by individual institutions (Walker and Bacon 1987), a UK National Committee suggested a more standardised methodology and terminology (Keene 1991). As described by Keene (1996) (Chapter 28), subsequent assessments have normally achieved much greater rigour through using standardised terms and had a firmer statistical basis for the process. The condition survey has proved useful, since it could be adapted to answer a range of questions. Thus, when combined with environmental monitoring information, it could show the impact of environmental conditions on the collections; when combined with curatorial (value) priority, it could provide a powerful tool for prioritisation of resources such as conservation; and when combined with information on storage materials and labour costs, it enabled accurate estimates to be created of the resources required for improving storage. Though it is widely appreciated that there is potentially some subjectivity in the process (Taylor and Stevenson 1999), through staff training and a calibration process (a collection of objects which all assessors survey and for which they then standardise their results to ensure that they score the condition of the same objects in the same way) the variation between assessors is minimised. The ready availability of spreadsheets and databases on laptop computers means that nowadays data is often entered directly onto a computer; consequently it is now easier and quicker to conduct such surveys than when Keene wrote about this process in 1991. However, problems remain, such as the limited skills of conservators and curators in materials identification.

A clear demonstration of how to adapt a condition survey to meet the demands of a large and very varied collection of objects in non-standard storage systems spread over multiple sites is provided by Helen Kingsley and Rob Payton (1994) (Chapter 29). Breaking the complete assemblage into a series of smaller sub-collections, dividing these up by storage locations, even a floor grid, and adapting the sampling strategy to the nature of the sub-collections, enables the data to be rigorously collected and, through appropriate mathematical correction of the differently sampled parts of the collection, to be combined to give an accurate picture of the state and nature of the whole collection. Though collection condition surveys provided information on the extent and nature of the artefacts in a collection, the amount of conservation and storage work identified as needing to be done was invariably so large that some form of prioritisation was required. Diane Dollery (1994) (Chapter 30) provided one of the first published examples from the UK of combined condition and curatorial assessments. In addition to a collection condition assessment, the National Museum of Wales set about giving the objects values for the information they could provide about the past or their ability to form a displayable object. A similar classification of the 'cultural and historic value' of objects was also devised in the early 1990s by the Dutch for their Delta Plan (Cannon Brooks 1993). Ultimately this approach enabled objects with high display potential and significant historical meaning but in poor condition to be prioritised over the badly damaged but less informative or the attractive but relatively historically meaningless objects. This enabled teams of curators and conservators to establish a prioritised order for conservation and storage work which maximised the preservation of the archaeological value of the collections of the museum.

References

Cassar, M. (1995) *Environmental Management,* London: Routledge.

Cannon Brooks, P. (1993) 'The "Delta Plan" for the Preservation of Cultural Heritage in the Netherlands', *Museum Management and Curatorship* 12: 303–317.

Dollery, D. (1994) 'A Methodology of Preventive Conservation for a Large Expanding and Mixed Archaeological Collection', in A. Roy and P. Smith (eds), *Preventive Conservation: Practice, Theory and Research, IIC Ottawa Congress 12–16 September 1994,* Ottawa: IIC, pp. 69–72.

Keene, S. (1991) 'Audits of Care: Framework for Collections Condition Survey', in M. Norman and V. Todd (eds), *Storage,* preprints for the UKIC Conference 'Restoration '91', pp. 6–16.

Keene, S. (1996) *Managing Conservation in Museums,* London: Butterworth-Heinemann, pp. 136–158.

Kingsley, H. and Payton, R. (1994) 'Condition Surveying of Large Varied Stored Collections', *Conservation News* 54: 8–10.

Taylor, J. and Stevenson, S. (1999) 'Investigating Subjectivity within Collection Condition Surveys', *Museum Management and Curatorship* 18(1): 19–42.

Walker, K. and Bacon, L. (1987) 'A Condition Survey of Specimens in the Horniman Museum: A Progress Report', in J. Black (ed.), *Recent advances in the Conservation and Analysis of Artifacts,* London: Summer Schools Press.

Chapter 27

Environmental Management: zonation, building management and environmental conditioning

May Cassar

[. . .]

Environmental zoning

SEPARATE ZONES MAY BE created within a building by comparing and matching their environmental characteristics. The most environmentally stable areas can then be allocated to the most sensitive parts of the collection. At its simplest, environmental zoning can be established by keeping doors and windows closed to isolate different rooms. More sophisticated zoning will depend on monitoring to discover which areas of the building have the most stable climatic conditions. It may be possible to extend the results from monitored areas to other areas with similar physical characteristics. Already stable areas will require less effort, energy and money to control than rooms subject to significant external and internal heat gains and losses.

Critical and non-critical areas

The concept of critical and non-critical areas is valuable for the assessment of plans for zoning and active environmental control. Not all areas in the museum need to be controlled to the level required by the most sensitive object (see Figure 27.1). Critical areas are the galleries, storage areas and conservation laboratories. These spaces are designated primarily for objects, so the environmental conditions in them can be geared to the needs of the collection. Non-critical areas include offices, corridors and shops. These spaces are mainly used by people, and therefore need to be controlled

Source: *Environmental Management*, London: Routledge, 1995, pp. 39–41, 77–87, 94–108.

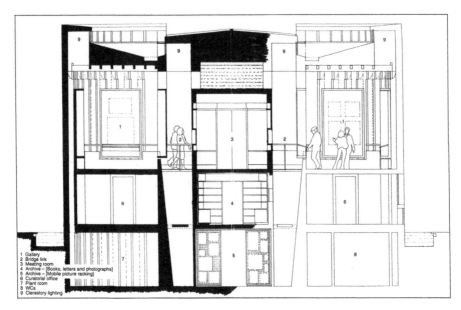

Figure 27.1 Proposed library for the Ruskin Collection: vertical cross-section through a new building which clearly zones critical and non-critical areas at the design stage. The Ruskin Library project is a project of the University of Lancaster, UK, and is intended to house the archive, reading room and display area for the collection of papers, books, paintings and water-colours associated with John Ruskin (Acknowledgement: McCormac, Jamieson Pritchard)

only to maintain the comfort of office staff and visitors. Museums should not exhibit environmentally sensitive objects in non-critical areas.

Critical zoning in the design or renovation of a museum space can be achieved through a two-stage process:

- All museum staff draw up 'room profiles' listing the facilities, services and activities that will be provided in each room.
- Use the room profiles to create functional groupings: which spaces have to be near to each other to function effectively?

This exercise will distinguish the people-priority and object-priority areas, permitting a rationalisation of environmental controls.

[. . .]

Controlling from the centre: building management and environmental conditioning

I do not like ducts, I do not like pipes. I hate them really thoroughly, but because I hate them thoroughly I feel that they have to be given their place. If I hated them and took no care, I think that they would invade the building and completely destroy it. I want to correct any notion you may have that I am in love with that kind of thing.

(Louis Kahn, World Architecture 1 (1964), London)

Centralised environmental systems are characterised by museum-wide systems of control and regulation. The two most important components of this kind of system are the air-conditioning plant and the building management system – both described later in this chapter. Be careful of the terminology: building-wide centrally controlled systems are not necessarily synonymous with air-conditioning. Mechanical ventilation is a familiar form of centralised environmental control that should not be confused with full air-conditioning.

A central control system is one response to a building that cannot provide enough passive control on its own. The museum building may have a short thermal lag or be poorly insulated; there may be too much unshaded glazing or too little ventilation control; or the problem may be external air pollution, or excessive internal heat and moisture gains from large numbers of people and heat-producing light sources.

These problems can be attacked by other means, however; and new buildings will be designed to reduce their effects to a minimum. An expensive, complex and space-hungry central control system is not a quick fix. A bankrupt museum is not a safe environment for any object.

Is a centralised system really necessary?

If full environmental control is never an automatic choice – or necessarily the best option – what are the alternatives? At the very least, there must be a cost comparison with partial air-conditioning and a non-conditioned building. (Table 27.1 lists some comparative running costs obtained from a 1991 English survey.) Does the whole building need full environmental control to reach into its furthest corner? And if the building really is so bad that a powerful system is the only way to make it tolerable, why is the museum still there? How much would a move or a new building cost?

An expensive option

Centralised systems are always expensive. First, there is the considerable capital outlay, and with an existing building the cost of disruptive alterations. Then there are high operating costs of energy consumption and maintenance. And in the future, by which time the collection will have become accustomed to its lavishly controlled environment, there will be replacement costs. If a high degree of flexibility – more

Table 27.1 Museum energy use, 1991

Environmental control with year-round usage	Running cost (£ per square metre per year)
More than 70% air-conditioning	11.64
Less than 70% air-conditioning	9.11
Not air-conditioned	5.94

Source: Oreszczyn, Mullany and Riain (1994)

control within different areas – is required of mechanical services, there is a cost to be paid in operational efficiency and running costs.

Maintenance and replacement costs over the life of a system are more difficult to predict than running costs, and there are few published data from museums. Cost data are available from air-conditioned commercial offices, however, and provide a good first estimate. A recent survey of sixty offices in the UK concluded that annual running costs and maintenance costs are very nearly the same; in the summer of 1989, for example, average annual air-conditioning running costs and maintenance costs for the surveyed offices were £11.21 and £10.56 per square metre, respectively.

Air-conditioning systems

The largest, most obvious – and often the most expensive – component of a modern centralised control scheme is the air-conditioning system. Air-conditioning is a permanently installed system of providing and maintaining an internal atmospheric condition within predetermined limits, irrespective of external conditions. This is a specialist area of environmental control requiring the permanent attention of building services engineers. As a rule of thumb, it costs about four times as much to air-condition a building, even without humidification, as it does simply to heat it.

A confusion of terms

The term 'air-conditioning' is often used without a clear understanding of what it implies. To building services engineers, it is synonymous with refrigeration, that is, cooling and dehumidification, but need not imply full control over relative humidity. On the other hand, museums often use the term to refer to a ducted system of conditioned air, with priority control over relative humidity in areas where the collection is housed. Beware of confusion, particularly at the planning stage of an air-conditioning project.

Full air-conditioning

'Full air-conditioning' describes a system that is capable of a comprehensive range of conditioning (see Figure 27.2). Within the limits imposed by the design specification, the full system can:

* clean the air by filtration;
* control the air temperature by heating and cooling;
* control the moisture content of the air, either by humidification or dehumidification; and
* distribute the air to where it is needed.

Air-conditioning can be centralised or decentralised. The choice will depend on the available space to site all the equipment and the environmental zoning that is planned within the building. All types of systems are unavoidably bulky; even where components like boilers, refrigeration units, fans, and filters can be reduced in size, the

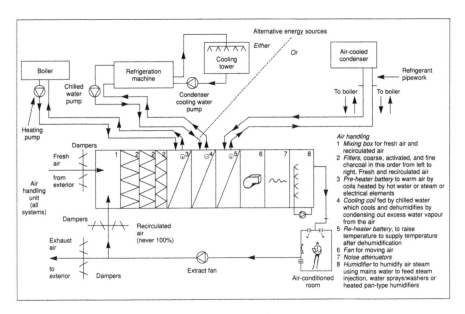

Figure 27.2 Typical air-conditioning system configurations

distribution ducting must retain its bulk. Large volumes of air at or near atmospheric pressure cannot be distributed through small-bore pipes.

When is full air-conditioning necessary?

Full air-conditioning can counter the effects of a polluted site or a severe climate. In temperate climates, a good building will buffer extremes of climate, leaving pollution – particularly in urban areas – as the most likely 'push' factor in favour of a full system. The chief 'pull' factor is the potential for very precise control of relative humidity, temperature and ventilation rates over large volumes of air; only full air-conditioning can achieve this.

There are disadvantages, besides the glaring issue of high costs: the plant and ducting eat up space, which in most museums is often in short supply; there is the risk that objects will be damaged if the system goes wrong; and there may be health risks, highlighted in recent years by outbreaks of Legionnaires' disease.

As every site is different, feasibility is another issue. An existing building may be unable to cope with the plant and ducting, particularly if it is historically or architecturally significant and legally protected against extensive alteration. External factors may also make a proposed system less viable: the air intakes will have to take account of the prevailing wind direction, and be kept away from potential pollution caused by restaurant or café services, car exhausts at parking sites, and the proximity of adjacent factories.

System requirements

A museum's management will install an air-conditioning system only if:

- the costs are sustainable;
- the system is designed to meet the needs of the collection; and
- the spatial impact of the system is tolerable.

The control set-point, that is, the value to which an automatic control must be pre-set so that a desired value is achieved – and the allowable variation from this pre-set level – will primarily reflect the conditions required by the collection, though many museums have to compromise in the face of the equipment's accuracy limits, and restrictions on capital, running and maintenance costs.

The new system must also be easy to operate and maintain, or its performance will drift and costs will escalate. It is easy to blame the equipment when it goes wrong or fails to perform to specification. Sometimes the equipment is to blame; ageing systems may be inefficient and prone to breakdown, and replacement will be the most cost-effective solution. But other possible causes should not be overlooked – these include faulty commissioning (see below), lack of maintenance, and failure to calibrate the control system. Museum staff should make it their business to know the operating sequence of an air-conditioning plant in order to be able to tell at least whether equipment is running.

Testing and commissioning the system

Thorough testing of new buildings or services takes time, which must not be swallowed up by other activities running behind schedule. Unless all commissioning tests are fully carried out, there is a danger that the museum will take over a development that does not meet the intended performance targets.

Commissioning tests are not all esoteric technical checks; there are many accessible trials that can and should be performed in the presence of museum staff, for example in a new building extension:

- Shutting down the air-conditioning plant, monitoring conditions and then measuring how quickly the plant can re-establish the required set levels after it is switched on again.
- Using simulated loads, testing the environmental control systems under load conditions before objects are installed in new exhibition spaces. (Thermal loads are simulated by arrays of 60 watt lamps distributed evenly about each room, each lamp representing the heat given off by one person. Moisture evaporating from people is simulated by electric kettles wired to release a person-equivalent amount of water vapour into the air.)

Under the Joint Contracts Tribunal, a 'Practical Completion Certificate' is issued by the architect once the system is installed, commissioned and running satisfactorily; after this has been signed by a person authorised by the museum (the architect, or the curator managing the project, for example), the contractor is required to correct defects which appear during the 'Defects Liability Period', normally twelve months from the issue of the certificate. It makes sense therefore to give the contractor responsibility also for routine servicing and maintenance during the period.

The certificate should not be signed on behalf of the client before the completion of the contract terms; before the building has been inspected, and system testing and commissioning are complete; or before the museum, as client, has agreed that all is well. The end of the commissioning process is reached when the commissioning sheet is issued; this verifies that the installation complies with the design requirements. The museum should insist on being provided with comprehensive operation and maintenance (O&M) manuals for all of the installed services, both for new and refurbishment projects and this should be specified in the contract. The manuals must be explicit in their detailed content, and the installation subcontractor must include 'as fitted' drawings showing the system in situ – manufacturer's component drawings will not suffice.

In practice, O&M manuals can be difficult to obtain; those that are provided, unless they have been supplied under the terms of the contract, often contain insufficient and even incorrect information. A Practical Completion Certificate should not be issued until the O&M manuals are received, checked by the consultants and the museum for the client's use.

Training and operating procedures

An air-conditioning system will require trained personnel on the museum staff to ensure its smooth operation. The staff who will operate the new system will need appropriate technical training, which could usefully begin during equipment installation – especially where the system is extensive or complex. These staff members are crucial to the successful operation of the system. Effective training demands adequate time and resources, which should be written into the original tender conditions for the air-conditioning project. Other staff such as conservators and curators will benefit from demonstration sessions, using the O&M manuals as reference.

Ideally, a museum should have direct control over its environmental systems, which should be regulated from within the building. Contracting out the day-to-day management of environmental systems must not imply opting out of responsibility for their performance. In a large institution, control and maintenance of the system will probably be vested in a building manager, who will need to confer regularly with the curatorial or conservation staff; they will provide him or her with assessments of the exhibition and storage environments.

Sooner or later, the system will suffer a partial or total breakdown; this will not be the best time to start thinking about what to do next. The emergency procedure should be in place right from the start, as should procedures to cover planned shutdowns for maintenance and repair.

Shut-down procedures, whether for emergency purposes or not, must aim to preserve environmental stability for as long as possible, particularly in the critical zone. Simple measures can be very effective: isolate affected areas by shutting the doors, and exclude the public from these areas until control is restored. Where an extensive system is being used to compensate for a poor building, shut-downs will have a marked effect: the building's weak buffering ability will allow a more rapid – and a potentially more damaging – environmental change. Under these circumstances, it is almost essential to include back-up equipment at the design stage.

Space: where will it all go?

Centralised control systems now almost universally employ air-conditioning equipment. This occupies large volumes of space, which cannot be recouped by skimping on the size of the plant. The heating and cooling capacity, the supply and extract fans, the humidifier and dehumidifier capacities, the filtration systems must all be large enough to deal with the expected load. An undersized system will be perpetually straining to meet the set-point conditions, and will suffer from poor accuracy and reliability. On the other hand, an oversized system running almost continuously on partial loads will present the museum with correspondingly oversized energy bills.

Volume, height and weight

The space requirements of a full air-conditioning plant can be designed into a new museum building – with compromises from both the architect and the consulting engineer. Museums in older buildings are less fortunate. Once again, there is no published information on the space required by air-conditioning plant as a percentage of the floor area in museums, but office and laboratory data suggest that up to 15 per cent of the volume of a building may be needed for full air-conditioning plant and ducting.

Ducting simply takes up space, but there are other problem dimensions, particularly height and weight. Hot and cold water storage tanks, boilers, refrigeration units, AHU (air handling units) can be tall and are always heavy.

Water tanks in suitable housings at roof level provide a good head of water, but in a museum the risk of leaks outweighs any advantages, with the result that pressurisation vessels are sometimes placed in the basement and serviced by pumps and leakage alarm systems. Some of the measures that can be taken to avoid water leaks are: using microbore systems of pipes, ensuring that there are no joins in the pipework under floors and installing a leak detection system. Mains-fed hot and cold water services eliminate the need for water storage tanks. Mains water systems save on costs and space, and also improve safety as they are less prone to bacterial infection. Some water supply authorities require users to hold water in tanks. This reserve storage can be an advantage when supplies are interrupted – safeguarding the water supply to the environmental control systems, and minimising the disruption to museum activities such as restaurant and toilet facilities.

The size of the AHU will depend on the volume of air it has to move; it too can be sited on the roof, where the air is cleaner, at the expense of additional ducting and weatherproofing. Even boilers can be moved upwards, away from their traditional home in the basement, in order to prevent their large-diameter flues from penetrating floors and occupying space. Safe floor and roof loadings must, of course, be assessed before any equipment can migrate to the roof or upper floors.

Air-conditioning in historic buildings

Space for equipment is hard to find in museums occupying buildings with historic interiors. Here, the system's designers must minimise visual intrusion and structural alteration, a demand that often calls for innovative approaches in both design and installation. Each building will have to be considered as an individual and legal and planning requirements will reduce the possibilities still further, but there are some general guidelines:

- Obtrusive equipment such as external condensers and fresh-air intake louvres must be carefully sited; the large size of AHUs, for example, means that they will almost certainly have to be located outside the building.
- Vertical runs of pipes, ducts and cables can be installed in cupboards and wall cavities.
- To minimise disruption, the original services should be used wherever possible.

Nevertheless, the installation of extensive control systems will always cause some disturbance to the historic house museum; it is the museum's responsibility to decide whether the installation is absolutely necessary, or whether conditions for the collection can be relaxed instead so that the impact of extensive control equipment on the fabric of the building is reduced. Because the historic building is the 'largest object in the collection', it may be more appropriate to seek a compromise between the needs of the contents, the building and its occupants. The best solution may be to forgo the provision of tightly controlled conditions for the building's contents.

Indoor air quality

Normal outdoor air contains widely varying concentrations of particulate matter and pollutants produced by natural processes of erosion and evaporation, and by human activity – particularly from combustion emissions and uncleaned industrial waste gases. There are also indoor contaminants generated by building, decorating and furnishing materials, and again by human activity; these include odorants, non-odorous gases and particulates.

Museum air must be clean. The question is, how clean? What would the cost implications be of accepting that all pollutants are harmful and that, therefore, there is no acceptable threshold? There are undoubtedly types of objects that are highly vulnerable to pollutants; it is equally true that an undirected 'filter anything and everything' decision will prove intolerably expensive. Air quality must depend on the level of protection required by the objects. Unfortunately, not enough is yet known about the precise effects of a range of pollutants on museum objects, so conservators are faced with an array of different recommendations for permissible pollutant concentrations and appropriate filter grades. When planning an air-conditioning system, it is important to establish whether filtration is needed by carrying out a pollution survey of the site. After appropriate measures are taken, monitoring of internal pollutant levels should be carried out in a similar way to monitoring relative humidity and temperature to check that the measures are giving the desired result.

Filtration systems

Air-conditioning and mechanical ventilation systems are designed to accept filters at suitable points in the air path. Filters come in a variety of types and degrees of fineness; some are mechanical – simple meshes that block particles of a certain size – others are 'active' or absorption filters – in which harmful gases are absorbed by special fillings, typically activated charcoal (Figure 27.3).

In practice, filters are installed in sets, increasing in fineness in the downstream direction. A very fine mechanical filter will stop all particles down to the size of its mesh, but if used on its own would soon become clogged or damaged by larger debris. A coarse filter is therefore installed first, followed by a sequence of other filters determined by the incoming air quality and the intended degree of protection. An ideal sequence is: coarse pre-filter, main particulate filter, gaseous pollution filter and lastly a fine particulate filter. Replacements must be installed in the same order.

All filters installed as part of a larger air handling system should be monitored for pressure drop, and not simply changed on a fixed time-interval basis. Filters should have positive sealing frame mechanisms, so that all incoming air passes through the filter; this allows monitoring instruments to read positively and ensures the best filter performance and air quality.

Particulate filters

The particulate filtration system most commonly used in museums is Eurovent 4/5, with coarse and fine filter grades in the categories EU1 to EU9. Under the Eurovent system, 'coarse' filter grades range from EU1 to EU4, and 'fine' filters from EU5 to EU9. The ultra-fine high-efficiency filters in the range EU10 to EU14 are rarely used outside the clinical and surgical environments.

For museums on severely polluted sites, the following recommendations still apply:

- particulates to be removed to 80 per cent efficiency on Eurovent 4/5;
- sulphur dioxide and nitrogen dioxide to be removed to below 10 micrograms per cubic metre;
- ozone to be removed to below 2 micrograms per cubic metre.

(Note: Eurovent is the European Committee of Manufacturers of Air Handling Equipment.)

Gaseous pollution

Methods that have been used to remove gaseous pollutants are alkaline washes, activated carbon, copper impregnated activated carbon and potassium permanganate on activated alumina filters. Activated carbon filters are preferred by many museums, and tests have indicated that they are reliable.

Figure 27.3 Basic filtration guide

Filters can be very expensive to maintain, so a good case must be made for their use. Although some can be recharged by the manufacturers, most are disposable and should be changed, as part of a regular maintenance programme, by the museum's own or contracted-in building personnel. The pressure drop across a filter is a much better guide to its condition than the elapsed time since the last service; filters – and indeed any other disposable components of an environmental control system – that are replaced on a rigid time-interval basis may still be serviceable, resulting in wastage and unnecessary costs.

Other methods of pollution control

In many museums, air filtration may be impossible or simply uneconomic, yet some simple housekeeping practices can reduce pollution to acceptable levels:

- If mechanical ventilation is available, it can be adjusted to produce a slightly positive (greater than ambient) air pressure in the exhibition galleries, which will help to keep dirt out; air movements will be outwards, not inwards. (This remedy may lead to higher than expected energy bills.)
- Good building maintenance, housekeeping and museum practices will prevent the generation of particulate pollution such as dust and grit.
- Dirt brought in by visitors on outdoor clothing can be limited by the provision of cloakrooms, and the use of large looped-pile mats in exterior doorways.
- Materials sensitive to gaseous pollution should be located far away from entrances. Well-regulated ventilation in the exhibition spaces will help to dilute gaseous pollutant concentrations, but filtration provides the only effective control of external gaseous pollution.
- Particularly vulnerable objects can be protected by a well-sealed display case containing an absorbent activated carbon material. All construction materials must be tested for stability before use.
  [. . .]

Building management systems

Truly centralised regulation of environmental control systems has recently become a practical reality, thanks to microprocessor technology. Microprocessors are now the main control component in a wide range of environmental equipment, from air-conditioning systems to transportable humidifiers.

The building management system (BMS) extends microprocessor control throughout the building, and beyond, to regulate virtually any number of services, from monitoring the internal environment to controlling lighting, heating, ventilation and air-conditioning systems, plant and energy management, and leak detection and response. Monitoring and control systems can even be interlinked, producing an automated system of self-regulating building control.

BMSs can integrate many other functions. Plant and equipment status can be monitored, and breakdowns or unexpected environmental variations reported; the system can be programmed to give priority to relative humidity control in display areas, but temperature in the museum's commercial area. A BMS can also monitor and record the status of security and fire alarms, though it is wise to keep alarm and environmental systems on separate circuits.

Is BMS a worthwhile investment?

A BMS installation is expensive: it will involve computer hardware and specialised software; a cable network around the building, together with suitable interfacing units; and sensors (for monitoring) and actuators (for controlling). Costs will vary with the complexity of the system, and whether the system is going into a new building or an existing one. It requires proper commissioning and trained and dedicated staff who fully understand the system to ensure smooth operation. Extensive environmental systems such as air-conditioning in new buildings will nowadays almost certainly be under BMS control.

Quoted equipment costs may not cover the building work associated with installation, which may be extensive and disruptive in an existing building; it may therefore be sensible to defer the work until other refurbishment – electrical rewiring, say – is due. Alternatively, a simple BMS could be installed to overcome the problems caused by the uncoordinated operation of existing equipment.

The system will need detailed planning, as every BMS is tailored to its own location and environmental equipment. When planning the system, do take the opportunity to extend it to as many areas as possible: transportable equipment can be brought into the network, provided there are interfaces near all potential operation sites; and remote stores and other sites can be linked through dedicated lines, the telephone system, or radiotelemetry.

Specialist advice on a potential project will be needed from the start. There has to be a clear design brief, accessible to all interested parties, including:

* the software designer (who may not know anything about psychrometry, or the demands on a museum environment);
* the subcontractor, who will install the system;
* the commissioning agent, who will test the installation and operation of the system;
* the museum, whose staff must be trained to operate the system.

While BMSs appear to provide a solution to the problem of co-ordinating and controlling a number of different functions within a museum, their complexity can make them unmanageable for the majority of museums – especially those that fail to recognise the need for highly skilled and trained staff to ensure the smooth day-to-day operation of a BMS.

Asset management systems

BMS installations can be enhanced by another layer of control in the form of a maintenance management programme, also called an asset management system. Particularly suited to large museums, the programme monitors the duty cycles of all equipment, including main and stand-by systems, so that maintenance can be related to time in service rather than an arbitrary calendar date. This brings substantial savings, especially for large installations, as infrequently used equipment is not subjected to unnecessary maintenance.

Energy efficiency and environmental control

For the collection's sake, a large, centralised environmental control system often has to run continuously for twenty-four hours a day, seven days a week. If its energy consumption is too high, the simplest 'cure' – shut-down – is not a realistic option, since museums are conditioned primarily for objects, not for people. The alternative is to improve efficiency – to obtain the same environment at a lower energy cost. This can be done through zoning of critical and uncritical areas, particularly since approximately 30 per cent of the floor area of museum buildings is not used for the display or storage of objects.

Up-to-date air-conditioning systems under BMS control can be fine-tuned to achieve a balance between energy cost and acceptable environmental controls. Savings can be made if the BMS is programmed to allow 'free cooling' (unaided by the refrigeration plant) whenever outdoor ambient conditions are suitable; if frequency inverters are installed to adjust fan speeds; and a high level of air recirculation is used in storage areas and at night in display areas. But there are other more general measures available to all museums, whatever their size and control methods.

[. . .]

Room-based environmental systems

For many museums, centralised systems and building-wide environmental control will be unattainable: perhaps the collection is too small to justify a large expense; or the building cannot be altered because it is old, historically important, or shared with another user. Whatever the reason, it is still possible to offer visitors a pleasing environment that conforms to the best principles of preventive conservation. Environmental management is not an all-or-nothing matter that can be resolved only by the expenditure of vast amounts of money.

At all scales and levels of resources, large and small, the approach to environmental management remains the same: discover the needs of the objects in the collection; monitor the existing environment, especially for relative humidity, temperature and light levels; and improve conditions that do not match the targets. When the centralised option of full and flexible control is not available, the solution will lie with a combination of existing building services and individual control units.

Heating and lighting equipment will probably already be in place; there may be scope for adding or replacing lighting circuits, or supplementing the existing heating system with portable units. Even where a museum's control over an existing building is very small, there is probably some potential for improving the lighting and heating controls. Relative humidity control presents a difficult problem; here, existing building services offer limited improvements in control, and transportable humidifiers and dehumidifiers will be needed.

Maintaining environmental stability in old or converted buildings can be difficult and time consuming when using transportable control units. Independent units
need delicate adjustment to achieve a level of wider co-ordination, and their integral
sensors have hitherto been crude, often creating a localised climate around the units
themselves. Fortunately, the development of microprocessor controls will bring
a new order of reliability and co-ordination to room-based environmental equipment (Figure 27.4). The new generation of electronic controllers can be positioned
away from the immediate influence of the unit, and should enable individual units to
be interlinked – which will at least banish the common (and absurd) spectacle of a
humidifier and a dehumidifier battling for control of the same space.

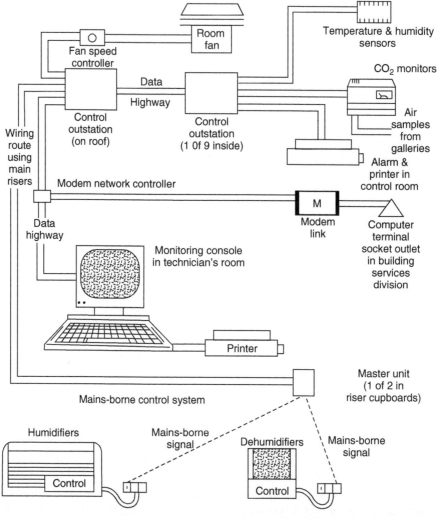

Figure 27.4 Synchronising the operation of a variety of independent environmental
control equipment within a space can be a complex and time-consuming
task

In refurbished buildings where some permanently installed climate control equipment can be used, it may be possible to install a simple BMS networking the operation of otherwise independent equipment. Even a modest scheme, perhaps controlling central heating, ventilation plant and transportable humidity control units, would provide an improvement in environmental stability.

Environmental control can also affect the building itself – something that may be particularly important where a museum shares an old building with another user. Where the museum and the other occupier maintain different environments in their respective spaces, and the museum requires tight humidity control, then if the other user turns off all the heating at night in winter and there is no vapour barrier in the walls that separate them, moisture may travel through the fabric and cause damage by interstitial condensation.

Controlling humidity

In the absence of an air-conditioning system, humidity is controlled by humidifiers, which add moisture to the air, and dehumidifiers, which remove it. There are several different kinds of both types of machine, each with advantages and disadvantages that will affect their suitability for a particular application. The type of unit has to be addressed at the planning stage of an installation, because it will determine whether, for example, units have to be plumbed into the mains water supply. Free-standing units may have reservoirs of water that need to be manually filled or emptied at regular intervals, so staff supervision may be a factor. Size is another variable: humidifier and dehumidifier capacities must be correctly matched to the volume of air and the air exchange rate of the room.

One very important consideration is the potential health risk: bacteria breed in water that is allowed to stand at room temperature, bringing a remote risk of the notorious Legionnaires' disease, and a much higher risk of the influenza-like 'humidifier fever'. An assessment of the risk and a strategy for illness prevention will be needed for all water-using environmental control equipment.

Another cause for vigilance is a more familiar one where water is stored near museum objects: the danger of leaks and flooding. The water supply, whether from unit reservoirs or a mains source, must always be carefully managed, especially where the units are located on upper floors. If the units do not have a failsafe device, leak detectors must be installed.

Humidifiers

Humidifiers increase the moisture content of the air by atomising water or by evaporating it. Atomising and ultrasonic humidifiers use the former approach, physically breaking the water into tiny droplets, so that whatever is in solution in the water supplied to the unit will find its way into the conditioned air. Distilled or demineralised water should therefore be used in these humidifiers, as any hard-water salts in tap water, for example, would be distributed unchanged into the environment. Faulty humidifiers of this type can still go on emitting moisture into the air, and where plumbed into a water supply could produce serious condensation on nearby surfaces.

As their name suggests, evaporative and steam humidifiers convert water into vapour before dispersing it, and therefore avoid the problem of water-borne mineral contamination. Tap water can be used but entails frequent cleaning of the equipment, so water softening may be necessary in hard-water districts. Evaporative humidifiers, the type most frequently used in museums, evaporate water from a small reservoir under the apparatus or from the water supply, depending on type. Larger evaporative units also incorporate a fan and temperature control, and air filters that need to be kept clean to maintain air flow and the required humidification effect. Unfortunately, evaporative units are less effective in naturally ventilated spaces, and do not reliably provide accurate control.

Although evaporative humidifiers are less likely to cause humidifier-related illness than atomising types, they still require particular care in cleaning, maintenance and inspection. Biocide treatment programmes may be advisable, but specialist advice should be sought first. Steam humidifiers are often recommended on health and safety grounds because they present less of a health risk than other types when correctly operated and maintained. Free-standing steam humidifiers are available but are not widely used in museums, principally because they emit steam into the space being conditioned. Most existing steam humidification equipment is part of larger permanent installations, where the steam is mixed with air in the duct before being diffused into the space.

One final caveat: the introduction of humidification in a historic building requires very careful planning. There could be a risk of structural problems associated with a change in the moisture equilibrium of the fabric, particularly where structural timber is concerned.

Dehumidifiers

There are two main types of dehumidifiers used in museums. The more costly desiccant type draws moist air over a drying agent carried on a rotating drum. The desiccant – preferably silica gel – is continually regenerated by warmed air, which should be then vented externally with its load of moisture at a safe distance from the space under treatment. The warm air required to regenerate the desiccant can raise ambient temperature near the unit by about 2°C when in operation.

Refrigerant dehumidifiers condense excess moisture out of the air by drawing it across refrigerant pipes; the water is collected in a pan, and the cooled dry air is warmed back to ambient temperature by heating coils before being returned to the room. The production of water means that the pan will need to be emptied regularly to avoid bacteriological contamination, flooding or the unit switching itself off when full; or a machine in a permanent position can be plumbed in to a suitable drain.

Desiccant dehumidifiers ordinarily use more energy than refrigerant types, but are more effective at lower temperatures because the drying agent's moisture capacity increases. In practice, the desiccant unit's higher running costs are offset by the additional energy refrigerant units use to auto-defrost their coils to retain efficiency at lower temperatures. For this reason refrigerant dehumidifiers should preferably not be used in spaces which are unheated in winter. At normal ambient internal conditions in the UK both types work well, the desiccant type being particularly useful because it does not need to be plumbed in to a drain.

Controllers

The simple humidistat

A humidistat is to humidity control what a thermostat is to temperature control. The simple humidistat often fitted to transportable humidifiers and dehumidifiers consists of a humidity sensor coupled to a switch. The sensor may be no more than a fibrous membrane – which should not be adjusted – and control is not particularly accurate; when the humidity rises to the set-point, the dehumidifier switches on (or the humidifier switches off), and vice versa when the humidity drops below the required point. The desired humidity is therefore only approximated by a sequence of on–off operations.

Control is made even more unreliable by the physical position of the humidistat; in the majority of transportable units, and in some wall-mounted steam units, it is close to the source of humidification. This is an unfortunate side-effect of transportability, which requires that a machine has its own sensor built in, but the effect is similar to that of a central heating thermostat mounted next to a radiator. The humidity in the room as a whole changes only slowly, whereas the humidity 'seen' by the sensor is influenced by the peculiar conditions near the unit. The result is poor environmental control, and wasted energy whenever the 'misled' units run for longer than the general humidity level requires.

Microprocessor-based controllers

Microprocessors bring an improved accuracy to the sensor system of transportable humidity control units. Their 'intelligence' means that they are programmed to look beyond the immediate humidity reading, resulting in a more accurate control of the environmental conditions and less sharp variations from the set-point. Compact and reliable microprocessor-based controllers are gradually replacing crude humidistats, and are already fitted as standard in some large transportable humidifiers.

Museum-specific controllers

The most recent development is a museum-specific, microprocessor-based electronic controller. Mounted away from the unit it controls, the device is designed to measure and control ambient humidity. The unit can be a humidifier, a dehumidifier or an electric radiator, which is controlled to give priority to humidity control while varying ambient temperature.

With the arrival of this new and advanced technology, it is now possible for controllers to regulate the flow temperatures of hot water and to control the heating valves on some conventional systems to give priority to ambient humidity, or more locally to synchronise the operation of a humidifier and a dehumidifier within the same space.

Heating

Heat can damage museum objects – either directly, through a simple excess, or indirectly, when it is suddenly introduced to a previously unheated space and destabilises the relative humidity. Existing heating and proposed new systems alike must therefore be carefully assessed as part of the museum's environmental strategy.

Heat has two – usually incompatible – functions in the museum environment:

- 'conservation heating', which draws on psychrometric principles to control relative humidity using heat;
- 'comfort heating', designed to provide pleasant surroundings for staff and visitors.

Heating can reduce high ambient relative humidity: empirical studies have shown that, in the UK, heating to a temperature of about 5°C above outside conditions is enough to reduce relative humidity below 65 per cent, which is the critical level for the growth of mould and fungi; but this is practicable only in unoccupied areas in a building that do not need to be heated to comfort conditions. Because this 5° difference has been achieved by experimentation, this temperature difference may have to be increased if there is damp present in the fabric of the space. In these conditions, dehumidification and not heating is the answer during the summer – and even then the space must ideally be unoccupied, and the windows and doors draughtproofed and kept closed, before high ambient humidity levels can be reduced satisfactorily. Dehumidification rather than heating to control relative humidity is cheaper to run but it does require a space to be sealed or a room to be located away from the effect of external conditions for it to achieve the desired result.

The familiar conflict between object needs and people needs soon arises, particularly in the exhibition areas: in a closed space, heat gains from people and lighting, quite apart from any heating services, cause a rise in temperature which in turn reduces relative humidity unless moisture is introduced from another source. Low relative humidity can damage many objects, so the temperature required for visitors' comfort in exhibition areas often entails some form of humidification during the winter heating season.

Providing and controlling heat

Modern heating systems will probably be based on the design of conventional domestic systems using water-filled radiators serviced by a central boiler. The heating system boiler should be separate from the water heating boiler and its distribution system. Radiator spurs should be capable of being shut off independently, and leak detection equipment is desirable; although leak detection and response sensors are expensive, they may one day earn their keep – especially if water pipes pass through areas in the critical zone. Temperature control will probably be managed by thermostats.

'Conservation heating' attempts as far as possible to manage the system so that it produces the desired level of ambient relative humidity, which reduces the need for dedicated humidity control equipment. The conservation approach is provided by dedicated humidity and temperature sensors; these feed information back to the heating system through the controllers, which may be both weather-compensating controllers located outside to measure the external temperature and regulate the flow temperature of the water in the system, and humidistatic controllers near the radiators in the system. The cost of this kind of pragmatic engineering system will vary with its complexity. A simple BMS installation may be justified, for example, in a store housing thousands of objects, or in an old museum building where the only form of environmental control is the existing heating system. However, this is likely to require dedicated and trained staff to operate it. Any alterations to an existing heating system must include, as a priority, separate heating circuits for the critical and non-critical zones.

Ideally, the heating system in the critical zone will never be turned off. If it is under 'intelligent' control, the temperature changes for an annual cycle can be programmed. For example, for the transition between the unheated and heated season to give the most stable possible temperature in northern temperate climates – and after advice from a building services or control engineer – the heating is turned on in the autumn at the same temperature as external conditions; the temperature setting is then incremented weekly by equal fractions of a degree to maintain as stable a temperature indoors during the coldest months as in the autumn. After a steady phase during January and February, the setting is decremented at the same weekly rate until the spring, when it is turned off. This procedure slows down – as far as is practicable – the adverse impact of a sudden temperature change on indoor relative humidity, but it still provides conditions that meet human comfort needs.

Where simple controllers on radiators are installed, they should be set to the autumn temperature throughout the year; this ensures that the heating will switch on only when the indoor temperature drops below the autumn ambient level. This type of control does not produce as much stability and more 'cycling' of the ambient relative humidity is likely, but it is cheap and easy to install. One advantage of old cast iron radiators is the slowness with which they heat up and cool down. This limited control can be lost if heat loss takes place along the system due to the fact that pipes are not lagged: all heating pipes, not only the ones hidden from sight, should be insulated.

The need for regulated ventilation

If a museum only had to care about the collection, ventilation rates could be reduced to a minimum to stabilise the internal environment. But a museum also welcomes the public, sometimes in very large numbers, and is an employer of staff. The air circulating inside the building therefore has to perform several functions: the basis of human respiration and thermal comfort, the dilution and removal of airborne pollutants, a medium for waste moisture and heat – indeed, it is the principal vehicle for the whole indoor environment.

Correct ventilation is the provision of sufficient air to a space to meet the criteria associated with its use. As usual, the museum is faced with conflicting requirements of humans and objects in many of its spaces, and ventilation is also the subject of a mass of laws and regulations in most developed countries. There is unlikely to be much freedom to ignore the requirements of the visitor in favour of the collection, and most ventilation problems will involve, first, the satisfaction of human needs and the appropriate legislation, followed by the establishment of the best available conditions for the collection. A building services engineer and a conservator will probably be needed to resolve any conflicting requirements.

Air change rates and general ventilation requirements, allowable pollution concentrations, carbon dioxide levels and other standards can usually be found in legislation governing health and safety in workplaces and public spaces; no ventilation provision can be created without knowledge of the appropriate rules. For example, a British health and safety regulation specifies that the long-term (eight hours) exposure limit for carbon dioxide is 0.5 per cent by volume (5000 parts per million), which requires approximately 2 litres of fresh air per second per person to achieve the required dilution.

Ventilation is another area where microprocessors can achieve a whole new order of control. BMSs and other computerised control networks can be designed to monitor air quality through carbon dioxide sensors and adjust air volume dampers or fan speeds accordingly, thereby creating a versatile, energy-efficient system of control capable of coping with widely varying visitor numbers and patterns of use. BMS-controlled ventilation can be as complex as full air-conditioning or as simple as fans located in the lined chimney flues of historic buildings.

Bibliography

Oreszczyn, T., Mullany, T. and Riain, C. N. (1994) 'A survey of energy use in museums and galleries', in M. Cassar (ed.) *Museums Environment Energy*, London: MGC.

Chapter 28

Collections Condition

Suzanne Keene

IT IS ARGUABLE THAT the first duty of museums is to care for and preserve the collections, since these are the physical assets, owned by the public, for which the organization is accountable, and on which all other museum activities are based. Condition monitoring can be seen as an audit, based on clear definitions, which allows the condition of different collections to be compared one with another, between different institutions, or over time. Such audits should take as little valuable conservation time as possible, and the results will be analysed and expressed numerically. Successive comparable surveys over time are the only obvious way to establish whether collections are deteriorating or not.

[. . .]

Surveying collections

Surveys can have a variety of objectives (Table 28.1). At least three types of survey are needed to provide a truly comprehensive view of collections preservation.

Preventive conservation assessments

In order to diagnose and eliminate the causes of deterioration, the preservation environment needs to be assessed in the broadest sense, covering institutional policies, procedures, available staff and skills, the history of the collections and space and physical resources for their preservation. Work on this has been completed in America,

Source: *Managing Conservation in Museums*, London: Butterworth-Heinemann, 1996, pp. 112–135, 136–158.

Table 28.1 The objectives of surveys, factors relevant to these, and data that need to be collected

Survey objective	Relevant factors	Data needed
Audit condition Identify causes of deterioration	Condition of individual objects Statistics on collections condition Environment: space, enclosures, supports/mounts, growth of collection, humidity, temperature, light, contaminants, pests, provenance Use: display, handling, repairs/conservation, examination, running/demonstration of objects	Condition audit Damage types and severity Observations Environmental records: past, present Damage types and severity Records of use
Diagnose trend	Condition: past vs. present Likelihood and rate of future change i.e. vulnerability and stability Factors which have caused/likely to cause damage	Condition past (?inferred) Condition present Condition predicted future (= stability) Present and likely future environment Present and likely future use
Affect trend	Change environment (see above) Modify use (see above): display conditions, handling/use procedures, conservation procedures, running or demonstration Modify object: treat or restore	Most potent causes of deterioration
Assess resources needed	Space, buildings, plans (HVAC etc.) Equipment (racks, cupboards, etc.) Materials (for mounts, etc.) Time, skills Finance	Size of task (e.g. number of objects, volume, storage area, etc.) Nature of task (e.g. mounting, treatment, refit store, new store) Account/cost of resource (e.g. conservator/years, sq. ft. of storage)
Assess benefits	Present use of objects, potential use, information potential, relevance to institution's purpose, monetary value, uniqueness, quality of workmanship, physical quality (e.g. wholeness), aesthetic quality	Present use (e.g. objects displayable, books readable, drawings accessible) Curatorial assessments of worth Numbers of objects being successfully preserved (i.e. in condition defined acceptable)
Recommend priorities	Institutional objectives Resources vs. benefits Consequences of 'do nothing'	Conservation/preservation policies Cost/benefit calculations using above data Vulnerability of objects/collections Judgements re will deteriorate or not

where the 'Conservation Assessment' is intended to be used for 'planning, implementing, and fund raising' (Getty Conservation Institute and National Institute for Conservation, 1991). In the UK, the Museums and Galleries Commission's 'Standards in the Museum Care of Collections' perform this function. Stores assessments (Keene 1996) are part of a conservation assessment.

Collections condition audits

Data on the condition of objects and collections themselves – the subject of this chapter. These complement preventive conservation assessments.

Curatorial assessments

Curatorial assessments of the importance of the object as part of the collection, i.e. of its significance for the intellectual dimension of the collection. This sort of assessment is clearly essential when setting priorities for action to be taken as a result of condition surveys, and for allocating resources. Despite current concerns with the refinement of collections through disposals, the only published work so far found on this emanates from the Dutch government, on the Delta Plan, a national initiative to address the backlog of collections management work in Holland (Directorate-General for Cultural Affairs 1992; Cannon-Brookes 1994).

As well as these general audits, object-by-object surveys will still of course be required for other purposes. For example, to plan remedial conservation projects, one will need to know which objects are the highest priority, and for this an object-by-object survey is essential. The observations made in sample surveys may be extended by instrumental or microscopic examination of objects in the sample: see for example the Library of Congress survey, in which the selected sample was tested for pH and fold strength (Wiederkehr 1984).

Existing work

Most earlier published work on surveys concentrates either on detailed condition reports on individual objects or on every-object surveys of collections undertaken to decide which objects should have priority for conservation (e.g. Walker and Bacon 1987). There are some general surveys of regions or collections types (e.g. Kenyon 1992; Storer 1989). Forms for collecting survey data are usually tailored to a particular type of collection, which makes it difficult to compare the condition of different collections. The first published report of a condition survey which collected the same categories of data for a diverse collection is to be found in Walker and Bacon (1987), an every-object survey for the Horniman Museum. Where only a sample of objects has been inspected, the selection has not been statistically designed but informal, e.g. every tenth object. However, a survey of the Library of Congress used statistically designed sampling to infer the condition of the twenty million books from a sample of 1000 (Wiederkehr 1984).

Most reports cite only an analysis of objects by type and conservation condition grade; not, for instance, condition by damage. This is because it is scarcely feasible to cross-tabulate two or more data variables by hand. Many extant surveys have not yet had their data analysed at all. This does not mean that they are useless: the information is also used as a complete collections inventory, as a basis for future condition monitoring, and as an immediate source of information about environmental problems. In most cases the information collected informally by observing storage conditions and obvious causes of damage has been drawn on and used, both in survey reports and in taking action, at least as much as the survey data itself.

Collections surveys are required to answer not the question, 'which objects need conservation?' but the even more important question, 'is the institution succeeding in its basic duty to preserve the collections?' This can be seen as an audit, based on clear definitions, which allows the condition of different collections to be compared one with another, between different institutions, or over time. Such audits should take as little valuable conservation time as possible, and give results which can be analysed and expressed numerically. Condition and damage can be categorized in standard ways that can apply to all types of collection. It is not necessary to examine every object in a large collection: statistical techniques can be used to design sample audits, as they are for sociological research, marketing, etc. Results can be calculated for the whole collection, and presented in simple and understandable ways.

Defining the data

Museum collections are extremely diverse, ranging from beetles to traction engines; flints to oil paintings; costumes to spacecraft. At first sight, it seems impossible that the condition of such a variety of objects could be described by a common set of terms. But it was found on studying surveys from different institutions that the terminology to describe 'condition' in different types of object was in fact quite similar.

Administrative data

These are the main terms used in analysing data and reporting results. Because museum collections are so diverse, even these seemingly obvious terms need to be defined to take account of collections which are often only partly inventoried, disorganized in store, and have no factual estimate of collections size.

- Collection. An administrative unit within the overall collection of the institution. There can be collections and sub-collections within collections.
- Store. A self-contained room in which collections are kept.
- Store location. An important concept, on which the survey design rests. The smallest identifiable grouping of objects within a store, e.g. a shelf, a box on a shelf, a group of objects on the floor, each drawer within a cabinet of drawers. If a shelf has some freestanding objects, and others contained in a box, then the freestanding objects would count as one store location, the box another.
- Object. The concept of objects-within-objects is a familiar problem in museum data definition: for example, is the object the tea set, or the individual cups and saucers? For condition audit purposes, the auditors decide what is most appropriate and record the rule they establish. Normally, an object made up of component parts is taken to be a single object.
- Object identification. The inventory or acquisition number. Though desirable, particularly for repeat surveying over time, for a collections condition audit objects do not need to have individual numbers.
- Descriptive of object. How much data are collected on this is optional, and may vary according to individual institutions' or collections' needs. It may include:

- Simple name
- Materials
- Manufacturing processes
- Type (e.g. photographic process)
  Data which might relate to, but do not describe, condition may optionally be included here: fragility (the object may be fragile but in perfectly good condition); completeness; working or not. These terms do not necessarily reflect deterioration.

Describing damage

The selection of existing survey forms which had been collected contained altogether 77 different terms to describe damage and deterioration, many of which were synonyms. They can be grouped within eight broad terms (Table 28.2):

- Major structural damage
- Chemical deterioration
- Minor structural damage
- Biological attack
- Surface damage
- Bad old repairs
- Disfigurement
- Accretions.

A survey which extended the framework described here defined the broad terms by listing the detailed ones they included. This survey also recorded the more detailed damage terms (relating to the condition of books) as sub-codes within the codes for the main headings (a Victoria and Albert Museum survey in 1991). For example, 'major structural damage' included: boards off; boards missing; spine off; spine missing; spine split; sewing broken; leaves detached; corners broken; boards severely misshapen; boards broken.

Describing condition

- Condition grade 1 GOOD   Object in the context of its collection is in good conservation condition, or is stable.
- Condition grade 2 FAIR   Fair condition, disfigured or damaged but stable, needs no immediate action.
- Condition grade 3 POOR   Poor condition, and/or restricted use, and/or probably unstable, action desirable.
- Condition grade 4 UNACCEPTABLE   Completely unacceptable condition, and/or severely weakened, and/or highly unstable and actively deteriorating, and/or affecting other objects: immediate action should be taken.

Table 28.2 The eight main terms under which types of damage can be grouped, and terms relating to some collections

	Structural damage		Surface damage	Disfigurement	Chemical/internal	Biological	Accretions	Bad old repair
	Major structural	Minor structural						
General	Separate pieces/part; Loose crack; Large tear likely to spread; Large holes; Major splits; Parts missing; Mechanical disorder	Crack; Small tear; Puncture; Small holes; Small splits; Obviously weak; Loose attachment; Bent; Warped; Creased; Distorted elements e.g. feathers	Flaking/lifted paint, etc. Peeling; Paint/surface looses; Bruised; Cupped; Delaminated; Crazed; Dented	Scratched; Stained; Abraded; Discoloured; Faded; Tarnished; Colours bled	Crumbling; Friable; Desiccated; Exudations; Grease; Salts	Insect attack; Moth; Woodworm; Foxed; Rodent damage; Mould; Mildew	Dirty; Encrusted; Surface salts; Deposits; Greasy	Adhesive; Misalignment; Staples; Sellotape; Patches
Furniture	Very loose joint; Separated attachment		Lifted veneer					
Paper	Very badly crumpled with split; Very badly creased with split; Very badly distorted/rolled	Cockled; Crumpled; Folded			Acid; Yellowed; Chemically changed edges; Matt burn; Redox spots; Metal impurity; Acid paper; Red rot			Tape; Sellotape
Books	Separated or nearly separated spine/cover							

Category						
Textiles, fibre	Split seam; Badly creased with split; Seriously crumpled; Crushed	Shrunken; Detached fibres		Deteriorated silk; Acid dyes		Clumsy stitching; Alterations
Pictures			Cupped paint; Losses; Flaking paint; Lifted paint	Blanched; Deteriorated canvas		
Ceramics/ glass		Chipped; Small crack		Salt damage; Crizzled	Encrustations	
Metals				Corroded; Rusted	Solder	

'Action' means something done to the object itself, rather than to its surroundings or environment.

There are several different aspects to 'condition', which have been used in different (or even in the same) surveys (Buck 1971; Walker and Bacon 1987; Keene 1991 and other survey reports):

- Insecurity (Buck 1971, and the V&A in early surveys): mechanical stresses, stability or vulnerability
- Disfigurement (Buck 1971, and the V&A): appearance of object
- Conservation priority (Horniman, Museum of London, British Museum, and others): how urgently is conservation needed?
- Condition rating (National Maritime, Public Records Office): e.g. good, fair, poor.

All the factors listed are valid aspects of 'condition'. They can be combined in the definitions of broad summarizing terms, as in Figure 28.1. The worse the condition of the object, the more terms descriptive of deterioration are likely to be applicable (Figure 28.2).

What conservators are really doing when they describe 'condition' is predicting the rate at which an object is likely to change, assuming that change in a museum object implies deterioration. The concept of 'stability', then, is central to the definition of 'condition'. Even when an object, although otherwise stable, is graded 'highly unstable' (or its equivalent) because of a detached fragment, which would be common practice, this is a prediction that the object will suffer serious change due to the fragment's permanent loss.

The condition of an object needs to be defined in the context of its particular collection. For example, a pot which is in separate sherds may be in GOOD condition as part of an archaeological archive, while the definition for an applied arts ceramic collection may place it in the UNACCEPTABLE category.

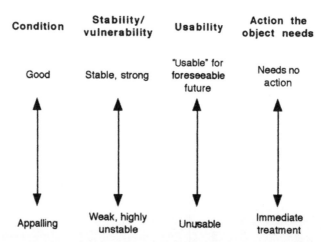

Figure 28.1 Aspects of the condition of an object

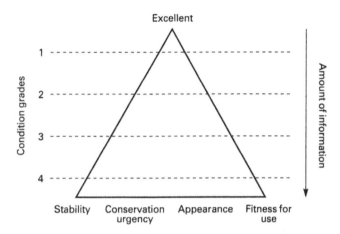

Figure 28.2 The amount of data needed to describe condition. The worse the condition of the object, the more description is needed

Data on damage will give information on why the object has been assigned its condition grade. For example, 'biological deterioration' combined with condition grade 4 implies pest infestation or active mould growth; grade 4 coupled with 'major physical damage' implies an insecure break or a detached part.

There is debate about the number of grades: between three and five. Four grades have been used in many institutions (British Museum, Horniman, Museum of London, National Museum of Wales). Allowing a fifth grade means that the majority of objects are assigned the middle, indeterminate grade, which does not give very useful information. Three grades do not allow sufficient discrimination between different grades of condition, and again have the disadvantage of an indeterminate grade.

Other possible data

Other useful data can be collected as part of the audit process. It would be simple to record the suitability of the object's store location. It is also easy to record what work is needed to render the condition of the object acceptable. If additional data are collected it is strongly advisable to design a restricted number of terms or categories, like those for damage or condition, so as to expedite the process of analysis.

The audit method

The basis of the sampling design arrived at is statistical method, by which we can learn what we want to know about the population (the whole collection) from statistics gathered about a sample (Rowntree 1981: 83). If the sample is selected randomly from the population, then it is possible to predict the accuracy of the estimate about the population, and also how confident we can be that the results from the audit can be applied to the whole collection (the confidence level).

There are several advantages in using a statistical sampling method. Audits take less time, which is important, because conservators are in short supply, and auditing itself does nothing directly to improve the condition of the collection. Fewer objects, examined more carefully, will give more reliable results than many objects examined only cursorily. If large quantities of data are collected, it is very difficult to make sense of them, whether they are analysed by hand or by computer.

Audit procedures and sampling

There are six distinct stages in an audit:

- Specify the objectives and scope of the audit, and decide on the time available.
- Undertake a pilot audit, to establish the variability of the collection and quantify the task.
- Analyse the pilot audit results, design the sampling procedure.
- Collect the data (conduct the audit itself).
- Analyse the data.
- Report the results.

Audit specification

If the results of the audit are to be adopted and used ('owned') by the institution generally, it is most important that both curators and conservators cooperate in as many stages as possible. Some obviously suitable tasks for cooperation are: to establish the objectives and scope of the audit, describe the nature of the collection, and note particular aspects of it which are of interest and which should be covered by the audit; to agree the administrative data which will be used in analysing the audit; to define the audit variables (what is 'an object' in the context of this collection? Does condition grade 4: UNACCEPTABLE need more precise definition?). The amount of time to be spent on the audit must be decided in advance; it is important to the statistical design.

Pilot audits

A pilot audit collects together the necessary information to design the sample and tests out the audit procedures. Necessary information will include information about the collection(s), information about how they are organized in store, quantifications of the size of the task (typically, how many store locations, and how many objects can be examined per day), and data on the statistical 'variability' of the collection (see below, Audit sampling design). It gives an opportunity to test out the means of data collection – whether paper forms or computer. It enables the data definitions to be tested in the context of the particular collection, and rules on their application to be agreed. For example, inexperienced auditors can find themselves to have set the criteria for condition grade 4: UNACCEPTABLE condition too low, so that they add 'even more urgent' classifications as the audit proceeds!

The pilot audit can be expected to take up to 20 per cent of the total time available for auditing (Kingsley and Payton 1994). It needs to be carefully thought out, so that all parts of the collection are covered evenly. The pilot audit procedure can be changed if necessary during its course (in the main audit, the procedure that has been designed should be rigidly adhered to unless it becomes clear that the design is seriously faulty).

Audit sampling design

The statistical method adopted is a two-stage systematic sampling procedure, with storage location as the first stage and individual objects the second. This allows samples to be designed to allow for different levels of between- and within-location variability. This is comparable to selecting every nth street, and within that street, every xth house to survey. The notation and formulae used are set out in Exhibit 9D (Keene 1996). Sampling design is discussed in detail in Keene and Orton (1992), and its application in practice in Kingsley and Payton (1994).

How many objects in the sample?

It seems paradoxical, but the primary determinant of sample size is not the size of the collection, but its variability (Rowntree 1981: 100; Cochran 1963). Thus, it is incorrect to assume that surveying a particular percentage of a collection will give results that can be extrapolated to the whole. The factors that determine sample size are:

The variability of the collection

'Variability' in audit terms means the number of objects per location, and the proportion of objects in the different grades of condition within different locations. The more variable the collection, the larger the sample required.

For example, if most store locations contain one badly damaged object and nine in good condition that collection is not very variable. If the number of objects per location varies from 1 to 1000 then the collection is variable. Variability must be established from a prior pilot survey. The results of the pilot survey will show how large a standard deviation (i.e. ±20 per cent) would result from the analysis; if it is too large, then the time allowed may have to be increased.

The confidence limits required and the standard deviation (range) in which the results are to be expressed, which are linked

Confidence level is expressed as a percentage, such as '95 per cent confidence level, applying to objects in condition grade 4'. It indicates the degree of confidence in calculating the condition of the whole collection from a sample, as in 'we can be 95 per cent certain that between 79 and 105 objects are in unacceptable condition'. Ninety-five per cent is a good level to choose.

The amount of time allocated to the audit

It is actually useful in designing an audit to allocate a specific amount of time for the process. Two person-months is probably enough, whatever the size of the collection, i.e. one month if two people are doing the inspection, as is good practice. The time allowance should include a person-week for a pilot survey and a person-week for analysing and writing up the results.

The statistical design of the audit

The statistical design (i.e. every fifth object from every ninth store location) is calculated by applying the formulae contained in Exhibit 9D (Keene 1996) to the pilot audit results. A computer program has been written to do this. The process is not very simple, however, and many audits thus have an informal design, i.e. one in ten objects. Informal audit designs are acceptable for small collections, but for those such as photography or libraries months of time could be wasted. Alternatively, most statistically designed audits turn out to use a sample of around 1000, as you will notice from opinion polls. The Library of Congress audit covered twenty million books in a sample of about 1000. The question here is, how should the 1000 be selected?

The objective of the sampling design can be expressed as:

> To design the most effective way of selecting a sample of objects to inspect, given that x objects can be examined in the time available (figure from the pilot survey), in order to calculate the proportion of objects in condition grade 4, to 95 per cent confidence limits. If there are too few objects in condition grade 4 condition, then condition grade 3 + condition grade 4 can be designated.

The aim is to achieve a balance between the sampling fractions f1 (the proportion of the locations sampled) and f2 (the proportion of objects sampled within each selected location) (Keene and Orton 1992). For example, for an audit of a social history collection every fourth location was sampled, and within those, every eighth object, both counts starting from a randomly selected first location or object (Exhibit 9A, Audit designs). Or, for a varied collection including both single large objects and groups of objects, object types were separately sampled (Kingsley and Payton 1994).

Whether the sample is statistically designed or informal, it is still very important to select objects at random. Only if they are, can statistics about the sample be used to calculate parameters for the collection. In an informal sample (say every tenth object) the first object must be selected randomly by drawing a ticket, etc., and subsequent objects must be chosen according to a predetermined systematic procedure. You can invent your own rules, but you must record them and stick to them.

Using an informal method with only one stage of sampling (e.g. every tenth object) has the advantage that it is very simple to extrapolate the results from the sample to the collection as a whole. Statistical techniques can still be used, if wished, to calculate the range and the confidence limit for the whole collection. The disadvantages are that considerably more objects may have been audited than necessary; scarce specialist time may not have been put to the best use; and unnecessary quantities of data may have to be analysed.

Data collection

There is a choice between recording audit data on paper or on computer. Paper records are permanent, accessible, and some analysis is easily done by hand (Figure 28.3 is a typical audit form). The disadvantage of paper is the bulk that quickly accumulates, and that statistical analysis beyond simple counts and percentages is in practice impossible.

Simple computer databases can provide an electronic form for entering audit records, which can then be listed and counted. Simple analyses such as percentages can be performed, using pre-designed report formats.

Data analysis and presentation

Data from audits can be analysed in several main ways.

Descriptive information

The data analysed here are the administrative information which has been collected. These variables can by analysed in as much detail as required. For example, photographic collections might be analysed by type of object: negative, print, etc., and by photographic process. These data would be held in an inventory of the collection, but if an inventory does not exist they will be invaluable.

Information on fragility, completeness, whether in working order, etc. can be analysed if the need for this has been anticipated in audit data design and data coding. Though not directly relevant to condition, this information is useful for collections care and management generally.

COLLECTIONS CONDITION AUDIT

Condition grades:
1: GOOD: Good conservation condition, stable
2: FAIR: Disfigured or damaged, no immediate action
3: POOR: Probably unstable, needs remedial work
4: UNACCEPTABLE: Actively deteriorating

Damage categories:
MAJor structural damage
MINor structural-cracked, bent, loose
SURFace flakes, crazing, lifting
DISFigurement - stains, scratches
CHEMical - acid paper, corrosion, rubber breakdown
BIOlogical - mould, insect, rodent
OLD - sub-standard repairs
ACCretions of dirt, grease, deposits

Survey code: 1995-C Initials: SK Date: 21.7.95
Collection: COSTUME
Sub-collection: ACCESSORIES
Store: BH-1-36
Location: SC3 S4

Inventory no.	Object name	Materials	MAJ	MIN	SURF	DISF	CHEM	BIO	OLD	ACC	COND	Remarks
			Tick								1-4	
1294-36	Hat	Straw, silk	✓								3	
A5437	Hat	silk		✓							1	
A21052	Hat	Wool						✓			4	Live moth
A5549	Hat	Wool						✓			4	"
1890-154	Gloves	Leather		✓	✓						1	
1995-55	Gloves	Wool									1	
		Totals for damage categories:	1	2	1			2			Cond:	1: 3; 2: ; 3: 1; 4: 2

Figure 28.3 An example of an audit form used to collect the data described here

- Analysis: Simple lists.
- Output: Lists of object types, stores, collections, etc. Because a sample only is collected, 'object type' has to be fairly broad; for instance, if 'object name' were to be analysed then lists would be too detailed to be meaningful, and many named objects would not be represented. Even so, 'object type' is a very quick way of producing an outline description of a collection.

Quantitative information

Sample audits are designed to enable quantitative information about whole 'populations' to be calculated from data about smaller samples. Quantitative information can be derived about the collections, including:

- Numbers of objects in collections, sub-collections, object types
- Numbers of objects in stores
- Numbers of objects in different condition grades (therefore needing or not needing conservation)
- Numbers of objects which have suffered different types of damage
- Numbers of objects needing mounting or other particular types of work
    and as a spin-off . . .
- Numbers of objects lacking a valid inventory number.

The results of this quantitative analysis can be combined with information on resources, i.e. work rates – numbers of objects conserved/mounted/cleaned, etc. in a year; materials, such as amount of mount board required to cut n mounts; prices of boxes, to quantify the resources needed to improve the condition of collections to some target state.

- Analysis: Counts of cases (object records) by different groups; statistics – standard deviation, maximum number, minimum number; cross-tabulations; application of the statistical formulae designed for audit analysis.
- Output: Quantified lists, tables, histograms, bar graphs. Information on resource requirements: price of required packaging, conservator/years to treat all objects in condition grade 4, etc. Examples of statistics as graphs are illustrated in Figure 28.4 (a) and (b).

Comparative information

Both numbers and proportions of objects analysed by different variables can be used to make comparisons of collections size, collections condition, etc. The proportion of objects grade 3 and grade 4 combined may be used as an index of condition. Comparing proportions of damage types may assist in understanding the causes of deterioration.

- Analysis: Cross-tabulations of object type (or other grouping: e.g. store) by condition grade, with percentages. Log-linear or contingency analysis to compare

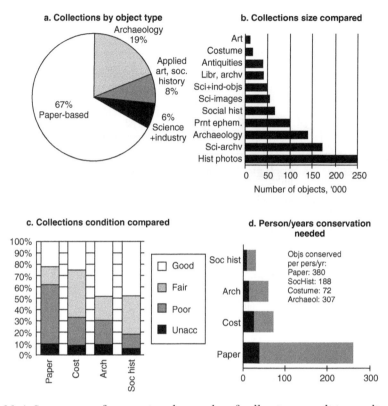

Figure 28.4 Some ways of presenting the results of collections condition audits

the condition of different object groupings. The chi-squared test of significance (if required). Percentages of objects with different types of damage.

- Output: Tables and figures. Percentage and other bar graphs; pie charts. See Figure 28.4, especially (c) and (d).

Correlational information

Information on how statistics relating to condition grade correlate with those for damage factors will undoubtedly be of interest. It can be expected that the relationship will be indicative of the causes of deterioration.

- Analysis: Scatter diagrams, correlation coefficient (if necessary).
- Output: Tables, but principally graphs.

Conclusions on audit data analysis

All this is very simple information, invaluable for collections care and management, and planning conservation. However, it is characteristic of collections information generally that it can be analysed in the same way at many different hierarchical levels (Figure 28.5). This means that many separate, though similar, audit analyses need to

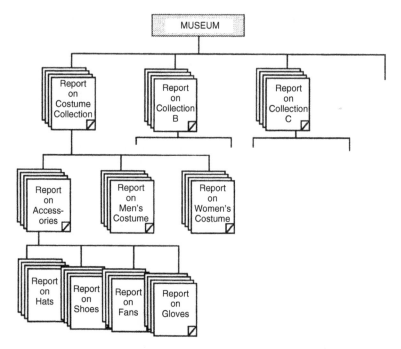

Figure 28.5 The hierarchical nature of museum collections data. Large or complex institutions will have more organizational tiers in their collections

be performed. These in turn result in piles of tables, diagrams, etc. It can be a daunting task to make full use of the information, to draw conclusions, and to quantify and plan work. It is also quite an undertaking to extract a general view. The complexity of actually making use of the information from audits is the main reason for urging that only really essential data be collected.

Reports of audits

The presentation of data and information from audits should follow the rules of good practice set out by Chapman (1986). The readership of the report should be considered. If it is a detailed report to a curator or within the conservation department it can be full, but if it is a high-level report to councillors or trustees it should be much briefer. Ask yourself, 'What do I expect to happen when the [trustees] have read this?', or, 'If I were a [trustee], what would I need to know so as to understand the significance of this report?' A collections condition audit report could potentially include a lot of information, but much of it can be brief. Some areas, particularly those relating to the causes of deterioration, would be explored in depth through a complementary preventive conservation survey. To avoid duplication they should only be touched on in a collections condition audit report. See also Table 28.1. Different collections often need separate, mini-reports of their own. The digestion and summarizing of many separate reports, even if they follow a common format, is (like really understanding the data) a considerable task.

Monitoring condition over time

If a new random sample of the collection were to be taken for each re-auditing exercise, few if any objects would be common to both audits. Any real change in the overall state of the collection might be masked by the variability introduced by the sampling procedures. The best way around this may be for subsequent audits to include a subset of the original sample in the new sample, probably about a third of the original. More detailed logging of data on the subset may be required in order to spot differences more easily. The subset would provide a benchmark against which the other parts of the audit can be measured. The subset itself would have to be randomly selected. There is some work based on this, and on using particular types of object as tell-tales on condition. This is especially relevant for mineral or fossil specimens, many of which become unstable outside a particular range of relative humidities (SPNHCC-CC Assessment Sub-Committee 1990).

Conclusions

A lot of time and effort has been put into surveys: time which could be spent on treating and caring for collections. In the past, very large amounts of data have been collected, and too little use has been made of them. Major reasons are that surveyors launch into form design and data collection – surveying itself – without evaluating sufficiently carefully what it is they want to discover, and without undertaking a trial, or pilot, survey to try out the process from start right through to analysis and report stage. Without an overview, information at individual object level assumes more importance to the surveyor than information about collections. Yet it is information at collections level that really enables us to manage their preservation.

References

Buck, R. D. (1971) 'What is condition in a work of art?', *Bulletin of the American Group-IIC* 12.

Cannon-Brookes, P. (1994) 'The "Delta Plan" for the preservation of cultural heritage in the Netherlands', *Museum Management and Curatorship* 12: 303–307.

Chapman, M. (1986) *Plain figures,* London: HMSO.

Cochran, G. W. G. (1963) *Sampling Techniques* (2nd edn), New York: Wiley.

Directorate-General for Cultural Affairs (1992) *Delta Plan for the Preservation of Cultural Heritage,* Fact Sheet C-ll-E 1992, Ministry of Welfare, Health and Cultural Affairs, P.O. Box 5406, 2280 HK Rijswijk, The Netherlands.

Getty Conservation Institute and National Institute for the Conservation of Cultural Property (1991) *The Conservation Assessment. A Tool for Planning, Implementing, and Fundraising,* Washington, DC: GCI.

Keene, S. (1991) 'Audits of care: collections condition surveys', in *Storage. Preprints of the RAI Conference,* London: UKIC.

Keene, S. (1996) *Managing Conservation in Museums,* Oxford: Butterworth-Heinemann.

Keene, S. and Orton, C. (1992) 'Measuring the condition of museum collections', in G. Locke and J. Moffett (eds) *CAA91: Computer Applications and Quantitative Methods in Archaeology,* Oxford: British Archaeological Reports.

Kenyon, J. (1992) *Collecting for the 21st Century. A Survey of Industrial and Social History Collections in the Museums of Yorkshire and Humberside*, Leeds: Yorkshire and Humberside Museums Service.

Kingsley, H. and Payton, R. (1994) 'Condition surveying of large varied stored collections', *Conservation News* 54 (July): 8–10.

Rowntree, D. (1981) *Statistics without Tears*, Harmondsworth: Penguin Books.

SPNHCC-CC Assessment Sub-Committee (1990) 'Defining standard procedures for assessing the condition of a fluid-preserved collection', in *Preprints of the 9th ICOM-CC, Triennial Meeting, Dresden*, Marina del Ray, CA: ICOM-CC, GCI.

Storer, J. D. (1989) *The Conservation of Industrial Collections*, London: Conservation Unit/ The Science Museum.

Walker, K. and Bacon, L. (1987) 'A condition survey of specimens in the Horniman Museum: a progress report', in *Recent Advances in the Conservation and Analysis of Artifacts,* London: Summer Schools Press.

Wiederkehr, R. R. V. (1984) *The Design and Analysis of a Sample Survey of the Condition of Books in the Library of Congress, Library of Congress Report*, Washington DC: Library of Congress (unpublished, but whence the introduction on the methodology is obtainable).

Chapter 29

Condition Surveying of Large Varied Stored Collections

Helen Kingsley and Robert Payton

T HE APPLIED ARTS SECTION of the conservation department at the Museum of London carried out a condition survey of applied arts, social and working history items (excluding paper and textiles) in 1992 of one of the Museum's largest outstores at the docklands in London. Instigated by Suzanne Keene, the then Head of Conservation, several surveys have been carried out over the last five years in the Museum of London and have been developed into a sophisticated tool for conservation management purposes, giving such information as: the state of the collections at a point in time; estimates of the resources needed to improve the overall state of the collections to a certain level; and to which parts of the collection conservation resources need to be directed. All of these can be assessed using the survey results as a solid framework of information.[1,2]

Problems in assessing varied collections

The survey of the Docklands collection, described here, is a good example of what can be achieved using a well planned and executed condition survey strategy for assessing large and varied collections. These collections, because they were port and dock-related, as well as containing working history items, were extremely mixed – from samples of narwhal tusk to steam engines; from large groups of identical objects, e.g. tools, to large single items, e.g. a boat. Because collected groups of objects, e.g. workshop materials, were kept together the mixtures of objects within these groups was extremely varied. The surveying strategy possibilities were made that much more complex by the fact that some of the larger objects were dismantled into

Source: *Conservation News* 54: 8–10. This is an article whose final and definitive form has been published in *Conservation News*, Volume 54 © 1994 Institute of Conservation.

parts, whilst others were still intact but were complex composite objects made from several materials, often in a variety of conditions. To summarise, the problems presented by the collection were: Variety of types of objects – Mixture of grouping and location of the objects – Complex nature of many of the objects. Conventional surveying techniques, of sampling X amount of objects in one in every Y locations would have given fairly meaningless and inaccurate results here because of the difficulty of assigning locations and, secondly, whole important sub-groups of these varied collections could have been missed out by a strict locational sampling strategy (Figure 29.1). Such surveying techniques, however, have been found to be valid for other surveys carried out in the Museum of London, where the storage systems and collections themselves are usually more regular and uniform. It was therefore decided to adopt a more pragmatic approach, tailoring the survey strategy to the need of the Docklands collection.

Developing a strategy for a difficult condition survey

The location of the collections

The Docklands and Working History collections, numbering up to 80,000 items, were stored in and around two warehouses, W and K annexe, and at the Port of London Authority (PLA) Library. Objects were housed on three floors of Warehouse W: half the ground floor area exhibited individual workshop displays, while the remaining area and the first and second floors were crowded with objects. The methods of storage were varied, e.g. boxes, containers, tea-chests, etc., also many were placed loosely on shelves and on the floor, leaning against or on top of each other, often with mixtures of storage methods within one location. The approximate storage area was 3,840 m². Warehouse K annexe was a very large storage facility. As with W, many objects were crowded together in boxes, containers or stacked loosely (Figure 29.1). The collection stored at K was mostly machinery, whole or in parts. The approximate

Figure 29.1 A large store, K warehouse, in the London Docklands. A strict location-based survey would not be suitable for such a mixed store

storage area was $3,250 \text{ m}^2$. The PLA Library comprised of three rooms housing most of the paper collection and objects, including signs and frames, which were stored leaning up against each other, stacked on the floor or on bay shelving.

The pilot survey

A pilot survey is used in condition surveying to assess the type, storage and approximate numbers of objects contained in the collection. It is also used to help form, or check, a condition sampling design enabling the survey to be completed in the time available and within the resources allocated to the project. For this particular survey the project was allocated 9 weeks in which a pilot survey, the main survey and inputting of the results onto a computer disk had to be accomplished. Initially it was decided to subdivide the main survey into four separate ones, due to the widely different facilities and environments existing in the two warehouses, the objects outside and the library. A method of defining 'locations' proved particularly difficult because of the variety of storage techniques and grouping of objects. A method was eventually devised and tested in the pilot survey, the results proving successful: a ground plan of the storage areas in the W and K annexe stores was drawn up; each floor was then subdivided into 16 equal areas using the structural floor pillars as guides. Each of these areas was given a code number for future reference. Within each area, storage groups were recorded and allocated a further number defining bays of shelves, shelf within bays, drawers within cabinet or cupboard, boxes, containers and loose objects grouped together on the floor or other surfaces. To describe uniformly the 3-dimensional array of these objects, each location was systematically counted from left to right and from top to bottom (Figure 29.2). All the 34 objects stored outside the warehouses were surveyed. The PLA Library was divided into 3 units denoting each of the 3 rooms. The storage locations were recorded and numbered by rows and/or bays and shelves within the bays. To avoid the problems previously mentioned with strict locational surveys and to ensure that the survey covered a representative sample

Figure 29.2 Trolleys in the Docklands store. An example of repeated single units of a sub-collection

of objects, the collection was divided into sub-collection categories, e.g. vehicles, tools, machine attachments, etc. The objects in Warehouse W were grouped into 24 sub-collections; Warehouse K into 12; outside objects into 3 and those at the PLA Library into 8. These sub-collections where they occurred in the stores were noted on the plans. Having defined locations and the groupings of types of objects to be surveyed, a choice of sampling design had to be made, given that not all of the collections could be feasibly surveyed. But one problem in condition surveying is that the larger the amount of variables within the collection, for example of types of objects and conditions, then the greater the sample size has to be. However, in this survey this problem was solved by sampling each of the sub-collections separately, thereby reducing the variables encountered with sampling all the sub-collections mixed together. As a result it also meant that the sample size could be reduced. A pilot survey was carried out on six sub-collection locations where the number of objects exceeded 30. Here a 20% and a 10% sample were tested on the same groups. The results from these were so similar that this suggested that the less time-consuming 10% survey sample could be used in the main survey. The only minor discrepancy was noted with the results from surveying composite objects; however, these were close enough to the 10% sample results for this lower percentage to be chosen.

The sample strategy eventually devised for the collections was as follows:

- Single units, i.e. objects of an individual type, e.g. vehicles: a survey was taken of all the objects, unless greater than 20 existed of any one type, in which case a 10% sample was surveyed. Of these a random number was pre-selected, e.g. every nth (1–10), for the choice of object location (Figure 29.3).

Figure 29.3 A variety of sub-collections stored in the same location of shelving units

- Collective units, i.e. bulk objects under the same category heading stored together in various locations, e.g. boxes, containers or groups of machine attachments: this took on a two-stage sampling design. First one in five (20%) storage locations were chosen, then within that location a 10% sample of the objects were surveyed. As above, a random number was pre-selected for choice of location and sample. Where there were only 1–5 sample objects in the chosen location these were disregarded as being statistically insignificant; in these instances the next nth location was used. Where there were less than 20 storage locations all were surveyed. Shelves, boxes and groups of completely mixed material, miscellaneous objects and one-off objects within the collections were not surveyed.

The main condition survey

The results from the pilot survey, when processed, indicated that the survey could be carried out within the allocated resources. Because of the safety aspects of working in out-stores and because of the difficulty of getting to the objects, it was necessary to have two people working together, one selecting and giving a verbal condition report on an object, the other specifying locations and recording the condition. The conditions of sampled objects were recorded on a form developed at the Museum of London, which asks for identification number; simple name; materials involved; damage categories; condition grade and comments. Also on each form the collection category (sub-group); exact location, using the prepared storage coordinates; and storage type were noted. The four condition grades were: 1 = Good, 2 = Fair, 3 = Poor, 4 = Unacceptable. If there was doubt as to which category the condition of the object fitted into, then, between the choice of two condition category numbers, the higher number was chosen, equating to a slightly worse condition since the objects, without conservation, cannot improve in condition in storage of their own accord. The form was designed to incorporate all information needed for the 'Microsoft Works' computer program. The overall time of the survey could have been reduced if the condition records had been entered directly onto the computer. However, this was not possible in this survey because of the immense areas to be covered when surveying each sub-collection and, more importantly, the absence of electrical sockets for attaching leads to the computer (the battery life of the computer would not have been sufficient). Practical problems encountered during the survey included the inaccessibility of some of the objects – a problem arising with all condition surveys of tightly packed collections. In these cases the next nth sample had to be taken. Also. complex composite objects were difficult to assess where each part was in a different condition. It was decided that rather than choosing a condition grade that equated to the part in the worse condition (analogous to the 'weakest link'), a more objective assessment equivalent to the overall state of the object be chosen. However, remarks about deteriorated parts were noted in the comments section of the survey form. The inputting of the results, including familiarisation with the software program, was quite time consuming, taking almost a fifth of the total survey time. However, once a routine was set up between 80–150 condition forms could be input in a day. The 'Microsoft Works' program that was used offered five report facilities:

- Statistics by store location;
- Object condition and counts by store location;
- Table of condition grades by damage types;
- List of objects as input;
- Statistics by sub-location.

The analysis of survey results using a computer is obviously quicker and can be better comprehended than by using the paper records.

Adjustment of the results

The sampling strategy, as carried out, gave undue emphasis to the results recorded from single objects compared to those of groups of objects, where in a 10% survey sample only results from one in ten were recorded. The situation became even more unbalanced when the single object's results were compared to those from a 10% sample of one in five locations, used for the bulk collections of objects. To give a better idea of the state of the whole of the collection, the results from the bulk collections had to be adjusted (weighted). After discussion with Dr Clive Orton of the Institute of Archaeology London, the following simple method of adjustment was formulated: for the 10% sampled results, these were multiplied by a factor of 10 to give a 1:1 relationship between the results and the number of objects. For the 10% samples of one in five locations, the results were only multiplied by a factor of five. A multiplication factor of fifty would have given the correct 1:1 relationship between results and objects, but this would have given undue prominence to, and tilted the emphasis of the overall results of the survey towards the bulk items. It was interesting to note that the adjustment of the results gave only a minor shift in emphasis of the final figures, with adjustments of only 5–6% average noted.

Interpretation and presentation of the results

The interpretation of survey results requires much skill. A fixed idea of what the information is going to be used for and the level of detail that is needed in the final report are critical when viewing the results. It is quite easy to get bogged down with thousands of figures and lose track of what is the ultimate aim of the survey. Computer-generated reports as listed above showing the results in different ways are invaluable in sifting through the mass of information. If, as in the case of this survey, the results were being read by mostly non-conservators, then they needed to be edited down to concise packets of information, with a summary to emphasise the salient points, i.e. the overall state of the collections and what conclusions could be drawn to improve the collection's condition. The use of pie and bar charts has been found to be particularly effective in getting over large amounts of the information in an easily readable form. Information from an earlier set of surveys of the state of the Museum of London's stores was combined with the collections condition survey results to give clear indications as to why the collections were in their present state and what was needed to improve the storage environment and the condition of the collections. This has been found to be more informative than reporting on the collection's condition in isolation. Estimates of time needed to improve the collections up to a certain standard could be carried out in the future by extrapolating the time taken to conserve samples of the relevant sub-groups – though as with the surveys themselves, the results from such estimates are indications only and cannot be used to give absolute figures.

Survey logistics

The following is a break-down of how much time the parts of the survey took to complete:

Activity	Days	People
Pilot survey/sample strategy	12	2
Analysing results	3	1
Undertaking condition survey:		
Warehouse W	11	2
Warehouse K	2.5	2
Outside	0.5	2
PLA Library	1	2
Inputting computer data and generating reports	14	1
Adjusting results	1	1
Analysis and writing the final report	3	1
Total	75 person days	

Conclusions

The survey technique described above shows that it is possible to rationalise even the most complex of collections to give meaningful and useful results. Not every museum can afford to, or even want to store their collections in strictly ordered locations. By adapting the existing condition survey technique from a location-based to a collections-based one, it is possible to survey all parts, or sub-groups, of the collection in a thorough way. The results can then be used, with a good degree of confidence, to indicate the state of the collections and, with curatorial input, to prioritise future collections care work.

References

1   Keene, S. (1990) *Assessing Collections Condition: Sampling and Surveying*, Museum of London, Conservation Department Research Report.
2   Keene, S. (1991) *Collections Condition Surveys* (project funded by the Office of Arts and Libraries), Museum of London, Conservation Department Research Report.

Chapter 30

A Methodology of Preventive Conservation for a Large, Expanding and Mixed Archaeological Collection

Diane Dollery

Introduction

IN 1990, THE NATIONAL MUSEUM OF WALES began to survey its collections, in response to widely expressed concern, both internal and external (Committee of Public Accounts 1989), that in the past insufficient resources had been allocated to their care and that, as a consequence, parts were at risk of being lost. Accordingly, the Museum has collected an immense quantity of data on the state of its collections. However, there is little long-term benefit in having this information unless it is utilized to improve collections management.

This paper examines and illustrates in a case study how the information obtained has been used in the Department of Archaeology and Numismatics to establish a realistic rolling programme of conservation and management for the reserve collections. The convergence of a number of factors has ensured that the emphasis of this programme is on preventive measures, the aim being to stabilize and/or improve the condition of as many objects as possible with the limited time and money available. The paper is in four parts. The first considers how the data were collected and interpreted; the second considers the concept of conservation in this context; the third is concerned with the relationship between these two, demonstrated in a case study. Fourth, some attention is given to the role of documentation in preventive conservation.

The survey

The aim of the survey was to gather information about the condition of the collections to facilitate sound management of their conservation by the establishment of prioritized work programmes.

Source: A. Roy and P. Smith (eds), *Preventive Conservation: Practice, Theory and Research, IIC Ottawa Congress 12–16 September 1994*, Ottawa: IIC, 1994, pp. 69–72.

Collection of data

The conservation staff in the Department of Archaeology and Numismatics undertook a sampled condition survey during 1991. A cluster sampling method (Keene 1991) was adopted, using storage locations as primary units. The sample was designed on a rule-of-thumb basis to consider 25% of the collection. However, because of the repetitive nature of the material within the collection, the time required to undertake the survey, and the boredom factor (Keene 1991), this was later reduced to 5%. For each item, nine different factors were assessed and scored from 1 to 5 (Figure 30.1).

In numerical terms, the surveyors looked at some 34,000 items; bags of pot sherds, flints and nails were taken as one item. The major problems were found to be with those materials which are inherently unstable: metalwork, especially iron, and bone, notably from Pleistocene deposits (generally sub-fossil). By considering only the data relating to conservation urgency, 0.03% of material surveyed required immediate treatment for survival and a further 10% required treatment in the near future. Although the percentage of material requiring attention was relatively small, the implications in terms of resources were significant. It was calculated that, allowing two days per item, these 4,500 items would take approximately 40 conservator-years to conserve, that is, to stabilize, assuming current storage conditions were maintained. It should be noted that the survey did not include any numismatic material, anything on display, or any non-accessioned material from excavations.

Interpretation and discussion

The basic aim of the survey was to assess the condition of the collection to enable it to be managed and conserved more effectively. It is therefore questionable whether some of the factors that were assessed were appropriate to (a) the context of the survey and (b) the context of the collections. For example, although damage and disfigurement may be pertinent in the context of a fine art collection, it is doubtful whether their assessment has any true meaning for an archaeological collection, where most items have been damaged or disfigured by burial. The inclusion of such factors resulted in the accumulation of a great deal of extraneous data which was later ignored. This is not only expensive in terms of collection time, but also disheartening for the surveyors, who see their efforts being discarded.

The three most important factors in relation to the aims of the survey are found in the last three columns of the Condition Survey form (Figure 30.1). The storage conditions of a collection have a direct bearing on its conservation requirements. Appropriate packing is perhaps the most effective way of preventing deterioration. Rationalization of the data at this stage was further impeded by a lack of curatorial information. The curatorial assessment box was left blank in many cases, or filled in arbitrarily; this may well have been a conscious decision on the part of the surveyors but, as will be demonstrated later, it is crucial in translating the survey into a work programme. It would, perhaps, have been better to leave it out at this stage, to prevent any misinterpretation. With the benefit of hindsight, it might also have been useful to consider whether items had been treated before. Assessing the efficacy of

National Museum of Wales

Condition Survey

Dept										
Date										
Location										
Sublocation										

Identity No.	Description	Completeness	Integrity	General Condition	Stability	Damage	Disfigurement	Cons urgency	Storage Conditions	Curatorial assessment

Figure 30.1 Survey form used in the Department of Archaeology and Numismatics, National Museum of Wales

previous treatments is important in deciding the best way to proceed should deterioration occur again.

Conclusion

The survey amassed a large amount of data, most of which has been ignored subsequently as it is considered to be of no relevance either to the aims of the survey or in the context of the collection. In order to utilize the information to generate a work programme, a secondary survey considering curatorial assessments and conservation history must be superimposed on the existing body of data.

Conservation in context

Conservation is the process by which the true nature of an object is preserved, including evidence of its origins, construction and use (UKIC 1983). There is a great desire among conservators to conserve everything, regardless of the logic of doing so. The level and type of conservation work required depend on a number of factors, the most basic of which is: why is this object being conserved? Are we merely attempting to maintain it in its current state, or should we be trying to enhance it, either aesthetically or by our understanding of it?

Conservation can be both active and passive. All 'active' conservation treatments interfere to a greater or lesser extent with the chemistry and equilibrium of an object; in the long term this can further compromise its integrity. For example, by cleaning an iron object with air-abrasion to enhance its appearance or expose surface detail, one can remove naturally protective corrosion crusts with which the object has reached equilibrium. Lacquering the surface may afford some protection, but will complicate the situation should corrosion occur subsequently. Moreover, the presence of lacquers or consolidants may in fact mask the true condition.

Such an approach may be initially appropriate for artifacts which can be considered aesthetically pleasing. But for the bulk of the collection, which can be perceived as an educational resource, such an approach probably represents a misdirection of conservation resources; 'untreated objects may constitute a better source of archaeological evidence than treated ones' (Keene 1990). In many situations, the object can be best conserved by non-interventionist preventive measures such as improving documentation, handling procedures and storage conditions. Here, the artifact is considered in relation to the 'big picture' – the environment within which the collection is housed. Although improving the storage/display environment may require an initially large financial outlay, this should be justified by the long-term benefits as fewer objects will deteriorate. The most effective use of resources to maintain condition is by preventing deterioration (Keene 1990). Conservation of individual artifacts is an expensive and stressful business.

For some artifacts – those that are rare within either the broad archaeological or the collection context – a combination of active and preventive measures will probably be required.

The case study

Introduction

Using the available data an attempt was made to establish a prioritized work programme by considering material type and then further subdividing into units by site.
This clearly demonstrated where conservation efforts should be targeted, but it created a daunting workload. Given that the laboratory staff must devote approximately
30% of their time to current excavations, it would be some time before any impact
was made on the reserves. Further rationalization therefore became imperative, if the
survey was to be used as a basis for generating a work programme and to avoid the
misdirection of resources.

As mentioned earlier, curatorial input had so far been limited. It soon became
clear from discussions that curatorial assessments had a fundamental impact on the
interpretation of the data. Several collections of material were immediately removed
from the list; however, none was added, which suggested that the survey had covered
the collection satisfactorily.

Selecting the case study

The ironwork from Prysg Field was chosen for the case study. This Roman material
represents approximately 20% of the total ironwork collection stored at the Roman
Legionary Museum, Caerleon. It is a large enough unit to produce useful results
in terms of estimates for the rest of the collection. It displays a range of problems
expected to be encountered in the rest of the collection: poor condition, old conservation treatments, poor storage, and lack of documentation.

The timetable

After initial discussions and cursory examination, the following timetable was established for the case study:

- Curatorial assessment   by mid November 1992
- Conservation assessment   by end November 1992
- Conservation treatment   by end February 1993
- Repackaging and storage   by end March 1993.

The timetable was seen as important in giving overall shape and direction to the
project.

The assessments

Curatorial and conservation staff were independently asked to address specific issues
relating to (a) collection status and (b) conservation type. The information obtained
in this way was then superimposed on the existing database to produce a viable
programme.

Curatorial input

Having identified in general terms an area of the collection requiring attention, it was now necessary to look at the material in closer detail, from both a curatorial and a conservation point of view. Initially, this involved producing a conservation assessment, identifying (a) those objects which could be conserved and (b) those that had deteriorated to a point where conservation might not be cost-effective, for example, a bag containing numerous small flakes of corroded iron with no obvious 'core'. Those objects which could not immediately be identified were X-rayed. The curatorial staff were then asked to add their assessments. It was found, however, that conservation information clouded an objective approach and objects were perceived to be of greater importance if they were known to be conservable.

Therefore, the strategy was altered. A form was compiled at curatorial level (Figure 30.2) to assess the importance of an object on curatorial grounds alone. High-priority items are those which are published, or of national or local rarity. Low-priority items are those which form the basis of the study collection, for example, good examples of common items. Those of negligible importance are bags of iron nails, pot sherds, cremated bone and so on. A column was included to indicate whether the item needed to be X-rayed to assist in establishing curatorial importance.

Conservation input

Once curatorial assessment had been completed, a further conservation assessment was carried out (Figure 30.3) in which all objects with a curatorial score of 1 or 2 were examined individually. As different levels of treatment have different implications in terms of resources, this assessment was based on the need for conservation and the type of conservation required. Very few objects fell into the categories 'object is stable' and 'no treatment required'. An extra column was included to note whether objects had been treated in the past. All curatorial high-priority objects with a

Curatorial Assessment Form for Ironwork				
X-ray scores: 1 – essential for assessment; 2 – desirable before discard; 3 – not necessary for assessment.				
Curatorial assessment scores: 1 – high priority (published items, etc.); 2 – low priority; 3 – negligible importance; ? – assessment awaits X-ray.				
Acc. no.; Box no.	Item no.	Description & publication details	X-ray? 1–3	Curatorial

Figure 30.2 Curatorial assessment form devised to prioritize items from individual sites

Conservation Assessment						
Conservation need scores: 1 – treatment essential for object survival; 2 – desirable but not essential; 3 – object is stable.						
Treatment: 1 – active treatment required (e.g. air abrading, consolidation); 2 – minimum passive conservation for stability (e.g. repacking); 3 – no treatment required; Previously treated ? – has it been conserved in the past.						
Acc. no.; Box no.	Item no. (bag no.)	Description	Curatorial assessment	Cons. need 1–3	Cons. treat. 1–3	Previously treated?

Figure 30.3 Conservation assessment form on which curatorial and conservation requirements are combined to produce a work programme

conservation need of 1 or 2 and in treatment category 1 were brought to the conservation laboratory for radiography and treatment. They were then subdivided into those that had been treated before and those which were in an 'as excavated' state.

At each stage of the process there was discussion between conservation and curator.

Conservation treatment

Objects previously treated

It had been noted in the original survey that a large number of artifacts from this and similar collections had been heavily lacquered. Some of these objects were very bulbous, and concern had been expressed that the large volume was due to corrosion in depth. It was decided to investigate these pieces to discover whether this was indeed the case, because removing the lacquer had serious implications in terms of time and possible further damage to the objects.

Two methods of removal were utilized: (a) immersion in a bath of industrial methylated spirits (IMS), this having been established by empirical testing as an appropriate solvent, and (b) mechanical cleaning using air-abrasion. In both cases, the lacquer was successfully removed, revealing that:

- the bulbous appearance of the objects was due to the fact that burial corrosion had never been fully removed;
- in the majority of cases, the lacquer was in fact holding the objects together.

It was interesting to note that all the lacquered items were clearly identifiable artifacts, for example spears. This probably explains why they were only partially cleaned. The objects did not appear to be deteriorating any more than those which were totally untreated. The problem appeared to be one of aesthetics. It was decided not to remove the lacquer mechanically, because improving the aesthetic quality of the artifacts fell outside the scope of this project.

Untreated objects

Minimum conservation was carried out to preserve the material. The bulk of the material was cleaned mechanically to remove active corrosion, using either air-abrasion or glass bristle brush. Fragmentary objects were only reassembled if necessary for the stability of the item. Several pieces were consolidated with epoxy resin to ensure structural integrity. The material was then divided into three groups. The first was simply repackaged; the second was lacquered, using Paraloid B-72 in propanone, and repackaged; and the third was washed in the Soxhlet, lacquered and repackaged. A control group of material in each category was placed on a shelf in the laboratory under ambient conditions to compare the efficacy of these approaches. After 10 weeks, none of the items had corroded. This raises the question of whether washing the material is of any benefit. Also, is lacquering necessary if the material is rarely handled? If an object is lacquered and then deteriorates further, the removal and replacement of the lacquer are potentially more damaging than if the object had never been lacquered. Obviously there is an advantage in lacquering if the object is to be handled regularly.

Results

Of 299 iron objects from Prysg Field, 58 were given high curatorial priority. Of these, 20 urgently required active conservation, for 15 it was desirable that they should be treated actively, and 23 required minimum passive conservation for stability, that is, suitable packaging and storage. This compares with 118 objects prioritized for treatment based on the 1991 condition survey.

Time spent on this case study was as follows:

- Planning · 2 people · 0.25 day
- Curatorial assessment · 2 people · 0.75 day
- Conservation assessment · 1 person · 0.50 day
- Conservation · 2 people · 7.50 days
- Packaging and storage · 1 person · 1.00 day

Total: 18.5 person days

This compares with 236 days on a basis of two days per object, proposed in the 1992 preliminary work programme devised on the basis of conservation need.

Collections management

It became apparent that a great deal of deterioration was due to poor packing. Objects were originally packed in plastic bags, which had been placed in plastic boxes. The plastic bags offered no protection against abrasive damage, especially when items were removed. Indicating silica gel was found in most of the boxes. This was mainly pink, indicating high humidity and a breakdown or lack of a micro-environmental monitoring and maintenance programme.

A general guide to the packaging of iron objects was produced and circulated to curatorial staff. As a further guide, a selection of objects was returned to the storage area packed in the appropriate fashion. A monitoring programme for silica gel was established, to ensure regeneration and replacement on a continuous basis. Repackaging was included as a conservation treatment method (minimum passive conservation for stability) but this need not be, and indeed is not, carried out by conservation staff.

The environmental conditions within the storage area were assessed and recommendations were made (MGC 1992). It was discovered that the relative humidity was higher than desirable for a storage area containing mainly metals, although the air-handling system was operating within its design tolerances. Poor maintenance was partly to blame and this has now been rectified.

Documentation

Certain types of documentation have a key role to play in preventive conservation. The initial survey amasses a body of data against which future changes can be measured. The project generates information about the collection which can be added to the existing database. It also provides further documentation to improve the use and interpretation of the collection. For example, X-rays add to the corpus of information about collections of metal objects and are a valuable study tool. The student or researcher, presented with a suitably packaged object and an X-radiograph, can extract much information without handling the artifact. The staff become more familiar with the collections and their value as an educational resource.

Obviously, conservation records are also generated. How detailed these should be is open to debate. As this paper has shown, collected and stored information is only of value if it can be used. Traditional conservation records can be very detailed but almost impossible to interpret: it is often much quicker to employ empirical tests to find solvents for an adhesive than to plough through records to discover what was originally used. If conservation information is included in databases for future reference, records should be 'user-friendly'. As such records are an important element of the collections database, the existence of conservation documentation should be included as a criterion in future surveys.

Conclusion

This exercise has demonstrated the importance of communication between conservators and curators in ensuring effective management of collections. The methodology devised was effective in reducing the number of objects which required interventive conservation; it also highlighted aspects of collections management that needed to be considered. The separation of conservation and curatorial assessments minimized confusion between what could be conserved and what needed conserving.

The incorporation of more documentary sources in the collections database decreases the need to handle artifacts directly in order to gather information; this obviously helps to preserve them. Finally, assessing the collection into prioritized categories was a useful curatorial exercise, and could be used to repackage material according to its importance. This would aid in the retrieval of material from the storage areas in the event of a disaster.

[. . .]

References

Committee of Public Accounts (1989) *Management of the Collections of the English National Museums and Galleries. First Report. House of Commons: Session 1988–89*, London: HMSO.

Keene, S. (1990) 'Management information for conservation' in *Preprints of the 9th ICOM-CC, Triennial Meeting, Dresden*, Marina del Ray, CA: ICOM-CC, GCI.

Keene, S. (1991) 'Audits of care: a framework for collections conditions surveys', in *Storage*, London: United Kingdom Institute for Conservation, 6–16.

MGC (Museums and Galleries Commission) (1992) *Standards in the Museum Care of Archaeological Collections*, London: MGC.

UKIC (United Kingdom Institute for Conservation) (1983) *Guidance for Conservation Practice*, London: United Kingdom Institute for Conservation.

Introduction to Part Three – Section Two

Chris Caple

Ethical considerations

THOUGH IT MAY BE IMAGINED that preventive conservation is completely benign
to objects, avoiding the damaging effects of light by storing them in the dark or
preventing insects from damaging them by freezing, this is not always the case. As
Miriam Clavir (1994) shows, simply preventing damage to the physical form of the
object fails to take into account the non-physical (intangible) aspects of the object.
In cultures where the object is believed to have personal or human traits, freezing the
object, even storing it with other inappropriate objects or allowing it to be handled
by inappropriate people may be considered to have harmed the spiritual or cultural
aspects of the object's identity, and thus its conceptual integrity.

Clavir's Chapter 31 reminds those undertaking preventive conservation of the
wider context of museum developments in the 1990s, especially the increasing awareness of the social context of collections. The need for museums to engage with the
public and to be aware of the conceptual integrity (intangible social and cultural
attributes) of objects is emphasised. The implications of a holistic approach to artefacts that includes dealing with the intangible social and cultural attributes of Native
American artefacts is explored. The steps that the Museum of New Mexico has taken
to develop storage facilities which preserve the conceptual integrity of the object,
even enabling ceremonies such as ritual feeding of objects to take place safely, are
described.

The increasing awareness of the intangible aspects of cultural heritage has continued and is reflected in the adoption of the UNESCO Convention for the Safeguarding
of the Intangible Cultural Heritage in 2003, the implications of which were discussed
in *Museum International* 56, 1–2 (May 2004). This awareness has also been reflected

by conservators in their development of ethical policies, such as the Burra Charter (rev. 1999) (Jokilehto 2009). However, the practical difficulties of knowing what the cultural significance is of many of the objects in our museum collections remains a considerable problem (Clavir 2009).

Different museums have been more or less active in tackling this issue. The National Museum of the American Indian (NMAI) has a mandate to 'consult, collaborate and cooperate with Native American peoples'. This applies as much to preventive conservation work as to any other aspect of the museum's activities. In the same way that modern health and safety legislation modifies what activities and materials can be used in a conservation laboratory, so the NMAI curators and conservators modify what preventive conservation work is done to objects to ensure that it accords with the beliefs of the tribes to whom the objects are ascribed. As Drumheller and Kaminitz (1994) describe in Chapter 32, this means identifying objects over which there are rules or taboos, identifying accurately what those rules and taboos are, then establishing what should or should not be done to the objects and, finally, working out how this can be reconciled with modern museum practice.

Clavir's 'conceptual integrity' does not only apply to ethnographic objects, but includes all artefacts, especially those that have an artistic, religious or working role. Child (2006) (Chapter 33) explores how objects in the Big Pit Museum, and even the mine itself, not only exist as physical examples of a particular type of tool or engine, but together form part of the complete picture/experience of a twentieth-century coal mine. They are integral parts of a working mine and form the context for every object in the museum. Removed from their present positions (context) or having their appearance altered (to better preserve them), they would lose their role as part of that picture and degrade the larger picture/experience and context. Thus, they need to stay in their present position and in their present (less than ideal) conditions or lose part of their conceptual integrity. They are, however, also functioning parts of a working coal mine governed by mining regulations designed to ensure safe working underground. In order to meet current mining regulations this machinery will need to be maintained, modified and, in some instances, replaced. Seeking to preserve such objects in their present state must be measured against these other requirements. Wherever possible, compromises are sought, but if coal mining is to be fully appreciated and understood, that means going underground in a realistic context, and it means seeing all the objects together in working condition, as they would have been in the past, degraded but, where required, amended to maintain their functional condition. Preventive conservation must be reconciled with visitor safety and the quality of context and conceptual integrity of the mine site as a whole. In similar museums, such as Beamish in Northern England, the museum often seeks to possess a minimum of two examples of each object, one to use as a working object and one to be stored for research and evidential purposes.

As with ethnographic objects (McGhee 1994), the materials of which a work of art is made can be important for their cultural or social meaning. However, those materials, as in the case of ice sculptures, may be impermanent. This impermanence may be part of their meaning, though this will depend both on the meaning of the artwork and the views of the artist or creator of the artwork. The same materials may also be present in the museum collections, without symbolic meaning, simply as a record of the material used at a given time and place. The preventive conservation approach to such impermanent materials may thus vary from artwork to artwork and collection to collection. One example of such a material is chocolate. Glenn Wharton, Sharon Blank and Claire Dean (1995) (Chapter 34) provide details of the chemistry and decay of chocolate and provides examples of a number of museum artefacts made of chocolate. Their paper details how conservators have enacted interventive and preventive conservation measures on these chocolate objects. Threats from insects, pests, vandalism and the environment are countered with a series of avoiding, blocking and eradication actions, often determined by the artists' wishes.

References

Child, B. (2006) 'Conserving a Coal Mine: Keeping Our Industrial Heritage Working', in C. Butler and M. Davis (eds), *Things Fall Apart . . .*, Cardiff: National Museum of Wales, pp. 24–31.

Clavir, M. (1994) 'Preserving Conceptual Integrity: Ethics and Theory in Preventive Conservation', in A. Roy and P. Smith (eds), *Preventive Conservation: Practice, Theory and Research, IIC Ottawa Congress 12–16 September 1994*, Ottawa: IIC, pp. 53–57.

Clavir, M. (2009) 'Conservation and Cultural Significance', in A. Richmond and A. Bracker (eds), *Conservation: Principles, Dilemmas and Uncomfortable Truths*, London: Butterworth-Heinemann, pp. 139–149.

Drumheller, A. and Kaminitz, M. (1994) 'Traditional Care and Conservation, the Merging of Two Disciplines at the National Museum on the American Indian', in A. Roy and P. Smith (eds), *Preventive Conservation: Practice, Theory and Research, IIC Ottawa Congress 12–16 September 1994*, Ottawa: IIC, pp. 58–60.

Jokilehto, J. (2009) 'Conservation Principles in the International Context', in A. Richmond and A. Bracker (eds), *Conservation: Principles, Dilemmas and Uncomfortable Truths*, London: Butterworth-Heinemann, pp. 73–83.

McGhee, R. (1994) 'Ivory for the Sea Woman: the Symbolic Attributes of Prehistoric Technology', in S. M. Pearce (ed.) *Interpreting Objects and Collections*, London: Routledge, pp. 59–66.

Wharton, G., Blank, S. and Dean, C. (1995) 'Sweetness and Blight: Conservation of Chocolate Works of Art', in J. Heuman (ed.), *From Marble to Chocolate: The Conservation of Modern Sculpture*, London: Archetype, pp. 162–170.

Chapter 31

Preserving Conceptual Integrity: ethics and theory in preventive conservation

Miriam Clavir

Introduction

THIS PAPER HAS DEVELOPED from the author's changing practice as an ethnographic conservator. Conservation work at the University of British Columbia
Museum of Anthropology, Vancouver, is chiefly concerned with preventive conservation. The author has come to realize that work in this area is situated as much in the
dynamic social environment of the object as in the dynamic physical environment.

Situated to the tangible as well as the intangible

Many museums in North America are currently undergoing significant changes.
One theoretical development which will affect conservation is the rethinking of the
role of the object. There is currently a re-evaluation of the primacy of collections as
the basis for a museum. George MacDonald, Director of the Canadian Museum of
Civilization, has described his museum as a presenter of history rather than a presenter of objects.[1] Delivering a positive visitor experience while presenting history,
or art, or whatever the particular mandate of the museum may be, is a major goal of
today's museums. This goal is accomplished by better visitor services and enhanced
museum interpretation, for example through interactive computer technologies,
or performance, or through graphic or oral presentations which highlight what the
original owners or makers of the objects wish to say. Interpretation is not necessarily
based solely on the objects themselves.

→ good quote.

In conjunction with the object losing (some would say simply changing) its place
in the theory of the museum, serious funding cutbacks have created a climate where
the standards and costs of object care and collections management are being ques-
tioned. A second major factor, therefore, driving the current changes in museums

Source: A. Roy and P. Smith (eds), *Preventive Conservation: Practice, Theory and Research, IIC
Ottawa Congress 12–16 September 1994*, Ottawa: IIC, 1994, pp. 53–57.

is the continuing financial deficit. The financial environment has direct implications for conservation funding but, as mentioned above, has also influenced the thinking of curators, directors and trustees about standards in preventive conservation.

A third factor causing major changes in museum practice in North America, specifically for museums holding collections from First Peoples, is requests by the First Peoples regarding objects originating in their communities. These requests may be for repatriation, for borrowing for use in ceremonies, for storage and display that is culturally sensitive, or for increased access to and co-management of these collections. It is recognized that First Peoples have a legitimate stake in these museums,[2] and this is backed by the force of law in the USA (through NAGPRA, the Native American Graves Protection and Repatriation Act)[3] and by the report of the Task Force on Museums and First Peoples in Canada,[4] which has been accepted by the Canadian Museums Association as a guiding document.

To summarize, the concept of what a museum is, what a museum does, and how, is undergoing radical rethinking. There are direct consequences for conservation practice, including preventive conservation. The subject of this paper is how one of these changes, requests from First Peoples, has an impact on ethnographic conservation and is creating new ways of thinking for conservators.

Preserving the cultural significance of ethnographic objects

How objects are seen: conceptual integrity

For ethnographic conservators in Canada, conceptual integrity has become a key phrase in the Code of Ethics published by the IIC-Canadian Group and the Canadian Association of Professional Conservators (CAPC). The Code states that 'all actions of the conservator must be governed by a respect for the integrity of the cultural] property, including physical, historical, conceptual and aesthetic considerations'.[5] Conceptual integrity was added to the Code in order to clarify the fact that the conservator's decision-making process includes consideration of the non-material properties of objects, properties such as religious or cultural significance, or the intention of the artist. These properties are included even if they are not physically evident to us through the object.[6, 7] Cultural significance is also a key concept in the Canadian Code of Ethics. The purpose of conservation is 'to study, record, retain and restore the culturally significant qualities of the object with the least possible intervention'.[5]

How objects are seen: viewpoints from the originating peoples

Ethnographic objects, like other collections in museums, have been seen by museum collectors, visitors and staff primarily as artifacts, relics, specimens, curios, souvenirs, art objects or the 'national heritage'. For an Aboriginal staff member or visitor, the objects might be seen as family regalia or community heritage. Intellectual and emotional content are both part of the viewing experience.

It is not surprising if First Peoples experience ethnographic museums very differently from Euro-Canadians or Euro-Americans. Apart from the larger symbolism of the museum as repository and presenter of a history of Native/non-Native relationships, there can be an important difference in the way the objects are seen from within their Native cultures, as illustrated by these quotations and others which follow in the text.

> 'In our way of thinking, everything is a significant event, and the past is as real as us being here right now. We are all connected to the things that happened at the beginning of our existence. And those things live on as they are handed down to us.' (Parris Butler, Fort Mohave)[8]

> 'When you get to the level of sacred objects, they shouldn't even be in collections with a curator. They should be back among the people who handle and care for them. They were given to us, each one of them was given to us by our Creator and they are for us. They are not for the general public.' (Pete Jemison, Seneca)[8]

> 'We are asking for things back which have been with us for thousands of years.' (Bill Tallbull)[9]

The way in which ethnographic objects are seen by conservators, whether as having fundamental ties to living peoples and a part of their continuing living culture, or primarily as works from the past preserved in a museum, will determine to what extent their practice reflects the preservation of cultural significance as defined by the culture of the originator or by the museum culture.

Impact of the world views of First Peoples on preventive conservation

Some requests to museums by First Peoples challenge the fundamentals of standard conservation practice and modern museum thinking. For example, repatriation, even to another professional museum repository such as a Native community museum, signifies that the objects have meaning to and serve the originating people. It may be decided that the objects can be handled or used in this service. For instance:

> The elders spoke of the importance for young people to know and touch their past if they are to have an identity in the future. . . .
> As soon as the formalities were over, a crowd gathered around the table where the artifacts lay. Looking, touching, admiring, shedding tears, they clearly felt empowered by their very presence.[10]

Apart from repatriation, non-Native museums which hold objects from First Peoples receive other requests which challenge conservation. For example, museums have been requested to allow religious ceremonies in storage areas, and some of these ceremonies leave materials in contact with the object or on the shelving which could attract insects. In one example, from New Mexico, the museum was asked not to save certain objects in the event of a natural disaster.[9] In an example of the most fundamental nature for conservators, First Peoples state that some objects now in museums were never intended to be preserved and should not now be preserved.

> Curation is not only a problem of outsiders caring for objects that they have no right to touch; curation also changes the character of an object by artificially prolonging its life.[8]

Ed Ladd stated that there is not a single item in Zuni culture which is used for religious or ceremonial purposes which is meant to be preserved in perpetuity. All are gifts to the Gods which are meant to disintegrate back into the earth to do their work.[9]

Examples of First Peoples/museums 'problem solving'

What are the implications for preventive conservation of these differences between the way some First Peoples look at ethnographic objects in museums and the way conservators do, especially considering the surrounding museum climate, mentioned earlier, which already appears to be working against the interests of preserving collections? The following section will give examples of requests from First Peoples which affect different areas of preventive conservation. It is interesting to note that there is often a compromise solution which can be developed through discussion. In addition, a consensus among conservators on the detailed application of concepts in the Code of Ethics such as 'conceptual integrity', 'responsibility to the originator' and 'maintaining a balance between the need of society to use a cultural property and the preservation of that cultural property'[5] will determine if the compromises are workable for us.

Sensitive storage

The Laboratory of Anthropology at the Museum of New Mexico in Santa Fe has a room which has been re-designed, through consultation, as storage for culturally sensitive objects. The objects which are culturally sensitive have been named as such by representatives from the pueblos. Several such objects from the Museum's collections have already been returned to the pueblo of origin, both before, and now in accordance with, the Native American Graves Protection and Repatriation Act. This Act mandates, inter alia, that sacred objects and inalienable, communally-owned objects must be returned to the tribe of origin if a museum wishes to continue to receive federal funding.

In certain cases, the originating people do not want the object back at this time. This may be, for example, because there are no cultural mechanisms in place to accept such a sacred or powerful object back home after being so long without traditional care. It may be because the appropriate guardian of the object is no longer alive or the appropriate ritual is not known. It may be that the tribe has elected, for whatever period of time, to leave the object in the safekeeping of the museum, in a 'stewardship' relationship in which the museum takes museum-type care of the object and allows access to appropriate tribal members for traditional care.

The room for culturally sensitive objects at the Museum of New Mexico (MNM) is set apart from the rest of the collections and includes the following features:

- It is like a traditional pueblo storage room in that
  - the person who enters must cross a threshold
  - the shelves are open
  - there is access to fresh air: the objects are considered to be living and therefore have a need to breathe.

- Blinds can be pulled down over the shelves or here are dust-covers so that all the objects do not have to be on view at the same time. By this means, the MNM has tried to avoid giving offence to people from the pueblos, who might otherwise see objects from a culture other than their own. It is a compromise which enables the MNM to use a single room for material from several different cultures.
- The objects are arranged by culture. Within each group, the objects are arranged in a certain order, and sometimes piled, on the advice of the consultants. The consultants also suggested interleaving piled objects with paper or cloth bags, as they do at home.
- The room is sealed off from the rest of the collections, so objects can be 'fed' (see point 1, referring to living things) or 'smudged' as required.[20, 21]

This room succeeds in achieving a workable compromise in preserving both the conceptual integrity of the objects, according to the wishes of the originators, and the physical integrity of the objects according to museum practice. For example, if corn-meal is left in the vicinity of the objects, the room is at least isolated from the rest of the collections. The use of dust-covers is a museum practice as well as a pueblo practice. There are, of course, compromises: conservators may not like the fact that objects are 'piled'. Undoubtedly there are also compromises in conceptual integrity that have been accepted by the pueblos. Such is the nature of a negotiated solution.

A very important feature of this room is that it was achieved through consultation and negotiation.[11, 12] An additional positive result for preventive conservation is that if a crisis arises, for example, insect infestation, or if the physical environment in the room becomes extreme in some way and affects the condition of the objects, then the avenues are there to consult quickly with the appropriate tribal people and to resolve the issue in a culturally appropriate manner.

Finally, a comment from Catherine Sease at the Field Museum in Chicago.[13] For one request to 'feed' objects, the conservators were able to meet the tribal religious representatives in advance and discuss the fact that the use of cornmeal creates the potential for an insect infestation. The conservators received permission to freeze the cornmeal before it was used.

Access and restricted access

Museums regularly restrict physical access to objects on display, for example by putting them in locked cases; this is a basic preventive conservation measure to prevent theft, handling, breakage, and other human actions destructive to the collection. Even for objects in storage, certain handling procedures, such as the use of gloves, are employed to minimize object deterioration. Museums are in the process of democratizing. One aspect of this is increased access to collections for the general public in order to reach a wider audience and gain broader support, including financial support. This involves 'lessening rather than increasing institutional arrangements between object and viewer'.[2] Each year, the UBC Museum of Anthropology receives visitors from at least half a dozen other museums wishing to implement a form of Visible Storage, the Museum's system where the storage racks are locked glass cases in the public galleries. The public at least has visual access to the majority of the museum's collections, even if they do not have physical access to them. For the public, 'access to heritage is a democratic right'.[2]

At the same time, the First Nations segment of the population is seeking broader, less rule-bound, access to collections. The Task Force on Museums and First Peoples made 'legitimate right of access by Aboriginal peoples' a key recommendation.[4] They also recommended that Aboriginal peoples 'recognize the legitimate concerns of museums with respect to the care, maintenance and preservation of their holdings'.[4]

It has been pointed out that 'One of the consequences of the increasing professionalization of museum work is that members of this developing profession begin to consider it their special responsibility and privilege to control and structure the relations between collections and the public . . . Curatorial staff who hold this view present themselves as the necessary agents not only for the care but also for the interpretation of heritage, just as teachers consider their curricula a necessary condition for learning.'[2] Conservators practising preventive conservation can consider themselves as being criticized, as being among the self-appointed intermediaries who show their power and privilege by restricting access to collections. Professional norms of collections care are being challenged in the arena of current museology, and to this arena have been added requests from First Peoples for increased access to objects from their heritage.

At the same time, there may be requests from First Peoples which are contrary to this trend to democratization. General access to collections is not necessarily being sought, except in the sense of repatriation of collections. In terms of collections which are housed in urban museums, it may be appropriate access which is being requested.

Appropriate access, however, may challenge the norms of standard museum and western cultural practice. For example, certain objects in both Makah and Zuni societies should not be seen or handled by women, including museum staff if these objects are in a museum. Certain objects from the US Southwest should not be seen outside of their religious context. Many medicine bundles from the Plains should not be opened and the contents seen, except by the person who has the ceremonial right to open and use that bundle. Some objects should not be seen by people from the community who are uninitiated; this may affect objects on display or in Visible Storage, which might be seen by school groups. Navaho museum staff-members need to know in advance if they will be exposed to objects associated with the dead, including archaeological objects. In addition, there are often rituals which must be performed when certain objects are accessed.[9]

In the background, as a philosophical basis underlying the access debates, are the western and First Peoples' points of view concerning right of access to the world's bank of knowledge and the right to keep knowledge private. Since the Enlightenment (c. 1865), there has been a western scholarly notion that 'people have a need and a right to learn freely and to have free access to knowledge'.[2]

'The concept in the white world is that "everyone's culture is everyone else's".
That's not really our concept.' (Pete Jemison, Seneca)[8]

Regarding the identification of Native American sacred sites in US National Parks, which has had the effect of increased tourism and inappropriate use of these sites,

Gilbert Sanchez of San Ildefonso pueblo said, 'You have to be responsible to us, so that the general public doesn't know'.[9]

For conservators, what is viewed as appropriate access will depend on how conceptual integrity is conceived and balanced with the preservation of physical integrity. If 'conceptual integrity' gives First Peoples moral rights similar to the moral rights artists and their estates are given in copyright law, then appropriate access can be more clearly defined and negotiated.

Storage equipment

The new National Museum of the American Indian (NMAI) has conducted extensive consultations with First Peoples to determine how the museum can best serve and express Native cultures. Some of their research concerned storage systems. Storage for culturally sensitive objects has been discussed above, using the Museum of New Mexico as an example. It has been reported that recommendations gathered by NMAI on storage for the general collections showed that half the respondents were in agreement with standard museum storage units, and almost two-thirds accepted museum standards for storage rooms. The rest varied according to particular cultural preferences; for example almost all the respondents from the northwest coast preferred to have their objects stored on wooden shelves or in wooden boxes. The nature of the object/shelf contact was important.[15]

These recommendations are workable within normal preventive conservation guidelines. For example, a number of objects from the northwest coast would be unaffected by the use of wooden shelves. If physically sensitive objects are present, the nature of different types of wood and the use of sealants would become a primary topic of discussion with the community representatives concerned.

Powerful objects

Certain objects from some cultures are not just significant or sensitive, but are also believed to embody power. These objects are seen as dangerous to those, even those outside the belief system, who do not know about and respect the power or, in some cases, do not know how to care for the objects in a traditionally respectful way. Non-Native conservators and other museum professionals may or may not be very concerned about beliefs in the spiritual and physical danger posed by certain objects, but sensitivity to this issue will affect standard preventive conservation practice. If there is, in the culture, a belief in the power inherent in certain objects, this will affect the interactions of those First Nations with the museum, and the interaction of First Nations staff-members with particular objects. For example, certain spiritual objects, such as some medicine bundles, may not be repatriated because there is no one in the community today with sufficient knowledge to control the power in the bundle. The museum, however, must still care for these objects, and provide appropriate access. Museums are concerned with safety in the workplace and safety for visitors; for some, there are spiritual as well as physical dimensions to this.

Inherent power may affect not only individuals in a museum but, in a different sense, communities. Objects which are 'out in the world', that is, in museums, and not being appropriately cared for, are, according to some First Peoples, a cause of problems in their communities.[8]

Traditional care

Some objects are regarded by First Peoples as best cared for by those who have the traditional spiritual authority to do so.[16] This care may be in the form of prayer or ceremony, but it also may take the form of remaking or renewing parts of an object. Object preservation is part of cultural preservation both in the sense of bringing harmony to the world, which is part of the power of the object mentioned above, and in the sense of passing down the 'conceptual integrity' – the songs, ceremonies and so on needed for the appropriate preservation of both the object and a way of life.

There are few museums which have achieved a sharing of 'care' for objects between non-Native conservators and Native authorities. When this has happened, it has usually been done on a consultative basis, and most often involving arrangements between curators, not conservators, and the First Peoples concerned.

In some cases, non-Native museum professionals have been given traditional training in the daily maintenance of certain objects.[14] At the same time, there are several Aboriginal museum professionals in Canada and, with five training programs now developed nationally for First Peoples intending to work in museums or Native cultural centers with a museum component, there will be many more.

One Native museum professional, Judy Harris, has written about the museum concept of care and conservation and the First Nations concept of traditional and ritual care. She discusses the 'divided loyalties' these engender for her, and the policies of her museum to give clear guidelines in this area.[17] John Moses, a First Nations conservator at the Canadian Museum of Civilization, has written on the question of traditional care and use of traditional materials in the conservation of objects from First Peoples.[18]

Environment

Environmental knowledge can be included in the subject area of traditional Native care; traditional 'conservation care' may be able to bring together different concepts to create a new and mutually satisfactory program for object preservation. A Native American basket-maker, Julia Parker, related how traditional basket repair took into account the environmental conditions to which the objects had been exposed.[9] In addition, opinions have been expressed by First Peoples that contemporary facilities for storing objects need to meet standard preventive conservation guidelines.[8, 19] Again, there is not necessarily a conflict between Native cultural viewpoints and non-Native preventive conservation viewpoints.

Conclusion

Preventive conservation has always recognized the dynamic physical environment to which objects are subject. This paper has attempted to highlight a dynamic social environment that affects the perception of objects, and to discuss how preventive conservation of the material culture of First Peoples can include preservation of the conceptual integrity as well as the physical, historic and artistic integrity of the objects.

Although, in current museological theory, the central role of the object to the concept of a museum is being rethought, the centrality of the ethnographic object to its originating community is becoming increasingly recognized. In museums there is an increasing awareness of the necessity for, and examples of, collaborative arrangements between museums and First Peoples. Aspects of preventive conservation such as care, storage, access, handling, environment and job safety are important components of this development.

Notes

1 MacDonald, G. (1993) remarks made at an MOA staff meeting, 20 September 1993.
2 Ames, M. M. (1992) *Cannibal Tours and Glass Boxes: The Anthropology of Museums*, Vancouver: UBC Press.
3 Native American Graves Protection and Repatriation Act (Act No. PL 101–601; 104 Stat. 3048; 25 USC 3001–3013), US Congress, Washington DC (1990).
4 Task Force on Museums and First Peoples (1992) *Turning the Page: Forging New Partnerships between Museums and First Peoples* (2nd edn), Ottawa: Assembly of First Nations and the Canadian Museums Association.
5 IIC-CG and CAPC (1989) *Code of Ethics and Guidance for Practice for Those Involved in the Conservation of Cultural Property in Canada* (2nd edn), Ottawa: IIC-CG and CAPC.
6 Costain, C, personal communication (1992).
7 Hodkinson, I. S. (1990) 'Man's effect on paintings' in B. A. Ramsay-Jolicoeur and I. N. M. Wainwright (eds) *Shared Responsibility: Proceedings of a Seminar for Curators and Conservators*, Ottawa: National Gallery of Canada.
8 Parker, P. (1990) *Keepers of the Treasures: Protecting Historic Properties and Cultural Traditions on Indian Lands*, Washington DC: US Department of the Interior.
9 Clavir, M. (1992) *IPAM: International Partnerships among Museums Report*, Vancouver: UBC Museum of Anthropology.
10 Morrison, B. (1993) 'Church returns native artifacts', *Anglican Journal* 119(9): 1, 6.
11 Bernstein, B. (1991) 'Repatriation and collaboration: the Museum of New Mexico', *Museum Anthropology* 15(3): 19–21.
12 Bernstein, B. (1992) 'Collaborative strategies for the preservation of North American Indian material culture', *Journal of the American Institute for Conservation* 31: 23–29.
13 Welsh, E., Sease, C., Rhodes, B., Brown, S. and Clavir, M. (1992) 'Multicultural participation in conservation decision-making', *Western Association for Art Conservation Newsletter* 14(1): 13–22.
14 Conaghty, G., lecture, Simon Fraser University, 10 February 1993 (unpublished).
15 Nason, J., lecture, UBC Museum of Anthropology, 12 February 1993 (unpublished).
16 Hill, R. (1991) 'Beyond repatriation', *History News*, March–April: 9–10.
17 Harris, J. (1993) 'Cultural function versus conservation: preserving the sacred artifact', in *Ontario Museum Annual* 11: 31–33.

18 Moses, J. (1993) 'First Nations traditions of object preservation' in K. Spirydowicz (ed.) *First Peoples Art and Artifacts: Heritage and Conservation Issues* (Eighteenth Annual Conference, Art Conservation Training Programs), Kingston, Ontario: Art Conservation Department, Queen's University.

19 Matas, R. (1993) 'The day Ottawa gutted a culture', *Globe and Mail,* 16 January: A1, A4.

20 Fed: placing ritual food on or near certain objects, as part of a ceremony.

21 Smudged: used here to mean the use of ritual smoke near an object, as part of a ceremony.

Chapter 32

Traditional Care and Conservation: the merging of two disciplines at the National Museum of the American Indian

Ann Drumheller and Marian Kaminitz

Introduction

A CURRENT ISSUE FOR MANY museums with ethnographic collections is the question of preservation of living cultures as opposed to preserving cultural material out of context and physically distanced from the lives of its makers.[1,2,3,4]

The National Museum of the American Indian (NMAI) is an institution of living cultures, dedicated to the preservation, study and exhibition of the life, language, literature, history and arts of the Native Peoples of the western hemisphere. NMAI's mission is to 'recognize and affirm to Native communities and the non-Native public the historical and contemporary cultures and cultural achievements of the Natives of the Western Hemisphere by advancing . . . in consultation, collaboration, and cooperation with Native Peoples, knowledge and understanding of Native cultures, including art, history, and language, and by recognizing the museum's special responsibility, through innovative public programming, research and collections, to protect, support and enhance the development, maintenance and perpetuation of Native cultures and communities.'[5]

Collections management and conservation measures are greatly affected by the museum's mission, which states that the collections policy respects and endeavors to incorporate the cultural protocols of Indian people that define:

- the cultural and religious sensitivities, needs and norms;
- the utilization of cultural knowledge and information;
- the restrictions outlined by specific tribal groups.[5]

Source: A. Roy and P. Smith (eds), *Preventive Conservation: Practice, Theory and Research, IIC Ottawa Congress 12–16 September 1994*, Ottawa: IIC, 1994, pp. 58–60.

Museum perspective

> Native cultures and the collections viewed within their cultural context con-
> stitute a rich part of the museum. The wishes of Native American peoples
> with respect to access, treatment and use of ceremonial and religious materi-
> als needed in the practice of their religion must be granted.[5]

Currently in the design phase are plans for NMAI's new storage and research facility, to be located at the Smithsonian Institution's Museum Support Center in Suitland, Maryland. This Cultural Resources Center will house the collections, archives,
library, resource center, conservation laboratory, registration department, curatorial department, collections management and other services. The architectural layout
and services of the building will respond directly to the input and needs of Native
Americans. Native and non-Native visitors, including scholars, will be accommodated by supporting traditional Native American care and renewal practices as well as
the more typical study and research projects.

Traditional care issues

A part of NMAI's consultations with Native American tribes throughout the western
hemisphere is the gathering of information regarding traditional care and storage concerns. Over the past three years, NMAI has accumulated information in the form of
traditional knowledge regarding the care of Native American materials. As a result of
the consultations, the museum decided to conduct a 'traditional care' survey of the
objects in the collection. The consultations and survey formed the foundation for the
types of question and kinds of information that the museum needed to be asking of
and gathering from Native Peoples.

The survey

From November 1992 through March 1993, a traditional care survey was conducted
by a Native American sub-contractor to Wendy Jessup and Associates (WJ&A).[6]
WJ&A was already under contract to perform an analysis of collections storage needs
for the NMAI's Cultural Resources Center. The sub-contractor and the museum's
collections staff worked as a team to identify 'everyday' and culturally sensitive,
sacred/ceremonial materials. The team also specified any particular traditional handling and storage requirements.

   Due to the size of the collection, the survey took several months and was completed in two stages. Surveying the South and Central American collections comprised the first stage of the project. These collections were chosen as a representative
sample for creating the project database. After the team had affirmed the categories
of data required for the survey, stage two – surveying the North American collections – was conducted. The data were then used to assist the architects in planning the
necessary storage configurations for the Suitland facility.

   It should be stated that the Native American sub-contractor did not work entirely
alone. Many times throughout the survey, the sub-contractor was in contact with

various Native Peoples to acquire additional information. 'In order to appease every tribe that is represented', the sub-contractor noted that 'good, strong, in-depth research must be done on their individual beliefs and people. The more information gained in this manner will be the only way to achieve our [NMAI's] final goal, unity.'[6] Everyone has their own solutions to storage problems. The museum is trying to incorporate all opinions, both traditional Native viewpoints and current museum standards, for the benefit of the objects.

Handling Native American materials

Most of the sacred and ceremonial materials in the NMAI collection are still very important to Native Peoples of the western hemisphere. For many Native Peoples, these objects, whether they be 'everyday' or ceremonial, are considered to be living. The staff at NMAI is conscious of the traditional nature of almost every object and holds the utmost respect for it. This is a major component of handling Native materials – having respect for them.

One facet of respect is the proper placement of tribal materials. Tribal objects must be thoroughly researched in order to place them properly in storage. For example, objects of tribal allies rather than those of tribal enemies should be adjacent to each other in storage. This is to prevent any disturbance between the objects themselves. These ideas are very relevant, even in modern Native thinking; to this day, some tribes still do not acknowledge each other's existence.

A second facet of respect is proper orientation with regard to the cardinal points. For example, some of the tribes along the Pacific coast have stated that the eastern direction is the most important, especially in the configuration of their ceremonial headgear. The importance of these directions varies between different tribes.

A third facet of respect is the acknowledgement of gender complexities within Native societies. Some tribes are concerned about men's things – fish-hooks, bows, shields and so on – being stored in the same location as women's things – scrapers, cradleboards, bowls and so on. This affects what can be stored above, below, adjacent to or between certain gender-related materials.

For women to handle certain sacred/ceremonial materials is problematic for some tribes, especially if the woman is menstruating. Many tribes believe that when women are menstruating they carry a very powerful energy. In the old days, menstruating women were segregated from their villages so that this energy would not negate or override any daily ceremonies which might be taking place. This traditional concept still holds in the way contemporary Native Peoples regard sacred and ceremonial objects in museum collections. With this in mind, the museum staff asks that female visitors respect and comply with this belief.

Pest management

An important aspect of preventive conservation and collections management is the pest control program. In the past, arsenic, DDT (1,1,1-trichloro-2,2-bis(4-chlorophenyl)ethane), cyanide, dibromomethane, dichlorvos (2,2-dichlorovinyl dimethyl phosphate) and other very toxic substances were used as fumigants or residual insecticides by many museums; in most cases there are very scanty records of the substances' used. Now that museums are turning to methods which are non-toxic to humans and non-damaging to objects, the National Museum of the American Indian has its own extra criteria to consider when deterring or eliminating active insect infestation.

While it may be acceptable to use standard enclosure and pest-treatment methods for most everyday artifacts, this is not appropriate for the culturally sensitive materials. Many, perhaps all, of the sensitive objects in the NMAI collections are considered to be living, breathing, individual members of the Native American cultures. This effectively eliminates the possibility of enclosing them in plastic bags as a barrier to discourage insects. Freezing is not available as an option for much tribal material, nor are carbon dioxide or low-oxygen/inert gas atmospheres with oxygen scavengers. All of the aforementioned methods would 'suffocate' a living entity. Storage cabinets must include air circulation if objects are to be kept inside them, and some objects can only be housed on open shelving. The logistical and practical implications in the above types of situation are heavily challenged when objects are actively infested.

With this task before them, the collections and conservation staff at NMAI have begun investigating traditional Native American fumigation techniques as an alternative to current conventional museum methods. Being developed is a research project involving several aromatic botanical substances traditionally used by Native Americans and the toxic effectiveness of these substances on museum pests. Also in the developmental stages is a design for a safe and effective vapor-permeable capsule containing traditionally used aromatic botanicals. These capsules may be included, where appropriate, as sachets in the storage areas. While the primary reason for including these botanicals is to accommodate the traditional care needs of certain collections, conservation and collections management staff will be evaluating this traditional storage method for its ability to repel insect pests.

It is possible that, if infestation occurs, consultation with the Native Americans concerned would result in agreement to use current standard museum techniques, such as freezing. However, consultation is essential before proceeding with this or any method, to see if it is acceptable to the particular tribe and appropriate for the object in question. This is consistent with the NMAI collections policy with regard to incorporating cultural protocols of Indian people that define their cultural and religious sensitivities, needs and norms.[5]

Treatment of sensitive materials

'Everyday' objects do not usually present handling restrictions and therefore can be examined and treated by conservators. But within many Native cultures there are concerns about whether sacred/ceremonial materials should be handled at all except by designated individuals within the tribe. This affects conservation. NMAI is trying to implement both traditional and standard conservation practices when dealing with sacred/ceremonial materials.

Treatment or, rather, repair and stabilization of culturally sensitive and sacred objects at NMAI are not undertaken without consultation and consent of the Native American group concerned. Most of these objects would not be treated at all, as their spiritual and cultural significance outweighs any need for conservation treatment. Working with the Native community as much as possible can make this transition easier for the museum.

The recent repatriation of sacred Jemez objects is an example of conservators being asked to assist.[7] Of the 86 objects repatriated to the Jémez Pueblo by NMAI, one shield was chosen by the Jémez religious leaders and tribal governors as the only object to be shared visually (or in any other way) with the public.

This shield was in need of a supplementary support so that it could be carried in procession back into the Pueblo. The elders requested that the support be attached by the NMAI's conservation staff. In discussion with the staff, the elders identified an appropriate support material and an acceptable method of attaching it to the shield. The conservators were then allowed to carry out the work.

Conclusion

It is very important for all people to understand the respect due to sensitive materials. In particular, it is of the utmost importance to acknowledge that there is no single answer or treatment which can be applied. The complexities involved in carrying out preservation or treatment of sensitive materials are multifaceted and ever changing.

Philosophically, the beliefs of most Native Peoples are cyclical in nature. All objects of material culture reflect that from which they come; however, their divine journey is not always evident.

NMAI conservation and collections management staff are guided by these beliefs. It is their responsibility to strive to incorporate these procedures by merging them with current museum standards of care and maintenance of collections.

References

1   Clavir, M. (1993) 'Per Guldbeck Memorial Lecture', *IIC-CG Bulletin* 18(3): 1–12.

2   Sease, C., Rhodes, A. B., Brown, S. and Clavir, M. (1992) 'Multicultural participation in conservation decision-making', *WAAC Newsletter* 14(1): 13–22.

3   Wolf, S. J. and Mibach, L. (1983) 'Ethical considerations in the conservation of Native American sacred objects', *Journal of the American Institute for Conservation* 23: 1–6.

4   Mibach, L. (1986) 'The Native North American approach to conservation', in R. Barclay, M. Gilberg, J. C. McCawley and T. Stone (eds) *Symposium 86: The Care and Presentation of Ethnological Materials*, Canadian Conservation Institute: Ottawa.

5   'National Museum of the American Indian, Smithsonian Institution collections policy', in A. Tabah (ed.) *Technical Information Services Forum: Occasional Papers on Museum Issues and Standards: Native American Collections and Repatriation*, Washington, DC: American Association of Museums.

6   Bad Bear, F. G. (1993) 'Report on traditional care consideration for collections storage', in Wendy Jessup & Associates, *National Museum of the American Indian Collections Storage Requirements for the Cultural Resources Center to be Constructed in Suitland, MD*, Draft Volume III, Alexandria, VA.

7   Personal conversations with Paul Tosa, Governor of the Pueblo of Jémez, and William Watley, Director of the Department of Archaeology and Preservation of the Pueblo of Jémez.

Chapter 33

Conserving a Coal Mine: keeping our industrial heritage working

Robert Child

W ALES WAS THE WORLD'S first industrialised country, that is, a country where more than half the population was involved in industrial work. Although it had an ancient history in mining for metals such as gold, tin and copper, by the eighteenth and nineteenth centuries coal mining and iron working were predominant. The parallel development of these industries was one of the key dynamic forces of the world's first industrial revolution. The south Wales valleys were transformed from an agricultural backwater to an industrial society.

The area around Blaenafon in south Wales is one of the finest surviving examples in the world of a landscape created by coal mining and iron working in the late eighteenth and early nineteenth centuries. In the late eighteenth century the ironworks were built and by 1812 they were claimed to be among the most productive in the world. In recognition of this, in December 2000, Blaenafon was designated a World Heritage Site and acknowledged as an area of outstanding universal value by UNESCO; it is the duty of the international community to co-operate to protect such sites.

In 2000, the National Museum of Wales took over the running of Big Pit, a former working coal mine in Blaenafon. The site at Big Pit is of great historical value, owing to its accessible underground workings and its above-ground complex (Figure 33.1). There are substantial conservation problems associated with preserving such a site, from the ethical considerations of the preservation versus presentation dichotomy, and the additional impositions from government listed building regulations and World Heritage Site status.

Source: C. Butler and M. Davis (eds), *Things Fall Apart . . .*, Cardiff: National Museum of Wales, 2006, pp. 24–31.

Figure 33.1 Big Pit when it was an active coal mine

Big Pit, until its closure, was the oldest working coal mine in south Wales, dating from 1860 when the original shaft was sunk. Originally supplying coal to the adjacent Blaenafon Company ironworks, it was operated commercially by the Blaenafon Company from 1873, and was nationalised by the National Coal Board in 1947. Its value as an historical site was recognized from the early 1970s, and measures were introduced then to preserve the authenticity and integrity of the site. It also acted as a collecting area for surplus equipment from other mines as an alternative to their disposal.

On its closure in 1980, Big Pit was one of approximately forty pits still working in the south Wales area; when it was first opened to the public in 1983 it was not so much as a 'museum' but as a 'job-creating' tourist attraction (Walker 1997). However, by the early 1990s deep coal working was virtually extinct in south Wales and Big Pit's significance as the survivor of an earlier age became apparent. In recognition of this, Cadw: Welsh Historic Monuments listed many of the above-ground buildings and structures, with the rationale that 'Big Pit was the most functionally complete colliery complex remaining in South Wales'. Big Pit became part of the National Museum of Wales as part of our industrial strategy, and became the National Coal Museum of Wales. With this takeover and concomitant grant applications to the Heritage Lottery Fund, fundamental ethical questions had to be considered on how the site should be conserved.

Preservation principles: what should we preserve?

Since the massive de-industrialisation of the 1980s and 1990s much of the structural landscape has changed. Mines have disappeared, coal tips have been flattened and grassed over and houses no longer burn coal, but North Sea gas. Too much of the social and local economic landscape has gone, and it would be inappropriate to resurrect or recreate it in order to set the Big Pit complex in 'authentic' surroundings. The Management Guidelines for World Cultural Sites (ICCROM 1998) emphasise the criteria for consideration as ones of 'historical integrity' and 'authenticity'. They define 'authenticity' as 'Original or genuine, as it was constructed and as it has aged and weathered in time, and should not be confused with "identical"; e.g. modern reconstruction'. Therefore, the Big Pit site and buildings should be preserved and maintained in their present format and not 'enhanced' with reconstructions of other 'typical' buildings. The interpretation and exhibition of the site should be based on the current contents, which represent the mine at its closure in 1980. This view-point is echoed by Cadw's decision to list twelve surface structures in 1995. This prevents any destruction or alteration of the buildings without prior consent and ensures that they receive adequate and proper care and maintenance. However, as Jones (1983) notes in his discussion paper on the conservation of the coal heritage in south Wales, 'scheduling is essentially negative' and does not initiate positive measures of conservation.

Big Pit sits in an exposed situation 1,400 feet above sea level, in an area of high rainfall and bleak winters. The principal causes of deterioration of the collections are therefore moisture and high humidity, causing corrosion, paint flaking and failure of metals and rotting wood. The effects are exacerbated by general air pollution (despite its rural position), off-gassing from the coal itself, dirt and the effects of sunlight.

The argument for preservation of the site as it stands is easy to justify and has great ethical merit. More debatable is the degree of activity that should be allowed, as working machinery, visitor tours and demonstrations are a balance between preservation and active interpretation. It is self-evident that a mine complex that demonstrates how it operated when it was a working mine is more realistic and more of a visitor experience than a fossilised, static exhibit (Figure 33.2). Current debate on the ethics of conservation notes the advantages of continuing to run machinery, as it

Figure 33.2 The famous Big Pit underground tour, accompanied by a former miner

aids interpretation and maintains specialist skills in the maintenance, care and repair of such machinery (Paine 1994).

How should the material be preserved?

Coal mines are part of special socio-economic areas that breed unique communities and foster particular virtues and vices. The operation of the mines in Wales developed into a traditional activity with a strong personal base. Apprentices joined a particular mine, often as boys, and developed skills and knowledge specific to their area. When these mines ceased to be active as producing industrial units, the workforce was dispersed either through redundancy and early retirement or by taking alternative jobs outside the industry. The few mines preserved as museums rely on a mix of ageing miners – usually former employees – and others who have more general experience of heavy engineering. There is a concern that, increasingly, these specialist skills and experience will be lost as the ex-employees retire and are not replaced by upcoming apprentices.

In order to maintain the concept of authenticity, we consulted widely on the future conservation of the contents of Big Pit. First and foremost in the discussions was the point that Big Pit is classified as a working mine and perforce must conform to the requirements of the Management and Administration of Safety and Health at Mines Regulations 1993 (MASHAM) and other demanding health and safety legislation. Additionally, the licence-holder of a coal mine (nominally the owner) must abide by the extensive number of Acts of Parliament, Approved Codes of Practices and Guidance on Regulations that govern operational practices, maintenance and repair regimes, monitoring and documentation procedures. All of which are good preventative conservation measures. The weight of coal-mining legislation makes most of our ethical decisions for us. If a 'working' mine is the favoured interpretative format, the appropriate laws must be adhered to. This approach is supported by Guidelines to Safety in Working Museums (Walker 1997), which takes a pragmatic view on operating machinery in heritage settings. There is, however, a large amount of material in a coal-mining setting that is not necessarily operational and is not covered by any specific legislation, but is still vulnerable and needs conservation. Big Pit coal mine is a contextual site that achieves its relevance as an historical document of post-war industrial conditions that existed there until its closure as a working mine in 1980. The objects seen on a public visit to the site are the 'tools of the trade' and their traditional use, maintenance and repair by the mining workforce play an integral part in the geographical, historical and socio-economic scene. They fall into three categories (Child 1997). First, the working machinery that needs to be maintained to a legal and safe standard only by professional and trained operatives. Second, the static and unused machinery, which provides the context to the site and can be conserved by trained staff. Finally, the collections and individual items that have importance as museum objects through rarity, age or cultural value and must be conserved by qualified conservation staff.

Ethical conservation

Owing to the special nature of the Big Pit collections in the context of the site, conservation methods need to be considered with care and ethical guidelines drawn up.

The overriding priority is the safety of staff and visitors. It is considered preferable to improve the environment by better drainage, ventilation and coverings rather than applying protective coatings, which may be inappropriate to the context and be visually unacceptable. Preventative conservation measures should be unobtrusive where possible, using measures such as hard-standings, good ventilation and canvas covers. Protective coatings such as grease or paint will only be used where they had some traditional use in the former working mine. If treatments are required they must be unobtrusive and, where possible, based on existing traditional methods of maintenance and repair, and preferably be carried out by local staff. 'Museum' conservation methodologies should only be used for objects in 'museum' type storage or displays, where additional conservation measures are necessary for their long-term preservation. Restoration may be necessary but only where there is a need for that object to be re-used in the mine context in a condition that better illustrates its use or appearance and its interpretation. Any restoration should use traditional crafts, techniques and standards, and be fully documented.

Preservation of the underground workings

Big Pit is a wet mine with over 100,000 gallons of water draining through it every day. Luckily, it has few problems from sulphur or methane gas emissions from the coal face itself, and so most of the problems are from very high ambient relative humidities. Being underground, the ambient temperatures are temperate at about 15°C throughout the year. Conservation of the underground machinery can only be satisfactorily achieved with effective protective coatings. Where possible, this is being done using original and traditional materials, including paint systems and grease. In some areas, to maintain an authentic appearance we are considering full paint systems but with an artificial weathering and corroded surface finish. The underground mining areas of Big Pit were excavated over the past one hundred years both for ironstone and coal. Some of the workings are not only of interest historically, but also geologically and biologically. We are fortunate in having departments concerned with geology and biological sciences as well as industry and commerce, and therefore monitoring and documentation of the mine workings is an ongoing exercise. As some underground areas have been inactive and unused for a long time, they are now considered in the same light as historic caves and as such are viewed according to the guidelines of the National Caving Association's Guidelines.

Future considerations

Big Pit is one of the foremost cultural heritage centres in the south Wales valleys. It attracts large numbers of local visitors, especially schoolchildren who wish to learn about their local history and its now defunct industry. Many visitors from further afield are delighted with the experience of going down 'a real coal mine with real coal miners'. The challenge for the conservation of Big Pit is not just the preservation of its structures and machinery, but also the knowledge, experience and working practices of its workforce – a resource that without forethought and planning will die out with the last miner.

References

Child, R. E. (1997) 'Ethics and conservation', in G. Edson (ed.) *Museum Ethics*, London and New York: Routledge.

ICCROM (1998) *Management Guidelines for World Cultural Heritage Sites*, Rome: ICCRIOM.

Jones, W. D. (1983) 'The coal mining industry in Wales: its conservation, preservation and interpretation', National Museum of Wales Discussion Paper. Unpublished.

Paine, C. (ed.) (1994) *Standards in the Museum Care of Larger and Working Objects*, London: Museums and Galleries Commission.

Walker, P. (1997) 'Maintenance of working objects at Big Pit Mining Museum', in D. Dollery and J. Henderson (eds) *Industrial Collections: Care and Conservation*, Cardiff: Council of Museums in Wales & United Kingdom Institute of Conservation.

Chapter 34

Sweetness and Blight: conservation of chocolate works of art

Glenn Wharton, Sharon D. Blank and J. Claire Dean

I needed something that would assert a really, really primal physicality that would also be on that edge of alluring, delicious and repulsive. And I just thought, yes, chocolate.

Helen Chadwick[1]

Introduction

Chocolate as a fine arts medium

The conservation of chocolate is a messy business. It is a challenging material for conservators not only because of its complex chemistry, but because of its potent symbolism. Artists who work in chocolate have usually chosen it as a medium for very specific reasons. An understanding and respect for the artist's concerns should govern the conservator's approach to chocolate.

The fascination with sculpting in chocolate appears to have begun early after its first manufacture in Europe. A surprisingly large number of contemporary artists have incorporated chocolate into their work. Some have sculpted and painted with it to create 'permanent' art, while others have melted it, poured it, gnawed it, and licked it during temporary installations and performances. Among the artists who have recently employed chocolate as a sculpture medium is Dieter Roth, who has sculpted self-portraits in the medium and used it in some of his paintings. Claes Oldenburg has created a number of works with chocolate candies covered with paint. Joseph Beuys has adhered painted chocolates to paper supports.

Source: J. Heuman (ed.), *From Marble to Chocolate: The Conservation of Modern Sculpture*, London: Archetype, 1995), pp. 162–170.

Many artists have also used chocolate in installation and performance pieces. Why do these artists work with chocolate? Not surprisingly, the answers are as diverse as the artists who have chosen it as a medium. Helen Chadwick associates it with mud and clay and primal soup. She describes it as having 'this smell, sweet, like death, and associations with romance, intoxication and addiction, excess, sickness . . . excremental pleasure.'[2] Janine Antoni sculpted lipstick containers by gnawing and spitting from 600 pound blocks of chocolate and lard. She has also made chocolate busts of herself, personally licked into shape. Her focus on chocolate is to explore notions of female sexuality and body image.[3] She refers to the way women experience their bodies, especially as manifested in eating disorders such as anorexia nervosa and bulimia.[4] Similarly, Karen Finley describes chocolate and other materials she applies to herself during performances as representing the violation perpetrated on women's bodies.[5] Paul McCarthy has used chocolate and other foodstuffs in his performances as 'paint', with his body as the canvas, to invoke bodily fluids such as blood, semen and excrement.[6] Anya Gallaccio's chocolate painted walls are allowed to alter during the course of the installation, to 'transform the work from something serene and beautiful to something repellent, and yet morbidly alluring'.[7] Edward Ruscha, also seduced by the qualities of chocolate, created a room lined shingle-style with 360 chocolate silkscreened papers for the Venice Biennale of 1970.[8]

The public often has a strong reaction to chocolate in art. Many pieces have been vandalized, particularly by biting and licking. Sue Hubbard describes the experience of viewing a phallic chocolate fountain by Helen Chadwick: 'for a chocoholic the smell is as seductive as that of a brewery to an alcoholic. As you enter, it permeates the gallery, sickly-sweet, cloying, drawing you towards the bubbling glutinous mass. The brown liquid pulses from the erect penile center in a constant ejaculation, slurping into the seething pool beneath. It is every wickedness and excess rolled into one. Other allusions encompass over indulgence, a regressive Freudian interest in coprophilia, a comment on first-world uses of the third-world resources (cocoa is a major third-world export), and the poisonous pollution of the planet with noxious industrial effluvia, within a delightfully witty and seductive context.'[9]

Our contemporary symbolism and associations with chocolate have been attributed to cocoa throughout its history. The Aztecs believed that Quetzalcoatl, who was born of a god and a virgin mortal, brought the cocoa bean from heaven. They believed that chocolate brought universal wisdom and knowledge. When cocoa was imported to Europe, it was promoted as a medicine that would cure all ills. The Spaniards referred to the beverage as a 'divine drink', which offered resistance to disease and guarded against fatigue. Casanova claimed that it was an inducement to romance. The word 'chocolate' is apparently synthesized from a combination of the words choco (foam) and tatl (water). In 1753, the Swedish botanist Carolus Linnaeus named the cocoa tree Theobroma cacao, Greek for 'food of the Gods'.

Chocolate history

The cocoa bean, from which chocolate is derived, was first cultivated by the Mayans about 600 AD, when it was brought to the Yucatan from the Amazon or Orinoco valleys of South America. The Aztecs later planted cacao trees throughout Central

America. They ground the beans into a fine powder, then mixed it with water to make a frothy, bitter drink called chocolatl by the Aztecs, and xocoatl by the Mayans.

The Spanish explorers encountered the chocolate beverage in the sixteenth century. The Aztec Emperor Montezuma provided Cortéz with lavish banquets where chocolate beverages were served. Cortéz carried cocoa beans back home, thereby introducing chocolate to Spain, where sugar was eventually added to the drink. The secret of its preparation was guarded for nearly a century.

Eventually, a taste for hot chocolate spread to Italy, Germany and France. As an expensive luxury, fashionable chocolate houses developed during the seventeenth century in the major capitals of Europe. In about 1700, the English further improved the drink by adding milk. This greatly reduced the price of the beverage, which led to more widespread consumption. The first chocolate bar is thought to have been made in England in 1847. Over time, various recipes developed by combining cocoa butter, chocolate liquor, sugar and other additives.

Chocolate manufacture

A full description of chocolate manufacture may be found in the many texts on chocolate processing (see further reading section). In essence, the cocoa beans are harvested from the cocoa tree and allowed to ferment. The beans are then dried and cleaned prior to roasting. It is in the fermentation and roasting that the true art of chocolate manufacture lies, for this is where the chocolate flavour is developed. After roasting, the cocoa bean nib is ground to produce a coarse but flowing substance known as cocoa liquor.

At this point, various production processes take place, depending on the desired product. Cocoa liquor may be pressed to extract the cocoa butter (a naturally occurring fat), then dried into a cake and ground to produce cocoa powder. If baking chocolate is to be made, the butter is not removed and the liquor is allowed to harden to a solid. Sweet chocolate (including semi-sweet and bitter chocolate) is cocoa liquor to which sugar and additional cocoa butter are added. Milk chocolate includes the addition of milk or milk solids. The shelf life of chocolate depends mainly on the way in which the fat in the newly made liquid chocolate is tempered and cooled.

Of course chocolate is not only tempered, but tampered. There are no internationally accepted standards for what ingredients can be added and it still be marketed as chocolate. The exact same product that can be sold as chocolate in one country may have to be called 'chocolate flavoured' if manufactured and retailed elsewhere. That blasphemous product 'white chocolate' has only sugar, milk, and cocoa butter, with no cocoa liquor at all. Even farther removed are products such as confectionery coating, which may contain wax and an astonishing variety of vegetable fats. Of the materials added to cocoa liquor to make chocolate, the sugars and fats are of most concern to the conservator. One must be prepared to encounter sugars of all forms and fats other than cocoa butter.

Chocolate chemistry

Chocolate is a complex organic material, one that modern manufacture has increased in its complexity. To the cocoa liquor, already a rich stew of organic molecules, a wide variety of fats, sugars, flavourings, preservatives and emulsifiers have been added. Structurally, chocolate is an aggregate with solid bits of sugars and cocoa beans surrounded by a fatty layer or 'binder'. This structure accounts for many of the phenomena observed in working with chocolate. The fat-based binder, ideally cocoa butter, but too frequently a nasty admixture of cheapening ingredients, allows the chocolate to flow during production, but also contributes mightily to the all-important 'mouth feel' of the chocolate.

The fermentation and roasting of the cocoa bean creates a fragrant array of over five hundred different molecules and a significant amount of acid. The primary acid is acetic, most of which is volatilized during processing, although enough acid can remain in chocolate to accelerate degradation of the wrappings and inclusions. The flavour of chocolate changes after manufacture, actually reaching its peak after a few months, as some of the molecules which create a bitter or sour taste escape. The loss of chocolate taste becomes noticeable after about a year, as more of the many organic molecules that create chocolate flavour are lost to the air and through oxidation. The interior of a chocolate belies that smooth, unperturbed surface. There is an astonishing amount of migration occurring on a molecular level. Volatile flavour molecules and fats migrate out, undesirable outside flavours and smells migrate in.

Perhaps some of the most interesting trace molecules found in chocolate are those capable of affecting our physiology. The phenylethylamine component of chocolate experienced its fifteen minutes of fame when it was found to be present in large amounts in the brain of those in passionate love, and not detectable after falling out of love. Although there was a brief rush on chocolate by chemically minded suitors hoping to induce a state of ardor in their beloved, phenylethylamine was subsequently found not to be psychoactive when eaten. Theobromine, on the other hand, has a very profound effect on the canine community. It stimulates the heart and decreases blood flow to the brain in dogs. A pound of chocolate can be lethal to a twenty-pound dog. In humans, large doses of theobromine have been known to cause headaches.

Chocolate is primarily defined by its fat content. Cocoa butter has six crystalline forms, the most physically stable of which is the beta form, with a melting point of 34.5°C. Chocolate is tempered to increase the percentage of the beta crystals. Tempering heats the chocolate to 48°C, at which point it is completely melted. The chocolate is then cooled to allow the formation of crystals and avoid bloom formation, and then slowly heated to a temperature, 32°C, at which only the beta form remains. Thus seeded, the cocoa butter will be primarily in the beta state. One can begin to grasp the extreme degree of temperature control required in the many steps leading to a finished chocolate.

As one may suspect, emulsifiers are often added to chocolate, lecithin being the most commonly used. However, manufacturers may add up to 1% surfactant in their efforts to produce a smooth, stable chocolate that resists chocolate bloom.

Chocolate deterioration

Chocolate bloom (or fat bloom) (Figure 34.1) is the result of exposure to warm temperatures and other phenomena which allow the less stable fractions of the cocoa butter (or other fats) to migrate to the surface of the chocolate. Bloom signifies dire

Figure 34.1 Fat bloom deposits on a chocolate sculpture of a cocoa bean. Presented
to chocolate historian William Mobley by the Chocolate Lovers Hall of
Fame in 1990. Collection of William Frost Mobley, Chocolate Historian,
Schoharie, New York

consequences within the chocolate. In addition to the unattractive appearance created
by the bloom, the structure of the chocolate itself has been weakened. In the most
advanced cases, the fatty binder that once held the solid particles together has been
lost, the plasticizer that gave the chocolate its flexibility and resilience is no longer in
place. The resulting material is a powdery, crumbling mass. Milk chocolate is not as
susceptible to bloom.

A more innocuous type of deterioration is sugar bloom. Sugar bloom is the relatively rare but unsightly and grainy white deposit that may form on the surface of
chocolate as the result of exposure to high humidities or moisture. Water allowed
to condense on the surface of chocolate will draw the sugar out of the chocolate and
deposit it on the surface.

How long will chocolate 'keep'? Cocoa butter is among the most stable fats, and
chocolate at low humidities is prone to few biological pests, discounting the human
and canine varieties. Chocolate keeps astonishingly well, and is more stable than many
of the materials used by contemporary artists. Although there is loss of flavour and
various oxidation products will have developed, including fatty acids, the chocolate
can still be structurally sound. Trace metallic contaminants, primarily iron and copper, serve as catalysts to degradation, as they will for many organic materials.

The presence of inclusions can also contribute to the degradation of chocolate.
Inclusions are frequently the point of attack for insect and mould infestations. Nuts
are probably the worst offender when it comes to fatty bloom, for the oils from the
nuts tend to migrate out through the chocolate layer; fatty biscuits will do the same
thing. Absorbent materials such as marshmallow have exactly the opposite effect,
sucking fats out of the chocolate. High-moisture centers can shrink with age or cause
sugar bloom. Hard centers which do not allow the chocolate to expand and react
with temperature changes will cause cracking in the chocolate enrobing. Centers that

have become hosts to bacteria can literally burst with fermentation products. Weak points in the chocolate coating, poor seams or thin walls, are focal points for releasing the stress of containing the center. Cracking of the coating only increases with time as the chocolate becomes more brittle. Liqueur centers are prone to the escape of alcohol through the chocolate, and leaching of sucrose to the surface. Armed with this knowledge, a conservator may come to view a box of mixed chocolates as a ticking time bomb.

Ethics, artist's intent and artist's rights

A basic understanding of the artist's intent is fundamental to the conservation of all modern and contemporary works of art, and chocolate is no exception. Some artists, such as Joseph Beuys, incorporate time into their work, thus allowing self-destruction to be part of the piece. For other artists, such as Dieter Roth, Helen Chadwick and Janine Antoni, the edibility or aroma of foodstuffs is critical to their conception.

It is difficult for conservators to refrain from consolidating, filling and inpainting, since these techniques are at the core of their training. Fortunately there is a growing body of conservation literature which helps conservators navigate between professional ethics and respect for the artist's intent. Heinz Althöfer has written about the conservation of decaying works of art, arguing that great demands are made on the conservator to correctly interpret objects made from found and deteriorating materials.[10]

As conservators we are often concerned with preserving the appearance of a work of art. This focus on appearance is appropriate for traditional art in which the viewer's experience is purely visual. More complex issues are presented by functional objects, where much of the meaning lies in the very functionality. If functional objects are preserved but not allowed to function, then arguably the intent of the object has been lost. Conversely, if the object is allowed to function, but is destroyed in the very functioning, then we have lost that object for posterity. Although these issues are raised with the preservation of all but the most traditional of art forms, with edible art they are raised to new poignancy.

If the process of deterioration is considered integral to the work of art, as is the case with Dieter Roth, Joseph Beuys, and others, physical interference with this process may be considered inappropriate. In a visit to the Tate Gallery, Dieter Roth was asked about his paintings, which were actively deteriorating. His reply was that he expected the paintings to deteriorate and that, although it should not be encouraged, they should be allowed to do so. 'The idea and not the object' should be preserved. In the process of investigating one of his paintings, he poked his finger in a chocolate element, which he sniffed to identify.[11]

Other artists have accepted modifications of their work by the public. Teeth marks appeared during the exhibition of Lisa Brown's chocolate cast of her own body. The artist decided to leave the teeth marks, saying 'nothing's sacred'.[12]

The nature and extent of modification may influence whether the artist accepts it or not. According to Janine Antoni, 'When I showed *Lick and Lather* in Venice, a 16-year-old schoolgirl bit off three of my noses.' The artist had thought about biting the noses off herself, but decided not to do it. The incident caused her to take the vandalized sculptures off display.[13]

In addition to respecting the intent of the artist, conservators should protect themselves by being aware of local legislation governing the rights of artists and their estates. In the United States, both federal and state laws protecting artists and their estates exist, but their validity regarding foodstuffs in art has not been tested in the courts. The law has in fact been hesitant to allow copyrighting of anything that is edible. If an artist could copyright a chocolate sculpture, it would be difficult to prevent a chocolatier or indeed a chef from copyrighting their specialized desserts. The distinction between fine art, craft, and culinary art is indeed a fine line.[14]

There have been a number of law suits regarding the alteration of works of art by well-meaning custodians. Among these is a suit filed against the Düsseldorf Academy, brought by Johannes Stuttgen over the destruction of a Joseph Beuys sculpture *Fettecke*.[15] The cleaning crew of the Academy removed an eleven-pound glob of fat and felt from a wall installation which Beuys had created.

Prior to performing a major conservation treatment on a deteriorated chocolate work of art, the conservator should strive to obtain a written statement of intention from the artist or artist's representative. Preventative measures should be taken to slow the deterioration of chocolate by exhibiting and storing it in a stable environment, and establishing good housekeeping policies for control of pests.

Environmental controls

Unquestionably, the most important factor in chocolate preservation is the maintenance of a cool environment. As previously mentioned, exposure to elevated temperatures will induce internal migration of fats within chocolate. It follows that chocolate should not be handled for an extended length of time because of this sensitivity to temperature. A storage environment that has been suggested for the ultimate preservation of chocolate is a heat-sealed plastic envelope with a nitrogen atmosphere, deep frozen at minus 20°C.[16] In the chocolate industry, 16 to 20°C is generally accepted as a standard. Lower temperatures of 8 to 10°C controls have been proposed in the industry, but these temperatures necessitate very careful control of relative humidity. A stable temperature of 20°C is recommended as realistic for the museum environment.[17]

The moisture content of the air is less critical to chocolate than temperature, although excessive moisture may cause partial dissolution of sugar and surface redeposition, known as sugar bloom. High levels of moisture may lead to mould formation. A relative humidity of below 50% has been recommended for museums.[18]

In 1990, samples from the painted chocolate component of *Two Frauleins with Shining Bread* by Joseph Beuys was brought to the Canadian Conservation Institute for analysis of deterioration products. The work was analyzed by R. Scott Williams.[19] The object was left untreated by the conservators of the Art Gallery of Ontario, in keeping with the artist's intent.[20,21] It was placed in a permanent display case with very little air volume, at ambient gallery environmental conditions of 45% (plus or minus 5%) relative humidity and 21°C.

Chocolate pests

Who can forgive the large range of pests that are attracted to chocolate? The best method of avoiding pests is good housekeeping. Regular cleaning and inspection are essential for any collection prone to insect attack, infested objects should be quarantined and the insect identified. If possible, contact should be made with the artist or artist's agent. Fumigation of a chocolate work of art with toxic substances will render it inedible, which may be in direct conflict with the artist's intent. Controlled freezing may risk water condensation on the surface of the chocolate. If freezing is the most practical option, careful use of desiccants will reduce condensation during thawing. Oxygen deprivation through exposure to nitrogen, carbon dioxide or Ageless™ may be safely employed.[22–24]

Claes Oldenburg's *Earthquake* (see Figure 34.2) was constructed as a model for a ride at Disneyland, where giant chocolate bars would shift precariously, crack open and settle back. It consists of a pile of Hershey Almond Chocolate bars with enamel paint and polyurethane resin poured over them. After an initial infestation by cigarette beetles, *Lasioderma serricorne*, the owner was left with the fragile shell of enamel paint and polyurethane, as well as thousands of carcasses (larvae) and a mountain of frass (reprocessed chocolate). It was decided to eradicate the insects by controlled freezing.[25] Unfortunately, the sculpture suffered a second infestation by varied carpet beetles, *Anthrenus verbasci*. The owner and conservator decided to fumigate the sculpture on the second occasion with methyl bromide.

Heinz Althöfer at the Düsseldorf Restoration Center has refused to treat an infested chocolate bust by Dieter Roth because it would render it inedible. The piece is being kept under Plexiglas (polymethyl methacrylate) cover in the conservation laboratory. 'I don't know how long it will take,' he said, 'but one of these days all we'll have left is a pile of powdery chocolate, and eventually that too will be gone. They'll eat it.'[26]

Figure 34.2 Earthquake by Claes Oldenburg, 1969. The sculpture was infested twice in recent history. First by cigarette beetles, then by varied carpet beetles. The beetles bored entrance and exit holes and ingested most of the chocolate. Collection of Maurice Tuchman

A sculpture by Dieter Roth containing yogurt and one by Anselm Kiefer incorporating poppy seeds arrived at the National Gallery of Art in Washington with pests. The artists and their agents were consulted, and neither artist was displeased upon learning about the infestation. In both cases a compromise treatment was reached. The Roth was fumigated, but the insect carcasses, frass and other detritus were preserved in situ. The poppy seeds in the Kiefer will be removed, frozen and replaced.[27]

Chocolate conservation techniques: the theory

The use of traditional conservation materials for cleaning, adhesion, gap filling and consolidation of chocolate is limited because of the sensitivity of sugar and fat to most classes of solvents. The selection of conservation materials should be based on the specific materials employed in the work of art, their condition, and the results from testing in small areas. The application of all solvents and heat should be used with caution.

Chocolate, being an emulsion of sorts, is soluble in a wide range of solvents. The sugar is affected by the extremely polar water, and the organic portions, primarily fat, are affected by less polar solvents. Theoretically, the somewhat polar vegetable fats in chocolate should be unaffected by non-polar solvents. However, a test of the solubility properties of an unaged semi-sweet chocolate revealed solubility in petroleum distillates, throwing theory out the window and wasting a perfectly good piece of chocolate. Chocolate never has an opportunity to age in our testing facility, thus precluding testing the solubility of aged fats. As the fats in chocolate oxidize with time, they effectively become more polar, and thus may be unaffected by non-polar solvents.

The high mobility of materials within the chocolate matrix may pose additional problems for the conservator. Not unlike efflorescence in stone or porous ceramics, fats and sugars may crystallize under coatings and force them from the surface. Adhesives may be plasticized by fats from the chocolate, and molecules from conservation materials may be found to migrate deep within the chocolate.

Adhesives and consolidants from the conservator's traditional arsenal are all likely to be effective at adhering to chocolate due to the range of functional chemical groups to be found within the matrix. The question of how much harm is done is a sticky one. The presence of solvents or even solvent vapours can be expected to increase the mobility of the fats, as the crystalline structure will be disrupted. The deleterious effects of water are well known.

Application of warmed confectionery coatings or wax provides an interesting question, that of disruption to the crystalline structure of the fats. The degree to which this is a problem is unclear. The authors are unaware of studies of the crystalline forms present in aged chocolate, and given the confectionery industry's obsession with freshness, such a study seems improbable. However, technical examination of a freshly made, tempered chocolate found only 50% of the stable beta form of cocoa butter. One suspects the percentage in an aged, degraded chocolate exposed to a range of temperatures would be significantly lower. Thus, again at the risk of mobilizing fatty components, heat below the 32°C melting point of beta prime should not further destabilize the crystalline structure.

Chocolate conservation techniques: the practice

The cleaning of chocolate art may include the removal of sugar bloom, fat bloom, accretions from oozing cream-filled interiors, and superficial dust and soiling. A clean, soft bristle brush, possibly aided by low vacuum pressure, should be employed to remove dust and bloom that is not well adhered. Pointed wood or plastic skewers and tweezers may assist in removal of more tenacious deposits.

Despite the temptation to simply lick the problem, the use of any solvent should be carefully tested prior to use. In some cases, minimal use of de-ionized water, saliva, ethanol or a clean petroleum solvent such as Naphtha VM&P solvent on a small cotton swab may be appropriate. The use of any of these solvents may cause the surface to partially dissolve. Water may induce the formation of sugar bloom. As Helen Cox warns, 'Wet cleaning should be avoided where chocolate has become friable and open textured, as the solvent may migrate into the structure and cause sub-surface melting.'[28]

An example of chocolate cleaning was the removal of reprecipitated sugar from a painted chocolate surface by gently scraping with wood skewers.[29] *Chocolates* (see Figure 34.3) by Claes Oldenburg consists of cream-filled Black Magic candies (Rowntree manufacture) in their original plastic container which is adhered to a cardboard support and set on green velvet-covered pressed wood (Masonite). The candies are covered with brown enamel paint. The cream fillings had oozed out of two of the candies, and deposited white reprecipitated sugar on the surface of the paint.

A wide range of adhesives bond well to chocolate, including acrylics, acrylic emulsions, and wax. Soft, powdery surfaces of broken edges may require pre-consolidation prior to adhesion of chocolate. As with cleaning, limitations are posed primarily by the sensitivity of chocolate to heat and most solvents, including water. If water, alcohol and acetone based adhesives cannot be used because of the risk of damage to the object, microcrystalline wax may be considered as an adhesive or fill

Figure 34.3 Detail of *Chocolates* by Claes Oldenburg, late 1960s. Expansion of cream-filled interior caused surface paint to crack. Reprecipitated sugar was deposited on the surface of some of the candies

material. Its tackiness may be adjusted by selection of a wax with an appropriate melting point or modification with a small amount of polyethylene wax.

Because of the narrow range of options imposed by chocolate, the use of high-quality chocolate has been suggested as an adhesive by Helen Cox.[30] Cadbury's 'Bournville' plain chocolate was used to repair a broken pair of chocolate pliers from a set of Victorian chocolate carpentry tools at the Doncaster Museum Conservation Laboratory.

Most of the chocolate in the Claes Oldenburg sculpture *Earthquake* had been eaten by insects (see Figure 34.2).[31] The voids were filled with brown-pigmented wax to simulate chocolate. A low melting-point micro-crystalline wax was gently manipulated into the entrance and exit holes bored into the hollow shell of paint by the insects. The wax was applied in a warmed and soft state, rather than a liquid state, in order not to affect the fragile shell of paint. The treatment was approved by the artist, who jokingly requested that the wax be strawberry scented if possible.[32]

Conclusion

As we have seen, chocolate is a stimulating material for the artist as well as the conservator. It has enjoyed an elevated status throughout its history, from its divine associations in Mayan and Aztec cultures to its symbolic use in contemporary art installations. The conservator must approach chocolate art with an understanding of the individual artist's philosophy and intent. Recognition of the artist's intent may force the conservator to consider preservation secondary to other issues. In some instances, a traditional conservation approach to eradicate pests, consolidate, fill and inpaint may be in direct contradiction with the artist's concept. Because of the sensitivity of chocolate to most solvents, the choice of any conservation material must certainly be made after careful testing. Since few active treatments are suitable for chocolate, emphasis should be placed on preventative conservation measures, such as good storage methods, handling procedures and pest management programs.

[. . .]

References

1   Chadwick, H., quoted in Vincent. S. (1994) 'Sweet excess', *Sunday Times*, 24 July 1994, London.
2   Vincent, S. (1994) op. cit.
3   Fielding, H. (1994) 'Part of sleep's rich tapestry', *Independent*, 27 March 1994, London.
4   Schwendenwien, J. (1992) 'Cravings: food into sculpture', *Sculpture* 11 (November–December): 44–49.
5   Santé, Luc. (1990) 'Blood and Chocolate', *The New Republic*, 203:16, 15 October 1990: 34–38.
6   McCarthy, P. Personal communication, 9 January 1995.
7   Alberge, D. (1994) 'Tasty art exhibit doomed to rot', *Independent*, January 1994, London.
8   Poncy, P. (of Edward Ruscha's studio) Personal communication, 9 January 1995.

9 Hubbard, S. (1994) 'The pulse of brown liquid', *New Statesman & Society*, 7:313, 29 July 1994: 34. (Review of exhibition by Helen Chadwick, Serpentine Gallery, London.)

10 Althöfer, H. (1977) *Fragmente und Ruine. Kunstforum International* 19:1: 57–170.

11 Tate Gallery Conservation Record, interview with Dieter Roth in 1977.

12 Alberge, D. (1994) 'Chocolate nude proves good enough to eat', *The Times*, 22 July 1994, London.

13 Fielding, H. (1994) op. cit.

14 This information on U.S. laws regarding artist's rights was synthesized from personal communication with Ann M. Garfinkle and Janet Fries of Garfinkle & Associates, Attorneys at Law, 1100 New York Avenue, N.W. Suite 630, Washington D.C. 20005–3934 on 4 January 1995.

15 Dornberg, J. (1989) 'Beuys Butter Battle', *ARTnews* 88:4, April 1989: 23.

16 Cruikshank, D. (1994) 'Conservation of Chocolate', *Scottish Society for Conservation and Restoration Journal* 5:1: 6–8.

17 Cruikshank, D. (1994) op. cit.

18 Cruikshank, D. (1994) op. cit.

19 Williams, R. S. (1990) 'Exudations on "Two Frauleins With Shining Bread"', *CCI Analytical Report No. ARS 2907 File No. 5070–1*, Ottawa: CCI.

20 Personal communication with the conservator, Barry Briggs, on 3 January 1995, Art Gallery of Ontario, 317 Dundas St., West, Toronto, Canada M5T 1G4. To further understand the dynamics of the materials which Beuys employed, the conservator created three different samples of similar milk chocolate candies, one with no paint, one with paint on the top, and one with paint on the top and the bottom. Since September 1991, the surfaces of the chocolate have developed light spots, which could relate to differences in content distribution. Otherwise the samples are in good condition.

21 A discussion of Beuys' interest in both physical and metaphysical change in his work may be found in: Kuspit, 'D. B. Beuys: Fat, fell and alchemy', *Art in America* 68 (May 1980): 79–89.

22 Florian, M. E. (1986) 'The freezing process: effects on insects and artifact materials', *Leather Conservation News* 3: 1–17.

23 Daniel, V., Hanlon, G. and Maekawa, S. (1993) 'Eradication of insect pests in museums using nitrogen', *WAAC Newsletter* 15:3 (September 1993): 15–19.

24 Gilberg, M. (1990) 'Inert atmosphere disinfestation using AGELESS oxygen scavenger', in *Preprints of the 9th ICOM-CC, Triennial Meeting, Dresden*, Marina del Ray, CA: ICOM-CC & GCI.

25 The sculpture was wrapped with several layers of paper, placed in a cardboard box, then frozen for forty-eight hours at –15°C. It was thawed for twenty-four hours at room temperature before repeating the freezing cycle for forty-eight hours. The paper and cardboard were used to prevent the precipitation of moisture on the surface.

26 Dornberg, J. (1991) 'Intensive care', *ARTnews* 90:1 (January 1991): 128–133.

27 Personal communication, 6 January 1995, with Shelley Sturman, Head of Object Conservation, National Gallery of Art, Washington, DC 20565. Treatment of Dieter Roth, *Insel* 1968 (Vogel promised gift) was performed by Judy Ozone, Object Conservator. Treatment of Anselm Kiefer. *Poppies and Memories* 1989 (1994.75.1) has not yet been carried out.

28 Cox, H. (1993) 'The deterioration and conservation of chocolate from museum collections', *Studies in Conservation* 38: 217–223.
29 Treatment performed by Wharton & Griswold & Associates Inc. in 1989.
30 Cox, H. (1993) op. cit., p. 221.
31 Treatment performed by Wharton & Griswold & Associates Inc. in 1989.
32 Personal communication with Claes Oldenburg, 1989.

Introduction to Part Three – Section Three

Chris Caple

All together now

THE PROBLEMS OF PREVENTIVE CONSERVATION never occur in isolation. Large collections located in historic buildings and comprising objects made of numerous different materials (with differing ideal storage conditions), each object having multiple social and contextual meanings, are normal. The collections are stored, exhibited, and used to support research; consequently, all proposed preventive conservation measures must be considered together and alongside the uses of the collection.

The scientific knowledge underpinning preventive conservation increased during the twentieth century, as did the availability of specialist skills, materials and equipment. This meant that the disparity between the highest and lowest standards of museum collection care increased. Museum councils had been established in the UK from 1963 to raise standards in museums. In the 1990s the museum councils oversight body, the Museums and Galleries Commission (MGC), commissioned a series of publications, *Standards in the Museum Care of . . .*, which described the appropriate conditions for preserving particular types of museum collections: Archaeological, Biological, Geological, Larger and Working Objects, Photographic, Musical Instrument, Costume and Textile and Touring Exhibitions. These can be downloaded from the Collections Link website.[1]

They helped to raise the collections care standards in UK museums and, as part of that process, in 1998 the MGC (1998) produced the *Levels of Collections Care: Self-Assessment Checklist* (Chapter 35). It enabled museums to assess their own standards of collections care and appreciate what was required to raise their standards to those described in the 'Standards' series. This publication also emphasised the need for a holistic approach to collections care and helped museums to recognise that, for example, whilst their humidity and temperature monitoring system met the 'Best Practice' requirement, their maintenance procedures for their buildings barely made the 'Basic' standard. Potentially, this enabled museums to better focus their resources so as to achieve the greatest preventive conservation benefit for their collection. These 'Levels of Collections Care' can be seen as having the same aim of a holistic approach to preventive conservation, as the Canadian Conservation Institutes' *Framework for Preservation*. The incremental approach of moving from 'Basic' to 'Best Practice' in the *Levels of Collections Care* corresponded well with the aspirations of museums and their staff, and thus encouraged their adoption and use.

National and international heritage agencies recognise that collections care needs to be fully integrated into the core activities of every museum. This is often best achieved through a teamwork approach involving a wide range of museum staff, not merely conservators or curators. Organisations such as ICCROM seek to emphasise this through relevant publications (Putt and Slade 2004). A similar strategy is also seen in the UK, where cultural collections management publications (Resource 2002; British Standards Institute 2009) have drawn from the earlier *Levels of Collections Care* work and used its checklist format to encourage self-awareness in integrating collections care into museums' core curatorial activities.

The term 'holistic approach to preventive conservation' is easy to use; the challenge is to manage all the different processes of obtaining information, making informed decisions, getting agreed priorities and then implementing them. Keene (1996) (Chapter 36) shows through a number of examples how a holistic approach to preventive conservation can be effected in practice. Key points include:

- The organisation must want to achieve high standards of care for its collections and have developed appropriate policies and the mechanisms to implement them if it is to achieve the standards of care that ensure the long-term preservation of its collections.
- There is a need to turn data into useful improvements in collections care. To do this, data on humidity, temperature, light, pollution and pest levels must be developed into information that can be readily understood by colleagues and can be used to formulate decisions which lead to actions that reduce the risks faced by objects in the museum environment.
- Engage with the reality of buildings, their operation and maintenance. There is a need to appraise critically the fabric of buildings and analyse critically the process of monitoring and maintaining the buildings' environments, to ensure that what is supposed to happen actually occurs. It is essential that staff understand accurately and completely every step in the process if the museum environment is to effectively controlled.

Resources are a key issue in determining the extent and nature of preventive conservation work that can be done. Good organisation and planning can minimise the problem of limited resources. Catherine Nightingale's paper (2005–6) (Chapter 37) explores the problems, particularly that of dust, faced by conservators, designers and curators in seeking to create an exhibition of fashion clothing in the Linbury Gallery of the Museum of London with insufficient funds to build museum cases for all the clothing. This meant dealing with the problems of costume on open display. Nightingale's paper shows that, by understanding in detail dust distribution patterns and the risks to the objects from visitor touch, through the use of simple precautions such as plinths, high and low barriers and locating objects at distances greater than 1.5m from the visitors, the risks to the objects could be minimised. Crucially, through monitoring the dust levels, conservators were able to assure the museum that dust-level mitigation strategies were effective. The light levels, in the 50–100 lux range, were higher than the normally recommended 50 lux maxima for textiles, though, as the exhibition ran for only 9 months, the annual light doses for the objects were, in practice, well below recommended annual levels. Interestingly, although the gallery was air conditioned, in practice the RH levels were between 45% and 65% for only 70% of the time. The extremes of RH were not recorded, though the temperature fluctuations between 28°C and 11°C in this gallery may go some way to explain the RH fluctuation. There may be concern that for 30% of the time the objects were outside the 46–65% band, but most unconfined textiles can cope with some RH fluctuation and the more 'at risk' objects were in glass cases, and so protected from the RH extremes. This paper demonstrates how modern conservators and curators are engaging actively with the concept of risk, which is increasingly being judged at an individual object level.

The realities of museum life mean that there are regular instances of collections remaining in museums buildings in which building work is being undertaken. The case study by Siobhan Watts, Janet Berry, Amy de Joia and Fiona Philpott (2002) (Chapter 38) of building work undertaken in Liverpool Museum and the Walker Gallery explores the threats from vibration and dust to the collections whilst they remained stored or displayed in the building under renovation. It demonstrates the steps that are appropriate to take, such as pragmatic risk assessment; identifying and removing objects at greatest risk from vibration damage before work starts; putting into place vibration and dust monitoring procedures and establishing 'working' maxima of 0.5G for vibration and 5 soiling units per week (soiling unit = 1% reduction in light reflection), based on previously published work. Despite initial testing to ensure that building activities did not exceed working standards, active monitoring during the process showed failures to control both dust and vibration by the contractor. This demonstrated both the need for regular meetings between museum staff and building contractors and the requirement, on occasion, for direct intervention to halt potentially damaging situations. The importance of communication and the need for management and control of building work as part of a preventive conservation approach is very clearly demonstrated.

The challenges of preventive conservation are, perhaps, at their greatest for objects on open display in unheated buildings such as those at St Fagan's, the National Folk Museum of Wales. Sue Renault (2006) (Chapter 39) describes how all the 'agents of deterioration' are present and active, with the additional handicap of curatorial neglect, seen in the form of previous inexpert cleaning, which has damaged a number of the objects. The benefits of authentic, powerful and sensory stimulating displays in open-air museums (Shafernich 1993) need to be balanced with the damage to arte-facts that open coal fires and human contact bring. The risks to the object from con-tinued open display are assessed with reference to the extent of visitor access. Smaller objects are considered sufficiently safe from theft behind 'roped off' areas, but they are removed from display areas with unrestricted visitor access, as the risk of theft is assessed as too high (see Chapter 9). This creates false visual differences between displays in different buildings or different areas of the same building, thus affecting visitors' perceptions of life in post-medieval rural Wales.

Renault also describes how at St Fagan's one of the key elements in the assess-ment of risk of open displays is the number of visitors a property receives; the higher the visitor numbers, the greater the damage (intentional and unintentional) that is done. The damage they cause varies from property to property, depending on its con-tents and the materials from which they are made. This leads to restrictions on access and closing of properties and is a good example of risk assessment in action and the concept of the 'carrying capacities' of historic properties: the numbers of people who can visit the property with minimal risk to the historic fabric and contents. The ques-tion of carrying capacities has been discussed in detail by Helen Lloyd (2006).

Note

1   http://www.collectionslink.org.uk/?ct=search.home/catList/2

References

British Standards Institute (2009) *PAS197:2009 Code of Practice for Cultural Collections Management*, London: BSI Keene, S. (1996)

Lloyd, H. (2006) 'Opening Historic Houses', in National Trust, *Manual of Housekeeping*, London: Butterworth-Heinemann, pp. 671–685.

Museums and Galleries Commission (1998) *Levels of Collections Care: A Self-Assessment Checklist for UK Museums*, London: MGC.

Nightingale, Catherine (2005–6) 'Designing an Exhibition to Minimise Risks to Costume on Open Display', *The Conservator* 29: 35–50.

Putt, N. and Slade, S. (2004) *Teamwork for Preventive Conservation*, Rome: ICCROM, http://www.iccrom.org/pdf/ICCROM_01_Teamwork_en.pdf

Renault, Sue (2006) 'Make Yourself at Home: Looking After an Open-Air Museum', in C. Butler and M. Davis (eds), *Things Fall Apart . . .*, Cardiff: National Museum of Wales, pp. 6–14.

Resource (2002) *Benchmarks in Collections Care for Museums, Archives and Libraries*, London: Resource.

Shafernich, S. M. (1993) On Site Museums, Open Air Museums, Museum Villages and Living History Museums: Reconstructions and Period Rooms in the United States and the United Kingdom, *Museum Management and Curatorship* 12: 43–61.

Watts, Siobhan, Berry, Janet, de Joia, Amy and Philpott, Fiona, 'In Control or Simply Monitoring? The Protection of Museum Collections from Dust and Vibration during Building Works', in R. Vontobel (ed.), *ICOM-CC 13th Triennial Meeting Rio de Janeiro 22–27 September 2002*, London: James & James, 2002, pp. 108–115.

Chapter 35

Levels of Collections Care: a self-assessment checklist

Museums and Galleries Commission

Introduction

THE MUSEUMS AND GALLERIES COMMISSION (MGC) has produced this handbook with the intention of setting out clear and realistic benchmarks for the care of museum collections. *Levels of Collection Care* aims to help museums and related organisations evaluate how well they are caring for their collections, giving an indication of where and what improvements might be needed and providing a benchmark against which future progress can be measured. The *Levels of Care* provide a guide, but should be considered alongside factors such as the significance of the collections and the way in which a museum uses them.

The scheme operates at three discrete levels, using the MGC's Registration Scheme as a framework. The minimum criteria set out for Registration constitute the foundation from which increasingly higher levels of collection care are developed. Complementary sets of levels of achievement for other aspects of museum activity can be developed using the same basic structure.

The three levels of collection care are:

*   Basic Practice – a minimum standard laid out in the MGC Registration criteria, which all museums should be able to achieve. Conservation and collection care issues that are not directly addressed in the Registration Scheme have been developed, making this a more comprehensive document.
*   Good Practice – this describes a good standard that is achievable by the majority of museums. This level represents a consensus of current professional opinion of best practice, tempered with realistic expectations.

Source: *Levels of Collections Care: A Self-Assessment Checklist for UK Museums*, London: MGC, 1998.

- Best Practice – this is the highest standard to which a museum can aspire and reflects a consensus of current professional opinion of best practice, much of which is enshrined in the MGC's series of publications, Standards in the Museum Care of Collections.

These three levels are consistent with the standards matrix developed by the MGC, which is also reflected in other MGC initiatives and publications. The general approach used in the Levels of Collection Care scheme is first describing the current situation in order to raise awareness, then identifying action to be taken and, finally, implementation and review. The levels are presented in table format, with the same headings as those used in the MGC's Registration Scheme. The Registration criteria are presented in the left-hand columns and the text is taken directly from the Registration Guidelines, with a few minor additions to ensure clarity and comprehension. The collection care levels are presented in the right-hand columns: Basic, Good and Best Practice. Each change in level is a discrete enhancement from the preceding one. The changes in level are cumulative – each building on the one below and subsuming it. It is important to realise that these levels underline the quality and breadth of collection care activities rather than relating to the size or type of museum, the nature of the collections or the staffing. The highest levels could equally be achieved by a well-managed museum run entirely by volunteers as by a large, national museum with a full-time staff.

The *Levels of Care* are descriptive and recognisable. A museum can use them as a self-assessment checklist, working through the tables to assess their current level of achievement. The outcome can be used in the development of a Forward Plan, or as an element in preparatory work for an application for Registration, Recognition, Designation or a Heritage Lottery Fund Grant. A more formal assessment might be required to meet a museum's needs, or as part of a local, regional or national assessment programme which may require the use of an external adviser. The MGC welcomes comments and suggestions from museums who have used this self-assessment scheme. The scheme will be reviewed approximately one year after publication and a decision made on whether further documentation, guidelines or support programmes should be developed.

REGISTRATION REQUIREMENTS AND GUIDELINES AND LEVELS OF COLLECTIONS CARE

The Museum

- Meeting the UK Museums Association's definition of a museum (Guideline 1.1) 'A museum is an institution which collects, documents, preserves, exhibits and interprets material evidence and associated information for the public benefit.'
- Meeting the MGC's definition of a 'national' museum in those cases where a museum uses the term 'national' or equivalent in its title (Guideline 1.2).

Basic Practice	There are no specific Levels of Collection Care for these elements of Museum Registration.
Good Practice	
Best Practice	

Museum management

- An acceptable constitution (Guideline 2.1).
- Evidence that the collections are, as far as possible, secured in the long term for the public benefit (Guideline 2.2).
- Formal arrangements to manage the collections (Guideline 2.3).
- Professional museum input into policy development and operational management (Guideline 2.5).

Basic Practice	There are no specific Levels of Collection Care for these elements of Museum Registration.
Good Practice	
Best Practice	

- The museum's statement of purpose and key aims (Guideline 2.4).

Basic Practice	This should include a reference to conserving for future generations the collections and associated evidence of our history, culture and environment.
Good Practice	
Best Practice	

Access to professional advice

- Adequate staff, whether paid or unpaid, temporary, permanent or contracted, to fulfil the museum's responsibilities (Guideline 3.1).

Basic Practice	An individual is assigned responsibility for caring for the collections. An individual is assigned responsibility for managing volunteers who work on the collections.
Good Practice	The individual assigned responsibility for caring for collections has a written job description. Museum has written policy on use of volunteers for collection care activities. All consultants working for the museum on collection care related issues have a written brief.
Best Practice	Conservation or collection care professionals operating at decision-making level of management. All individuals who work on the collections have written job descriptions outlining area and level of responsibility within collection care.

- Access to professional curatorial advice (Guideline 3.2).

Basic Practice	There are no specific Levels of Collection Care for this element of Museum Registration.
Good Practice	
Best Practice	

- Access to professional conservation advice (Guideline 3.3).

Basic Practice	There is an adequate number of conservation or collection care staff to enable the museum to meet the collection care requirements of the MGC's Registration Scheme. The museum seeks and receives on a regular basis advice from an experienced conservation or collection care professional on the museum's general performance in all areas of collection care. All conservation or collection care professionals providing advice or services should be members of a professional organisation and adhere to the code of conduct/ethics appropriate to their field. Any conservation or collection care practice that is contracted to provide advice or services should normally be included on the MGC's Conservation Register.
Good Practice	A professionally trained and/or experienced conservator is consulted as part of a planned approach to collection care to give advice, guidance and/or training on all aspects of collection care.
Best Practice	The governing body/management committee receives a written annual report on the general condition of the collection, which includes a description of areas of concern or specific problems and an action plan containing recommendations on how the situation can be improved.

- Staff training and development (Guideline 3.4).

Basic Practice	Staff training needs in the field of collection care are assessed periodically. All staff receive basic training in care and handling of objects as part of induction training.
Good Practice	Ongoing collection care training, education and awareness-raising needs identified. Training policy formulated based on identified needs. Training programme implemented to develop appropriate collection care skills.
Best Practice	Training needs and provision reviewed as part of museum's forward planning cycle.

Collecting policy

- Description of the museum's collection including significant loans (Guideline 4.1).

Basic Practice	There are no specific Levels of Collection Care for this element of Museum Registration.
Good Practice	
Best Practice	

- Acquisition and Disposal policy which meets the Registration requirements (Guideline 4.2).

Basic Practice	The museum's Acquisition and Disposal Policy states any limitations on collecting, including acceptance on loan, imposed by factors such as inadequate staffing, exhibition facilities, storage (quality or capacity) or conservation resources.
Good Practice	Only items which the museum has the resources to care for in the long term are collected or accepted on loan.
	Advice is sought from a conservator or other collection care specialist familiar with the museum's facilities and resources when drafting or revising Acquisition and Disposal Policy.
	Advice is sought from a conservation or collection care professional about any items being considered for acquisition or disposal by the museum.
Best Practice	A museum intending to revise its Acquisition and Disposal Policy addresses any inadequacies in conservation and collection care that have restricted collecting in its Forward Plan.

Documentation

- Maintenance of basic documentation records (Guideline 5.1).

Basic Practice	Any cleaning, repair, restoration, conservation or equivalent processes to items in the collections recorded.
	Results of all inspections or surveys of collections are recorded.
	Record kept of the use/status of objects in the collection.
	Museum has access to documentation records covering conservation, repair or restoration work undertaken both in-house or commissioned.
	Museum stores conservation documentation as securely as other object documentation.
	Conservation documentation records are cross-referenced to object number.
Good Practice	Documentation records for Condition Checking, Conservation or other relevant procedures conform to SPECTRUM: The UK National Documentation Standard.
	Museum possesses documentation describing all conservation or restoration treatments undertaken either in-house or contracted out.
	Record kept of all monitoring of environmental parameters e.g. light, relative humidity, temperature, pollutants, pests, etc.
	Record kept of calibration and maintenance of all environmental monitoring equipment.

	Record kept of any monitoring and treatments for pest infestation, whether to individual objects, collections or the museum building. Record kept of all operating (playing, running or working) of objects, where appropriate. Documentation recorded using archival standard methods and material, and stored in environment designed to ensure its long-term preservation.
Best Practice	Record kept by museum of all building works, maintenance and inspections. Record kept by museum of all inspections, maintenance, upgrades and repair of plant and equipment. Record kept of special events held in museum and visitor numbers. The level of technical information required to describe any remedial conservation work undertaken on objects is specified, and this information provided to those undertaking the work. Documentation Procedures Manual lists standard conservation and related procedures and provides guidance on recording. Procedures in place to initiate routine inspections of buildings, stores and galleries, and of condition surveys of objects or collections.

- Planned programme to eliminate backlogs, if they exist, within a stated timescale (Guideline 5.2).

Basic Practice	
Good Practice	
Best Practice	Museum has programme to obtain any relevant conservation treatment records of objects in the collection, which it does not currently have.

Care of collections

- Evidence that a museum has taken reasonable steps to preserve the collections (Guideline 6.1).

Conservation

Each museum should aim to store, handle, display and use its collections in such a way as to minimise risk of damage and deterioration and thereby increasing long-term access to, and appreciation of, the collection.

Storage

Basic Practice	An individual is assigned responsibility for stores and objects housed in them. Procedures in place to manage access to the stores.

Access to stores normally restricted to staff and approved researchers.
If at all possible, objects are not stored in a building that is not
under the control of the museum's governing body/management
committee. Where this does happen, then suitable management
procedures are in place, agreed by both parties.
Assessment made of potential hazards such as high-level water
pipes, drains etc.
Potentially flammable material isolated from rest of collection.
Clear, flat working area available in storage area for examination/
sorting of objects.
All small objects are kept separate and contained.
Objects protected from dust.
Large objects stored on racks or pallets.
Objects are not stacked on top of or inside one another.

Good Practice   Objects with special storage needs identified.
The museum has at least one separate area dedicated to object
storage.
Space is sufficient to provide indoor storage of existing collection.
Preventive measures taken to protect objects from identified haz-
ards such as water or drain pipe-work passing through store.
There is a store plan near the entrance showing the layout of the
store.
All bays, cabinets, shelves and boxes are clearly numbered and
labelled with light- and water-resistant ink.
All objects are accessible and easily retrievable.
All objects/containers are on shelves or on pallets raising them
above the floor sufficiently to permit cleaning and to protect from
flooding.
Shelving is padded to prevent damage to objects.
Doorways and aisles are sufficiently wide to allow passage of large
objects and trolley/transporter.
Objects are not stored in aisles.

Best Practice   All object storage areas are physically separate from any public and
administrative areas.
Special controlled environments provided for objects identified as
requiring this.
Separate space used for storage of non-collection items.
Temporary holding area available, separate from main storage and
exhibition areas.
All storage furniture and materials are as inert as possible and do
not give off vapours which are harmful to objects in direct contact
or close proximity.
Objects are stored in accordance with recommendations in relevant
MGC specialist Care of Collections Standards, where appropriate.

Handling

Basic Practice	All staff have basic knowledge of how to handle and transport collection items. Some equipment available for moving objects. Some equipment available for gaining access to objects. Protective clothing available and used where necessary.
Good Practice	Objects requiring special care when being handled or moved are identified (or programme in place to complete in specified time-scale) and this information added to object history file. Objects requiring special care are physically identified (label, box etc). Advice taken from specialists when large or unusual objects are to be moved. Researchers are supervised at all times.
Best Practice	Objects are handled in accordance with recommendations in relevant MGC specialist Care of Collections Standards, where appropriate.

Display

Basic Practice	Advice is sought about appropriate display techniques and materials when setting up an exhibition/display or building a display case. Programme of checking condition of objects on display that are considered particularly vulnerable. Physical access to objects on display for museum staff is kept as simple as possible without compromising security.
Good Practice	Conservation or collection care professional is part of exhibition team. Programme in place for routine checking of all objects on display. Materials and techniques used in the construction of displays/exhibits are approved by a conservation or collection care professional. Exhibition areas can be isolated from other areas of the museum. Access is possible to allow periodic cleaning and maintenance of 'dead' areas. Light fittings can be changed or adjusted without the need for access via display volume. Display cases incorporate appropriate features to protect objects.
Best Practice	Objects displayed in accordance with recommendations in relevant MGC specialist Care of Collections Standards, where appropriate.

Use of collections

Basic Practice	Upon acquisition, all objects are assessed to determine their use/status in the museum and this information recorded in the object's documentation.

Good Practice	The use/status of objects is reviewed periodically and any change approved by museum management.
Best Practice	Objects are used in accordance with recommendations in relevant MGC specialist Care of Collections Standards, where appropriate.

Operating or playing

Basic Practice	No object is played or worked unless the museum's governing body/management committee have formally approved this activity.
Good Practice	Museum has a written policy on who can operate or play objects that have been designated as suitable. Information on playing or working kept in object conservation file.
Best Practice	Individual operating/playing log maintained and kept with object's documentation.

Display outdoors

Basic Practice	No object is displayed outdoors unless it has been assessed as being suitable for such use by a conservation or collection care professional, or a person who has experience in the long-term, outdoor preservation of the type of object.
Good Practice	The decision to display an object outdoors is reviewed annually by museum management.
Best Practice	

Reserve/study collection

Basic Practice	Facilities for researchers/students include clear flat surface of adequate size in non-public area, provided with appropriate personal protective equipment.
Good Practice	Written guidelines on the care and handling of objects provided for researchers.
Best Practice	Member of staff supervises researchers at all times when they are studying objects.

Handling/schools loan service

Basic Practice	No object is made available for handling by visitors or schools' loans service unless it has been assessed as being suitable for such use. Items in Handling Collection are clearly identified as having this status.
Good Practice	Museum has written policy on use of objects for handling/schools loan collections and the provision of non-accessioned objects or use of replicas. Written guidelines on care and handling provided for non-museum professionals.
Best Practice	The special status of objects in handling collections is clearly demonstrated to all users.

Loans

Basic Practice	Condition of objects assessed as part of procedure for considering loan.
Good Practice	Loan agreement for any loaned object specifies conditions under which it is handled, transported, displayed and stored, and its condition assessed and reported to owner.
Best Practice	The museum applies the conditions described in the MGC publications Standard for Touring Exhibitions, Care of Collections Standards series and, where appropriate, the Government Indemnity Scheme Conditions for objects it loans.

Conservation off-site

Basic Practice	All items sent off-site for conservation treatment are handled, transported and housed in conditions to the same standard as those in the museum.
Good Practice	
Best Practice	

Measures to care for the collections

Museums must provide information on the measures that they currently take to care for their collections, together with their conservation plans and policies. Information may be submitted on the application form or by reference to a separate Collections Management Plan. Details where available should be provided in the following areas.

Collection condition assessments

Ensuring that you have a good overview of the condition of all items in your collection.

Basic Practice	Sensitive or vulnerable items in the collection identified.
Good Practice	Simple condition survey of collection completed, or planned programme in place to complete in specified time-scale.
	Condition reports exist for items identified as being particularly sensitive or vulnerable.
	Condition surveys undertaken by conservation or collection care professional.
Best Practice	Collection care plan, or equivalent section of Forward Plan, prioritises collections requiring more detailed condition surveying and proposes action plan.

Environmental monitoring

This includes temperature, relative humidity, light and pollutants. Monitoring can be carried out with simple as well as sophisticated instruments.

Basic Practice	An individual is assigned responsibility for monitoring the museum's environment.
	Basic environmental data is collected.
	Monitoring equipment is stored and calibrated as recommended by manufacturer.
Good Practice	A programme is in place to measure relative humidity, temperature and light levels (visible and ultraviolet), in galleries and object stores.
	Environmental monitoring programme is based on the environmental conditions the museum has identified it wishes to achieve.
Best Practice	Data from the environmental monitoring programme is examined periodically and a summary prepared.
	Data from the environmental monitoring programme is used to inform decision-making during planning for any improvement scheme or major development to the museum.
	Periodic assessments are made of the ongoing environmental monitoring needs of the museum.
	An assessment is made of potential atmospheric pollutants and a programme of spot checks is in place.

Assessment of building conditions

Whether the building is sound and can provide the best possible environmental conditions for your collection. (NB – Plant, equipment, utilities should also be included in this section though they are not specified in the Registration Guidelines.)

Basic Practice	Buildings are inspected periodically by staff.
	Plant and equipment is inspected periodically by staff.
	Funds are available for building maintenance.
	Funds are available for maintenance of plant and equipment.
	Museums that close and are unoccupied for periods of the year are visited and inspected regularly.
Good Practice	Buildings are regularly inspected by architect, surveyor or other competent person.
	Schedule for the routine maintenance of building and utilities is in place.
	Schedule for inspection and service of plant/equipment is in place.
	Museums that are closed for long periods during the year have a programme of actions to ensure the safety and well-being of the collection and the building during this period.
Best Practice	Reports on building condition used in the planning of improvements or major developments to the museum, and to revise Forward Plan.
	Museum has in place a comprehensive operational and maintenance programme for its buildings, services and plant.
	Museum has in place guidelines on the behaviour of contractors/service providers on site.

Environmental control

Control can be achieved by using simple as well as sophisticated measures.

Basic Practice	The building in which the collection is housed is wind- and water-tight, and can provide basic protection to the collection.
	Museum has determined the level of control of the environment (temperature, relative humidity, light and pollutants) it wishes to achieve.
	Simple measures are taken to control environment to the levels the museum has determined it wishes to achieve
Good Practice	The building in which the collection is housed can act as a buffer against unfavourable weather conditions outside.
	An individual is assigned responsibility for overseeing control of the museum's environment.
	Controlled environments established for some vulnerable objects.
	Bulk of collection housed to protect from extreme conditions.
	Housekeeping inspection of all areas of museum undertaken periodically.
	Maintenance programme for environmental control equipment (including UV filter replacement) is in place.
	Museum staff has management control over operational settings of all environmental control equipment/plant.
	Products used by cleaning and maintenance staff are selected to avoid those which give off gas or fumes potentially hazardous to collections (e.g. chlorine, hydrogen peroxide) and this is specified in contract if appropriate.
	All internal building surfaces are finished with a seal, where appropriate, to reduce dust.
Best Practice	The building in which the collection is housed has high insulation properties and is built or improved to a high specification.
	Special environments established for all objects/collections identified as requiring this, or planned programme of improvements to achieve this in specified time-scale.
	Developments to achieve improved environmental conditions are based on assessment of needs of the collection, environmental monitoring data and building inspections.
	The environment is controlled in accordance with recommendations in relevant MGC Care of Collections Standard, where appropriate.

Pest control

This can be achieved through simple good-housekeeping.

Basic Practice	An individual is assigned responsibility for monitoring and control of pests.
	'Ad hoc' inspections made of building and collections.

All objects and associated packing materials entering the museum
building are inspected for possible pest infestation.
Any pesticide treatment is done in compliance with the relevant
Health & Safety Regulations.

Good Practice   Objects/collections/areas at highest risk are identified and there is
a programme of visual checking for infestations.
Museum has reviewed types of pest that could potentially harm the
collection, building or museum operations.
Access points for potentially harmful pests identified.
Museum has isolation area to house all items coming into the build-
ing prior to examination for possible pest infestation.
A pest-monitoring programme is in place.
All trapped insects identified.
Advice is taken from a conservation or collection care professional
before pest treatment is undertaken on museum object or collec-
tions, or part of museum buildings housing objects.

Best Practice   Integrated pest management programme in place.

Maintenance of conservation treatment records

These constitute a significant part of an object's documentation and should be retained
by the museum whether its own staff carries out the work, or outside specialists.

Basic Practice   See **Documentation**
Good Practice
Best Practice

Planned programme to institute improvements in collections

Where deficiencies are identified, whether in the condition of individual items or in
the conditions in which they are housed, displayed or used, the museum should plan
to institute improvements over time, and on the basis of priority. These objectives
should be reflected in the Forward Plan.

Basic Practice   Periodic reviews evaluate the condition of the collection and
summarise priorities for improvements.

Good Practice   Identified priorities for improvements to collection care are under-
pinned by action plan to make improvements within a specified
time period.
Periodic reviews of collection care use a consistent methodology,
such as the MGC's Levels of Collection Care, that enables direct
comparisons to be made and so monitor progress.

Best Practice   There is a periodic review of collection care strategy which
contributes to the revision of policies and programmes, ensuring a
planned approach to improvements in overall collection care.

• Evidence that a museum has taken reasonable steps to ensure the security of the
collections.

Basic Practice	Any independent practice taking responsibility for an object for the purpose of undertaking conservation or related work (including transportation to off-site facility) meets the criteria for security, insurance and good care required of those practices that are accepted on to the MGC's Conservation Register.
Good Practice	An assessment is made by a member of staff, or someone acting on the institution's behalf, that the level of security is appropriate for any object that is transported or housed off-site whilst undergoing conservation or related treatment.
Best Practice	

Risk assessment and security systems (Guideline 6.2)

Details must be provided of the measures that the museum has taken to assess the risks to collections from such threats as fire, water, theft, and vandalism, and the appropriate steps to address these. This will include such measures as the identification of particularly vulnerable collections, the installation of physical protection and alarm systems, staff invigilation, key security systems, inventory check procedures and insurance arrangements. Where problems are identified, museums should make an assessment of additional requirements and plan to meet these within an appropriate time-scale. Specialist advice should be sought as necessary.

Basic Practice	Assessment of risk to the collection care of objects is incorporated into the Levels described elsewhere in this section.
Good Practice	
Best Practice	

Emergency planning (Guideline 6.3)

Each museum should aim to develop emergency planning systems for the protection and rescue of the collections in the event of emergencies, such as theft, fire, flood or other catastrophes. An emergency planning system might include compiling and updating a manual (recording details of suppliers of specialist equipment and services), floor plans (identifying key features of the building and its contents to help salvage and loss control) and checklists (to regulate routine maintenance to reduce risks). Museums should indicate whether they have drawn up such plans or are considering doing so.

Basic Practice	Museum has identified need to draw up an emergency response plan and has programme to complete this in a reasonable time-scale.
Good Practice	Disaster recovery equipment and materials available. Museum has details of suppliers of specialist equipment and services for use in an emergency. Floor plans (identifying key features of the building and its contents) are available to help salvage and loss control. Local police and fire service are informed about potential risks to

collection when responding to an emergency.

Assessment made of potential hazards to collections such as high-level water pipes, drains, flammable materials etc.

Best Practice   An emergency planning system for the protection and rescue of the collection in the event of emergencies is in place.

There is a programme for the regular updating of the plan and associated information.

Rehearsals of emergency response procedures carried out regularly.

Public face of the museum

- Opening hours and access arrangements appropriate to the nature and location of the museum (Guideline 7.1).

Basic Practice	There are no specific Levels of Collection Care for this element of Museum Registration.
Good Practice	
Best Practice	

- A range of public services appropriate to the nature and scale of the museum (Guideline 7.2).

Basic Practice	Museum is able to respond to public enquiries on the basic care of objects.
Good Practice	Museum takes measures to explain to visitors the risks and special needs of objects on display. Conservation and collection care are integrated into the museum's public education programme where these exist.
Best Practice	Museum has a programme to communicate to visitors how it cares for its collections and to raise awareness of the wider applications.

- A range of visitor facilities appropriate to the nature and scale of the museum (Guideline 7.3).

Basic Practice	There are no specific Levels of Collection Care for this element of Museum Registration.
Good Practice	
Best Practice	

Financial management

- Budgets or accounts for the past two years (Guideline 8.1).

Basic Practice	There are no specific Levels of Collection Care for this element of Museum Registration.
Good Practice	
Best Practice	

- A planned approach to budgeting (Guideline 8.2).

Basic Practice	Collection care projects prioritised.
	Resources required for collection care identified.
	All contracted out conservation work is undertaken on the basis of the 'Guidelines for competitive tendering and professional practice' produced by UKIC on behalf of the Conservation Forum.
Good Practice	Resources allocated to collection care projects.
Best Practice	Annual review of museum's resources, facilities and activities used to identify and prioritise collection care projects.
	Review used to identify resources needed to maintain and develop levels of collection care.

- Long-term security for the museum building (Guideline 8.3).

Basic Practice	There are no specific Levels of Collection Care for this element of Museum Registration.
Good Practice	
Best Practice	

Authorisation of information

- Formal approval of:
  - the museum's statement of purpose and key aims
  - the museum's acquisition and disposal policy
  - the appointment of a curatorial adviser if appropriate (Guideline 9.1).

Basic Practice	
Good Practice	
Best Practice	Formal approval of Collections Management Plan or equivalent.

- Declaration that the museum's governing body has complied with all relevant legal, safety and planning requirements (Guideline 9.2).

Basic Practice	COSHH assessments completed for all processes covered by the legislation.
	Museum has copies of hazard data-sheets for all chemicals, products etc. used or stored on the site.
Good Practice	
Best Practice	

MODEL ASSESSMENT CHECKLIST

Assessment made using the MGC's Level of Collection Care

MGC Registration Scheme Section	Levels of Collection Care		
	Basic	Good	Best
The Museum			
• Meeting the UK Museums Association's definition of a museum	Shading indicates where Levels of Collections Care are not applicable		
• Meeting the MGC's definition of a 'national' museum			
Museum management			
• An acceptable constitution			
• Collections secured in the long-term for the public benefit			
• Formal arrangements to manage the collections			
• Professional museum input into policy development and operational management			
• Museum's statement of purpose and key aims			
Access to professional advice			
• Adequate staff and appropriate training			
• Access to professional curatorial advice			
• Access to professional conservation advice			
Collecting policy			
• Description of museum collection			
• Acquisition and Disposal policy			
Documentation			
• Maintenance of basic documentation			
• Planned programme to eliminate backlogs			
Care of collections			
• Preserve the collection			
Conservation			
Storage			

Handling			
Display			
Use of collections			
Operating or playing			
Display outdoors			
Reserve / study collection			
Handling / schools loan service			
Loans			
Conservation off-site			
Measures to care for the collection			
Collection condition assessments			
Environmental monitoring			
Assessment of building condition, assessment of plant, equipment etc.			
Environmental control			
Pest control			
Maintenance of conservation treatment records			
Planned programme to institute improvements in collections			
• Evidence that a museum has taken reasonable steps to ensure the security of the collections			
Risk assessment and security systems			
Emergency planning			
Public face of the museum			
• Opening hours and access arrangements			
• Range of public service			
• Range of visitor facilities			
Financial management			
• Budgets or accounts			
• Planned approach to budgeting			
• Long-term security for the museum building			

Authorisation of information			
• Formal approval of policies			
• Compliance with relevant legal requirements			

Chapter 36

Information for Preservation

Suzanne Keene

[. . .] Preservation – preventive conservation – is not easy. Like rigorous total quality management, preservation will affect procedures and work practice in practically every museum operation. It includes raising awareness of what can be done to avoid damage to objects. Many necessary measures are negative ones – 'thou shalt not' – and attempting to implement them unfortunately gives conservators a reputation for being negative spoil-sports.

Conservators are often urged to compromise. This notion could do with some examination. Compromise in these terms can be taken to mean giving permission for objects to be displayed or housed in conditions that are less than optimal. This is not the conservator's role. The conservator's role is to be a source of expert knowledge of the effects on objects of various physical and climatic factors, and of how these factors can be modified, and to give their opinion and advice accordingly. This advice may be taken or not taken; but the conservator cannot say that in their opinion a watercolour will not fade if displayed at 2000 lux if it is their opinion that it will fade. As a designer once remarked to me, dealing with conservation requirements is no better and no worse than dealing with building or fire regulations. They exist for the wider benefit and have to be worked with, if the organization so decides.

Where the notion of compromise enters is in accepting that the risk from imperfect conditions over a finite period may be minimal. Risks from environmental factors may in fact be less serious than we previously thought. Innovative ways are being found to address requirements. The watercolour could be exhibited at 2000 lux for ten days and still be within Thomson's standards if it was stored for the rest of the year. In fact, the conservator cannot say that the watercolour will not fade if it is displayed at 50 lux,

Source: *Managing Conservation in Museums*, London: Butterworth-Heinemann, 1996, pp. 112–135.

the accepted limit for sensitive material. Fifty lux was chosen as the light limit for sensitive materials not because it does no damage, but because that is the lowest light level at which people can effectively perceive colour. Recent studies have indicated that people aged over fifty need higher light levels, and so the standard should be adjusted to take account of that. Conservators' efforts might be better spent ensuring that security lighting was minimal out of visiting hours – something that nobody could disagree with.

If they are to be expert advisers, then there is a strong obligation on conservators to be genuinely expert. One of the first duties of the preservation conservator is to keep up with the latest thinking on the effects of climatic factors. These are likely to become less significant, not more, as real life effects are assessed. Recent work by Michalski and by Mecklenberg is establishing this new view (Michalski 1990; Mecklenberg and Tumosa 1991a, b; Michalski 1993). As Christoffersen (1993) observes, there is now 'no overwhelming evidence that a perfectly steady climate is necessary for the stability of . . . objects'.

Conservators are highly knowledgeable and intelligent, and they come from a wide variety of technical backgrounds. Because the profession is not very large, they are also very good at networking on an international scale, and do not suffer from information overload to the degree that is experienced elsewhere. This means that in conservation there really is a great deal of real understanding of the effects of environmental factors on objects, of how these factors can be controlled, and of highly innovative ways in which this can be done; more than is found in most heating and ventilating engineering companies. The trouble is that conservators lack credibility with these other professionals, because they do not hold their recognized qualifications, and because contractors can be sued (though in my experience this is rare) if what they install fails to provide the specified conditions. An excellent example of this situation, and of what can be achieved by applying understanding and imagination, is set out by Cassar and Clarke in their work on environmental control for the Courtauld Gallery in Somerset House (Cassar and Clarke 1993).

Standards and policies

Standards for the museum environment should, ideally, express the results of expert work and knowledge in a form that can be easily communicated and the application of which can be monitored. Outside standards for museum operations can be used as a valuable counterweight to the drive for accountability based on finance and public activities alone. Conservators should seize on standards; they are an official validation of professional knowledge and opinion. The relevance of standards to museums generally is discussed by Caton (1991), and specifically to conservation by Cassar and Keene (1990). Fortunately, there are many recognized standards and guidelines for the conservation of collections. Standards may exist, however, but the organization needs to express its organizational will to apply them by specifically adopting as policy those it considers most relevant.

Standards and specifications for the environment for collections are thoroughly dealt with by Thomson (1986), and in the extensive literature (see Section B1 in the *Art and Archaeology Technical Abstracts*). These now include the curatorial standards and museums registration schemes being developed by the Museums and Galleries Commission (1988; Paine 1992a,b, 1993, 1994) for different types of collection. They are discussed in Cassar and Keene (1990).

Standards do have to be used with circumspection. While many authors advocate the use of fixed standards, another view, put forward by Michalski (1990), is that standards are too rigid and encourage institutions to disregard the undeniable fact that some objects will deteriorate even though standards are adhered to. For example, he says, in the case of maximum light (lux) limits, standards for maximum exposure may be too high for some objects, and needlessly low for others. Michalski is extending his critical appraisal of standards into those for relative humidity and temperature.

The concepts embodied in these approaches differ more than do their use in the management of deterioration. In both, it will be necessary for the institution to set policies for the environment for its objects, and apply these to the spaces in which they are kept by means of specifications. If standards are to be used, then the particular ones to be adhered to will need to be stated: for instance, BS 5454 for paper and archive collections; Thomson (1986: 33) Class I for sensitive objects. If standards are not to be used, then the policy must specify the procedure for setting parameters for the storage or display environment for each class of object or individual object. But either way, parameters still have to be set, and a formal record of them maintained.

While standards are commonly set for temperature, humidity and light, parameters for gaseous and particulate pollution are less often specified, because they are much more difficult to measure and expensive to control. While Thomson does give parameters for these factors, they are not included in, for example, BS 5454: 1989 (British Standards Institution 1989), the British Standard specification for library buildings, other than for mechanical air handling; or in the Museums and Galleries Commission *Standards in the museum care of . . . collections* (Paine 1992a,b, 1993, 1994) other than for particulates such as dirt and dust.

Special reports

From time to time, it will be useful to take an overview of preservation in the museum. This will entail special investigations, to draw together the results of ongoing monitoring, and to assess factors such as storage quality that it is not useful to monitor continuously. Investigations like this will form the basis for strategies for preservation. Examples are assessments of the standard of stores, and audits of collections condition. Information for conservation strategies and planning will need to be collected to answer the questions:

*   What is the size of the tasks we will be addressing?
*   What are we aiming to achieve?
*   What do we need to do to achieve it?
*   How should we plan to do it?

Judgements and assessments of quality

To a conservator, environmental monitoring usually means logging temperature, humidity and light; but many of the most drastic effects on the well-being of objects are brought about by aspects of the environment that can only be assessed by making a visual judgement. Examples are the adequacy of space in stores, whether buildings are sound or have leaks, whether conditions are clean or filthy dirty, whether objects are adequately enclosed or supported, and whether organizational procedures are satisfactory, such as those for putting objects away after use. The Museums and Galleries Commission's *Standards in the museum care of . . . collections* (for instance, Paine 1994) set out desirable standards for these aspects. They are further discussed below, under Stores assessments.

Like numerical information, this more qualitative information should be collected at regular intervals. In order to set targets for improvement, and measure progress, these non-numerical assessments need to be categorized in some way.

Stores assessments

Appropriate storage is the foundation for effectively preserving collections. There are several models for stores assessments. In the USA, the Department of the Interior is responsible for archaeological collections and archives held by the National Parks Service. Special Directive 80–1, issued in 1986, requires any National Parks site having collections to assess the standard of storage annually, to declare what improvements are necessary, and to report action since the report the previous year. Also in the USA, the Getty Conservation Institute (GCI) and National Institute for Conservation (NIC) have jointly developed a procedure and published guidelines for 'conservation assessment' (Getty Conservation Institute and National Institute for the Conservation of Cultural Property 1991). This is an explanatory checklist, which takes a holistic view of the care of collections. It is meant to be used by independent consultants, from another institution or working privately, who are commissioned by a museum to visit it and report on the care of its collections. The report then forms the basis for action and for seeking grants.

Other more general views of the care and management of collections, again in the USA, are gained through the Museum Assessment Program (MAP). This is run by the Association of American Museums (Association of American Museums 1985), and encourages assessment and improvement among museums in a similar way to that described for the Conservation Assessments. In the UK, we have the *Standards in the museum care of . . . collections* which are being issued by the Museums and Galleries Commission (e.g. Paine 1994). These standards do not include assessment checklists, but they do provide detailed guidelines on how collections should be cared for.

Case study: stores assessments

The Conservation Department in the Historic City Museum was becoming much more outgoing, and as they all made more visits to the stores, the conservators became very aware of what a tiny proportion of objects in the collection they were able to treat. Each conservator was familiar with some stores, those that housed their particular type of collection, but few of them had even visited all of the stores. They knew that, as in many museums, while storage for some collections was exemplary, storage for others verged on disastrous.

Storage improvements were in the air, because the museum was in the early stages of specifying a large new off-site store, which would take the contents of many of the existing stores. The Conservation Department had been encouraged by the senior management team to develop a strategy for collections preservation. They decided that as part of this strategy development all the museum's stores should be surveyed, necessary actions identified, and the results summarized and included in the strategy as recommendations to the museum's senior management.

The conservators debated how to collect and analyse the information. The museum had many different stores – altogether about thirty separate spaces. From attending conferences and visiting museums abroad, the conservators were familiar with developments in America, in particular, the Conservation Assessment and Museum Assessment Program, and the National Parks Service Special Directive (Getty Conservation Institute and National Institute for the Conservation of Cultural Property 1991; US Department of the Interior 1986). They also consulted the recent survey of science and industry collections in Yorkshire and Humberside (Kenyon 1992), which had assembled this sort of information.

The Head of Conservation would be the person to draw together the results and draft the report, so she strongly favoured a uniform format for assessing the stores, with minimal text. The American formats, although recording much useful information, seemed rather wordy. However, a very useful feature of the National Parks Service Special Directive was that major deficiencies of stores had to be declared, and progress on rectifying them reported each year. The Yorkshire and Humberside survey was the result of a consensus of many people in the surveyed museums; it offered a format that was quick to complete and analyse, but it omitted information about the store building itself, which is an extremely important factor. Therefore, a new Stores Assessment Form was devised that combined, the conservators hoped, the best features of the existing variants (Figure 36.1). To give the survey the maximum authority, the assessment elements were checked against the Museums and Galleries Commission's *Standards in the museum care of . . . collections* (e.g. Paine 1994).

Assessing the stores using these new forms was a rapid exercise. After some experimentation, the Head of Conservation decided to supplement the written report with graphic summaries, as in Figure 36.2.

The Head of Conservation felt that there was an opportunity here to encourage cohesion within the department as well as to broaden people's perspectives. A seminar was therefore arranged for the whole department, in which each section in turn presented their results and findings. This proved to be an excellent experience for some, but was perhaps more appreciated by the heads of section than by everyone. There proved to be an immense amount of material to digest – too much for a consensus view to form – and some conservators felt that it had resulted in little progress. However, with the results from the completed forms fortified by the many suggestions and observations that had arisen in discussion, the Head of Conservation was able to go away and write what she felt was a coherent and realistic strategy, one that it would be difficult for the museum to reject. The conservators as a whole were now the best informed group in the museum on the general state of the collections, as was proper to their role.

STORES ASSESSMENT FORM Museum: .... Store name/i.d.: ....

Floor area, m2: .... Location: .... Collections type/names: ....

Usable volume, m3: .... Fullness (%): 0 25 50 75 85 95 100 Over 100% ....

Most urgent action?:

	Good	Adeq	Poor	Unac		Good	Adeq	Poor	Unac
Building type Overall rating for collec. type:					Storage equip't Overall rating for collec. type:				
Purpose store					Racks				
"Office" type					Containers				
Light industrial building					Sufficiency of space for objects				
Open air					Access for moving, inspection, etc.				
Airtightness					Small overspill to floor				
Thermal mass or insulation					Access adequate				
					Moving equipment				
Action needed?:					**Action needed?:**				
Maintenance Overall rating for collec type:					Environm. control Overall rating for coll. type:				
Structural condition					Temperature control				
- walls, plaster, etc					Humidity control				
- roof					Dust pollution control				
- drains, gutters					Gaseous pollution control				
Decoration					Monitoring				
Preventive maintenance schedule					Light control				
Services					(Air conditioning - Y / N)				
Energy efficiency					(Local heat, humidity control - Y / N)				
Action needed?:					**Action needed?:**				
Action summary:					Object protection Overall rating for collec. type:				
1.					Containers				
					Acid free or suitable mounts				
2.					Objects supported by packing, etc.				
					Dust or dirt contamination				
3.					Pests or bird ingress				
					Action needed?:				
4.									

Figure 36.1 Stores assessment form. Although detailed and comprehensive, this can rapidly be filled in. Actions are to be noted at all points

Stores assessment data

Store name	Area, m2	Volume, m3	% Full	Collectn. type(s)	Building type	Maint-enance	Environ control	Storage equipm't	Object protect'n	Action needed
Anvil La yard				Large objs	U	U	U	U	U	Open air: unsatisfactory
Anvil La. 1.1	710	3,900		Large objs	G	G	A	G	G	
Anvil La. 2	460	2,300		Vehicles etc	A	A	A	A	P	Works need completion
Anvil La.1.2	47	150		Misc objs	A	A	A	A	A	
Anvil La.1.3	39	105		Smll. objs	A	G	A	G	A	
Anvil La.1.4	18	49		Misc objs	A	G	G	U	P	Objects for disposal?
Anvil La.1.5	41	110		Models	A	G	G	G	G	Some objs to be boxed
Archive sort	115	300		Paper	A	G	G	G	G	-
Brossay				Vehics	U	U	U	A	U	Open air: unsatisfactory
Drawing store	223	583		Paper	A	G	G	G	A	Monitor
Film store	21	48		Films	A	A	P	A	A	Temp. store; upgrade/relocate
Lib. plant rm	57	171		Library	A	A	P	P	P	Environm. control
Library st	123	492		Library	A	A	A	A	A	Better containers
Neg store 2	60	150		Photos	A	G	P	A	P	Better containers
New Rd. 1	168	424		Paper	A	A	P	A	P	Unsuitable store
New Rd. 2	120	240		Misc objs	A	A	A	A	A	Risk of leak/flood
New Rd. 3	48	112		Misc objs	A	G	G	G	G	Sort + stock check
New Rd. 4	58	151		Library	A	A	P	P	P	Undertake maintenance
New Rd. 5	88	229		Paper	A	A	P	U	P	Improve housekeeping
New Rd. 7	105	410		Misc objs	A	G	A	G	G	Sep. office from store
New Rd. 9	36	140		Textiles	A	G	A	G	G	-
Photo negs.	65	163		Photos	G	G	G	G	G	Monitor; improve containers
Pict/print	91	228		Paper	A	A	G	A	G	Roof repairs
Stitch row	500	2,000		Rail equip	A	A	A	P	P	?
East Yard				Vehics	U	U	U	U	U	Open air: unsatisfactory
West Yard	1,600	1,600		Veh equip	U	U	U	U	U	Open air: unsatisfactory
Totals:	*4,793*	*14,055*								

STORAGE QUALITY:	
E	Excellent
F	Fair
P	Poor
U	Unacceptable

Data sorted by object size

Store name	Obj size	Collectn. type(s)	Building type	Maint-enance	Environ control	Storage equipm't	Object protect'n	
New Rd. 9	S	Textiles	F	E	F	E	E	Storage good to adequate
Anvil La.1.5	S	Models	F	E	E	E	E	
Anvil La.1.3	S	Smll. objs	F	E	F	E	F	
New Rd. 7	M	Misc objs	F	E	F	E	E	
New Rd. 3	M	Misc objs	F	E	E	E	E	
New Rd. 2	M	Misc objs	F	F	F	F	F	
Anvil La.1.4	M	Misc objs	F	E	E	U	P	
Anvil La.1.2	M	Misc objs	F	F	F	F	F	
Photo negs.	P	Photos	E	E	E	E	E	
Archive sort	P	Paper	F	E	E	E	E	
Drawing store	P	Paper	F	E	E	E	F	
Pict/print	P	Paper	F	F	E	F	E	
Library st	P	Library	F	F	F	F	F	
Film store	P	Films	F	F	P	F	F	Storage poor or unacceptable
New Rd. 1	P	Paper	F	F	P	F	P	
Neg store 2	P	Photos	F	E	P	F	P	
New Rd. 4	P	Library	F	F	P	P	P	
Lib. plant rm	P	Library	F	F	P	P	P	
New Rd. 6	P	Paper	F	F	P	U	P	
West Yard	L	Veh equip	U	U	U	U	U	
East Yard	L	Vehics	U	U	U	U	U	
Stitch row	L	Rail equip	F	F	F	P	P	
Brossay	L	Vehics	U	U	U	F	U	
Anvil La. 2	L	ehicles etc	F	F	F	F	P	
Anvil La. 1.1	L	Large objs	E	E	F	E	E	
Anvil La yard	L	Large objs	U	U	U	U	U	

Shaded areas designate poor or unacceptable standards of storage.

54% of stores are good to adequate, including all newly established ones. These stores are occupied mainly by medium to small objects.

46% of stores are in some aspects poor or unacceptable These stores are occupied mainly by large objects and by paper, library and film

Figure 36.2 Diagrams summarizing the results of stores assessments. This proved to be an excellent way of communicating with senior management

Collections condition audits

A third area which may be the subject of special investigations and reports is the condition of the collections: how successful is the museum in discharging its duty to preserve them? [See Chapter 28, 'Collections condition'.]

Environmental monitoring

Temperature and humidity were found in 'The Survey' (Corfield et al. 1989) to be recorded in about half of all the museums and galleries which responded. In the present most common method of data collection – the clockwork thermohygrograph – one instrument must be left in each location being recorded; and each instrument produces one paper chart per week, fortnight, or month, depending on the interval selected (Figure 36.3). Instruments and systems that record digital measurements on

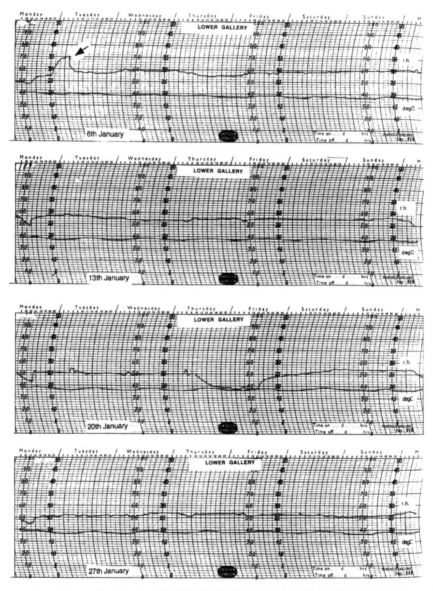

Figure 36.3 Recordings from weekly clockwork thermohygrograph charts for a gallery during January. The arrow indicates a distinctive peak in relative humidity, due to temporary failure of the chiller unit

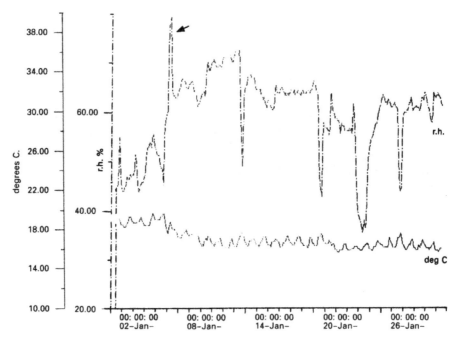

Figure 36.4 Chart from digital recordings using a Squirrel electronic data logger. The arrow indicates the same peak as in Figure 36.3

electronic media are being used much more commonly (e.g. the Squirrel data loggers made by Grant Instruments, the Findlay Irvine monitoring system, the MEACO Museum Monitor, and a variety of building management systems). Some options are discussed in Saunders (1989). Figure 36.4 shows an example of a chart produced from a Squirrel data logger.

Light is usually monitored by single measurements taken with an electronic lux meter, rather than continuously. Standards are expressed in terms of a maximum level of lux or ultraviolet light, so this is often sufficient. Continuous recording is necessary if the object is lit by natural light, since the levels of this will vary and a single reading will not suffice (e.g. Staniforth 1990). Continuous readings also make the alternative form of standard, for kilolux-hours per year (Thomson 1986: 30 and 268), more feasible to administer. Other simple ways of logging cumulative light exposure are described by Tennant et al. (1982), and Kenjo (1986). Instruments are becoming available to continuously or cumulatively log light exposure (e.g. the Elsec and Hanwell instruments, manufactured respectively by Littlemore Scientific Engineering Co. and Exeter Environmental Services). Cumulative light exposure can also be monitored by the Blue Wool Standard test (BS 1006 1978), in which pieces of textile dyed with colourants with known fading characteristics are exposed. These can give a highly graphic picture of the effects of light on an object.

Pollution, whether gaseous or particulate, is seldom measured; 'The Survey' (Corfield et al. 1989: 81, Q. 5.1) recorded only fifteen museums out of 938 as doing this. Some simple test strips for measuring some pollutants are described in

Kenjo (1986). Other passive sampling devices are described by Grzywacz (1993). The Museum of London has employed passive monitoring for nitrogen dioxide using diffusion tubes. The tubes are sent to a laboratory for analysis. Hackney (1984) has reviewed other methods of monitoring gaseous pollution.

Pests. An excellent example of pest monitoring and its use is given in Florian (1987). The variables recorded included those for time, geographical location and insect species. All were used to diagnose the problem, eradicate active infestations, set up new procedures for prevention, and design ongoing monitoring.

Presenting and using environmental data

Analysis over time

Temperature and humidity may be recorded either in analogue form by a recording pen on a paper chart (Figure 36.3), or else as digital measurements taken at set intervals (printed out as a chart, Figure 36.4). In the case of analogue thermohygrograph records, each chart contains a wealth of data (and one can quickly accumulate a filing cabinet full), but it is extremely difficult to make much general sense of this. In management terms, we need answers to questions such as:

- For what proportion of the time is the environment within/outside the set parameters? (This monitors whether set standards are being attained.)
- What is the variation per hour/day/week/year? (Fluctuations are sometimes more damaging than even sustained levels at an inappropriate relative humidity or temperature.)
- Is there a diurnal or other regular pattern to variations? (If so, there may be a cause that can easily be corrected.)

The first and second questions can potentially be answered if measurements are recorded digitally instead of graphically, since computer software is supplied with the instrument with which to analyse the data. The software that is supplied by the digital instrument manufacturers facilitates graphic presentation (e.g. Squirrel-soft, supplied by Grant Instruments), and will give some statistical information. None of the software supplied with data loggers fully meets requirements as yet, although it is improving. To really undertake the necessary statistical analysis, the data needs to be downloaded into a spreadsheet and manipulated as an entirely separate operation.

Although records from clockwork thermohygrographs are very difficult to use to gain an overall picture over any length of time, they do have particular advantages, because the readings are continuous (i.e. analogue) rather than being taken at a series of fixed intervals, as are those from electronic data loggers. For example, the clockwork thermohygrograph chart in Figure 36.3 shows a record of a period in a gallery. The distinctively shaped peak (indicated by an arrow) to 70 per cent relative humidity at the beginning of the week '7th January' indicates a failure or cut-out of the heating and ventilating system chiller unit, but this could not be deduced from the data logger chart, Figure 36.4 which simply shows a peak at that point (again indicated by an arrow). This illustrates a loss of information, because the readings on the thermohygrograph chart are continuous, whereas the data logger was recording at set intervals of half an hour. Although electronic data loggers can potentially save a lot of time, analogue instruments may still have their place, because of the richness of the information they offer to an experienced interpreter.

Thermohygrograph charts can be drawn on in various simple ways to give approximate answers:

Proportion of time within set parameters: visual estimates can be made of time outside parameters and regularly recorded as figures, and a summary chart (e.g. Figures 36.5, 36.7) can be drawn to give an idea of fluctuations over a longer period of

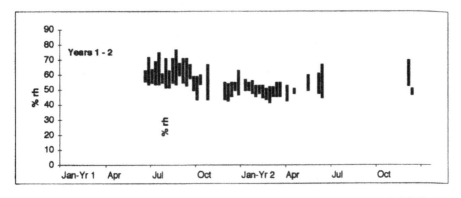

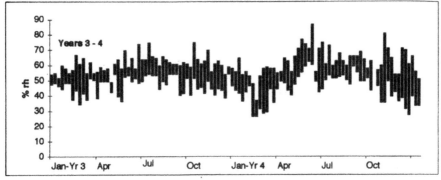

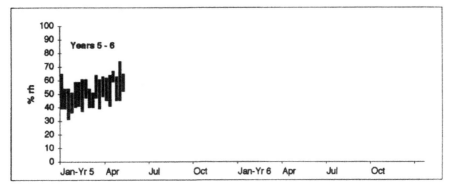

Figure 36.5 Chart summarizing weekly maximum and minimum relative humidity over five years

time. Digitally recorded output can be presented in charts with the time axis compressed (e.g. Figure 36.6a).

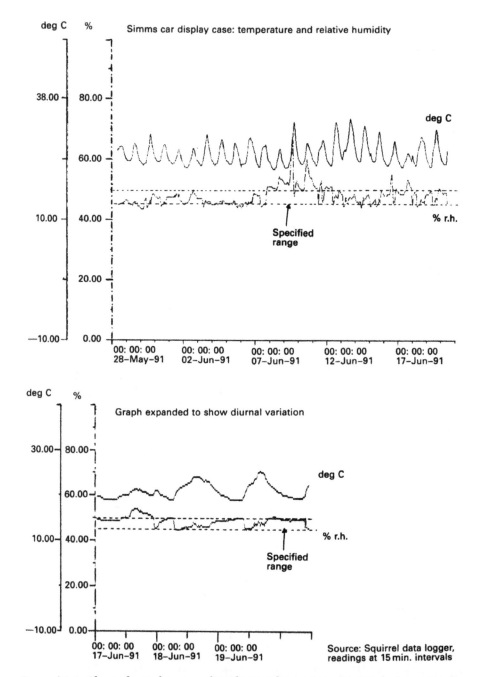

Figure 36.6 Charts from the same digital recording using a Squirrel electronic data
logger. (a) Four weeks, drawn with the time (x) axis compressed. (b)
Four days, drawn with the time (x) axis extended

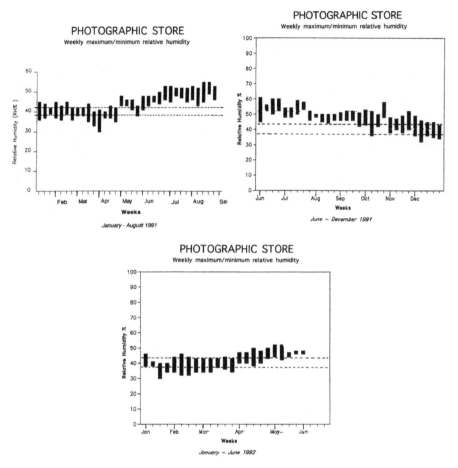

Figure 36.7 Chart summarizing weekly maximum and minimum relative humidity over three six-month periods. Seasonal fluctuation is clearly shown

Variation per hour/day/week/year: normal paper charts are adequate for short periods; but a summary chart (see Figures 36.5 and 36.7) is needed if variation over a longer period is to be shown.

Monitoring recurrent variation: the same chart can be left in place: as several traces accumulate, trends become apparent.

The great plus point of thermohygrograph charts is that, because they have been so widely used for such a long time, they form a universal means of communication between curators, conservators and air-handling engineers alike. Summary max–min charts (Figures 36.5, 36.7) are an obvious derivation of the familiar thermohygrograph charts. The most effective forms of management information seem to be these or line graphs with the time (x) axis compressed (Figure 36.6a).

Analysis by area

Environmental monitoring can be displayed spatially, showing the state of the environment at a point in time in the form of a plan of the building (e.g. Saunders 1989).

Although useful for analysing causes and effects, this is less crucial for understanding the effects on objects.

In the case of pest management, it is recommended that observations are recorded not only by time of year but also on a building plan; a visual pattern quickly builds up (Florian 1987). The same is the case in monitoring gaseous pollution: trends over time are of interest, since one would wish pollution levels to be decreasing, rather than increasing; but to understand what is happening it is also necessary to reveal pollution gradients by comparing levels in different areas: e.g. outdoors, in the entrance hall, deep within the display galleries, inside a showcase (Hackney 1984).

Building management systems

Monitoring, presentation and control can be done in other ways. Building management systems are becoming more common. Such systems are like networked data loggers and control systems combined. The spaces in the building are monitored for whatever factors are of interest, as is the state of the plant and the controls. Every aspect of the plant can be individually controlled, provided that it is connected to the system. Computer screens can display the state of the environment at a point in time in the form of a plan of the building (e.g. Saunders 1989). It is fairly new for such systems also to continuously log environmental parameters and to store the results over time, but this can now be specified.

Discussion

Is one method of monitoring better than another? Figures 36.3 and 36.4 are copies of charts from analogue thermohygrographs (clockwork instruments with hair hygrometers) and digital data loggers (Squirrel, Grant Instruments) for the same four weeks in January. The specified environmental parameters were 50 to 55 per cent relative humidity, 20°C. Although the traces look at first sight reassuringly level, close inspection shows that a high proportion of the time is outside specifications: up to nearly 60 per cent relative humidity for most of the week of 6th January, and down to 40 per cent relative humidity for most of a day in the week of the 20th January, with other sharp deviations from time to time. The charts, especially if seen one at a time at weekly intervals, do not permit an overall view of conditions, although they do provide a rich source of data.

In the Squirrel data logger (Grant Instruments) chart, for one of the same galleries during January (Figure 36.4), the vertical scale has been expanded, giving a much more dramatic picture. The same features can be seen as on the analogue thermohygrograph trace, but in addition, the regular drops in relative humidity which occur every Monday (when the plant was switched off for maintenance) stand out clearly – on the normal charts they are less obvious because they occur at the beginning of the chart. This is a digital recording, and any area of the graph could be shown at an expanded scale for closer inspection.

The summary max–min graph (Figure 36.5) shows the maximum and minimum relative humidity. It is a very effective means of indicating overall seasonal variation and departures from specified parameters, but it gives no indication of how long deviations from specifications lasted. Like the Squirrel data logger presentation (Figure 36.4), it makes deviations from specification much more apparent than do weekly thermohygrograph charts.

The question is, which visual impression is closest to the effects of such deviations on objects? Work is only beginning on this central question: how much do environmental fluctuations matter? Is there a Pareto curve (80 per cent of the benefit comes from 20 per cent of the effort) for the benefits of a non-fluctuating environment? Padfield's theoretical data (1990) seem to show that in wood there is little response to short-term fluctuations. Michalski (1993) gives evidence that some objects can sustain prolonged drops of as much as 40 percentage points in relative humidity, but that others will be damaged by a fall of 25 percentage points. The effect of falls of much less than 25 percentage points he finds to be negligible. If, at any time in its history, an object has been kept for any length of time in a widely fluctuating environment, then most of the damage that can occur will already have done so. Only a few objects, particularly composite ones, and ones with a laminar structure such as paintings, will be damaged by drops in relative humidity. More will be damaged by biological activity arising from elevated relative humidity. As Michalski says,

> Drops of −40 per cent relative humidity do not constitute an emergency for loose skins, fur, textiles, costumes, metals, botanical specimens, or most archival material. In fact, it is a period of reduced decay . . . . For collections dominated by rigid organic materials (wood and paint), we must accept that the data support common sense, not magic numbers. Safe relative humidity is a broad valley . . . if total control sacrifices reliability of the 25–75 per cent relative humidity limits, or other issues like fire and pests, I believe it is counter-productive to the total well-being of most collections.
>
> (Michalski 1993)

Do we then assume that fluctuations such as that on 7th January, shown both on the thermohygrograph chart (Figure 36.3) and on the Squirrel chart (Figure 36.4) do not matter? In this particular case, the objects in these galleries had been exposed to many such fluctuations, and worse, over time. For example, on a previous occasion, the air-handling system failed completely at the height of the summer, and the galleries were exposed to humidities of 80 to 90 per cent for over two weeks. Rigorous inspection found only one case of damage to objects clearly attributable to this: some medieval coal, in which the sulphide mineral had decayed, causing its total disintegration.

Case study: managing the environment

The Historic City Museum had about fifteen recording thermohygrographs producing either weekly or monthly charts. From these records, it was obvious that environmental conditions in some of the stores and galleries were far from meeting generally accepted standards. Yet, although records had been kept for a number of years, it had proved to be almost impossible to bring about much improvement to conditions.

The problem fell into two parts. First was the nature of the buildings and spaces themselves. The museum building had been constructed in the 1920s. It was a substantial concrete and masonry structure in which ventilation was mainly natural, with mechanical air supply only to a few specific galleries. There was no possibility of large-scale investment in air-handling plant for most of the museum. Some of the stores were located in this same building, but others were in a substantial brick-built warehouse not far from the museum.

The second part of the problem was to do with people and organizations. The museum's buildings, plant and services were maintained and managed by the Buildings and Estates Department of the local authority. The services engineers were often found to be slow to act, and to have little interest in tackling the museum's problems.

It was decided that it might help the situation if a regular forum for communication were set up. A committee was therefore established, to meet quarterly to review problems (and successes!) and agree on and monitor action. As well as the engineers and the Head of Conservation, the museum's house manager was included, as she controlled the museum's own in-house maintenance budget.

The first thing to emerge was that the engineers had in fact never been given specifications for the museum spaces, apart from the few galleries with mechanical ventilation. Simple specifications of relative humidity and temperature were drawn up for each of the spaces for which the engineers were responsible.

Next, a conservator was designated Environmental Liaison Conservator. This person would coordinate environmental monitoring by the different conservation sections, monitor and analyse the results, and be a single channel of communication with the engineers. As well as contacting the engineers informally when necessary, she prepared summary charts for the two-monthly museum environment meetings, and reported on them (e.g. Figure 36.7).

As soon as the state of the environment on the central site could more clearly be understood, a programme was set up to review the environmental control packages, particularly for the stores, and modify them or install new ones as necessary. The cost of this turned out to be much less than had been supposed: in the region of £3000 to £4000 per store if new equipment was needed.

Through these meetings and information, the museum was at last communicating its requirements clearly and creating a forum which decided on, planned, and monitored the necessary action. It would be satisfactory to report a dramatic improvement in environmental conditions. It is true that some newly installed plant was brought up to correct operation fairly rapidly. But, in spite of much genuine cooperation by the local authority's senior representative, hardly any of the new equipment which had been planned had been installed eighteen months after it had been agreed. The environment in the galleries, never good, was deteriorating, if anything, still further.

The reasons for this apparent lack of success were several. The museum had no real power over the local authority, because the authority was also a major funding body for the museum. The local authority personnel suffered from organizational problems of their own, as well as a general underestimation of the need for engineering and technical expertise in the field of environmental control. The museum building was old, and the local authority was reluctant to invest money in a structure which it saw as having a finite life. Information may be necessary for effective operation, but alone it is not sufficient.

Nevertheless, the foundation of understandable, accurate and sufficient information and data on the environment will benefit the museum, both as the basis for firmer diplomatic action with the local authority and also if the maintenance and operation of the environmental control plant is contracted out under compulsory competitive tendering. It was of great benefit when planning and specifying the new store, as environmental records for areas with mechanical ventilation in the museum could be compared (unfavourably!) with those for a naturally stable off-site warehouse store. As a result, the museum was able to decide with some confidence that the expense of mechanical HVAC would not be necessary for the new store if certain structural design principles were adhered to. The building should if possible be a substantial masonry one; storage spaces should if possible be enclosed by offices, ceilings and roof spaces, and circulation corridors; and storage spaces should be as completely sealed as possible, so as to obtain the fullest benefits from the thermal mass of the building.

Tales of the environment

It is a cause of particular difficulty that architects and services engineers are familiar with environmental control by means of mechanical air handling, to the exclusion of all other possibilities. Stories about over-reliance on expensive mechanical and computerized systems are commonplace, and a few of them illustrate the principles described above.

Story 1: No connection

A small-scale ventilation system was designed and installed to control the environment in three large sealed showcases. A computerized building management system was set up for the whole building, with a monitor in each showcase, but the individual monitors for each case were not properly identified. The conservators in any case monitored the cases independently using Squirrel data loggers. They found that the environment in the cases rarely met the specifications. After two or three years with no improvement, an important loaned object had to be returned to its owner, and a trusted and reliable engineer was called in. He found the root of the problem to be that the air-handling ducts passing air from the ventilation plant to the showcases had never been connected to the plant.

Story 2: Not invented here

A medium-sized museum had always had problems with its air conditioning plant, which failed to produce the specified environment. To try to tackle this, the museum employed a consultant engineer to review the design of the part of the system for each gallery as it was redesigned. For one gallery, due to house particularly delicate objects, the engineer produced drawings which would fundamentally alter and improve the supply and extract systems. Having produced the design, he was unfortunately not called on to monitor the installation of the system, which was undertaken by sub-contractors. When he reappeared on the scene he was horrified to find his drawings in a torn dusty heap in the corner, with the redesigned system bearing no relationship to them. As installed, it would not work. The project suffered thousands of pounds' worth of delay while the worst mistakes were rectified.

Story 3: Separate spaces

The temporary exhibition gallery in a museum was renowned for its fluctuating and damp environment, despite supposedly having full air-conditioning. When an exhibition including important borrowed paintings was planned, it was decided to make greater efforts to improve conditions. The engineers were asked to run the plant for a month before the exhibition to allow for acclimatization. They did so, but for two weeks, despite all their efforts, the environment fluctuated wildly. Eventually they investigated thoroughly and discovered that, during the construction of a previous exhibition, the air-conditioning control sensors had been completely enclosed in a sealed space against a poorly insulated outside wall.

Conclusions

There is a general and generic problem with the standard of expertise and people who work on building and services maintenance. This makes it extremely difficult to tackle environmental problems at their root, but with persistence and accurate information one can sometimes succeed. If you find an architect or a services engineer who really understands the principles of environmental control and is willing to be imaginative in their application, treasure them and never let them disappear into the wilderness.

Conservators need to be highly alert to developments in the understanding of the effects of the environment on objects. While they should stand firm in their expression of their expert opinion, they should make sure that they are expert, and be very aware of the different ways in which desirable conditions can be created. Conservators need to evolve preventive conservation into preservative conservation.

Conservators have often succumbed to the temptation to put their time and effort into monitoring the environment, rather than into investigating what real, simple improvements are possible through changing procedures and communicating with engineers and maintenance staff. The difficulty of effecting improvements, even though obvious, should not be underestimated. It is easy for conservators to be seen as encroaching on other people's patches, as indeed we do. Patience, persistence and time are needed. Always try applying brains and imagination, and the inherent characteristics of buildings and materials, to a problem before reaching for the mechanical environmental control plant. Always synthesize data into information before acting.

Finally, it is worth remembering that it is not changes in relative humidity and temperature that cause the worst damage to collections, but much more serious risks, such as grossly unsuitable storage – dirty, overcrowded, with buildings not even wind- and weather-proof; catastrophe when contractors are working in the building which houses the collections; or leakage or flood due to a badly chosen site or services routed through stores.

References

Association of American Museums (1985) *Museum Assessment Program: MAP 1 and MAP II questionnaires*, Washington DC: AAM.

British Standards Institution (1978) *BS 1006: 1978 Methods for the Determination of the Colour Fastness of Textiles to Light and Weathering, International Organization for Standardization Recommendation R105*, Milton Keynes: BSI.

British Standards Institution (1989) *BS 5454: 1989. The Storage and Exhibition of Archival Documents*, Milton Keynes: BSI.

Cassar, M. and Clarke, W. (1993) 'A pragmatic approach to environmental improvements in the Courtauld Institute Galleries in Somerset House', in *Preprints of the ICOM-CC 10th Triennial Meeting, Washington, DC*, Marina del Ray: Getty Conservation Institute/ICOM-CC.

Cassar, M. and Keene, S. (1990) 'Using standards', in S. Keene (ed.) *Preprints Managing Conservation Conference*, London: UKIC.

Caton, J. (1991) 'Setting standards', *Museums Journal* (January): 34–35.

Christoffersen, L. D. (1993) 'Resource-saving storage of historical material', in *Preprints of the ICOM-CC 10th Triennial Meeting, Washington, DC*, Marina del Ray: Getty Conservation Institute/ICOM-CC.

Corfield, M., Keene, S. et al., eds (1989) *The Survey*, London: UKIC.

Florian, M. (1987) 'Methodology used in insect pest surveys in museum buildings – a case history', in *Preprints of the ICOM-CC 8th Triennial Meeting, Sydney, Australia*, Marina del Ray: Getty Conservation Institute/ICOM-CC.

Getty Conservation Institute and National Institute for the Conservation of Cultural Property (1991) *The Conservation Assessment. A Tool for Planning, Implementing, and Fundraising*, Washington, DC: GCI & NICCP.

Grzywacz, C. M. (1993) 'Using passive sampling devices to detect pollutants in museum environments', in *Preprints of the ICOM-CC 10th Triennial Meeting, Washington, DC*, Marina del Ray: Getty Conservation Institute/ICOM-CC.

Hackney, S. (1984) 'The distribution of gaseous air pollution within museums', *Studies in Conservation* 29: 105–116.

Kenjo, T. (1986) 'Certain deterioration factors for works of art and simple devices to measure them', *International Journal of Museum Management and Curatorship* 5: 295–300.

Kenyon, J. (1992) *Collecting for the 21st Century. A Survey of Industrial and Social History Collections in the Museums of Yorkshire and Humberside*, Leeds: Yorkshire and Humberside Museums Service.

Mecklenberg, M. F. and Tumosa, C. S. (1991a) 'An introduction into the mechanical behaviour of paintings under rapid loading conditions', in *Art in Transit, Conference Proceedings, London*, Washington: National Gallery of Art.

Mecklenberg, M. F. and Tumosa, C. S. (1991b) 'Mechanical behaviour of paintings subjected to changes in temperature and relative humidity', in *Art in Transit, Conference Proceedings, London*. Washington: National Gallery of Art.

Michalski, S. (1990) 'Towards specific lighting guidelines', in *Preprints of the ICOM-CC 9th Triennial Meeting, Dresden*, Marina del Ray: Getty Conservation Institute/ICOM-CC.

Michalski, S. (1993) 'Relative humidity: a discussion of correct/incorrect values', in *Preprints of the ICOM-CC 10th Triennial Meeting, Washington, DC*, Marina del Ray: Getty Conservation Institute/ICOM-CC.

Museums and Galleries Commission (1988) *Guidelines for a Registration Scheme for Museums in the UK*, London: Museums and Galleries Commission.

Padfield, T. and Jensen, P. (1990) 'Low energy control in museum stores', in *Preprints of the ICOM-CC 9th Triennial Meeting, Dresden*, Marina del Ray: Getty Conservation Institute/ICOM-CC.

Paine, C., ed. (1992a) *Standards in the Museum Care of Archaeological Collections. Standards in the Museum Care of Collections, no. 1*, London: Museums and Galleries Commission.

Paine, C., ed. (1992b) *Standards in the Museum Care of Biological Collections. Standards in the museum care of collections, no. 2*, London: Museums and Galleries Commission.

Paine, C., ed. (1993) *Standards in the Museum Care of Geological Collections. Standards in the museum Care of collections, no. 3*, London: Museums and Galleries Commission.

Paine, C., ed. (1994) *Standards in the Museum Care of Larger and Working Objects. Standards in the museum care of collections, no. 4*, London: Museums and Galleries Commission.

Saunders, D. (1989) 'Environmental monitoring – an expensive luxury?', in *Environmental Monitoring and Control, Dundee, Conference Preprints*. Glasgow: Scottish Society for Conservation and Restoration.

Staniforth, S. (1990) 'The logging of light levels in National Trust houses', in *Preprints of the ICOM-CC 9th Triennial Meeting, Dresden*, Marina del Ray: Getty Conservation Institute/ICOM-CC.

Tennant, N. H., Townsend, J. H., et al. (1982) 'A simple integrating dosimeter for ultraviolet light', in N. S. Brommelle and G. Thomson, eds, *Science and Technology in the Service of Conservation*, Preprints IIC Washington Congress, London: IIC.

Thomson, G. (1986) *The Museum Environment* (2nd edn), London: Butterworth.

US Department of the Interior (1986) *Special Directive 80–1*, Washington DC: United States Department of the Interior.

Chapter 37

Designing an Exhibition to Minimise Risks to Costume on Open Display

Catherine Nightingale

Introduction

I N OCTOBER 2004, the Museum of London opened a major exhibition celebrat-
ing the history and creativity of London fashion, 'The London Look: Fashion from
Street to Catwalk', in which a large proportion of 120 costumes, both contemporary and historical, were put on open display. It was a unique opportunity to show
a large part of the comprehensive costume collection otherwise not on public view,
but a limited budget meant there was little money for new showcases. In light of
this, the traditional thinking behind the displaying of costume in the Museum was
reviewed, taking into account recent investigations into dust deposition and experiences of other institutions of placing costume on open display. Working closely with
the Museum's designers, an innovative design was created which aimed to minimise
the identified risks to the objects whilst still creating an exciting and visually stimulating experience.

Access

Recent government documents (DCMS 2005) and publications including the
Museums Association's *Collections for the Future* (Wilkinson 2005) remind museums
of their obligation to place as much of the nation's heritage as possible where it can
be seen and appreciated by the public, 'to continue to improve and broaden access'
(DCMS 2005: 12). Initiatives such as the Museums, Libraries and Archives Council's Renaissance in the Regions (Resource 2001) also aim to open up collections
to the general public. The financial situation of many museums is putting pressure

Source: *The Conservator* 29 (2005/6): 35–50.

on them to find ways of placing their collections in positions where they can be appreciated in ever more efficient ways. The Museum of London is no exception to this.

Approximately 1% of the Museum's collections are on display and, although there have been many successful initiatives to encourage visitors to see the stored collections, in terms of numbers of visitors and information learned, it could be argued that at present the most effective and informative way to increase access is to put objects on display. This is becoming more of a challenge; the budget for the first exhibition in the newly opened temporary exhibition gallery (the Linbury Gallery), '1920s The Decade that Changed London', was £500,000 (£1,000 per square metre). By 'The London Look', a year later, this had been reduced to £350,000 (£700 per square metre), especially challenging to those involved, given the generally relatively high costs of costume exhibitions.

The limited available budget meant that purchasing new showcases was not possible, and the existing cases were not numerous or large enough to accommodate the 120 outfits proposed for the exhibition. Approximately £65,000 had been spent on cases for the previous exhibition in the gallery, and it was estimated that, if re-used, they could house only about a fifth of the costume proposed for the exhibition. This implied that purchasing sufficient cases for the whole exhibition would cost approximately £260,000.

In the past, the concept of placing historic costume on open display would probably not have been considered by either conservators or curators at the Museum of London but, given more recent moves to make accessible as many objects as possible, it was felt that everything should be done to facilitate the exhibition in spite of the lack of resources. Since the main potential obstacles were the conservation concerns, the opportunity was taken to review policies on the display of historic textile items, hitherto placed in showcases.

The Museum of London has numerous objects on open display, in room settings and on plinths, but these are chosen for their more robust nature and are made of materials which can be dusted and cleaned with relatively little risk of damage. There was not a precedent for putting historic costume on open display; the Museum's only comparable experience was the holding of an exhibition of contemporary fashion consisting entirely of loan items belonging to a private individual who was happy for the costume to be on open display. The fact that an internal designer was appointed who had previous museum experience and knowledge of conservation issues greatly helped in the decision to consider open display as an option, in that it allowed for the creation of a design which could be used in a crucial way to help minimise risks to the costume.

Risk factors

In the early stages of exhibition planning, research was done into the potential risks to the costume if it were to be put on open display. There had been several exhibitions in other institutions in the recent past which had set a precedent, notably Versace at the Victoria and Albert Museum, and Giorgio Armani: A Retrospective at the Royal Academy of Arts, as well as the opening of the Fashion and Textile Museum in south

London. Information on the experiences gained from these was very useful in high-lighting the areas of concern. Information was also gathered from the experience of displaying other forms of textile items in historic houses.

The main potentially damaging factors which emerged were physical damage and soiling from visitor touching and dust, the latter being a problem not only in the visible distraction it could cause, but also in the potential damage caused by removing it from the costume, especially if this were to be done frequently. Both institutions reported having to regularly clean the items on display and had experienced visitors touching garments. At the Victoria and Albert Museum, it was necessary to clean the costumes every two weeks following visitor comments regarding visual dust, particularly on the darker items; the Royal Academy were also regularly cleaning and checking items on a weekly basis.

There had been leaks in the Linbury Gallery during its inaugural exhibition, mainly found to be caused by faulty drains. These had been repaired but, in a relatively new gallery, this was a risk to any object on open display, and particularly items made of textile. In addition, it was felt that attack from insects such as clothes moths, known to exist in the Museum of London, was more likely if items were not sealed in a case. Relative humidity and temperature fluctuations would also be more difficult to buffer.

Comparisons were complicated by the fact that historic costume was to be included in the exhibition as well as many twentith-century pieces, whereas these previous exhibitions consisted primarily of twentith-century or contemporary costume; the Royal Academy were able to dry-clean all items on display both before and after the exhibition, which would not be possible for the items on display in 'The London Look'. Some of the earlier costumes were very delicate and included vulnerable dresses, such as one with applied beetle wing decoration, and a painted Hartnell dress. Conversely, some of the contemporary items were seen as more vulnerable either to fading or potential theft. Overall though, the majority of the costume, even if historic, was felt to be robust. However, it was clear from the outset that a variety of strategies would be required, depending on the vulnerability of the objects.

Major institutions such as the Victoria and Albert Museum and the Royal Academy attract very large numbers of visitors compared to the Museum of London. The Versace exhibition at the Victoria and Albert Museum received 160,543 visitors in a three-month period whereas the 1920s exhibition at the Museum of London had 116,000 over a period of nine months. As will be discussed below, many potentially damaging factors can be linked to the volume of visitors passing through an exhibition; consequently, it was felt that the Museum of London would be at an advantage in terms of object preservation.

One of the other key factors in the decision to consider open display for the exhibition was the amount of time the items would be on show. 'The London Look' was to last for six months and was not planned for the summer months, when insect activity might be at its highest. The relatively short time-span would at least give a finite limit to dust deposition and cleaning regimes although these could only be estimated. In the event, the exhibition was extended to nine months, after consultation and agreement with conservation staff.

Dust

Recent research and projects such as the Leverhulme-funded project, as detailed by Lithgow et al. (2005), have greatly increased our understanding of the mechanisms of dust deposition and the nature of museum dust as well as how visitors perceive dust (Lithgow et al. 2003). Development of relatively straightforward monitoring systems (Adams 1997; Adams et al. 2001; Kibrya 1999) means that information about levels of dust in a particular area can be readily acquired. Combined with a basic understanding of the dynamics of the proposed exhibition space, it is possible to use this knowledge to predict something of the nature of the dust problem that can be anticipated.

The Linbury Gallery, the exhibition space used for 'The London Look', is two floors below the main visitor entrance and, like the rest of the Museum, has filtered air conditioning (fitted in this case with synthetic panel primary filters, glass fibre bag secondary filters and activated carbon filters). These factors should minimise the amount of dust from outside the building such as soil or street dust and atmospheric pollutants likely to be deposited. Research suggests that most visible dust deposited on objects is made up of fibrous particles, since they are by far the larger (Yoon and Brimblecombe 2000b), but that smaller particles may be more difficult to remove and more damaging in the long term (Tetreault 2003; Hatchfield 2002; Phenix and Burnstock 1990). The larger particles appear to come mainly from visitors' clothing and are found at highest levels in the areas of a gallery adjacent to the routes that visitors use, peaking around the entrance area of a given space. Dust levels fall off as the distance increases between visitor and object, falling by 50% with every metre (Lloyd et al. 2002). Dust from floor level, brought in on shoes, seems to be re-deposited at up to 30 cm from the floor, but very little above this height. There are also increased levels of dust found at a height of between 80 and 150 cm, probably caused by friction detaching fibres from visitors' clothing (Yoon and Brimblecombe 2000a; Lloyd et al. 2002).

During the preceding exhibition, monitoring was carried out in the gallery to establish the levels of dust deposited on objects on open display. Using the method modified by Adams (1997), glass microscope slides were placed horizontally in three locations and replaced on a weekly basis. They were sent to be analysed using Adams's method based on measuring the loss of reflective surface, also referred to as the loss of gloss method. This gives an indication as to the levels of dust deposited rather than the exact nature of the particles of which it consists. The percentage of loss of reflectance is used to calculate the results, which are expressed in soiling units per week (su wk^{-1}). A 1% reduction in reflectance after seven days' exposure is equivalent to 1 su wk^{-1}. There is an error of ± 1. Results from the monitoring (Figure 37.1) suggested what are regarded as being low levels; generally those under 5 su wk^{-1} are seen as low, 5–10 medium and 10–15 very high, of the levels to be expected outdoors. The results were encouraging, especially given the fact that the gallery had been completed just before the opening of the exhibition and it was anticipated that there would be a certain amount of building dust residue in the area.

The objects on open display in the previous 1920s exhibition included a car and furniture with polished surfaces. These had to be regularly dusted (every two weeks)

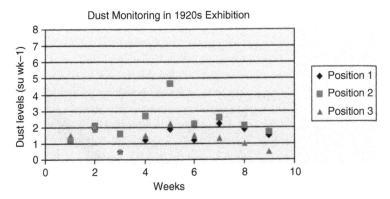

Figure 37.1 Results of dust monitoring in '1920s The Decade that Changed London' exhibition at the Museum of London

throughout the exhibition, due to very noticeable levels of dust; this suggested that, in spite of perceived low levels of dust, the same might be necessary in 'The London Look', especially on any dark polished surfaces. A visit from Peter Brimblecombe, currently working on the Leverhulme-funded project looking at many aspects of dust deposition, provided important insight into the nature of the dust. A visual inspection by him suggested that, as suspected, the visible dust was made up primarily of clothing fibres. There was little that could be done to reduce the levels of dust generally in the exhibition space but, taking all the above factors into consideration, it was felt that the design could help significantly in protecting the costumes on display.

Dust removal

It is not within the remit of this paper or the author's area of expertise to provide an in-depth discussion of the disadvantages or otherwise of cleaning textile objects. However, in general, it is agreed that any form of dust removal is potentially harmful to even the most robust textile. The main methods of non-wet cleaning involve the use of brushes and/or vacuum cleaners and will, inevitably, result in some loss of the textile fibre (Landi 1992). To what extent and at what point this becomes unacceptable is a matter for debate (Ashley-Smith 2003), but obviously damage will increase with frequency of cleaning. This must be balanced against evidence that certain particles, if left for any length of time, may form irreversible bonds with the surface (Tímár-Balázsy and Eastop 1998; Lithgow et al. 2005).

Estimates were made of the potential amount of time that would have to be devoted to cleaning the costume by conservation staff, as it was felt that this would be a dominant aspect of the maintenance of the exhibition. It was calculated that a thorough clean of all the costume on open display with brushes and vacuum cleaners would take approximately 30 hours and it was felt that this would possibly be necessary every four weeks. This estimate was based on the experience at the Victoria and Albert Museum during the Versace exhibition, when staff were cleaning every two weeks. Since our visitor figures were not expected to be nearly as high, it was thought that the same frequency would not be necessary.

Visitor touching

This can fall into several different categories, both accidental and intentional. There was some concern by the curators that certain items, particularly the more recent ones, would be targets for collectors and vulnerable to theft. The main risk to the costume, however, would probably be from casual touching, either by brushing past or intentional feeling of fabric texture and costume detail. This is a recognised effect of putting objects on open display; it is accepted that all objects on open display in the galleries at the Museum will be touched and consequently only those which can have any moving parts secured, and are robust enough to withstand any potential damage or to endure cleaning to remove greasy fingerprints or graffiti are chosen for display. Surfaces of objects are frequently coated with waxes or resins, where applicable, for protection. Textile items are equally, if not more, susceptible to touch; fabrics are created as much for the way they feel as for the way they look and the temptation to use the sense of touch to explore the exhibition was recognised as a factor in the risks to the clothing on display. Conversely, the damage caused by frequent touching to vulnerable costumes would be less reversible as well as potentially much greater, the staining harder to remove, and the physical damage more difficult to repair than on metal or wooden objects.

Conservation guidelines

Based on our understanding of the nature of dust deposition in the Linbury Gallery, and the other main risk factors, a list of conservation criteria was created for the designer to try to integrate into her initial design concepts for the exhibition (see Appendix 37.1). The key points of this were:

Plinths

All objects on open display should be placed on plinths approximately 30 cm high. This would serve a variety of purposes; it would minimise the amount of dust re-deposited from floor level on to the objects; it would create a physical and mental differentiation between visitor path and object display areas, thus reducing the temp-tation to brush past the costumes and it would protect the objects from potential damage during cleaning of the floor.

Barriers

These should be placed around all objects on open display to dissuade visitors from touching the objects and to reduce levels of deposited dust. They should be at least 1.5 metres from the object, as dust levels caused by visitors fall off greatly beyond this distance and this was felt to be the distance beyond which it would be difficult for curious visitors to reach out and touch the costumes. They should preferably be solid to the floor to catch dust, and should ideally be around 1 metre high to minimise the dust deposited at shoulder height; however, it was felt that the distance from visitor to costume was the most important factor.

Cases

All items of costume judged by the textile conservators to be too vulnerable to damage by touching or by cleaning to remove dust deposits should be displayed in cases. All accessories and smaller objects should be placed in cases for security reasons.

Positioning

As far as possible, objects deemed to be more sensitive to dust levels should be placed some distance into the exhibition area to avoid the higher levels of dust associated with the entrance. Account should also be taken of the need to place some more vulnerable items towards the centre of a given plinth rather than round the edges, where they could be touched; that way, the conservators could identify items which might appear more tactile to visitors or more vulnerable to physical damage to be positioned accordingly. There should be enough room between mannequins to allow access for cleaning and pest monitoring during the display.

Lighting

It was known from the outset of the project that the light levels would need to be kept relatively low to protect vulnerable dyes and delicate fabrics on display, but it was felt that the design could do much to compensate for this and create a bright rather than gloomy atmosphere.

Design of 'The London Look' exhibition

The eventual design of the exhibition was a result of several discussions and amendments as the project developed. Although there were some variations from the guidelines, these were always in consultation and agreement with the project conservator and the textile conservators. The importance of the clarity and achievability of the initial conservation guidelines cannot be over emphasised; this enabled them to be built in to the design concept right from the start, rather than is so often the case, an existing design having to undergo adaptation following conservation comments. The end result was felt to put the costumes in as safe an environment as was necessary to minimise the risks, whilst creating a design which fulfilled the Museum's requirements.

The concept of the design aimed to put a spotlight on the fashion industry in London from all angles and centred around the way in which the public view or access fashion, i.e. through the photographer's lens, by reading a magazine, watching catwalks on television or through advertising. There was a strong desire to recreate something of the glamorous mood and ostentatious atmosphere of the catwalk, and therefore to avoid traditional cases and conventional mannequins. Open display methods allowed garments from high fashion houses to be placed next to high street fashion and had the added intention of presenting the industry not just from a designer's point of view but also from the maker's or distributor's perspective. It was hoped that the exhibition would attract not only traditional museum visitors, but also young students of fashion and other fashion aficionados. More detailed information regarding individual costumes was presented in magazine-style booklets, reflecting the design concept of methods of accessing fashion. The practice of the fashion industry of using materials in unexpected ways was mirrored in the use of latex rubber as a wall divider and lace for defining the interactive areas.

With potential visitors accustomed to seeing outfits close-up on billboards and television, the design aimed to maximise the sense of openness of the exhibition whilst still allowing visitors to get close to the costumes. Wherever possible, each item on open display could be seen without viewing through glass from at least one point in the gallery. All the costume items on open display were placed in groups on plinths. Each main theme of the exhibition had a separate triangular-shaped plinth, with wide walkways splitting them into different sections, but also creating viewing points from a variety of angles. This enabled the garments to be seen from different perspectives and distances. The grouping of costume created maximum visual impact where colours might otherwise have been seen as dull to the casual observer, for example with suits or work wear (Figure 37.2). The plinths were a minimum of 20 cm high and were usually stepped to 40 or 60 cm high, enabling items towards the back to be seen clearly whilst still allowing large groups of costumes to be displayed together, maximising the number of garments that could be put on show. At the same time, the quantity of low-level dust deposited on the costume was kept to a minimum and objects were protected during floor cleaning. The disadvantage of this display method was that those items in the middle of the group could not be viewed close up.

Two types of barriers were used, all made of laminated glass. Approximately 50% of the plinth edges were surrounded by high glass panels set into the edge of the

Figure 37.2 The 'Tradition' section of the 'London Look' exhibition. The costume was arranged on a stepped plinth to allow groups of objects to be clearly seen, and high glass barriers around the rear two edges enabled visitors to get close to the items around the edges

plinth (Figure 37.3). At 2350 mm from floor level they were higher than all items on display, providing protection without interfering with the sight lines. The panels were 1000 mm wide and were attached at ceiling level with tension cables, although these were not felt to be structurally necessary once construction was complete. There were gaps between each barrier of 10 mm, which added to the sense of openness without enabling the objects to be touched. The height of the barriers allowed many objects to be displayed up close to the glass so that details on clothing could be easily viewed. It was hoped that this would compensate for the fact that in other areas items were placed a certain distance from the viewer.

Low glass barriers, 700 mm from floor level, were employed for approximately 40% of the plinth edges, usually along the main viewing point in the centre of the plinth next to the caption rails. The caption stands were placed immediately in front of them to further dissuade visitors from reaching or stepping over. Low-level cases displaying accessories and ephemera were used as barriers where possible on the corners or edges of the plinths, allowing open views.

The mannequins behind the low-level barriers were positioned so that the central pole was 1.5 metres from the plinth edge. This placed them well out of reach. Those behind the high barriers adjacent to the lower barriers were positioned 1 metre from where visitors would stand, as it was felt that most visitors would not reach round the edge of the higher pieces of glass. Beam alarms were used in strategic areas in the exhibition to protect items from theft, although anything felt to be easily removable was stitched to the mannequins, which were adapted to make this possible. No objects were situated in areas where leaks had previously occurred; the designer had positioned the plinths a safe distance from the vulnerable areas.

Cases were used for approximately one fifth of the costumes and for almost all accessories and ephemera, including shoes and handbags. Most vulnerable costume

Figure 37.3 Part of the 'Alternative' section of 'London Look'. High glass barriers were used to enable objects to be placed at the edges of plinths and to protect those felt to be more vulnerable

was placed in large re-used cases, especially around the introductory area, where dust levels were expected to be highest, and in the final contemporary section, which included a high proportion of fragile items such as painted fabrics. In other areas, where it was not always possible to position cases due to the themed nature of the exhibition, the higher glass barriers were used to increase protection where needed. Any costume items deemed too sensitive for open display which could not be put in cases were removed from the exhibition object list at early stages.

The necessary low light levels were compensated for by the design, which created what was perceived as a bright space even though the light levels on the costume were at 50–100 lux. The idea of the fashion photographer's flash was the inspiration for the large gloss-white angular plinths on which the bulk of the mannequins were displayed. The white reflected light and brightened the space. White mannequins blended into the background and helped focus attention on to the garments themselves as well as contributing to the lightness of the whole. From a design perspective, the simplicity of the plinths provided a blank canvas, allowing a Teddy boy outfit to be displayed next to a punk outfit, for example. Lighting around the edges of the plinths helped create contrast without jeopardising the objects, and in other areas, globe lights were hung above the cases without shining directly on to the objects. The use of film showing many of the costumes on live models added light and movement as well as giving another dimension to the exhibition.

Strategically placed interactive displays in clearly defined areas encouraged visitors to try on garments and touch and examine tailoring details and fabric samples (examples of the latter can be seen on the front of the plinths in Figures 37.2 and 37.3). It was hoped this would create a contrast with the real museum costume and discourage touching of objects whilst fulfilling the natural desire to feel the textile. It was necessary to replace or repair several of these during the exhibition, suggesting that they were well used by the visitors.

Exhibition maintenance

Throughout its duration, the exhibition was checked on a daily basis during weekdays by a member of the conservation department and a log was kept of any concerns. The inspection involved visual assessment of dust levels and looking out for any damage to the clothes on open display. Visitor numbers totalled 39,000, approximately half what they were for the previous exhibition; this may have had an impact on the levels of dust.

Cleaning of floors and plinths

The cleaning staff were given detailed instructions of methods to be used to clean the floors and cases. Floors were cleaned every morning with vacuum cleaners and damp cloths. This helped keep dust levels within the gallery to a minimum so that any at floor level would not be redistributed elsewhere as visitors walked through the exhibition.

The plinths were cleaned by conservation staff when necessary; care was needed to work round the mannequins and lift parts of dresses which were resting on the floor and it was seen as an opportunity to inspect the costumes close up. Dust Bunnies™ were found to be the most effective way of removing dust whilst keeping redistribution to a minimum. A log was kept of each clean. Generally, the plinths required dusting every two to three weeks. This was assessed on purely visual criteria: when dust balls could be seen in the corners or dust was judged to be distracting. Inevitably, the dust was more noticeable on the black plinths than the white and, on occasion, it was found necessary to give them an additional clean. In addition, as these plinths were situated in the introductory area, the levels of dust were likely to have been higher.

Cleaning and monitoring of the costume

Cleaning of the costume was carried out only twice in the nine-month period of the exhibition. Despite the fact that the plinths were noticeably dusty every two weeks, the costume did not appear so and it was felt more beneficial for it to remain uncleaned than for small amounts of dust to be removed unnecessarily. The lack of visible dust may be explained by the fact that the horizontal surfaces of the clothes, where large particles of dust are more likely to be deposited, were that much higher than the plinth surfaces and less dust was being deposited, or simply that it showed up less on the fabric of the clothes than on the polished flat surfaces of the plinths.

Dust on some items, such as a Paul Smith painted velvet jacket and a dark blue velvet dress, appeared obtrusive at an earlier stage than on other items; this was used as an indicator of when to clean. The extension of the exhibition from six to nine months confirmed the decision for the first clean; it was concluded that it would not be possible to leave the costume for the entire nine months, so it was decided to clean all items on open display half way through the exhibition and then again prior to de-installation. This was achieved using a Museum Vac®, or brushes. As predicted, each clean took staff approximately 30 hours in total. Each item was also thoroughly examined for any moth infestation. Significantly, the cleaning regimes roughly mirrored those of institutions such as the National Trust, who deal with textile items on display in historic houses. There, floors are cleaned daily when properties are open to the public and less accessible fragile objects are inspected only on an annual basis and cleaned if necessary (Lloyd et al. 2002). Since most properties are closed over the winter months, the frequency of cleaning is similar to that of 'The London Look'.

Samples of the dust removed from some of the costumes were retained; small squares of lightweight non-woven interfacing were placed between the two sections of the hose on the Museum Vac®, to trap any particles removed from a particular object. These were then stored in sealable plastic bags. This enabled comparisons to be made between the earlier and final cleans, and also provided a useful archive of the types of particles deposited and to what extent fibres from the objects were removed during the cleaning process. Inspection under magnification of the samples removed from the vacuum cleaner revealed that some fibres from the items had been removed as anticipated, but by keeping the dusting to a minimum it was judged to have caused minimal, acceptable levels of damage. The samples examined also confirmed that, as expected, the majority of the dust was fibrous clothing particles.

Thorough inspection of the costume at the conclusion of the exhibition revealed that there was no noticeable damage to any of the items on display. There were no reported incidents of touching of the costumes during the exhibition. In addition, there were no visible indications of any insect attack; all wool items were treated by freezing to ensure that this was the case.

Monitoring of dust

Weekly dust monitoring was continued in the Linbury Gallery throughout the exhibition. Slides were placed in a variety of locations on one plinth ('Fusion') so that comparisons could be made between areas behind the low barriers and behind the high glass panels; between the front of the plinth and towards the back; and also between shoulder level and base level on the mannequins. In the final month, further slides were positioned on two other plinths ('Introduction' and 'Innovation') to give a wider variety of information (Figure 37.4).

The results are shown in Figures 37.5 and 37.6. Overall, as anticipated, dust levels were low and this seems to be borne out by the fact that the costume required cleaning only twice. It is difficult to draw many firm conclusions about the function of the barriers and panels; the general low levels of dust recorded may [be the reason for] the variation between the results being insignificant. The 'Fusion' plinth chosen for the bulk of the monitoring was situated near the end of the visitor route through the exhibition, so it is likely that the dust levels were lower than in other areas of

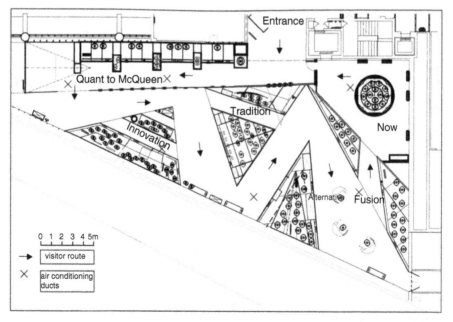

Figure 37.4 Plan of the Linbury Gallery in the Museum of London during the 'London Look' exhibition showing the anticipated visitor route and locations of the ducts for the air conditioning system

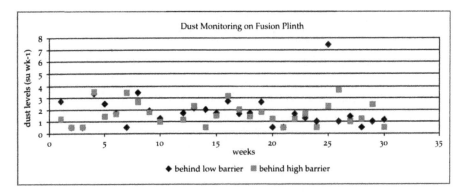

Figure 37.5 Results of dust monitoring immediately behind barriers on the 'Fusion' plinth in the 'London Look' exhibition

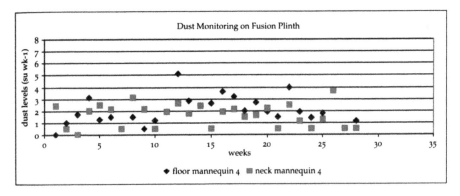

Figure 37.6 Results of dust monitoring on the 'Fusion' plinth in the 'London Look' exhibition from slides placed on the floor next to mannequin 4 and on the back of the neck

the gallery. In addition, air conditioning ducts (positions marked on Figure 37.6) or a nearby fire exit may have been providing enough air movement to interfere with results. Specifications for the air conditioning system state airflow rates at the ceiling outlets to be 2.83 m³s⁻¹.

There does not appear to be any relationship between the dust levels recorded and relative humidity or temperature. Monitoring of environmental conditions revealed that the relative humidity was between 45% and 65% RH for 70% of the time and the temperature averaged 21°C. The fluctuations (maximum 24°C and minimum 11°C) did not correspond to any changes in dust levels. The weather was not recorded, as it was not felt to have been significant, due to the distance between the exhibition area and the entrance of the Museum. Visitor numbers are recorded monthly by the Museum, rather than by week, so it is difficult to establish a direct link with the dust slide results, but the weeks when there appear to be increased levels of dust tend to correspond to bank holidays, when visitor numbers are generally higher in the Museum.

Figures 37.7 and 37.8 show the results obtained in the final month on the 'Introduction' and 'Innovation' plinths and, although again the levels are low, some indications are given as to the effectiveness of the barriers. The slide placed in front of the barrier on the 'Innovation' plinth has recorded higher levels than that immediately behind the barrier. Interestingly though, there is little variation between the low-level barrier and the high glass panels. In addition, the slides placed on the 'Introduction' plinth show that dust levels are higher at the front of the plinth than at the back, as would be expected. The costume on this plinth was positioned at the back.

Conclusion

From a conservation standpoint as well as from a design perspective, the exhibition can be deemed to have been a great success; damage to the costume on open

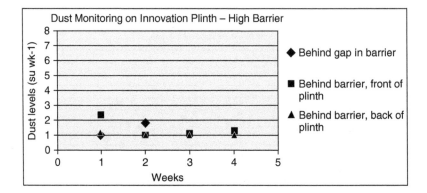

Figure 37.7 Results of dust monitoring on the 'Innovation' plinth of the 'London Look' exhibition behind high barrier

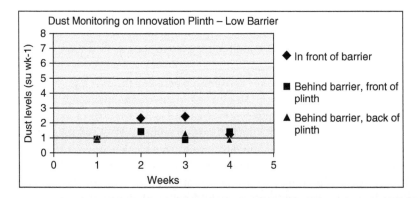

Figure 37.8 Results of dust monitoring on the 'Innovation' plinth of the 'London Look' exhibition behind and in front of low barrier

display was judged to be minimal and acceptable and at the same time the content of the exhibition was displayed in a manner which enhanced its meaning and conveyed the desired atmosphere to the visitor. Exit surveys conducted during the exhibition found that 92% of visitors found the design of the exhibition attractive or very attractive. In addition, the project was delivered within budget and enabled objects to be put on display which would otherwise have remained far less accessible in storage, given the limitations of the budget.

For many years the Conservation Department has contributed to the guidelines supplied to external designers and contractors by the Museum of London, providing specifications on case construction and materials (Ganiaris and Sully 1998), as well as working closely with internal designers and technicians. This project was able to build on that valuable relationship. The collaboration between Conservation and Design departments was a very productive one for both parties; the designer appreciated the clear guidelines and felt that she was able to work within these to create a stimulating and memorable design that fulfilled her ambitions. The integration of a collection care risk assessment into the design of the exhibition was felt to have greatly contributed to minimising dust levels on the costume. This was confirmed to a certain extent by the dust monitoring carried out. A monitoring technique involving use of sticky traps might reveal additional information about dust deposition; it would be interesting to note the levels of dust on vertical surfaces as well as horizontal, especially given that woven fabrics will trap more dust on this plane than other, smoother materials. Open display should not be viewed as a feasible method of display of costume in more permanent galleries or if large numbers of visitors are anticipated, but, as far as temporary exhibitions are concerned, it would appear that it can be successful, given certain parameters. If the risks are seen to be acceptable, especially for those exhibitions containing reasonably robust objects, and the area and settings are well designed, costume can be displayed even where funds are unavailable to purchase new showcases.

If museums are to fulfil the obligation to make more of their collections easily accessible to the general public, to get more of their collections out of store in order to 'extend the possibility of people encountering objects' (Wilkinson 2005: 4), especially with increasingly limited resources, it may be that conservation will need to re-assess traditional display guidelines. Information gathered from the emerging body of conservation research and an awareness of risks in a given situation should be used to assess the real impact of particular display methods on objects. This is particularly applicable for temporary exhibitions, where often the same strict criteria are stipulated as for permanent displays.

Appendix 37.1: 'London Look' – conservation guidelines for design

Main potential causes of damage to objects if on open display

- touching – may lead to irreversible physical damage – also dirt/grease deposits impossible to remove
- dust – particularly difficult to remove from textile objects without damaging them

- moth attack – results in irreversible damage – objects will attract them into exhibition area – difficult to detect until too late
- theft – smaller parts of costume may be removed
- vandalism – costume/textiles are particularly vulnerable as often impossible to reverse damage
- routine cleaning of gallery – may result in physical damage
- damage from light (this is also true for cased items)

Suggested solutions

Barriers around all costume items on open display

- at least 1.5 metres from objects (dust levels produced by people fall off greatly above this distance)
- rigid, not rope
- 1 m high

Plinths for all objects on open display

- at least 30 cm high (reduces dust levels from floor and minimises risk of damage during cleaning)
- suspending objects/mannequins is a possibility for some items but creates complications with mounting so should be done in consultation with conservation staff

Lighting

- will have to be below 70 lux for majority of textile items, i.e. fairly dark over most of the space
- contemporary textile items should have low light levels too – modern dyes are susceptible to light damage
- accessories can be brighter

Positioning of more vulnerable objects on open display

- away from entrance (this is where dust levels are generally higher)
- as far from barriers as possible (dust levels decrease the further from visitors they are)
- raised (dust levels fall off with height)

If cases are to be used, certain considerations should be made for costume items

- access inside cases will be required throughout the exhibition for checking for possible moth infestation
- lighting to be external wherever possible – if internal may have to be fibre optic to reduce heat levels inside cases (access required)

Conservation [are] to monitor [the] dust levels and moth activity in [the] Linbury Gallery once [the] 1920s [exhibition] is open – this may result in identification of certain black spots – [and] may influence layout of objects on open display if causes cannot be rectified. Textile conservation [are] to identify any particularly vulnerable items, during object list compilation, which will require cases. There may be some borrowed items which will have to be in cases.

Bibliography

Adams, S. (1997) 'Dust deposition and measurement – a modified approach', *Environmental Technology* 18: 345–350.

Adams, S., Brimblecombe, P. and Yoon, Y. H. (2001) 'Comparison of two methods for measuring the deposition of indoor dust', *The Conservator* 25: 90–93.

Ashley-Smith, J. (2003) 'A model for the degradation of textiles on open display and the risks of vacuum cleaning', in M. Ryhl-Svendsen (ed.) *Indoor Air Quality in Museums and Historic Properties 2003: 5th meeting of the Indoor Air Pollution Working Group. Presentation Abstracts and Additional Notes*, IAQ at www.iap.dk/iap/iaq2003/2003_contents.htm, presentation 24.

DCMS (2005) *Understanding the Future: Museums and 21st Century Life*, London: Department for Culture Media and Sport.

Ganiaris, H. and Sully, D. (1998) 'Showcase construction: materials and methods used at the Museum of London', *The Conservator* 22: 57–67.

Hatchfield, P. B. (2002) *Pollutants in the Museum Environment, Practical Strategies for Problem Solving in Design Exhibition and Storage*, London: Archetype Publications.

Kibrya, R. (1999) 'Surveying dust levels', *Museum Practice* 12 (4:3): 34–36.

Landi, S. (1992) *The Textile Conservator's Manual* (2nd edition), Oxford: Butterworth-Heinemann.

Lithgow, K., Brimblecombe, P., Knight, B. and Julien, S. (2003) 'Visitor perception of dustiness', in M Ryhl-Svendsen (ed.) *Indoor Air Quality in Museums and Historic Properties 2003: 5th meeting of the Indoor Air Pollution Working Group. Presentation Abstracts and Additional Notes*, IAQ at www.iaq.dk/iap/iaq2003/2003_contents.htm, presentation 5.

Lithgow, K., Lloyd, H., Brimblecombe, P., Yoon, Y. H. and Thickett, D. (2005) 'Managing dust in historic houses – a visitor/conservator interface', in I. Verger (ed.) *ICOM Committee for Conservation, Preprints 14th Triennial Meeting, The Hague, Vol II*, London: ICOM-CC.

Lloyd, H., Lithgow, K., Brimblecombe, P., Yoon, Y. H., Frame, K. and Knight, B. (2002) 'The effects of visitor activity on dust in historic collections', *The Conservator* 26: 72–82.

Phenix, A. and Burnstock, A. (1990) 'The deposition of dirt: a review of the literature with scanning electron microscope studies of dirt on selected paintings', in S. Hackney, J. Townsend and N. Eastaugh (eds) *Dirt and Pictures Separated*, London: UKIC.

Resource (2001) *Renaissance in the Regions: A New Vision for England's Museums*, London: Resource.

Tetreault, J. (2003) *Airborne Pollutants in Museums, Galleries and Archives: Risk Assessment, Control Strategies, and Preservation Management*, Ottawa: CCI.

Timár-Balázsy, Á. and Eastop, D. (1998) *Chemical Principles of Textile Conservation*, Oxford: Butterworth-Heinemann.

Wilkinson, H. (2005) *Collections for the Future*, Report of a Museums Association inquiry chaired by Jane Glaister, London: Museums Association.

Yoon, Y. H. and Brimblecombe, P. (2000a) 'Contribution of dust at floor level to particle deposit within the Sainsbury Centre for Visual Arts', *Studies in Conservation* 45: 127–137.

Yoon, Y. H. and Brimblecombe, P. (2000b) 'Dust at Felbrigg Hall', *Views* 32 (National Trust): 31–32.

Chapter 38

In Control or Simply Monitoring? The protection of museum collections from dust and vibration during building works

Siobhan Watts, Janet Berry,
Amy de Joia and Fiona Philpott

Introduction

T HERE HAS RECENTLY BEEN a dramatic increase in the number of large-scale construction projects in U.K. museums, largely as a result of lottery funding. This has led to the development and application of new techniques for monitoring dust and vibration during building works (Ford and Adams 1999; Kibrya 1999; Saunders et al. 1999; Eremin et al. 2000). Over the last few years, the National Museums and Galleries on Merseyside (NMGM) have undertaken major refurbishment works in two of its eight public venues, the Liverpool Museum and the Walker Art Gallery. [. . .] In both instances, a proportion of the collections remained on site during building works. Dust and vibration were monitored throughout the construction programme, but it was the controls within the building contract and the degree to which these were implemented, together with the general level of site supervision, that proved to be the decisive factors in controlling dust and vibration levels.

[. . .]

Monitoring vibration

[. . .]

Relatively little has been published on the risk of damage to museum collections from vibration during construction works transmitted through the building by pneumatic drills, saws and other tools. Vibration affecting paintings during transit has been studied in detail, both to determine levels of vibration at which damage

Source: R. Vontobel (ed.), *ICOM-CC 13th Triennial Meeting Rio de Janeiro 22–27 September 2002*, London: James & James, 2002, pp. 108–115.

may occur and to assess the levels of vibration to which works of art are exposed in different forms of transport (Mecklenburg 1991; Saunders 1998). The results of this work have been applied to suggest a 0.5 G limit for the vibration to which paintings are exposed during building work (Saunders et al. 1999; Tear 1999). Measurements of vibration affecting other collections, particularly objects with friable paint surfaces and pre-existing weaknesses, have suggested that damage to the most sensitive objects can occur at vibration levels exceeding 0.2 G (Thickett 1999).

[. . .]

For the Walker Art Gallery, [. . .] to investigate how far vibration was transmitted through the building, a series of tests were undertaken before the main work was due to start. The effect of two pneumatic drills operating simultaneously was tested for a variety of demolition activities, such as the breakout of walls to insert extract grilles, and the excavation of concrete slabs for the formation of padstones. Vibration was measured by fixing Tinytag high-sensitivity shock loggers to walls in galleries adjoining the building site. [. . .] The vibration levels recorded during these initial tests were all below the specified limit of 0.5 G. In the buffer zone, vibration levels up to 0.4 G were measured during drilling at the base of walls adjoining the building site (Figure 38.1), but vibration at this level was not transmitted to areas further from the site where collections were stored.

[. . .] During the major demolition works, [data from] vibration loggers were downloaded daily. Contractors provided regular briefings to staff on activities likely to cause vibration, so that loggers could be sited accordingly and the risk assessed at each stage. On several occasions, the contractor started work in a new area or used new percussive tools that exposed the collections to vibration above 0.5 G (Figure 38.2), and work was stopped while methods were reviewed. In these instances, consideration was given to the use of alternative equipment (diamond cutters as opposed

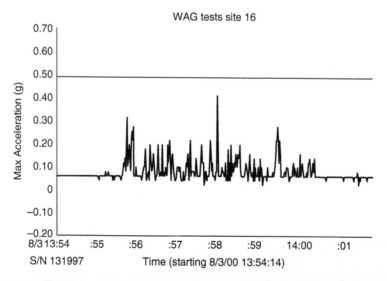

Figure 38.1 Vibration measured at the Walker Art Gallery during tests of excavation work using two pneumatic drills adjacent to the buffer zone

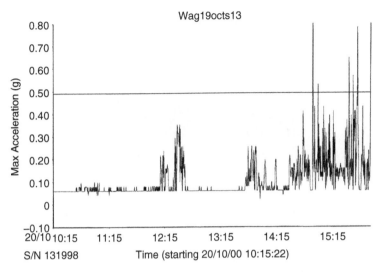

Figure 38.2 Vibration measured on the wall in one of the collections stores at the Walker Art Gallery during building works. On this occasion, work was stopped and methods were revised

to percussive tools) or to whether collections could be easily and safely moved for the duration of the activity.

Monitoring dust

Dust deposition was monitored at a number of sites throughout the period of the building contract at both the Liverpool Museum and the Walker Art Gallery. The method used was the glass deposition gauge technique developed by Brooks and Schwar (1987) and modified by Adams (1997). Glass microscope slides were measured for surface reflection and exposed at designated sites for one week. Following exposure, the slides were measured again, and the percentage reduction in reflection was calculated and recorded as 'soiling units per week' (su wk^{-1}), where 1 su wk^{-1} is equivalent to a 1% reduction in gloss after seven days of exposure. This method for dust deposition has been used to monitor dust at other museums (Ford and Adams 1999; Kibrya 1999; Eremin et al. 2000) and at historic houses (Lithgow and Adams 1998).

Control of the dust at the Liverpool Museum during the building works proved difficult. In the initial weeks of the contract (January 2000), there was an incident in which the contractor neglected to implement the specified sealing methods before commencing work adjacent to the gallery, causing clouds of plaster dust to be deposited. During this week, the rate of dust deposition in the nearby first floor gallery was measured as 30 su wk^{-1} (Figure 38.3), compared to a proposed acceptable threshold of 5 su wk^{-1} for museums (Ford 1997). Analysis of the dust using SEM-EDS (Scanning Electron Microscope with Energy Dispersive X-Ray Spectroscopy) indicated that approximately 95% of the dust consisted of inorganic particles. Particles rich

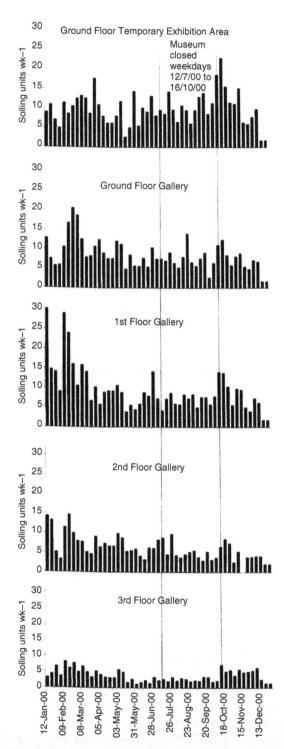

Figure 38.3 Weekly dust deposition rates in galleries at the Liverpool Museum during one year of construction works (January to December 2000)

in calcium and sulfur, aluminium and silicon, and titanium were identified, which is typical of the inorganic debris from demolition works. The results of the dust monitoring were used to pursue a claim against the contractor, to cover remedial cleaning and conservation of objects in the gallery following the incident.

[. . .]

Management and implementation of monitoring methods

One of the more difficult aspects of both projects was the control of subcontractors' activities through the main contractor. The production of clear, informative material by the museum for distribution to all subcontractors may be one way of communicating the particular risks to the collections. In reality, a more effective way of overseeing their activities is to have a representative on the ground repeatedly checking and questioning working methods and practices, either through strong site-level contract administration and/or through the appointment of a clerk of works.

[. . .]

References

Adams, S. (1997) 'Dust deposition and measurement: a modified approach', *Environmental Technology* 18: 345–350.

Brooks, K. and Schwar, M. J. R. (1987) 'Dust deposition and the soiling of glossy surfaces', *Environmental Pollution* 43: 129–141.

Eremin, K. Adams, S. and Tate, J. (2000) 'Monitoring of deposited particle levels within the Museum of Scotland: during and after construction', *The Conservator* 24: 15–23.

Ford, D. (1997) 'Slides and Frisbees – determining dust deposition rates', *V&A Conservation Journal* January 1997: 19–21.

Ford, D. and Adams, S. (1999) 'Deposition rates of particulate matter in the internal environment of two London museums', *Atmospheric Environment* 33: 4901–4907.

Kibrya, R. (1999) 'Surveying dust levels', *Museum Practice* 12: 34–36.

Lithgow, K. and Adams, S. (1998) 'Monitoring methods of dust control during building works', *National Trust – View* 29: 26–28.

Mecklenburg, M.F. (ed.) (1991) '*Art in Transit: Studies in the Transport of Paintings, Proceedings of the International Conference on the Packing and Transportation of Paintings*', Washington: National Gallery of Art.

Saunders, D. (1998) 'Monitoring shock and vibration during the transportation of paintings', *National Gallery Technical Bulletin* 19: 64–73.

Saunders, D., Slattery, M. and Mulder, I. (1999) 'Building work, vibration and the permanent collection' *Conservation News* 68 (March): 10–13.

Tear, P. (1999) 'Protecting the works of art during the Centenary Project works', unpublished report, London, The Wallace Collection (www.the-wallace-collection.org.uk).

Thickett, D. (1999) 'Assessment of vibration damage levels', The British Museum unpublished Conservation Research Report No. 1996/7.

Chapter 39

Make Yourself at Home: looking after an open-air museum

Sue Renault

S T FAGANS NATIONAL HISTORY MUSEUM in Cardiff is the longest established open-air museum in the UK. The Earl of Plymouth donated St Fagans Castle, a late sixteenth-century manor house, and its surrounding gardens to the National Museum of Wales in 1946, and it opened to its first visitors in July 1948 as the Welsh Folk Museum, with an entry fee of a shilling (5p). Since then, buildings have been collected from all over Wales and re-erected on the site, each furnished to a particular period with items from the national collections. Over the past fifty years it has inspired millions of visitors with an appreciation of Welsh history and traditions.

The ethos of the Museum has been to make the visitor feel that the interiors they are seeing are as believable as possible, and physical access has been a priority. Very few restrictions have been placed on the visitor, and the friendly welcome they traditionally receive is a strong feature of the Museum's attraction. However, the cracks, quite literally, began to show as years of handling and display in uncontrolled environments began to take their toll on the individual objects.

Agents of decay

Even in the most perfect museum environments, objects can still decay. In the majority of cases a combination of factors causes the damage. Probably the easiest way to understand the inter-relationships between these factors is to consider a single object. For example, a simply constructed wooden table. Four planks of pine form the top, with two nails at each end of the planks to hold them to the frame below. The four legs are bolted onto the frame. The top of the table, the outer surfaces of the frame and all

Source: C. Butler and M. Davis (eds), *Things Fall Apart . . .*, Cardiff: National Museum of Wales, 2006, pp. 6–14.

surfaces of the legs are finished with a polyurethane varnish. To begin with, the heat and ultraviolet light from any sunlight falling on the tabletop cause the varnish to yellow as it becomes chemically degraded. If subjected to constant fluctuations of temperature and relative humidity, the planks of the tabletop begin to split and warp. The warping results because the upper surfaces of the planks are sealed by the varnish and are therefore no longer affected by changes in the moisture content of the air, whilst the lower surfaces can still expand and contract. Where the nails are restricting the freedom of the planks to undergo expansion and contraction, cracks will appear. The high relative humidity that causes the wood to swell will also cause the nails and bolts to corrode. This corrosion will be quickened by the natural acidity of the wood. As the metal corrodes, metal oxides begin to form on the outer surfaces of the nails, leaching into the surrounding wood and causing staining of the wood and slow loss of the nail.

As well as physical and chemical decay, the table is also susceptible to biological decay. High relative humidity can result in mould growth, and the pine is also susceptible to attack by woodworm. The larvae of this beetle munch away inside the wood, forming innumerable empty corridors before pupating just below the surface and then emerging through the tell-tale holes. Once it has undergone a woodworm attack the wood becomes more susceptible to moisture changes and, depending on the extent and the location of the damage, can become structurally unstable. If the table stands on an uneven floor for a long period of time, settling occurs whereby the table shapes itself to compensate for some of the legs being on lower ground than the others. If the table were then to be moved to an even surface, it would wobble. All this damage can easily occur if the table is displayed in an uncontrolled environment.

The table is an example of a composite object, constructed from more than one material. The major concern with all composite objects is the effect their materials of construction will have on one another. Treating these objects usually means having to compromise. The best example of this is in choosing the optimum relative humidity at which to display the object. For a wooden-handled knife, the wood, being organic, is best kept at approximately 55 to 60 per cent relative humidity, whilst to prevent the blade from corroding the knife would need as low a relative humidity as possible, preferably below 20 per cent. Without physically separating the handle from the blade, which is an option but would make interpretation difficult, the only solution is to choose a relative humidity in the middle.

Perhaps the most awkward composite objects we deal with at St Fagans are the buildings themselves. They are part of the national collections, and they are in constant use. In 2001, free entry was introduced to all National Museum of Wales sites and since then the number of visitors to St Fagans has doubled to nearly 700,000 a year. The daily wear and tear by the visitors on buildings originally intended for a handful of occupants now exacts a heavy toll on their fabric. Even on the stone floors it is possible to see the visitor tracks where the floor has eroded; this is even more visible in the buildings with traditional-recipe mud floors. In the parlour of a seventeenth-century farm house, the central table and chairs now sit on an island of solid floor, formed as the surrounding area has been literally walked away. However, year-round opening means that it is impossible to undertake the required maintenance outside of opening hours. Instead, the buildings have to be closed on a rota basis to cause least impact on visitor enjoyment.

Display of the collections

A common feature of all the display environments at the Museum of Welsh Life, with the exception of the galleries in the main building, is the juxtaposition of the objects. The dressers have plates on them (Figure 39.1), the beds are dressed and the shelves and sideboards are laden with knick-knacks. In choosing a dresser for display, its condition needs to be considered: will it bear the weight of the items on it? Could the items chosen to sit on the dresser scratch it? How can we minimise the risks? This type of analysis of individual objects is preventative conservation at a micro level.

The types of display can be loosely divided into three. The first of these is the more conventional museum gallery, with objects displayed in cases or in roped areas. Here, the objects are protected from handling and are displayed in a controllable climate. Security is also less problematic and the objects tend to be the best examples, often of higher monetary value and historical status. The same can be said of the second display type, the interior of St Fagans Castle. This is similar to the way the National Trust displays the contents of country houses, with the majority of objects of higher quality mainly on view behind barrier ropes.

The third type of display is the re-erected buildings themselves, located over much of the site. These displays have one major common feature: the public – up close and personal. The objects are reachable and all are fair game for handling. In fact, observations on site have shown that the more recognizable objects are to the visitor, the more likely they are to handle them.

Before any building is opened to the public, careful consideration is given to an object's proximity to the visitor route, weighed against its fragility. Certain types of material are particularly vulnerable: the textiles and many of the paper-based exhibits in the cottages are not accessioned, and are regarded as relatively expendable. These are items used as 'set dressing', in the certain knowledge that they will be worn away by handling and/or decay in the harsh environment of the historic interiors. The open fires that make the buildings so inviting and aid interpretation are actually depositing acidic soot on the contents, corroding the metals and dirtying everything. Combine

Figure 39.1 A Welsh dresser on display at St Fagans

this with the greasy, acidic deposits left after handling and the high moisture content in the buildings and you have a recipe for decay.

The environments within these buildings can be loosely separated into two further subdivisions: those with electricity and those without. In buildings with no electricity, the fire is our only means of environmental control. Unfortunately, because the fire can only safely be alight during visitor hours when it can be attended (Figure 39.2); the relative humidity can vary by as much as 30 per cent. For a bulky piece of furniture this is not too serious because it takes a couple of days for the change to register, but for smaller and less dense organic objects these fluctuations can cause serious damage. This is particularly true of objects that are restricted by their construction: the swelling and contraction of an organic material around a fixed point creates internal stresses that often result in cracks or tears. Of course this is not immediately noticeable to the visitor, since the lighting in these buildings is low. Without electricity, illumination is provided by authentic period systems such as candles and oil lamps, or by the harsher modern gas camping lanterns, all of which have their own particular limitations.

The cleaning staff have the unenviable task, using brushes and lint-free dusters, of trying to rid these buildings of the soot produced by fires and lighting methods and the dust emanating from the hundreds of visitors per day. Despite heroic efforts this can sometimes be little more than a disturbance rather than a removal.

Where a building has electricity available it is possible to alleviate the effects of dampness by using low background heat and installing dehumidifiers. The first experiments in this area were carried out using night storage heaters hidden beneath the counters in two reconstructed shops. Their success was limited because of the accessibility of the controls. On a cold day, there was always the temptation for staff to adjust the boost control, so that on subsequent days the temperature within the building would soar. The most effective approach to date has been the introduction of underfloor heating. When the 1940s prefab house was recently erected this discreet form of heating was installed under the floorboards. It now runs night and day through the cold months at a constant 10°C, acting as background heating and ironing

Figure 39.2 A farmhouse heated by an open fire, and with no electricity

out the temperature fluctuations between night and day. This allows a greater range of objects to be displayed (see Figure 39.3 on p. 540).

The preventative conservation policy

The advent of free entry to the Museum has made all members of staff re-evaluate why things are done and how. It has become obvious that if we are to present the site to its best advantage, not just to today's visitors but also to future visitors, then we cannot simply continue as we are; we have to make changes. Through collaboration and consultation we have written a preventative conservation policy specifically for St Fagans. The stated intention is to allow access to the collection whilst substantially reducing the risk of damaging the accessioned objects.

For the policy to work it is necessary to deliver relevant and continued training. The next step therefore is to devise and implement training schemes for any member of staff handling the collection. Controlling handling will to a degree limit physical damage to the collection, but it cannot work in isolation. Despite the best will in the world, accidental damage is inevitable in overcrowded buildings. As mentioned earlier, the buildings on site are now subjected to a use that is above and beyond that for which any of them were designed. Of necessity, agreed visitor limits exist for all display areas. Until recently the implementation of this preventative measure has been the sole responsibility of the staff on duty in the building. We have now begun to experiment with the use of signs and all areas are currently under assessment with regard to the use of channelling systems. Such measures lift the weight of responsibility from the individual member of staff, providing them with a supervisory role and making it clear to the public that their authority comes from the institution. Signs also allow us to explain why numbers have to be limited, so that the visitor can understand the reasons for the policy.

Implementation of the visitor limits has another advantage. Not only is accidental damage to the collection reduced, whether this is through bumping against furniture or knocking and smashing ceramics, but it also makes security easier. By reducing the numbers inside the building at any one time, it is now possible for staff to watch the collection and thus fulfil their security role.

With such a vast array of objects on open display, constructed from a wide variety of materials, keeping the collection clean is no easy task. Specialist knowledge of the cleaning methods to be employed in individual buildings is essential to avoid unintentional damage. During the process of writing the policy it was recognized that the damage caused by inappropriate cleaning far outweighs any that dust sitting on an object will do whilst waiting for a trained cleaner to become available. It has shifted the balance from the apparent all-consuming need to clean for the sake of it towards cleaning in a controlled and informed way.

It has long been recognized that frequent polishing of plated metals causes the irreversible loss of the plating, so that the silver-plated trophy turns to brass; but the same idea holds true for many materials within the collection. Stone floor erosion is in part attributable to the frequent mopping that has occurred over many years, with over-wetting assisting the breakdown of the surface.

Discontinuing inappropriate cleaning methods and zoning the displays into areas that need daily, weekly or monthly cleaning makes the whole process more manageable. It also opens up the possibility of giving the cleaning staff ownership of the buildings they are trained to clean, and using them for tasks such as insect monitoring to aid the 'housekeeping' conservators in their constant battle to prevent infestation. In order to cement this bond between the cleaners and the housekeeping conservators, we are piloting an induction training scheme whereby any new cleaner will spend their first week working alongside one of our housekeepers. During this week, the housekeeper can impart the conservation aims within the individual buildings, the role of good preventative conservation, and the importance of the cleaner in the process.

The housekeeping conservators have a pivotal role in safeguarding the collection. It is essential that they are informed of all activities, events and maintenance requirements at the planning stage so that they can ensure that appropriate safeguards are in place and all the relevant staff are consulted. This has to include every member of staff, because no matter what job we do, whether curator, cleaner, typist or electrician, the collection is what makes us a museum. On the basest level, safeguarding the collection is, in effect, protecting our jobs: on the noblest level, safeguarding the collection is protecting the cultural heritage of Wales.

Fundamental to the protection of the collection is the provision of an appropriate display environment. Despite being based on an open-air site, the conservation staff constantly strive to achieve the best standards set out by the Museums, Libraries and Archives Council. We are driven by the belief that we must continuously review and adapt the methods of environmental control at our disposal. Discussions surrounding the formation of the conservation policy made everyone aware of how vital electricity is to the care and protection of the collection. As a result, agreement has been reached that consideration will be given to finding the most beneficial heating system for all new buildings, and the installation of electricity is an absolute necessity. More than this, there is now an undertaking to install electricity in all the existing buildings on the site as soon as practicable, given the constraints of resources available, and also to draw up a plan for installing heating systems.

One of the hardest concepts to get across to both staff and the public is that once an object becomes part of the collection there has to be a separation of form from function. It is all too easy to forget this when there is not a clear visual separation of objects for public or staff use from objects in the collection. For example, accessioned furniture is widely used for storing the newspapers used to light the fires. Hinges are being worn by daily use, the weight of the newspapers is causing structural stress, and this is magnified as the papers absorb moisture from the atmosphere, creating a damp microclimate inside the cupboard and encouraging mould growth. Clearly, a change of practice is required. For some buildings, storage of such materials could be accommodated in an area out of public view. Alternatively, the answer may be a return to authentic fire-lighting methods, appropriate to the period of the house. Whatever the solution in the individual buildings, the result will be that the public will no longer see staff opening pieces of furniture and they will therefore no longer feel encouraged to follow suit. This is one example of many mixed messages we currently send out to the public and which, through the policy, we hope to address.

The policy in practice

St Fagans has always sought to display its buildings as realistically as possible. Over time the interiors have slowly lost this realism as objects fell apart, were withdrawn – or simply stolen. Sparse interiors have slowly become the trend because they have proved to be more sustainable. The visitor goes away with the sense that people from earlier periods lived with next to no possessions, and so we are creating a false impression.

In the bedroom of Kennixton farmhouse, dating to the seventeenth century, despite the occupants having been relatively prosperous, there are no small personal items on display (Figure 39.4). How did they amuse their children, brush their hair or

Figure 39.3 The bedroom of the Museum's 1940s prefab

Figure 39.4 The upstairs bedroom in Kennixton farmhouse

even light their rooms? With such items being too rare, valuable, fragile or portable, they could not be risked on open display in a building with five rooms and only one member of staff present for security. The result is a sterile room relieved only by the replica textiles adorning the bed.

Compare this to the bedroom in the prefab. Here the room is adorned with personal items (Figure 39.3). This is not just possible because items from the 1940s are more easily available, but mainly because they have the protection of being in a roped off area. In this sense, it can be argued that slightly restricted physical access to the collection in the form of a barrier actually makes a much larger proportion of the collection visually accessible. We do not intend to use the preventative conservation policy as a tool to separate the visitor from the collection, but rather to use it to enhance their experience. In terms of implementing the policy, we are only just beginning, but, if we get it right, the visitor will be impressed by the care all our staff lavish on the collection and they will take away a sense of how highly we value the objects, not simply for themselves, but for the history and culture they represent.

Preventive Conservation: the future

Introduction to Part Four

Chris Caple

The future

W HILST THE FUTURE CANNOT BE known, it is possible to identify some of the new
and emerging issues in preventive conservation, such as preservation 'in situ',
DNA and climate change, which appear likely to represent significant challenges for
the future.

Our ability to travel, our desire for more intense experiences, our need for context
so as to make buildings and objects more meaningful, and our recognition of the rights
of individual nations, regions and groups have meant that historic sites and their contents are increasingly likely to be preserved 'in situ' rather than to be brought back to
the 'treasure house' museums of major European and North American cities. As our
technical skills and the resources available for heritage work increase, so does our ability to preserve artefacts in challenging environments and remote locations. The most
extreme examples of this phenomenon would appear to be the huts and their contents
from the 'heroic period' of Antarctic exploration (1899–1917) located on Ross Island
in Antarctica. Julian Bickersteth, Sarah Clayton and Fiona Tennant (2008) (Chapter 40) describe the extremity of the challenge of mitigating the effect of extreme
climatic conditions and practising preventive conservation in such an inhospitable
environment. Though it would be possible to transfer these huts and their contents in
their entirety to Australia, New Zealand or Europe, the context of seeing them in the
desolate wilderness of Antarctica conveys the importance and meaning of these huts
far more eloquently than any label ever could. They are an important monument to the
history and development of the Antarctic: an early twentieth-century wooden shed has
infinitely less meaning in the museum of a large urban conurbation than when it is only
one of a handful of buildings present on a continent. The practical difficulties of enact-

ing preventive conservation on these buildings and their contents rests not simply with the extreme climatic conditions, but also with the problems of distance, the numerous different materials of which they are composed and the surrounding presence of a fragile, protected natural environment which cannot be disturbed. There are also major managerial challenges, wrestling with a number of different organisations, the complexity of international politics, the lack of a national funding body and the fact that research has often not been done into the decay mechanisms and conservation of materials in these extreme climatic conditions (Barr and Chaplin 2004).

It is tempting to think that through implementing our present preventive conservation measures we are preserving our museum collections in perpetuity; however, this may only be true at a macro visual level. As Julian Carter (2006) (Chapter 41) suggests, this may not be the case at the molecular level. Developments in microbiological and molecular research have meant that it is now appreciated that museum collections, especially natural history collections, contain an invaluable information resource in the form of DNA, whose decay cannot be seen, but which it is essential to preserve as a unique research resource for the future. Similar arguments can be advanced for the need to preserve the microscopic traces of body fluids on textiles (Eastop and Brooks 1996), organic residues on archaeological ceramics (Evershed et al. 2001), insect traces in the dirt on archaeological artefacts (Fell 1996) and organic material impressions preserved in metal corrosion (Janaway 1984). The chemical composition, molecular make-up or microscopic physical traces of museum objects are as much part of the physical evidence of our past as the shape and decoration of the object. As we develop the capacity to analyse this information, it is increasingly important that we develop preventive conservation techniques for preserving this evidence of our past. This is a new and challenging technical frontier for conservators and curators, which is expanding as our technical ability to recover molecular and microscopic information increases.

Though we may be slowly coming to grips with many of the preventive conservation problems presented by our present collections in our existing museum buildings, the present situation will not continue, as we live in an ever-changing world. One of the most fundamental changes we potentially face is that of changes to our climate. The initial work on the impact of climate change on heritage in the UK has been spearheaded by May Cassar (2005). It is clear that more extreme weather events will occur and they will do so with increased frequency. May Cassar and Robyn Pender (2005) (Chapter 42) explore some of the challenges this will bring. For example, the predicted infrequent but occasionally high levels of rainfall will lead to an increased risk of flooding to museums and their collections, as well as to historic houses and their interiors. To meet such threats, we will need to engineer solutions such as building additional overflows for gutters. However, if this means altering the fabric and appearance of historic buildings, ethical questions such as 'what is the point of preserving an inaccurate, partially truthful past?' are raised.

Climatic changes will particularly affect building exteriors and objects exposed to the elements: thus the increasing temperature levels in the tundra mean that archaeological remains preserved by the permafrost in places such as Greenland are already beginning to be lost as the permafrost levels thaw. The changing temperatures in Europe are predicted to lead to greater damage to the stonework of historic buildings through salt crystallisation and biological growth (Sabbioni 2008). Although we are still collecting the data and developing the models to determine the effect of increased temperature and relative humidity changes on collections within buildings, it is already clear that it will make greater demands on HVAC (heating, ventilation and air conditioning) systems when we are seeking to increase sustainability and reduce the use and cost of such systems (Cassar 2008).

As the levels of knowledge about preventive conservation are growing, so the expectations of museum directors, curators and conservators are rising and the decisions for those practising preventive conservation are becoming more complex. Rob Waller and Stefan Michalski (2004) have started to explore how we may manage this situation through developing and using 'expert systems' which could utilise all the available information and express risk in mathematical terms on a common and understandable scale, such as annual (object) loss rate. Such risk management systems are perhaps getting nearer, but the reality of finite resources will invariably leave us choosing between preserving less, well, or more, badly.

References

Barr, S. and Chaplin, P. (2004) *Cultural Heritage in the Arctic and Antarctic Regions*, Oslo: ICOMOS IPHC.

Bickersteth, J., Clayton, S. and Tennant, F. (2008) 'Conserving and Interpreting the Historic Huts of Antarctica', in D. Saunders, J. H. Townsend and S. Woodcock (eds), *Conservation and Access, Contributions to the London Congress 15–19 September 2008*, London: IIC, pp. 218–220.

Carter, J. (2006) 'Breaking the Code: Conserving DNA – New Demands on Natural Science Collections', in C. Butler and M. Davis (eds), *Things Fall Apart . . .*, Cardiff: National Museum of Wales, pp. 16–22.

Cassar, M. (2005) *Climate Change and the Historic Environment*, London: Centre for Sustainable Heritage.

Cassar, M. (2008) 'Climate Change and the Collection Environment', a presentation at *Climate Change and Museum Collections, IIC Dialogues for the New Century, A Climate Change Panel Discussion*, July 2008, IIC London Conference.

Cassar, M. and Pender, R. (2005) 'The Impact of Climate Change on Cultural Heritage: Evidence and Response', in A. Paterakis et al. (eds), *ICOM-CC 14th Triennial Meeting, The Hague 12–16 September 2005*, pp. 610–616.

Eastop. D. and Brooks, M. (1996) 'To Clean or Not to Clean: The Value of Soils and Creases', *ICOM-CC 11th Triennial Meeting, Edinburgh 1996*, Edinburgh: ICOM-CC, pp. 687–691.

Evershed, R. P., Dudd, S. N., Lockheart, M. J. and Jim, S. (2001) 'Lipids in Archaeology', in D. R. Brothwell and A. M. Pollard (eds), *Handbook of Archaeological Sciences*, London: Wiley, pp. 331–350.

Fell, V. (1996) 'Washing Away the Evidence', in A. Roy and P. Smith (eds), *Archaeological Conservation and its Consequences, 1996 IIC Copenhagen Congress*, London: IIC, pp. 121–126.

Janaway, R. (1984) Textile Fibre Characteristics Preserved by Metal Corrosion: the Potential of SEM Studies, *The Conservator* 7: 48–52.

Sabbioni, C. (2008) 'Climate Change and Cultural Heritage Research', a presentation at *Climate Change and Museum Collections, IIC Dialogues for the New Century, A Climate Change Panel Discussion*, July 2008, IIC London Conference.

Waller, R. and Michalski, S. (2004) Effective Preservation: From Reaction to Prediction, *Getty Conservation Institute Newsletter* 19(1), Spring: 1–4.

Chapter 40

Conserving and Interpreting the Historic Huts of Antarctica

Julian Bickersteth, Sarah Clayton and Fiona Tennant

Introduction

THE FOUR ANTARCTIC HUTS IN THE Ross Sea Dependency built during the Heroic Age of Antarctic exploration (1899–1917) contain some 15,000 artifacts. A program for their conservation and long-term care has been developed over the last six years, culminating in the placement of a conservation laboratory at New Zealand's Scott Base and the employment of conservators to 'winter over' in the Antarctic while conserving the artifacts.[1]

There is arguably no more challenging current conservation project, requiring coordination and planning of equipment, supplies, transport of artifacts from the huts to Scott Base, employment of contract conservators and development of cold climate conservation treatment methodologies. Heavily international in focus, to date conservators from Australia, New Zealand, Britain, Canada and Germany have wintered over.

[. . .]

This paper outlines with the background to this long-running project, which has been under planning since 2002 and fully underway since early 2006, with completion expected c. 2013. [. . .] It discusses the way in which the project is developing site interpretation solutions to provide ongoing access to the huts and the program. This latter issue is a vital opportunity for promoting conservation components of the project, given continuing limited visitor access and the way in which modern telecommunications can provide real-time access to the conservators.

Source: D. Saunders, J. H. Townsend and S. Woodcock (eds), *Conservation and Access, Contributions to the London Congress 15–19 September 2008*, London: IIC, 2008), pp. 218–220.

Background

The Heroic Era huts in Antarctica

At the end of the nineteenth century the Antarctic region was largely unknown beyond the whaling industry based on small outlying islands. Exploration of the area became popular at the turn of the twentieth century with the race to conquer the Antarctic mainland and to reach the South Pole. This period became known as the Heroic Era of Antarctic exploration, lasting from 1899 to 1917.[2] The Ross Dependency of Antarctica contains 34 historic sites,[3] including four of the five original expedition bases left from the Heroic Era of exploration (Figure 40.1).[4] Nowhere else on the Antarctic continent holds such a number of historic huts.[5] Explorers chose this part of Antarctica as a base from which to launch their expeditions, due to its proximity to the South Pole. One base is on the Antarctic mainland at Cape Adare, the other three are on Ross Island. Ross Island is attached to the Antarctic mainland by the Ross Sea Ice Shelf.

The huts on Ross Island are:

- Discovery Hut (Hut Point), from Captain Scott's first expedition 1901–1904.
- Nimrod Hut (Cape Royds), from Ernest Shackleton's expedition 1907–1909.
- Terra Nova Hut (Cape Evans) from Scott's last expedition 1910–1913; see Figure 40.1 for hut locations.

All the huts were pre-fabricated kits from England and Australia. They were packaged for travel and erected by the crew when they arrived on the ice. The crew slept,

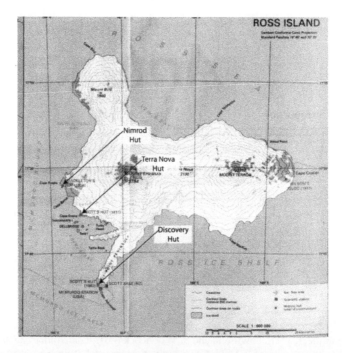

Figure 40.1 Ross Island, Antarctica (courtesy of Antarctic Heritage Trust 2006)

Figure 40.2 Interior of Shackleton's Hut at Cape Royds (image from J. Bickersteth)

ate and worked in the huts (Figure 40.2). Each of the expedition bases had working space for at least one biologist, geologist, meteorologist and physicist,[6] and a dark-room for the expedition's photographer to process images. Together these four huts remain an "astonishingly powerful evocation of the men who risked their lives on those early expeditions".[7]

Project management and funding

The conservation project, the Ross Sea Heritage Restoration Project, is managed by the Antarctic Heritage Trust of New Zealand (AHT), which was formed in 1987 to "care for the heritage of the Heroic Era located in the Ross Sea region of Antarctica on behalf of the international community".[8] The AHT is an independent, not-for-profit body that operates closely with the New Zealand crown entity, Antarctica New Zealand (AntNZ) in Christchurch. The relationship between the two bodies is critical, as AntNZ provides all the logistical support to enable AHT to operate in Antarctica, including air and ground travel, accommodation on the ice and all clothing and food. Combined with the hut conservation program, which works in tandem with the artifact conservation program, the project is one of the largest programs supported by AntNZ.

The AHT is not funded by AntNZ beyond the latter providing logistical support. The AHT raises the necessary funds for the historic huts conservation project through a variety of means. This has included grants from NZ Lotteries, direct grants from the NZ Government, philanthropists in the USA, UK and NZ, and fund raising in NZ and the UK (where the AHT has a sister organization known as UKAHT). Through a carefully built up program of developing relationships with key international play-ers in the heritage field, such as the Getty Conservation Foundation and the World Monuments Fund, the AHT continues to be highly successful in raising both funds and profile for the huts, and can be cited as a model of how to build a fund-raising program for such a project.

The conservation challenge

As unique tangible evidence of world exploration and human endurance from over 100 years ago, these huts are exceptionally special, but showing the signs of environmental and human impact. The huts and their contents are suffering from physical deterioration caused by several factors, including the environment, human access and natural causes. The Antarctic Treaty system includes the Protocol on Environmental Protection to the Antarctic Treaty. This recognizes the importance of Antarctic historic sites and establishes a management framework for them.[6,9] Within this framework, the huts are allocated the highest protection status possible, Antarctic Specially Protected Areas (ASPAs). Each ASPA has a conservation plan that includes maximum visitor levels and codes of conduct. All of the Heroic Era huts are ASPAs.[5]

Physical deterioration

No more than 2000 people are allowed to visit each hut per year,[8] as required by the ASPA conservation plan, to minimize human impact on the sites and huts.[10] It is unlikely that these limits will change. They will not be raised, due to concerns about visitor impact.[10] They will not be lowered, as it is believed that the current levels are sustainable. A balance of visitation is the key and the benefits of allowing visitation should not be underestimated.[2] Visiting and experiencing the historical sites creates great advocates for the ongoing need for preservation,[2,11] and some become a major source of funds for the preservation program.[2] However, despite established protocols for pre-briefing of visitors, limitation of numbers in the huts at any one time and the provision of guides, there is evidence that visitation is contributing to damaging the huts and sites.[2,6] with resulting preservation concerns.[11,12] Damage includes ingress of snow and scoria (the lava gravel around the huts) carried in on visitors' boots. This causes physical damage to the floorboards and linoleum floor coverings. Further damage has been caused by visitors handling and moving artifacts.

Environmental deterioration

The Antarctic environment is incredibly harsh. Extreme temperatures and wind speeds, humidity and salt are having a brutal effect on the huts and their contents, both inside and out. Wind and ice abrasion are gradually weakening elements of the hut structure and external movable heritage items as well.

Freeze–thaw cycles between winter and summer are affecting most materials, including textiles, leather, metals, timber and glass. Artifacts placed adjacent to floor or wall surfaces tend to form ice crystals on the surface, particularly in the case of food cans, where the contents remain frozen while the packaging thaws.

Data logging of temperature and relative humidity (RH) conditions has been undertaken for nearly 10 years, and shows a consistent pattern of above-freezing temperatures and high RH levels in summer. However, there has been no conclusive evidence that the presence of visitors exacerbates these environmental levels. The high humidity during summer also has the effect of encouraging copious mould growth in damp sections of the inside of the huts.

Salts, primarily sodium chloride, come from a number of sources. Firstly all the Heroic Era huts are in close proximity to the sea. Salt from sea spray has accumulated in the environment, as there is no rain to wash it away. It is so abundant that the black scoria gravel surrounding the huts often appears to have a light dusting of frost, but on closer inspection it is identified as salt crystals. When the wind picks up, both the fine scoria and salt is blown into every crevice. Secondly, all the huts and contents traveled to Antarctica aboard ships. Some ships leaked badly and many of the provisions were stored on the top deck of the ships. A third factor that may pose a minor salt issue is the proximity of Mount Erebus, an active volcano.

[. . .]

Access and interpretation

Apart from several permanent exhibitions around the world that contain original material from the Heroic Era of Antarctic exploration, the only way of currently accessing the collections is by visiting them physically. Each summer (December/ January) small tour groups, either from visiting cruise ships or from the US Scientific Base at McMurdo, adjacent to Scott Base, are taken to one or several of the huts. This visitation will continue as the conservation program proceeds. However, the conservation program has been the catalyst to create further access to the huts and the conservation program by virtual means. This has included live telephone hook-ups with conferences, a presentation of a webcast and, most prominently, the writing of a blog hosted on London's Natural History Museum's website. It is the museum's second most popular blog, already visited by tens of thousands of online visitors. It provides a mixture of entertaining and technical information about the conservation program and life at Scott Base. More locally, the Canterbury Museum in Christchurch, which holds the world's strongest collection of Heroic Era Antarctic artifacts, is actively collaborating with AHT to promote the project. This involves both looking after those artifacts which for various reasons of security and fragility have been removed from the ice, and managing AHT's Vernon collection management system. AHT itself is active in promoting the conservation project to visitors to the site through publications of books, guides to the historic sites and conservation plans, lectures on visiting cruise ships and by holding open days at Scott Base for the nearby US Antarctic program at McMurdo.

This has resulted in a number of benefits. Not only has it helped to promote the conservation program and the stories behind the huts, and thus indirectly help fund-raising, it has also assisted conservators who may have struggled with the isolation of Antarctica to recognize the international interest in the project and the value of the work they are undertaking.

As the artifacts are returned to the huts, their layout is being refined to reflect more accurately the period of first occupation, based upon physical and written documentation. While this is an important part of the project, the fundamental interpretive value of the huts lies in the physical survival of the structures and their contents, leading the World Monuments Fund to call Scott's Hut at Cape Evans "The world's most evocative heritage building".[13]

[. . .]

Notes

1   Tennant, F., and Bickersteth, J., 'Conserving in the deep freeze. Saving and interpreting the Heroic Era huts of the Ross Dependency in Antarctica', conference paper presented at the AICOMOS 2007 Conference Extreme Heritage. James Cook University, 19–21 July 2007.
2   Chaplin, P. (2004) 'Polar heritage sites at risk – politics, principles and practical problems', in *Cultural Heritage in the Arctic and Antarctic Regions*, Oslo: ICOMOS & IPHC.
3   Antarctic Heritage Trust (2004) *The Historic Huts of the Ross Sea Region*, Christchurch: Antarctic Heritage Trust.
4   Chaplin, P., and Barr, S. (2004) 'An overview of polar heritage sites', in *Cultural Heritage in the Arctic and Antarctic Regions*, Oslo: ICOMOS & IPHC.
5   Tennant, F. (2007) 'Creating educational and inspirational experiences with geographically remote cultural collections: Opportunities for the Heroic Era explorer huts in Antarctica'. MA dissertation. University of Leicester (unpublished).
6   Farrell, R., Blanchett, R., Auger, M., Duncan, S., Held. B., Jurgens, J., and Minasaki, R. (2004) 'Scientific evaluation of deterioration in historic huts of Ross Island. Antarctica', in *Cultural Heritage in the Arctic and Antarctic Regions*, Oslo: ICOMOS & IPHC.
7   Antarctic Heritage Trust (2004) *Conservation Plan for Discovery Hut, Hut Point*, Christchurch: Antarctic Heritage Trust.
8   Antarctic Heritage Trust, www.heritage-antarctica.org/indcx.cfm (accessed 21 April 2008).
9   Pearson, M. (2004) 'Artefact or rubbish – a dilemma for Antarctic managers', in *Cultural Heritage in the Arctic and Antarctic Regions*, Oslo: ICOMOS & IPHC.
10 Wills, F., personal communication, 24 January 2007.
11 Barr, S. (2004) 'Polar monuments and sites', in *Cultural Heritage in the Arctic and Antarctic Regions*, Oslo: ICOMOS & IPHC.
12 Hughes. J. (2004) 'Deterioration of Antarctic historic sites – effects of Antarctic climates on materials and implications for preservation', in *Cultural Heritage in the Arctic and Antarctic Regions*, Oslo: ICOMOS & IPHC.
13 World Monument Fund, '2008 world monuments watch list of 100 most endangered sites', http://wmf.org/pdf/Watch_2008_list.pdf (accessed 21 April 2008), now at http://www.wmf.org/sites/default/files/press_releases/2008%20Watch%20List.pdf

Chapter 41

Breaking the Code: conserving DNA – new demands on natural science collections

Julian Carter

O VER THREE MILLION BIOLOGICAL SPECIMENS are housed at the National Museum of Wales, including thousands of different species of plants, animals and fungi. Museums hold some of the most important collections of natural science material in the UK, with some institutions holding specimens collected over 300 years ago. The collections were originally put together as 'curiosities', but were subsequently developed by dedicated scientific expeditions. These specimens have been used to form the basis of our ideas on issues such as evolution, ecology and taxonomy and they continue to play an important role in research and education. As the pressure on our natural environment and its flora and fauna increases, these collections are becoming an ever more important resource for both traditional morphological studies and modern genetic studies. Museum collections are particularly useful in that, as well as containing many different species, they also span time and geography. They become of even greater value when many of the species collected are now either extinct or so highly endangered that further collection is not possible, or not viable, due to financial or political reasons. The result is that many of these specimens form an irreplaceable record that is vital in developing our understanding of various biological processes, especially in key issues such as biodiversity and climate change.

Preserving biological material can be very difficult. Upon death, physiological and cellular control processes are lost and autolytic decay sets in. This decay causes the destruction of cells by enzymes produced by the organism itself and, if unchecked, this results in rapid degradation. Museum fixation and preservation treatments are aimed at halting the processes of autolytic decay, allowing the long-term preservation

Source: C. Butler and M. Davis (eds.) *Things Fall Apart . . .*, Cardiff: National Museum of Wales, 2006, pp. 16–22.

of biological material. This can involve the specimens being passed through a series of treatments before reaching the final method of preservation.

The preservation of natural science material was initially only possible for dry inert materials. It was not until the development of fluid preservation that it became possible to preserve moist, soft biological material. The practice of fluid preservation dates back to 1644, when Croone presented to the Royal Society two whole puppies preserved in the 'spirit of wine' (ethyl alcohol). Later, towards the end of the nineteenth century, the properties of formaldehyde were discovered. Formaldehyde is used to fix biological tissue chemically in order to stop it degrading, and its use has become widespread in museums. These practices have changed very little over the last century, and alcohol and formaldehyde solutions are still amongst the most important techniques available for the preservation of biological tissue. The result is that many of the methods used in museums are based on what appears to have worked, rather than hard scientific evaluation.

Recent years have seen the development of new demands on museum biological collections. There has been a rapid development and improvement in the technology and techniques used in microbiological research. Of particular note is the development of the Polymerase Chain Reaction (PCR), which has enabled researchers to replicate and amplify very small amounts of DNA for subsequent analysis. DNA, or deoxyribonucleic acid, is a long double-helix molecule that carries the genetic coding information for a species, and is contained in every cell of an organism. The result is that very small quantities of DNA can now be extracted from museum specimens, and then replicated until there is sufficient DNA for a researcher to work with. The DNA is used in many areas of study, such as evolution, species identification and ecology. This new accessibility to the genetic information of species, and the growing crisis in the world's biodiversity, means that museum collections are now being increasingly used as a resource for microbiological studies. Examples of such studies include:

- Work on the extinct Tasmanian wolf to see how it related to existing marsupials.
- Identification of difficult groups of organisms such as mosquitoes, allowing the accurate identification of malaria-carrying species.
- The identification and the distribution of Lyme's disease by examining the blood in preserved ticks for the DNA of the bacteria responsible for it. The disease is characterised in humans by neuralgic, cardiac and rheumatic conditions and can be fatal.

The result is that there is now a need for those caring for biological collections to have a better understanding of how the methods used to conserve the specimens affect the integrity of the DNA held within them. By improving this understanding it should be possible to improve specimen preservation for both morphological and molecular study as cost-effectively as possible.

Many factors will affect the condition of the DNA in a specimen. These include the preservation history and the age of the material. Autolytic decay causes the rapid degradation of DNA molecules from the effects of enzymes and reactive molecules in the tissues. Preservation treatments aim to halt the decay processes, but can themselves have an effect on the condition of the DNA. The DNA can also be affected by factors such as hydrolysis, oxidation, radiation and temperature. All these processes can cause structural changes to the DNA molecules including:

- Denaturation, where the duplex DNA molecule becomes separated into single-stranded DNA, which is more open to chemical attack.
- Cross-linking reactions, which bond the duplex DNA to each other or other molecules such as proteins, making the DNA less accessible.
- Strand breakages or nicks in the sugar phosphate backbone of the DNA molecules, causing fragmentation.
- Chemical modification of nucleotides which carry the genetic coding, through addition, removal, or replacement of chemical groups. This can cause changes in the nucleotide sequence or alter the way the DNA reacts chemically.

The best method we currently have for the storage of specimens for molecular analysis is freezing, known as cryo-preservation. This can be done in liquid nitrogen, or by the use of –80°C freezers. However, cryo-preserved collections require constant monitoring and are expensive to maintain. For these reasons they are not a practical consideration for many natural history museums. In addition cryo-preservation will not preserve the morphology of a specimen, at least not in a way that makes the specimen accessible. So how do other methods of fixation and preservation used with natural science collections affect the condition of the DNA?

Some of the first published DNA studies using museum specimens looked at extinct or rare animals. The material used for these studies was dried muscle, skin, feather or bone and tended to provide DNA that was around 200–300 base pairs long. Whilst this DNA was essentially degraded, it proved usable for cloning, hybridisation and PCR. During this period, workers were also beginning to look at using the DNA stored in archival histopathological material fixed in formaldehyde (Figure 41.1) or some other chemical fixative, and then embedded in paraffin. The successful

Figure 41.1 A deep sea spider (*Pygnogonida*) preserved in formaldehyde

extraction of DNA surviving in such material demonstrated that biological tissue that had been exposed to a whole range of chemical treatments could still have a viable use in DNA studies. This view has been further reinforced from studies with ancient DNA obtained from archaeological and subfossil remains.

The establishment of usable DNA in museum specimens that were originally collected for their gross morphological features has led to the consideration of a wide range of museum-preserved specimens for subsequent molecular work, including fluid-preserved material. As the use of preserved material in DNA studies increased, consideration began to be given to the effects of museum preservation treatments on the condition of the DNA and the reliability of any analysis carried out, such as the reading of DNA sequences. Some of the resulting studies showed that the DNA that could be extracted from formaldehyde-fixed material tended to be of low molecular weight, whereas ethanol-fixed and preserved material potentially yielded high molecular-weight DNA. It is thus considered that fixatives such as formaldehyde either badly degrade the DNA or alter it chemically, making extraction and analysis of the DNA difficult. The preservative action of ethanol on DNA is thought to be related to its dehydrating and 'pseudo-fixative' effect on proteins, in which water is removed and proteins are preserved by structural, rather than chemical, changes. Ethanol, however, does not preserve the external morphology, histology and internal anatomy as well as formaldehyde does.

Drying is also a widely used method of preservation in museums (Figure 41.2). Many different groups of organisms can be preserved in a dry form, and many

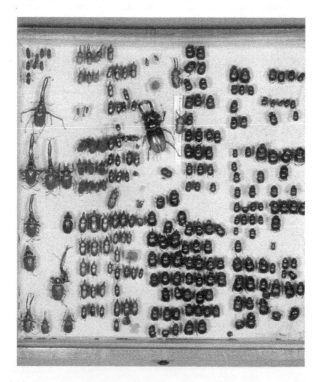

Figure 41.2 Dried entomological specimens

specimens are subsequently dried following fluid preservation. Drying is a particularly useful method with many groups of insects. How the specimen is dried can
affect the integrity of the DNA; for example entomologists use ethyl acetate to kill
and prepare specimens for dry pinning, and this has been found to preserve DNA
very poorly. Specialised drying techniques such as Critical Point Drying, and certain
chemical drying methods potentially give both good morphological and good DNA
preservation.

We have been further assessing many of the preservation processes listed in Table
41.1. The results obtained from this research have reaffirmed many of the findings
of previous studies considering the problems of molecular preservation. However,
some additional observations have been noted, especially with the use of ethanol-
based solutions. One of the most important methods of preservation we use involves
the use of Industrial Methylated Spirits (IMS). The use of methyl alcohol in IMS, to
make it unfit for consumption, allows the alcohol duty costs to be dropped, making it considerably cheaper to purchase than absolute ethanol. A growing concern
is whether the use of IMS as a preserving fluid is as good as ethanol preservation for
the condition of whole genomic DNA. Recent work suggests that IMS preservation
does have an effect on the condition of the DNA within a specimen. While high

Table 41.1 A summary of the effects of various preservation protocols on inverte-
brate specimens (after Thomas 1994, Reiss et al. 1996, Dillon et al. 1996, Quicke
et al. 1999)

Mode of fixation	Subsequent preservation	External morphology	Histology	Internal anatomy	DNA
Cryo preservation	Freezer at −70°C or below	Can be Good	Poor	Fair to Good	Good
Absolute ethanol	Absolute ethanol	Poor to Good	Poor to Fair	Poor to Fair	Good
70–80% IMS	70–80% IMS	Fair to Good	Fair to Good	Fair to Good	Fair to Good
70–80% IMS	CPD or chemical drying	Good	Poor	Good	Fair to Good
70–80% IMS	Air drying	Good for certain groups	Poor	Variable	Fair
4% formaldehyde	70–80% IMS	Fair to Good	Fair	Fair	Poor to Fair
4% formaldehyde	4% formaldehyde	Good	Fair to Good	Good	Poor
Ethyl acetate	Air dried	Fair to Good	?	Variable	Very Poor
Formaldehyde-based histological	Same	Fair to Good	Good	Good	Very Poor to Poor
Mercury-based histological	Same	Fair to Good	Good	Good	None or Very Poor

molecular-weight DNA can be extracted, analysis suggests that the IMS preservation process has weakened the DNA, although it remains usable in molecular analyses. Using IMS also causes similar morphological preservation problems to absolute ethanol. These problems can be reduced by diluting the IMS solutions to 80 per cent IMS, and by using additives such as propylene glycol. However, the use of 80 per cent IMS solutions causes an immediate drop in the quantity of DNA that can be extracted, and whilst high molecular-weight DNA is present, significant degradation has occurred. The use of propylene glycol in the solution does not appear to affect the overall preservation of the DNA in 80 per cent IMS solutions. Archival samples that had been preserved in 80 per cent IMS for over fifteen years still yielded extractable DNA, but this was significantly degraded. From this it can be deduced that the action of water is likely to be the main contributing factor to the degradation of the DNA. Thus there is evidence to suggest that although the level of denaturant additives (i.e. methyl alcohol) in IMS is low, their effect on the preservation of DNA is potentially significant, especially over time. In addition, the presence of water in the preserving solution will also add significantly to the degradation of the DNA

Whilst our current methods of preservation do have the potential to preserve DNA (Table 41.1), the major problem is still that when an organism dies the cellular protection mechanisms are no longer effective. By investigating possible methods for improving fluid preservation treatments it should be possible to enhance both morphological and molecular preservation in museum-preserved specimens. Current research at the National Museum of Wales is considering such factors.

In the meantime, the standard methods we use are likely to preserve DNA in a condition suitable for molecular studies, especially as the procedures used in these studies continue to improve. Our biological collections are an important resource, and their value is increased by the development of molecular analytical methods.

Bibliography

Dillon, N., Austin, A. D. and Bartowsky, E. (1996) 'Comparison of preservation techniques for DNA extraction from hymenopterous insects', *Insect Molecular Biology* 5: 21–24.

Quicke, D. L. J., Belshaw, R. and Lopez-Vaamonde, C. (1999) 'Preservation of hymenopteran specimens for subsequent molecular and morphological study', *Zoology Scripta* 1–2: 261–267.

Reiss, R. A., Schwert, D. P. and Ashworth, A. C. (1995) 'Field preservation of coleoptera for molecular genetic analysis', *Environmental Entomology* 24: 716–719.

Thomas, R. H. (1994) 'Analysis of DNA from natural history museum collections', in B. Schierwater, B. Streit, G. P. Wagner and R. Desalle (eds) *Molecular Ecology and Evolution: Approaches and Applications*, Basel: Birkhäuser Verlag AG.

Chapter 42

The Impact of Climate Change on Cultural Heritage: evidence and response

May Cassar and Robyn Pender

Introduction

A RCHAEOLOGICAL SITES AND some buildings have survived at least two periods of global warming (around 1500–1200 BC and 800–1200 AD) and intervening cold periods. With international scientific evidence mounting and the reliability of future climate predictions increasing, in 2002 English Heritage commissioned research to gather evidence on climate change as a possible cause of environmental instability of cultural heritage and to inform present and future planning (Cassar 2005).

Climate change modelling and prediction

Climate change predictions are based on climate models which are constructed from studies of the current climate system, including atmosphere, ocean, land surface, cryosphere and biosphere, and the factors that influence it such as greenhouse gas emissions and future socio-economic patterns of land use. A climate model is a mathematical formulation of the effects of all the key processes operating in the climate system, and the effectiveness of any particular model is assessed by seeing how well it reproduces past climate behaviour. Additionally, extrapolating the models to future climates incorporates not only the scientific uncertainties inherent in modelling complex weather systems, it implies that the broad operation of the climate system will remain constant and not undergo dramatic shifts and the much less quantifiable uncertainties in future emissions and land use. Advanced global models typically have a coarse resolution (a few hundred kilometres), which does not allow for useful local climate change projections where local weather is heavily influenced by local topography and land use.

Source: A. Paterakis et al. (eds), *ICOM-CC 14th Triennial Meeting The Hague 12–16 September 2005*, London: James & James, 2005, pp. 610–616.

More detailed regional climate models (RCMs) are constructed for limited areas and shorter time periods. The United Kingdom's Meteorological Office supports the Hadley Centre for Climate Prediction and Research, which has several such regional climate models. This study used the UKCIP02 projections (Hulme et al. 2002) from the output of the regional climate model HadRM3, whose resolution is 50 km over Europe, with the model run over the periods 1961–90 and 2070–99 for a range of emission scenarios. The confidence levels in the key predictions are qualitative because they are based on expert understanding of complex science, observed data, the ability to predict and the consistency of the model (Table 42.1).

Table 42.1 Summary statements of UK weather changes and relative confidence levels for the UKCIP02 climate change scenarios

Key predictions Temperature:	Confidence level
Annual warming by the 2080s of 1–5°C, depending on region	High
Greater summer warming in the southeast than the northwest of England	High
Variability: years as warm as 1999 becoming very common	High
Greater warming in summer and autumn than in winter and spring	Low
Greater day-time than night-time warming in summer	Low
Summer and autumn temperatures become more variable	Low
Precipitation:	
Generally wetter winters for the whole United Kingdom	High
Greater contrast between summer (drier) and winter (wetter) seasons	High
Snowfalls decrease significantly everywhere	High
Substantially drier summers for the whole United Kingdom	Medium
Variability: summers as dry as 1995 become very common	Medium
Winter and spring precipitation becomes more variable	Low
Storminess:	
Winter depressions become more frequent, including the deepest ones	Low
Humidity:	
Specific humidity increases throughout the year	High
Relative humidity decreases in summer	Medium
Soil moisture levels:	
Decrease in summer and autumn in southeast England	High
Increase in winter and spring in northwest England	Medium
Sea level rise:	
Continuation of historic trends in vertical land movements introduces significant regional differences in relative sea level rises around the United Kingdom	High
Storm surge: for some coastal locations and some scenarios, return periods will reduce an order of magnitude by the 2080s	Medium
Changes in storminess, sea level and land movement mean that storm surge heights will increase by the greatest amount off southeast England	Low
Solar radiation:	
Reduction in summer and autumn cloud, especially in the south, and increase in radiation	Low

Focussing on the high-confidence projections for 2080, the United Kingdom is likely to experience a rise in temperature, an increase in variability leading to some very warm years, and an increase in wetter winters everywhere; greater contrast between summer and winter seasons and a decrease in soil moisture levels in summer and autumn in southeast England; increased regional differences in sea level rises and a significant decrease in snowfalls everywhere.

To manage a wide array of climatic variables and heritage types in an integrated research project is a huge challenge. A decision was made to concentrate on two specific contrasting regions, the northwest and the southeast of England. Both had already been extensively studied by Cranfield University's RegIS project (Holman et al. 2001), which was the only published integrated assessment of climate change impacts in the UK and was therefore of unique importance.

Methodology

The risks inherent in gathering and interpreting observed evidence made it essential to design a methodology that allowed access to a diverse range of sources, so that data could be verified before being accepted as evidence. The methodology made empirical evidence more robust by cross-checking different types of data.

Project teamwork

A multidisciplinary team of investigators was assembled, including conservators, building physicists, archaeologists and a climate modeller. The widest possible list of likely climate-related problems for cultural heritage was brought together, the UKCIP02 climate change scenarios (Hulme et al. 2002) were evaluated and the variables most likely to impact on cultural heritage in the two study areas were selected.

Questionnaire

The purpose of the questionnaire was to gather data, but also to be an information source for the recipients. It was constructed around 18 central questions, one for each issue of concern identified by the project team, namely seasonal and diurnal temperature changes, seasonal and extreme rainfall, sea level rise, storm surge, river flooding, water runoff and erosion, soil moisture content, water table height and chemistry, relative humidity, wind, solar radiation and cloud cover, lightning and fire risk, plant physiology and distribution, pest and diseases, human comfort and health and safety. Each question was accompanied by a text synopsis of the climate change impact projected for that issue, using predictions from the UKCIP02 climate change scenarios (Hulme et al. 2002) and the RegIS project (Holman et al. 2001) and comparing the projections for 2080 with the baseline years of 1961–90, making it possible to see the likely degree of future change. The questionnaire was circulated widely to national, regional and local scientific and heritage experts, and local site managers, requesting evidence of links between climate change and its impact on cultural heritage, the likely future effect on heritage of current climate change predictions and the planning and preparation that would be needed to ensure a timely management response.

Site visits

The questionnaire was followed by visits to 17 buildings, archaeological sites, parks and gardens with contrasting climates, flood risk, accessibility, urbanization, types of buildings, archaeology and gardens. The choice was made in consultation with regional and local heritage experts, managers, advisers and custodians. The visits were intended to see and hear at first hand the climate change threats to the sites, to examine examples of damage attributed to climate change and to discuss how these were impacting on local stewardship decisions.

Regional workshops

Two regional workshops were organized in Cambridge and Manchester, representing two areas affected differently by climate change. Regional experts and managers discussed the questionnaire and site visit data, future protection plans and likely conflict over the different ways in which heritage might respond to climate change. On the basis of the cross-referred evidence from the questionnaire, site visits and workshops, the original list of climate-related problems was distilled into five issues central to the cultural heritage, namely: temperature (maximum temperatures rising markedly); soil moisture (levels dropping markedly and summer drought); extreme rainfall and high winds (torrential rainfall becoming common and damaging winds probably becoming common); river flooding (floods increasing in frequency and severity); and coastal flooding (sea level rises and storm surges exacerbating coastal flooding and loss).

Policy makers' workshop

A policy makers' workshop met to discuss and prioritize the five issues. Maps overlaid the locations of vulnerable sites and their susceptibility to patterns of local climate change produced from regional climate models (Cassar 2005). They helped make complex risk data accessible and provided a direct and effective means of perceiving the overall scale of climate change problems and the risks to individual sites (Figures 42.1 and 42.2). The policy makers' workshop distilled several recommendations as well as some general conclusions on how cultural heritage could adapt to a changing climate.

Evidence of threat and observed changes to cultural heritage

This evidence was based on specific observations by heritage managers of changes attributed to climate change and on experience, knowledge and understanding of the sites in their care. The climate change factors identified as the greatest threat to cultural heritage were reached by consensus and almost all heritage managers had already noticed progressive changes in the climate patterns of their sites and associated increases in deterioration.

Buildings and their contents

The inability of historic rainwater disposal systems to handle torrential or wind-driven rain was highlighted as a contributory factor in the wetting of walls. Solar radiation

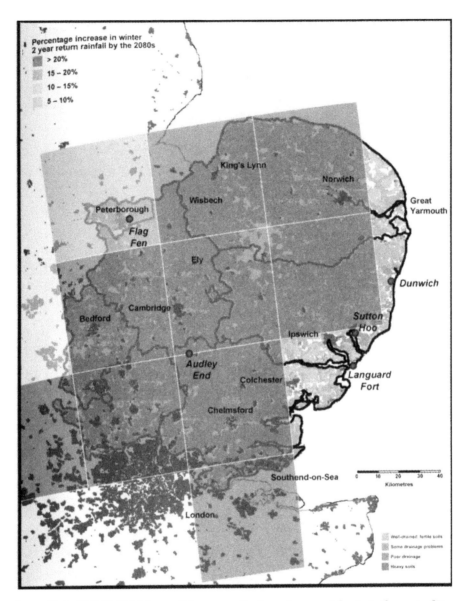

Figure 42.1 UKCIP02 high-confidence prediction of torrential rain in the east of England superimposed on visited sites

drives moisture and salts inside walls, leading to damp and the risk of efflorescence on internal surfaces. The problems of river flooding necessitating extensive repairs to buildings and the risk of disturbance to buried archaeology of improvements to drainage systems to cope with flood risks were emphasized. Audley End House, a historic property with gardens in southeast England, was highlighted as an example where there have been problems with rainwater disposal, damp penetration, damage to decorative plasterwork and river flooding of the gardens. Although the UKCIP02

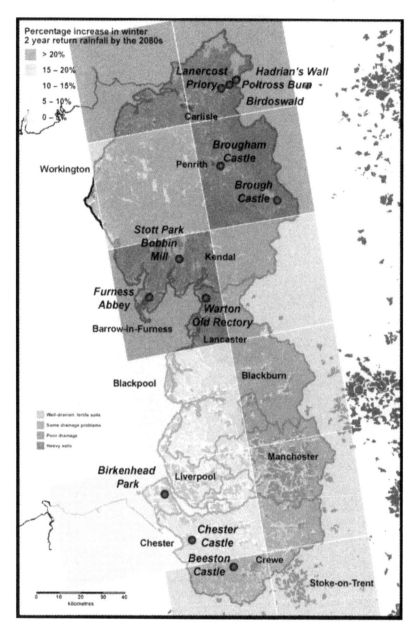

Figure 42.2 UKCIP02 high-confidence prediction of torrential rain in the northwest
        of England superimposed on visited sites

climate change scenarios have a low confidence level for predictions of storminess and
high winds, these issues were flagged up as problems already being experienced with
historic roofs, windows, awnings, verandas, large trees close to buildings, ruins and
excavated archaeology. The high confidence level predicting a decrease in soil moisture levels also puts buildings at risk from subsidence. The increased erosion of the

ruins of Furness Abbey on the Cumbrian peninsula in the northwest of England was linked to wind throw, increased storminess and gales, whereas coastal loss in southeast England continues to affect the medieval town of Dunwich, which has virtually disappeared into the sea. Predicted changes in temperature and relative humidity were considered to be small and gradual enough for vulnerable materials to accommodate them. However, concern was expressed over the indirect future effect of these changes, namely increased demand for mechanical cooling in summer, requiring meticulous environmental monitoring of conditions and a set of baseline values. Evidence of the change in distribution of existing pest species across the United Kingdom and the introduction of new pest species suggest that isolated opportunities alone cannot account for these changes in the past decade.

Buried archaeology

Changes in soil moisture and chemistry were unanimously considered a threat to preservation in situ, as baseline knowledge of the effect of changes in soil chemistry on preservation is poorly understood: for example the loss of certain data types only preserved in waterlogged/anaerobic/anoxic conditions, the loss of archaeology presently preserved close of the ground surface and the effect on the archaeological record of the drying of soil causing the loss of stratigraphic integrity. The increase in sea level and storminess is a danger for many sites vulnerable to erosion, such as the Sutton Hoo barrow site, because of the disturbance of the metastable equilibrium between artifacts and soil. On the other hand, in areas that lie below sea level, such as the Fenland area in southeast England where many prehistoric and Roman fenland sites were built and decayed under tidal influence, flood-risk alleviation schemes could cause more damage to buried archaeology than flooding, though the occurrence of torrential rain would cause erosion. Changes in plant physiology and distribution were of concern for a variety of reasons: drought causing loss of vegetation exacerbating erosion, deep root penetration damaging structures causing subsidence and sediment boundaries and changes in vegetation cover affecting the survival of artifacts and ecofacts.

Parks and gardens

The effect of climate change on parks and gardens has been documented elsewhere (Bisgrove and Hadley 2002). The evidence from this research confirmed that many factors that affect buildings and archaeology also affect historic parks and gardens. Wind and rainfall are a key concern. Mature tree specimens are particularly susceptible to wind damage. Storms have already damaged or destroyed many historic landscapes, but there is concern that in the future climate change can make identical replacements difficult to grow. Excessive rainfall has caused trees to become unstable and to topple during gales, while the planting that can cope successfully with dry summer conditions is at risk from waterlogged soils in winter. The predicted rise in temperature could see a dramatic change in the appearance of the English landscape, where daffodils and apples need frost to germinate or set seed. Warmer temperatures have already increased the risk from pests, such as the year-round presence of Canada geese at Birkenhead Park in northwest England destroying grassed areas. Changes in the chemistry and height of water tables would affect water supplies to ornamental lakes, fountains and other water features, whereas the after-effects of high tides and river flooding can be exacerbated by salinity of the flood water, as for example at Westbury Court Garden on the River Severn in the west of England, where yew hedges hundreds of years old are at risk.

Strategies for adapting cultural heritage to climate change

Planning time-scales

Convincing policy makers to include climate change impacts in planning and, moreover, cultural heritage can be difficult. The questionnaire revealed, and the workshops confirmed, that planning time-scales in the heritage sector are often much longer than conventional planning cycles (Figure 42.3).

Out of 57 questionnaire respondents, only 13 indicated a planning timeframe of five years, whereas 21 respondents indicated a timeframe of over 100 years. This 'long view' is vindicated by the emphasis on preparation and adaptation in the Third Assessment Report of the United Nations Intergovernmental Panel on Climate Change (McCarthy et al. 2001), which advises policy makers that adaptation is a necessary strategy at all scales to complement climate change mitigation efforts and that 'Adaptation has the potential to reduce adverse impacts of climate change and to enhance beneficial impacts, but will incur costs and will not prevent all damages'. Heritage professionals can make a positive contribution to longer-term planning for climate change by other authorities, can ensure that cultural heritage is integrated into these plans and more specifically in conservation plans directly affecting cultural heritage. However, caution must be exercised, as confidence in longer-term predictions is lower overall than short-term predictions.

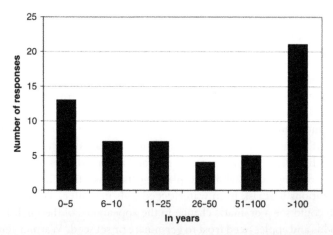

Figure 42.3 Heritage managers' questionnaire responses on planning time-scales

Monitoring, management and maintenance

The research did not reveal new problems for cultural heritage but it drew attention to long-standing conservation issues. Maintenance and condition monitoring will become more critical as climate change takes effect. Where there is concern that drainage and rainwater disposal systems in historic buildings may not have the capacity to deal with torrential rain, it will be important to keep all gutters, hoppers and down pipes, even the most difficult and inaccessible, meticulously clean so that an increase in rainfall can flow away safely. Crucially, there was consensus among heritage experts and managers that non-invasive or concealed improvements might not be possible, requiring difficult choices on what to sacrifice and a preference for funding to be directed towards maintenance instead of new building work.

Loss and obsolescence

The issue of acceptance of loss of some heritage elements to save the rest was raised in the context of coastal archaeological sites. One heritage manager stated: 'We'll never save everything, so hard decisions are needed as to which to let go', with an emphasis on assessments of value, significance and life expectancy. There was a different view from some stewards of the natural environment, with measures being taken to reverse the loss of natural habitats by reinstating salt marshes in southeast England. The question of environmental obsolescence was raised for ageing buildings that will need adapting to survive climate change and to remain relevant to modern use. As the historic building fabric interacts with rather than excludes moisture, the issue that needs addressing is whether there might ever be sound environmental reasons for demolition.

Policy actions

In conclusion, several key policy recommendations emerged from the research to indicate the way forward for understanding the impact of climate change on cultural heritage.

Cooperation

The different strands of cultural heritage need to cooperate, share information and speak with unity on the issue of climate change and that there are benefits from integration with the natural environment. Cultural heritage cannot stand alone and common concerns are an opportunity for cross-disciplinary cooperation.

Funding

Maintenance emerged as a key concern, necessitating a more equitable balance between funding for repair and maintenance, tax incentives for sustainable maintenance, the formation of partnerships with other interested parties such as the insurance industry and support for skills training for upgrading, repairing and maintaining cultural heritage.

Research

The lack of good data on the effects of environmental change and the lack of under-standing of the behaviour of the materials, worsening with the shift of climate goal posts, was a significant issue. Research is needed on monitoring change and devel-oping appropriate sustainability indicators, with outputs being used to drive policy, develop strategies and disseminate knowledge and awareness.

Education

The public needs educating on the impact of climate change on cultural heritage and on the importance of cultural heritage as a climate change indicator. At a local level, site logbooks are needed to record impacts of climate change as part of the imple-mentation of conservation plans. At an international level, a mechanism for sharing knowledge and experience would enable information, resources and good examples of adaptation to be shared.

[. . .]

References

Bisgrove, R. and Hadley, P. (2002) Gardening in the global greenhouse: the impacts of climate change on gardens in the UK, Technical Report, Oxford: UKCIP. http://www.ukcip.org.uk/publications/

Cassar, M. (2005) *Climate Change and the Historic Environment*, London: English Heritage. http://discovery.ucl.ac.uk/2082/

Holman, I., Hollis, J., Bellamy, P., Berry, P., Harrison, P., Dawson, T., Audsley, E., Annetts, J., Debaets, A., Rounsvell, M., Nicholls, R., Shakley, S. and Wood, R. (2001) *The REGIS Project (CC0337) Regional Climate Change Impact and Response Studies in East Anglia and in North West England (RegIS)*, Cranfield, UK: United Kingdom Climate Impacts Programme, Department of the Environment, Food and Rural Affairs and United Kingdom Water Industries Research. http://www.cranfield.ac.uk/sas/naturalresources/research/projects/regis.html

Hulme, M., Jenkins, G. J., Lu, X., Turnpenny, J. R., Mitchell, T. D., Jones, R. G., Lowe, J., Murphy, J. M., Hassell, D., Boorman, P., McDonald, R. and Hill, S. (2002) *Climate Change Scenarios for the United Kingdom: The UKCIP02 Scientific Report*, Norwich, UK: Tyndall Centre for Climate Change Research, School of Environmental Sciences, University of East Anglia. http://www.ukcip.org.uk/ukcp09/ukcip02/

McCarthy, J. J., Canziani, O. F., Leary, N. A., Dokken, D. J. and White, K. S. (eds) (2001) *IPCC Climate Change 2001: Working Group II: Impacts, Adaptation and Vulnerability. Summary for Policymakers, 2.7*, Cambridge: UK, Intergovernmental Panel on Climate Change. http://www.grida.no/climate/ipcc_tar/wg2/index.htm

Index